MODELLING ECONOMIC SERIES

Readings in Econometric Methodology

Edited by

C. W. J. GRANGER

ADVANCED TEXTS IN ECONOMETRICS

General Editors

C. W. J. GRANGER   G. MIZON

CLARENDON PRESS · OXFORD

Oxford University Press, Walton Street, Oxford OX2 6DP

Oxford New York Toronto
Delhi Bombay Calcutta Madras Karachi
Kuala Lumpur Singapore Hong Kong Tokyo
Nairobi Dar es Salaam Cape Town
Melbourne Auckland Madrid
and associated companies in
Berlin Ibadan

Oxford is a trade mark of Oxford University Press

Published in the United States by
Oxford University Press Inc., New York

First published 1990
Reprinted 1990
First issued in paperback 1991
Paperback reprinted 1992

British Library Cataloguing in Publication Data
Data available

Library of Congress Cataloging in Publication Data
Modelling economic series: readings in econometric methodology /
edited by C. W. J. Granger.
p. cm.
Includes bibliographical references.
1. Econometrics. I. Granger, C. W. J. (Clive William
John),
1934–
HB139.M624 1989 330'.01'5195—dc20 89-16203
ISBN 0-19-828689-9
ISBN 0-19-828736-4 (pbk)

Printed in Great Britain
on acid-free paper by
Biddles Ltd
Guildford and King's Lynn

Contents

General Introduction

Where are the Controversies in Econometric Methodology?

C. W. J. Granger

1. Introduction

The novice empirical modeller faces many difficulties and problems concerned with the evolving specification, evaluation, and interpretation of the model. The advice that econometric modelling is an activity that should not be attempted for the first time is unhelpful but contains a useful warning. Good modelling is probably both an art and a science. A sound knowledge of theoretical econometrics and the availability of an efficient and flexible computer program is not enough to ensure success.

The purpose of this book is to bring together advice and discussions by prominent thinkers in the area of econometric methodology. There is certainly no one generally acceptable path to a good model. In fact, the papers included here are partially chosen to illustrate the deep differences of opinion between various groups of econometricians, concerning the modelling process and the interpretation of models. One ends with several different modelling strategies, each with supporters and critics. At the present stage of development in economics it is probably an advantage to have different groups look at the same problem from different viewpoints, so that their models and conclusions can be compared and possibly then form the basis for a new, comprehensive model. The fact that one model dominates another under some criterion, such as forecasting ability, does not necessarily imply that the better model should be retained and the lesser one totally discarded, as both models may contain elements of 'truth' and so should be combined.

The book is concerned with the process of modelling a group of economic time series for some specific purpose. It will concentrate on the strategy of modelling, the choice of *specification* and its evaluation when alternatives are considered, and also the *evaluation* of the model. Very little attention is paid to the question of how best to *estimate* the parameters of the model, a question to which econometricians have paid an undue amount of attention in the past 50 years.

The modelling exercise will have a dependent variable y_t, which may be a vector, to be explained by the contents of an information set I_t. This information may contain just numerical information, such as the values of y_{t-j}, x_{t-j}, $j > 0$ where x_t is a vector of explanatory series. I_t can be called 'improper' if it does *not* contain y_{t-j}, the past of the dependent variable. Generally, only proper information sets will be considered. An information set J_t: y_{t-j}, $j > 0$, x_{t-j}, $j \geq 0$, may be called a contemporaneous set as it contains values of x_t measured at the same time as the dependent variable. This information can be augmented by personal beliefs or implications from some theory which is accepted as having value. The choice of the information to use in constructing a model is clearly of considerable importance. This choice is discussed further below.

As the values of all major economic variables are announced regularly it is easy to believe in the existence of a generating mechanism. In this introductory chapter, and in most of the papers in this collection, a true generating mechanism is assumed to exist and an objective of the model-ling process is to make statements about this mechanism. It is an interesting philosophical point whether a complete representation of the true mechan-ism can be given, but I doubt if this question has much practical relevance.

The true mechanism is likely to be extremely complex as in some cases it is constructed from the original decisions of many millions of economic agents aggregated both cross-sectionally and temporally to the observed macro series. The effects of aggregation are also discussed later. Because of the complexity of the actual economy, the following axiom will be taken as being true.

AXIOM A   Any model will be only an approximation to the generating mechanism, with there being a preference for the best available approxi-mation that is available. It follows that several models can all be equally good approximations. How one can judge the quality of the approximation means further discussion.

The objective of modelling is usually stated to be either the testing of economic hypotheses, to form forecasts or to suggest policies. However, it will be assumed here that the basic objective is:

AXIOM B   The basic objective of a modelling exercise is to affect the beliefs – and hence the behaviour – of other research workers and possibly other economic agents. These beliefs may be about the size or signs of certain coefficients (relating to a hypothesis from an economic theory), the quality of a forecasting technique or the relevance of some policy strategy, for example. The degree of belief, about the correctness of some hypo-thesis say, may be measured as a probability and can be affected by the outcome of an empirical investigation. For example an economist may say that his or her belief about the statement 'inflation can be controlled by using a policy of money supply being attached to pre-announced slowly growing monetary targets is 0.4'. A carefully conducted empirical study may obtain results that change this economists' belief to 0.6 and consequentially change his or her behaviour. Of course, this purpose is not limited to econometric modelling and can also apply to a new economic theory at all levels of sophistication.

It follows that there will be producers of models and also *consumers* of these models, and the two groups will generally view the modelling process quite differently. What is an important problem or a controversial question for one group may be of little interest to the other group. Because of the need to communicate the quality of a model by the producers to the consumers, the following definition is suggested:

DEFINITION   A transferable model consists of:

(1) a set of equations, with estimates of the parameters, and
(2) the results of a comprehensive *evaluation* exercise.

A model is called transferable if one research worker can communicate its content to another worker. Throughout this book this will be taken to mean that the model can be presented in a precise, mathematical form. However, because of Axiom B, it is *not* enough to just present the estimated equations, it will also be necessary to provide evaluation statistics, comparisons with other models, the results of specification tests, out-of-sample evaluation, and so forth. The more comprehensive these evaluation statistics the more likely another researcher will find the model to be useful and acceptable, provided the statistics are favourable to the model.

The evaluation should be sufficiently detailed and be constructed to convince the consumer that the model has enough quality to be relevant for reconsideration of the consumer's belief. Some discussions of modelling methodology concentrate on (1), that is the specification and estimation of the model, but many of the papers in this collection also contain extensive discussions of evaluation. Some of the elements of the evaluation process are discussed later in this introductory chapter.

It is less clear whether the process by which a model specification is achieved is relevant to its evaluation. If a professional psychic just produces a model from his or her mind, complete with estimated parameters, then such a model is unlikely to be given much credence, but if it performs really well on a wide battery of evaluation procedures, then it will start to become acceptable and be relevant for changing beliefs. If one changes the word 'psychic' to 'theorist' here, this remark has particular relevance. An example is the suggestion by I. M. D. Little (1962) that firms' profits follow a random walk, an idea which met with considerable disbelief until his model was found consistently to outperform other forecasts of profits. One of the main worries about the present methods of model formulation is that the specification search procedure produces models that fit the data spuriously well, and also make standard techniques of inference unreliable. This is a kind way of saying that the model may be achieved due to an effective method of data mining. However, this is less of a concern if the evaluation techniques are effectively orthogonal to the model specification procedure. This could be true of some encompassing tests and out-of-sample forecasting evaluations, for example.

2.   Outline of the Contents of the Book

The papers in the book have largely been chosen to encourage applied economists and users of econometric methodology to *think* about the process of modelling. A simplistic form of the classical modelling procedure starts with a theory, restates this in the form of estimable equations, the parameters are then estimated, some simple evaluation information given, such as R^2, t-statistics and possibly the Durbin – Watson statistic, finally the resulting model is interpreted and its 'policy implications' explored. Anyone trying to follow this sequence is likely to meet several problems. Should one use an equilibrium or a disequilibrium theory? How does one decide which variables are exogenous and which endogenous? What does one do about endogenous variables for which there is no theory, or for which there are satisfactory alternative theories? What does one do if it becomes clear that the model is not data coherent – that is, does not fit the data well or explain some of its main features, such as a trend or a seasonal component? How should one react if a specification test suggests that a variable is missing, or if an encompassing test finds some other model is superior in some way? Many of the papers have been selected because they attempt answers to these and the many others faced in the modelling process. They suggest strategies, defend their own positions, and criticize others.

The papers in the first part of the book point out some of the difficulties faced by modellers, the specification of the model, its evaluation and interpretation. The first five papers both criticize and defend commonly used time series modelling processes. The real problem is that certain vital parameters of a model, which are important for hypothesis testing or policy implications, may be very unstable as model specification changes. Leamer points out that the plausible range of values of one of these parameters, the so-called 'extreme bounds', can be very large. By ignoring this problem of interpretation, or of evaluation of the model, it is suggested that interpretation is very dubious. There are some difficulties with Leamer's argument, as discussed by the other authors. These papers are included to point out that there are real controversies in econometric methodology and

that a simplistic approach may well not be sufficient to arrive at a satisfactory model.

Pagan's paper (Chapter 6) briefly reviews this discussion and critically
outlines three alternative methodologies that have been proposed, one
based on vector autoregressions, using little economic theory, one involving
both economic theory and time series methods (called here the LSE methodology) and a third making heavy use of economic theory and also Bayesian
techniques. This paper is useful as it gives a clear overview of these major
modelling strategies. The final two papers of this section discuss fundamental questions of modelling, such as the practical usefulness of identifiability
conditions, whilst also presenting particular strategy viewpoints.

The second part of the book contains papers discussing three particular
strategies, that used by constructors of large-scale econometric models
(Fair, Chapter 9), the vector autoregression models, using Bayesian priors
(Todd, Chapter 10) and Bayesian techniques, an application by Leamer
(Chapter 11) and a spirited discussion of their relevance through a series of
challenges by Zellner (Chapter 12).

Part III of the book consists of three papers discussing the LSE methodology, associated with Sargan, Hendry, Wallis, Mizon and various of
their colleagues. This seems to be the most carefully thought through and
thus comprehensive modelling strategy currently available. The papers
give different accounts of this methodology varying in depth, viewpoint
and ease of comprehension.

The final part is specifically concerned with model evaluation. White
(Chapter 16) suggests an automated procedure of model selection, based
on specification tests, and Chong and Hendry (Chapter 17) are particularly
concerned with evaluation.

Before each of these parts there is a brief discussion of their contents.

The papers probably will not provide answers to all the questions faced
by modellers. It is still very difficult to answer the question 'how would you
teach a student to model an economic relationship?', as it is difficult to
anticipate all of the problems that can occur when actually performing an
empirical study. No one strategy is advocated in this collection, but rather
more weight has been given to papers concerned with the LSE approach,
as I think that they state the questions to be faced rather more clearly than
the alternatives. It is certainly good that different strategies exist, so that
different research workers can arrive at different models. Probably only by
comparing, and combining, models using different viewpoints can really
good models be achieved.

If a reader wants a quick overview of the main points in the book, at a
less technical level, I recommend starting with Chapters 6 (Pagan), 7
(Hendry and Mizon), 10 (Todd), 13 (Gilbert) and 17 (Chong and Hendry).

The next four sections of this introductory chapter discuss some fundamental issues, such as the form of the data generation process (henceforth DGP), the consequences of data mining, which involves the actual or conceptual consideration of many possible models, and whether or not one should look at the data before starting the modelling process. It is suggested that to achieve properly balanced model specifications, this pre-analysis is essential. The chapter then discusses some of the controversies in model construction and then in model evaluation.

The contents of this chapter, and most of the papers in the readings, consider just models of time series. Some of the results and suggestions also apply to cross-sectional and to panel data models but these types of data are not specifically considered.

3.   The Data Generating Process

The variables that are used to describe and to characterize an economy originate in the decisions made by the components that comprise the economy, the numerous individuals or consumers, companies, governments and institutions. For example, families make decisions about what to consume and when, how many hours to work, and in what to invest; firms make decisions about employment, production, pricing, marketing, borrowing, investment, and so forth. The decisions produce components of important macrovariables such as total consumption and production and are based on inputs such as previous wages, current prices, and interest rates. The input and output variables of all the decision-makers may be considered the basic variables of the economy, although there may be deeper variables involved which help determine the decision rules leading to the potentially observable decision outcomes. In any major economy there may be several billion such variables. The eventual outcomes of the decisions will often not be quite what was planned, poor health may disrupt a decision to work a full week, or a machine breakdown or supply shortages result in a lower production then expected, for example. If we had a vector of the decision outputs, it could be written as a function of all the input variables plus a stochastic residual vector. As decisions inevitably take time to formulate and propagate, the outputs will occur *after* the inputs. Whether or not the economy at this level is best described by a continuous time model or a short-interval discrete time model is only of philosophical interest when faced with the pragmatic question of how to build a model using available data.

Suppose that one is performing an empirical study to achieve a specific, stated purpose and to achieve this purpose a model is required for some set of variables, called the variables of interest and denoted Y_t. These variables are all assumed to be observed at the same time interval, say a month for ease of discussion. In a macroeconomic study some of these variables of interest will be cross-sectional aggregates such as consumption, profits, or production for an industry or a whole economy. Decisions may be made more frequently than monthly, so to go from the basic decision input and output variables to the observed variables of interest will involve both cross-sectional and temporal aggregation. Without being specific, this will just be called the 'aggregation window'. Both types of aggregation can have very important effects on the relationships between variables, as discussed in Granger (1987, 1988), Weiss (1984) and elsewhere. Some of the effects are briefly discussed in later sections.

Suppose that in addition to the variables of interest, there are another set of variables, denoted $\mathbf{X}_t$, which will be used to explain $\mathbf{Y}_t$. Thus, the original, very large set of input and output decision variables used by the micro-level individual and institutional decision-makers, denoted $\mathbf{W}_t$, is replaced by the variables $(\mathbf{Y}_t, \mathbf{X}_t, \mathbf{S}_t) \underset{1-1}{\longleftrightarrow} \mathbf{W}_t$, where $\mathbf{S}_t$ are a group of variables such that there is a one-to-one relationship between the two complete sets, i.e. knowing $\mathbf{W}_t$ *gives* $\mathbf{Y}_t$, $\mathbf{X}_t$, $\mathbf{S}_t$ and vice-versa. In the modelling process one is interested in the joint distribution of (Y_t, X_t) conditional on the past of these series. To get to this distribution one starts with the joint distribution of $\mathbf{Y}_t$, $\mathbf{X}_t$, $\mathbf{S}_t$ for all t, and then marginalizes out $\mathbf{S}_t$ and past $\mathbf{S}_t$.

The 'true generating process' for the economy is characterized by the joint distribution of all the $\mathbf{W}_t$, or better by the conditional distribution of $\mathbf{W}_t$ on past $\mathbf{W}_t$. To get from here to the modelling situation one has to go to $\mathbf{Y}_t$, $\mathbf{X}_t$ via the cross-sectional and temporal aggregation window and then marginalize out past and present $\mathbf{S}_t$. The model thus achieved will clearly be an approximation of the true generating process. Any theory upon which the model is based also has to pass through this same approximating process if some of the $\mathbf{S}_t$ variables, that are not being used, are actually relevant to the relationship between $\mathbf{Y}_t$ and $\mathbf{X}_t$, then it is well known that biased estimates of parameters can result (for the linear regression case see Theil, 1957; Leamer, 1987). As much of $\mathbf{S}_t$ is unobserved, it thus becomes difficult to put a precise interpretation on any individual coefficient of the model, without using some heroic assumptions about the simplification of the DGP.

The majority of the papers in this collection discusses how to characterize or approximate the joint distribution of $\mathbf{Y}_t$ and $\mathbf{X}_t$ conditional on their past, or the distribution of $\mathbf{Y}_t$ conditional on the past of $\mathbf{Y}_t$ and the past (and possibly also the present) of $\mathbf{X}_t$. In fact, most attention is paid to the conditional expectation of $\mathbf{Y}_t$ given past Y_t and past (and present) $\mathbf{X}_t$, often with the further assumption that these explanatory terms enter the expectation only linearly. The possible distance between the model actually constructed and the true generating process is seen to be considerable.

There are yet further reasons for worrying about this distance between model and actuality. The data measurement procedure is inexact, often based on samples with only partial response, so that measurement error is usually present, although its importance is usually unclear. Further, the raw data may be filtered and altered in various ways, for example, 'outliers' may be removed by some automated procedure or the series may be seasonally adjusted. The method of seasonal adjustment may be particularly troublesome, as a different filter is often used for recent data compared to historical data and the historical filters may involve data at times $t + h$, with h both positive and negative, to obtain a seasonally adjusted value of the series at time t.

As the original decisions of agents made at time t can only involve information available at that time, so that conditioning on the past is a natural procedure when modelling, the data available for analysis may have lost this useful simplification.

The natural distinction between past and present is also confused by temporal aggregation. If, for data observed daily, $\mathbf{X}_{t-1}$ causes or explains $\mathbf{Y}_t$ and $\mathbf{X}_t$ contains no further useful information, this will not be true in general for the same series observed only monthly. Temporal aggregation will induce contemporaneous relationships and will produce apparent two-way causality from a true one-way causal situation. It will also, generally, weaken relationships between a stationary series and its past and also most explanatory relationships between stationary series. On the other hand integrated ($I(1)$) series retain this property on temporal aggregation and co-integration remains (for a pair of $I(1)$ series having a linear combination that is $I(0)$).

Cross-sectional aggregation can often produce much simpler relationships between aggregates than between typical disaggregated series. For example, time-varying parameters can become (virtually) constant, heteroskedasticity can be (virtually) removed and the strength of a non-linear relationship reduced. However, the strength of relationship can change in either direction as one goes from the typical micro-relationship to that found between macro variables depending on whether the variables contain common factors or not (see Granger, 1987, 1988).

4.   Data Mining

With a limited amount of data available and a huge number of possible models there is always a possibility that, if enough models are fitted to the data, one will appear to fit very well but in fact will not be useful. The classical example is having a time series of twenty terms, fitting a polynomial in t of order 19 (which has twenty parameters), thus getting a perfect fit. However, this model will typically forecast very poorly. Although this type of data mining is 'clearly' unacceptable, there are more subtle forms which are difficult to detect and which produce models that are difficult to interpret.

It is useful to consider a simple example discussed by Lovell (1983). Suppose that Y_t is a white noise series, independent of all of a set of potential explanatory white noise series $X_{jt}, j = 1, \ldots, N$. Suppose that all models of the form

$$Y_t = \beta_0 + \beta_1 X_{it} + \beta_2 X_{jt} + \varepsilon_t$$

are estimated by ordinary least-square for all pairs (i, j) and the equation that fits 'best' in terms of R^2, is selected. Clearly, if N is large, it will be likely that the best equation will have apparently significant R^2 value and that one or more of the explanatory variables will have t-values that are apparently significant. Here 'significance' is determined in the traditional way, using standard t-tables, for example. Lovell provides the results shown in Table 1, using a nominal significance level of $\alpha = 5$ per cent. Thus, with five explanatory variables and choosing the best pair, on 23 per cent of occasions at least one of β_1 and β_2 will appear to be significant using the standard t-test at a 5 per cent level. For twenty explanatory variables this figure increases to 74 per cent. These results assume the explanatory variables are orthogonal to each other and are white noises. If the series are temporally correlated, the probability of spurious relationships being found increases. Granger and Newbold (1974) show that regressions built on independent random walks have a high probability of obtaining high R^2 values, 'significant' t-values, but can often be detected by the regression having low Durbin–Watson statistics.

Returning to the white noise case, Lovell (1983) suggest a simple *rule of thumb* for interpreting significance levels of regressions obtained from data mining. If the reported regression contains k explanatory variables, selected from a set of N available variables, using a claimed significance level $\hat{\alpha}$ then these variables should be viewed as actually being significant at the $\alpha = (N/k) \hat{\alpha}$ level. Thus, if $k = 2$, $N = 20$ and $\hat{\alpha} = 1$ per cent, the approximate true significance level is 10 per cent. This approximation may

Table 1.

N	5	10	20	100
Probability of at least one coefficient significance	0.23	0.40	0.74	0.99
True significance level	4.9%	22.6%	60.1%	92.3%

not be very useful when the explanatory variables are not orthogonal and when they are correlated over time.

These results illustrate the difficulty of interpreting the modelling procedure of an individual dedicated data miner and when the model evaluation uses the same data as used for the model specification and estimation. The difficulties are somewhat reduced if the researcher admits to the mining and the various models attempted. The problems are more difficult if there is a 'mining industry', as pointed out by Denton (1985). If there are many independent workers, each producing a single regression but probably with a different specification than the others, one will eventually obtain the same 'best' equation as found by the individual data miner.

There are several forms of data mining, as pointed out by Leamer (1978), who uses the less provocative description 'specification searching'. He discussed six different types of such searches but just three will be mentioned here, called by him proxy search, data-selection search and simplification search. Consider a simple log demand model

$$\log D = \beta_0 + \beta_1 \log Y + \beta_2 \log P + e$$

where Y is income and P is price. Using some appropriately defined variables and some obtained data it would be easy to fit such a model, using any one of a variety of estimating procedures. A 'proxy search' occurs when alternative definitions of income, say, are used in the model in the hope of obtaining a better fitting model. A 'data-selection search' occurs if, starting with the basic model, other variables are added, which may be vaguely suggested by some theory, again in the hope that a better goodness-of-fit is obtained. This is a less extreme case of data mining than that considered by Lovell, but is similar in spirit. Finally a 'simplification search' would occur if terms with 'insignificant t-values' are dropped from the model or if terms are combined, for example to give an equation

$$\log D = \beta_0 + \gamma \log (Y/P).$$

A desire for simplicity can be equated to the belief in the usefulness of parsimony, as discussed in Section 8.

Leamer prefers the term 'specification search' because such searching can produce both good and bad aspects of models. On the positive side, search may produce a superior model, under various criteria, particularly if important explanatory variables are discovered that are not clearly suggested by current theory. On the negative side, unstructured searching may result in apparently good models and certainly change the methods of statistical inference that are appropriate. As classical inference is based on a single regression using clear data derived from a random experiement, the effect of economic reality and the case of a sequence of models selected by data analysis is potentially profound. R^2 and t-values need to be viewed with caution and used as guides rather than precise ways of stating the quality of a model. This is particularly true when the method of selection of a model (maximizing R^2, say) is related to the evaluation procedure (the size of maximum t-value). The situation may become less difficult if other evaluation methods are used, including out-of-sample data, as discussed later.

Acceptable specification search is the process of moving from a current model to a better one, using sensible criteria to determine 'better'. It is this process that is discussed by several papers in this volume. 'Data mining' should be reserved for use, perhaps, with models that are derived from a very widespread, randomized search, which may lead to well-fitting but inappropriate models. However, procedures such as stepwise regressions can produce good models, as shown by Lovell (1983) using a simulation study. The dangers associated with data mining suggest that the specification search cannot end with a 'best model'. What is needed is also a battery of specification tests and evaluation procedures. Without these, the consumer of the model may not be convinced of its usefulness and quality.

5. Looking at the Data

A purist may prefer not to look at the data before starting the modelling process, being worried that a subtle form of data mining can occur. In practice, it is essential at least to look at plots of the individual series against time to establish what are the major features of the data that the model must capture. If the series contains a strong upward trend in mean, then a model that is unable to capture this trend is clearly not a good candidate to be an acceptable model. Some possible dominant features are trends in mean or variance, strong seasonal components or the long swings associated with unit root components.

The plots may also suggest various kinds of data problems, such as outliers, missing data, sudden changes in level or variance (suggesting a possible change of definition of a variable or a policy change). Each of these problems have to be considered and resolved. Missing data can be handled by the use of dummies or by interpolation, for example. Outliers can either be dealt with by sophisticated techniques or by simple ones. What exactly is an outlier is often a judgement made by the researcher who also has to decide whether the outlier is part of the usual generating mechanism or something extraordinary. Whether or not outliers are removed from the data can make an enormous difference to the analysis – a pair of outliers k time units apart produces a considerable autocorrelation of lag k for a series, for example. The first phase of dealing with an outlier is to ask if the value really occurred or if it is a data handling error. If it is real, it is useful to know why it occurred, is it the result of a strike or extreme weather, or in the case of silver prices in late 1979, an attempt by some speculators to corner the silver market. If the reason for the outlier is some real, rare event which disrupts the usual generating mechanism, it is usual to remove the disturbed values and then to treat the gap as missing data. However, the context is important – if extreme weather disrupts house building, this can be viewed as useless data, but if one is modelling the effect of weather on residential electricity demand, then the extreme weather case may contain very valuable information about this relationship.

The plotting of series, both individually and jointly, is an essential step in the modelling process that is all too frequently missed by inexperienced researchers. Similarly, plots of residuals from models may well contain important information.

6. Balanced Equations

If the variable being explained by a model, the dependent variable, has some dominant features, a minimum condition for the model to be satisfactory is that the explanatory variables should be capable of explaining this feature. Examples of such dominant features are strong autocorrelation and long swings (particularly a unit root at zero frequency in the autoregressive part of the generating mechanism), a strong seasonal (particularly unit roots at season frequencies), a trend in mean (perhaps defined as a monotonic component in the unconditional mean), or a trend in variance. In a linear model,

$$Y_t = \beta X_t + \text{residual} \tag{1}$$

if Y_t has any of these features, the X_t also will have to contain similar features for X_t to explain Y_t, otherwise these strong features will have to appear in the residual, which will then have undesirable features for estimation and inference. An equation which has X_t having the same dominant features as Y_t will be called *balanced*. Thus if X_t is I(0), Y_t is $I(1)$, the equation will not be balanced, but if the dependent variable is ΔY_t, the equation is then balanced. It is a necessary condition that a specified model be balanced for the model to be satisfactory. However, it is not a sufficient condition, as has been pointed out by Yule (1926), Granger and Newbold (1974) and Phillips (1987) when discussing spurious regressions. It is pointed out in these papers that if X_t, Y_t are *independent* $I(1)$ series and a regression of the form (1) is estimated by ordinary least-squares, then frequently one gets apparent significant relationships (with large t and F values). It is also found that the Durbin-Watson statistic is very low, which is an important warning signal that a spurious regression has been obtained and that the residual is far from white noise.

The existence of these dominant features can either be determined by the prior viewing of the data, as discussed in the previous section, or in some cases by formal testing, especially for unit roots (see for example Phillips and Perron, 1988; Dickey and Fuller, 1981; and Hylleberg, Engle, Granger and Yoo (1988).

It might be noted that if X_t is Y_{t-1}, or includes this or other lags of the dependent variable, the equation is automatically balanced. This clearly illustrates the advantage of using dynamic specifications and proper information sets.

Some of the consequences of balanced equations can be illustrated using the zero frequency unit root dominant component. Suppose that Y_t has a univariate model

$$a(B) (1 - B)^d Y_t = c(B) \varepsilon_t$$

where $a(1) \neq 0$, $c(1) \neq 0$, and ε_t is a zero mean, white noise process. Further suppose that all the roots of $a(z) = 0$ lie outside the unit circle $|z| = 1$, so that $(1 - B)^d Y_t$ is stationary. Y_t is called integrated of order d, denoted $Y_t \sim I(d)$ and the only values of d used here are 0 and 1. An $I(1)$ process contains long-swings, has long memory and dominates an $I(0)$ process, in that an $I(1)$ plus an $I(0)$ process is always $I(1)$.

A pair of unbalanced equations of form (1) are (i) $Y_t \sim I(1)$, $X_t \sim I(0)$ and (ii) $Y_t \sim I(0)$, $X_t \sim I(1)$. If the models are augmented, balanced equations are quickly found, by adding Y_{t-1} as an explanatory variable in (i) and X_{t-1} in (ii). When there are a pair of explanatory variables X_{1t}, X_{2t} and an equation is formed as

$$Y_t = \beta_1 X_{1t} + \beta_2 X_{2t} + \text{residual} \tag{2}$$

then if $Y_t \sim I(0)$, X_{1t}, X_{2t} both $I(1)$ generally the equation is unbalanced, but balancing may occur if X_{1t}, X_{2t} are cointegrated. If there exists a linear combination $Z_t = X_{1t} - A X_{2t}$ that is $I(0)$, then the X's are said to be cointegrated and a balanced form of (2) occurs:

$$Y_t = \gamma Z_t + \text{residual}.$$

Cointegration is discussed in Granger (1986) and a number of tests for cointegration are available.

If a dynamic explanatory equation is considered of the form

$$\alpha(B)Y_t = \beta(B)X_t + \text{white noise residual}$$

(with a single explanatory variable X_t), where Y_t, X_t are both $I(1)$ then it follows that either X_t, Y_t are cointegrated, or that $\alpha(1) = 0$ and either $\beta(B) \equiv 0$ or $\beta(1) \equiv 0$. This is easily seen by writing $\alpha(B) = \alpha_0 + \alpha(1 - B)\alpha^*(B)$ and $\beta(B) = \beta_0 + (1 - B) \beta^*(B)$ where it may be assumed that $\alpha^*(1) \neq 0$ and $\beta^*(1) \neq 0$.

Gathering terms gives

$$(\alpha_0 Y_t - \beta_0 X_t) = -\alpha^*(B)\alpha\Delta Y_t + \beta^*(B)\Delta X_t + \text{residual}.$$

The conclusion arises because all terms must be $I(0)$.

7. Where Are the Controversies?

A convenient way to introduce a number of important topics is to consider areas of controversy in the econometric methodology literature.

A. *Controversies concerning the modelling process.*

(a) Start big or start small?   Should a modeller start with a small model, test for missing variables and then expand the model, or should a large model be the starting point and then tests for simplification applied?

(b) Should models be simplified?   In a search for simplicity – or parsimony – should 'insignificant' terms be dropped from the model. Will the simpler model generally perform better than the original model?

(c) How should the information set be chosen?   How should the information set used in the modelling process be selected, should it be large or small, how should one choose between alternative definitions of some possible explanatory variable? Should the information set be selected by the use of some economic theory or less formally?

(d) Should Bayesian priors be used?   Should a Bayesian technique be used, such as tight priors on coefficients? Should such priors be used on all coefficients, including covariances of residuals, or just on a few selected coefficients? Should the chosen priors be carefully justified?

(e) Should the model specification be based on economic theory?   Should the model be based on some well-founded theory, such as an optimizing typical agent theory? Should the model be constrained so that the theory must hold or merely so that the theory can be true? What if there are several competing theories? What happens to the theory when it is passed through the aggregation window?

(f) How to choose the functional form?   What functional forms to consider and which to use?

(g) Number of equations?   Should a single equation or multiple equation model be constructed, if the latter, how many equations?

(h) Should the model include contemporaneous explanatory variables? Should the dependent variable at time t be explained by other variables also measured at time t, or should only reduced forms be specified? Temporal aggregation will suggest that contemporaneous variables should be used but spurious relationships may be found.

(i) Do different objectives lead to different models?   Should different models be constructed for forecasting, control and hypothesis testing?

There are also some questions concerning evaluation and interpretation.

B. Controversies concerning evaluation and interpretation

(a) Out-of-sample evaluation?

Should an 'out-of-sample' evaluation be used, such as a forecasting comparison or a cross-validation exercise?

(b) Diagnostic tests?

Should a battery of diagnostic tests be used to check the specification and to suggest respecification?

(c) Usefulness of extreme bounds analysis.

Should an extreme bounds analysis be used to check the fragileness of the model? Leamer has pointed out that alternative specifications of a model can produce quite different estimates of some key parameter, thus making interpretation of this parameter different. The idea has been strongly attacked in the literature but other papers give support for the idea. A discussion occurs before Part I of the readings.

(d) How should models be compared?

Should the producer specify his own alternative models or use those of others in a comparison exercise?

It can be argued that the decisions made about these various questions will affect producers and consumers differently. Provided that the producer

Table 2.   Who Cares?

Controversy	Producer	Consumer
(1) Modelling		
a. Starting big or small	yes	no
b. Model simplification	yes	no
c. Choice of information set	yes	yes
d. Bayesian priors used	yes	no
e. Use of theory	yes	yes
f. functional forms	yes	yes
g. Single or multiple use	yes	yes
h. use of contemporaneous	yes	no
i. objective relevance	yes	yes
(2) Evaluation		
a. Out-of-sample	no	yes
b. Diagnostic tests	yes	no
c. Extreme bounds	no	yes
d. Compare with other models	yes	yes

undertakes a complete evaluation exercise for his or her model, the consumer should not care about the modelling strategy that produced the model. For example, if tight Bayesian priors were used in making the model, this should be of no concern to the consumer provided an alternative model is also produced using weaker priors and found to be inferior. Similar arguments exist for the other controversies. A tentative listing of who cares about the various controversial questions is shown in Table 2, all based on the assumption that a complete evaluation exercise *was conducted and reported*. If no such exercise is available, the consumer should care a great deal about all of the questions.

A brief discussion of controversies (a), (b) and (c) is given in Section 8, (d) and (e) are discussed in Section 9. Topics (f) and (g) are not discussed as they are standard, but very important modelling decisions. Section 10 considers topics (h) and (i) and evaluation questions are considered in Section 11.

8. Big or Small? Parsimony

There are quite different strategies available concerning the 'size' of the initial model. The now traditional pure time series modelling techniques, associated with Box and Jenkins (1970), goes from simple to complex. Starting with a single series, so that Y_t is explained by just its own past, simple AR(p) or MA(q) models are considered, with increasing p, q values. Next, bivariate models might be considered, with some 'obvious' explanatory variable X_t used in a dynamic specification, with both Y_t and X_t explained by the past values of these series. The next stage might be to build vector autoregressive (VAR) models, VARMA models, using three or more variables, modelled jointly, using perhaps the techniques discussed in Granger and Newbold (1987). The increasingly complex models can be compared by the ability to forecast one or more pre-specified variables, for example.

Many writers prefer a quite different tactic, of starting with a large information set, or vector of explanatory variables, using initially a rich specification and then testing for simplification. This process, of going from large to small, is supported by the LSE group, for example.

A more conservative approach, which is frequently used, is to start with a moderately sized model and to consider both simplifications and also expansions of the model, using various specification tests.

The idea of 'size' used has two dimensions, the number of explanatory variables and the number of lags used with these variables. At the two extremes, a time series model might use no explanatory variables but consider many lags of the dependent variable whereas the constructor of a large-scale econometric model may use thousands of variables but only a few lags. Clearly there are many strategies available and there seems to be no clear dominance of one over the others. The bigger the model, the more parameters have to be estimated, more specifications have to be considers topics (h) and (i) and evaluation questions are considered in Section 11.

If one has many possible explanatory variables which can enter a model at many lags, it is easy to suggest plausible models containing too many parameters for successful estimation to be likely. A vector autoregression involving N variables and p lags involves in the order of N^2p parameters, so that if $N = 10$, $p = 4$ there are 400 parameters to be estimated from 2000 pieces of data, say, if 200 terms are available for each series. It is clear why there is a desire for simpler models.

A strategy applied by many modellers is the principle of parsimony.

The Principle of Parsimony

If two models appear to fit the data equally well, choose the simpler model (that is the one involving the fewest parameters). This principle is proposed by Box and Jenkins (1972) when considering the modelling of time series. They suggest that the fewer parameters that have to be estimated, the better estimates will result. Parsimony is related to Ockham's Razor and the Jeffreys–Wrinch simplicity postulate discussed by Zellner (1986). Jeffreys (1967, p. 47) says that 'simpler laws have the greater prior probabilities' and earlier that laws 'should ... be put in an order of decreasing prior probability'. Zellner says that scientists may have the belief that 'sophistically simple hypotheses or models will probably work well in explaining facts and in prediction'. He goes on to challenge anyone to find a very complicated model in any area that has performed well in explanation or prediction. These ideas do not necessarily mean that scientists believe that the world is simple; merely that simple but sophisticated models can provide very good approximations to the actual DGP, and that going on to more complicated models will not buy much in terms of extra performance.

Naturally, their views are not unchallenged. A univariate time series modeller can claim that a few lags is no worse than using many lags, a large-scale macro modeller may argue that one involving fifty equations will fit the economy as well as a model having a thousand equations. As most simple models can be nested in a larger one, in principle both can be estimated and their relative specifications tested by a likelihood ratio test.

It is certainly true that a simple model is easier to appreciate and to interpret, and so is more likely to be influential in changing peoples beliefs about some topic or hypothesis. There is thus probably a preference for such simple models by both the contractors of models and their consumers.

9.   The Use of Additional Information: Theory Priors

It is obviously appropriate for the constructor of a model to utilize any information that is considered to be relevant. This information can be numerical, such as the outcome of a consumer's buying intention survey, may take the form of a belief and thus be expressible as a Bayesian prior on some parameter, or can be a particular specification suggested by some economic theory. The problem with using such additional information is that the model producer has to convince the potential consumer of the model that the information is relevant and that the model is improved by using it. I will consider the three examples given above from the viewpoint of a consumer. If an unconventional explanatory series is used, such as the Michigan index of consumer sentiment, for example, the consumer's attitude towards this use may depend on the way that the model will be utilized. For purposes of forecasting, any information that produces better forecasts is probably acceptable (provided that, in practice, the information is available quickly so that forecasts can be easily formed). However, if the model is to be used for policy purposes or to test some theory, more careful justification is required. The new explanatory variables can be thought of as surrogates for missing expectations by consumers, say, but this has to be shown to be reasonable and also that more conventional expectation estimates are not superior. If a model using the unconventional variables is shown to be superior in various dimensions to ones not using them, their use will be justified.

Similarly, a model using tight Bayesian priors should be shown to be superior to one using weak priors or none at all. The producer may well not be able to be convincing about why a particular prior is used but if the resulting model is better, using a 'fair' test, it may well be acceptable to the consumer. Clearly, it is helpful to be a good Bayesian, so that one's experiences help produce useful priors, but a poor Bayesian is inferior to a non-Bayesian in terms of the quality of the model produced. A good Bayesian essentially increases the effective sample size by excluding certain parts of the parameter space from analysis.

The use of economic theory is very controversial. Some writers insist that a model be based on an optimizing behaviour of individual economic agents, whereas others largely reject the usefulness of such theory (see Sims, Chapter 8, for example). The first group need consider not just a theory relevant to a 'typical agent' but clearly need to discuss the effect of passing the results of this theory through the aggregation window.

Most writers seem to agree that an economic theory is useful to provide an initial model specification, realizing that this theory will almost certainly be insufficient for a complete, dynamic specification, with some missing or poorly measured variables. It seems to be generally agreed that a theory should not be binding on the model, but should be allowed to be true within the model. It then becomes an empirical question as to whether or not the theory is true. If a producer insists on building a model based on a binding theory, this model needs to be shown to be superior to models not so constrained.

In all of these cases the consumer needs to be shown that the extra information is helpful for the quality of the model, so that the evaluation exercise becomes again of critical importance.

10. Modelling Objectives and the Use of Contemporaneous Variables

The three objectives usually given for modelling are, of course, to provide forecasts, to suggest policies and to test a hypothesis about the economy. An important question to ask is – should one build different models for different objectives? If one believed in the existence of a true generating mechanism that was attainable, then only one model is required, but given that models are only approximations to the truth, and perhaps inadequate ones, then different models may be appropriate. Suppose that there are two models, A built for policy purposes and B for forecasting. One can ask if A is a plausible model if B produces the better forecasts? What would the reverse question be, given that it is extremely difficult to evaluate a policy model? An adequate evaluation is not 'this is what would have happened if policies had been based on this model' unless actual policies were so based, and then to what would the outcomes be compared? In all cases the use of the model is only optimal conditional on the model specification being correct, and if the estimation method is sound. If models are only approximations it is unclear how to evaluate them for objectives other than for forecasting.

The situation is made more difficult if the producer of the model uses contemporaneous variables. As the inputs to a decision process necessarily temporally precede the observed outputs to this process, it can be argued that explanatory variables should enter a model with lags. However, temporal aggregation removes this argument, and suggests the use of contemporaneous explanatory variables. A difficulty arises because the direction of explanation, or causality, is disrupted by temporal aggregation. Thus, if one is comparing the two models

$$Y_t = \beta_0 X_{t-1} + \beta_1 Y_{t-1} + \text{residual}$$
$$Y_t = \gamma_0 X_t + \gamma_1 Y_{t-1} + \text{residual}$$

the second may appear to fit better because it is nearer to the truth or because $Y_{t-\varepsilon}$ is a good explanation of X_t, where ε is small (at least much less than one in size). If the purpose of the model is to provide forecasts, the two specifications will be (asymptotically) identical given an optimal forecasting model for X_t. (Rob Engle has an unpublished theorem to this effect.) However, for the other objectives, the implications may be quite different whether or not contemporaneous variables are used. I think that this is a question deserving a great deal more discussion both by producers and consumers of models.

11. Evaluation Questions

There are many ways of evaluating models ranging from the inadequate and simplistic, such as comparing R^2 values, to the inventive and ambitious, such as encompassing tests, discussed in chapters 7 and 17, for example. Evaluation is used both by the producer to decide if the current form of the model is adequate and by the consumer to judge the relative quality of the model compared to others.

To meet the basic objective of being able to influence consumers the evaluation exercise should probably contain discussion of:

(1) What pre-analysis was conducted, such as trend removal, seasonal adjustment, removal of outliers and missing values, how definitional changes of recorded variables were dealt with and such like? There may also be an investigation into some stylized facts for the variables, such as their order of integration or whether or not they contain a strong seasonal.
(2) What specification search was undertaken to reach the 'final model'?
(3) What assumptions were made for the analysis (e.g. normality); what theory was assumed to be in force, if any; what identification or other constraints were applied to the model; and what Bayesian priors were used, plus convincing reasons?
(4) The results of using different estimation procedures.
(5) The quality of the data used.

The evaluation analysis may also include for

(1) Single models: goodness of fit statistics, correlogram of residuals, diagnostic tests for various problems (time-varying parameters, missing variables, heteroskedasticity) plus an 'out-of-sample evaluation', such as the properties of out-of-sample forecasts or the results of a cross-validation exercise.
(2) Comparison with other models: comparison of post-sample forecasts, perhaps by considering combining of forecasts, and encompassing tests.

Table 3.

No. of models	Percentage, best in-sample model, also best out-of-sample
3	62
4	35
5	37
6–13	18

It is, of course, important to have good alternative models against which to compare one's own. This suggests that the consumer is better off having several producers each carefully constructing models using quite different strategies. Consumers would be worse off if one particular modelling technique becomes dominant and generally adopted. At this time such a situation is not in sight, as there are many sensible alternatives, as seen in the papers that follow.

The use of out-of-sample data in the evaluation exercise is somewhat controversial. If a model has been specified and estimated on some given set of data, it is unclear whether or not the same data should be used to evaluate the model. A time series model may be identified and estimated using data for the period $t = 1, \ldots, N$ and then evaluated using the period $N + 1, \ldots N + H$. Alternative models can be compared using their forecasting ability over the later period ('out-of-sample'). For example, using the specification achieved from the first period ('in-sample'), true forecasts can be made at times $N + 1, N + 2, \ldots, N + H - h$ for horizons $1, 2, \ldots, h$ steps ahead. Each forecast uses just data up to the time of the forecast, the forecasts can be compared to actuals, and sums of squared forecasts errors obtained separately for each of the horizons. If a model has been obtained from an extensive data mine of the sample, its in-sample error will underestimate the out-of-sample forecasting ability of the model and the 'best' in-sample model may not prove best out-of-sample. Mayer (1975) reviews a number of actual empirical projects in which several models are constructed in-sample and then are compared out-of-sample. He found the percentages shown in Table 3.

It would be interesting to know the percentage of times that the best in-sample model was significantly worse than the model that performed best out-of-sample. These results could suggest that several models performed almost equally well in-sample, or that data mining had occurred, or that there was parameter instability between the in- and out-of-sample periods.

The best division of the available data into 'in' and 'out' of sample periods seems to be unclear at this time.

12. Conclusions and Basic Readings

This introductory chapter has attempted to raise questions about the modelling process rather than suggest solutions. Some solutions are proposed in the following papers, although a great deal of further work is required on virtually every aspect of econometric methodology.

A reader will require a sound basic knowledge of econometrics to appreciate the papers fully. A list of a few appropriate books and journals is given below.

A reasonable starting point in learning econometrics is the text *Econometrics*, by G. S. Maddala (McGraw-Hill, 1977) which takes a practical, fairly modern viewpoint. A much more comprehensive account is *The Theory and Practice of Econometrics*, by G. G. Judge, W. E. Griffith, R. C. Hill, H. Lutkepohl and T-C. Lee (Wiley, 2nd edn, 1985), which is particularly useful on specification tests. For time series econometrics the obvious places seem to be *The Econometric Analysis of Time Series*, by A. C. Harvey (Philip Allan, Oxford, 1985) and C. W. J. Granger and P. Newbold's *Forecasting Economic Time Series*, Academic Press (2nd edn, 1987). The three-volume *Handbook* of *Econometrics*, edited by Z. Griliches and M. D. Intrilligator (North Holland, 1986) contains a wealth of information, including a very useful discussion on 'Wald, likelihood ratio and Lagrange multiplier tests', by R. F. Engle (Chapter 13, Volume II). A clear history and overview of econometrics has been provided by M. H. Pesaran in the *New Palgrave Dictionary of Economics*, edited by J. Eatwell, M. Milgate and P. Newman (Macmillan, 1987).

The journals containing most articles in econometrics are the *Journal of Econometrics, The Journal of Applied Econometrics*, and *Econometric Theory*. *Econometrica* occasionally publishes papers in the area.

Two recent discussions on econometric methodology at conferences are reported in journals: the Lake Arrowhead Econometrics Conference in the *Journal of Econometrics*, and the Australian Bicentennial Conference at the Australian National University will appear in the *Economic Record*, both in 1989.

References

Box, G. E. P. and Jenkins, G. M. (1970), *Time series analysis, forecasting and control*. Holden-Day, San Francisco.

Denton, F. T. (1985), Data mining as an industry, *Review of Economics and Statistics*, 67, 124–7.

Dickey, D. A. and Fuller, W. A. (1981), Likelihood ratio statistics for autoregressive time series with a unit root, *Econometrica*, 9, 1055–72.

Granger, C. W. J. (1986), Developments in the study of co-integrated economic variables, *Oxford Bulletin of Economics and Statistics*, 68, 213–28.

Granger, C. W. J. (1987), Implications of aggregation with common factors, *Econometric Theory*, 3, 208–22.

Granger, C. W. J. (1988), Aggregation of time series variables – a survey. Institute for Empirical Macroeconomics, Discussion Paper 1, Federal Reserve Bank of Minneapolis.

Granger, C. W. J. and Newbold P., (1974), Spurious regressions in econometrics, *Journal of Econometrics*, 2, 111–20.

Granger, C. W. J. and Newbold, P. (1987), *Forecasting economic time series*. Academic Press, San Francisco.

Hylleberg, S., Engle, R. F., Granger, C. W. J. and Yoo, S. (1988), Seasonal integration and co-integration. UCSD Department of Economics Working Paper.

Jeffreys, H. (1967), *Theory of probability*. Oxford University Press, Oxford.

Leamer, E. E. (1978), *Specification searches, ad hoc inference with non-experimental data*. John Wiley Sons, New York.

Leamer, E. E. (1987), Specification problems in econometrics, *The Palgrave, A Dictionary of Economics*, ed. by J. Eastwell, M. Milgate and P. Newman. Mac millan Press, London.

Little, I. M. D. (1962), Higgledy, piggledy growth, *Oxford Bulletin of Economics and Statistics*, 24, 387–412.

Lovell, M.C. (1983), Data mining, *Review of Economics and Statistics*, 65, 1–12.

Mayer, T. (1975), Selecting economic hypothesis by goodness of fit, *Journal of Political Economy*, 86, 877–83.

Phillips, P. C. B. (1986), Understanding spurious regressions in econometrics, *Journal of Econometrics*, 33, 311–40.

Phillips, P. C. B. and Perron P. (1988), Testing for a unit root in time series regression, *Biometrika*, 75, 335–66.

Theil, H. (1957), Specification errors and the estimation of economic relationships, *Review of the International Statistical Institute*, 25, 41–51.

Weiss, A. (1984), Systematic sampling and temporal aggregation in time series models, *Journal of Econometrics*, 26, 271–81.

Yule, G. U. (1926), Why do we sometimes get nonsense correlations between time series? *Journal of the Royal Statistical Society*, 89, 1–64.

Zellner, A. (1986), Bayesian analysis in econometrics. MRG Working Paper No. M8610, University of Southern California.

PART I

Basic Methodological Issues

Introduction

Doing econometrics is like trying to learn the laws of electricity by playing the radio. (Guy Orcutt)

That applied econometrics is not currently in the most robust of health is hard to deny. (McAleer, Pagan and Volker – paper 2)

In order to draw inferences from data as described by econometric texts, it is necessary to make whimsical assumptions. (Leamer – paper 1)

It is easy to be critical of applied work, perhaps particularly in econometrics which tries to be sophisticated in both model development and in application. The point of being critical is not merely to indicate real problems with current research but to provoke responses from those who believe that they have answers. The papers in this first section illustrate both the critical questions about the quality of the present work and also the responses. In the first paper Leamer discusses many important and relevant problems with the usual modelling process and the interpretation of the resulting model. He describes these as being both fragile (small changes in specification lead to big changes in important parameters) and whimsical (the models are based on assumptions and procedures that are difficult to defend). He suggests the use of 'extreme bounds analysis' (EBA), discussed further below, to help interpret models with such problems. In their response, McAleer, Pagan and Volker (paper 2) attack the usefulness of EBA, suggest a process of modelling that is less arbitrary, and propose criteria for judging the quality of a model. They then suggest that an earlier critical discussion of time series modelling by Cooley and LeRoy fails to meet these criteria. Paper 3, by Breusch, presents a simple proof of Leamer's extreme bounds analysis. Papers 4 and 5 are the responses by Cooley and LeRoy and by Leamer to paper 2. There is not a great deal of agreement between the two sides.

The final three papers in this section present a more optimistic approach to the problems of modelling. Pagan (paper 6) critically discusses three particular approaches, due to Leamer (essentially Bayesian), to Sims (vector autoregression), and the LSE group (progressive time series modelling). He seems to believe that all three methods have useful qualities and also real practical difficulties. Hendry and Mizon (paper 7) suggest that acceptable models can be achieved but that 'serendipity ... is desirable if we are to break out of the straitjacket of received theory'. They discuss papers 1, 2 and 4 but claim that 'whimsy has no role in the modelling process'. They also emphasize the difference between producers and consumers of models. The final paper in this section, by Sims, presents a very strong criticism of the identification constraints used in classical simultaneous models. He then advocates the use of VAR models and suggests that they have useful interpretations.

Leamer's paper 1 quickly gets to a main difficulty in interpretation of any statistical model, much of statistical methodology is based on experimental design and randomization, whereas economic data are not generated in this fashion. If one had a correctly specified model, or a good approximation to the generating mechanism, this would not be a problem, but Leamer contends that the specifications used by actual researchers are whimsical, being based on assumptions or procedures that are difficult to define. As different researchers will use different specifications based on their own views of what models are reasonable, the literature may potentially generate a wide variety of models. Leamer points out that this may lead to a fragility of important parameter values in the model. To illustrate the basic ideas, suppose that a variable Y_t is explained by X_{ot} and possibly also a group of other explanatory variables X_{jt}, $j = 1, \ldots, n$. Suppose that all workers use X_{ot} but can use any part of the group X_{jt}, $j > 0$. If the parameter on X_{ot} is of particular interest, to test a theory or for determining a policy, and if the model is linear and estimated by OLS, a wide variety of estimated values of the parameter of interest can arise from the alternative specifications. The maximum and minimum values of these estimates give the extreme bounds of the parameter. The theory of these extreme bounds is given by Breusch in paper 3. The bounds can be very wide but their usefulness is discussed critically by McAleer, Pagan and Volker (paper 2) and by Breusch. One problem is that the bounds may come from models that might be viewed as having quite unreasonable specifications by most researchers. A recent paper, not included here, by Granger and Uhlig (1988), considers the extent of the extreme bounds using model specifications having R^2 values only K per cent less than the maximum R^2 achievable, using all the X_{jt} variables, $j > 0$. For quite low values of K, say 4 or 10 per cent, the range of the extreme bounds can still be rather wide, so that the model is still fragile in Leamer's terminology.

The sequence of papers in this section will introduce the reader to some of the controversies and difficulties in econometric methodology, plus some of the strategies to circumnavigate these problems. These papers set up the modelling strategies and the evaluation procedures discussed in the later papers.

Reference

Granger, C. W. J. and Uhlig Harold F. (1988), Reasonable extreme bounds analysis. Discussion Paper 2, Institute for Empirical Macroeconomics, Federal Reserve Bank of Minneapolis.

1

Let's Take the Con out of Econometrics

Edward E. Leamer

Econometricians would like to project the image of agricultural experimenters who divide a farm into a set of smaller plots of land and who select
randomly the level of fertilizer to be used on each plot. If some plots are
assigned a certain amount of fertilizer while others are assigned none, then
the difference between the mean yield of the fertilized plots and the mean
yield of the unfertilized plots is a measure of the effect of fertilizer on
agricultural yields. The econometrician's humble job is only to determine if
that difference is large enough to suggest a real effect of fertilizer, or is so
small that it is more likely due to random variation.

This image of the applied econometrician's art is grossly misleading. I
would like to suggest a more accurate one. The applied econometrician is
like a farmer who notices that the yield is somewhat higher under trees
where birds roost, and he uses this as evidence that bird droppings increase
yields. However, when he presents this finding at the annual meeting of the
American Ecological Association, another farmer in the audience objects
that he used the same data but came up with the conclusion that moderate
amounts of shade increase yields. A bright chap in the back of the room
then observes that these two hypotheses are indistinguishable, given the
available data. He mentions the phrase 'identification problem', which,
though no one knows quite what he means, is said with such authority that
it is totally convincing. The meeting reconvenes in the halls and in the bars,
with heated discussion whether this is the kind of work that merits
promotion from Associate to Full Farmer; the Luminists strongly opposed
to promotion and the Aviophiles equally strong in favour.

One should not jump to the conclusion that there is necessarily a
substantive difference between drawing inferences from experimental as
opposed to non-experimental data. The images I have drawn are deliberately prejudicial. First, we had the experimental scientist with hair neatly
combed, wide eyes peering out of horn-rimmed glasses, a white coat, and
an electronic calculator for generating the random assignment of fertilizer
treatment to plots of land. This seems to contrast sharply with the non-

This article first appeared in *American Economic Review*, Vol. 23, no. 1, March 1983,
pp. 31–43.

experimental farmer with overalls, unkempt hair, and bird droppings on his boots. Another image, drawn by Orcutt, is even more damaging: 'Doing econometrics is like trying to learn the laws of electricity by playing the radio'. However, we need not now submit to the tyranny of images, as many of us have in the past.

1.   Is Randomization Essential?

What is the real difference between these two settings? Randomization seems to be the answer. In the experimental setting the fertilizer treatment is 'randomly' assigned to plots of land, whereas in the other case nature did the assignment. Now it is the tyranny of words that we must resist. 'Random' does not mean adequately mixed in *every* sample. It only means that, on the average, the fertilizer treatments are adequately mixed. Randomization implies that the least squares estimator is 'unbiased', but that definitely does not mean that for each sample the estimate is correct. Sometimes the estimate is too high, sometimes too low. I am reminded of the lawyer who remarked that 'when I was a young man I lost many cases that I should have won, but when I grew older I won many that I should have lost, so on the average justice was done'.

In particular, it is possible for the randomized assignment to lead to exactly the same allocation as the non-random assignment, namely, with treated plots of land all being under trees and with non-treated plots of land all being away from trees. I submit that, if this is the outcome of the randomization, then the randomized experiment and the non-randomized experiment are exactly the same. Many econometricians would insist that there is a difference, because the randomized experiment generates 'unbiased' estimates. But all this means is that, if this particular experiment yields a gross overestimate, some other experiment yields a gross underestimate.

Randomization thus does not assure that each and every experiment is 'adequately mixed', but randomization does make 'adequate mixing' probable. In order to make clear what I believe to be the true value of randomization, let me refer to the model

$$(1) \qquad\qquad Y_i = \alpha + \beta F_i + \gamma L_i + U_i,$$

where Y_i is the yield of plot i; F_i is the fertilizer assigned to plot i; L_i is the light falling on plot i; U_i is the unspecified influence on the yield of plot i, and where β, the fertilizer effect, is the object of the inferential exercise. We may suppose to begin the argument that the light level is expensive to measure and that it is decided to base an estimate of β initially only on measurement of Y_i and F_i. We may assume also that the natural experiment produces values for F_i, L_i, and U_i with expected values

$E(U_i|F_i) = 0$ and $E(L_i|F_i) = r_0 + r_1F_i$. In the more familiar parlance, it is assumed that the fertilizer level and the residual effects are uncorrelated, but the fertilizer level and the light level are possibly correlated. As every beginning econometrics student knows, if you omit from a model a variable which is correlated with included variables, bad things happen. These bad things are revealed to the econometrician by computing the conditional mean of Y given F but not L:

$$
\begin{aligned}
(2) \qquad E(Y|F) &= \alpha + \beta F + \gamma E(L|F) \\
&= \alpha + \beta F + \gamma(r_0 + r_1 F) \\
&\equiv (\alpha + \alpha^*) + (\beta + \beta^*)F,
\end{aligned}
$$

where $\alpha^* = \gamma r_0$ and $\beta^* = \gamma r_1$. The linear regression of Y on f provides estimates of the parameters of the conditional distribution of Y given F, and in this case the regression coefficients are estimates not of α and β, but rather of $\alpha + \alpha^*$ and $\beta + \beta^*$. The parameters α^* and β^* measure the bias in the least squares estimates. This bias could be due to left-out variables, or to measurement errors in F, or to simultaneity.

When observing a non-experiment, the bias parameters α^* and β^* can be thought to be small, but they cannot sensibly be treated as exact zeroes. The notion that the bias parameters are small can be captured by the assumption that α^* and β^* are drawn from a normal distribution with zero means and covariance matrix M. The model can then be written as $Y = \alpha + \beta F + \varepsilon$, where ε is the sum of three random variables: $U + \alpha^* + \beta^*F$. Because the error term ε is not spherical, the proper way to estimate α and β is generalized least squares. My 1974 article demonstrates that if (a, b) represent the least-squares estimates of (α, β), then the generalized least squares estimates $(\hat{\alpha}, \hat{\beta})$ are also equal to (a, b):

$$
(3) \qquad \begin{pmatrix} \hat{\alpha} \\ \hat{\beta} \end{pmatrix} = \begin{pmatrix} a \\ b \end{pmatrix},
$$

and if S represents the sample covariance matrix for the least squares estimates, then the sample covariance matrix for $(\hat{\alpha}, \hat{\beta})$ is

$$
(4) \qquad \mathrm{Var}(\hat{\alpha}, \hat{\beta}) = S + M,
$$

where M is the covariance matrix of (α^*, β^*).

The meaning of equation (1.3) is that unless one knows the direction of the bias, the possibility of bias does not call for any adjustment to the estimates. The possibility of bias does require an adjustment to the covariance matrix (1.4). The uncertainty is composed of two parts: the usual sampling uncertainty S plus the misspecification uncertainty M. As sample size grows, the sampling uncertainty S ever decreases, but the misspecification uncertainty M remains ever constant. The misspecification matrix M that we must add to the least-squares variance matrix is just the (prior) variance of the bias coefficients (α^*, β^*). If this variance matrix is small, the least-squares bias is likely to be small. If M is large, it is correspondingly probable that (α^*, β^*) is large.

It would be a remarkable bootstrap if we could determine the extent of the misspecification from the data. The data in fact contain no information about the size of the bias, a point which is revealed by studying the likelihood function. The misspecification matrix M is therefore a pure prior concept. One must decide independent of the data how good the non-experiment is.

The formal difference between a randomized experiment and a natural experiment is measured by the matrix M. If the treatment is randomized, the bias parameters (α^*, β^*) are exactly zero, or, equivalently, the matrix M is zero matrix. If M is zero, the least-squares estimates are consistent. If M is not zero, as in the natural experiment, there remains a fixed amount of specification uncertainty, independent of sample size.

There is therefore a sharp difference between inference from randomized experiments and inference from natural experiments. This seems to draw a sharp distinction between economics where randomized experiments are rare, and 'science' where experiments are routinely done. But the fact of the matter is that no one has ever designed an experiment that is free of bias, and no one can. As it turns out, the technician who was assigning fertilizer levels to plots of land, took his calculator into the fields, and when he was out in the sun, the calculator got heated up and generated large 'random' numbers, which the technician took to mean no fertilizer; and when he stood under the shade of the trees, his cool calculator produced small numbers, and these plots received fertilizer.

You may object that this story is rather fanciful, but I need only make you think it is possible, to force you to set $M \neq 0$. Or if you think a computer can really produce random numbers (calculated by a mathematical formula and therefore perfectly predictable!), I will bring up mis-measurement of the fertilizer level, or human error in carrying out the computer instructions. Thus, the attempt to randomize and the attempt to measure accurately ensures that M is small, but not zero, and the difference between scientific experiments and natural experiments is difference in degree, but not in kind. Admittedly, however, the misspecification uncertainty in many experimental settings may be so small that it is well approximated by zero. This can very rarely be said in non-experimental settings.

Examples may be ultimately convincing. There is a great deal of empirical knowledge in the science of astronomy, yet there are no experiments. Medical knowledge is another good example. I was struck by a headline in the 5 January, 1982 *New York Times*: 'Life saving benefits of low-cholesterol diet affirmed in *rigorous* study'. The article describes a randomized experiment with a control group and a treated group.

'Rigorous' is therefore interpreted as 'randomized'. As a matter of fact, there was a great deal of evidence suggesting a link between heart disease and diet before any experiments were performed on humans. There were cross-cultural comparisons and there were animal studies. Actually, the only reason for performing the randomized experiment was that someone believed there was pretty clear non-experimental evidence to begin with. The non-experimental evidence was, of course, inconclusive, which in my language means that the misspecification uncertainty M remained uncomfortably large. The fact that the Japanese have both less incidence of heart disease and also diets lower in cholesterol compared to Americans is not convincing evidence, because there are so many other factors that remain unaccounted for. The fact that pigs on a high-cholesterol diet develop occluded arteries is also not convincing, because the similarity in physiology in pigs and humans can be questioned.

When the sampling uncertainty S gets small compared to the misspecification uncertainty M, it is time to look for other forms of evidence, experiments or non-experiments. Suppose I am interested in measuring the width of a coin, and I provide rulers to a room of volunteers. After each volunteer has reported a measurement, I compute the mean and standard deviation, and I conclude that the coin has width 1.325 millimetres with a standard error of 0.013. Since this amount of uncertainty is not to my liking, I propose to find three other rooms full of volunteers, thereby multiplying the sample size by four, and dividing the standard error in half. That is a silly way to get a more accurate measurement, because I have already reached the point where the sampling uncertainty S is very small compared with the misspecification uncertainty M. If I want to increase the true accuracy of my estimate, it is time for me to consider using a micrometer. So too in the case of diet and heart disease. Medical researchers had more or less exhausted the vein of non-experimental evidence, and it became time to switch to the more expensive but richer vein of experimental evidence.

In economics, too, we are switching to experimental evidence. There are the laboratory experiments of Charles Plott and Vernon Smith (1978) and Smith (1980), and there are the field experiments such as the Seattle/Denver income maintenance experiment. Another way to limit the misspecification error M is to gather different kinds of non-experiments. Formally speaking, we will say that experiment 1 is qualitatively different from experiment 2 if the bias parameters (α_1^*, β_1^*) are distributed independently of the bias parameters (α_2^*, β_2^*). In that event, simple averaging of the data from the two experiments yields average bias parameters $(\alpha_1^* + \alpha_2^*, \beta_1^* + \beta_2^*)/2$ with misspecification variance matrix $M/2$, half as large as the (common) individual variances. Milton Friedman's study of the permanent income hypothesis is the best example of this that I know. Other examples are hard to come by. I believe we need to put much more effort into identifying qualitatively different and convincing kinds of evidence.

Parenthetically, I note that traditional econometric theory, which does not admit experimental bias, as a consequence also admits no 'hard-core' propositions. Demand curves can be shown to be positively sloped. Utility can be shown not to be maximized. Econometric evidence of a positively sloped demand curve would, as a matter of fact, be routinely explained in terms of simultaneity bias. If utility seems not to have been maximized, it is only that the econometrician has misspecified the utility function. The mispecification matrix M thus forms Imre Lakatos' 'protective belt' which protects certain hard-core propositions from falsification.

2.   Is Control Essential?

The experimental scientist who notices that the fertilizer treatment is correlated with the light level can correct his experimental design. He can control the light level, or he can allocate the fertilizer treatment in such a way that the fertilizer level and the light level are not perfectly correlated.

The non-experimental scientist by definition cannot control the levels of extraneous influences such as light. But he can control for the variable light level by including light in the estimating equation. Provided nature does not select values for light and values for fertilizer levels that are perfectly correlated, the effect of fertilizer on yields can be estimated with a multiple regression. The collinearity in naturally selected treatment variables may mean that the data evidence is weak, but it does not invalidate in any way the usual least-squares estimates. Here, again, there is no essential difference between experimental and non-experimental inference.

3.   Are the Degrees of Freedom Inadequate with Non-experimental Data?

As a substitute for experimental control, the non-experimental researcher is obligated to include in the regression equation all variables that might have an important effect. The NBER data banks contain time-series data on 2000 macroeconomic variables. A model explaining gross national product in terms of all these variables would face a severe degrees-of-freedom deficit since the number of annual observations is less than thirty. Though the number of observations of any phenomenon is clearly limited, the number of explanatory variables is logically unlimited. if a polynomial could have a degree as high as k, it would usually be admitted that the degree could be $k + 1$ as well. A theory that allows k lagged explanatory variables would ordinarily allow $k + 1$. If the level of money might affect

GNP, then why not the number of presidential sneezes, or the size of the polar ice cap?

The number of explanatory variables is unlimited in a non-experimental setting, but it is also unlimited in an experimental setting. Consider again the fertilizer example in which the farmer randomly decides either to apply F_1 pounds of fertilizer per acre or zero pounds, and obtains the data illustrated in Figure 1. These data admit the inference that fertilizer level F_1 produces higher yields than no fertilizer. But the farmer is interested in selecting the fertilizer level that maximizes profits. If it is hypothesized that yield is a linear function of the fertilizer intensity $Y = \alpha + \beta F + U$, then profits are

$$\text{Profits} = pA(\alpha + \beta F + U) - p_F AF,$$

where A is total acreage, p is the product price, and p_F is the price per pound of fertilizer. This profit function is linear in F with slope $A(\beta p - p_F)$. The farmer maximizes profits therefore by using no fertilizer if the price of fertilizer is high, $\beta p < p_F$, and using an unlimited amount of fertilizer if the price is low, $\beta p > p_F$. It is to be expected that you will find this answer unacceptable for one of several reasons:

(1) When the farmer tries to buy an unlimited amount of fertilizer, he will drive up its price, and the problem should be reformulated to make p_F a function of F.
(2) Uncertainty in the fertilizer effect β causes uncertainty in profits, Variance (profits) $= p^2 A^2 F^2 \text{Var}(\beta)$, and risk aversion will limit the level of fertilizer applied.
(3) The yield function is nonlinear.

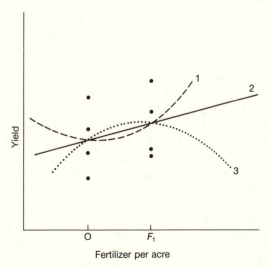

Figure 1   Hypothetical data and three estimated quadratic functions

Economic theorists doubtless find reasons (1) and (2) compelling, but I suspect that the real reason farmers don't use huge amounts of fertilizer is that the marginal increase in the yield eventually decreases. Plants don't grow in fertilizer alone.

So let us suppose that yield is a quadratic function of fertilizer intensity, $Y = \alpha + \beta_1 F + \beta_2 F^2 + U$, and suppose we have only the data illustrated in Figure 1. Unfortunately, there are an infinite number of quadratic functions all of which fit the data equally well, three of which are drawn. If there were no other information available, we could conclude only that the yield is higher at F_1 than at zero. Formally speaking, there is an identification problem, which can be solved by altering the experimental design. The yield must be observed at a third point, as in Figure 2, where I have drawn the least squares estimated quadratic function and have indicated the fertilizer intensity F_m that maximizes the yield. I expect that most people would question whether these data admit the inference that the yield is maximized at F_m. Actually, after inspection of this figure, I don't think anything can be inferred except that the yield at F_2 is higher than at F_1, which in turn is higher than at zero. Thus I don't believe the function is quadratic. If it is allowed to be a cubic then again there is an identification problem.

This kind of logic can be extended indefinitely. One can always find a set of observations that will make the inferences implied by a polynomial of degree p seem silly. This is true regardless of the degree p. Thus no model with a finite number of parameters is actually believed, whether the data are experimental or non-experimental.

4. Do We Need Prior Information?

A model with an infinite number of parameters will allow inference from a finite data set only if there is some prior information that effectively constrains the ranges of the parameters. Figure 3 depicts another hypothetical sequence of observations and three estimated relationships between yield and fertilizer. I believe the solid line A is a better representation of the relationship than either of the other two. The piecewise linear form B fits the data better, but I think this peculiar meandering function is highly unlikely on an a priori basis. Though B and C fit the data equally well, I believe that B is much more likely than C. What I am revealing is the a priori opinion that the function is likely to be smooth and single peaked.

What should now be clear is that data alone cannot reveal the relationship between yield and fertilizer intensity. Data can reveal the yield at sampled values of fertilizer intensities, but in order to interpolate between these sampled values, we must resort to subjective prior information.

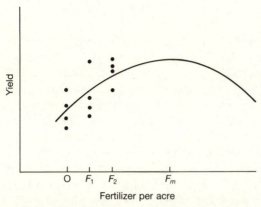

Figure 2   Hypothetical data and estimated quadratic function

Economists have inherited from the physical sciences the myth that scientific inference is objective, and free of personal prejudice. This is utter nonsense. All knowledge is human belief; more accurately, human opinion. What often happens in the physical sciences is that there is a high degree of conformity of opinion. When this occurs, the opinion held by most is asserted to be an objective fact, and those who doubt it are labelled 'nuts'. But history is replete with examples of opinions losing majority status, with once-objective 'truths' shrinking into the dark corners of social intercourse. To give a trivial example, coming now from California I am unsure whether fat ties or thin ties are aesthetically more pleasing.

The false idol of objectivity has done great damage to economic science. Theoretical econometricians have interpreted scientific objectivity to mean that an economist must identify exactly the variables in the model, the functional form, and the distribution of the errors. Given these assumptions, and given a data set, the econometric method produces an objective

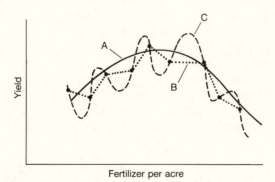

Figure 3   Hypothetical data and three estimated functions

inference from a data set, unencumbered by the subjective opinions of the researcher.

This advice could be treated as ludicrous, except that it fills all the econometric textbooks. Fortunately, it is ignored by applied econometricians. The econometric art as it is practised at the computer terminal involves fitting many, perhaps thousands, of statistical models. One or several that the researcher finds pleasing are selected for reporting purposes. This searching for a model is often well intentioned, but there can be no doubt that such a specification search invalidates the traditional theories of inference. The concepts of unbiasedness, consistency, efficiency, maximum-likelihood estimation, in fact, all the concepts of traditional theory, utterly lose their meaning by the time an applied researcher pulls from the bramble of computer output the one thorn of a model he likes best, the one he chooses to portray as a rose. The consuming public is hardly fooled by this chicanery. The econometrician's shabby art is humorously and disparagingly labelled 'data mining', 'fishing', 'grubbing', 'number crunching'. A joke evokes the Inquisition: 'If you torture the data long enough, Nature will confess' (Coase). Another suggests methodological fickleness: 'Econometricians, like artists, tend to fall in love with their models' (wag unknown). Or how about: 'There are two things you are better off not watching in the making: sausages and econometric estimates.'

This is a sad and decidedly unscientific state of affairs we find ourselves in. Hardly anyone takes data analyses seriously. Or perhaps more accurately, hardly anyone takes anyone else's data analyses seriously. Like elaborately plumed birds who have long since lost the ability to procreate but not the desire, we preen and strut and display our t-values.

If we want to make progress, the first step we must take is to discard the counterproductive goal of objective inference. The dictionary defines an inference as a logical conclusion based on a set of facts. The 'facts' used for statistical inference about θ are first the data, symbolized by x, second a conditional probability density, known as a sampling distribution, $f(x|\theta)$, and, third, explicitly for a Bayesian and implicitly for 'all others', a marginal or prior probability density function $f(\theta)$. Because both the sampling distribution and the prior distribution are actually *opinions* and not *facts*, a statistical inference is and must forever remain an *opinion*.

What is a fact? A fact is merely an opinion held by all, or at least held by a set of people you regard to be a close approximation to all.[1] For some that set includes only one person. I myself have the opinion that Andrew Jackson was the sixteenth president of the United States. If many of my

[1] The notion of 'truth by consensus' is espoused by Thomas Kuhn (1962) and Michael Polanyi (1964). Oscar Wilde agrees by dissent: 'A truth ceases to be true when more than one person believes it.'

friends agree, I may take it to be a fact. Actually, I am most likely to regard it to be a fact if the authors of one or more books say it is so.

The difference between a fact and an opinion for purposes of decision-making and inference is that, when I use opinions, I get uncomfortable. I am not too uncomfortable with the opinion that error terms are normally distributed because most econometricians make use of that assumption. This observation has deluded me into thinking that the opinion that error terms are normal may be a fact, when I know deep inside that normal distributions are actually used only for convenience. In contrast, I am *quite* uncomfortable using a prior distribution, mostly I suspect because hardly anyone uses them. If convenient prior distributions were used as often as convenient sampling distributions, I suspect that I could be as easily deluded into thinking that prior distributions are facts as I have been into thinking that sampling distributions are facts.

To emphasize this hierarchy of statements, I display them in order: truths; facts; opinions; conventions. Note that I have added to the top of the order, the category truths. This will appeal to those of you who feel compelled to believe in such things. At the bottom are conventions. In practice it may be difficult to distinguish a fact from a convention, but when facts are clearly unavailable we must strongly resist the deceit or delusion that conventions can represent.

What troubles me about using opinions is their whimsical nature. Some mornings when I arise, I have the opinion that Raisin Bran is better than eggs. By the time I get to the kitchen, I may well decide on eggs, or oatmeal. I usually do recall that the sixteenth president distinguished himself. Sometimes I think he was Jackson; often I think he was Lincoln.

A data analysis is similar. Sometimes I take the error terms to be correlated, sometimes uncorrelated; sometimes normal and sometimes non-normal; sometimes I include observations from the decade of the fities, sometimes I exclude them; sometimes the equation is linear and sometimes non-linear; sometimes I control for variable z, sometimes I don't. Does it depend on what I had for breakfast?

As I see it, the fundamental problem facing econometrics is how adequately to control the whimsical character of inference, how sensibly to base inferences on opinions when facts are unavailable. At least a partial solution to this problem has already been formed by practicing econometricians. A common reporting style is to record the inferences implied by alternative sets of opinions. It is not unusual to find tables that show how an inference changes as variables are added to or deleted from the equation. This kind of sensitivity analysis reports special features of the mapping from the space of assumptions to the space of inferences. The defect of this style is that the coverage of assumptions is infinitesimal, in fact a zero volume set in the space of assumptions. What is needed instead is a more complete, but still economical way to report the mapping of assumptions into inferences. What I propose to do is to develop a correspondence between regions in the assumption space and regions in the inference space. I will report that all assumptions in a certain set lead to essentially the same inference. Or I will report that there are assumptions within the set under consideration that lead to radically different inferences. In the latter case, I will suspend inference and decision, or I will work harder to narrow the set of assumptions.

Thus what I am asserting is that the choice of a particular sampling distribution, or a particular prior distribution, is inherently whimsical. But statements such as 'The sampling distribution is symmetric and unimodal' and 'My prior is located at the origin' are not necessarily whimsical, and in certain circumstances do not make me uncomfortable.

To put this somewhat differently, an inference is not believable if it is fragile, if it can be reversed by minor changes in assumptions. As consumers of research, we correctly reserve judgement on an inference until it stands up to a study of fragility, usually by other researchers advocating opposite opinions. It is, however, much more efficient for individual researchers to perform their own sensitivity analyses, and we ought to be demanding much more complete and more honest reporting of the fragility of claimed inferences.

The job of a researcher is then to report economically and informatively the mapping from assumptions into inferences. In a slogan, 'The mapping is the message.' The mapping does not depend on opinions (assumptions), but reporting the mapping economically and informatively does. A researcher has to decide which assumptions or which sets of alternative assumptions are worth reporting. A researcher is therefore forced either to anticipate the opinions of his consuming public, or to recommend his own opinions. It is actually a good idea to do both, and a serious defect of current practice is that it concentrates excessively on convincing one's self and, as a consequence, fails to convince the general professional audience.

The whimsical character of econometric inference has been partially controlled in the past by an incomplete sensitivity analysis. It has also been controlled by the use of conventions. The normal distribution is now so common that there is nothing at all whimsical in its use. In some areas of study the list of variables is partially conventional, often based on whatever list the first researcher happened to select. Even conventional prior distributions have been proposed and are used with non-negligible frequency. I am referring to Robert Shiller's (1973) smoothness prior for distributed lag analysis and to Arthur Hoerl and Robert Kennard's (1970) ridge regression prior. It used to aggravate me that these methods seem to find public favour whereas overt and complete Bayesian methods such as my own proposals (Leamer, 1972) for distributed lag priors are generally ignored. However, there is a very good reason for this: the attempt to form a prior distribution from scratch involves an untold number of partly arbitrary decisions. The public is rightfully resistant to the whimsical inferences which result, but at the same time is receptive to the use of priors in ways that control the whimsy. Though the use of conventions does control the whimsy, it can do so at the cost of relevance. Inferences based on Hoerl and Kennard's conventional 'ridge regression' prior are usually irrelevant, because it is rarely sensible to take the prior to be spherical and located at the origin, and because a closer approximation to prior belief can be suspected to lead to substantially different inferences. In contrast, the conventional assumption of normality at least uses a distribution which usually cannot be ruled out altogether. Still, we may properly demand a demonstration that the inferences are insensitive to this distributional assumption.

A. The Horizon Problem: Sherlock Holmes Inference

Conventions are not to be ruled out altogether, however. One can go mad trying to report completely the mapping from assumptions into inferences since the space of assumptions is infinite dimensional. A formal statistical analysis therefore has to be done within the limits of a reasonable horizon. An informed convention can usefully limit this horizon. If it turned out that sensible neighbourhoods of distributions around the normal distribution 99 times out of 100 produced the same inference, then we could all agree that there are other more important things to worry about, and we may properly adopt the convention of normality. The consistency of least-squares estimates under wide sets of assumptions is used improperly as support for this convention, since the inferences from a given finite sample may nonetheless be quite sensitive to the normality assumption.[2]

The truly sharp distinction between inference from experimental and inference from non-experimental data is that experimental inference sensibly admits a conventional horizon in a critical dimension, namely the choice of explanatory variables. If fertilizer is randomly assigned to plots of land, it is conventional to restrict attention to the relationship between yield and fertilizer, and to proceed as if the model were perfectly specified, which in my notation means that the misspecification matrix M is the zero matrix. There is only a small risk that, when you present your findings, someone will object that fertilizer and light level are correlated, and there is an even smaller risk that the conventional zero value for M will lead to

---

[2] In particular, least-squares estimates are completely sensitive to the independence assumption, since by choice of sample covariance matrix a generalized least-squares estimate can be made to assume any value whatsoever (see Leamer, 1981).

inappropriate inferences. In contrast, it would be foolhardy to adopt such a limited horizon with non-experimental data. But if you decide to include light level in your horizon, then why not rainfall; and if rainfall, then why not temperature; and if temperature, then why not soil depth, and if soil depth, then why not the soil grade; ad infinitum. Though this list is never-ending, it can be made so long that a non-experimental researcher can feel as comfortable as an experimental researcher that the risk of having his findings upset by an extension of the horizon is very low. The exact point where the list is terminated must be whimsical, but the inferences can be expected not to be sensitive to the termination point if the horizon is wide enough.

Still, the horizon within which we all do our statistical analyses has to be ultimately troublesome, since there is no formal way to know what inferential monsters lurk beyond our immediate field of vision. 'Diagnostic' tests with explicit alternative hypotheses such as the Durbin–Watson test for first-order autocorrelation do not truly ask if the horizon should be extended, since first-order autocorrelation is explicitly identified and clearly in our field of vision. Diagnostic tests such as goodness-of-fit tests, without explicit alternative hypotheses, are useless since, if the sample size is large enough, any maintained hypothesis will be rejected (for example, no observed distribution is exactly normal). Such tests therefore degenerate into elaborate rituals for measuring the effective sample size.

The only way I know to ask the question whether the horizon is wide enough is to study the anomalies of the data. In the words of the physiologist, C. Bernard:

A great surgeon performs operations for stones by a single method; later he makes a statistical summary of deaths and recoveries, and he concludes from these statistics that the mortality law for this operation is two out of five. Well, I say that this ratio means literally nothing scientifically, and gives no certainty in performing the next operation. What really should be done, instead of gathering facts empirically, is to study them more accurately, each in its special determinism . . . by statistics, we get a conjecture of greater or less probability about a given case, but never any certainty, never any absolute determinism . . . only basing itself on experimental determinism can medicine become a true science. (Bernard, 1927, pp. 137–8)

A study of the anomalies of the data is what I have called 'Sherlock Holmes' inference, since Holmes turns statistical inference on its head: 'It is a capital mistake to theorize before you have all the evidence. It biases the judgements.' Statistical theory counsels us to begin with an elicitation of opinions about the sampling process and its parameters; the theory, in other words. After that, data may be studied in a purely mechanical way. Holmes warns that this biases the judgements, meaning that a theory constructed before seeing the facts can be disastrously inappropriate and psychologically difficult to discard. But if theories are constructed after having studied the data, it is difficult to establish by how much, if at all, the data favour the data-instigated hypothesis. For example, suppose I think that a certain coefficient ought to be positive, and my reaction to the anomalous result of a negative estimate is to find another variable to include in the equation so that the estimate is positive. Have I found evidence that the coefficient is positive? It would seem that we should require evidence that is more convincing than the traditional standard. I have proposed a method for discounting such evidence (Leamer, 1974). Initially, when you regress yield on fertilizer as in equation (2), you are required to assess a prior distribution for the experimental bias parameter β^*; that is, you must select the misspecification matrix M. Then, when the least-squares estimate of β turns out to be negative, and you decide to include in the equation the light level as well as the fertilizer level, you are obligated to form a prior for the light coefficient γ consistent with the prior for β^*, given that $\beta^* = \gamma r_1$, where r_1 is the regression coefficient of light on fertilizer.[3]

This method for discounting the output of exploratory data analysis requires a discipline that is lacking even in its author. It is consequently important that we reduce the risk of Holmesian discoveries by extending the horizon reasonably far. The degree of a polynomial or the order of a distributed lag need not be data-instigated, since the horizon is easily extended to include high degrees and high orders. It is similarly wise to ask yourself before examining the data what you would do if the estimate of your favourite coefficient had the wrong sign. If that makes you think of a specific left-out variable, it is better to include it from the beginning.

Though it is wise to select a wide horizon to reduce the risk of Holmesian discoveries, it is mistaken then to analyse a data set as if the horizon were wide enough. Within the limits of a horizon, no revolutionary inference can be made, since all possible inferences are predicted in advance (admittedly, some with low probabilities). Within the horizon, inference and decision can be turned over completely to a computer. But the great human revolutionary discoveries are made when the horizon is extended for reasons that cannot be predicted in advance and cannot be computerized. If you wish to make such discoveries, you will have to poke at the horizon, and poke again.

5. An Example

This rhetoric is understandably tiring. Methodology, like sex, is better demonstrated than discussed, though often better anticipated than

---

[3] In a randomized experiment with $r_1 = 0$, the constraint $\beta^* = \gamma r_1$ is irrelevant, and you are free to play these exploratory games without penalty. This is a very critical difference between randomized experiments and non-randomized non-experiments.

experienced. Accordingly, let me give you an example of what all this ranting and raving is about. I trust you will find it even better in the experience than in the anticipation. A problem of considerable policy importance is whether or not to have capital punishment. If capital punishment had no deterrent value, most of us would prefer not to impose such an irreversible punishment, though, for a significant minority, the pure joy of vengeance is reason enough. The deterrent value of capital punishment is, of course, an empirical issue. The unresolved debate over its effectiveness began when evolution was judging the survival value of the vengeance gene. Nature was unable to make a decisive judgement. Possibly econometricians can.

In Table 1 you will find a list of variables that are hypothesized to influence the murder rate.[4] The data to be examined are state-by-state murder rates in 1950. The variables are divided into three sets. There are four deterrent variables that characterize the criminal justice system, or in economic parlance, the expected out-of-pocket cost of crime. There are four economic variables that measure the opportunity cost of crime. And there are four social/environmental variables that possibly condition the taste for crime. This leaves unmeasured only the expected rewards for criminal behaviour, though these are possibly related to the economic and social variables and are otherwise assumed not to vary from state to state.

A simple regression of the murder rate on all these variables leads to the conclusion that each additional execution deters thirteen murders, with a standard error of seven. That seems like such a healthy rate of return, we might want just to randomly draft executees from the population at large. This proposal would be unlikely to withstand the scrutiny of any macro-economists who are skilled at finding rational expectations equilibria.

The issue I would like to address instead is whether this conclusion is fragile or not. Does it hold up if the list of variables in the model is changed? Individuals with different experiences and different training will find different subsets of the variables to be candidate, for omission from the equation. Five different lists of doubtful variables are reported in Table 2. A right winger expects the punishment variables to have an effect, but treats all other variables as doubtful. He wants to know whether the data still favour the large deterrent effect, if he omits some of these doubtful variables. The rational maximizer takes the variables that measure the expected economic return of crime as important, but treats the taste variables as doubtful. The eye-for-an-eye prior treats all variables as doubtful except the probability of execution. An individual with the bleeding heart prior sees murder as the result of economic impoverishment. Finally, if

---

[4] This material is taken from a study by a student of mine, Walter McManus (1982).

Table 1. Variables used in the analysis

(a) Dependent variable
M = Murder rate per 100,000, FBI estimate.
(b) Independent deterrent variables
PC = (Conditional) Probability of conviction for murder given commission. Defined by $PC = C/\hat{Q}$, where C = convictions for murder, $\hat{Q} = M \cdot NS$
NS = state population. This is to correct for the fact that M is an estimate based on a sample from each state.
PX = (Conditional) Probability of execution given conviction (average number of executions 1946–50 divided by C).
T = Median time served in months for murder by prisoners released in 1951.
$XPOS$ = A dummy equal to 1 if $PX > 0$.
(c) Independent economic variables
W = Median income of families in 1949.
X = Percentage of families in 1949 with less than one-half W.
U = Unemployment rate.
LF = Labour force participation rate.
(d) Independent social and environmental variables
NW = Percentage non-white.
AGE = Percentage 15–24 years old.
URB = Percentage urban.
$MALE$ = Percentage male.
$FAMHO$ = Percentage of families that are husband and wife both present families.
$SOUTH$ = A dummy equal to 1 for southern states (Alabama, Arkansas, Delaware, Florida, Kentucky, Louisiana, Maryland, Mississippi, North Carolina, Oklahoma, South Carolina, Tennessee, Texas, Virginia, West Virginia).
(e) Weighting variable
$SQRTNF$ = Square root of the population of the FBI-reporting region. Note that weighting is done by multiplying variables by $SQRTNF$.
(f) Level of observation
Observations are for 44 states, 35 executing and 9 non-executing. The executing states are: Alabama, Arizona, Arkansas, California, Colorado, Connecticut, Delaware, Florida, Illinois, Indiana, Kansas, Kentucky, Louisiana, Maryland, Massachusetts, Mississippi, Missouri, Nebraska, Nevada, New Jersey, New Mexico, New York, North Carolina, Ohio, Oklahoma, Oregon, Pennsylvania, South Carolina, South Dakota, Tennessee, Texas, Virginia, Washington, West Virginia.
The non-executing states are: Idaho, Maine, Minnesota, Montana, New Hamphshire, Rhode Island, Utah, Wisconsin, Wyoming.

Table 2. Alternative prior specifications

Prior	PC	PX	T	XPOS	W	X	U	LF	NW	AGE	URB	MALE	FAMHO	SOUTH
Right winger	I	I	I	*	D	D	D	D	D	D	D	D	D	D
Rational maximizer	I	I	I	*	I	I	I	I	D	D	D	D	D	D
Eye-for-an-eye	I	I	D	*	D	D	D	I	D	D	D	D	D	D
Bleeding heart	D	D	D	*	I	I	I	I	D	D	D	D	D	D
Crime of passion	D	D	D	*	I	I	I	I	I	I	I	I	I	I

Notes: (1) *I* indicates variables considered important by a researcher with the respective prior. Thus, every model considered by a researcher will include these variables. *D* indicates variables considered doubtful by the researcher. * indicates *XPOS* treated as important, and one with it as doubtful. Each prior was pooled with the data two ways: one with *XPOS* treated as important, and one with it as doubtful.
(2) With five basic priors and *XPOS* treated as doubtful or important by each, we get ten alternative prior specifications.

Table 3.   Extreme estimates of the effect of executions on murders

Prior	Minimum estimate	Maximum estimate
Right winger	−22.56	−.86
Rational maximizer	−15.91	−10.24
Eye-for-an-eye	−28.66	1.91
Bleeding heart	−25.59	12.37
Crime of passion	−17.32	4.10

Note: Least-squares is −13.22 with a standard error of 7.2.

murder is thought to be a crime of passion then the punishment variables are doubtful.

In Table 3, I have listed the extreme estimates that could be found by each of these groups of researchers. The right-winger minimum of −22.56 means that a regression of the murder rate data on the three punishment variables and a suitably selected linear combination of the other variables yields an estimate of the deterrent effect equal to 22.56 lives per execution. It is possible also to find an estimate of −0.86. Anything between these two extremes can be similarly obtained; but no estimate outside this interval can be generated no matter how the doubtful variables are manipulated (linearly). Thus the right winger can report that the inference from this data set that executions deter murders is not fragile. The rational maximizer similarly finds that conclusion insensitive to choice of model, but the other three priors allow execution actually to encourage murder, possibly by a brutalizing effect on society.

I come away from a study of Table 3 with the feeling that any inference from these data about the deterrent effect of capital punishment is too fragile to be believed. It is possible credibly to narrow the set of assumptions, but I do not think that a credibly large set of alternative assumptions will lead to a sharp set of estimates. In another paper (Leamer, 1982), I found a narrower set of priors still leads to inconclusive inferences. And I have ignored the important simultaneity issue (the death penalty may have been imposed in crime-ridden states to deter murder) which is often a source of great inferential fragility.

6.   Conclusions

After three decades of churning out estimates, the econometrics club finds itself under critical scrutiny and faces incredulity as never before. Fischer Black (1982) writes of 'The trouble with econometric models.' David

Hendry (1980) queries 'Econometrics: alchemy or science?' John W. Pratt and Robert Schlaifer (1979) question our understanding of 'The nature and discovery of structure?' And Christopher Sims (1982) suggests blending 'Macroeconomics and reality'.

It is apparent that I too am troubled by the fumes which leak from our computing centres. I believe serious attention to two words would sweeten the atmosphere of econometric discourse. These are whimsy and fragility. In order to draw inferences from data as described by econometric texts, it is necessary to make whimsical assumptions. The professional audience consequently and properly withholds belief until an inference is shown to be adequately insensitive to the choice of assumptions. The haphazard way we individually and collectively study the fragility of inferences leaves most of us unconvinced that any inference is believable. If we are to make effective use of our scarce data resource it is therefore important that we study fragility in a much more systematic way. If it turns out that almost all inferences from economic data are fragile, I suppose we shall have to revert to our old methods lest we lose our customers in government, business, and on the boardwalk at Atlantic City.

References

Bernard, C. (1927), *An Introduction to the Study of Experimental Method*. Macmillan, New York.

Black, Fischer, (1982), The trouble with econometric models, *Financial Analysts Journal*, March/April 35, 3–11.

Friedman, Milton (1957), *A Theory of the Consumption Function*. Princeton University Press, Princeton.

Hendry, David (1980), Econometrics – alchemy or science?, *Economica*, November, 47, 387–406.

Hoerl, Arthur E. and Kennard, Robert W (1970), Ridge regression: biased estimation for nonorthogonal problems, *Technometrics*, February, 12, 55–67.

Kuhn, Thomas S. (1962), *The Structure of Scentific Revolutions*. University of Chicago Press, Chicago.

Lakatos, Imre (1969), Falsification and the methodology of scientific research programmes, in Lakatos, I. and Musgrave, A. (eds), *Criticism and the Growth of Knowledge*. Cambridge University Press, Cambridge.

Leamer, Edward E. (1972), A class of prior distributions and distributed lag analysis, *Econometrica*, November, 40, 1059–81.

Leamer, Edward E. (1974), False models and post-data model construction, *Journal of American Statistical Association*, March, 69, 122–31.

Leamer, Edward E. (1978), *Specification Searches: Ad Hoc Inference with Non-experimental Data*. Wiley, New Yolk.

Leamer, Edward E. (1981), Techniques or estimation with incomplete assumptions, *IEEE Conference on Decision and Control*, San Diego, December.

Leamer, Edward E. (1982), Sets of posterior means with bounded variance priors, *Eonometrica*, May, 50, 725–36.

McManus, Walter (1981), Bayesian estimation of the deterrent effect of capital punishment. Mimeo, University of California-Los Angeles.

Plott, Charles R. and Smith, Vernon L. (1978), An experimental examination of two exchange institutions, *Review of Economic Studies*, February 1978, 45, 133–53.

Polanyi, Michael, *Personal Knowledge*. Harper & Row, New York.

Prat, John W. and Schlaifer, Robert (1979), On the Nature and Discovery of Structure. Mimeo.

Shiller, Robert (1973), A distributed lag estimator derived from smoothness priors, *Eonometrica*, July, 41, 775–88.

Sims, C. A. (1980), Macroeconomics and reality, *Econometrica*, January, 48, 1–48.

Sims, C. A. (1982), Scientific standards in econometric modeling. Mimeo.

Smith, Vernon L. (1980), Relevance of laboratory experiments to testing resource allocation theory, *Evaluation of Econometric Models*, ed. by J. Kmenta and J. Ramsey. Academic Press, New York.

2

What Will Take the Con Out of Econometrics?

Michael McAleer, Adrian R. Pagan, and Paul A. Volker*

More than twenty years ago Carl Christ recounted a story about a new typist who rendered 'econometrics' as 'economic tricks'. No doubt this tale was greeted with some amusement at that time; equally without doubt, today it would probably only occasion wry and knowing smiles. Charting the course of this transition, and accounting for its direction, has been the concern of a number of recent articles. Perhaps the most perceptive of these has been Edward Leamer's article (1983). His contribution is of special interest, as it seeks not only to be descriptive but prescriptive; methods are outlined, the use of which Leamer sees as essential to the restoration of confidence in econometric research. Such techniques have now been promulgated and applied in a number of contexts. Thomas Cooley (1982), for example, looks at the impact of industry concentration upon profits; Louis Dicks-Mireaux and Mervyn King (1984) consider the effect of pensions on savings; Cooley and Stephen LeRoy (1981) are concerned with money demand. These constitute just three of the more prominent applications.

Although the number of applications of the methods is growing, and approving references are being made to them, surprisingly few have queried the basis of the contention that the procedures really do allay some of the suspicion greeting econometric results; a singular exception being Phoebus Dhrymes (1982). Yet the claims being made for this methodology are such as to demand a close investigation. As witnesses to these claims we quote Leamer and Herman Leonard:

> We propose that researchers be given the task of identifying interesting families of alternative models and be expected to summarize the range of inferences which are implied by each of the families. When a range of inferences is small enough to be

* McAleer and Pagan: Department of Statistics, The Faculties, Australian National University, Camberra, A. C. T. 2600, Australia; Volker: Bureau of Labour Market Research, Canberra. An earlier version of this paper appeared as a Working paper in Economics and Econometrics, No. 097, Australian National University. It is available on request. We thank all those who commented on that version. We believe that those comments sharpened our arguments considerably. Special thanks go to Ed Leamer, Tom Cooley, Trevor Breusch, David Hendry, Allan Gregory, Hashem Pesaran, Peter Schmidt, and Pravin Trivedi. This article first appeared in *American Economic Review*, Vol. 75, No. 3, June 1985, pp. 293–307.

useful and when the corresponding family of models is broad enough to be believable, we may conclude that these data yield useful information. When the range of inferences is too wide to be useful, and when the corresponding family of models is so narrow that it cannot credibly be reduced, then we must conclude that inferences from these data are too fragile to be useful.

The proper test of our proposals is whether they are useful in practice. We believe that researchers will find them to be efficient tools for discovering the information in data sets and for communicating findings to the consuming public. (1983, p. 306)

The aim of our paper is to consider possible answers to the question in the title. Because of its position as one proposed answer, and its strong advocacy by a number of authors (for example, Cooley and LeRoy, 1981, p. 827), we pay particular attention to Leamer's extreme bounds analysis (EBA). In our inquiry, contained in Sections I, II, and III; the discussion is structured along the lines of the three themes in the statement above: the effect of looking at different families of models, the determinants of a fragile inference, and the nature of the conclusions that may be drawn from the information provided by EBA. Based on the arguments of those sections, we conclude that EBA does not go very far in removing the con from econometrics. Furthermore, in most instances it can actively distract a researcher from asking important questions about an econometric model.

But just because the promise and the performance of EBA diverge, it does not obviate the need for a methodology aiming to dispel doubts arising over conventional research presentation and analysis. Accordingly, Section IV sets out our own prescription, the basic ingredients of which are the necessity for a clear and full disclosure of the process whereby a preferred model was selected, and the requirement that a thorough evaluation has been made of the properties of such a specification. Such an orientation is scarcely original, reflecting in its concerns an oral tradition that owes much to Denis Sargan's (1964) influential paper on wages and prices. Nevertheless, it is worth explicitly stating these principles, as our experience convinces us that, consistently applied, they can go a long way towards the 'de-conning' of econometrics. As an example of this approach, and to contrast our prescription with EBA, Section IV below re-examines the conclusions drawn by Cooley and LeRoy from their demand for money study.

1. The Problems in Families

Trying to define 'the family' nowadays is enough to give a sociologist a nervous breakdown. To keep things simple one is inclined to assign a few individuals to its core and then to generate a whole range of alternatives by adding on children, grandparents, aunts, uncles, and other 'relatives'. Such a homely analogy captures rather nicely the essence of the 'family of models' mentioned by Leamer and Leonard. At their core are variables classified as *important*. Added on are variables termed *doubtful*. What demarcates them is that *only the latter can be combined in an arbitrary linear fashion*. We emphasize this definition, since much of the discussion and use of EBA tends to proceed as if the division were based upon whether the associated coefficients are likely to be zero or not.[1] Because this is not so, the decision to assign variables to their respective classifications is not a trivial one, and we explore it in detail in Section III.

To complete the elements of EBA, the concept of a *focus* variable is needed. This derives from the assumption that the magnitude of one of the model coefficients is of special interest. By itself, this feature tells us nothing about the nature of such a variable; it may be free or doubtful. Examples of both are given by Leamer (1983). His 'bleeding heart liberal' regards the impact of execution probability upon murders as doubtful, while his 'right winger' treats the same variable as free.

Proponents of EBA work with the maximum and minimum point estimates of the focus coefficient as the set of restrictions upon the doubtful variables is changed. If the gap between these values is wide, readers are generally informed that no reliable inference can be drawn about the influence of the focus variable. Thus Cooley and Le Roy express the belief that almost nothing can be said about the value of the interest elasticity of the demand for money. Within one of their families of models this elasticity could lie anywhere between -6.27 and 2.24.

Now it is a rare family that does not have a member with problems at some stage or other. Families of models also share this characteristic, but this is rarely mentioned by EBA advocates. Notwithstanding that, it has to be the case that a consumer of the conclusion drawn from an application of the methodology must take some notice of the nature of the model that generated the extreme bounds. When this is done, there are at least two situations in which inferences drawn from EBA would have to be heavily discounted.

First of all, the restrictions that are being imposed upon the doubtful variables may be entirely unacceptable. Suppose that γ_1 and γ_2 are the parameters associated with the income and lagged dependent variable terms in a money demand function, and both variables are treated as doubtful. Then a restriction of the form $\gamma_2 - \theta\gamma_1 = 0$, with θ negative,

---

[1] Unfortunately, the terminology of 'important' and 'doubtful' tends to bolster this impression. For this reason we substituted 'free' for important, as that captures the nature of these variables much more closely. Ideally, a similar change would have been desirable for doubtful.

would offend against theoretical conceptions. An extreme bound generated with $\theta < 0$ in a money demand example would be of little interest, and yet there is nothing to safeguard against such a possibility. While Leamer himself is aware of this problem (see Leamer, 1978, p. 199), there have been few attempts at cautioning users of EBA about it. Cooley and LeRoy do not mention it at all, despite the fact that income and wealth elasticities associated with one of the extreme bounds of the ninety-day Treasury bill rate are actually negative.

Attempts have been made to limit such conflicts. Leamer (1982) restricts the feasible parameter space by requiring an investigator to put upper and lower limits on prior variances. It is hard to know what to make of this 'solution', as the choice of such limits is extremely difficult and essentially arbitrary. One person's view of what constitutes a reasonable bound is unlikely to coincide with another's, and there is always the residual suspicion that prior variances have been chosen to yield narrow or tight bounds. As a satisfactory alternative to current practice it leaves much to be desired. It re-introduces the very element of whimsy that EBA was supposed to ameliorate.

A second alternative is to ensure that the extreme bounds do not disagree too greatly with the sample. Cooley does this by invoking the constraint that estimates should lie within the α per cent confidence ellipsoid associated with the least-squares estimates of the complete model. A range of sample-modified bounds can then be generated by varying α. When $\alpha = 100$, the ordinary extreme bounds are found.

Once we introduce the sample evidence to constrain the alternative models, we are implicitly being asked to accept a number of conventions underlying EBA (at least as presented in the literature). Namely, that the errors in models be normally distributed, non-autocorrelated, and homoscedastic; that the regressors be predetermined; and finally, that sample sizes are large enough for 'confidence intervals' to be known with accuracy. No doubt these conventions may be appealing, but Leamer himself has pointed out the problem with their use: 'Though the use of conventions does control the whimsy, it can do so at the cost of relevance' (1983, p. 38). That principle is certainly applicable here, as the breakdown of any of these conventions means that the 'α per cent confidence intervals' are anything but, and exactly what constraint is being applied becomes increasingly hazy.

These considerations emphasize the absolute necessity of knowing the point estimates of all coefficients in the model generating the bounds. But such knowledge is still not sufficient to decide if we have just come across a problem child or not. It is perfectly possible for all point estimates to appear reasonable, but for the model to be rejected on other grounds, such as when it exhibits substantial serial correlation. An extreme value generated from such a model would not be of great interest, since an investigator would not regard it as a suitable candidate for conveying information about the focus coefficient. Without knowing the *full set of characteristics* of the models generating the extremes, it is impossible to know what weight should be placed on the latter. Mere provision of the bounds, as in Cooley and LeRoy for example, is not enough. Much more information is needed to assess whether these bounds are meaningful.

2.   When is an Inference Fragile?

In what has transpired so far we have been somewhat vague about exactly how the bounds are used to conclude that an inference is fragile. If left that way, EBA becomes a 'black box', and no understanding of the factors leading to an inference being fragile would be available. For this reason we have gleaned two interpretations of fragility from the literature applying EBA, each of which is sufficiently precise to enable analytical results to be established.

The first to these, henceforth referred to as Type A fragility, is given by Leamer and Leonard as follows:

These extreme values, $\hat{\beta}_{min}$ and $\hat{\beta}_{max}$, delineate the ambiguity in the inferences about β induced by the ambiguity in choice of model. If the interval $[\hat{\beta}_{min}, \hat{\beta}_{max}]$ is short in comparison to the sampling uncertainty, the ambiguity in the model may be considered irrelevant since all models lead to essentially the same inferences. (p. 307)

With the sampling uncertainty measured as k times the estimated standard deviation of the focus coefficient, k being a predetermined constant, such a definition has been adopted by Leamer–Leonard, Cooley, and Cooley–LeRoy. The first provide no guidance about k, Cooley selects a value of $k = 4$, while the last opt for $k = 2$. To investigate the consequences of adopting this definition of fragility, we provide Proposition 1 (proof available on request).

PROPOSITION 1:
   (a) When the focus variable is doubtful, the necessary and sufficient condition for Type A fragility to exist is that the chi-square statistic for the doubtful variable coefficients to equal their prior means (χ_D^2) exceeds k^2.
   (b) When the focus variable is free, the necessary condition for Type A fragility is that $\chi_D^2 > k^2$.

Proposition 1 is quite striking, as it shows that whether an inference is to be Type A-fragile or not depends upon two quantities: namely, the significance of the doubtful variables in the model and the value chosen for k. Regarding the first, its magnitude will depend crucially upon the prior means assumed for the doubtful variables. If the prior means are taken to be zero, whereas the OLS estimates lie a long way from that point, a large value of χ_D^2 is likely. The closer the means are to the OLS values, the smaller will be χ_D^2, and the less the evidence of fragility. Everything therefore depends upon the whimsy of the reporter in the choice of prior means for doubtful variables! Hardly a good method for getting rid of the con artists. Instead it gives them enormous scope for generating almost any result they like. In the examples of EBA usage available, only Fiebig (1981) attempts to spell out this sensitivity of bounds to prior mean specification.

Proposition 1 moreover tells us something else of importance: that inferences will only be fragile if doubtful variables are informative. Assuming for convenience that prior means are zero, a large value of χ_D^2 signals to a researcher that these variables should appear in any model from which inferences are to be drawn. From this perspective, EBA is just an inefficient (and incomplete) way of communicating to readers the fact that the doubtful variables are needed to explain the data; a better solution would be just to present estimates of the general model along with an associated χ_D^2 statistic, letting consumers of research judge whether any further simplification of the model is justified.[2]

The analytic results presented in Proposition 1 can also rationalize the findings of a number of different investigations in which EBA has been employed. Leamer and Leonard's nuclear reactor example treats as doubtful those variables with *t*-values all below 1.03, leading to a lack of Type A fragility. In contrast, Cooley's profits regressions exhibit four variables with *t*-statistics greater than 3.5, and three of the four *always* appear as doubtful variables. Is it any wonder then that he concludes that Type A fragility exists for a concentration/profits relationship?

Perhaps the ambiguities raised above could be dissipated by an alternative definition of fragility. Leamer and Leonard provide just that, and we will designate it as Type B fragility in what follows. They say: 'An alternative definition of shortness derives from a decision problem based on $\hat{\beta}$: the interval is short if all values in the interval lead to essentially the same decision' (p. 307, fn. 1).

When implemented by Leamer (1983), Type B fragility occurs if there is

---

[2] It is of interest to specialize k to 2. When only a single doubtful variable is present Type A fragility occurs when the *t*-statistic of the doubtful variable exceeds 2, which is a conventional rule of thumb for selection of regressors. As the number of doubtful variables grows, however, a constant value of $k = 2$ means that the comparison of χ^2 with 4 corresponds to larger and larger levels of significance. Most researchers would presumably find this implicit assumption in EBA a little odd.

a sign change implicit in the bounds. Ignoring, as Leamer does, the fact that these bounds themselves have standard errors, we proceed to analyze the nature of this type of fragility using Proposition 2 (proof available on request).

PROPOSITION 2:

(a) *When the focus variable is doubtful the necessary and sufficient condition for Type B fragility to exist is that $X_D^2 > \chi_{F0}^2$, where χ_{F0}^2 is the χ^2 statistic for testing if the focus coefficient is zero.*

(b) *When the focus variable is free, the necessary condition for Type B fragility is $\chi_D^2 > \chi_{F0}^2$.*

The movement from Type A to Type B fragility only changes the benchmark against which the significance of the doubtful variables is checked. It is no longer set by the reporter but determined by the data (χ_{F0}^2). Furthermore, when the focus variable is doubtful, it is always the case that χ_D^2 exceeds χ_{F0}^2 (ignoring singularities in the design matrix), and so Type B fragility is in evidence. While such a result is solely a consequence of the fact that zero is an admissible value for that doubtful variable coefficient, it serves to emphasize how Type B fragility may eventuate purely by a classification of variables. An example of this is provided by Leamer in his discussion of the impact of execution on murders. After placing the execution variable in the doubtful class, thereby producing an opposite sign to that from unrestricted least-squares, he concludes: 'I come away ... with the feeling that any inference from these data about the deterrent effect of capital punishment is too fragile to be believed' (p. 47).

Since the sign change did not depend in any way upon the data, we find such a conclusion a trifle hard to defend.[3]

3. When is a Variable Doubtful?

Propositions 1 and 2 strongly suggest that the conclusions on fragility drawn from EBA are intimately bound up with the classification of variables as doubtful and free. The polar case where the focus variable is orthogonal to all other regressors gives a striking demonstration of that fact. When treated as free, the gap between the bounds is zero, as the point estimate of the focus coefficient is entirely insensitive to combinations of other variables. But, when treated as doubtful, the width of the bounds

---

[3] Note that a sign change also occurred when the execution variable was free under the 'eye-for-eye' specification. With *eleven* doubtful variables, and a *t*-statistic of less than two for the execution coefficient, an application of Proposition 2(b) should leave us in little doubt over why that was so.

varies directly with χ_D^2; the more significant the focus variable the greater the degree of fragility inferred.

A concrete example may serve to highlight just how important this choice can be to the outcome. Accordingly we consider the model of murder rates set out in the April 1983 SEARCH manual (it resembles that in Leamer, 1982). Table 1 gives the extreme bounds, range (the absolute value of the difference between the bounds), and ratio of range to standard errors for the impact of execution on murders under different variable designations.

As the definition of Type A fragility reflected the relative magnitudes of the range and standard deviation, the last column of Table 1 contains the information that would be used to assess whether inferences about the impact of executions upon murders are fragile. Clearly the decision about which variables are doubtful can have enormous consequences for any conclusions. Such variation naturally poses the question of how we are to know which one of the four options is to be adopted? Or, when is a doubtful variable doubtful? The answer must be that there is no answer. A decision to nominate a variable as doubtful is a personalized one, resting very much upon the opinions and values of the nominator. Consensus is no more likely over this choice than in the traditional selection of regressors problem.

Having elicited this point, the most serious defect in EBA becomes transparent: unless extreme bounds are presented for *all* possible classifications of variables as doubtful and free, an observer cannot be certain that the selection does not constitute a 'con job'. *Selectivity in regression reporting therefore has as an exact analogue in EBA the different classifications of variables as doubtful and free.* EBA users report results for only particular variable categories and so are as arbitrary and selective

Table 1. Extreme bound information for execution coefficient (PX)

Free variables	Min	Max	Range	Range/SD
None	−2.87	2.72	5.59	115.0
PX	−0.45	1.35	1.8	37.0
PX, intercept	−0.40	0.10	0.5	10.3
PX, intercept, other variables with $t > 3$ (*S, PC, PCTPOOR*)	−0.22	−0.01	0.21	4.3

Note: *PC* = probability of conviction, *PX* = probability of execution, *S* = sentence, *PCTPOOR* = percentage poor, standard deviation of focus coefficent = 0.0486, SD = standard deviation.

in their modus operandi as the practices they criticize and claim to be improving on.

We can see this effect in Table 2.1. With nine variables in the regression there are 181,440 possible doubtful/free splits. Hence, inevitably some selection from this huge number will be made. Someone intent on demonstrating that executions deter murders would undoubtedly quote the final classification (or an augmented version), while those wishing to denigrate such a position would opt for the first two doubtful variable choices. There seems no reason to suppose that all of the classifications in Table 2.1 would be given by either protagonist, any more than one would anticipate each individual presenting the equivalent set of regressions composed of the different types of free variables. Thus there is little reason to believe that EBA provides a reporting style that is any better than that currently practised.

Section 2.1–2.3 can now be drawn together to highlight the fact that EBA is not a satisfactory solution to the question posed in the title of this paper.[4] Section 2.1 argued that the extreme bounds themselves are not enough to enable conclusions to be drawn regarding fragility; we need to know the characteristics of the models generating such bounds. Sections II and III demonstrated that EBA is as capable of manipulation as the traditional presentation it aims to replace; perhaps more so in one respect in that an additional arbitrary choice of prior mean must be made. Consequently, if one feels unhappy with the information provided by *selective regressions*, one should not be any more satisfied with extreme bounds obtained by *selective variable partitions*. A con man in one mode would have no fear of becoming deskilled in the other.

4. Cooley and LeRoy's Demand for Money Function: Contrasting the Methodologies

Given our belief that EBA cannot de-con econometrics, is there anything that might? Not generally, as there are almost certainly instances in econometrics, just as in science, of outright fraud. Nothing will detect such deception, except a vigorous critical tradition and a requirement that utilized data be either available or easily replicable. But our perception of the scepticism greeting many econometric studies is that it does not arise from a high incidence of such a phenomenon. Rather it stems from a

---

[4] It is important to emphasize that an answer to this question is our central concern. We do not quibble with the contention that EBA displays the impact of prior information on posterior means. To do so would be inconsistent with our Proposition 1. Nor do we argue that, *for a given variable partition*, EBA might not be useful. In Section IV we do, in fact, exploit it in exactly such a context.

feeling that the sins are venial rather than mortal; something has been left undone that should have been done.

Now EBA clearly addressed itself to this problem by indicating for a *given variable partition and universe of variables*, the worst outcomes if everything conceivable were done. What it leaves undetermined is both the process by which the partition it is conditional upon was arrived at, and the operating characteristics of models generating the extremes. Three points therefore always need to be considered in assessing an EBA. In turn, these three elements also occur in the traditional line of research and are, we believe, the source of much of the dissatisfaction with it. Because they are pivotal to the methodology advanced in this section, we list them below:

(1) Selection of a general model.
(2) How and why any general model was simplified to the preferred one(s).
(3) Quality control of the preferred model(s).

Selection of a general model is a problem with all research methodologies (including EBA) and we can do not better than concur with Leamer and Leonard when they say: 'But it is up to readers of research to decide if the reported family of models is credibly inclusive. If the researcher, for whatever reason, selects an incredibly narrow family of models, readers will properly ignore the results' (p. 307).

Even if we largely agree that the choice of variables considered in an investigation was commendably large, it is frequently the case that little discussion is provided of the strategy employed to obtain a more parsimonious representation of the data. Where a systematic reduction is possible, it should be followed; where it is not, detail should be sufficient to enable a consumer of the research to determine exactly the criterion adopted in performing the simplification. At a very minimum this forces the presentation of an estimated general model and some analysis of how the preferred model relates to it.

Our final category focuses upon the quality control exercised on the models presented. Frequently, this is little short of abysmal and, as James Ramsey comments, 'it is amazing that so little is done to evaluate the model and the results' (1983, p. 242). Yet, ultimately, quality control is as important for the econometrics profession as it is for automobile manufacturers. A gradual realization of this point has in fact stimulated the development of criteria for the formal evaluation of models. For later reference it is useful to summarize the outcome of that research by classifying derived methods into five major categories:

(1) Consistency with theory.
(2) Significance, both statistical and economic.

(3) Indexes of inadequacy.
(4) Fragility or sensitivity.
(5) Whether a model can encompass or reconcile previous research.

These five categories can be viewed as a regrouping of the criteria suggested in David Hendry and Jean-François Richard (1982) for settling upon a 'tentatively adequate' model. Categories 1 and 2 have tended to dominate in past evaluative analysis and even now constitute the corpus of most applied econometrics courses and texts. Increasing attention has, however, been paid to the necessity of item 3, with Hendry (1980) giving a general perspective and Hendry (1983) a detailed application. Robert Engle (1982b) and Pagan and Anthony Hall (1983) provide an account of much of the technology, emphasizing that these methods aim to extend the horizon in directions where errors might be anticipated. Some indexes, such as the Durbin–Watson statistic, have been routinely used in applied work. But, as the articles referenced above demonstrate, the set of indexes *conventionally* reported is much too small to be completely effective.

Item 4 encompasses considerations raised by EBA. However, in contrast to the emphasis placed by EBA upon sensitivity of point estimates to a change in the menu of included variables, there is an older tradition of assessing the fragility of models by reference to new data. This is done either through predictive failure, recursive estimation, or interaction with other parts of a model as in simulation analysis. Fragility as an important criterion for model evaluation is therefore not a novel idea. Rather it is the emphasis EBA places upon variation in point estimates of a particular coefficient under model respecification, which is novel. In fact, an EBA would seem to constitute an important part of the evaluative process. It must be a rare instance in which some arbitrariness does not creep into the simplification process, particularly when working with cross-section data. The extreme bounds then provide useful information upon the effects of such arbitrary decisions, at least in respect of the focus coefficient. Such is the way we employ EBA in the following case study.

The final category distinguished above challenges a model to encompass or explain alternative models, particularly those originating from past endeavours. Lack of reconciliation between studies is a glaring defect in much current applied research, and this requirement, whether interpreted formally as in Grayham Mizon and Richard (1982), or rather more informally as in James Davidson et al. (1978), must become an essential cornerstone for applied econometric research. Only if it is met can one be truly satisfied that progress has been made in understanding an empirical phenomenon.

In order to contrast the methodology outlined above with the approach of those viewing EBA as the cornerstone of econometric work, we will look at the money demand function inquiry presented in Cooley and

Table 2. Extreme bounds for long-term interest elasticity (*RTB*)

Free variables	Min	Max
None	−12.14	12.15
RTB	−6.27	2.24
RTB, intercept	−0.375	0.019

LeRoy. This paper has been cited approvingly by a number of authors, both for what it said about econometric practice and for its claim about the likely magnitudes of interest elasticities. In doing our comparison we have presumed that the study was meant to be a serious application of the EBA methodology, rather than just illustrative. Certainly, there is support for this hypothesis in the stress Cooley and LeRoy laid upon the conclusions drawn from their analysis.

One fact that should by now by apparent from our assignation of EBA to a group of methods for model evaluation, is our belief that exclusive attention to the results from it can lead to quite erroneous conclusions about the robustness of parametric inferences. Such tunnel vision tends to distract researchers from the other vital questions needing to be asked. A primary example would be whether the model upon which EBA is being practised is comprehensive enough. Later it is argued that, in Cooley and LeRoy's case, there is ample evidence of it not being so.

For the moment we accept their formulation of the problem, turning instead to one of the items in the list assembled earlier as bedevilling EBA; namely, the way in which conclusions on fragility are attendant upon the assumed doubtful/free division. Our Table 2.2 shows how important such selections were for Cooley and LeRoy's conclusions concerning their second specification (see their Table 2, p. 836).

The extreme bounds shrink dramatically when the intercept is made a free variable. (Note that Cooley and LeRoy, Table 1, p. 835, do not indicate it as doubtful but the bounds of −6.27 and 2.24 from their Table 2 only occur when it is so treated.) With a *t*-statistic of −3.96 such an outcome should not be surprising, given our Proposition 1 above. Building a case for the treatment of the intercept as doubtful rather than free would, to our minds, be quite difficult, but the most important lesson from Table 2 is how misleading it is to give the extreme bounds for a single doubtful/free partition of the variables.[5]

---

[5] In fact, Cooley and LeRoy present a broader range of bounds than those in Table 2.2. invoking the extra constraint that coefficient estimates must lie in a specified confidence ellipsoid. Those in Table 2 correspond to the 100 per cent ellipsoid, and represent wider bounds than most contained in their Table 2.

Table 2 shows that any of the conclusions drawn by Cooley and LeRoy about the magnitude of interest elasticities must be treated with scepticism, even if the output of EBA is taken as the dominant source of information on these parameters. The wide bounds relied upon for their critique appear to have been manufactured solely by a particular variable classification. But the inadequacies in their work are even more serious than that. No attention was paid by them at all to the quality of the model used for EBA, and it is therefore appropriate that we briefly review it.

In Cooley and LeRoy's specification the demand for real money ($M1$) is held to be a function of two interest rate variables, the savings and loan passbook rate (RSL) and the ninety-day Treasury bill rate (RTB), real GNP (nominal GNP divided by the GNP deflator, P), the current inflation rate (INF), the real value of credit card transactions (VCC), and real wealth (W). They use seasonally adjusted quarterly data for the period 1952:II to 1978:IV, and present (p. 834) estimates for a loglinear specification. Our estimates of their model are shown in Table 3.[6]

To evaluate Cooley and LeRoy's estimated equation, it is sufficient to note that the most basic index of inadequacy, the Durbin–Watson statistic, is 0.063. This is an example of the situation condemned by Granger and Newbold (1974), in which the Durbin–Watson statistic is markedly exceeded by the R^2 and in which arises the danger of the 'spurious regression' phenomenon. It is clearly not sensible to investigate fragility with such an inadequate model.

From the above discussion one is entitled to be dubious of the validity of Cooley and LeRoy's claim that the interest elasticity of the demand for money cannot be known with much precision. Nevertheless, it could be correct. Moreover, in view of the prominence of the topic in the literature, and the particular stand taken by Cooley and LeRoy on the issue, it is interesting to see what type of model would have eventuated, *given only the data series used by Cooley and LeRoy as input*, if a proper modelling strategy had been followed.[7] That strategy involves the three stages described at the beginning of this section.

A.   Selection of the General Model

Under the restriction on the universe of available variables, the main direction in which generalization of Cooley and LeRoy's model can take

---

[6] Cooley kindly made their data available to us. We were able to reproduce their results with the exception that the real wealth elasticity should be -0.107 rather than $+0.107$, and the inflation rate should not be in logarithms since negative rates were observed over the sample period.

[7] The restriction seems necessary to avoid the situation where differences in any conclusions we reach to those of Cooley and LeRoy are simply a consequence of our using information not available to them.

Table 3. Alternative estimates of the money demand function[a]

	M1	RTB	RSL	INF	GNP	VCC	W[b]
Cooley and LeRoy		-0.010 (0.011)	-0.175 (0.069)	-0.036 (0.167)	0.372 (0.081)	-0.009 (0.055)	-0.107 (0.096)
			SEE = 0.028, D-W = 0.063				
Simplified model							
Lag 0		-0.003 (0.003)	-0.111 (0.040)	-0.156 (0.029)	0.048 (0.051)	-0.009 (0.018)	0.178 (0.045)
Lag 1	0.866 (0.054)	-0.005 (0.003)	0.053 (0.043)	-0.012 (0.026)	0.062 (0.058)	0.007 (0.017)	-0.178 (0.048)
	SEE = 0.0031, D-W = 1.938, $\varrho_1 = 0.306$, $\varrho_2 = -0.219$, $\varrho_3 = 0.194$						
				(0.133)	(0.129)	(0.131)	
Preferred model	0.835[c] (0.047)	-0.009 (0.002)	-0.074 (0.021)	-0.146 (0.026)	0.126 (0.027)		0.178 (0.041)
	SEE = 0.0031, D-W = 2.024, $\varrho_1 = 0.391$, $\varrho_2 = -0.301$						
				(0.118)	(0.112)		

[a] All regressors except the inflation rate are in logs. Constant term is not shown. Standard errors are shown in parentheses. SEE = standard deviation of residuals, D-W = Durbin–Watson statistic.
[b] For the preferred regression this column is $\Delta \ln W$.
[c] Coefficient of lagged real money (in logs).

place is in the order of dynamics. Given the wide use of distributed lags in modelling money demand, it seems extraordinary that the authors chose to ignore Christopher Sims' maxim that 'a time series regression model arising in econometric research ought in nearly every case to be regarded as a distributed lag model until proven otherwise' (1974, p. 289). The omission of dynamics is even stranger in the light of Cooley and LeRoy's own comments: 'Such lagged endogenous variables as the lagged money stock ... cannot plausibly be excluded from the demand side either explicitly as observable explanatory variables for the demand for money or implicitly through the time dependence of the error' (p. 840).

Our general model therefore has the same variables as Cooley and LeRoy, but with four lags on all variables (including the dependent). This lag structure seems reasonable considering the data used are quarterly. The period selected for study was, however, shorter than that used by Cooley and LeRoy. Judd and Scadding (1982) have recently noted that a large number of studies have experienced difficulty in estimating conventional money demand functions for the post-1973 period. Not only do these models predict poorly, but in a large number of cases such models are dynamically unstable. Various reasons for the poor performances of the models are canvassed by Judd and Scadding. Among them, the most likely cause of the observed instability in the demand for money after 1973 is innovation in financial arrangements' (p. 1014), which originated from the rapid rise in inflation during the period. In accordance with this view, we restricted ourselves to the subsample 1952:II to 1973:IV, with the first four observations used for constructing up to four lags on all variables.[8]

B.   Simplification of the General Model

Our first step in simplification of the general model represents an attempt to determine the order of dynamics on each of the variables through a sequence of nested tests. The procedure we use was proposed by Sargan (1980), and has been termed the COMFAC algorithm, due to the fact that it seeks to determine common factors in the distributed lag polynomials associated with each variable. Briefly the logic of the method is as follows.

Suppose the general model had the form

(1) $y_t = b_1 y_{t-1} + \ldots + b_4 y_{t-4} + c_0 x_t + \ldots + c_4 x_{t-4} + e_t.$

With the aid of lag operators, (1) can be rewritten as

(2) $b(L)y_t = c(L)x_t + e_t,$

where $b(L) = 1 - b_1 L \ldots -b_4 L^4$ and $c(L) = c_0 + c_1 L + \ldots + c_4 L^4$ are

---

[8] The counterpart to Cooley and LeRoy's model over this shorter period gives parameter estimates -2.90, -0.021, -0.382, -0.009, -0.616, -0.017, and -0.052 with standard error of estimate 0.0083.

polynomials in the lag operator L. If the term $(1 - \varrho_1 L)$ is a common root of both polynomials, (2) can be re-expressed as

$$(3) \qquad b^*(L)y_t = c^*(L)x_t + u_t,$$

with
$$b(L) = (1 - \varrho_1 L)b^*(L),$$
$$c(L) = (1 - \varrho_1 L)c^*(L),$$

and
$$(1 - \varrho_1 L)u_t = e_t.$$

An examination of (3) shows that the presence of a common factor has created a new model with maximum lag of three in y_t and x_t and first-order serial correlation $(AR(1))$ in the errors. As there were nine parameters in (2) and only eight in (3), a restriction has been imposed, whose validity may be tested. If the restriction is accepted, the model is capable of being simplified. Moreover, if ϱ_1 turns out to be zero, the original model must have had both the orders in y_t and x_t overstated.

In our general model there are six regressors apart from the intercept. Hence, in the analogous move from (2) to (3), *six* restrictions are being imposed in the first attempt at simplification. If the first common factor is accepted, imposing the second leads to a further six restrictions, with the equation error now given as $AR(2)$, $u_t = \varrho_1 u_{t-1} + \varrho_2 u_{t-2} + e_t$. In this way, each additional common factor restriction leads to six fewer estimated coefficients. Since we have a sequence of nested tests, we set the level of significance of each test at 1 per cent so as to have an overall level of significance of approximately 4 per cent.[9]

There are two difficulties that can arise in using the F-test to test the common factors. First, there will generally be multiple minima for the sums of squares (see Sargan, 1980) and, second, there is no guarantee that the common roots in the polynomials attached to the variables are real. In order to guard against complex roots, we test for two common factors initially, and then test for one common factor only if two are rejected. Thus, in testing for the first two common factors in Table 2.4, the calculated F-statistic is 1.7555, the unrestricted (restricted) lag length is 4(2) and 12 restrictions are being tested (6 associated with each common factor).

Compared with the critical value of $F(12, 48, 0.01) = 2.59$, the calculated statistic is not significant. At this stage, then, the lag length has been reduced from 4 to 2 and the equation error can be expressed as $AR(2)$. Testing third and fourth common factors gives a value of 3.904 for the F-statistic which is significant at 1 per cent. Therefore, the third and fourth

---

[9] To test the restrictions, we used the standard F-test given by $F = [(\bar{e}'\bar{e} - \hat{e}'\hat{e})/\hat{e}'\hat{e}] \cdot [(T - \hat{k})/r]$, where $\bar{e}'\bar{e}$ is the sum of squared residuals from the restricted model, $\hat{e}'\hat{e}$ is its unrestricted counterpart, $(T - \hat{k})$ is the degrees of freedom of the unrestricted model, and r is the number of restrictions to be tested. In this way some allowance is made for the number of parameters estimated in the unrestricted model.

Table 4   Tests of Common Factors (83 observations)

Common factor	Unrestricted lag length	Restricted lag length	F-statistic	D.F.	Critical F(0.01)
1,2	4	2	1.755	(12,48)	2.59
3,4	2	0	3.904	(12,60)	2.50
3	2	1	0.426	(6,60)	3.12

common factors are rejected. Returning to the second-order lag and testing for the third common factor only gives a value of 0.426 for the *F*-statistic. Since the calculated value is significantly less than 3.12, three common factors are accepted. The model can now be expressed as one lag on all variables, with an equation error given as $AR(3)$. The resulting model is referred to as the 'simplified' one in Table 3.

The following observations are relevant to the simplified dynamic specification given in Table 3. Of the four interest rates, only current *RSL* is significant, and, apart from the lagged dependent variable, the only significant lagged variable is real wealth. Moreover, current and lagged wealth have coefficients which add to zero exactly. Neither the current nor lagged real value of credit card transactions exerts a significant effect on real balances. Finally, the third common factor (ϱ_3) is not significantly different from zero, thereby reducing the implicit lag length of the specification by one.

It is fairly clear that the model is still overparameterized. Accordingly, we imposed a further eight restrictions, namely zero coefficients for VCC and the lagged values of RTB, RSL, INF, GNP, and VCC, a zero sum for the wealth coefficients, and a zero value for the third common factor. The calculated *F*-statistic of 1.001 is signficantly less than $F(8, 66, 0.01) \simeq 2.8$, leading to acceptance of the restrictions. Our preferred model is therefore the last one listed in Table 3.

C.   *Quality Control: Is the Model a Lemon?*

How does the estimated model in Table 3 stand up to the five criteria for quality control listed at the beginning of this section? With the exception of the term $\Delta \ln W_t$, it constitutes a very traditional specification of money demand. The presence of the change in, rather than the level of, wealth is, however, consistent with theoretical considerations. If transactions requirements are held constant, that is, GNP_t is fixed, the fact that money ($M1$) is an asset dominated for portfolio purposes by interest-bearing deposits of near equal liquidity suggests that the long-term wealth effect should be zero. In the short run though, it has been frequently noted that changes in wealth are initially held as demand deposits before reallocation, and the combination of $\Delta \ln W$, and the lagged dependent variable

Table 5. Indexes of adequacy for the preferred model

Statistic type		Statistic value						Critical value
RESET[a]		3.27						$F(2, 74, 0.01) \simeq 4.9$
Diff. Test[b]		2.59						$\chi^2(8, 0.01) = 20.09$
Normality Test[c]		1.74						$\chi^2(2, 0.01) = 9.21$
Hetero. Test[d]		1.82						$\chi^2(1, 0.01) = 6.63$
ACF of squared	(1)	−0.68	(3)	0.51				SND $(0.01) = 2.33$
residuals[e]	(2)	0.49	(4)	0.36				
ACF of	(1)	1.22	(3)	0.73	(5)	1.62	(7)	0.22
residuals[f]	(2)	1.17	(4)	0.53	(6)	0.28	(8)	1.12

[a] The F-test that the coefficients of the predictions squared and cubed in the regression of the residuals against these and the derivatives are zero. Computation was done via partitioned inversion to avoid serious numerical inaccuracy.

[b] The differencing test of Charles Plosser et al. (1982). One iteration of Sargan's (1959) AIV estimator upon the differenced model was performed from the estimates in Table 3. Instruments for the derivatives with respect to the coefficients of M_{t-1} and u_{t-1} were constructed as in Plosser et al. (fn. 7).

[c] The joint normality test of Bowman and Shenton (1975), or Bera and Jarque (1981).

[d] the LM test that $\gamma = 0$ in $\sigma^2 = \sigma^2(E(y_t))^\gamma$ where y_t is the dependent variable of a regression. Pagan et al. (1981) derive this LM test but it was proposed originally as a test for heteroscedasticity by Anscombe (1961).

[e] The t-statistics were formed by regressing the squared residuals against their lagged values. This approach was used by Granger and Andersen (1978) for the detection of non-linear models but can also be used to check for Engle's (1982a) ARCH effects or as a general specification error test.

[f] Writing the model as a non-linear regression $y = f(X; \theta) + \varepsilon$, the t-statistics that the coefficient of the lagged residuals $\hat{\varepsilon}_{t-j}$ are zero in the regressions of $\hat{\varepsilon}_t$ against $\hat{\varepsilon}_{t-j}$ and $\partial f_t / \partial \theta$ for $j = 1, \ldots, 8$.

describes such a process, the implied lag distribution being 0.178, −0.029, −0.025, etc. Perhaps the only difficulty with such an interpretation is that the portfolio reallocation process is not faster.

Table 5 investigates whether there are any obvious inferential monsters lurking beyond the horizon, by augmenting the moments of the preferred model with a number of variables designed to capture inadequacy. No striking deficiencies are in evidence. A number of other experiments were conducted to determine whether it was possible to reject the chosen model by the addition of particular variables. These included a number of lags in real GDP, RSL, etc., time trend, seasonal dummies, and estimation with up to seventh-order serial correlation pattern. None of these augmentations was found to contribute anything of signficance. A final point worth mentioning is that t-statistics, made robust to heteroscedasticity as suggested by White (1980), were about 10 per cent higher than those in Table 3. The only exception to this rule – that for inflation – was only slightly smaller.

A check on parameter constancy is available by examining the size of prediction errors made when an equation is estimated over a particular sample and then used to forecast out of sample.[10] In this vein, the preferred model was estimated to 1970:IV and one-step prediction errors were generated from 1971:I to 1973:IV by augmenting the preferred equation with the Type B constructed variables in Pagan and Nicholls (1984). The '*F*-test' that the coefficients on the twelve constructed variables were jointly zero was 1.58, well below the critical $F(12, 62, 0.01)$ value of 2.49. Although an examination of the individual errors does reveal one large error, namely that for 1972:I, where the *t*-value was 2.58, the prediction errors for 1971–73 were much the same as the sample errors, with an average absolute value of 0.4 per cent.[11]

D.   *Are Interest Elasticities of Money Demand Zero?*

As our model was of satisfactory quality to 1973:IV, it is reasonable to utilize it to shed light on the question of whether data is uninformative about interest elasticities, as alleged by Cooley and LeRoy.[12] Conditional upon the structure of the final model being valid, we can say that all variables in the estimated relationship (including *both* interest rates) are highly significant, and to adopt their hypothesis of a zero interest rate effect as an acceptable interpretation of the data would be totally inappropriate. To be sure, this final specification was arrived at after a decision in which an arbitrary group of variables was dropped because of insignificance. To assure readers that the well-defined interest elasticities found in our preferred model were not dependent upon this action, and to illustrate what we believe is the place of EBA, we computed the extreme bounds for the two long-run interest elasticities. This was done by making the coefficients on either RSL or RTB the focus, treating all excluded variables are doubtful, and using the estimates of parameters on $\ln M_{t-1}$, $\ln RTB_t$ (or $\ln RSL_t$), $\ln RTB_{t-1}$ (or RSL_{t-1}) associated with the bounds to obtain long-run responses. To be consistent with Cooley and LeRoy, we concentrate upon the long-run elasticities as they summed lagged coef-

---

[10]   A more detailed analysis is available in our earlier working paper.

[11]   Although our model gave satisfactory performance up to 1973, just like automobiles, age finally caught up with it, and after that date its predictive performance declined dramatically. For the twelve quarters after 1973:IV, the *F*-test that prediction errors were zero was 5.69, with only the errors for 1974 not being significantly different from zero individually. The absolute error was 1.7 per cent over this three-year period. Thus Goldfeld's (1976) puzzle of the 'missing money' is certainly not resolved by working with Cooley and LeRoy's data alone.

[12]   Encompassing tests were also advocated to assess model quality. These are not really possible here given the restriction placed upon the data set, although it is clear that our model dominates those which exclude either RSL or RTB, the inflation rate, wealth or explicit dynamics. In Hendry and Richard's terminology, our model strongly variance-encompasses Cooley and LeRoy's as is apparent from the standard errors of estimate in our fn. 8 and Table 3.

ficients when dynamics were admitted. These bounds were extremely narrow, being -0.053 to -0.068 (RTB) and -0.400 to -0.441 (RSL), indicating that the effect of interest rates upon money demand was not sensitive to our decision to exclude certain variables.

5. Conclusions

That applied econometrics is not currently in the most robust of health is hard to deny, and it would be difficult to find as entertaining or as perceptive an analysis of its ills as that found in Leamer's various articles. What concerns us is that the prescriptions made in those articles are inappropriate, in part because of faulty diagnosis. Extreme bounds analysis (EBA) is most emphatically *not* the medicine to cure an ailing patient.

Section 1 argued that extreme bounds are generated by the imposition of highly arbitrary, and generally unknown, restrictions between the parameters of a model. Exactly why such bounds should be of interest therefore becomes something of a mystery. Furthermore, as shown in Sections II and III, the methodology is flawed on other grounds. EBA demands a general, adequate model from which the bounds may be derived, and a consensus over which variables are critical to a relationship. These are highly questionable conventions and we demonstrated, both theoretically and empirically, that deviations from them almost completely negate the utility of EBA.

After largely rejecting EBA, Section IV of the paper moved on to our own diagnosis and prescription. Both are founded on the belief that many of the difficulties applied econometrics currently faces originate in the very poor attempts currently made to accurately describe the process whereby a model was selected, and to ascertain its adequacy. Acceptance of this proposition leads to the necessity for the establishment and promulgation of standards with which to conduct applied research. Many other disciplines have faced and taken steps to solve this problem, and movement in this direction is long overdue in econometrics. With these considerations in mind we proposed a three-stage approach to modelling, involving the selection and subsequent simplification of a general model and a rigorous evaluation of any preferred model. Under the latter heading, five ways of performing such an evaluation were distinguished. It may not be too fanciful to think of such criteria as a 'checklist' to be applied when reviewing or performing applied work. Only if a model passes most items on the list should it be seriously considered as augmenting our knowledge.

Having set up some yardsticks with which to evaluate models, Section IV applied them to the money demand example in Cooley and LeRoy. Their specification was found to fail even the simplest of these criteria, making any conclusions drawn from it highly suspect. In sharp contrast to this failure, the application of a modeling strategy beginning with a general model and progressively constraining the parameter space led to a representation which passed all items of the checklist. This example highlighted the benefit of a systematic approach to modelling and model evaluation.

In closing, a confession. We are only too aware that what has been described are the necessary rather than sufficient conditions for taking the con out of econometrics. As any users of corporate accounts will be aware, there are many ways around standards. But that is not to deny their value. It serves only to highlight the need.

References

Anscombe, F. J. (1961), Examination of residuals. *Proceedings*, Fourth Berkeley symposium on Mathematical Statistics and Probability, Vol. 4, pp. 1–36.

Bera, Anil K. and Jarque, Carlos M. (1981), An efficient large sample test for normality of observations and regression residuals. Working Papers in Economics and Econometrics, No. 040, Australian National University.

Bowman, K. O. and Shenton, L. R. (1975), Omnibus contours for departures from normality based on $\sqrt{b_1}$ and b_2, *Biometrika*, No. 2, 62, 243–50.

Christ, Carl F. (1967), Econometrics in economics: some achievements and challenges, *Australian Economic Papers*, December, 6, 155–70.

Cooley, Thomas F. (1982), Specification analysis with discriminating priors: an application to the concentration profits debate, *Econometric Reviews*, No. 1, 1, 97–128.

Cooley, Thomas F. and LeRoy, Stephen F. (1981), Identification and estimation of money demand, *American Economic Review*, December, 71, 825–44.

Davidson James E. H. et al. (1978), Econometric modelling of the aggregate time-series relationship between consumers' expenditure and income in the United Kingdom, *Economic Journal*, December, 88, 661–92.

Dhrymes, Phoebus J. (1982), Comment, *Econometric Reviews*, No. 1, 1, 129–32.

Dicks-Mireaux, Louis and King, Mervyn (1984), Pension wealth and household savings: tests of robustness, *Journal of Public Economics*, February/March, 23, 115–39.

Engle, Robert F. (1982a), Autoregressive conditional heteroscedasticity with estimates of the variance of United Kingdom Inflation, *Econometrica*, July, 50, 987–1007.

Engle, Robert F. (1982b), A general approach to Lagrange multiplier model diagnostics, *Journal of Econometrics*, October, 20, 83–104.

Fiebig, D. G. (1981), A Bayesian analysis of inventory investment, *Empirical Economics* 6, 229–37.

Goldfeld, Stephen M. (1976), The case of the missing money, *Brookings Papers on Economic Activity*, 3, 683–730.

Granger, C. W. J. and Andersen, A. (1978), *An Introduction to Bilinear Time Series Models*. Vandenhoeck and Ruprecht, Gottingen.

Granger, C. W. J. and Newbold, P. (1974), Spurious regressions in econometrics, *Journal of Econometrics*, July, 2, 111–20.

Hendry, David F. (1980), Econometrics: alchemy or science?, *Economica*, November, 47, 387–406.

Hendry, David F. (1983), Econometric modelling: the consumption function in retrospect, *Scottish Journal of Political Economy*, 30, 193–220.

Hendry, David F. and Richard, Jean-François (1982), On the formulation of empirical models in dynamic econometrics, *Journal of Econometrics*, October, 20, 3–33.

Judd, John P. and Scadding, John L. (1982), The search for a stable money demand function: a survey of the post-1973 literature, *Journal of Economic Literature*, September, 20, 993–1023.

Leamer, Edward E. (1978), *Specification Searches: Ad Hoc Inference with Nonexperimental Data*. Wiley & Sons, New York.

Leamer, Edward E. (1981), SEARCH, a linear regression computer package. Mimeo, University of California–Los Angeles.

Leamer, Edward E. Sets of posterior means with bounded variance priors, *Econometrica*, May, 50, 725–36.

Leamer, Edward E. (1983), Let's take the con out of econometrics, *American Economic Review*, March, 73, 31–43. (reprinted as Chapter 1 in this volume).

Leamer Edward E. and Leonard, Herman (1983), Reporting the fragility of regression estimates, *Review of Economics and Statistics*, May, 65, 306–17.

Mizon, Grayham E. and Richard, Jean-François (1982), The encompassing principle and its application to non-nested hypotheses. Paper presented to the European meeting of the Econometric Society, Dublin.

Pagan, A. R. and Hall, A. D. (1983), Diagnostic tests as residual analysis, *Econometric Reviews*, No. 2, 2, 159–218.

Pagan, A. R. and Nicholls, D. F. (1984), Estimating predictions, prediction errors and their standard deviations using constructed variables, *Journal of Econometrics*, March, 24, 293–310.

Pagan, A. R., Hall, A. D. and Trivedi, P. K. (1981), Assessing the variability of inflation. Working Papers in Economics and Econometrics, No. 049, Australian National University.

Plosser, Charles I., Schwert, G. William and White, Halbert (1982), Differencing as a test of specification, *International Economic Review*, October, 23, 535–52.

Ramsey, James B. (1983), Perspective and comment, *Econometric Reviews*, No. 2, 2, 241–8.

Sargan, J. D. (1959), The estimation of relationships with autocorrelated residuals by the use of instrumental variables, *Journal of the Royal Statistical Society*, Series B, No. 1, 21, 91–105.

Sargan, J. D. (1964), Wages and prices in the United Kingdom: a study in econometric methodology, *Econometric Analysis for National Economic Planning*, ed. by P. E. Hart Butterworths, London, pp. 25–63.

Sargan, J. D. (1980), Some tests of dynamic specification for a single equation, *Econometrica* May, 48, 879–97.

Sims, Christopher A. (1974), Distributed lags, *Frontiers of Quantitative Economics*, North-Holland, Amsterdam, pp. 289–338.

White, Halbert (1980), A heteroskedasticity-consistent covariance matrix estimator and a direct test for heteroskedasticity, *Econometrica*, May, 48, 817–38.

3

Simplified Extreme Bounds

Trevor S. Breusch

Abstract. Alternative derivations are given of Leamer's 'extreme bounds' in regression models. Emphasis is placed on connections between the bounds and the usual least squares estimates, standard errors, and test statistics. Simple calculation of the bounds without a special computer program is shown, but some doubts are raised about the value of the information obtained.

1. Introduction

Leamer (1985) complains that his 'extreme bounds analysis' meets with little approval or understanding, either in the Bayesian guise from which it is motivated or after his attempts to translate it to language that is more widely understood. He fears it is the translation that causes the problems. This note is an attempt at an alternative translation, using different methods and giving different emphasis. The main objective is to clarify the connections between information provided by reporting of extreme bounds and the usual output and summary statistics of regression analysis. As far as possible, derivations are in straightforward algebra and there are minimal references to Bayes' theorem, prior distributions or the geometry of ellipsoids.

The next section below contains Bayesian and non-Bayesian derivations of the bounds, with the former in just sufficient detail to motivate the exercise and to show its equivalence with the latter. The extreme bounds will be seen to depend on familiar point estimates, standard errors and test statistics.

McAleer, Pagan and Volker (1983, 1985) make a spirited criticism of the bounds analysis, particularly in its applications by Cooley and LeRoy (1981) and Leamer (1983). They provide two propositions that connect indices of 'fragility' to be found in the literature using the bounds analysis with conventional test criteria. These propositions are restated in Section 3 with some clarification, and given particularly simple proofs.

This article first appeared as an unpublished Working Paper, Economics Department, University of Southampton, October 1985. The support of the ESRC under grant HR8323 is gratefully acknowledged, as are the comments from Michael McAleer.

In Section 4 some computational aspects are examined. Leamer (1978, p. 194) offers a computer program 'SEARCH' to calculate the bounds, but it will be seen that a simple calculation with the output of an ordinary least-squares program is sufficient.

Section 5 has some comments relating to the bounds as a way of packaging conventional criteria and to the Bayesian formulation of the problem.

2. Derivation

The setting is the linear model $y = X\beta + u$ where u is distributed as $N(0, \sigma^2 I)$. There are prior linear constraints $R\beta = r$, which refer to a subset (of linear combinations) of the coefficients. Coefficients (or linear combinations) that are assigned particular values by the constraints are called 'doubtful'; coefficients not so restricted are 'free'. The object of primary interest is a particular coefficient (or linear combination), $\beta_0 = \psi'\beta$, called the 'focus' coefficient. The focus coefficient may be doubtful, in which case $\psi = R'\alpha$ for some α, or may be free (or a combination of the two).

This terminology (which is the refined form of Leamer, 1985) is more natural in a special case that arises frequently in practice. The free co-efficients belong to explanatory variables that will definitely remain in the model; the doubtful coefficients belong to variables that may be dropped. Thus, there is a partitioning that gives $X\beta = X_F\beta_F + X_D\beta_D$, and the prior constraints $\beta_D = 0$ are a special case of $R\beta = r$ with $R = (0,I)$ and $r = 0$. Although the free/doubtful terminology is less natural, the mathematics is no more difficult for the general $R\beta = r$ form of constraints.

Given the constraints $R\beta = r$, the restricted least-squares estimate is

$$\hat{b} = b - VR'A^{-1}(Rb - r), \qquad (1)$$

where $b = (X'X)^{-1}X'y$ is the unrestricted estimate, $V = \sigma^2(X'X)^{-1}$ and A

$A = RVR'$. It is convenient to define V so that $V = \text{var}(b)$, but the scale factor σ^2 in fact cancels from (3.1). A compact form for the restricted estimate of the focus coefficient $\beta_0 = \psi'\beta$ is

$$\begin{aligned} \hat{b}_0 &= \psi'b - \psi'VR'A^{-1}(Rb - r) \\ &= b_0 - x'y, \end{aligned} \qquad (2)$$

where b_0 is the unrestricted estimate of the focus coefficient,

$$x = A^{-1/2}RV\psi \quad \text{and} \quad y = A^{-1/2}(Rb - r) \qquad (3)$$

with $A^{-1/2}$ the unique symmetric square root of A^{-1}.

The extreme bounds are the smallest and largest values that can be obtained as estimates of the focus coefficient β_0, under a set of different treatment of the prior constraints $R\beta = r$. In the Bayesian formulation –

which for Leamer motivates the whole exercise – the constraints are interpreted as specifying some aspects of a prior distribution on β. The interpretation is that the (doubtful) linear combinations $R\beta$ are given a prior mean vector of r but no prior variance matrix, while the remaining (free) linear combinations have prior distributions that remain diffuse. Different estimates of the focus coefficient are obtained as the marginal posterior mean (or mode) of β_0, when the prior variance (or the precision) of $R\beta$ ranges over all positive semidefinite matrices. Let the prior precision of $R\beta$ be $M'M$, where M can be assumed without loss of generality to have full row rank. Then the prior precision for the full β vector is $R'M'MR$, and the usual formula gives the posterior mean of β as

$$\tilde{\beta} = (X'X + R'M'MR)^{-1}(X'y + R'M'Mr).$$

Upon some rearrangement, this can be expressed as

$$\begin{aligned}
\tilde{\beta} &= b - (X'X + R'M'MR)^{-1}R'M'M(Rb-r) \\
&= b - (X'X)^{-1}R'M'[I + MR(X'X)^{-1}R'M']^{-1}M(Rb-r) \\
&= b - VR'M'(\sigma^2 I + MAM')^{-1}M(Rb-r).
\end{aligned}$$

The posterior mean of the focus coefficient $\beta_0 = \psi'\beta$ is then

$$\begin{aligned}
\beta_0 &= b_0 - x'A^{1/2}M'(\sigma^2 I + MAM')^{-1}MA^{1/2}y \\
&= b_0 - x'W(\sigma^2 I + W'W)^{-1}W'y, \tag{4}
\end{aligned}$$

where $W = A^{1/2}M'$. Note that a particular choice of W uniquely determines M, and conversely, so the bounds are the extreme values of β_0 as W ranges over all (full column rank) matrices.

Another characterization of the bounds, which does not have the Bayesian motivation, refers to the different estimates of the focus coefficient when *implications* of the given constraints are imposed in restricted least-squares estimation. Thus the bounds are the smallest and largest values of $\hat{\beta}_0 = \psi'\hat{\beta}$, where $\hat{\beta}$ is the least-squares estimate subject to $M(R\beta-r) = 0$, with R and r taken as given and M free to vary. Since redundant constraints are irrelevant, it can again be assumed without loss of generality that M has full row rank. Then

$$\begin{aligned}
\hat{\beta}_0 &= b_0 - \psi'R'M'(MAM')^{-1}M(Rb-r) \\
&= b_0 - x'W(W'W)^{-1}W'y, \tag{5}
\end{aligned}$$

where again $W = A^{1/2}M'$. In this form the bounds are the extreme values of β_0 as W ranges over all (full column rank) matrices.

LEMMA   For given vectors x and y and all symmetric matrices P such that P and $I - P$ are positive semidefinite,

$$\tfrac{1}{2}x'y - \tfrac{1}{2}(x'x\, y'y)^{1/2} \leqslant x'Py \leqslant \tfrac{1}{2}(x'y + \tfrac{1}{2}(x'x\, y'y)^{1/2}, \tag{6}$$

and both bounds can be attained for some P.

Proof   For any scalar θ, the stated properties of P imply that

$$(x - \theta y)' P(x - \theta y) + (x + \theta y)' (I - P)(x + \theta y) \geq 0, \qquad (7)$$

which simplifies on cancellation to

$$x'x + 2\theta x'y + \theta^2 y'y - 4\theta x' Py \geq 0.$$

Now suppose $x \neq 0$ and $y \neq 0$ (else the result is trivial) and let $\theta = (x'x/y'y)^{1/2}$. Then dividing through by 4θ gives

$$\tfrac{1}{2}[x'y + (x'x\, y'y)^{1/2}] - x'Py \geq 0,$$

which yields the upper bound on $x'Py$ as stated in (3.6). It is readily verified that the upper bound can be attained: for example by $P = w(w'w)^{-1}w'$, where w is proportional to $x + \theta y$, and θ is as given above. The proof of the lower bound and its attainment is exactly the same, except with $-\theta$ in place of θ in (7) and in the definition of w.

THEOREM The extreme values of $\bar{\beta}_0$ in (4) and $\hat{\beta}_0$ in (5) over all choices of W are

$$b_0 - \tfrac{1}{2}x'y \pm \tfrac{1}{2}(x'x\, y'y)^{1/2}, \qquad (8)$$

where the minus sign gives $\beta_0^{(\min)}$ and the plus sign gives $\beta_0^{(\max)}$. Both bounds can be attained by $\hat{\beta}_0$, and can be approached arbitrarily closely by $\bar{\beta}_0$, for some choice of W.

Proof Both $\hat{\beta}_0$ and $\bar{\beta}_0$ have the form $b_0 - x'Py$ for some P such that P and $I - P$ are positive semidefinite, so the Lemma is directly applicable. Attainment of the bounds by some $\hat{\beta}_0$ follows directly from the Lemma. Furthermore, any $\hat{\beta}_0$ defined as in (3.5) with, say, $W = W^*$, may be approximated arbitrarily closely by defining $\bar{\beta}_0$ in (4) with $W = aW^*$ for some scalar a, and letting $a \to \infty$.

Other characterizations are possible of the same bounds, $\beta_0^{(\min)}$ and $\beta_0^{(\max)}$, involving subsets of implications of the constraints $R\beta = r$. For example, W may be restricted to have just one column (so that $\hat{\beta}_0$ may be described as the result of imposing just one implied constraint), or W may be restricted to have just one column less than the number of rows of R (so that $\hat{\beta}_0$ may be described as the result of replacing the doubtful variables by a single linear combination of them that has its coefficient estimated freely). Clearly the same bounds are applicable to these restricted sets of $\hat{\beta}_0$ values. And the bounds are still attainable for some W, since attainment requires only that W be chosen so that its columns are all orthogonal to one given vector but its column space includes another given vector that is orthogonal to the first one.

Various alternative expressions for the bounds in (8) can be obtained from recognizing the properties of the vectors x and y. In particular:

$$x'y = \psi' VR'A^{-1}(Rb - r) = b_0 - \hat{b}_0 \qquad (9)$$

is the difference between the unrestricted and fully restricted estimates of the focus coefficient;

$$y'y = (Rb-r)'A^{-1}(Rb-r) = \chi_D^2 \qquad (10)$$

is the χ^2 statistic for testing the full set of constraints $R\beta = r$; and

$$x'x = \psi'VR'A^{-1}RV\psi = \text{var}(b_0) - \text{var}(\hat{b}_0) \qquad (11)$$

is the reduction in variance of the estimate of β_0 due to imposing the constraints $R\beta = r$. These alternative expressions are useful for interpreting and computing the bounds.

3. The 'Straw-Man' Propositions

McAleer et al. (1983, 1985) consider two indices of 'fragility' that may be found in applications of extreme bounds analysis. Their two propositions, which connect the fragility indices with conventional test criteria, may be simplified, particularly in the proofs.

Proposition 1 refers to 'Type A' fragility, which is said to exist when the distance between the bounds exceeds the standard deviation of the unrestricted least-squares estimate of the focus coefficient by more than some predetermined multiple, i.e. when for some k

$$\beta_0^{(max)} - \beta_0^{(min)} > k(\text{var}(b_0))^{1/2}.$$

The proposition states that the condition $\chi_D^2 > k^2$ is:

(a) necessary and sufficient when the focus coefficient is doubtful;
(b) necessary in general.

Proof   From the bounds expression (8),

$$\begin{aligned}
\beta_0^{(max)} - \beta_0^{(min)} &= (x'x\,y'y)^{1/2} \\
&= (\phi\,\text{var}(b_0)\chi_D^2)^{1/2}, \qquad (12)
\end{aligned}$$

where $\phi = x'x/\text{var}(b_0) = [\text{var}(b_0)-\text{var}(\hat{b}_0)]/\text{var}(b_0)$. Thus Type A fragility occurs if and only if $\phi\chi_D^2 > k^2$. Since $0 \le \phi \le 1$, the condition $\chi_D^2 > k^2$ is necessary, and so part (b) is proved. When the focus coefficient is doubtful $\psi = R'\alpha$ for some α, and the restricted estimate of the focus coefficient is exactly specified by the constraints as $\hat{b}_0 = \alpha'r$. Hence $\text{var}(\hat{b}_0) = 0$, which implies $\phi = 1$. The condition $\chi_D^2 > k^2$ is then necessary and sufficient, and so part (a) is proved.

Proposition 2 refers to 'Type B' fragility, which is said to exist when possible estimates may be positive or negative, i.e. when $\beta_0^{(max)}$ and $\beta_0^{(min)}$ have opposite signs. The proposition states that the condition $\chi_D^2 > t_0^2 = b_0^2/\text{var}(b_0)$ is:

(a) necessary and sufficient when the focus coefficient is doubtful;
(b) necessary in general.

(McAleer, Pagan and Volker (1983) set $r = 0$ in their proofs 'without loss of generality'. However, it will be seen that $r = 0$ is required for Proposition 2(a) to be true generally).

Proof When the focus coefficient is doubtful, $x'x = \text{var}(b_0)$ and $x'y = b_0 - a'r$. The bounds from (3.8) can then be written as

$$\tfrac{1}{2}(b_0 + a'r) \pm \tfrac{1}{2}(\text{var}(b_0)\chi_D^2)^{1/2}. \tag{13}$$

Since $c \pm d$ have opposite signs if and only if $d^2 > c^2$, the bounds have opposite signs if and only if

$$\chi_D^2 > (b_0 + a'r)^2/\text{var}(b_0). \tag{14}$$

The result in part (a) follows when $a'r = 0$, which holds when $r = 0$ but not in general otherwise.

For part (b), with any focus coefficient and possibly inhomogeneous constraints, consider weaker bounds that may not be minimal. The Cauchy–Schwarz inequality $|x'y| \leq (x'x\, y'y)^{1/2}$ implies that the bounds (8) are contained within the bounds

or equivalently, $$b_0 \pm (x'x\, y'y)^{1/2}$$

$$b_0 \pm (\phi\, \text{var}(b_0)\, \chi_D^2)^{1/2}.$$

Since $0 \leq \phi \leq 1$, these are contained within the bounds

$$b_0 \pm (\text{var}(b_0)\, \chi_D^2)^{1/2}. \tag{15}$$

These later bounds have opposite signs (if and) only if $\chi_D^2 > b_0^2/\text{var}(b_0)$, which is therefore a necessary condition for Type B fragility, as stated in part (b).

Actually, Proposition 2(a) is trivial, because the stated condition holds with probability one when the focus coefficient is doubtful and $r = 0$. Then, since $\hat{b}_0 = 0$ gives $x'y = b_0$ and $x'x = \text{var}(b_0)$, and as always $y'y = \chi_D^2$, it follows from the Cauchy–Schwarz inequality that

$$\chi_D^2 \geq b_0/\text{var}(b_0), \tag{16}$$

with strict inequality unless x is proportional to y. Except in the case of a single constraint in $R\beta = r$ (when the outcome is also trivial because the focus coefficient is the only one that is doubtful), the continuous random variable vector y is proportional to the fixed vector x with probability zero. Thus (16) will be the strict inequality with probability one, and the condition for Proposition 2(a) will be automatically satisfied. As noted by Leamer (1985, p.318): 'If there are two or more doubtful variables, a coefficient on a doubtful variable may be positive or negative, regardless of the degree of correlation between the variables.'

4. Computational Matters

All of the development so far has followed Leamer (1978) in treating the variance parameter σ^2 as known and referring to χ^2 statistics, etc., based on known σ^2. It is straightforward to replace σ^2 throughout with s^2, the degrees-of-freedom-corrected residual variance estimate from the unrestricted model. Then $(\text{var}(b_0))^{1/2}$ becomes $\text{SE}(b_0)$, the usual standard error for b_0, and χ_D^2 become qF_D, where F_D is the usual F statistic for testing the q independent linear constraints in $R\beta = r$.

Alternative expressions for the bounds in (8) enable them to be calculated from the information printed out by most least-squares computer programs. The only minor complication is that typically a revised estimate of σ^2 would be computed from the restricted model for use in the standard errors of the restricted coefficient estimates. (This would happen if the restricted model was estimated by ordinary least-squares after reparameterizing, if necessary, and dropping of doubtful variables.) If the revised σ^2 estimate is called $\hat{s}^2$, the bounds may be calculated as

$$\tfrac{1}{2}(b_0 + \hat{b}_0) \pm \tfrac{1}{2}[[\text{SE}(b_0)^2 - \text{SE}(\hat{b}_0)^2 s^2/\hat{s}^2]qF_D]^{1/2}. \tag{17}$$

Other forms that may be more useful can be obtained by substituting for s^2, $\hat{s}^2$ and F_D in terms of unrestricted and restricted residual sums of squares. There are further simplifications when the focus coefficient is doubtful, since then $\hat{b}_0$ is specified by the constraints and $\text{SE}(\hat{b}) = 0$.

5. Comments

One view of the extreme bounds is that they summarize, in a readily understandable metric, information that would otherwise lead to the same conclusions about 'fragility', but which would be more difficult to report and assimilate in another form. Note that the mid-point between the bounds is determined by the simple average of the unrestricted and restricted least-squares estimates of the focus coefficient. The distance between the bounds depends, multiplicatively, on the decrease in sampling variance of the estimated coefficient due to imposing the constraints and the relative loss of fit (or equivalently the F ratio). Narrow bounds arise when there is not much gain in sampling precision or there is not much loss of fit; in either case there is the implication that unrestricted and restricted least-squares estimates are similar in value. Thus in the extreme cases where the focus variable is orthogonal to the doubtful variables, or where the unrestricted estimates exactly satisfy the constraints, the bounds coincide at the (unrestricted equals restricted) estimate of the focus coefficient. (In the notation of Section 2, $x = 0$ or $y = 0$ implies $x'y = 0$ and hence $b_0 = \hat{b}_0$.) However, similar values for unrestricted and restricted estimates do not necessarily lead to narrow bounds. (Neither $x = 0$ nor $y = 0$ is implied by $x'y = 0$.)

Some of the sharpest criticisms by McAleer, Pagan and Volker (1983, 1985) refer to analyses in which the focus coefficient is classified as doubtful. In that situation Type A fragility is equivalent to a large value of the usual test statistic, as indicated by Proposition 1(a), and a finding of Type B fragility is a foregone conclusion, as indicated by the discussion of Proposition 2(a). The bounds analysis does not allow sample evidence to overcome prior doubts about the relevance of a variable of interest; any such inference is automatically judged to be 'fragile'. While Leamer (1985) is unmoved by these criticisms, and even lists the passage quoted above in connection with the necessary finding of Type B fragility as an 'altogether desirable' property, the Bayesian credentials of the analysis do seem to be undermined. There is something wrong with an inference methodology that allows the Bleeding Heart of Leamer (1983) to cry 'fragile' whenever the data contradict his prior view that capital punishment has a doubtful effect on the murder rate!

One suggestion by McAleer, Pagan and Volker is to restrict the bounds analysis to situations where the focus coefficient is not among those classified as doubtful. While this would avoid cases in which there appear to be obvious anomalies, it does lack a rationale. In Leamer's Bayesian characterization of the bounds, the doübtful/free distinction relates to the prior information, whereas the focus/other distinction reflects the objectives of the research. There is no reason in principle for any relationship between the prior and the loss function.

However, there are other interpretations that might be made. A researcher who is prepared to set a doubtful coefficient to zero or some other value, irrespective of the strength of evidence in the data, does seem to reveal a lack of interest in learning about that quantity. It is implausible that a parameter that can be given such a cavalier prior specification could ever be an object of interest in the research. The translation in the bounds analysis of possible constraints into prior distributions might make sense for nuisance parameters that do not enter the loss function, but letting the focus coefficient be free seems essential for the analysis to be coherent.

Even then, there are aspects of the bounds analysis that are unconvincing as a characterization of actual research practice. The fact that different researchers would typically have different constraints on the 'soft' part of the specification does not necessarily reveal divergent prior views, and certainly not ones that might be held dogmatically. There are many reasons for imposing constraints, with model simplicity and estimation precision ranked high among them. Of course, one's confidence in the results would be enhanced if these different treatments of the subsidiary part of the model made no operationally or statistically significant difference. But in the bounds analysis, constraints are interpreted as revealing a family of priors, and the only robust inference is one that can be sustained under all possible extreme combinations of these priors. This chain of translation – from constraints to 'doubt', from doubt to prior views, and particularly to prior views that might be held dogmatically – has weaknesses at every link.[1]

Appendix

The methods used above yield a short algebraic proof of the main result in Leamer (1975), as an alternative to the geometric argument that is used there. The most general statement there is Theorem 2 which says, in the notation of this paper, that restricted ($\hat{b}_0$) and unrestricted (b_0) estimates of a regression coefficient are related by

$$|\hat{b}_0 - b_0| \leq \text{SE}(b_0)(qF_D)^{1/2}. \tag{A1}$$

A proof of this is immediate, since from (3.2) in the text above, and the Cauchy–Schwarz inequality, it follows that

$$
\begin{aligned}
|\hat{b}_0 - b_0| &= |x'y| \\
&\leq (x'y \, y'y)^{1/2} \\
&= \phi^{1/2}\text{SE}(b_0)(qF_D)^{1/2} \\
&\leq \text{SE}(b_0)(qF_D)^{1/2},
\end{aligned}
$$

where the last line follows from $0 \leq \phi \leq 1$.

The familiar result from Leamer (1975) is that, when a variable is dropped from a regression equation, there can be no change in the sign of any coefficient that is more significant than the coefficient of the omitted variable. This follows from the general result above, since the estimates $\hat{b}_0$ and b_0 can differ in sign only if $|b_0| < |\hat{b}_0 - b_0|$, which in view of (A1) requires $|t_0| < (qF_D)^{1/2}$, where $t_0 = b_0/\text{SE}(b_0)$. In the case of a single constraint, $q = 1$ and $(qF_D)^{1/2} = (F_D)^{1/2} = |t_D|$, so that $|t_0| < |t_D|$ is necessary.

References

Cooley, T. F. and LeRoy, S. F. (1981), Identification and estimating of money demand, *American Economic Review*, 71, 825–44.

Leamer, E. E. (1975), A result on the sign of restricted least-squares estimates, *Journal of Econometrics*, 3, 387–90.

Leamer, E. E. (1978), *Specification Searches*. Wiley, New York.

Leamer, E. E. (1982), Sets of posterior means with bounded variance priors, *Econometrica*, 50, 726–36.

[1] Leamer (1982) develops the bounds that result when the prior variance matrix of the doubtful coefficients has a restricted range. The requirement to accommodate dogmatic priors is replaced by a need to supply more information on the extremes of the strength of the prior views.

Leamer, E. E. (1983), Let's take the con out of econometrics, *American Economic Review*, 73, 31–43.

Leamer, E. E. (1985), Sensitivity analyses would help, *American Economic Review*, 75, 308–13.

McAleer, M., Pagan, A. R. and Volker, P. A. (1983), Straw-man econometrics? Working Paper in Economics and Econometrics No. 097, Australian National University.

McAleer, M., Pagan, A. R., and Volker, P. A. (1985), What will take the con out of econometrics?, *American Economic Review*, 75, 293–307.

4

What Will Take the Con Out of Econometrics?
A Reply to McAleer, Pagan, and Volker

*Thomas F. Cooley and Stephen F. LeRoy**

Our 1981 paper, criticized by Michael McAleer, Adrian Pagan, and Paul
Volker (1985), made two points. First, we argued that specification uncertainty renders suspect practically any but the weakest inference about
the interest elasticity of money demand. Second, we contended that there
is no credible reason to imagine that simultaneity problems are adequately
dealt with in existing studies of money demand. Now, if McAleer et al. had
wanted to make a truly effective criticism of our paper, they might have
pointed out that if the second point is granted, the first does not follow.
The Leamer–Leonard method for ascertaining fragility is based on the
maintained assumption that the error is orthogonal to all the candidate
regressors – precisely the assumption that we criticized in the second half
of our paper. Had McAleer et al. argued along these lines, we would have
been hard put to come up with a convincing reply. It is true that we
suggested (p. 827) that extreme fragility is evidence of serious simultaneity
problems. We suspect, however, that this argument would not bear close
examination, except perhaps in special cases or as a loose statement of why
we were motivated to think about simultaneity problems. Our argument
reflected the rhetorical exigencies of a difficult transition, rather than any
line of reasoning we could readily make precise. We are surprised that no
one has called us on this point.

McAleer et al., of course, could not pursue these lines without in-
validating their own purported contribution, which consists of attempting
to rehabilitate one-equation-at-a-time estimation despite the fact that the
equations being estimated are presumably embedded in simultaneous
equation systems. It is therefore no surprise that McAleer et al. ignored
our invitation to engage in a serious discussion of macroeconometric
practice, given that their ox would be gored more than ours.

McAleer et al. either have an understanding of the nature of simultaneous equations estimation very different from ours, or they completely

* University of California, Santa Barbara, CA 93106. We are indebted to Andrew Rose for
helpful comments.

This article first appeared in *American Economic Review*, Vol. 76, No. 3, June 1986,
pp. 504–7.

misunderstood our argument. For example, consider their Section IV, Part A, where they found it strange that we deleted the lagged value of the money stock as an explanatory variable for the current money stock despite our expressed opinion that 'such lagged endogenous variables as the lagged money stock . . . cannot plausibly be excluded from the demand side either explicitly as observable explanatory variables for the demand for money or implicitly from the time dependence of the error' (p. 840). Our intention in the passage just cited, contrary to McAleer et al.'s interpretation, was not to criticize estimates of money demand (such as our own) that exclude the lagged dependent variable. Rather, it was to cast doubt on the presumption that lagged money could plausibly serve as an instrument for the interest elasticity of money demand, as has widely been recommended. Despite the simplicity of this argument, McAleer et al. completely misread it, finding only that it is 'strange' that even though we conceded that m_{-1} should in principle enter the money demand equation, we nonetheless suppressed it from an ordinary least-squares equation.

I

Let us suppose, contrary to what we argued in our 1981 paper, that simultaneity problems can magically be assumed away. Thus assume that even though we do not know what the correct explanatory variables are, we are nonetheless sure that the unobserved determinant of money demand is statistically independent of these variables. Thus there is no problem with ordinary least-squares. These were the conditions assumed in the first half of our paper, and throughout by McAleer et al. Our suggestion was simply that specification uncertainty be explicitly acknowledged, and that the sensitivity of the estimated interest elasticity to respecifications be assessed using the methods developed by Leamer and others. Our idea was to encourage econometricians to report priors explicitly so that readers can compare their own priors to those of the econometrician and evaluate the results accordingly.

This suggestion appeared uncontroversial to us, but apparently not to McAleer et al. They are troubled by the fact that different extreme bounds can result from different classifications of variables as doubtful or free. They conclude that since assessments of fragility depend on a 'whimsical' choice of priors, such assessments are altogether unreliable. We are mystified by this criticism. It is indeed true that different priors lead to different posteriors – what would be the point of Bayesian econometrics if it were otherwise? Prior beliefs are by definition treated as given; what is gained by calling them whimsical? McAleer et al. appear to suppose that there is some way to dispense with prior beliefs in doing statistical inference, so that a data set can be made to reveal a single correct inference with the appropriate application of statistical technique. On the contrary, both Bayesian and classical statistics of the Cowles variety depend essentially on prior information. The conclusion that an inference is fragile is not some kind of descriptive fact, as McAleer et al. presume, the validity of which can be impugned if it is shown to depend on a whimsical choice of priors. Rather, the fragility of an inference is conditional on the choice of prior. It is precisely the virtue of Leamer's method, not its fault, that it relates fragility to prior beliefs.

McAleer et al. found fault with extreme bounds analysis because no account is taken of prior beliefs about the signs of coefficients; instead variables are classified only as doubtful or free. Here again we are unpersuaded. One of the most important tasks of empirical econometrics is the verification (or falsification) of sign priors. Now, if the reader knows that in the process of arriving at a preferred specification the econometrician has incorporated his (or her) prior beliefs about the signs of coefficients, as by deleting variables which have 'wrong' signs, will he (or she) be persuaded by a report of an estimated equation in which all coefficients have the 'right' sign? We doubt it. It is exactly because it is (in many contexts) so easy to find in the parameter space a regression that reproduces prior beliefs that readers are routinely unimpressed by reports of 'success' in estimation.

Having demonstrated, at least to our satisfaction, that McAleer et al.'s reservations about extreme bounds analysis are without substance, we must acknowledge that one of their criticisms of our application of extreme bounds analysis is correct, and it is not minor. Just as they suggested, we treated the constant term as doubtful. This was inadvertent; since we are not aware of any theory that could justify suppression of the constant, it should be treated as free. McAleer et al. repeated our calculations with this correction and found that the extreme bounds are near zero. The interpretation is that our data and priors justify a confident conclusion that the interest elasticity of money demand is approximately zero, not that any inference about this parameter is fragile. Since McAleer et al. successfully duplicated our results, we have no doubt that their calculation is correct. But the conclusion that the interest elasticity of money demand is zero reflects the exclusion of lagged terms from our regressions. We suppressed dynamics because their inclusion would only widen extreme bounds which, we (incorrectly) believed, were already very wide. Since we have not re-calculated the extreme bounds under a less stringent restriction on priors, we must concede that we have not demonstrated the correctness of our contention that, on reasonable priors, any inference about the interest elasticity of money demand is extremely fragile.

II

The question arises whether McAleer et al.'s rejection of our strictures on conventional estimation practices means that they accept these practices. Although there is no necessary reason for one to imply the other, examination of McAleer et al.'s proposed procedure for arriving at a 'tentatively adequate' money demand equation reveals that they do in fact accept received practice, subject to some new bells and whistles which are discussed below. They ignore simultaneity problems, and see nothing undesirable in the informal and unsystematic infusion of prior information during the estimation process. Indeed, they recommend it. Our 1981 paper, of course, criticized received practice on exactly these two points. As an example of McAleer et al.'s casual incorporation of prior information, we need do no more than consider their choice of sample period. Their data set ended twelve years ago. Why not use more recent data? Because 'a large number of studies have experienced difficulty in estimating conventional money demand functions for the post-1973 period' (p. 302). This explanation, accompanied by a nod in the direction of financial innovation (the alleged cause of the unruly money demand equations estimated from more recent data), appears to McAleer et al. sufficient to justify truncating the data set to the convenient 1952–73 period for which 'satisfactory' estimated money demand equations are a dime a dozen. *Plus ça change, plus c'est la même chose.*

Beginning with this informal choice of an adequate data set, McAleer et al. approach the problem of modelling money demand as a four-step process: (1) begin with an overparameterized model; (2) attempt to restrict the number of parameters in that model using tests for common dynamic structure in the variables; (3) set to zero all coefficients in the restricted model that are insignificant; (4) perform a battery of diagnostic tests to see if the model passes quality control. The first three steps in this process reflect McAleer et al.'s version of David Hendry's (1980, 1983) philosophy of modelling 'from the general to the specific'. The line of reasoning that underlies this approach is that sequences of properly nested tests can be treated as independent. Thus, by nesting tests in this way, the overall significance level of the tests can be controlled. This feature, however, is not going to be very important when the tests at each stage have low power against reasonable alternatives, as do those used by McAleer et al. Moreover, properly nesting tests requires setting in advance fixed criteria for accepting restrictions, not looking at a collection of t-statistics and making arbitrary decisions about which variables to delete. The end result of the McAleer et al. procedure is a simplified model that represents just one of many possible paths through the thicket of restrictions.

It should also be clear that the general-to-the-specific approach, while it may have some benefits when properly executed, is philosophically at odds with structural econometric estimation. The latter requires one to begin with a model that is subject to identifying and possibly overidentifying restrictions. In the former approach one begins from an overparameterized model and identification and exogeneity restrictions play no particular role. Viewed as a nonstructural model, however, the initial single equation considered by McAleer et al. is too narrowly conceived. Considering that the variables being modelled consist of money, GNP, interest rates, inflation rates and wealth, all likely to be jointly endogenous, a vector autoregression would be a more appropriate overparameterized non-structural model.

The final step of the modelling procedure advaocated by McAleer et al. is designed to confront the model with a variety of problems and performance criteria to see how well it holds up. Here the authors make a complete about-face on modelling philosophy. They switch to a specific-to-the-general modelling approach by testing whether the model should be generalized to include a group of variables not considered previously; seasonal variables, additional lags, trends and so on. It is not clear (because it is never discussed) why these variables were not included in the initial overparameterized model. At this stage, McAleer et al. also act as though they have been dealing with a structural model by reporting the results of a test for simultaneous equation bias even though the test requires candidate instrumental variables, and is consequently applicable only in the presence of identifying restrictions.

Finally, McAleer et al. report the fact that although their model 'gave satisfactory performance up to 1973, just like automobiles, age finally caught up with it, and after that date its predictive performance declined dramatically' (p. 305 fn. 11). This might lead the unwary reader to conclude that their equation fails one of the diagnostic tests the importance of which they stress: out-of-sample prediction. On the contrary; McAleer et al. report no problems in this respect. To arrive at such a startling conclusion they truncated the data set at 1970, re-estimated their model, and then compared out-of-sample forecasts with the data through the end of 1973. The fact that the prediction errors had variance comparable to that of the sample errors then led them to report success in the out-of-sample prediction! The breakdown of the model after 1973 apparently has no bearing here. It appears as if McAleer et al. see no need to hold themselves to the demanding standards of model adequacy that they recommend to us.

References

Cooley, Thomas F. and LeRoy, Stephen F. (1981), Identification and estimation of money demand, *American Economic Review*, December, 71, 825–44.

Cooley, Thomas F. and LeRoy, Stephen F. (1985), Atheoretical macro-econometrics: a critique, *Journal of Monetary Economics*, November, 16, 283–308.

Hendry, David F. (1980), Econometrics: alchemy or science?, *Economica*, November, 47, 387–406.

Hendry, David F. (1983), Econometric modelling: the consumption function in retrospect, *Scottish Journal of Political Economy*, 30, 193–220.

McAleer, Michael, Pagan, Adrian R. and Volker, Paul A. (1985), What will take the con out of econometrics?, *American Economic Review*, June, 75, 293–307.

5

Sensitivity Analyses Would Help

Edward E. Leamer

A fragile inference is not worth taking seriously.

All scientific disciplines routinely subject their inferences to studies of fragility. Why should economics be different? It hasn't been different up to now. Now do I think it ever will be, notwithstanding the comments of Michael McAleer, Adrian Pagan, and Paul Volker (1985).

Decentralized studies of fragility are common whenever an inference matters enough to attract careful scrutiny. When Isaac Erlich (1975) claims to have demonstrated that capital punishment deters murders, he elicits a great outpouring of papers that show how the result depends on which variables are included (Forst, 1977), which observations are included (Blumstein et al., 1978), how simultaneity problems are dealt with (Passell, 1975), etcetera, etcetera. These disorganized studies of fragility are inefficient, haphazard, and confusing.

What we need instead are organized sensitivity analyses. We must insist that all empirical studies offer convincing evidence of inferential sturdiness. We need to be shown that minor changes in the list of variables do not alter fundamentally the conclusions, nor does a slight reweighting of observations, nor correction for dependence among observations, etcetera, etcetera.

I have proposed a form of organized sensitivity analysis that I call 'global sensitivity analysis' in which a neighbourhood of alternative assumptions is selected and the corresponding interval of inferences is identified. Conclusions are judged to be sturdy only if the neighbourhood of assumptions is wide enough to be credible and the corresponding interval of inferences is narrow enough to be useful. But when an incredibly narrow set of assumptions is required to produce a usefully narrow set of conclusions, inferences from the given data set are reported to be too fragile to be believed.

In dramatic conflict with real data analyses, theoretical econometricians behave as if a given data set admitted a unique inference. This priesthood

* Department of Economics, University of California, Los Angeles, CA 90024. Helpful comments from Sebastian Edwards, John Riley, and especially Harold Demsetz are gratefully acknowledged.

This article first appeared in *American Economic Review*, Vol. 75, No. 3, June 1985, pp. 308–13.

takes as their self-appointed task the uncovering of the elaborate method by which the unique inference can be squeezed from a data set. Indeed, this is the reaction of McAleer et al., who offer a method of squeezing Thomas Cooley and Stephen LeRoy's (1981) data set. They propose to deal with specification ambiguity by charting one *ad hoc* route through the thicket of possible models. Complicated *ad hoc* searches like the one they suggest have no support in statistical decision theory, and virtually none in classical sampling theory. What is to be made of a procedure that sets scores of parameters to zero if they are not 'statistically significant' at arbitrarily chosen levels of significance? And what inferences are allowable after a model passes a battery of 'specification error' tests that are sometimes more numerous than even the set of observations? This recommendation of McAleer et al. merits the retort: 'There are two things you are better off not seeing in the making: sausages and econometric estimates', to which they might reply: 'It must be right, I've been doing it since my youth.'

1. Extreme Bounds Analysis

McAleer et al. direct their criticisms at what they call 'extreme bounds analysis'.[1] Since most of their concerns stem from misunderstandings about the setting in which this applies, I will begin my reply with a careful description of the specification ambiguity that properly gives rise to this form of sensitivity analysis. This setting is most accurately described in Bayesian terms, but to communicate with non-Bayesian readers I often adopt the more familiar language of the specification searcher. I fear it is the translation that causes the problems.

In Bayesian terms, the 'extreme bounds' are applicable when the prior distribution for a subset of coefficients is located at the origin but is otherwise unspecified, and the prior distribution for the other coefficients is 'diffuse'. A sensitivity analysis is then performed to determine if features of the posterior distribution depend importantly on the way this partially defined prior distribution is fully specified. It is particularly easy to search over the set of alternative posterior distributions to find the extreme posterior modes of linear combinations of coefficients, ergo 'extreme bounds'.

---

[1] I prefer to use the words 'extreme bounds' to refer to the largest possible set of inferences that a given data set will admit. This largest possible set of inferences depends on the largest possible family of models cum priors that the researcher is willing to entertain. The family of models that give rise to what McAleer et al. call 'extreme bounds analysis' may or may not be the widest set under consideration. In order to bring attention to this difference in language, I will put quotation marks around the words when used in the sense of McAleer et al.

It has been my experience that this Bayesian description of the 'extreme bounds analysis' meets with equally small amounts of approval and understanding. To combat this ignorance and suspicion, I have tried to market the idea in the following disguise. Imagine the estimation of a regression in a setting in which there are a few variables that are always left in the equation (the free variables), and some others that the researcher feels comfortable experimenting with (the doubtful variables).[2] Normally, this experimentation is limited to a small subset of the possible models that could have been estimated. Suppose instead that we consider the whole continuum of models in which the free variables and any one linear combination of the doubtful variables are included in the model. If it turns out that inferences about issues of interest are essentially the same for all choices of the linear combination of doubtful variables, then there need be no debate about which doubtful variables ought to be deleted. If, as is often the case, this bound turns out to be uselessly wide, then either the inferences are reported to be too fragile to be useful, or the bounds are narrowed in one way or another.

This disguised treatment of the sensitivity issues is quite alright up to this point, but an explicitly Bayesian framework is required to discuss sensibly any attempt to narrow the bounds. Unfortunately, the transition to the proper Bayesian foundation of the analysis is not easy for many people. For example, McAleer et al., and others as well, remark that the extreme estimates come from a model that includes a very strange linear combination of the doubtful variables. To cure this 'problem', it is often proposed to restrict the bounds to the set of regressions that exclude subsets of the doubtful variables, a procedure that can be called 'all subsets regression'. But this advice depends on the parameterization of the model, which is usually chosen by whim rather than design. In a distributed lag model the 'all subsets regressions' would be different if $x(t)$ and $x(t-1)$ are doubtful variables than if $x(t)$ and $x(t) - x(t-1)$ are doubtful variables, since in the former case the omission of $x(t)$ leaves $x(t-1)$ as the included variable, whereas in the latter case $x(t) - x(t-1)$ is retained.[3]

How should the parameters be defined? The subject of sensitivity analysis provides an answer. Regression coefficients should be defined about which prior opinions are independent. If, before the data are

---

[2] A terminological error that was first made in my earlier study (1978, p. 194) and adopted vigorously by myself and H. B. Leonard (1983) is the use of 'focus' rather than 'free' to describe the variables that are always in the equation. It is often but not always the case that the free variables are also the focus variables. An earlier version of the paper by McAleer et al. had comments that rested on this terminological error, and at my suggestion they have adopted the word free.

[3] As a matter of fact, unless you are prepared to commit to a particular coordinate system, the restriction to all subsets regression is vacuous since all subsets in all coordinate systems will reproduce exactly the extreme bounds.

observed, opinions about $b(1)$ do not depend on information about $b(2)$, then these are suitable choices for the pair of coefficients but $b(1)$ and $b(1)$ + $b(2)$ are not. The reason for defining the model with a priori independent coefficients is that, if the prior distribution cannot be more fully specified, the 'all subsets' bound applies (see Chamberlain and Leamer, 1976) and is generally narrower than the 'extreme bounds'. For the distributed lag example the model should be written as $y = b(1) \times (x(t) + x(t - 1)) + b(2) \times (x(t) - x(t - 1))$ if the best guess of $b(1)$, the steady-state responsiveness of the dependent variable, is unaffected by information about $b(2)$, the responsiveness to changes in the level of the stimulus. In that event, if both variables are regarded to be doubtful, it makes sense to see what happens to the estimate of $b(1)$ when $b(2)$ is set to zero, and it makes sense to see what happens to the estimate of $b(2)$ when $b(1)$ is set to zero.

Classical inference offers no advice on how to choose a parameterization. It is altogether immaterial whether $x(t)$ and $x(t - 1)$ are the explanatory variables, or $x(t)$ and $x(t) - x(t - 1)$, or $(x(t) + x(t - 1))$ and $(x(t) - x(t - 1))$. As a result, there is total confusion in the literature about anything that depends on the coordinate system, the multicollinearity problem being the prime example.[4]

'All subsets' regression replaces the extreme bounds if the prior distribution is suitably restricted. There are many other bounds that could be computed depending on how fully the prior distribution is specified. the restricted family of prior distributions that I often find appealing has a fixed prior mean and an 'interval' of prior covariance matrices (see my 1982 article). The 'extreme bounds analysis' is one special case with an unbounded interval of covariance matrices for a subset of coefficients and a sharply defined covariance matrix for the others. This somewhat unusual interval of prior distributions is often and properly criticized for being too wide on one subset and too narrow on the other. Indeed that is the criticism of McAleer et al., though of course they don't use this language to express their concerns.

McAleer et al. offer some useful caveats about 'extreme bounds analysis', pointing out the important point that the bounds depend on the family of prior distributions. I am confident that on reflection the properties that seem to bother them will be judged to be altogether desirable, and I welcome the glare of publicity that they offer. These properties are:

---

[4] After all, there is always a coordinate system in which the 'variables' are orthogonal and in which by traditional standards there is no multicollinearity problem. I have repeatedly but unsuccessfully tried to explain this simple point. Expressed most dramatically, since orthogonality is a happenstance of the coordinate system, there may still be a multicollinearity problem if the explanatory variables are orthogonal, though it is more accurate to say that there is a problem of dimensionality. For more, see my earlier articles (1973 or 1978, or 1983).

(1) The bounds depend on the choice of variables that are treated as doubtful.
(2) If coefficients are set to values other than zero, different bounds will result. (This amounts to saying that the bounds depend on the location of the prior distributions.)
(3) The bounds for the free coefficients will be wider the more statistically significant are the doubtful variables.
(4) If a variable is treated as doubtful, a zero estimate for its coefficient is necessarily obtainable.
(5) If there are two or more doubtful variables, a coefficient on a doubtful variable may be either positive or negative, regardless of the degree of correlation between the variables.

If you do find these properties undesirable, it must be that you are implicitly rejecting the family of prior distributions on which they are based. It is no surprise that 'extreme bounds analysis' does not apply in all cases. As a matter of fact it rarely applies. I use it primarily as a warm-up device for introducing the kind of bounds that I think are truly applicable. I welcome this kind of criticism of the 'extreme bounds analysis' since it affords me the opportunity to enrich the vocabulary of the conversation by demonstrating the proper Bayesian foundation of the analysis. With this enriched vocabulary it is possible to demonstrate how other, more relevant bounds may be computed.

2. Global Sensitivity Analysis

The real point of disagreement between myself and other econometricians is that I believe the only 'model selection' game in town ought to be the global sensitivity game. Except for issues associated with data-instigated models and simplification problems, both of which are dealt with in my earlier study (1978), a sensible and general characterization of the problem of inference begins with a broad family of alternative models and a representative, but hypothetical, prior distribution over that family. Because no prior distribution can be taken to be an exact representation of opinion, a global sensitivity analysis is carried out to determine which inferences are fragile and which are sturdy. A neighbourhood of prior distributions around the representative distribution is selected and inferences that depend in a significant way on the choice of prior from this neighbourhood are judged to be fragile. Ideally, the neighbourhood of distributions is credibly wide, and the corresponding interval of inferences is usefully narrow. But if it is discovered that an incredibly narrow neighbourhood of prior distributions is required to produce a usefully narrow set of inferences, then inferences from the given data set are suspended, and pronounced too fragile to serve as a basis for action.

I don't pretend that this research strategy is easy. It certainly is not a comfortable one for those trained in and wedded to classical inference. It isn't something that can be done by a computer without the aid of a human. I recognize that it will take some considerable experience with these methods until we can decide what constitutes a 'credibly' wide set of assumptions. One thing that is clear is that the dimension of the parameter space should be very large by traditional standards. Large numbers of variables should be included, as should different functional forms, different distributions, different serial correlation assumptions, different measurement error processes, etcetera, etcetera.

In principle, a global sensitivity study should be carried out with respect to all dimensions of the model in one grand exercise. Alas, the mathematical/computational problems in dealing with the list of etceteras are very severe. But since the longest journey begins with a single step, a piecemeal approach is proposed in which the sensitivity analysis is carried out with respect to a limited number of dimensions of the model. The parameters that lend themselves to the most congenial analysis are regression coefficients, but I can given you some interesting and useful results on errors in variables (Klepper and Leamer, 1984), and on the distribution of residuals (Leamer, 1981, 1983a, 1984 articles, and C. Z. Gilstein and Leamer, 1983a, b).

When you review a global sensitivity analysis, you need ask yourself two important questions: is the dimension of the model space adequate? Is the neighbourhood of prior distributions the right width – wide enough to include all sensible distributions but not so wide that it includes nonsensical ones? I interpret the comments on Cooley and LeRoy by McAleer et al. to amount to a healthy discussion of exactly these two issues. This I believe is precisely the form that debates about empirical results ought to take. McAleer et al. find Cooley and LeRoy's space of models inadequate because it includes no parameters for the dynamics, and they find the neighbourhood of priors to be both too wide (allowing funny linear restrictions) and too narrow (some of the free variables might be doubtful). The very fact that they are able to make these comments reveals the value of the global sensitivity framework for focusing the issues.

McAleer et al.'s 'most serious' charge is:

Unless extreme bounds are presented for *all* possible classifications of variables as doubtful and free, an observer cannot be certain that the selection does not constitute a 'con job.' *Selectivity in regression reporting therefore has as an exact analog in EBA the different classifications of variables as doubtful and free.* [p. 298]

This charge seems to be based on the belief that the distinction between free and doubtful variables is altogether arbitrary. Actually the split should be selected to represent as accurately as possible the other relevant information that is required to draw sensible inferences from the given data set. When readers differ concerning their willingness to believe and/or to use other relevant information, then a menu of inferences should be presented, and as clear as possible a statement should be made about the assumptions that are necessary to make one inference or another. When the menu isn't broad enough to suit your tastes, there is no reason to believe the inferences claimed by the author. For example, McAleer et al. find the menu of inferences offered by Cooley and Leroy to be un-interesting because the models include no parameters for dynamics. McAleer et al. seem not to have been 'conned'. Why are they worried about the intelligence of the rest of us? Thus I think a global sensitivity analysis is neutral at worst with respect to dishonesty. After all, the finding that a data set does not admit a sturdy inference is news worthy of publication. On the other hand, current institutions clearly encourage, and have produced, either delusion or deceit.

3.   A Sugar Pill for a Nearly Terminal Patient

An epidemic of overparameterization debilitates our data analyses. We need strong medicine to combat this disease. I know a global sensitivity analysis is a bitter pill to swallow. But try it, I think it's going to make us all feel much better. Maybe not entirely well, but better anyway. The sugar pill that McAleer et al. offer has the pleasant taste of the familiar, but past experience suggests that it won't do any good.

Global sensitivity analysis can deal in principle with all varieties of parameters. 'Extreme bounds analysis' is one example of a global sensitivity analysis. In order to make clear how the proposal of McAleer et al. compares with 'extreme bounds analysis', we need to focus on the problem for which the 'extreme bounds analysis' is intended, namely the choice of variables. The comments that follow apply equally well to other parameter spaces, since the competing methodological approaches are the same regardless of the nature of the statistical assumptions selected by different parameters. In particular, the complaint that 'extreme bounds analysis' doesn't deal with serial correlation, non-normality, etcetera, is quite irrelevant. After all, it is hardly reasonable to complain that brain surgery can't cure a hangnail.

What McAleer et al. propose for the problem of choice of variables is a combination of backward and forward step-wise (better known as unwise) regression. The variables are divided into three groups, say $x(1)$, $x(2)$, and $x(3)$. The first equation that is estimated includes all the variables from the sets $x(1)$ and $x(2)$ and excludes all the variables from the set $x(3)$. This 'general model' is subjected to a sequence of tests to determine if subsets of the variables comprising $x(2)$ can be omitted. The order for imposing the restrictions and the choice of significance level are arbitrary, though in some cases set by convention. Thus results a 'preferred model'. Then this preferred model is subjected to a battery of 'specification error' tests to determine if variables in the subset $x(3)$ should be included. Again the order and the levels of significance are arbitrary. So is the split into the subsets $x(1)$, $x(2)$, and $x(3)$. What meaning should be attached to all of this?

References

Blumstein A., Cohen, J. and Nagin, D. (1978), *Deterrence and Incapacitation: Estimating the Effects of Criminal Sanctions on Crime Rates*. National Academy of Sciences, Washington.

Chamberlian, Gary and Leamer, Edward E. (1976), Matrix weighted averages and posterior bounds, *Journal of the Royal Statistical Society*, No. 1, 38, 73–84.

Cooley, Thomas F. and Leroy, Stephen F. (1981), Identification and estimation of money demand, *American Economic Review*, December, 71, 825–44.

Erlich, Isaac, (1975), The deterrent effect of capital punishment: a question of life and death, *American Economic Review*, June 65, 397–417.

Forst, B. (1977), The deterrent effect of capital punishment: a cross state analysis of the 1960's, *Minnesota Law Review*, May. 61, 743–67.

Gilstein, C. Z. and Leamer, E. E. (1983a), Robust sets of regression estimates, *Econometrica*, March, 51, 321–33.

Gilstein, C. Z. and Leamer, E. E. (1983b), The set of weighted regression estimates, *Journal of the American Statistical Association*, December, 78, 942–8.

Klepper, Steven and Leamer, Edward E. (1984), Consistent sets of estimates for regressions with errors in all variables, *Econometrica*, January, 52, 163–83.

Leamer, Edward, E. (1973), Multicollinearity: a Bayesian interpretation, *Review of Economics and Statistics*, August, 55, 371–80.

Leamer, Edward E. (1978), *Specification Searches*. Wiley & Sons, New York.

Leamer, Edward E. (1981), Sets of estimates of location, *Econometrica*, January, 49, 193–204.

Leamer, Edward E. (1982), Sets of posterior means with bounded variance priors, *Econometrica*, May, 50, 726–36.

Leamer, E. E. (1983a), Let's take the con out of econometrics, *American Economic Review*, March, 73, 31–43.

Leamer, E. E. (1983b) Model choice and specification analysis, *Handbook of Econometrics*, Vol. I, ed. by Z. Griliches and D. Intriligater. North-Holland, Amsterdam, pp. 285–330.

Leamer, E. E. (1984) Global sensitivity results for generalized least squares estimates, *Journal of the American Statistical Association*, December, 79, 867–70.

Leamer, E. E. and Chamberlain, Gary (1976), A Bayesian interpretation of pretesting, *Journal of the Royal Statistical Society*, No. 1, 38, 85–94.

Leamer, E. E. and Leonard, H. B. (1983), Reporting the fragility of regression estimates, *Review of Economics and Statistics*, May, 65, 306–17.

McAleer, Michael, Pagan, Adrian R. and volker, Paul A. (1985), What will take the con out of econometrics?, *American Economic Review*, June, 75, 293–307.

Passell, P. (1975), The deterrent effect of the death penalty: a statistical test, *Stanford Law Review*, November, 28, 61–80.

6

Three Econometric Methodologies:
A Critical Appraisal

Adrian R. Pagan

Abstract. Three econometric methodologies, associated respectively with David Hendry, Christopher Sims and Edward Leamer have been advocated and practised by their adherents in recent years. A number of good papers have appeared about each methodology, but little has been written in a comparative vein. This paper is concerned with that task. It provides a statement of the main steps to be followed in using each of the methodologies and comments upon the strengths and weaknesses of each approach. An attempt is made to contrast and compare the techniques used, the information provided, and the questions addressed by each of the methodologies. It is hoped that such a comparison will aid researchers in choosing the best way to examine their particular problem.

Keywords. Econometric methodologies; Hendry; Sims; Leamer; extreme bounds analysis; vector autoregressions; dynamic specification.

Methodological debate in economics is almost as long-standing as the discipline itself. Probably the first important piece was written by John Stuart Mill (1967), and his conclusions seem as pertinent today as when they were written in the nineteenth century. He observed that many practitioners of political economy actually held faulty conceptions of what their science covered and the methods used. At the same time he emphasized that, in many instances, it was easier to practise a science than to describe how one was doing it. He finally concluded that a better understanding of scope and method would facilitate the progress of economics as a science, but that sound methodology was *not* a necessary condition for the practice of sound methods. 'Get on with the job' seems the appropriate message.

It is interesting that it was not until the 5th World Congress of the Econometric Society in 1985 that a session was devoted to methodological issues. There are good reasons for this. Until the mid-1970s it would have been difficult to find a comprehensive statement of the principles guiding

This article first appeared in *Journal of Economic Surveys*, Vol. 1, No. 1, January 1987, pp. 3–24. Much of this paper was presented in the symposium on 'Econometric Methodology' at the World Econometric Congress at Boston in August 1985. I am grateful to Ed Leamer for his extensive comments upon the paper.

econometric research, and it is hard to escape the conclusion that econometricians had taken to Mill's injunction with a vengeance. Even the debate between 'frequentists' and 'subjectivists' that prevailed in statistics was much more muted in econometrics. It is true that there was a vigorous attempt to convert econometricians to a Bayesian approach by Zellner (1971) and the 'Belgian connection' at CORE (see Drèze and Richard, 1983). But this attempt did not seem to have a great impact upon applied research.

All of this changed after 1975. Causes are always harder to isolate than effects, but it is difficult to escape the impression that the proximate cause was the predictive failure of large-scale models just when they were most needed. In retrospect it seems likely that the gunpowder had been there for some time, and that these events just set it off. Most, for example, will know Ed Leamer's (1978, p. vi) account of his dissatisfaction with the gap between what he had been taught in books and the way practitioners acted, and it seems likely that many others had felt the same way about the type of econometrics then prevalent. But these misgivings were unlikely to have any impact until there was evidence that there was something to complain about.

Since 1975 we have seen a concerted attempt by a number of authors to build methodologies for econometric analysis. Implicit in these actions has been the notion that work along the prescribed lines would 'better' econometrics in at least three ways. First, the methodology would (and should) provide a set of principles to guide work *in all its facets*. Second, by codifying this body of knowledge it should greatly facilitate the transmission of such knowledge. Finally, a style of reporting should naturally arise from the methodology that is informative, succinct, and readily understood.

In this paper we look at the current state of the debate over methodology. Three major contenders for the 'best methodology' title may be distinguished. I will refer to these as the 'Hendry', 'Leamer' and 'Sims' methodologies, after those individuals most closely *identified* with the approach. Generally, each procedure has its origins a good deal further back in time, and is the outcome of a research programme that has had many contributors apart from the named authors above. But the references – Hendry and Richard (1982), Leamer (1978), and Sims (1980a) – are the most accessible and succinct summaries of the material, and therefore it seems appropriate to use the chosen appellations. Inevitably, there has been some convergence in the views, but it will be most useful to present them in polar fashion, so as to isolate their distinct features.

1.   The 'Hendry Methodology'

Perhaps the closest of all the methods to the 'old style' of investigation is the 'Hendry' methodology. It owes a lot to Sargan's seminal (1964) paper, but it also reflects an oral tradition developed largely at the London School of Economics over the past two decades. Essentially it comprises four 'steps'.

(1) Formulate a general model that is consistent with what economic theory postulates are the variables entering any equilibrium relationship and which restricts the dynamics of the process as little as possible.
(2) Re-parameterize the model to obtain explanatory variables that are near orthogonal and which are 'interpretable' in terms of the final equilibrium.
(3) Simplify the model to the smallest version that is compatible with the data ('congruent').
(4) Evaluate the resulting model by extensive analysis of residuals and predictive performance, aiming to find the weaknesses of the model designed in the previous step.

Steps (i) and (ii)

Theory and data continually interplay in this methodology. Unless there are good reasons for believing otherwise, it is normally assumed that theory suggests which variables should enter a relationship, and the data are left to determine whether this relationship is static or dynamic (in the sense that once disturbed from equilibrium it takes time to re-establish it).

It may help to understand the various steps of Hendry's methodology if a particular example is studied. Suppose that the investigator is interested in the determinants of the velocity of circulation of money. Let m_t be the log of the money supply, p_t be the log of the price level and y_t be the log of the real income. Theoretical reasoning suggests that, for appropriately defined money, $m_t - p_t - y_t$ should be a function of the nominal interest rate (I_t) along any steady-state growth path. With $i_t = \log(I_t)$, we might therefore write $m_t^* - p_t^* - y_t^* = \delta i_t^*$ where the starred quantities indicate equilibrium values.

Of course equilibrium quantities are not normally observed, leading to the need to relate these to actual values. For time series data it is natural to do this by allowing the relations between the variables m_t, p_t, y_t and i_t to be governed by a dynamic equation of the form

$$m_t = \sum_{j=1}^{p} a_j m_{t-j} + \sum_{j=0}^{q} b_j p_{t-j} + \sum_{j=0}^{r} c_j y_{t-j} + \sum_{j=0}^{s} d_j i_{t-j}. \qquad (1)$$

The first step in Hendry's methodology sets p, q, r and s to be as large as practicable in view of the type of data (generally $p = q = r = s = 5$ for quarterly data), and to then estimate (1). This model, the general model, serves as a vehicle against which all other models are ultimately compared.

Now (1) could be written in many different ways, all of which would yield the same estimates of the unknown parameters, but each of which packages the information differently and consequently may be easier to interpret and understand. Generally, Hendry prefers to re-write the dynamics in (1) as an 'error correction mechanism' (ECM). To illustrate this point, the simple relation

$$x_t = ax_{t-1} + b_0 x_t^* + b_1 x_{t-1}^*, \tag{2a}$$

where x_t^* is the equilibrium value of x_t, has the ECM

$$\Delta x_t = (a - 1)(x_{t-1} - x_{t-1}^*) + b_0 \Delta x_t^* + (a - 1 + b_0 + b_1)x_{t-1}^*$$
$$= (a - 1)(x_{t-1} - x_{t-1}^*) + b_0 \Delta x_t^*, \tag{2b}$$

since steady-state equilibrium in (2a) implies $x = ax + b_0 x + b_1 x$ or $a + b_0 + b_1 = 1$. Although (2b) is no different to (2a), Hendry prefers it since Δx_t^* and $(x_{t-1} - x_{t-1}^*)$ are closer to being orthogonal and he is able to interpret its elements as equilibrium (Δx_t^*) and disequilibrium $(x_{t-1} - x_{t-1}^*)$ responses.

Moving away from this simple representation we can get some feeling for the type of equation Hendry would replace (1) with by assuming that m_t adjusts within the period to p_t, making the log of real money $m_t - p_t$ the natural analogue of x_t in 2(a). The equilibrium value is then $x_t^* = yt + \delta i_t$, and by appeal to (2b) it is clear that a re-formatted version of (1) would involve terms such as Δy_t, Δi_t and $(x_{t-1} - x_{t-1}^*) = (m_{t-1} - p_{t-1} - y_{t-1} - \delta i_{t-1}) = (m_{t-1} - p_{t-1} - y_{t-1}) - \delta i_{t-1}$. Since $(m - p - y)_{t-1}$ is related to the lagged velocity of circulation, it may be easier to interpret this re-formulated equation. Terms such as $(m - p - y)_{t-1}$ frequently appear in studies of the demand for money by Hendry and his followers. For example, in Hendry and Mizon (1978), the following equation appears

$$\Delta(m - p)_t = 1.61 + 0.21\Delta y_t - 0.81\Delta i_t + 0.26\Delta(m - p)_{t-1} - 0.40\Delta p_t$$
$$- 0.23(m - p - y)_{t-1} + 0.61 i_{t-4} + 0.14 y_{t-4},$$

where I have replaced $\log(1 + i_t)$ with $- i_t$.

Thus, steps (i) and (ii) demand a clear statement of what the variables in the equilibrium relation should be, as well as a choice of parameterization. Hendry (1986) provides what is currently the most detailed explanation of his second step, but even a perusal of that source leaves an impression of the step being more of an art than a science, and consequently difficult to codify. To some extent the problem arises since Hendry tends to blur steps (ii) and (iii) in his applied work, with the re-formatted equation sometimes seeming to derive from an inspection of the parameter estimates in (1). In those cases (1) is both simplified and rearranged at the same time.

The idea of beginning with a general model as the benchmark against which others might be compared seems only common sense, but there is little doubt in my mind that it was a minority view in the 1960s (and may still be). One frequently saw (and sees) explicit rejection of this step on the grounds that it was impossible to do because economic variables were too 'collinear', with no attempt made to discover if there was even any truth in that assertion for the particular data set being used.[1] Over many years of looking at my own and students' empirical studies, I have found the rule of starting with a general model of fundamental importance for eventually drawing any conclusions about the nature of a relationship, and cannot imagine an econometric methodology that did not have this as its primary precept. As will be seen, all the methodologies analysed in this paper ascribe to that proposition.

Step (iii)

The first two steps in the methodology therefore seem unexceptionable. It is in the third that difficulties arise. These relate to the decision to simplify (1) and the reporting of this decision, i.e. how to go from the large model implicit in (1) to one that is easier to comprehend but which represents the data just as well. Normally, in Hendry's methodology this step involves the deletion of variables from (1), but it could also involve choosing to set combinations of parameters to particular values. For convenience our discussion will centre upon model reduction via variable deletion. To simplify at all requires a *criterion function* and a *decision rule*; how to use and report inferences from such information are the difficult issues in this third step.

First, the decision stage. It is rare to find a criterion that is not based upon the log likelihood (or its *alter ego*, in regression models, the sum of squares). Frequently, it is something equivalent to the likelihood ratio test statistic, $-2 \log (L_s/L_G)$ where L_s and L_G are the likelihoods of simplified and general models respectively. For regression models this is approximately the product of the sample size and the proportional change in the residual variance in moving from the general to simplified model. To know what is a 'big' change in the likelihood, it is common to select critical values from a table of the chi-square distribution by specifying a desired probability of Type I error. As is well known, one can think of this probability as indicating the fraction of times the simplified model would be rejected when it is true, given that the general model is re-estimated with data from many experiments differing solely by random shocks. Many see this myth as implausible in a non-experimental science such as economics, but myths such as this form the basis of many disciplines e.g. perfect competition in

---

[1] As is well known the importance of collinearity is a function of the parameterization used. Thus the data may be very informative about certain parameters, e.g. long-run responses, but not others, e.g. dynamics. It is not useful (or valid) to claim it is uninformative about everything.'

economics. What is important is that any framework within which analysis is conducted lead to useful results. If reliance upon the 'story' regularly causes error, it is then time to change it for something else.

On the whole, I believe that these concepts have served us well, but there are some suggestions of alternative decision rules that may prove to be more useful. Thus Akaike (1973) and Mallows (1973) derive decision rules that opt for the deletion of a variable in a linear model if the change in the residual variance is less than $\sqrt{2}$ times the inverse of the sample size.[2] Rissanen (1983), looking at the likelihood as an efficient way to summarize all the information in the data, formulates a decision rule that the change in residual variance must be less than a function of the sample size and difference in model dimensions. None of these is incompatible with the 'Hendry' methodology; to date they have not been used much, but that is a matter of choice rather than necessity.

Having made a decision what should be reported? My own attitude, summarized in McAleer et al. (1985), is that an exact description of the decisions taken in moving from a general to simplified model is imperative in any application of the methodology. Rarely does this involve a single decision, although it would be possible to act as if it did by just comparing the finally chosen simplified model and the original one, thereby ignoring the path followed to the simplified version. This is what Hendry seems to do in various applied studies; he normally only provides the value of a test statistic comparing the two models at each end of the path, with very little discussion (if any) of the route followed from one end to the other.

There seem to me to be some arguments against this stance. First, it is hard to have much confidence in a model if little is explained about its origin. Hendry's attitude seems to be that how a final model is derived is largely irrelevant; it is either useful or not useful, and that characteristic is independent of whether it comes purely from whimsy, some precise theory, or a very structured search (Hendry and Mizon, 1985). In a sense this is true, but it is cold comfort to those who are implementing the methodology, or who are learning it for the first time. Reading Hendry's applied papers frequently leaves only puzzlement about how he actually did the simplification. In Hendry (1986) for example, the transition from a model with thirty-one parameters to one with only fourteen is explained in the following way (p. 29):

---

[2] Problems emerge if a decision rule is employed based on keeping Type I errors constant – see Berkson (1938). As the test statistic is the product of the sample size by the proportional change in variance, even very small changes in the latter become large changes in the criterion when the sample size is large. Decision rules such as those in Rissanen (1983) and Schwartz (1978) overcome this, but it might be better to model formally the underlying conflict between Type I and Type II error as in Quandt (1980).

These equations ... were then transformed to a more interpretable parameterisation and redundant functions were deleted; the resulting parsimonious models were tested against the initial unrestricted forms by the overall F-test.

It is true that confidence in the simplified model is partly a function of the value of the F-test, but by its very nature this evidence can only mean that *some* of the deleted variables don't matter. To see why, consider a general model with three regressors x_1, x_2 and x_3, all of which are orthogonal. Suppose the F statistic for the deletion of x_3 is 5 and that for x_2 is 0.5. Then the F statistic for the joint deletion of x_2 and x_3 is 2.75, and joint deletion is likely, even though it is dubious if x_3 should be deleted at all. Thus an adequate documentation of the path followed in any simplification process is desirable, rather than just accompanying any simplification with a vague statement about it. More than that, I do believe in the possibility of situations in which simplication may be done in a systematic way, e.g. in choosing dynamics via COMFAC (as in Hendry and Mizon, 1978 or McAleer et al., 1985), polynomial orders within Almon procedures and various types of demand and production restrictions that form a nested heirarchy. As far as possible I am in favour of exploiting such well-developed strategies for simplification. Research should also be encouraged with the aim of developing new procedures or methods that require fewer assumptions.

Knowledge of the path may be important for another reason. As discussed above the critical value used in the decision rule is taken from the tables of the χ^2 or F distribution. But under the conditions of the story being used, this is only true if the simplification path consists of a single step. When there has been more than one step, the critical values cannot normally be taken from a χ^2 distribution, and it may be misleading if one proceeds as if it can. Some, for example Hill (1986), see this as a major flaw in the methodology, and others feel that the decision rule needs to be modified quite substantially in the presence of such 'data mining'. When the move from a general to a simplified model can be formulated as a nested sequence, adjustments can be made to obtain the requisite critical value (Mizon (1977) gives an account of this), but in the more common case where this is not possible theoretical analysis has made little progress. Nevertheless, numerical methods of Type I error evaluation, such as the bootstrap, do enable the tracing of Type I error for *any* sequence of tests and specified decision rules. Veall (1986) provides an application of this idea.

I am not certain that it is worthwhile computing exact Type I errors. Ignoring the sequence entirely produces a bias against the simplified model, but that does not seem such a bad thing. Moreover, the ultimate change in the criterion function is independent of the path followed. It is frequently the change in the criterion itself which is of interest, in that it displays the sensitivity of (say) the log likelihood to variation in parameter value for the deleted variables as these range from zero to the point estimates of the general model.

Step (iv)

Excellent accounts are available of the necessity of this step – Hendry and Richard (1982) – and the techniques for doing it – Engle (1984). Essentially, these procedures check if sample moments involving the product of specified variables with functions of the data (typically residuals) are zero. Very general treatments of diagnostic tests from this viewpoint have recently been given by Tauchen (1985) and Newey (1985).[3] These procedures fulfil a number of roles within the methodology. They are important within a modelling cycle for the detection of inadequate models, but they are also important in the reporting phase, where they provide evidence that the conventions underlying almost any modelling exercise are not violated by the chosen model. Routine examination of such items as the autocorrelation function and recursive estimation of parameters has proved to be indispensable both to my own modelling (Anstie et al., 1983; Pagan and Volker, 1981) and to those of a large number of students studying applied econometrics at the Australian National University over the past decade (Harper, 1980; Kirby, 1981, for example). More than anything else, it is step (iv) which differentiates Hendry's methodology from that which was standard practice in the 1960s.

2.   The 'Leamer Methodology'

Providing a succinct description of Leamer's methodology is a good deal more difficult than doing so for the Hendry variant. Basically, the problem lies in a lack of applications of the ideas; consequently it is hard to infer the general principles of the approach from any classic studies of how it is to work in practice. Despite this qualification, I have reduced Leamer's methodology to four distinct steps.

(1) Formulate a general family of models.
(2) Decide what inferences are of interest, express these in terms of

---

[3] Both papers treat only the case where the observations making up the sample moments are i.i.d., but it is clear that the analysis extends to the case where the 'orthogonality' relations follow a martingale difference process. This covers most cases of interest in econometrics. Note, however, that Tauchen's results require that the maintained model be estimated by maximum likelihood.

parameters, and form 'tentative' prior distributions that summarize the information not contained in the given data set.

(3) Consider the sensitivity of inferences to a particular choice of prior distributions, namely those that are diffuse for a specified subset of the parameters and arbitrary for the remainder. This is the extreme bounds analysis (EBA) of Leamer (1983) and Leamer and Leonard (1983). Sometimes step (3) terminates the process, but when it appears that inferences are sensitive to the prior specification this step is only a warm-up for the next one.

(4) Try to obtain a narrower range for the inferences. In some places this seems to involve an explicit Bayesian approach, but in others it seems just to involve fixing a prior mean and interval for prior covariance matrices. If the restrictions in this latter step needed to get a narrow range are too 'implausible', one concludes that any inference based on this data is fragile.

Collected as in (i)–(iv), Leamer's methodology seems to be just another sect in the Bayesian religion, and there is little point in my going over the debate in statistics concerning Bayesian procedures. Much of this is epistemological and I doubt if it will ever be resolved. In practice, the limited appeal of Bayesian methods to econometricians seems to have been based on the difficulties coming from a need to formulate high-dimensional priors in any realistic model, nagging doubts about the need to have precise distributional forms to generate posterior distributions, and the fact that many dubious auxiliary assumptions are frequently employed (for example, lack of serial correlation and heteroscedasticity in the errors). In theory, all of these doubts could be laid to rest, but the computational burden becomes increasingly heavy.

Viewed as basically an exercise in Bayesian econometrics, I have therefore very little to say about Leamer's method. It is not to my taste, but it may well be to others'. However, in attempting to sell his ideas, Leamer has produced, particularly in step (iii), an approach that can be interpreted in a 'classical' rather than Bayesian way, and it is this which one tends to think of as the 'Leamer methodology'. The reasons for such a belief lie in the advocacy of such ideas in Leamer's two most widely read articles, Leamer (1983) and Leamer and Leonard (1983), although it is clear from Leamer (1985, 1986) that he now sees the fourth step as the important part of his analysis. Nevertheless, applications tend to be of step (iii), and we will, therefore, analyse it before proceeding to (iv).

Returning to steps (i) and (ii), it is apparent they do not differ greatly from Hendry's methodology (HM); the main distinction is that in HM the emphasis is on building a model from which inferences will later be drawn, whereas Leamer focuses upon the desired inference from the beginning.

Because of this concern about a particular parameter (or, more correctly, a linear combination of parameters), it is not clear if Leamer has a counterpart to the simplification step in Hendry's methodology. In published applications he always retains the complete model for inferences, but he has suggested to me that some simplification may be practised as an aid to communication or in the interest of efficient prediction.

Thus, cast in terms of (1) the essential distinction in these early steps between the two methodologies is that Leamer would want a clear definition of what the issues in modelling money demand are at the beginning. Suppose it was the question of the impact of interest rate variations on money demand, the question raised by Cooley and LeRoy (1981) in one of the best-known applications of Leamer's ideas. Then either the size of individual d_j values or $(1 - \Sigma a_j)^{-1} \Sigma d_j$ (the long-run response) would be the items of interest, and the model would be reparameterized to reflect these concerns. In Hendry's case it is rare to find a particular set of coefficients being the centre of attention; it is variable interrelationships as a whole that seem to dominate. As in McAleer et al. (1985), questions about the magnitude of the interest rate response in (1) are answered after the final model is chosen.

Step (iii)

To gain a better appreciation of what is involved in step (iii), particularly as a contrast to HM, it is necessary to expose the link between them. Accordingly, take the general model

$$y_t = x_t\beta + z_t\gamma + e_t, \tag{3}$$

where z_t are a set of doubtful variables, and interest centres upon the point estimate of the first coefficient in the β vector, β_1. In terms of the variables in (1), x_t would relate to the interest rate variables while z_t would be the remainder. In step (iii) Leamer examines the extreme values of the point estimates of α_1 as all possible linear combinations of z_t are entered into regressions that always contain x_t (this being formally equivalent to diffuse priors upon β and arbitrary priors on γ). In McAleer et al. (1983, Appendix) it is shown that the absolute difference between these bounds, scaled by the standard deviation of the OLS estimate of β_1 from (3), is given by:[4]

$$\text{SD}\,(\hat{\beta}_1)^{-1}|\hat{\beta}_{1,\max} - \hat{\beta}_{1,\min}| = \phi\chi_D^2 \tag{4}$$

where $0 \leqslant \phi \leqslant 1$ and χ_D^2 is the chi-square statistic for testing if γ is zero.

Leamer refers to the left-hand side of (4) as 'specification uncertainty'. Let us first take the extreme case that $\phi = 1$ and ask what extra information is provided by an EBA that is not available to someone following HM. In

---

[4] Breusch (1985) has an elegant proof of this.

the latter, if χ_D^2 was small, the recommended point estimate of β_1 for someone following HM would be that from the model deleting z_t. From (4) an exactly equivalent statement would be that the 'specification uncertainty' is very small, and the point estimate of β_1 would not change very much as one moved from the general to the simplified model. This is to be expected since, following Hausman (1978), a large difference between β_1 for the simplified and general models must mean evidence against any simplification. Thus the two approaches provide a different packaging of the same information, and share exactly the same set of difficulties. In particular, all the problems of nominating a critical value for χ_D^2 have their counterpart in Leamer's methodology as providing critical values for specification agreement on the latter question by users of the EBA method, with a range of definitions being proposed. Another interesting concomitant of (4) is that if, $\gamma \neq 0$ in (3), $\chi_D^2 \to \infty$ as the sample size grows, and so, when $\phi \neq 0$, the range between the bounds tends to infinity. Thus Leamer's complaints about classical hypothesis testing apply also to his own methodology!

Now, in HM it is an *insignificant* χ_D^2 that is important, but this need not be *numerically small* if the dimension of z_t is large. Taking the previously cited example from Hendry (1986), where seventeen parameters were set to zero, $\chi^2(17,0.05) = 27.59$, allowing a potentially enormous gap between $\hat{\beta}_{1,\min}$ and $\hat{\beta}_{1,\max}$; point estimates of the simplified model might therefore depart substantially from those based upon other ways of combining the z_t. If it is point estimates of β_1 that are desired, it becomes very informative to perform an EBA (i.e. to compute ϕ); knowledge of χ_D^2 only sets an upper limit to the specification uncertainty, as it is the collinearity between regressors, reflected in ϕ, that determines the exact value of the 'specification uncertainty'.[5] Whenever a large number of variables are deleted in a simplification exercise, the provision of extreme bounds for any coefficients of interest seems desirable.

Where the two methodologies really part company is over the interpretation of a large χ_D^2. Followers of HM would argue that one should take point estimates of β_1 from the general model, concluding it would be an error to take them from the simplified model, as the data clearly indicate that the z_t appear in the relationship.[6] Leamer would presumably conclude

[5] This division shows that interpretations which see the differences between the methodologies as due to different attitudes to collinearity are incorrect. Bounds can be wide even if collinearity is weak (ϕ small).

[6] We have not dealt with the question of what inferences about β_1 might be then drawn from $\hat{\beta}_1$. Unfortunately, it is not uncommon in econometrics to see sharp conclusions drawn about the value of β_1 on the basis of a test of a sharp hypothesis such as $\beta_1 = 1$ or zero (Hall, 1978; Barro, 1977). All that can be concluded, however, is that a range of possible values for β_1 are compatible with $\hat{\beta}_1$, and this range is frequently found by examining $k\mathrm{SD}(\hat{\beta}_1)$, where k is some selected constant. Traditionally, k was set by stipulating the Type I error to be sustained, but Andrews (1986) has recently suggested a way of incorporating power requirements into the determination of k.

that 'Because there are many models which could serve as a basis for a data analysis, there are many conflicting inferences which could be drawn from a given data set' and therefore 'inferences from these data are too fragile to be useful' (Leamer and Leonard, 1983, p. 306). I confess that I cannot be convinced that our response to a situation where the data are clearly indicating that valid point estimates of β_1 will not be found by deleting z_t from (1) should be to conclude that the data are not informative about β_1!

There is no denying that there would be comfort in narrow bounds, as any conclusions that depend upon the precise value of β_1 would then be unchanged by variation in specifications. Some, for example Feldstein (1982), even see this as a desirable characteristic. But I think it hard to argue that the majority of modelling exercises can be formulated in terms of interest in the value of a single coefficient (or a linear combination of them). It is perhaps no accident that the examples Leamer provides in his articles do feature situations where single parameter inference is paramount, whereas Hendry's examples – money demand, consumption – are more concerned with the model as a whole. If the equation (3) was being developed as part of a policy model, or even to provide predictions, knowledge of χ_D^2 is important, as a large value would presumably imply that models which retained z_t would out-perform those that did not. Any model should be judged on all its dimensions and not just a few of them. One might argue for an extension of Leamer's methodology that chose 'β_1' as representative of many characteristics of a model. Since prediction errors can be estimated as the coefficients of dummy variables (Salkever, 1976) these might be taken as $\hat{\beta}_1$. Alternatively, why not look at the extreme bounds for the residual variance? But these must be the two estimates of σ^2 obtained by including and deleting all the z_t in (1), and so one is essentially re-producing the χ_D^2 statistics. Accordingly, once attention shifts from a single parameter to overall model performance EBA begins to look like a version of step (ii) of HM.

Step (iv)

The fourth step constitutes the clearest expression of Bayesian philosophy in Leamer's work. Until this step it is not mandatory to formulate a prior distribution, but now at least the mean and variance of it must be provided (only two moments are needed given the type of prior assumed in his SEARCH program). A proper Bayesian would then proceed to combine this prior knowledge with a likelihood, reporting the posterior distribution for the coefficient. If forced to give a point estimate of the coefficient, such an individual would probably give the mode, median, or mean of the posterior distribution. That would then be the end of the exercise, the data and prior beliefs having been optimally combined to provide the best information possible about the parameter value. Consequently, when modelling money demand as in (1), a Bayesian would need to formulate a $(p + q + r + s)$-dimensional prior distribution upon the parameters of this model. A daunting task, although some progress has been made in automating the process of prior elicitation in recent years, and Leamer (1986) is an excellent example of how to do this in a context similar to that in (1).

What differentiates Leamer from a standard Bayesian is his reluctance to follow the above prescription rigidly. Rather, he prefers to study how the mean of the posterior distribution changes as the prior variances change. In Leamer (1986) he stipulates a prior covariance matrix A, but then modifies it to V obeying the following constraint:

$$(1 - \lambda)A \leqslant V \leqslant \{1/(1 - \lambda)\}A \ (0 \leqslant \lambda \leqslant 1).$$

A λ ranges from zero to unity the precision of the prior information diminishes and, for any given value of λ, bounds for the posterior mean can be computed corresponding to each side of the inequality. What is of primary interest to Leamer is how these bounds change in response to variations in λ, rather than just the values at $\lambda = 0$. As he says in Leamer (1985), what he is concerned with is *sensitivity analysis*, and it is the question of sensitivity of inferences to variation in assumptions which should preoccupy the econometrician.

If step (iv) is thought of as a tool to provide a Bayesian analyst with evidence of how important prior assumptions are for conclusions based on the posterior, it seems unexceptionable and useful. Is this also true for an investigator not operating within the Bayesian paradigm? What is of concern to that individual is the shape of the likelihood. Step (iv) can provide some information on this aspect. On the one hand, if the likelihood is completely flat the posterior and prior means would always coincide. On the other hand, if the likelihood was sharply defined around a particular point in the parameter space, changing λ would cause the posterior mean to shift from the prior mean to this point. Unfortunately, it is not entirely reliable as a guide to the characteristics of the likelihood, as can be seen in the case of the linear model. With the prior mean set to $\hat{\beta}_{OLS}$ and A proportional to $(X'X)^{-1}$, the posterior and prior means always coincide, so nothing is learnt about the likelihood as λ is varied.

From the above, the intention of step (iv) seems good, even if in execution it may leave something to be desired. I think it certainly true that workers in the HM tradition do not pay enough attention to the shape of the likelihood (see fn 6). The provision of second derivatives of the log likelihood (standard errors) gives some feel for it, but they can be very unreliable if problems are non-linear. Whether Leamer's procedure is the best response is a moot point; at the moment it is one of the few methods we have of discovering information about curvature in the likelihood, and its strategy to overcome the problems caused by a high dimensional parameter space (index it by a single parameter λ) may well be the best way to proceed. Certainly, we can use all the help we can get when it comes to the analysis of data.

My main reservation about step (iv), however, is that it does not do *enough* sensitivity analysis, being restricted to the parameters of the prior distribution. As exemplified in his SEARCH program, there are many conventions underlying the methodology (just as there were in HM), but those applying it have made precious little attempt to query the validity of such conventions for the data set being analysed. This is odd since, in principle, there should be few difficulties in mimicking step (iv) of HM. Since most diagnostic tests can be formulated as measuring the sensitivity of the log likelihood to the addition of variables designed to detect departures from the conventions (Pagan, 1984) they should be readily adapted to Leamer's framework.[7] It seems imperative that this become part of the methodology. Leamer has indicated to me that he does see the need to examine the data for anomalies that suggest revision of the model space or of the initial prior distributions; the tools in this task ranging from unexpected parameter estimates and peculiar residual patterns to (possibly) goodness-of-fit statistics. But he emphasizes that adjustments must be made for any data-instigated revision of the model or prior. Because such adjustments are difficult his first preference is for an initial selection of prior and model extensive enough as to make any such revision unlikely. Nevertheless, when theory is rudimentary and underdeveloped, commitment to the original model and prior is likely to be low, and the need for revision correspondingly high.

3. Sims' Methodology

Interdependence of actions is one of the characteristics of economic studies. Hence, it might be argued that the evaluation of policy will normally need to be done within a framework that allows for such interdependence. In fact, a good deal of analysis, and the econometrics supporting it, is done in a partial rather than general equilibrium way – see Feldstein (1982), for example, where the impact of taxes upon investment is assessed in a series of single-equation studies. Traditionally, such questions were analysed with the aid of a system of structural equations:

$$By_t - Cx_t = e_t, \tag{5}$$

---

[7] In Pagan (1978) I used CORE's Bayesian Regression Program to check for serial correlation. Lagged residuals were added to the model and the posterior distribution for the coefficient of that variable was then calculated.

where y_t is a vector of endogenous variables, x_t a vector of predetermined variables, and e_t was the disturbance term. In (5), following the lead of the Cowles Commission researchers, both B and C were taken to be relatively sparse, so as to 'identify' the separate relations, i.e. it was assumed that an investigator could decide which variables appeared in which equations.

Both of the two previous methodologies would probably subscribe to this framework, aiming to calibrate the non-zero elements in B and C (Leamer might regard the exclusion restrictions as only approximately correct, but I know of nowhere that he has explicitly stated his preferred procedure). By contrast, the third methodology jettisons it. Sims (1980a) dissented vigorously from the Cowles Commission tradition, resurrecting an old article by Liu (1960), which insisted that it was 'incredible' to regard B and C as sparse. The argument touches a chord with anyone involved in the construction of computable general equilibrium models. If decisions on consumption, labour supply, portfolio allocations, etc. are all determined by individuals maximizing lifetime utility subject to a budget constraint, each relationship would be determined by the same set of variable. Consequently, theoretical considerations would predict no difference in the menu of variables entering different equations, although the quantitative importance of individual variables is most likely to vary with the type of decision.[8] Prescription of the zero elements in B and C therefore involves excluding variables with coefficients 'close' to zero. In this respect the action is little different to what is done in any attempt to model reality by capturing the major influences at work. This was Fisher's (1961) reply to Liu, and I find it as pertinent now as when it was written.

Much more could be said about this issue of identifiability, but this is not the place to do so. One cannot help wondering, however, if it is as serious as Sims suggests. There do not seem many instances in applied work where identification is the likely suspect when accounting for poor results. Despite the large amount of attention paid to it in early econometrics, it is hard to escape the impression that issues of specification and data quality are of far greater importance.

Nevertheless, it would be silly to ignore these arguments if it was indeed possible to do analysis without such assumptions. Sims claims that it is. In the Cowles Commission methodology, 'structure-free' conclusions would have been derived from the reduced form:

$$y_t = B^{-1}Cx_t + B^{-1}e_t = \Pi x_t + v_t, \qquad (6)$$

---

[8] Even within these models the existence of governments means that (say) prices entering demand relations will be different from those in supply relations by the presence of indirect taxes, and this gives an external source of variation. It should be noted that Sims gives a number of other arguments against identifiability, some relating to expectations and others, about our inability to specify the exact order of dynamics.

but Sims chooses instead to work with a vector autoregressive represen-
tation (VAR) for the endogenous and exogenous variables. Defining $z_t' = (y_t', \bar{x}_t')$, where $\bar{x}_t$ includes all members of x_t that are not lagged values of
variables, this has the form:

$$z_t = \sum_{j=1}^{p} A_j z_{t-j} + e_t. \tag{7}$$

Although it is (7) that is estimated, two further manipulations are made
for use in later stages of the methodology. First, (7) is inverted to give the
innovations (or moving average) form:

$$z_t = \sum_{j=0}^{\infty} \bar{A}_j e_{t-j} \tag{8}$$

where $\bar{A}_0 = \text{cov}(e_t)$. Since $\bar{A}_0$ is a positive definite matrix there exists a
non-singular lower triangular matrix P such that $P A_0 P' = I$, allowing the
definition $\eta_t = P e_t$, where η_t has zero mean and covariance matrix I. (8)
may then be rewritten in terms of η_t as:

$$z_t = \sum_{j=0}^{\infty} \bar{A}_j P^{-1} P e_{t-j} = \sum_{j=0}^{\infty} D_j \eta_{t-j}, \tag{9}$$

where the η_t are the *orthogonalized innovations*.

Having dispatched the preliminaries it is possible to summarize Sims's
methodology in four steps.

(1) Transform data to such a form that a VAR can be fitted to it.
(2) Choose as large a value of p and $\dim(z_t)$ as is compatible with the size
   of data set available and then fit the resulting VAR.
(3) Try to simplify the VAR by reducing p or by imposing some arbitrary
   'smoothness' restrictions upon the coefficient.
(4) Use the *orthogonalized* innovations representation to address the
   question of interest.

Step (i)

This is an important step. The idea that z_t can be expressed as a VAR has
its origins in the theory of stationary processes, particularly in the Wold
decomposition theorem. But that justification is not essential until the last
step; until then the VAR might well have unstable roots. However, stable
roots are indispensable to step (iv), as the coefficients $\bar{A}_j$ only damp out for
a stable VAR, i.e. $z_t = a z_{t-1} + e_t$ (z_t a scalar) becomes

$$z_t = \sum_{j=0}^{\infty} a^j e_{t-j}$$

and $a^j \to 0 (j \to \infty)$ only if $|a| < 1$. If step (4) is to be regarded as an
essential part of the methodology, the question of the appropriate
transformation to render z_t stationary must be faced at an early stage.

In Sims (1980a) and Doan et al. (1984), as well as most applications, this seems to be done by including time trends in each equation of the VAR. In the latter article the attitude seems to be that most economic time series are best thought of as a stationary autoregression around a deterministic trend: after setting up the prior that the series follow a random walk with drift (equation (3), p. 7) they then say: 'While we recognise that a more accurate representation of generally held prior beliefs would give less weight to systems with explosive roots'. It is not apparent to me that this is a 'generally held prior belief', particularly given the incidence of random walks with drift in the investigation of Nelson and Plosser (1982) into the behaviour of economic time series. If the series are of the random walk type, placing deterministic trends into a regression does not suffice to induce stationarity, and an innovations form will not exist for the series in question. Of course, the sensible response to this objection would be to focus upon growth rates rather than levels for variables that are best regarded as ARIMA processes. I suspect that this makes somewhat more sense in many contexts anyway. In macroeconomic policy questions, for example, interest typically centres upon rates of growth of output and prices rather than levels, and it therefore seems appropriate to formulate the VAR in this way. Consequently, the difficulties raised by the type of non-stationarity exhibited by many economic time series is not insurmountable, but it does suggest that much more care needs to be taken in identifying the format of the variables to be modelled than has been characteristic of past studies employing Sims's methodology.

Step (ii)

Both p and the number of variables in z_t need to be specified. The first parameter will need to be fairly large (the decomposition theorem sets it to infinity), and most applications of Sims's methodology have put p between four and ten. Doan et al. (1984, fn 3) indicate that, at least for prediction performance, conclusions might be sensitive to the choice of lag length. Stronger evidence is available that the selection of variables to appear in z_t is an important one – Sims's conclusion about the role of money in Sims (1980a) were severely modified in Sims (1980b) by expanding z_t to include an interest rate. Essentially step (ii) is the analogue of step (i) in the previous two methodologies, and the need to begin with a model that is general enough haunts all the methodologies. Perhaps the difficulties are greater in Sims's case, as he wants to model the reduced form rather than a single structural equation. To adopt such a position it would be necessary to respond to Sims's contention that structural equations should also contain a large number of variables, although what is really at issue is whether they are quantitatively more important to the reduced form analysis.

Step (iii)

Step (iii) is required precisely because of the fact that both p and $\dim(z_t)$ need to be large, and so the number of unknown parameters, $p \times \dim(z_t)$, can easily become too large to be estimated from the available data. In his original article Sims chose p via a series of modified likelihood ratio tests in exactly the same way as was done in step (ii) of Hendry's methodology. Because there are few degrees of freedom available in the most general model, this may not be a good way to select p. Accordingly, in Doan et al. (1984) a different approach was promoted that was 'Bayesian in spirit'. In this variant the A_j were allowed to vary over time as

$$\text{vec}(A_{j,t}^i) = \pi_8 \text{vec}(A_{j,t-1}^i) + (1 - \pi_8)\text{vec}(A_j^i) + v_{j,t}^i, \qquad (10)$$

where the i indicates the ith equation and $v_{j,t}$ is a normally distributed random variable with covariance matrix V that is a function of $\pi_1 \ldots \pi_7$. Fixing the A_j^i in (10) (at either unity, if the coefficient corresponds to the first lag of the dependent variable of the equation, or zero otherwise), there remain eight unknown parameters. (10) describes an 'evolving coefficient model'. The likelihood for (9) and (10) was derived by Schweppe (1965) and can be written down with the aid of the Kalman filtering equations. Two of the π parameters were then eliminated by maximizing this likelihood conditional upon the fixed values of the others.

One might well ask what the rationale for (10) is; Doan et al. claim (p. 6): 'What we do thus has antecedents in the literature on shrinkage estimation and its Bayesian interpretation (for example, the works by ... Shiller (1973)'. I would dispute this connection. In the Bayesian formulation of shrinkage estimators, shrinkage occurs only in a finite sample, since the prior information is dominated by the sample information as the sample size grows, i.e changes in (say) the prior variance have a negligible effect upon the posterior distribution in large samples. This is not true for (10); changes in π always have an effect upon the likelihood, since the variance of the innovations is always a function of the π (see equation (10) of Doan et al.) Reference to Shiller's work seems even more misleading. Shiller allows the coefficients to be 'random' *across the lag distributions, not across time*, i.e. he would have

$$\text{vec}(A_{j,t}^i) = \pi_8 \text{vec}(A_{j-1,t}^i) + (1 - \pi_8)\text{vec}(A_j^i)$$

and not

$$\text{vec}(A_{j,t}^i) = \pi_8 \text{vec}(A_{j,t-1}^i) + (1 - \pi_8)\text{vec}(A_j^i)$$

Thus, as (10) is a model for coefficient evolution, and not the imposition of prior information, it is hard to see why this procedure is any less objectionable than that followed by the Cowles Commission; Malinvaud's (1984) reaction to the idea is easy to sympathize with.

Step (iv)

As step (iv) has been the subject of a number of excellent critiques, particularly Cooley and LeRoy (1985), little will be said about it. There are two major objections. First, the move from innovations to orthogonal innovations raises questions. With the exception of the first variable in z_t, the orthogonal innovations are hard to give any sensible meaning to; resort is frequently made to expressions such as 'that part of the innovation in money not correlated with the innovations in other variables'. In many ways the difficulty is akin to that in factor analysis; the mathematics is clear but the economics is not. Unfortunately, many users of the technique tend to blur the two concepts in discussion, e.g. in Litterman and Weiss (1985) the 'orthogonalized' soubriquet is dropped.

A second query arises over the *use* of the orthogonalized innovations representation. As Cooley and LeRoy (1985) point out, to ascribe any meaning to impulse responses for these innovations, it is necessary that the latter be treated as exogenous variables, and that requires the imposition of prior restrictions upon the causal structure of the system in exactly the same fashion as was done by the Cowles Commission. The strong claims the methodology makes to being free of prior information therefore seem to be largely illusory.

As an aid to understanding the issues raised above it may help to return to (1) and the question of the response of money to interest rate variations. Sims would first choose a lag length and a set of variables to form the VAR. A minimal subset would be the variables m_t, p_t, i_t and y_t in (1), but because one is attempting to capture economy-wide interactions rather than just a money demand relation, extra variables that may need to be included could be world activity, the exchange rate, and fiscal policy variables. A lot of thought has to go into this choice. Making the set too small can seriously bias the answers, whereas making it too large renders the method intractable unless other restrictions are imposed upon the VAR coefficients as in step (iii). Once the latter strategy is followed the 'clean-skin' appeal of VARs begins to dissipate.

Granted that steps (i)–(ii) have provided a satisfactory VAR representation for m_t as in (7), it is then inverted to give the innovations representation (8) that expresses m_t as a linear function of the innovations in the interest rate $e_{i,t}$ and the other variables in the VAR: $e_{p,t}$, $e_{m,t}$, $e_{y,t}$, etc. The equation corresponding to m_t in (8) would be of the form

$$m_t = \bar{a}_{0,mm} e_{m,t} + \bar{a}_{0,mp} e_{p,t} + \bar{a}_{0,mi} e_{i,t} + \bar{a}_{0,my} e_{y,t} + \ldots$$

and the response of m_t to a unit innovation in the interest rate would be $\bar{a}_{0,mi}$. This is to be contrasted with the response of m_t to a unit innovation in the interest rate provided by $(1) - d_0 \bar{a}_{0,ii}$ – obtained by replacing i_t in (1) by $i_t = \bar{a}_{0,ii} e_{i,t} + \ldots$ (the interest rate equation in (8)). Therefore different answers to the question of the response of m_t to variations in i_t would be obtained from methodologies concentrating upon (1) alone from those that incorporate system responses; in (1) the response is estimated by holding prices and income constant, whereas Sims seeks the effects on the quantity of money without such cet. par. assumptions. To some extent the methodologies are not competitive, as they frequently seek to answer different questions.

Sims aims to analyse a much broader set of issues than Hendry or Leamer normally do, but there are difficulties commensurate with this breadth. Making the set of variables to appear in the VAR large enough is one of these, and his fourth step illustrates another. To speak of the response of m_t to a unit innovation in the interest rate it must be possible to carry out that experiment without disturbing current prices, incomes, etc. But that means the innovations $e_{i,t}$ must be uncorrelated with all the other innovations. When they are not, Sims invokes artificial constructs, the orthogonal innovations, $v_{i,t}$, $v_{p,t}$, $v_{y,t}$, etc. These are linear combinations of $e_{i,t}$, $e_{p,t}$, $e_{y,t}$ designed to be orthogonal to one another, and hence capable of being varied independently of each other. Just like principal components, it is uncertain what meaning should be attached to these entities, leading to the controversy recounted above in discussion of step (iv).

4.   Summing up

Our review of the methodologies now being complete, it is time to sum up. Ignoring the criticisms of details that have been offered, how effective are the methodologies in meeting the three criteria of 'goodness' listed at the beginning of this chapter, namely the provision of general research tools, the codification and transmission of principles, and the reporting of results?

None of the methodologies claims to be completely general. Sims's explicitly deals only with time series, while many of Hendry's concerns are specific to such series as well. Leamer's techniques are heavily based upon the OLS estimator. All have the common deficiency of a failure to address explicitly the burgeoning field of microeconometrics. Whilst it is true that the philosophies underlying Hendry's and Leamer's work transfers (see, for example, Cameron and Trivedi, 1986), the actual techniques employed would need extensive modification, particularly in light of the very large data sets that make traditional model selection methods inappropriate. There is clearly a lot to be done before any of the three methodologies provides a complete set of techniques for data analysis.

Part of the objective of this paper has been to try to set out the general principles of each methodology, so as to assist in the communication and teaching roles. But this was done at a high level of abstraction. When it comes to application many questions arise which currently seem to be resolved only by 'sitting at the feet of the master'. Hendry, for example, is very vague about how he manages to simplify his models, so little is learnt about how this is to be done by a reading of his articles. Leamer recommends formulating multi-dimensional priors, but provides little practical guidance on how (say) the covariance matrices featuring in them are to be selected. Sims's methodology seems clearest when it is applied to the big issues of macroeconomics such as the neutrality of money, but altogether vaguer when the question is of the much more prosaic kind such as the impact of a quota upon import demand. No doubt Sims would be able to handle such queries, but the personal ingenuity required seems a stumbling block to the transmission of knowledge.

What about reporting? Hendry's methodology seems to provide useful information in a concise form, although it is sometimes possible to be overwhelmed with the detail on the statistics presented when judging the adequancy of a model. Perhaps this just reflects a lack of familiarity and an early stage in learning about what are the most useful tests. Leamer's extreme bounds are easy to understand; however, the extensions in which prior variances are restricted become much harder to interpret. To my mind, it is Sims's methodology which is the worst when it comes to the reporting role, with pages of graphs and impulse responses being provided. Whether this reflects a transition stage, or the problems mentioned previously about step (iv), is still unclear, but a more concise method of reporting does seem to be needed.

Granted that no methodology has managed to obtain a perfect score, what have we learnt from all of this debate? First, a substantial clarification of the procedures of model selection and auxiliary concepts such as 'exogeneity'. Second, a pronounced recognition of the limits of modelling. Any reading of (say) Marschak (1953) makes it evident that the Cowles Commission researchers were not deficient in this respect (doubters might note the amount of space Marschak denotes to discussing the 'Lucas critique'), but somehow it got lost in the euphoria of the 1960s. The much more critical attitude towards econometrics that prevails today is generally a good thing, although there is a danger that the emergence of differing methodologies will be interpreted as a tacit admission of a complete failure of econometrics, rather than as constructive attempts to improve it.

What about the future? Constructing 'systematic theologies' for econometrics can well stifle creativity, and some evidence of this has already become apparent. Few would deny that in the hands of the masters the methodologies perform impressively, but in the hands of their disciples it is all much less convincing. It will be important to rid econometrics of the 'black box' mentality that always besets it. A poor modelling strategy is unlikely to give useful results, but a good one cannot rescue a project by rigidly following any methodology if it was badly conceived from the very beginning. What I see as needed is a greater integration of the different methodologies. Although it is convenient to draw demarcation lines between them in discussion, this should not blind a researcher to the fact that each methodology can provide insights that the others lack. Extreme bounds analysis is an important adjunct to Hendry's methodology if large numbers of parameters have been omitted in any simplification. Examining the residuals for model deficiencies should be as automatic in Leamer's and Sims's methodologies as it is in Hendry's. Checking if the restrictions imposed by a model selected by Hendry's or Leamer's methodologies upon the VAR parameters are compatible with the data should be part of any analysis involving time series. Our data are such that we cannot ignore the fact that the information therein may need to be extracted by a wide range of techniques borrowed from many different approaches.

References

Akaike, H. (1973), Information theory and the extension of the maximum likelihood principle. *2nd. International Symposium on Information Theory*, ed. by B. N. Petrov and F. Csaki. Akailseonia-Kindo, Budapest, pp. 227–81.

Andrews D. W. K. (1986), Power in econometric application. Mimeo, Yale University.

Anstie, R., Gray M. R. and Pagan A. R. (1983), Inflation and the consumption ratio. *The Effects of Inflation: Theoretical Investigations and Australian Evidence*, ed. by P. K. Trivedi and A. R. Pagan. Centre for Economic Policy Research, Canberra, Australia, pp.

Barro, R. J. (1977), Unanticipated money growth and unemployment in the United States. *American Economic Review*, 67, 101–15.

Berkson, J. (1938), Some difficulties of interpretation encountered in the application of the chi-square test. *Journal of the American Statistical Association*, 33, 526–42.

Breusch, T. S. (1985), Simplified extreme bounds. University of Southampton Discussion Paper No. 8515.

Cameron, A. C. and Trivedi, P. K. (1986), Econometric models based on count data: comparisons and applications of some estimators and tests. *Journal of Applied Econometrics*, 1, 29–54.

Cooley, T. F. and LeRoy, S. F. (1981), Identification and estimation of money demand. *American Economic Review*, 71, 825–44.

Cooley, T. F. and LeRoy, S. F. (1985) Atheoretical macroeconometrics: a critique. *Journal of Monetary Economics*, 16, 283–308.

Doan, T., Litterman, R. and Sims, C. (1984), Forecasting and conditional projection using realistic prior distributions. *Econometric Reviews*, 3, 1–100.

Drèze, J. H. and Richard, J. F. (1983), Bayesian analysis of simultaneous equation systems. *Handbook of Econometrics*, edited by North-Holland, Amsterdam.

Engle, R. F. (1984), Likelihood ratio, Lagrange multiplier and Wald tests in econometrics. *Handbook of Econometrics*, Z. Griliches and M. D. Intriligator. North-Holland, Amsterdam.

Feldstein, M. (1982), Inflation, tax rules and investment: some econometric evidence. *Econometrica*, 50, 825–62.

Fisher, F. M. (1961), On the cost of approximate specification in simultaneous-equation estimation. *Econometrica*, 29, 139–70.

Hall, R. E. (1978), Stochastic implications of the life cycle – permanent income hypothesis: theory and evidence. *Journal of Political Economy*, 86, 971–1007.

Harper, I. R. (1980), The relationship between unemployment and unfilled vacancies in Australia: 1951–1978. *Economic Record*, 56, 231–43.

Hausman, J. A. (1978), Specification tests in econometrics. *Econometrica*, 46, 1251–72.

Hendry, D. F. (1986), Empirical modelling in dynamic econometrics. Applied Economics Discussion Paper No. 1, University of Oxford.

Hendry, D. F. and Mizon, G. E. (1978) Serial correlation as a convenient simplification, not a nuisance: a comment on a study of the demand for money by the Bank of England. *Economic Journal*, 88, 549–63.

Hendry, D. F. and Mizon, G. E. (1985), Procrustean econometrics. Discussion Paper, University of Southampton.

Hendry, D. F. and Richard, J. F. (1982), On the formulation of empirical models in dynamic econometrics. *Journal of Econometrics*, 20, 3–33.

Hill, B. (1986), Some subjective Bayesian considerations in the selection of models. *Econometric Reviews*, 4, 191–246.

Kirby, M. G. (1981), An investigation of the specification and stability of the Australian aggregate wage equation. *Economic Record*, 57, 35–46.

Leamer, E. E. (1978), *Specification Searches*. Wiley, New York.

Leamer, E. E. (1983), Let's take the con out of econometrics. *American Economic Review*, 73, 31–44.

Leamer, E. E. (1985), Sensitivity analyses would help. *American Economic Review*, 75, 308–13.

Leamer, E. E. (1986), A Bayesian analysis of the determinants of inflation. *Model Reliability*, ed. by D. A. Belsey and E. Kuh. MIT Press, Cambridge, Mass.

Leamer, E. E. and Leonard, H. (1983), Reporting the fragility of regression estimates. *Review of Economics and Statistics*, 65, 306–17.

Litterman, R. and Weiss, L. (1985), Money, real interest rates and output: a reinterpretation of postwar U.S. data. *Econometrica*, 53, 129–56.

Liu, T. C. (1960), Underidentification, structural estimation, and forecasting. *Econometrica*, 28, 855–65.

McAleer, M., Pagan, A. R. and Volker, P. A. (1983), Straw-man econometrics. Working Paper in Econometrics No. 097. Australian National University.

McAleer, M., Pagan, A. R. and Volker, P. A. (1985), What will take the con out of econometrics? *American Economic Review*, 75, 293–307.

Malinvaud, E. (1984), Comment to forecasting and conditional projection using realistic prior distributions. *Econometric Reviews*, 3, 113–18.

Mallows, C. L. (1973), Some comments on C_p. *Technometrics*, 15, 661–75.

Marschak, J. (1953), Economic measurements for policy and prediction. *Studies in Econometric Method* (*Cowles Commission Research Monograph No. 14*), edited by W. C. Hood and T. C. Koopmans. Yale University Press, New Haven, pp. 1–26.

Mill, J. S. (1967), On the definition of political economy and on the method of investigation proper to it. *Collected Works*, Vol. 4. University of Toronto Press, Toronto.

Mizon, G. E. (1977) Model selection procedures. *Studies in Modern Economic Analysis*, edited by M. J. Artis and A. R. Nobay. Basil Blackwell, Oxford.

Nelson, C. R. and Plosser, C. I. (1982). Trends and random walks in macroeconomic time series: some evidence and implications. *Journal of Monetary Economics*, 10, 139–62.

Newey, W. (1985), Maximum likelihood specification testing and conditional moment tests. *Econometrica*, 53, 1047–70.

Pagan, A. R. (1978), Detecting autocorrelation after Bayesian regression. CORE Discussion Paper No. 7825.

Pagan, A. R. (1984), Model evaluation by variable addition. In *Econometrics and Quantitative Economics*, edited by D. F. Hendry and K. F. Wallis. Basil Blackwell, Oxford.

Pagan, A. R. and Volker, P. A. (1981), The short-run demand for transactions balances in Australia. *Economica*, 48, 381–95.

Quandt, R. E. (1980), Classical and Bayesian hypothesis testing: a compromise. *Metroeconomica*, XXXII, 173–80.

Rissanen, J. (1983), A universal prior for integers and estimation by minimum description length. *Annals of Statistics*, 11, 416–31.

Salkever, D. S. (1976), The use of dummy variables to compute predictions, prediction errors and confidence intervals. *Journal of Econometrics*, 4, 393–7.

Sargan, J. D. (1964) Wages and prices in the United Kingdom: a study in econometric methodology. *Econometric Analysis for National Economic Planning*, edited by P. E. Hart *et al.* Butterworth, London.

Schwarz, G. (1978), Estimating the dimension of a model. *Annals of Statistics*, 6, 461–4.

Schweppe, F. C. (1965), Evaluation of likelihood functions for Gaussian signals. IEEE *Transactions on Information Theory*, 11, 61–70.

Shiller, R. J. (1973), A distributed lag estimator derived from smoothness priors. *Econometrica*, 41, 775–88.

Sims, C. A. (1980a), Macroeconomics and reality. *Econometrica*, 48, 1–47.

Sims, C. A. (1980b), Comparison of interwar and postwar cycles: monetarism reconsidered. *American Economic Review*, 70, 250–7.

Tauchen, G. (1985), Diagnostic testing and evaluation of maximum likelihood models. *Journal of Econometrics*, 30, 415–43.

Veall, M. R. (1986) Inferences on the deterrent effect of capital punishment: bootstrapping the process of model selection. Mimeo, University of Western Ontario.

Zellner, A. (1971) *An Introduction to Bayesian Inference in Econometrics*. Wiley, New York.

7

Procrustean Econometrics: Or Stretching and Squeezing Data

David F. Hendry and Grayham E. Mizon

Abstract. Recent concern about the inadequacies of econometric models has led not only to the search for causes, but also to the proposal of constructive remedies for these difficulties. In this paper we analyse the links between econometric modelling methodologies and the performance of econometric models. We comment on a number of the constructive modelling strategies that have been proposed, and emphasise the importance of evaluating models, especially by checking whether they are congruent with the available information. This process of model evaluation is destructive rather than constructive, and the criteria it employs form a set of necessary, not sufficient, conditions for model adequacy.

Non-technical Summary

History warns us that the selective use of evidence to support theories can yield short-term confirmation, but that it may achieve no more than the corroboration of prejudice or whim. Positive simple correlations between money supply and inflation, or between unemployment and the level of real wages, have the appeal of simplicity, but do not provide a solid foundation on which to build a remedial economic policy. In this paper we emphasize the distinction between the context of discovery and the context of justification. In particular we argue that serendipity in the creation of theories and models is desirable if we are to break out of the straitjacket of received theory. There is, however, no role for whimsy in the use of evidence to assess the relevance of a theory; this should be done systematically and thoroughly. We describe criteria designed to ensure that a model is congruent with the available information. There are four main sources of information: a priori theory; sample data; properties of the measurement system used to collect the sample data; and data provided by

This paper originally appeared as discussion paper no. 68, October 1985, Centre for Economic Policy Research, 6 Duke of York Street, London SW1Y 6LA. We are indebted to John Aldrich, Chris Allsopp, Terence Gorman, John Muellbauer, Adrian Neale, Jean-Francois Richard, and John Vickers for helpful comments on the material herein. Financial support from the ESRC to Nuffield College and to Southampton University under grants B00220012 and HR8323 respectively is gratefully acknowledged.

and incorporated in alternative models. A model is said to be congruent when it is coherent with all four types of information.

Part of the purpose in designing a model to be consistent with the available evidence is to be able to persuade others of its value, by demonstrating that it is robust to minor changes in specification, and performs at least as well as any other available model. This latter property, that of requiring a model to encompass its rivals, imposes high demands on a model, but when satisfied provides impressive evidence in its favour.

The model design criteria which we discuss do not constitute a unique modelling strategy, rather they provide a set of *necessary* conditions to be satisfied if a model is to be worthy of serious consideration by people other than its originator. Whilst we know of no set of *sufficient* conditions for good model design, the ones we describe have proved to be valuable. They improve research efficiency because they do not require the estimation of thousands of models before finding a reasonable one, and they contribute to the durability of models which are less likely to suffer predictive failure when new information becomes available.

One of the difficulties encountered in arguing the case for econometrics is the fact that it is essentially destructive. The notable achievement of econometrics is the weeding out of inadequate models and economic theories. However, this destructive role of econometrics has a constructive purpose, namely isolating the best available models for a particular purpose at any point in time.

1.   1985: An Econometric Odyssey

Edward Leamer's lively style of writing makes it a welcome pleasure to read his various expositions, an enjoyment which is enhanced by so much of the content being agreeable. We share his qualms about the low professional standing and credibility of much empirical econometric evidence, and support his critical chastisement of many of the bad practices which have produced this nadir. Even when he strays from the righteous paths of critical appraisal and incisive analysis onto the rocky road of advocating a specific constructivist econometrics, the conviction of his views tends to reduce our lingering doubts to a covert guilt at failing to be counted among the believers. Although we knew that our own voyage had been closer to the combined wanderings of Theseus and Ulysses than the fast lane to nirvana, Leamer's message in 'Let's take the con out of econometrics'[1] prompted the dreadful thought that we too were quite literally all at sea.

Like earlier travellers weary of a peregrination strewn with models

---

[1] References below of the form 'Leamer, p.—' are to this paper.

wrecked on the Scylla of misspecification by steering too far from the supposed Charybdis of collinearity, we contemplated the proffered hospitality of one A. Priori Episteme, whose luxurious beds were many millions of potential hyperparameters long. But, at the sight of his previous guests, some stretched beyond their extreme bounds and the more fragile simply fragmented, we hurriedly sailed into the apparently enchanting refuge of his arch-rival, A. Posteriori Scientia, only to see her whimsically squeeze some of her visitors into parsimonious couches, built solely for those with suitably autocorrelated contours. Worse still, mimicking Procrustes, anything residual was lopped off, albeit by an anachronistic Occam's Razor.

Buffeted by a sudden squall gusting recently from Episteme's island, we were blown past our own familiar bed of nails which now looked surprisingly inviting given the alternatives. It at least was mainly designed for the discomfiture of con artists and unshapely models, although we confess it took stoical practice for even the most objective of empiricists to obtain temporary relief from its sharp spikes.

The four basic issues on which we wish to comment are all present in this parody:

(1) Is an inference *fragile*, or just 'fragile' as construed in Leamer (1983a), if stretching econometric estimates to their extreme bounds produces conflicting inferences? Are 'fragile' models useless or not? Here we draw on the debate between Leamer and Michael McAleer, Adrian Pagan, and Paul Volker (1985) who question the value of Leamer's extreme bounds analysis (EBA) as a method for investigating fragility, and offer a pertinent critique of EBA as a way of reducing any 'con' in econometrics.

(2) Relativity, quarks, and double helices all seem quite *whimsical* to us, as many scientific discoveries and inventions must do at the start of their careers; indeed Michael Faraday's first dynamo was actually called a 'plaything'! Whimsy is often an essential element in *discovery*. We see its condemnation by Leamer (1983a) as consequent on a methodology which implicitly assumes that nothing is contained in heaven and earth that is not already incipiently in his priors, notwithstanding his comments on p. 40.

(3) McAleer, Pagan, and Volker advocate extensive testing of any selected model as a means of 'quality control' in econometric modelling. We have considerable sympathy for this viewpoint. Where our views, Leamer's and McAleer, Pagan, and Volker's most closely coincide is in seeing the desirability of *critical evaluation* (of models and methods, including each other's). Where our respective views diverge most is in the promulgation of *con*structive remedies. It is here that the

'con' needs removing – to be replaced by 'de'. Such an outcome is neither the product of a nihilist outlook nor a chance event. Conditional on accepting a model or method as claimed by its protagonists, seeking refutation is almost universally a valid procedure, since (in principle) it only requires a single counter-instance. But whereas non-refutation is *necessary*, we know of no *sufficient* conditions to justify conjectures or constructive methodologies (*pace* Leamer's 'global sensitivity analysis' even combined with a 'grand universal prior' or the sequential simplification approach adopted by McAleer, Pagan, and Volker). Hence we remain sceptical of the possibility of developing any model selection procedures which could uniformly deliver valid models.

(4) Science is a *process* of accumulating empirical knowledge based on a data-instigated progressive research strategy in which the *model* is the message. Precisely how a model is obtained is a matter of research efficiency not germane to the validity or usefulness of the product. Thus, the debate noted in point (3) about model selection procedures is not crucial, whereas replicability and critical evaluation are fundamental. Whether it be by hunch, lucky guess, serendipity, inspiration, data mining, dreams, priors, or whatever, useful models can be, and in the history of science have been, developed, sometimes for the most outlandish reasons (see for example Mason, 1962).

Our note is structured as follows: although we can but sketch our approach in a comment on the debate about 'deconning' econometrics, Section 2 describes the main points. Readers interested in greater detail could consult *inter alia* Hendry and Mizon (1978), Hendry and Richard (1983) and Mizon (1984). Note that our analysis is specifically oriented to time-series data.

Then in Sections 3 and 4 we tackle the issues of 'fragility' and of whimsy respectively (points (1) and (2) above). The roles of construction and destruction (point (3) above) are noted throughout the discussion, whereas the concept of a progressive research strategy (point 4) merits a separate section (5). Section 6 concludes our comments.

2.   To Stretch or to Squeeze?: That is the Question

A *model* is a simplified representation intended to capture the salient features of some group of phenomena. Intrinsically, therefore, models embody the notions of design and a corresponding focus of interest, but are inherently approximations and inevitably 'false'. 'Thus, no model with a finite number of parameters is actually believed' (Leamer, p. 34). Nevertheless, models can differ radically in their *usefulness* (or otherwise!)

relative to the objectives for which they were constructed. The extent to which they are useful depends on their actual design, not on the origins or methods whereby that design was achieved.

As noted above, the sources of a model's *theoretical* specification lie in the realms of art and psychology. However, all *empirical* models must correspond to a reduction of whatever mechanism generated the observed data. The basic operations of reduction are transforming (which really precedes reduction), marginalizing (eliminating variables) and conditioning (treating certain variables as given); for example, aggregation corresponds to a set of linear transformations of the data followed by marginalization with respect to all non-aggregates. Naturally, there are associated transformations of the invariants, relative constancies, and/or parameters of the original mechanism. Thus, whenever an empirical econometric relationship is asserted, it implicitly entails a vast sequence of reductions from the economic data generation process comprising agents transacting, producing, consuming, and so on. For a discussion of the relationship between conditioning and the concept of exogeneity, see Engle, Hendry and Richard (1983).

An important consequence of empirical models being reductions, is that the 'error' on an econometric equation is a *derived* process only loosely connected with whatever autonomous shocks impinged on the economy. That error must represent 'everything not elsewhere specified' in the asserted equation. As such, it varies with the equation's formulation and, more pertinently, is susceptible to being *designed* to satisfy certain criteria. Most empirical economists are aware of such a possibility through the now 'classical' application of (e.g.) the Cochrane–Orcutt procedure to 'remove' residual autocorrelation – that is, to redesign the residual to produce a Durbin–Watson statistic of around 2. But we all know that while design can be deliberate or by default – and can be good, bad, or indifferent in either case – human artifacts must be designed. The first major step to taking whatever 'con' there is in econometrics out of it is to openly recognize modelling as a matter of design (like bridge-building) not of garnering 'truth' (like an exercise in quantitative logic).

The next stage is to recognize that so-called 'tests' are widely used as *design criteria* as with the Durbin–Watson example above. A numerical value for such a statistic near that anticipated under the conventional null hypothesis reflects only on the adequacy of the design, not on the 'validity' of the model. For instance, the 'COMFAC' procedure proposed by Denis Sargan (1980) and applied by McAleer, Pagan, and Volker, offers one route to testing the validity of an autoregressive error assumption against the alternative of a more general (linear) dynamic model. It is crucial to note that a reject outcome reveals both 'bad design' and 'invalidity' (subject to the usual statistical caveats) whereas a non-reject outcome only reflects 'not-bad-design'. We reiterate our view that COMFAC is best used as an evaluation device (checking data coherency) rather than as a constructive tool (for finding models, unless there are sound economic theory reasons for anticipating an error autoregression (see Hendry and Mizon, 1978; Mizon and Hendry, 1980).

Given that design is pandemic, and that 'tests' are used as selection devices to prefilter out poor designs, what status can be ascribed to 'data-instigated' model specifications? To answer this we first need a taxonomy of the available information and adopt an extension of that in Hendry (1983): (1) the data set used by the investigator; (2) theoretical (and other 'prior') information; (3) the structure of the measurement system and (4) data used by 'rival' investigators.

The two data sources (1) and (4) can be further partitioned relative to any point in time t into the past ($t - j$ for $j > 0$), the present, and the future ($t + h$ for $h > 0$). This creates eight information sets, associated with each of which is a criterion of model design. Many of these are already widely used, though often in different disguises. For example, the past of (1) leads to the notions of an innovation error (one which cannot be explained by the selected data set) and of a data-coherent model (i.e. a model whose fit does not deviate *systematically* from the observed data). The future in (1) leads to parameter constancy: a full discussion is provided in Hendry and Richard (1982, 1983). Theory-consistent is the term for satisfying (2), although theory might be used as a selection criterion, or treated as an aspect to be tested. A model is data-admissible (3) if its fitted and forecast values automatically satisfy the properties of the measurement system (e.g. unemployment is positive and less than 100 per cent). A model which can account for the results obtained by rival explanations is said to be *encompassing* (see Davidson, Hendry, Srba and Yeo 1978; Mizon, 1984; and Mizon and Richard, 1985). If an encompassing model exists, then other models are inferentially redundant conditional on it. As Florens and Richard (1985) demonstrate in a Bayesian framework, encompassing corresponds to the dual in parameter space of sufficient statistics in sample space. Parsimonious encompassing plays a pivotal role in our econometric methodology and we consider it to be an essential component of an empirically progressive research strategy in economics, even though no model is ever 'correct'. A model is called *congruent* if it is encompassing, data coherent, theory consistent, admissible and has constant parameters.

The thrust of this section is that most selection criteria can be satisfied *within-sample* by appropriate design with genuine testing occurring only on later evidence. Conversely, models already invalidated within-sample seem an unlikely basis for a useful econometrics. Thus, congruency provides a set of *necessary* conditions for good model design, although future research will undoubtedly extend the set of requirements for congruency. Much of the debate about 'methodology' in econometrics concerns the efficiency of alternative search strategies (which is important for the productivity of our profession), rather than the choice of design criteria (which is important for the usefulness of models). When a model is quoted with a subset (or even a battery) of 'insignificant' test statistics, this illustrates only the quality of its design, not its intrinsic validity, since generally (though perhaps not universally), a model would have been revised had apparent reject outcomes been observed during the construction process. Parenthetically, poor modelling strategies often lead to the need to run hundreds of regressions, irrespective of the design criteria. We have written separately on improving model-search procedures (see Mizon, 1977; Hendry, 1979; Hendry and Ericsson, 1983). Directionless or repeated searches may increase the probability of choosing poor models, but cannot affect the actual usefulness of the final selection, which is a property of the model, not of the mapping.

Once a model has been designed to an investigator's satisfaction, its claimed properties exclude a vast range of potential features of the world. For example, a congruent model excludes the errors being autocorrelated, or rival models fitting substantially better, and so on. *Conditional* on taking the putative congruent model as claimed by its protagonists (subject to reproducibility discussed in 4 below), a range of tests can be constructed, which the model's proprietors would agree had a given distribution. Discrepant outcomes on such tests clearly cast doubt on the credibility of the earlier claims. The attendent issue of the respective roles of construction and destruction is apparent: any particular method for the former (whether mechanistic, flair-driven or whatever) is not valid in general (although it may happen to work in some specific instance) whereas the conditional test strategy is valid,[2] and is especially powerful against new data, new models, and new tests.

Robustness raises issues which are related to, but distinct from, those of 'fragility' and collinearity. In our framework, models are robust in a given direction if small changes in that direction alter the specification only marginally. For particular directions, reasonable matrices usually can be agreed. As an example, extending the data set by more variables or more observations should leave the parameters of a robust model virtually unchanged. As Leamer (1983b) argues, collinearity is a property of a parameterization, not of a model. Nevertheless, 'common sense' and 'theory' often suggest that certain parameterizations are of greater interest for modelling purposes than others (including, say, separating impact

---

[2] Though not necessarily definitive as protective belts and anomaly-absorbing strategies are open to defenders of a theory or a model; the issue of progression is considered in 5 below.

effects from equilibrium responses in dynamic models). We call a parameterization 'near-orthogonal' if the corresponding variables have low mutual intercorrelations, and 'parsimonious' if of low dimensionality. *We seek to design congruent models with parsimonious, near-orthogonal parameterizations precisely because in practice we have found such models to be robust.* As one possible empirical illustration of many of the concepts just described, the model in Davidson et al. (1978) has constant parameters for far longer sample periods than that from which it was selected (see Davidson and Hendry, 1982 and Davis, 1982). Even so, it is encompassed by the model of Hendry and Ungern-Sternberg (1981), although the estimates of the original regression parameters are hardly altered by the addition of variables which significantly lower the equation standard error. Whether robust models can still be 'fragile' is the topic of the next section.

Finally, the question which began this section seems less well posed than Hamlet's: neither seems a correct response. Rather than stretching models as proposed by Leamer, or squeezing the data into an autocorrelated error representation as in McAleer, Pagan, and Volker, we suggest designing models to be congruent with the available information, progressively improving them as new information and ideas accrue.

3.   Are "Fragile" Models Fragile – or does Extreme Bounds Analysis Stretch our Credulity?

Everyone agrees that a sensitivity analysis to evaluate the fragility of a model is important – the only issues of potential disagreement concern how to undertake such an analysis, and what it should comprise. In their insightful dissection of EBA, McAleer, Pagan, and Volker highlight two vitally important limitations to its use as a method for evaluating fragility:

(1) the bounds obtained depend on which variables are treated as doubtful; *and*
(2) if a so-called 'doubtful' variable is actually crucial in accounting for the behaviour of the regressand, then 'fragile' results will be found.

It seems an odd method of analysing sensitivity to consider cases in which one is non-informative on the coefficients of the *interesting* variables, while being very informative about the coefficients of the 'doubtful' variables. If the 'doubtful' variables really do matter, then models which exclude them are manifestly invalid – how, therefore, can they constitute a *valid basis for criticism*? Certainly not simply because coefficients alter sign or greatly change in magnitude. Denote the 'free' variables by $\{\underline{x}_t\}$, the "doubtful" by $\{\underline{z}_t\}$ and the regressand by $\{y_t\}$ with the valid model being:

(1) $y_t|\underset{\sim}{x}_t, \underset{\sim}{z}_t \sim E(\beta'\underset{\sim}{x}_t + \gamma'\underset{\sim}{z}_t, \sigma^2)$, where $\beta \neq \underset{\sim}{0}$ and $\gamma \neq \underset{\sim}{0}$.

Now delete $\underset{\sim}{z}_t$, reducing the conditioning set to $y_t|\underset{\sim}{x}_t$, such that:

(2) $E(y_t|\underset{\sim}{x}_t) = \underset{\sim}{\lambda}'\underset{\sim}{x}t$.

Even *before estimating (2)*, whether the least-squares estimators $\hat{\lambda}$ and $\hat{\beta}$ will have the same or different signs for specific coefficients can be *deduced* from (1) and the auxiliary information about the 'regression' of $\underset{\sim}{z}_t$ on $\underset{\sim}{x}_t$. Neither the presence of sign changes *nor their absence* tells one anything about the fragility of (1). Indeed, (1) automatically encompasses (2), so (2) is inferentially redundant conditional on (1), and conversely, since $\gamma \neq \underset{\sim}{0}$, the 'parsimonious' model (2) does not encompass (1). EBA magnifies the confusion by stretching the set of priors from just $\gamma = 0$. It seems a dangerous tool which suggests that a robust, congruent model is 'fragile' just because some of its variables are important!

For time-series data, most relevant $\{\underset{\sim}{x}_t\}$, $\{\underset{\sim}{z}_t\}$ series are stochastic and autocorrelated – so changes in the residual process $u_t = y_t - E(y_t|.)$ can directly reveal the invalidity of derived submodels through autocorrelation, or heteroscedasticity or, increases in σ_u^2 and/or parameter non-constancy. Consequently, EBA is not *necessary* for model evaluation. Note that Leamer (1983a) not only fails to provide any description of how well the submodels characterize the data; none is offered for how well the overall model does so. Readers are left devoid of information for appraising either the general model, or the models supposedly demonstrating the 'fragility' of that general model. We cannot accept that EBA is a route towards increasing the credibility of econometric evidence, either constructively, as done by a researcher to help him select 'non-fragile' models, or destructively, since invalid models could well seem 'non-fragile' models, or destructively, since invalid models could well seem 'non-fragile' and excellent ones 'fragile'. Whether or not this occurs depends on the one hand on the irrelevance of 'doubtful variables' and on the other hand on possibly meaningless claims that essential variables are 'doubtful'. EBA has an unknown, variable, and apparently often large Type I error. Thus, we disagree with McAleer, Pagan, and Volker's implicit view that EBA has a role in econometrics (footnote 4), but concur with their statement that EBA is 'an inefficient (and incomplete) way of communicating to readers the fact that the doubtful variables are needed to explain the data'.

How then do we interpret the findings of 'fragility' of inference about interest elasticities in money demand as discussed by Cooley and LeRoy (1981)? Quite simply, we note that the *unconditional* standard deviation of the growth rate of real money over their sample period is under 1 per cent as against the standard error of their estimated model being greater than 2 per cent and we dismiss *all* inferences therefrom as invalid and irrelevant.

We would do so even if EBA had *not* revealed any fragility. Until a model adequately characterizes data, no inference from it meritis attention.

4.   Artificial Priors and Real Data: Are we on a voyage of discovery or do we know everything already?

Precedents for beliefs in a priori knowledge of the real world stem from at least the time of Plato's *Meno* (though there the *real* issue was virtue rather than fact!). Nevertheless, we do not consider Leamer's Bayesian viewpoint to be an adequate formulation for scientific discovery, which we see as the lifeblood of science, since creative ideas almost always lie outside currently accepted priors. Indeed, we believe Leamer has hoisted himself on the econometric equivalent of Morton's Fork[3]: if existing evidence is 'fragile' and 'whimsical' and hence lacks credibility – *what evidential basis is there from which to formulate useful priors*? Conversely, if existing evidence is a good basis for 'priors', what is wrong with current procedures? The counter that priors represent 'subjective beliefs', and need not be data-based, reopens Pandora's Box to set free unbounded ascientific scholasticism, unless *offset by rigorous testing of assertions*.

When evaluating models it is crucial to maintain a clear distinction between the 'context of discovery' and the 'context of justification' (as enunciated by John Herschel (1830) – see for example John Losee (1980). As Karl Popper (1974, p. 31) has argued, 'how it happens that a new idea occurs . . . is irrelevant to the logical analysis of scientific knowledge'. Thus it follows that no way is illegitimate, including those of Leamer, and of McAleer, Pagan, and Volker. Such an assertion does not imply that any model is legitimate, nor that any search strategy will be efficient, merely that how one found a model cannot affect its *intrinsic* usefulness. Consequently, we cannot agree with the first part of the assertion in McAleer, Pagan, and Volker that 'many of the difficulties applied econometrics currently faces originate in the very poor attempts currently made to accurately describe the process whereby a model was selected, and to ascertain its adequacy'; we fully endorse the last claim!

Where whimsy, whether in theories or in priors, is based on a flair which leads to new discoveries we are strongly in its favour. Whimsy in the context of justification, especially in the reporting of results, is another matter, but one where journal editors could play a substantial role by insisting on a minimum amount of descriptive information to allow readers to appraise

---

[3] Morton's Fork is the scheme devised by Archbishop John Morton (*c.* 1420–1500), in the reign of Henry VII, to increase the royal revenues. He levied contributions from the rich on the ground that they could afford to contribute, and from those who lived without ostentation on the ground that their economies must have made them rich.

empirical claims (viz., simple items like means and standard deviations of dependent variables and their growth rates, percentage equation standard errors, as well as interpretable indices of residual autocorrelation, heteroscedasticity, and parameter constancy). Alternatively expressed, whereas we are unconcerned about the origins of conjectures, we are very concerned about how much genuine effort has been devoted to attempted refutation. Leamer's (p. 37) statement that 'sometimes I take the error terms to be correlated, sometimes uncorrelated' has ambiguous referents, but if he is wandering into the arena of evaluation, we have a simple proposal: find out.

The replication and testing of others' claims plays an essential role in the physical sciences and should do so in economics. The recent explosion in the availability of powerful, standardized microcomputers with internationally compatible software and easy and accurate transfer of data between researchers will soon work wonders in rooting out 'con' artists. Already the evaluation of others' models has been reduced from a Labour of Hercules to a routine student exercise. We believe that much of the so-called 'con' is self-delusion not deceit, and hence that most researchers will welcome the next generation of friendly yet powerful software which not only releases the conduct of empirical research from drudgery but also offers really useful diagnostic information to help differentiate between whimsy that will remain capricious and that which might lead to greater understanding.

5. The Model is the Message – A Progressive Research Strategy in Econometrics

Although it is undoubtedly only one of many possible routes to developing useful empirical models with theoretical content, we obtained a large increase in our modelling efficiency by adopting an explicit progressive research strategy as follows:

At the outset the model is formulated with sufficient generality such that if a more general model were essential to adequately characterize the data, then one would have gained new knowledge from that information alone. This step necessitates comprehensive knowledge about previous models for the variables of interest in order to conduct encompassing tests. But it does *not* entail regarding every series in a massive databank as a potential candidate for inclusion in every relationship. Such a mindless approach seems most unlikely to lead to testable, let alone parsimonious, congruent models. Leamer's claim (p. 34) that 'the non-experimental researcher is *obligated* to include in the regression all variables that *might* have an important effect' (our italics) is sufficiently vague to allow us to choose the charitable interpretation. In the class of single-equation linear models, encompassing does *not* require embedding (or nesting), but does require variance dominance – that is, in large samples one model cannot encompass another unless it fits at least as well. Thus, goodness-of-fit is necessary but not sufficient for congruency in that class.

If the data base is inadequate to estimate the general model (e.g. the sample size is too small), any necessary presimplifications are recorded for later investigation and a feasible 'general unrestricted model' is estimated. The data series are transformed to create a near-orthogonal parameterization, selected to correspond to likely decision variables of the relevant economic agents, contingent on information they could have had available; frequently, the resulting parameters are of direct interest in that they have sensible theory interpretations. The transformed model is then simplified to eliminate redundant influences (which may be genuinely conditionally irrelevant, or may just lack variablity in the given data set). While no *unique* procedure can be specified, this does not concern us as later evaluation will reveal the quality of the design. Within-sample 'tests' are used as selection criteria to guide the modeller towards a congruent model. The products of such an approach have in practice tended to be parsimonious, robust, and reasonably constant, as well as successfully encompassing previous models. While the residuals are innovations against the information utilized, since modelling is a process (not a once-for-all event) it must be anticipated that later models will explain further components of those residuals leading to a progressive sequence of successively encompassing, congruent models. Each extension 'invalidates' previous efforts so that the sequence proceeds destructively, but with a constructive intention.

Even so, to quote Chalmers (1978, p. 83): 'given the obvious unpredictability of the outcome of scientific research, it is unrealistic, perhaps even absurd, to expect a methodology of science to be such that it offers definite rules for deciding the correct steps to take in the practice of science'. Surely the same argument must apply in economics. Intermittently, (whimsical) new ideas might lead to the overthrow of the entire framework in favour of another which presages more progression or greater excess corroborated content (see Thomas Kuhn, 1962 and Imre Lakatos, 1980). We do *not* claim to adjudicate on this context of discovery; we merely wish to suggest a progressive evaluation strategy in the context of justification.

6. Conclusions

To the extent that 'con' connotes 'trickery', let us banish it from econometrics (see Joseph Schumpeter, 1954, p. 209); to the extent that 'con' denotes 'learning', let it flourish in an econometrics progressing by learning from data.

The creation of theories and models for scientific evaluation is subjective and often whimsical, but the process of scientific advance remains objective. We certainly do not accept Leamer's claim (p. 37) that 'the false idol of objectivity has done great damage to economic science'; *per contra*, a subjectivist substitute is likely to have that consequence. We conjecture that such ostensible views on whimsicality and objectivity derive from a failure to distinguish clearly between:

(1) the process of discovery as against that of justification, and
(2) the research efficiency of various modelling strategies as against the associated design criteria.

Whimsicality in creation may be precisely what is needed to escape from the straitjacket of received theory, but by the same token, systematic and rigorous evaluation of empirical claims is crucial to avoid whimsical justifications. The design criteria discussed above provide a set of *necessary* conditions for a model to be congruent with the available information. Doubtless there are more ways to develop models than we could conceive, varying greatly in the efficiency with which they deliver congruent models. No single approach is likely to be universally valid, due to the manifest fact that we do not yet fully understand the world, and until we do, we cannot know what would have been the 'best' way to study it – even if a 'best' way were to exist. No route is necessarily vacuous. To the extent that the concepts of 'fragility' and 'whimsy' correspond to our notions of non-robustness and whimsical justification we applaud Leamer's arguments, and trust that our note may help to clarify precisely what such concepts entail. Equally, we strongly support the arguments of McAleer, Pagan, and Volker in favour of stringent evaluation of empirical claims, and would reiterate that replication, congruency, and especially encompassing are priorities for a progressive econometrics.

Nevertheless, we doubt that as a practical tool extreme bounds analysis has a useful independent role in econometric modelling of economic time series. Firstly, since it reveals nothing about the extent to which a model actually characterizes data, 'fragility' found in a given model is uninformative about the fragility of the underlying inference. For example, consider Cooley and Le Roy's finding concerning the 'fragility' of the anticipated negative influence of interest rates on a money demand. Certainly it is a fragile matter in their model; but since that model suffers from massive residual autocorrelation and parameter non-constancy within-sample, it is an invalid basis for any inferences beyond its own non-congruency. Conversely, the equilibrium solution of the alternative model proposed by McAleer, Pagan, and Volker satisfies the requirements of

EBA for non-fragility, yet also manifests predictive failure over the period 1974(I)–1978(IV). Thirdly, paraphrasing a point made by McAleer, Pagan, and Volker, a robust and congruent model could seem 'fragile' just because its main explanatory variables were claimed to be doubtful – the ultimate whimsicality in the context of justification.

In a study of $M1$ demand in the USA over the period 1958–84, Baba, Hendry, and Starr (1985) have used the modelling approach outlined in Section 2 above, seeking to develop a congruent model which could encompass both the successes and the failures of previous studies. The resulting model does not experience any significant predictive failure over the period 1974–77 (nor over 1982–4) and offers one explanation for the demise of the models due to Goldfeld (1976) and to McAleer, Pagan, and Volker. That study is predicated on the view that predictive failure is the most pertinent problem in time-series econometrics, but equally is of great value both in disposing of inadequate models and in revealing the substantial information content of data evidence. An important empirical point to note from the study of McAleer, Pagan, and Volker is that the predictive failure does not arise simply from dynamic misspecification, the second pandemic disease in econometrics. As a spin-off benefit, perhaps the role of autocorrelation might now be better understood.

There are, of course, many important analytical points in both their paper and in Leamer (1983a) and we would not wish to end with the impression that the econometrists themselves are in disarray. As newspapers long ago discovered, good news is no news, but scandal sells well. We have perforce focused on the areas of potential disagreement to enhance clarification and to avoid boring repetition of common ground. Most econometricians appear to be concerned to raise the efficiency of empirical econometrics research and the credibility of its products. Fearing that a strident chorus of 'don't-do-thats' will deter excessively, despite the best methodological prescription being 'think of the truth at the start', a variety of more constructive panaceas have been proposed, although destruction and criticism are really the jointly valid message. We at least are not pessimistic about the future of an econometrics which develops using critical evaluation within a progressive research strategy.

References

Baba, Yoshi, Hendry, David F. and Starr, Ross M. (1989), U. S. money demand, 1960–1984. Discussion Paper, University of San Diego.

Chalmers, Alan F. (1978), *What is This Thing Called Science?* University of Queensland Press, Queensland.

Cooley, Thomas F. and Le Roy, Stephen F. (1981). Identification and estimation of money demand, *American Economic Review*, December, 71, 825–44.

Davidson, James E. H. and Hendry, David F. (1981), Interpreting econometric evidence: consumers' expenditure in the U.K., *European Economic Review*, June, 16, 177–92.

Davidson, James E. H., Hendry, David F., Srba, Frank and Yeo, Stephen (1978), Econometric modelling of the time-series relationship between consumers' expenditure and income in the United Kingdom, *Economic Journal*, December, 88, 661–92.

Davis, E. Philip (1982), The consumption function in macro-economic models: a comparative study. Discussion Paper No. 1, Bank of England.

Engle, Robert, F., Hendry, David F. and Richard, Jean-François (1983), Exogeneity, *Econometrica*, March, 51, 277–304.

Florens, Jean-Pierre and Richard, Jean-François (1985), Encompassing. Discussion Paper, CORE, University of Louvain-la-Neuve.

Goldfeld, Stephen M. (1976), The case of the missing money, *Brookings Papers in Economic Activity*, 3, 683–730.

Hendry, David F. (1979), Predictive failure and econometric modelling in macro-economics: the transactions demand for money, *Economic Modelling*, ed. by P. Ormerod, Heinemann, London, pp. 217–42.

Hendry, David F. (1983), Econometric modelling: the 'consumption function' in retrospect, *Scottish Journal of Political Economy*, November, 30, 193–220.

Hendry, David F. and Ericsson, Neil R. (1983). Assertion without empirical basis: an econometric appraisal of 'Monetary Trends in ... the United Kingdom, by Milton Friedman and Anna Schwartz. Panel Paper 22, Bank of England.

Hendry, David F. and Mizon, Grayham E. (1978). Serial correlation as a convenient simplification, not a nuisance: a comment on a study of the demand for money by the Bank of England, *Economic Journal*, September, 88, 549–63.

Hendry, David F. and Richard, Jean-François (1982), On the formulation of empirical models in dynamic econometrics, *Journal of Econometrics*, October, 20, 3–33.

Hendry, David F. and Richard, Jean-François (1983), The econometric analysis of economic time series, *International Statistical Review*, June, 51, 111–63.

Hendry, David F. and von Ungern-Sternberg, Thomas (1981), Liquidity and inflation effects on consumers' expenditure, *Essays in the Theory and Measurement of Consumer Behaviour in Honour of Sir Richard Stone*, ed. by A. S. Deaton. Cambridge University Press, Cambridge, pp. 237–60.

Herschel, John (1830), *A Preliminary Discourse on the Study of Natural Philosophy*, Longman, Rees, Brown & Green and John Taylor, London.

Kuhn, Thomas S. (1962), *The Structure of Scientific Revolutions*. Chicago University Press, Chicago.

Lakatos, Imre (1980), *The Methodology of Scientific Research Programmes*, Vol. 1, ed. by John Worrall and Gregory Currie. Cambridge University Press, Cambridge.

Leamer, Edward E. (1983a) 'Let's take the con out of econometrics, *American Economic Review*, March, 73, 31–44.

Leamer, Edward E. (1983b), Model choice and specification analysis, *Handbook of Econometrics*, Vol. 1, ed. by Z. Griliches and M. D. Intriligator. North-Holland,

Amsterdam, pp. 285–330.

Losee, John (1980), *A Historical Introduction to the Philosophy of Science*. Oxford University Press, Oxford.

Mason, Stephen F. (1962), *A History of the Sciences*. Collier Books, New York.

McAleer, Michael, Pagan, Adrian R. and Volker, Paul A. (1985), What will take the con out of econometrics?", *American Economic Review*, 75, 293–307.

Mizon, Graham E. (1977), Model selection procedures", *Studies in Modern Economic Analysis*, ed. by M. J. Artie and A. R. Nobay. Basil Blackwell, Oxford, Chap. 4.

Mizon, Graham E. (1984), The encompassing approach in econometrics, *Econometrics and Quantitative Economics*, ed. by D. F. Handry and K. F. Wallis. Basil Blackwell, Oxford, 11, 135–72.

Mizon, Graham E., and Hendry, David F. (1980), An empirical application and Monte Carlo analysis of tests of dynamic specification, *Review of Economic Studies*, January, 47, 21–45.

Mizon, Graham E. and Richard, Jean-François (1985), The encompassing principle and its application to testing non-nested hypotheses, *Econometrica*.

Popper, Karl R. (1974), *The Logic of Scientific Discovery*. Hutchinson, London.

Sargan, J. Denis (1980), Some tests of dynamic specification for a single equation, *Econometrica*, May, 48, 879–97.

Schumpeter, Joseph A. (1954), *History of Economic Analysis*. George Allen & Unwin, London.

8

Macroeconomics and Reality

Christopher A. Sims

Existing strategies for econometric analysis related to macroeconomics are subject to a number of serious objections, some recently formulated, some old. These objections are summarized in this paper, and it is argued that taken together they make it unlikely that macroeconomic models are in fact over identified, as the existing statistical theory usually assumes. The implications of this conclusion are explored, and an example of econometric work in a non-standard style, taking account of the objections to the standard style, is presented.

The study of the business cycle, fluctuations in aggregate measures of economic activity and prices over periods from one to ten years or so, constitutes or motivates a large part of what we call macroeconomics. Most economists would agree that there are many macroeconomic variables whose cyclical fluctuations are of interest, and would agree further that fluctuations in these series are interrelated. It would seem to follow almost tautologically that statistical models involving large numbers of macro-economic variables ought to be the arena within which macroeconomic theories confront reality and thereby each other.

Instead, though large-scale statistical macroeconomic models exist and are by some criteria successful, a deep vein of scepticism about the value of these models runs through that part of the economics profession not actively engaged in constructing or using them. It is still rare for empirical research in macroeconomics to be planned and executed within the framework of one of the large models. In this lecture I intend to discuss some aspects of this situation, attempting both to offer some explanations and to suggest some means for improvement.

I will argue that the style in which their builders construct claims for a connection between these models and reality – the style in which 'identification' is achieved for these models – is inappropriate, to the point at which claims for identification in these models cannot be taken seriously.

This article first appeared in *Econometrica*, Vol. 48, No. 1, January 1980, pp. 1–48. Research for the paper was supported by NSF Grant Soc-76-02482. Lars Hansen executed the computations. The paper has benefited from comments by many people, especially Thomas J. Sargent and Finn Kydland.

This is a venerable assertion; and there are some good old reasons for believing it,[1] but there are also some reasons which have been more recently put forth. After developing the conclusion that the identification claimed for existing large-scale models is incredible, I will discuss what ought to be done in consequence. The line of argument is: large-scale models do perform useful forecasting and policy-analysis functions despite their incredible identification; the restrictions imposed in the usual style of identification are neither essential to constructing a model which can perform these functions nor innocuous; an alternative style of identification is available and practical.

Finally we will look at some empirical work based on an alternative style of macroeconometrics. A six-variable dynamic system is estimated without using theoretical perspectives. Under a sophisticated neo-monetarist interpretation, a restriction on the system which implies that monetary policy shocks could explain nearly all cyclical variation in real variables in the economy is tested and rejected. Under a more standard macroeconometric interpretation, a restriction which is treated as a maintained hypothesis in econometric work with Phillips curve 'wage equations' or paired wage and price equations is also rejected.

1. Incredible Identification

A.   *The Genesis of 'A Priori Restrictions'*

When discussing statistical theory, we say a model is identified if distinct points in the model's parameter space imply observationally distinct patterns of behaviour for the model's variables. If a parameterization we derive from economic theory (which is usually what we mean by a 'structural form' for a model) fails to be identified, we can always transform the parameter space so that all points in the original parameter space which imply equivalent behaviour are mapped into the same point in the new parameter space. This is called normalization. The obvious example is the case where, not having an identified simultaneous equation model in structural form, we estimate a reduced form instead. Having achieved identification by normalization in this example, we admit that the individual equations of the model are not products of distinct exercises in economic theory. Instead of using a reduced form, we could normalize by requiring the residuals to be orthogonal across equations and the coefficient matrix of current endogenous variables to be triangular. The

---

[1] T. C. Liu (1960) presented convincing arguments for the assertion in a classic article.

resulting normalization into Wold causal chain form is identified, but results in equations which are linear combinations of the reduced form equations. Nobody is disturbed by this situation of multiple possible normalizations.

Similarly, when we estimate a complete system of demand equations, we recognize that the set of equations, in which each quantity appears only once, on the left-hand side of one equation in the system, and all prices appear on the right of each equation, is no more than one of many possible normalizations for a system of equations describing demand behaviour. In principle, we realize that it does not make sense to regard 'demand for meat' and 'demand for shoes' as the products of distinct categories of behaviour, any more than it would make sense to regard 'price of meat' and 'price of shoes' equations as products of distinct categories of behaviour if we normalized so as to reverse the place of prices and quantities in the system. Nonetheless we do sometimes estimate a small part of a complete demand system together with part of a complete supply system – supply and demand for meat, say. In doing this, it is common and reasonable practice to make shrewd aggregations and exclusion restrictions so that our small partial-equilibrium system omits most of the many prices we know enter the demand relation in principle and possibly includes a shrewdly selected set of exogenous variables we expect to be especially important in explaining variation in meat demand (e.g., an Easter dummy in regions where many people buy hams for Easter dinner).

' While individual demand equations developed for partial equilibrium use may quite reasonably involve an array of restrictions appropriate to that use, it is evident that a system of demand equations built up incrementally from such partial-equilibrium models may display very undesirable properties. In effect, the shrewd restrictions which are useful for partial equilibrium purposes, when concatenated across many categories of demand, yield a bad *system* of restrictions.

This point is far from new, having been made, e.g., by Zvi Griliches (1968) in his criticism of the consumption equations of the first version of the Brookings model, and by Brainard and Tobin (1968) in relation to financial sector models in general. And of course this same point motivates the extensive work which has been done on econometrically usable functional forms for complete systems of demand equations and factor demand equations.

The reason for re-emphasizing the dangers of one-equation-at-a-time specification of a large model here is that the extent to which the distinctions among equations in large macromodels are normalizations, rather than truly structural distinctions, has not received much emphasis. In the version of the FRB-MIT model reported in Ando et al., (1972), for example, a substantial part of the interesting behavioural equations of the financial sector are demand equations for particular assets. Consumption, of course, is represented by demand equations, and the supply of labour and demand for housing also in principle represent components of a system of equations describing the public's allocations of their resources. Thus the strictures against one-equation-at-a-time specification which are ordinarily applied to the financial or consumption equations of a model as a sub-group, really apply to this whole set of equations.

If large blocks of equations, running across 'sectors' of the model which are ordinarily treated as separate specification problems, are in fact distinguished from one another only by normalization, what 'economic theory' tells us about them is mainly that any variable which appears on the right-hand side of one of these equations belongs in principle on the right-hand side of all of them. To the extent that models end up with very different sets of variables on the right-hand sides of these equations, they do so not by invoking economic theory, but (in the case of demand equations) by invoking an intuitive, econometrician's version of psychological and sociological theory, since constraining utility functions is what is involved here. Furthermore, unless these sets of equations are considered as a system in the process of specification, the behavioural implications of the restrictions on all equations taken together may be much less reasonable than the restrictions on any one equation taken by itself.

The textbook paradigm for identification of a simultaneous equation system is supply and demand for an agricultural product. There we are apt to speak of the supply equation as reflecting the behaviour of farmers, and the demand equation as reflecting the behaviour of consumers. A similar use of language, in which labour supply equations are taken to apply to 'workers', consumption equations to 'consumers', asset demand equations to 'savers', sometimes obscures the distinction in macromodels between normalized and structurally identified equations.[2] On the other hand, the distinction between 'employers' and 'investigators' on the one hand, and 'consumers' and 'workers' on the other, does have some structural justification. There certainly are policies which can drive a wedge between supply and demand prices for transactions between the 'business' and

---

[2] In Hurwicz's (1962) abstract discussion of structural systems it is apparent that an equation system identified by normalization is not an identified structure. An identified structural equation is one which uniquely remains invariant under a certain class of 'interventions' in the system. In the supply and demand paradigm, the natural class of interventions to consider is excise taxes. It is not impossible that a system of demand equations be structural in Hurwicz's sense – McFadden (1974) has provided an instance of a structural interpretation of a sort of demand equation, in which the identifying interventions are deletions or additions in the list of available commodities. But nothing like McFadden's analysis exists or is likely to be developed to justify structural distinction between labour supply and consumption, for example.

'household' sectors, which is roughly the distinction with which we are concerned. Furthermore, if business behaviour is taken to be competitive, the business sector simply traces out the efficient envelope of available technology in response to demand shifts. Then the distinction between business and households becomes the distinction between 'nature' and 'tastes' on which identification in the supply–demand paradigm rests. The idea that weather affects grain supply and not (much) grain demand, while the ethnic and demographic structure of the population affects grain demand but not (much) grain supply, is a powerful source of identifying restrictions. The same nature–tastes distinction is a source of powerful identifying restrictions in large macromodels, but the number of such restrictions available is not large relative to the number of equations and variables in large macromodels.

B.   Dynamics

The fact that large macroeconomic models are dynamic is a rich source of spurious 'a priori' restrictions, as we shall see below, but it also weakens the few legitimate bases for generating identifying restrictions alluded to in the previous section. If we accept the modern anti-interventionist school's argument that dynamic macroeconomic models ought not to violate the principle that markets clear,[3] then dynamics do not raise new problems in this respect; the business sector single-mindedly pursues profit, according to the directions of the observable price vector, so that the difference between the business sector of a dynamic model and that of a static model is only in whether the efficiency frontier traced out has dynamic elements. If instead we take the view that prices themselves may adjust sluggishly, we enter the wilderness of 'disequilibrium economics'. This phrase must, it seems to me, denote a situation in which we cannot suppose that business behaviour is invariant under changes in the public's tastes. The reason is that business behaviour, when markets don't clear, must depend not only on hypothetical business demands and supplies given current prices, but also on the nature of whatever rationing is currently going on – e.g. on the excess demand of Walrasian theory. If the degree of excess demand or supply in the labour market enters employer behaviour, then by that route any variable which we think of as connected to labour supply decisions enters the dynamic labour demand equation.

   J. D. Sargan (1961) considered the problem of simultaneous-equation identification in models containing both lagged dependent variables and serially correlated residuals. He came to the reassuring conclusion that, if a few narrow-looking special cases are ruled out, the usual rules for checking identification in models with serially uncorrelated residuals apply equally

---

[3] This position is set forth persuasively by Lucas (1972).

well to models with serially correlated residuals. In particular, it would ordinarily be reasonable to lump lagged dependent variables with strictly exogenous variables in checking the order condition for identification, despite the fact that a consistent estimation method must take account of the presence of correlation between lagged dependent variables and the serially correlated residuals. Though consistent estimation of such models poses formidable problems, Sargan's analysis suggested that identification is not likely to be undermined by the combination of lagged dependent variables and serial correlation.

Work by Michio Hatanaka (1975), however, makes it clear that this sanguine conclusion rests on the supposition that exact lag lengths and orders of serial correlation are known a priori. On the evidently more reasonable assumption that lag lengths and shapes of lag distributions are not known a priori,[4] Hatanaka shows that the order condition takes on an altered form: we must in this case cease to count repeat occurrences of the same variable, with different lags, in a single equation. In effect, this rule prevents lagged dependent variables from playing the same kind of formal role as strictly exogenous variables in identification; we must expect that, to identify an equation, we will have to locate in other equations of the system at least one strictly exogenous variable to serve as an instrument for each right-hand-side endogenous variable in the given equation.

Application of Hatanaka's criterion to large-scale macromodels would probably not suggest that they are formally unidentified. The version of the FRB-MIT model laid out in Hale (1975), e.g., has over ninety variables categorized as strictly exogenous, while most equations contain no more than six or eight variables. However the Hatanaka criterion, by focusing attention more sharply on the distinction between endogenous and strictly exogenous variables, might well result in models being respecified with shorter lists of exogenous variables. Many, perhaps most, of the exogenous variables in the FRB-MIT model (Hale, 1975) or in Fair's model (1976) are treated as exogenous by default rather than as a result of there being good reason to believe them strictly exogenous. Some are variables treated as exogenous only because seriously explaining them would require an extensive modelling effort in areas away from the main interests of the model-builders. Agricultural price and output variables, the price of imported raw

---

[4] By saying that it is evidently more reasonable to assume we do not know lag lengths and shapes a priori, I do not mean to suggest that one should not impose restrictions of a reasonable form on lag lengths and shapes in the process of estimation. However, we should recognize that truncating lag distributions is part of the process of estimation – lag length is itself estimated one way or another – and that when our model is not identified without the pretence that we know lag length to begin with, it is just not identified. A similar point applies to 'identifying' simultaneous equation models by imposing 'a priori' constraints that coefficients which prove statistically insignificant are zero. Setting such coefficients to zero may be a justifiable part of the estimation process, but it does not aid in identification.

materials, and the volume of exports are in this category in the FRB-MIT model. Other variables are treated as exogenous because they are policy variables, even though they evidently have a substantial endogenous component. In this category are the Federal Reserve discount rate, federal government expenditures on goods and services, and other variables. It appears to me that if the list of exogenous variables were carefully reconsidered and tested in cases where exogeneity is doubtful, the identification of these models might well, by Hatanaka's criterion, fail, and would at best be weak,[5] even if the several other sources of doubt about identifying restrictions in macromodels listed in this paper are discounted.

C.   *Expectations*

It used to be that when expected future values of a variable were thought to be important in a behavioural equation, they were replaced by a distributed lag on that same variable. Whatever else may be said for or against it, this practice had the advantage of producing uncomplicated effects on identification. As the basis in economic theory for such simple treatments of expectations has been examined more critically, however, it has become apparent that they are unsound, and that sound treatments of expectations complicate identification substantially. Whether or not one agrees that economic models ought always to assume rational behaviour under uncertainty, i.e. 'rational expectations', one must agree that any sensible treatment of expectations is likely to undermine many of the exclusion restrictions econometricians had been used to thinking of as most reliable. However certain we are that the tastes of consumers in the US are unaffected by the temperature in Brazil, we must admit that it is possible that US consumers, upon reading of a frost in Brazil in the newspapers, might attempt to stockpile coffee in anticipation of the frost's effect on price. Thus variables known to affect supply enter the demand equation, and vice-versa, through terms in expected price.

But though analysis of rational expectations raises this problem for us, by carrying through with that analysis we may achieve identification again by a new route. The rational expectations hypothesis tells us expectations ought to be formed optimally; by restricting temperature in Brazil to enter US demand for coffee *only* through its effect on the optimal forecast of price, we may again identify the demand equation. Wallis (1980) and Sargent (1978) (among others) have shown how this can be done. Lucas

---

[5] In this case of serial correlation of undetermined form and lagged dependent variables with undetermined lag lengths, the model is identified by the relation between structural parameters and the distributed lag regressions of endogenous variables on strictly exogenous variables. When the strictly exogenous variables have low explanatory power, estimates of the endogenous-on-exogenous regressions are likely to be subject to great sampling error, and the identification may be said to be weak.

(1972) in fact suggested that this be done in some of the earliest work on the implications of rational expectations for macro-economics.

It is my view, however, that rational expectations is more deeply subversive of identification than has yet been recognized. When we follow Hatanaka in removing the crutch of supposed a priori knowledge of lag lengths, then in the absence of expectational elements, we find the patient, though perhaps wobbly, re-establishing equilibrium. At least the classical form of identifying restriction, the nature-vs.-tastes distinction that identifies most supply and demand models, is still in a form likely to work under the Hatanaka criterion. In the presence of expectations it turns out that the crutch of a priori knowledge of lag lengths is indispensable, even when we have distinct, strictly exogenous variables shifting supply and demand schedules.

The behavioural interpretation of this identification problem can be displayed in a very simple example.[6] Suppose a firm is hiring an input, subject to adjustment costs, and that input purchase decisions have to be made one period in advance of actual production. Suppose further that the optimization problem has a quadratic–linear structure (justifying certainty-equivalence) and that the only element of uncertainty is a stochastic process shifting the demand curve. In this situation the firm's hiring decisions will depend on forecasts of the demand-shift variable. But suppose that the demand-shift process is a martingale-increment process – that is, suppose that the expected value of all future demand shifts is always the mean value of that variable. Then the expected future demand curve is always the same, input hiring decisions are always the same, and we obviously cannot hope to estimate from observed firm behaviour the parameters of the dynamic production function.

Special though it may seem, this example is representative of a general problem with models incorporating expectations. Such models will generally imply that behaviour depends on expected values of future prices (or of other variables). In order to guarantee that we can discover from observed behaviour the nature of that dependence on future prices, we must somehow insure that expected future prices have a rich enough pattern of variation to identify the parameters of the structure. This will ordinarily require restrictions on the form of serial correlation in the exogenous variables.

Of course, in a sense these problems are not fresh. If we want to estimate a distributed lag regression of y on x we must always restrict x not to be identically zero. The new element is that when we try to estimate a distributed lag regression of y on x and expected future x, the variation in the

----

[6] Robert Solow used essentially the same example in published comments (Solow, 1974) on earlier work of mine.

expected future x will always be less rich than that in the past x, so that the required restrictions are likely to be an order of magnitude more stringent in rational expectations models. To take a slightly more elaborate example, suppose our behavioural model is

$$(1) \qquad c*y(t) = b^{-*}\, p(t) + b^{++}\, \hat{p}_t(t),$$

where '*' denotes continuous-time convolution, $\hat{p}_t$ is the stochastic process of expected values of p given information available at time t, $b^+(s) = 0$ for $s > 0$, and $b^-(s) = 0$ for $s < 0$, and $c(s) = 0$, $s < 0$.[7] To be explicit about the notation, (1) could be written as

$$(2) \qquad c*y(t) = \int_0^\infty b^-(s)p(t - s)\, ds + \int_0^\infty b^+(-s)\hat{p}_t(t + s)\, ds.$$

Now suppose that the only information available at s is current and past values of p, and suppose further that p is a stationary first-order Markov process, i.e. that p can be thought of as generated by the stochastic differential equation

$$(3) \qquad \dot{p}(t) = -rp(t) + e(t),$$

with e a white noise process. It then follows that

$$(4) \qquad \hat{p}_t(t + s) = e^{-rs}p(t), \quad \text{all } s > 0.$$

Therefore (1) takes the form

$$(5) \qquad c*y(t) = b^{-*}p(t) + p(t)g(b^+),$$

where the function g is given by $g(b^+) = \int_0^\infty b^+(s)\, e^{-rs}\, ds$. While we can expect to recover $g(b^+)$ from the observed behaviour of y and p, knowledge of $g(b^+)$ will not in general determine b^+ itself unless we have available enough restrictions on b^+ to make it a function of a single unknown parameter. First-order Markov processes are widely used as examples in econometric discussions because of their analytic convenience, and they do not of course pose any identification problem for the estimation of b^- – the past of p will show adequately rich variation to identify b^- even if our parameter space for b^- is infinite-dimensional. This distinction, the need for enough restrictions to make b^+ lie in a one-dimensional space while b^- need only be subject to weak damping or smoothness restrictions for identification, is the order-of-magnitude difference in stringency to which I referred above.

At this point two lines of objection to the above argument-by-example may occur to you. In the first place, might we not be dealing with a hairline category of exceptional cases? For example, what if we ruled out all finite-order Markov processes for p in the preceding example? This is a small

---

[7] Though it does not matter for our argument, in actual examples, c, b^- and b^+ may be generalized functions, so that $c*y$, e.g., may be a linear combination of derivatives of y.

subset of all stationary processes, yet ruling it out would invalidate the dimensionality argument used to show b^+ not to be identified. In the second place, isn't it true that in most applications, c, b^+, and b^- are not separately parameterized, so that information about c and b^-, which we agree is available, will help us determine b^+? The latter line of objection is correct as far as it goes, and will be discussed below. The former line of objection is not valid, and the next paragraphs contain an argument that this identification problem is present no matter what stationary process generates p in the example. Since the argument gets technical, readers with powerful intuition may wish to skip it.

If, say, b^+ is square-integrable and p is a stationary process with bounded spectral density, then the term $b^{+}*\hat{p}_t(t)$ in (1) itself is a stationary process. Furthermore, the prediction error from using b^+ in (1) when b^+ is correct is a stationary stochastic process with variance given by

$$s^2(\hat{b}^+, b^+) = \|\hat{b}^+ - b^+\|_R^2, \quad \text{where}$$

(6)
$$\|f\|_R = \left[\iint f(s)f(u)R(s, u)\ ds\ du\right]^{1/2} \quad \text{and}$$

$$R(s, u) = E[\hat{p}_t(t + s)\hat{p}_t(t + u)].$$

Now under fairly weak restrictions requiring some minimal rate of damping in the autocorrelation function of p, we will have an inequality of the form

(7)
$$|R(s, u)| < R_1(s)R_2(u - s), \quad \text{for } u > s,$$

where $R_1(s) \to 0$ monotonically as $s \to \infty$ and R_2 is integrable.[8]

We define the translation operator by $T^s f(t) = f(t - s)$. Then from (7) and the definition of $\|\ \|_R$ in the second line of (6) we get, for $f(t) = 0, t < 0$,

(8)
$$\|T^s f\|_R^2 \leqslant R_1(s) \iint f(v)f(u)R_2(u - v)\ du\ dv.$$

Therefore $\|T^s f\|_R^2 \to 0$ as $s \to \infty$, and we have proved the following proposition.

PROPOSITION If the moving average representation of p has a weighting function which is $O(s^{-2})$, then no translation-invariant functional is continuous with respect to the norm $\|\ \|_R$ defined in the second line of (6).

Obviously this means that the L_2 and L_1 norms are not continuous with respect to $\|\ \|_R$. Putting this result in somewhat more concrete terms, we

---

[8] The process p has the moving average representation $p(t) = a*e(t)$, with e white noise. Then $R(s, u) = \int_s^\infty a(v)a(v + u - s)\ dv$ for $s < u$. If we then assume, for example, that $a(s)s^2$ is bounded, which would follow if p were assumed to have a spectral density with integrable fourth derivative, then it is not hard to verify that R_1 can be taken to have the form $A(1 + s)^{-3}$ and R_2 the form $B(1 + u - s)^{-2}$.

have shown that when p meets the conditions of the proposition, we can make the effect of estimation error on the fit of equation (1), given by $s^2(\hat{b}^+, b^+)$, as small as we like, while at the same time making the integrated squared or absolute deviations between b^+ and $\hat{b}^+$ as large as we like. The fit of equation (1) cannot be used to fix the shape of b^+, under these general conditions.

Somehow, then, we must use information on the relation of c and b^- to b^+ or other prior information to put substantial restrictions on b^+ a priori. Restriction on the relation of c and b^- to b^+ are especially promising, since c and b^- are in general identified without strong prior restrictions. For example, a symmetry restriction, requiring c^{-1} and b^+ to be mirror images, which does emerge from some optimization problems, would be enough to identify b^+. On the other hand, many behavioural frameworks leave parameters which economists would not ordinarily fix a priori dependent on the difference in shape between b^+ and c^-, which is precisely what will be hard to estimate. The following example illustrates the point.

Suppose firms maximize the expected discounted present value of revenue, given by

$$(9) \quad \int_s^\infty e^{-\varrho(t-s)}(Q(t) - P(t)(\delta K(t) + \dot{K}(t)) - \Theta(\dot{K}(t) + \delta K(t))^2) \, dt$$

subject to

$$(10) \qquad\qquad Q(t) = \alpha K(t) - \lambda K^2(t)$$

The interpretation is that $P(t)$ is the price of the fixed factor input K, δ is the depreciation rate, ϱ is the interest rate, and Θ determines the output forgone as the rate of gross investment increases.

The first order conditions for a solution to this equation give us

$$(11) \quad (D^2 - \varrho D - (\lambda/\Theta) - \delta\varrho - \delta^2)K = (\delta + \varrho - D)P/2\Theta - \alpha/2\Theta,$$

where D is the derivative operator. Firms taking P as exogenous will, at each s, choose a solution to (11) from time s onward, using $\hat{P}_s(t + s)$ in their computations in place of P itself. Since the P_s series and the problem's initial conditions change with s, (11) itself does not apply to observed K and P. If, however, we assume that firms have enough foresight not to choose solutions to (11) along which K diverges exponentially from its static optimum value, then we will find the following equation holding at each s:

$$(12) \quad (D + M_1)K(s) = (D + M_2)^{-1} (\delta + \varrho - D) \hat{P}_s(s)/2\Theta - (\alpha/2\Theta M_2),$$

where M_1 and M_2 are the two roots (with signs reversed) of the polynomial in D on the left of (11). These two roots will always be of opposite sign, and M_2 is negative, so that $(D + M_2)^{-1}$ operates only on the future of the function to which it is applied. It is not hard to verify that the roots have the form

(13) $M_1 = \frac{1}{2}[\sqrt{\varrho^2 + 4((\lambda/\Theta) + \varrho\delta + \delta^2)} - \varrho]; \quad M_2 = -\varrho - M_1.$

In the case $\varrho = \delta = 0$, we get $-M_1 = M_2$, so that from knowledge of M_1 we obtain M_2 and thereby the entire operator applied to expected future P in (12). The only way identification could be frustrated would be for expected future P to show no variation at all, so that K itself became constant. It should be noted that this could, of course, happen with P being constant. If P were a moving average process of the form $P = a^*e$, with $a(s) = 0$ for $s > T$, and if at time t firms know only the history of P up to time $t - T$, then $\hat{P}_s$ is identically equal to P's unconditional mean. In the more interesting case where the information set includes current P, identification problems arise only with ϱ and $\delta \neq 0$.

With ϱ and δ non-zero, equation (12) involves five coefficients, all functions of the five unknown parameters of the model. If $\hat{P}_s$ were a stationary process we would be justified in following our instincts in declaring all structural parameters identified. However, in fact identification depends on there being sufficient independent variation between the time path of expected future *levels* of P and expected future *derivatives* of P. With ϱ or δ non-zero, the operator applied to $\hat{P}_s$ on the right side of (12) differs from that applied to K on the left by more than a reflection. Even if we know ϱ a priori (by reading the financial press), first-order Markov behaviour for P implies that δ is not identified (assuming still that past P makes up the information set). In the first-order Markov case with $\dot{P} = -rP + e$, we have $(d/dt)\hat{P}_s(t) = -r\hat{P}_s(t)$ for all $t > s$. Thus (12) becomes, when we replace $\hat{P}_s$ by its observable counterpart,

(14) $(D + M_1)K(s) = -(\delta + \varrho + r)P(s)/2\Theta(M_2 + r) + (a/2\Theta M_2).$

The separate coefficients on $\hat{P}_s$ and its derivative in (12) have merged into one, leaving the structural parameters unidentifiable from the relation of the observable variables. In particular, one can see by examining (14) and (13) that one could vary δ, Θ, α and λ in such a way as to leave coefficients in (14) unchanged even for fixed ϱ and r, so that knowing r from the data and ϱ a priori will not suffice to identify the model.

D.   *Concrete Implications*

Were any one of the categories of criticism of large-model identification outlined in the preceding three sections the only serious criticism, it would make sense to consider existing standard methodology as a base from which to make improvements. There is much good work in progress on estimating and specifying systems of demand relations. Some builders of large models are moving in the direction of specifying sectoral behaviour

---

[9] For example, Fair (1976) takes this approach in principle, though his empirical equations are specified with a single-equation approach to forming lists of variables. Modigliani (1977) reports that the MPS model (like the Fair model) has interest rates turning up in many household behavioural equations.

equations as systems.[9] There is much good work in progress on estimating dynamic systems of equations without getting fouled up by treating knowledge of lag lengths and orders of serial correlation as exact. There is much good work treating expectations as rational and using the implied constraints in small systems of equations. Rethinking structural macro-model specification from any one of these points of view would be a challenging research programme. Doing all of these things at once would be a programme which is so challenging as to be impossible in the short run.

On the other hand, there is no immediate prospect that large-scale macromodels will disappear from the scene, and for good reason: they are useful tools in forecasting and policy analysis.

How can the assertion that macroeconomic models are identified using false assumptions be reconciled with the claim that they are useful tools? The answer is that for forecasting and policy analysis, structural identification is not ordinarily needed, and that false restrictions may not hurt, may even help a model to function in these capacities.

Textbook discussions sometimes suggest that structural identification is necessary in order for a model to be used to analyse policy. This is true if 'structure' and 'identification' are interpreted in a broad way. A structure is defined (by me, following Hurwicz, 1962 and Koopmans, 1959) as something which remains fixed when we undertake a policy change, and the structure is identified if we can estimate it from the given data. But in this broad sense, when a policy variable is an exogenous variable in the system, the reduced form is itself a structure and is identified. In a supply and demand example, if we contemplate introducing an excise tax into a market where none has before existed, then we need to be able to estimate supply and demand curves separately. But if there has previously been an excise tax, and it has varied exogenously, reduced form estimation will allow us accurately to predict the effects of further changes in the tax. Policy analysis in macromodels is more often in the latter mode, projecting the effect of a change in a policy variable, than in the mode of projecting the effect of changing the parameters of a model equation.

Of course, if macroeconomic policy-makers have a clear idea of what they are supposed to do, and set about it systematically, macroeconomic policy variables will not be at all exogenous. This is a big if, however; and in fact some policy variables are close enough to exogenous that reduced forms treating them or their proximate determinants as exogenous may be close to structural in the required sense.[10] Furthermore, we may sometimes be able to separate endogenous and exogenous components of variance in policy variables by careful historical analysis, in effect using a

[10] We shall see below, that in Germany and the US money supply, while not entirely exogenous, has an exogenous component which accounts for much of its variance.

type of instrumental variables procedure for estimating a structural relation between policy variables and the rest of the economy.

Lucas's (1972) critique of macroeconomic policy-making goes further and argues that, since a policy is not really just one-change in a policy variable, but rather a rule for systematically changing that variable in response to conditions, and since changes in policy in this sense must be expected to change the reduced form of existing macroeconometric models, the reduced form of existing models is not structural even when policy variables have historically been exogeneous – institution of a non-trivial policy would end that exogeneity and thereby change expectation formation rules and the reduced form.

There is no doubt that this position is correct, if one accepts this definition of policy formation. One cannot choose policy rules rationally with an econometric model in which the structure fails to include realistic expectation formation. However, what practical men mean by policy formation is not entirely, probably not even mainly, choice of rules of this sort. Policy-makers do spend considerable effort in comparing projected time paths for variables under their control. As Prescott and Kydlund (1977) have shown, making policy from such projections, while ignoring the effect of policy on expectation-formation rules, can lead to a very bad time path for the economy, under some assumptions. Or, as Sargent and Wallace (1975) have shown, it can on other assumptions be merely a charade, with the economy's real variables following a stochastic process which cannot be affected by any such exercises in choice of time paths for policy variables.

I do not think, however, that practical exercises in conditional projection of effects of policy are either charades or (usually) Prescott and Kydlund's case of 'Peter White' policy-making.[11] Suppose it were true that the policy rule did make a difference to the economy. There are many ways to argue that this is true in the face of Sargent's (1977) or Sargent and Wallace's (1975) analysis, all being suggestions for forms of non-neutrality of money. To be concrete, suppose that the real variables of the economy do follow a stochastic process independent of the money supply rule but that for some reason the rate of inflation enters the social utility function.[12] Then the optimal form for macropolicy will be stabilization of the price level.[13] If we

---

[11] Peter White will ne'er go right/ Would you know the reason why?/ He follows his nose where'er he goes/ And that stands all awry (nursery rhyme).

[12] It is a little hard to imagine why the rate of inflation should matter if it affects no real variables. A more realistic and complicated scenario would suppose that there are costs to writing contingencies into contracts, and enforcing contracts with complicated provisions, so that a macropolicy which stabilizes certain macroeconomic aggregates – prices, wages, unemployment rates, etc. – may simplify contract-writing and thus save resources. This has been made the basis of an argument against inflation by Arthur Okun (1975).

[13] Discussion of such a policy seems particularly appropriate in the Fisher–Schultz lecture,

could agree on a stable model in which all forms of shock to the aggregate price level were specified a priori, then it would be easy in principle to specify an appropriate function mapping past values of observed macro-variables into current levels of policy variables in such a way as to minimize price variance. However, if disturbances in the economy can originate in a variety of different ways, the form of this policy reaction function may be quite complicated. It is much easier simply to state that policy rule is to minimize the variance of the price level. Furthermore, if there is uncertainty about the structure of the economy, then even with a fixed policy objective function, widely understood, the form of the dependence of policy on observed history will shift over time as more is learned about (or as opinions shift about) the structure of the economy. One could continually re-estimate the structure and, each period, re-announce an explicit relation of policy variables to history. However it is simpler to announce the stable objective function once and then each period solve only for this period's policy variable values instead of computing a complete policy reaction function. This is done by making conditional projections from the best existing reduced form model, and picking the best-looking projected future time path. Policy choice is then most easily and reliably carried out by comparing the projected effects of alternative policies and picking the policy which most nearly holds the price level constant. Accurate projections can be made from reduced form models fit to history because it is not proposed to change the policy rule, only to implement effectively the existing rule.

In fact, it appears to be a mistake to assume that the economy's real variables follow a process even approximately unrelated to nominal aggregates. Thus stabilization of the price level alone is not likely to be the best policy. However, it is not clear that the existing pattern of policy in most countries, in which there is weight given to stabilization of inflation, unemployment, and income distribution, is very far from an optimal policy. Simply implementing policy according to these objectives in the way the public expects is a highly non-trivial task, and one in which reduced-form modelling may be quite useful.

To summarize the argument, it is admitted that the task of choosing among policy regimes requires models in which explicit account is taken of

as Irving Fisher supported such a policy: 'The more the evidence in the case is studied, the deeper will grow the public conviction that our shifting dollar is responsible for colossal social wrongs and is all the more at fault because those wrongs are usually attributed to other causes. When these who can apply the remedy realize that our dollar is the great pickpocket, robbing first one set of people, then another, to the tune of billions of dollars a year, confounding business calculations and convulsing politics, and, all the time, keeping out of sight and unsuspected, action will follow and we shall secure a boon for all future generations, a true standard for contracts, a stabilized dollar' (Fisher, 1918).

the effect of policy regime on expectations. On the other hand, it is argued that the choice of policy regime probably does have important consequences, and that an optimal regime and the present regime in most countries are both most naturally specified in terms of the effects of policy on the evolution of the economy, rather than in terms of the nature of the dependence of policy on the economy's history. Effectively implementing a stable optimal or existing policy regime therefore is likely appropriately to involve reduced-form modelling and policy projection.

But I have argued earlier that most of the restrictions on existing models are false, and the models are nominally over-identified. Even if we admit that a model whose claimed behavioural interpretation is spurious may have a useful reduced form, isn't it true that when the spurious identification results in restrictions on the reduced form, the reduced form is distorted by the false identifying restrictions? The answer is yes and no. Yes, the reduced form will be infected by false restrictions and may thereby become useless as a framework within which to do formal statistical tests of competing macroeconomic theories. But no, the resulting infection need not distort the results of forecasting and policy analysis with the reduced form. Much recent theoretical work gives rigorous foundation for a rule of thumb that in high-dimensional models restricted estimators can easily produce smaller forecast or projection errors than unrestricted estimators even when the restrictions are false. Of course very false restrictions will make forecasts worse, but in large macromodels restrictions very false in the sense of producing very bad reduced-form fits are probably usually detected and eliminated. Thus models whose self-proclaimed behavioural interpretation is widely disbelieved may nonetheless find satisfactory uses as tools of forecasting and policy projection.

Because existing large models contain too many incredible restrictions, empirical research aimed at testing competing macroeconomic theories too often proceeds in a single- or few-equation framework.[14] For this reason alone it appears worthwhile to investigate the possibility of building large models in a style which does not tend to accumulate restrictions so haphazardly. In addition, though, one might suspect that a more systematic approach to imposing restrictions could lead to capture of empirical regularities which remain hidden to the standard procedures and hence lead to improved forecasts and policy projections.[15]

Empirical macroeconomists sometimes express frustration at the limited amount of information in economic time series, and it does not

[14] Modigliani (1977) has used the MPS model as an arena within which to let macroeconomic theories confront each other, however.
[15] The work of Nelson (1972) and Cooper and Nelson (1975) provides empirical support for this idea.

infrequently turn out that models reflecting rather different behavioural hypotheses fit the data about equally well. This attitude may account for the lack of previous research on the possibility of using much less parsimoniously parameterized multiple-equation models. It might be expected that in such a model one would find nothing new except a relatively larger number of 'insignificant' *t* statistics. Forecasts might be expected to be worse, and the accurate picture of the relation of data to theory one would obtain might be expected to be simply the conclusion that the data cannot discriminate between competing theories.

In the next section of this paper we discuss a general strategy for estimating profligately (as opposed to parsimoniously) parameterized macromodels, and present results for a particular relatively small-scale application.

2. An Alternative Strategy for Empirical Macroeconomics

It should be feasible to estimate large-scale macromodels as unrestricted reduced forms, treating all variables as endogenous. Of course, some restrictions, if only on lag length, are essential, so by 'unrestricted' here I mean 'without restrictions based on supposed a priori knowledge'. The style I am suggesting we emulate is that of frequency-domain time series theory (though it will be clear I am not suggesting we use frequency-domain methods themselves), in which what is being estimated (e.g. the spectral density) is implicitly part of an infinite-dimensional parameter space, and the finite-parameter methods we actually use are justified as part of a procedure in which the number of parameters is explicitly a function of sample size or the data. After the arbitrary 'smoothness' or 'rate-of-damping' restrictions have been used to formulate a model which serves to summarize the data, hypotheses with economic content are formulated *and tested* at a second stage, with some perhaps looking attractive enough after a test to be used to further constrain the model. Besides frequency-domain work, such methods are implicit or explicit in much distributed lag model estimation in econometrics, and Amemiya (1973) has proposed handling serial correlation in time domain regression models in this style.

The first step in developing such an approach is evidently to develop a class of multivariate time series models which will serve as the unstructured first-stage models. In the six-variable system discussed below, the data are accepting of a relatively stringent limit on lag length (four quarters), so that it proves feasible to use an otherwise unconstrained (144-parameter) vector autoregression as the basic model. In the larger systems one will eventually want to study this way, some additional form of constraint, beyond lag length or damping rate constraints, will be necessary. Finding the best way to do this is very much an open problem. Sargent and I (1977) have published work using a class of restricted vector time series models we call index models in macroeconomic work, and I am currently working on applying those methods to systems larger than that explored below. Priestly, Rao, and Tong (1974) in the engineering literature, and Brillinger (1978), have suggested related classes of models. All of these methods in one way or another aim at limiting the nature of cross-dependencies between variables. If every variable is allowed to influence every other variable with a distributed lag of reasonable length, without restriction, the number of parameters grows with the square of the number of variables and quickly exhausts degrees of freedom. Besides the above approaches, it seems to me worthwhile to try to invent Bayesian approaches along the lines of Shiller's (1973) and Leamer's (1973) work on distributed lags to accomplish similar objectives, though there is no obvious generalization of those methods to this sort of problem.

The foregoing brief discussion is included only to dispose of the objection that the kind of analysis I carry out below could not be done on systems comparable in size to large-scale macromodels currently existing.

What I have actually done is to fit to quarterly, postwar time series for the US and West Germany (FRG) on money, GNP, unemployment rate, price level, and import price index, an unconstrained vector auto-regression. Before describing the results in detail, I will set out the two main conclusions, to help light the way through the technical thickets to follow.

Phillips curve equations or wage–price systems of equations are often estimated treating only wages or only wages and prices jointly as endogenous. The 'price' equation is often treated as behavioural, describing the methods firms use to set prices for the products, while the wage or Phillips curve equations are often discussed as if they describe the process of wage bargaining or are in some way connected to only those variables (unemployment in particular) which we associate with the labour market. In the estimated systems for both the US and FRG, the hypothesis that wage or price, or the two jointly, can be treated as endogenous, while the rest of the system is taken as exogenous, is decisively rejected. Estimates conditioned on this hypothesis would then be biased, if the equations did have a structural interpretation. On the other hand, the estimated equations, having been allowed to take the form the data suggest, do not take the forms commonly imposed on them. Unemployment is not important in the estimated wage equations, while it is of some importance in explaining prices. The money supply has a direct impact on wages, but not on prices.[16]

---

[16] Some empirical macroeconomists in the US have begun to reach similar conclusions. Wachter (1976) has introduced money supply into 'wage' equations, and Gordon (1977) has taken the view that equations of this type ought to be interpreted as reduced forms.

Sargent (1977) put forward a more sophisticated version of the rational expectations macromodel he had analysed in earlier work. He shows that the implication of his earlier model that a variable measuring real aggregate labour or output should be serially uncorrelated is not a necessary adjunct to the main policy implication of his earlier model: that deterministic monetary policy rules cannot influence the form of time path of real variables in the economy. We shall see that such an elaborate model can take two extreme forms, one in which the nature of cyclical variation is determined by the parameters of economic behavioural relations, the other in which unexplained serially correlated shocks to technology and tastes account for cyclical variation. The more satisfying extreme form of the model, with a behavioural explanation for the form of the cycle, implies that the real variables in the economy, including relative prices, ought to form a vector of jointly exogenous variables relative to the money supply, the price level, or any other nominal aggregate. This is very far from holding true in the system estimated here. For the US, money supply, and for the FRG the price level, shows strong feedback into the real economy.

A. Methodological Issues

Since the model being estimated is an autoregression, the distribution theory on which tests are based is asymptotic. However, for many of the hypotheses tested the degrees of freedom in the asymptotic χ^2 distribution for the likelihood ratio test statistic is not a different order of magnitude from the degrees of freedom left in the data after fitting the model. This makes interpretation of the tests difficult, for a number of reasons. Even if the model were a single equation and not autoregressive, we know that F statistics with similar numerator and denominator degrees of freedom are highly sensitive to non-normality, in contrast to the usual case of numerator degrees of freedom much smaller than denominator degrees of freedom, where robustness to non-normality follows from asymptotic distribution theory. This problem is worse in the case where some coefficients being estimated are not consistently estimated, as will be true when dummy variables for specific periods are involved. If constraints being tested involve coefficients of such variables (as do the tests for model stability below), even F statistics with few numerator degrees of freedom will be sensitive to non-normality. In the case which seems most likely, where distributions of residuals have fat tails, this creates a bias towards rejection of the null hypothesis.

There is a further problem that different, reasonable-looking, asymptotically equivalent formulas for the test statistic may give very different significance levels for the same data. In the single-equation case where k linear restrictions are being tested, the usual asymptotic distribution theory suggests treating $T \log (1 + kF/(T - k))$ as $\chi^2 (k)$, where F is the usual F

statistic and T is sample size. Where k is not much less than T, significance levels of the test drawn from asymptotic distribution theory may differ substantially from those of the exact F test. Of course k times the F statistic is also asymptotically $\chi^2(k)$ and a test based on k is asymptotically equivalent to the likelihood ratio test. Since treating kF as χ^2 ignores the variability of the denominator of F, such a procedure has a bias against the null hypothesis relative to the F test. The usual likelihood ratio test shares this bias. Furthermore, over certain ranges of values of F, including the modal value of 1.0, the usual likelihood ratio is larger than kF and thus even further biased against the null hypothesis.

In the statistical tests reported below, I have computed likelihood ratios as if the sample size were $T - k$, where k is the total number of regression coefficients estimated divided by the number of equations.[17] This makes the likelihood ratio tend to be smaller than kF in the single-equation case, though whether this improves the applicability of the distribution theory much is certainly debatable. In any case we shall see that most hypotheses entertained are rejected, so this modification of the usual likelihood ratio test in favour of the null hypothesis would not change the main results.

The procedures adopted here are obviously only *ad hoc* choices; and the problem of finding the appropriate procedure in situations like this deserves more study.[18]

B. Stability Over Time and Lag Length

The six data series used in the model for each country – money, real GNP, unemployment, wages, price level, and import prices – are defined in detail in the data appendix. Each series except unemployment was logged, and the regressions all included time trends. For Germany, but not the US, seasonal dummy variables were included. Most but not all the series were seasonally adjusted. The period of fit was 1958–76 for Germany, 1949–75 for the US.

---

[17] That is, the usual test statistic, $T(\log |D_R| - \log |D_U|)$ is replaced by $(T - k)(\log |D_R| - \log |D_U|)$, where D_R is the matrix of cross products of residuals when the model is restricted; D_U is the same matrix for the unrestricted model.

[18] Some readers have questioned the absence in this paper of a list of coefficients and standard errors, of the sort usually accompanying econometric reports of regression estimates. The autoregressive coefficients themselves are difficult to interpret, and equivalent, more comprehensible, information is contained in the MAR coefficients, which are presented in the charts. Because estimated AR coefficients are so highly correlated, standard errors on the individual coefficients provide little of the sort of insight into the shape of the likelihood we ordinarily try to glean from standard errors of regression coefficients. The various χ^2 tests on block triangularity restrictions which are presented below provide more useful information. However, it must be admitted that it would be better were there more emphasis on the shape of the sum-of-squared-residuals function around the maximum than is presented here. Ideally, one would like to see some sort of error bound on the MAR plots, for example; I have not yet worked out a practical way to do this.

The estimated general vector autoregressions were initially estimated with lag lengths of both four and eight, and the former specification was tested as a restriction of the latter. In both countries the shorter lag length was acceptable. The $\chi^2(144) = 166.09$ for the US and $\chi^2(144) = 142.53$ for the FRG. The corresponding significance levels are about 0.20 and 0.50. In all later work the shorter lag length was used.

The sample-split tests we are about to consider were all executed by adding a set of dummy variables to the right-hand side of all regressions in the system, accounting for all variation within the period being tested. The likelihood ratio statistic was then formed as described in Section 2.A, comparing the fit of the system with and without these dummy variables. Because non-normal residuals are not 'averaged' in forming such a test statistic, the statistics are probably biased against the null hypothesis when degrees of freedom in the test statistic are small. On the other hand, they are probably biased in favour of the null hypothesis when the degrees of freedom approach half the sample size, at least when compared with the single-equation F statistic.

For both West German and US data, splitting the sample at 1965 (with the dummy variables applied to the post-1965 period) shows no significant difference between the two parts of the sample. However, again for both countries, splitting the sample at the first quarter of 1971 or 1958 (using dummy variables for the smaller segment of the sample) shows a significant difference between the two parts of the sample. For the 1971 split the marginal significance levels of the test are 0.003 for Germany and less than 10^{-4} for the US. However, as can be seen from Table 1, in both countries the difference between periods is heavily concentrated in the equation for price of imports. Testing the five other equations in the system, treating the import variable as predetermined, yields marginal significance levels of 0.07 for the US and 0.15 for Germany.[19]

The 1971 date was originally chosen to correspond to the beginning of a period of price controls in the US. It appears, however, that in both the US and Germany the major source of difference between the periods comes out of the 1973–4 commodity price boom, with little evidence of a strong effect of price controls in the US.

---

[19] While the test statistics used in this case have the same form as those for other hypotheses tested in this paper, they differ in not exactly being likelihood ratio tests. This is because they use conditional likelihood given the price of imports, even though it is admitted that the price of imports is only predetermined, not exogenous. The asymptotic distribution theory continues to apply (or not apply) to these statistics as for the bona-fide likelihood ratios, however. It may affect the reader's interpretation of these results to know that, if the import price variable is omitted from the system in the US the significant change at 1971 appears more evenly spread across the five equations. My initial work with US data was with such a five-equation system, and the import price variable was added to the system with the suspicion that it might concentrate the structural shift.

Table 1.   Test for model homogeneity: 1953–71 vs. 1972–6 (Germany), 1949–71 vs. 1972–5 (US)[a]

Equation	US	Germany
M	$F(16, 54) = 1.84$	$F(20, 47) = 2.88$
RGNP	$= 1.10$	$= 1.94$
U	$= 0.92$	$= 0.76$
W	$= 0.61$	$= 0.42$
P	$= 1.75$	$= 0.74$
PM	$= 5.10$	$= 4.10$
Overall first five	$\chi^2(96) = 160.05$	$\chi^2(120) = 170.76$
equations	$\chi^2(80) = \ \ 99.16$	$\chi^2(100) = 114.58$

[a] All χ^2 test statistics are computed as reported in footnote 17. They are likelihood ratio test statistics conditioned on the initial observations. The "unrestricted" model is one in which a separate parameter is introduced to explain each variable in each of the periods of the latter time interval. The *F* test statistics are the corresponding single-equation test statistics computed in the usual way. They are, of course, not actually distributed as *F* here because of the presence of lagged dependent variables.

For the sample split at 1958, the marginal significance levels are 0.0007 for the US and 0.003 for Germany ($\chi^2(216) = 286$ and $\chi^2(120) = 178$, respectively). However as can be seen from Table 2 the shift is again concentrated in the price-of-imports equation for the US. For the US the marginal significance level of the test for the five other equations is 0.15, though four of the five equations have considerably lower significance levels when we consider the individual *F* tests. For the German data the 1958 sample split was chosen because Robert J. Gordon, working with similar data in recent research, had forgone attempting the interpolations and splices necessary to extend the period of fit back before 1958. Thus it is quite possible that the shift we detect is mainly caused by non-comparability in the data for the earlier period. At least some of the shift comes from changed coefficients of the seasonal dummy variables in the wage equation, which fits the explanation of non-comparable data.

These tests suggest that, though the equations for price of imports show strong effects of other variables no matter the period to which they are fitted, the equations are not stable. In computing tests of hypotheses, therefore, I have in each case avoided relying on a maintained hypothesis that there is a stable import price equation. On the other hand, in preparing projections of responses of the system to shocks, I have always included an import price equation fit, one way or another, to the whole

Table 2. Test for model homogeneity: 1953–7 vs. 1958–76 (Germany), 1949–57 vs. 1958–75 (US)

Equation	US	Germany
M	$F(36, 46) = 0.69$	$F(20, 47) = 1.56$
RGNP	$= 2.57$	$= 0.92$
U	$= 1.83$	$= 3.77$
W	$= 1.94$	$= 3.71$
P	$= 2.81$	$= 3.00$
PM	$F(36, 30) = 6.31$	$= 0.97$
Overall first five	$\chi^2(216) = 286.69$	$\chi^2(120) = 178.00$
equations	$\chi^2(180) = 199.92$	$\chi^2(100) = 152.08$

[a] Same comments apply as for Table 1.

sample, because the responses of import prices to other variables, though not stable, are strong.

Even when the import price equation is excluded, it is apparent that individual equations often show suspiciously large *F* statistics for the sample split hypothesis. Whether it is better to treat these mainly as due to non-normality – occasional outlier residuals – while maintaining the hypothesis of a stable linear structure, is a question which deserves further exploration. With as many parameters as are estimated in this model, it is probably not possible without longer time series than are yet available to distinguish clearly between instability in the form of occasional outlier residuals and instability in the form of parameter shifts.

C. General Descriptions of the Estimated Systems

Autoregressive systems like these are difficult to describe succinctly. It is especially difficult to make sense of them by examining the coefficients in the regression equations themselves. The estimated coefficients on successive lags tend to oscillate, and there are complicated cross-equation feedbacks. The common econometric practice of summarizing distributed lag relations in terms of their implied long-run equilibrium behaviour is quite misleading in these systems. The estimated US system, for example, is a very slowly damped oscillatory system. For the first forty quarters or so of a projection, nominal variables move in phase, as one would expect. But after this period (which is about half a cycle for the system's long oscillations) the cycles in the various nominal variables move out of phase. Clearly the infinitely long-run behaviour of this system is nonsensical, though over any reasonable economic forecasting horizon the system is quite well behaved.

The best descriptive device appears to be analysis of the system's response to typical random shocks. Except for scaling, this is equivalent to tracing out the system's moving-average representation by matrix polynomial long division. As will be seen below, the resulting system responses are fairly smooth, in contrast to the autoregressive lag structures, and tend to be subject to reasonable economic interpretation.[20]

The 'typical shocks' whose effects we are about to discuss are positive residuals of one standard deviation unit in each equation of the system. The residual in the money equation, for example, is sometimes referred to as the 'money innovation', since it is that component of money which is 'new' in the sense of not being predicted from past values of variables in the system. The residuals are correlated across equations. In order to be able to see the distinct patterns of movement the system may display it is therefore useful to transform them to orthogonal form. There is no unique best way to do this. What I have done is to triangularize the system, with variables ordered as M, Y, U, W, P, PM. Thus the residuals whose effects are being tracked are the residuals from a system in which contemporaneous values of other variables enter the right-hand sides of the regressions with a triangular array of coefficients. The M equation is left unaltered, while the PM equation includes contemporaneous values of all other variables on the right. An equivalent way to think of what is being done is to note that what we call the M innovation is assumed to disturb all other variables of the system instantly, according to the strength of the contemporaneous correlation of other residuals with the M residual, while the PM residual is only allowed to affect the PM variable in the initial period.

The charts at the end of the paper display, for each shock in the triangularized system, the reponse of all variables in the system.

The biggest differences between countries which emerge from perusal of the charts are as follows.

(1) In the US money innovations have very persistent effects on both money and other nominal variables. In Germany money innovations, though larger, are much less persistent. The peak effect of the money

---

[20] The moving-average representation having smooth weights, in the sense of having weights whose Fourier transform is relatively small in absolute value at high frequencies, is equivalent to the spectral density being relatively small at high frequencies, and thus to the stochastic process itself being smooth. An autoregressive representation having smooth weights yields almost exactly the opposite condition on the spectral density. Thus we ought to expect nonsmooth 'lag distributions' in these vector autoregressions. The idea that the moving-average weights should be smooth in this sense suggests a possible Bayesian approach to estimating these systems which deserves further investigation.

innovation on real GNP is much bigger for the US than for Germany.
(2) Real GNP; innovations are associated with substantial inflation in the FRG, not the US.
(3) An unemployment innovation is followed by an apparent expansionary reaction from the monetary authority in the US, with a corresponding rise in real GNP and a fall in unemployment to a point farther below trend than the initial innovation was above trend. No such expansionary reaction in the money supply appears in Germany, where instead an unemployment innovation is followed by a drop in the money supply and a period of deflation and below-trend GNP.
(4) Wage innovations are much bigger in Germany, and generate a temporary accommodating response there, unlike the US. The sustained negative movement in real GNP is smaller in Germany than in the US.[21]
(5) Price innovations are of negligible importance in the US system. In the German system, price innovations are a major source of disturbance. There they produce a large, sustained drop in real GNP and persistent decline in the real wage, despite a temporarily accommodating response from the money supply.
(6) Import price innovations have bigger and more persistent real effects in Germany where the peak effect nearly matches that of price innovations and exceeds that of money innovations.

Common elements of the responses in the two countries are as follows.

(1) Money innovations tend temporarily to increase the real wage and real GNP and to reduce unemployment, with an opposite swing in these variables following.
(2) Real GNP innovations are of similar magnitude and decay rapidly in their real effects in both countries.
(3) Wage innovations are followed by sustained drops in real GNP in both countries.
(4) Import price innovations are followed by movements of the same sign in prices and wages in both countries.

Price, wage, and import-price innovations induce patterns of response in both countries which are consistent with their representing supply shocks – they are followed by declines in real GNP. Under this interpretation it is not surprising that the real variables in Germany's smaller and more open

---

[21] For reasons I have not yet discovered, the response to a wage innovation is quite different in a system fit to Gordon's data, which differ from mine mainly in the methods he used for interpolation and splicing. Gordon's data have wage innovations followed by much bigger negative movements in real GNP, and have somewhat smaller negative movements in GNP following a price innovation.

Table 3. Proportions of forecast error k quarters ahead produced by each innovation: US 1949–75[a]

Forecast error in	k	Triangularized innovation in:					
		M	Y/P	U	W	P	PM
M	1	1.00	0	0	0	0	0
	3	0.96	0	0.03	0	0	0
	9	0.73	0	0.24	0.02	0	0
	33	0.54	0	0.27	0.09	0	0.09
Y/P	1	0.15	0.85	0	0	0	0
	3	0.35	0.59	0.04	0.01	0.01	0
	9	0.30	0.18	0.37	0.13	0.00	0.02
	33	0.28	0.15	0.33	0.16	0.02	0.06
U	1	0.02	0.35	0.63	0	0	0
	3	0.14	0.49	0.32	0	0.03	0
	9	0.26	0.20	0.41	0.09	0.02	0.02
	33	0.34	0.14	0.34	0.13	0.03	0.03
W	1	0.08	0.05	0.04	0.84	0	0
	3	0.17	0.06	0.07	0.55	0.09	0.06
	9	0.45	0.02	0.05	0.25	0.08	0.16
	33	0.64	0.02	0.19	0.07	0.02	0.07
P	1	0	0.04	0.15	0.24	0.56	0
	3	0.04	0.01	0.14	0.36	0.33	0.12
	9	0.14	0.02	0.12	0.25	0.11	0.36
	33	0.60	0.02	0.20	0.07	0.02	0.09
PM	1	0	0	0.06	0.05	0.08	0.81
	3	0.01	0.01	0.02	0.13	0.10	0.75
	9	0.06	0.02	0.13	0.08	0.03	0.68
	33	0.54	0.03	0.20	0.04	0.01	0.18

[a] The moving-average representation on which this table was based was computed from a system estimate in which the PM equation was estimated by generalized least-squares in two steps. An initial estimate by ordinary least-squares was used to construct an estimate of the ratio of residual variance in PM during 1949–71 to the residual variance in 1971–5, and this ratio was used (as if error-free) to re-estimate the equation by generalized least-squares. This procedure is not in fact efficient, since once the break in residual variance in the PM equation is admitted, the usual asymptotic equivalence of single-equation and multiple-equation autoregression estimates breaks down.

economy should show greater sensitivity to such shocks than the real variables in the US economy. This in turn might in part explain the German money supply's tendency temporarily to accommodate such shocks more than does the US money supply. The German money supply tends to return more quickly to its trend path when it moves away from trend for any reason, and shows no indication of being used as a policy instrument to counteract unemployment. These differences could reflect differences in

Table 4. Percentages of forecast error k quarters ahead produced by each innovation: West Germany 1958–76[a]

Forecast error in	k	Triangularized innovation in:					
		M	Y/P	U	W	P	PM
M	1	1.00	0	0	0	0	0
	3	0.84	0.04	0.05	0.01	0.04	0.02
	9	0.53	0.04	0.14	0.08	0.20	0.01
	33	0.39	0.05	0.13	0.07	0.27	0.09
Y/P	1	0.07	0.93	0	0	0	0
	3	0.14	0.79	0.01	0.05	0	0
	9	0.15	0.47	0.03	0.06	0.03	0.25
	33	0.13	0.22	0.05	0.04	0.42	0.14
U	1	0	0.03	0.97	0	0	0
	3	0.19	0.09	0.67	0.03	0.02	0
	9	0.15	0.10	0.37	0.02	0.08	0.29
	33	0.09	0.11	0.15	0.02	0.50	0.14
W	1	0	0.03	0.01	0.96	0	0
	3	0.11	0.18	0.01	0.59	0.03	0.09
	9	0.23	0.23	0.02	0.23	0.24	0.05
	33	0.21	0.13	0.08	0.15	0.31	0.12
P	1	0.02	0.02	0	0.10	0.86	0
	3	0.03	0.06	0.05	0.09	0.76	0
	9	0.05	0.13	0.03	0.05	0.68	0.06
	33	0.08	0.10	0.04	0.05	0.67	0.06
PM	1	0.06	0	0.02	0	0.02	0.89
	3	0.04	0	0.02	0.01	0.08	0.85
	9	0.10	0.04	0.09	0	0.16	0.61
	33	0.06	0.08	0.04	0.02	0.57	0.23

[a] Here the moving-average representation was computed from a system estimate which made no allowance for non-stationarity over the period. Since stability over the sample period is sharply rejected by a test, the results here have to be taken as a kind of average of the different regimes which prevailed in the sample. The numbers reported here, like the plotted MAR's, apply to data with the two-sided interpolation referred to in the data appendix for price. Correction of the interpolation method to make it one-sided would make small but noticeable changes in the T table. The largest change would be increases of between 0.05 and 0.07 at the 33-quarter horizon in the proportion of variance in all variables but money and price itself accounted for by price innovations. For the U and PM rows these increases in the P column come almost entirely from the PM column, so that there are corresponding decreases in the proportion of variance accounted for by PM.

philosophy of money management, or in the costs and effectiveness of monetary policy actions between the two countries.

Tables 3 and 4 provide a type of summary which is useful in locating the main channels of influence in the model. A variable which was strictly exogenous would, if there were no sampling error in estimates of the system, have entries of 1.00 in its diagonal cell in these tables, with zeroes in all other cells in its row of the tables. Exogeneity is equivalent to this condition that a variable's own innovations account for all of its variance. The price variable in Germany and the money supply variable in the US both have more than half their variance accounted for by own-innovations at all time horizons shown, and the German money supply variable has more than 40 per cent of its variance accounted for by own-innovations at all time horizons shown. No other variables have so much variance accounted for by own-innovations, indicating that interactions among variables are strong. The main source of feedback into money supply in the US is unemployment innovations, while in Germany it is price innovations. Feedback into prices in Germany is diffused across all variables in the system. The responses of price to innovations in other variables are reasonable in form, tending to keep price roughly in line with the wage variable, so that it seems unreasonable to impose price exogeneity as a constraint on the system.[22]

In the US, over long horizons, money innovations are the main source of variation in all three price variables – wages, prices, and import prices. This is not true in Germany, reflecting the fact that money innovations do not persist long enough in Germany to induce the kind of smooth, neutral response in the price variables which eventually dominates in the US data.

Table 5 displays the forecast standard errors over various forecasting horizons implied by the model when sampling error in the estimated coefficients is ignored. Actual forecast errors will of course be substantially bigger, even if the model's parameters do not change, because the statistical estimates are imperfect. Yet even pretending, as this table does, that the estimated trend coefficients are known exactly, we see that forecast error rises steadily as the forecasting horizon lengthens, for nearly every variable. For a stationary process, forecast standard error tends to some upper bound as the horizon increases. Only real GNP and unemployment in the US, show much sign of this sort of behaviour in this table, indicating that the estimated system is very slowly damped.

D.   *Tests of Specific Hypotheses*[23]

Suppose we treat (y, m) as a vector process, where y is a vector of quantities and relative prices determined in the private sector and m is the money supply. Assuming that (y, m) has no perfectly linearly predictable components, we can write

$$(15) \qquad\qquad y(t) = a^*e(t) + \lambda c^*f(t),$$

---

[22] In fact, a test of the hypothesis that price is exogenous in West Germany yields an $F(20, 47) = 2.28$ and thus a marginal significance level of 0.01.

[23] The ideas expressed in this section are in part due to Thomas J. Sargent.

Table 5. Forecast standard errors, k quarters ahead[a]

	k	US	West Germany
M	1	0.004	0.011
	3	0.010	0.020
	9	0.022	0.029
	33	0.055	0.036
Y/P	1	0.008	0.009
	3	0.016	0.013
	9	0.032	0.018
	33	0.036	0.032
U	1	0.002	0.003
	3	0.005	0.003
	9	0.010	0.006
	33	0.012	0.011
W	1	0.004	0.008
	3	0.008	0.013
	9	0.016	0.023
	33	0.037	0.033
P	1	0.004	0.007
	3	0.009	0.011
	9	0.018	0.023
	33	0.043	0.035
PM	1	0.014	0.015
	3	0.038	0.029
	9	0.075	0.043
	33	0.158	0.077

[a] These figures are computed from the same MARs used in computing Tables 3 and 4. They use the formula for the t-step-ahead expected squared forecast error in variable i:

$$s^2(i, t) = \sum_{j=1}^{p} \sum_{v=0}^{t-1} a_{ij}(v)^2 s_j^2,$$

where there are p variables in the system, $s_j^2 = s^2(j, 1)$ is the variance of the jth innovation, and $a_{ij}(v)$ is the coefficient on the vth lag of the jth innovation in the MAR equation for variable i.

where $f(t) = m(t) - \varepsilon[m(t)|m(t - s), y(t - s), s > 0]$ is the innovation in $m(t)$ and $e(t) = y(t) - \varepsilon[y(t)|m(t), m(t - s), y(t - s), s > 0]$ is that part of the innovation in $y(t)$ which is orthogonal to $f(t)$. Here '$\varepsilon[X|Z]$' means 'best linear predictor of X based on Z', which coincides with conditional expectation only under normality assumptions.

There is a class of classical rational expectations models which imply that no form of policy rule for determining m can affect equation (15) except by affecting $a(0)$, the matrix λ, and the variance in f. Further these models imply that when the variance in f is kept at zero, $a(0)$ is invariant to changes in the policy rule.

To see how this conclusion might be derived, suppose that the ith type of economic agent chooses $x_i(t)$ according to an attempt to maximize some objective function which depends on $x_i(s)$ and $p_i(s)$ for all j and s (p_i is a price relative to some fixed numeraire). It is critical to this argument that money balances, even real money balances, not be included in X. This is a strong neutrality assumption. (If real money balances were in X, *nominal* interest rates would have to enter p.) We assume the first-order conditions describing the solution to the jth agent's maximization problem are given by

(16) $G_j(p, x, u_j, t) = 0,$

where u is a vector of shifts in the objective functions of various agents in the economy. The whole past and future of p, x, and u_j enter (16) in principle, and we assume that the only effect of the t argument is to change the time origin of decision making – i.e. if $Lp(s) = p(s-1)$, then $G_j(Lp, Lx, Lu_j, t+1) = G_j(p, x, u_j, t)$.

We take the symbol 'E_{tj}' to mean 'expected value conditional on the information available to agents of type j at time t'. If there is uncertainty, we assume that actual values of $x_j(t)$ are chosen by solving

(17) $E_{tj}[G_j(p, x, u_j, t)] = 0,$

as would be appropriate if the jth type of agent has an objective function which is a von Neumann-Morgenstern utility function. The system of equations of the form (17) together with market-clearing conditions (determining which 'supply' x_j's have to add up to which sums of 'demand' x_j's) are assumed to determine $x(t)$ and $p(t)$ at each t. In general the solution for $y(t) = (x(t), p(t))$ will involve all aspects of all the individual conditional distributions for future u_j's which enter the system. To reach our conclusions we need the drastic simplifying assumption that only the first moments of these conditional distributions affect decisions, as would be true if all the objective functions in the system were quadratic. Thus we assume that (17) can be solved to yield a system of the form

(18) $y(t) = H_t({}_{tj}\hat{u}, \text{ all } j, {}_{tj}\hat{y}(s), \text{ all } s < t, \text{ all } j)$

where ${}_{tj}\hat{u}$ is a vector of functions of time with ith element ${}_{tj}\hat{u}_i(s) = E_{tj}[u_i(s)]$ and ${}_{tj}\hat{y}(s) = E_{tj}[y(s)]$. As with G in (17), we assume that H_t depends on time only through shift of time origin, so that

$$H_t(u, y(s), s < t) = H_{t+1}(Lu, Ly(s), s < t + 1).$$

The economic substance of (18) can be summarized as an assertion that the only route available by which monetary policy can influence the levels of real variables in the system is by its possible effects on expected future levels of real shocks to the economy (the u's). Such effects are possible, according to this type of model, because some agents may observe some prices in terms of money more quickly than they observe relative prices. Thus if the monetary authority has a richer information set than some agents, it may be able to improve private-sector forecasts by making the money supply (and hence the aggregate price level) move in appropriate ways. Also, by introducing fluctuations in the aggregate price level which are not related to movements in u, the monetary authority can reduce the quality of private forecasts.[24] The versions of these models which imply that monetary policy is impotent assume that every private information set in the economy includes all the information available to the monetary authority.

Suppose we assume in particular that monetary policy is based on information contained in the history of the monetary aggregate, m, and the history of y alone. That is, $m(t) = F(y(t - s), m(t - s), s > 0) + f(t)$. Though we allow a random component $f(t)$ in $m(t)$, the assumption that the policy-makers' information set is restricted to the history of y and m is taken to mean that $f(t)$ is independent of $y(t + s) - E_{t-1}(y(t + s))$ for all s, where 'E_{t-1}' means 'conditional expectation given $y(s)$, $m(s)$ for $s \leqslant -1$'.

If equation (18) is linear and if $_{tj}\hat{y}(t - s)$ $y(t - s)$ for $s > 0$ (as is implied by our assumption that all private agents know the past history of y), we obtain from (18):

(19) $E_{t-1}[y(t)] = H_t(E_{t-1}(u(s)))$, all s; $y(t - s)$ for $s > 0$.

Under our assumptions about policy, knowledge of past values of m can be of no help in forecasting u once past u is known (u is causally prior as a vector, in Granger's sense, relative to m). Now equation (15) is part of the joint moving-average representation of the process (y, m), and we therefore have by construction

(20) $$E_{t-1}y(t) = \sum_{s=1}^{\infty} a(s)e(t - s) + \sum_{s=1}^{\infty} c(s)f(t - s).$$

By the definition of an innovation, we can use (19) to write

(21) $y(t) = H_t(E_{t-1}(u(s)))$, all s; $y(t - s)$ for $s > 0) + a(0)e(t) + \lambda c(0)f(t)$

where f is, as in (15), the innovation in m when (y, m) is treated as a vector process and e is the component of the innovation in y orthogonal to f. Under our assumptions about policy, $f(t)$ must be unrelated to the real disturbance process u. We assume further that from the past history of y and m, agents can calculate actual past values of u.[25] Then it is not hard to show that $e(t)$ must in fact be a linear transformation of the innovation vector for u. Thus the component of the right-hand side of (21) which depends on the $E_{t-1}(u(s))$ series is a fixed linear combination of past values

---

[24] It not obvious to me, however, that when different agents have different information sets the economy must be worse off with lower-quality private forecasts.

[25] This is probably not restrictive. If u could not be deduced from past y and m (e.g. if it was of too high dimension) it could probably be redefined to satisfy our assumption without altering the argument.

of $e(t)$. The weights in that linear combination depend on the structure of the u process only. Using these conclusions (and the linearity of H) to rewrite (21) we get

$$(22) \qquad b_1^* y(t) = b_2^* e(t) + a(0)e(t) + \lambda c(0)f(t).$$

Assuming b_1 is invertible, we arrive finally at an interpretation of (20): $b_1^{-1*}b_2(s) = a(s)$ for $s > 0$, $b_1^{-1}(s)c(0) = c(s)$ for $s > 0$. Since b_1 and b_2 do not depend on the form of the monetary policy rule, the main conclusion announced at the beginning of this section follows. That $a(0)$ is invariant to changes in deterministic policy rules follows from (18) and our information assumptions, since when all private information sets include the information on which policy is based and $f(t) = 0$, and t, (18) determines $y(t)$ without regard to the form of the policy rule.

Up to this point, the theory which has been invoked has generated no explicit restrictions on the joint autoregressive representation of m and y, despite the fact that the theory clearly has strong implications for policy. The theory does, however, allow us to interpret the estimated MAR. Note that b_1 in (22) is determined by the coefficients on lagged y in H_t in (21), and that H_t in turn has been determined by the coefficients of the G_j functions in (16). Thus b_1 is determined by the parameters of the utility functions and production functions of economic agents. The lag distribution b_2, on the other hand, arises from the forecasts of u which enter H_t in (21). While b_2 is affected by the form of H, and hence by utility and production functions, it is zero if $u(t)$ is serially uncorrelated, regardless of the form of H_t.

Since c, the time path of y's response to m innovations, is just $b_1^{-1}c(0)$, it follows that c can change only in limited ways (via changes in the vector $c(0)$) in response to changes in the money supply rule.

Obviously if b_2 is zero and b_1 is a scalar, (22) implies that $y(t)$ is serially uncorrelated. In words, if there are no dynamics in utility functions or production functions (b_1 scalar) and if the shocks to utility functions, production functions, and endowments are serially uncorrelated ($b_2 = 0$), then this model implies that real variables are serially uncorrelated. The notion that market-clearing rational expectations models imply that real variables are serially uncorrelated has received a good deal of attention in the literature. Hall (1975), e.g., explored it treating unemployment as the leading example of a real variable. Hall's simple model is a special case of the one considered here, in which b_1 is assumed to be scalar. Because of the scalar-b_1 assumption, Hall concludes that if real variables are in fact strongly serially correlated, then the market-clearing rational expectations model has to 'explain' serially correlated real variables via non-zero b_2. As he points out, this amounts to 'explaining' the business cycle as serial correlation of unexplained origin in unmeasurable influences on the economy;

such a theory does not really explain anything. Furthermore, it does in particular rule out the possibility that nearly all observed cyclical variation in real variables is attributable to monetary policy aberrations (i.e. to f) and therefore limits the potential gain to be expected from monetarist policy prescriptions.

The latter part of Hall's argument does make sense. However, Hall's conclusions depend on the notion that strong serial correlation in y is evidence of strongly non-zero b_2. In fact, it is easy to see from (22), as has been pointed out by Sargent, that large serially correlated movements in y can be explained without resort to powerful, serially correlated movements in u, simply by admitting the existence of dynamic elements in technology or tastes – i.e. non-scalar b_1. If serial correlation in y is explained by non-scalar b_1 without resort to non-zero b_1, however, a testable implication of the theory for the joint (y, m) autoregression still emerges; y should be causally prior relative to m. Formally, this is because with $b_2 = 0$, (22) expresses the innovation in y as a linear combination of current and past y's alone, without using past m's. Another way to put the same thing is to observe that, with $b_2 = 0$, the best linear one-step-ahead forecast of $y(t)$ is $\Sigma_{s=1}^{\infty} b_1(s)y(t-s)$. That this formula not involve lagged m is precisely Granger's definition of m not causing y.

A test for block-exogeneity of the real sector thus has special interest in the context of this model. If the test were passed, the implication would be either that variance in u is small relative to that in f or that u does not have large serial correlation. In either case, serially correlated cyclical movements would be accounted for largely by the parameters of the objective functions G_j. If the test were not passed, the implication would be that b_2 is non-zero and the parameters of G_j do not account for the observed pattern of serial correction. Note that this test does not bear on whether the rational expectations, market-clearing, neutral money theory is true – it only examines how well it accounts for the observed cyclical variability of the economy. It could be that b_2 is strongly non-zero and that u has large variance, yet still be true also that the model considered here is correct. In this case it could not be expected that changing monetary policy to reduce the variance in f, as most monetarists would suggest, would change the cyclical variability of the economy very much. But it would remain true that activist monetary policy could have only very limited effect in increasing the stability of the economy.[26]

---

[26] The model does not imply that policy has no real effects. By changing the variance of f, policy can in general affect $a(0)$ and λ, and with a given arbitrarily chosen objective function for policy it is unlikely that $f = 0$ will be the optimum choice. On the other hand, if the objective function of policy makers is related to those of economic agents in a reasonable way and important externalities ars not present, it is likely to turn out that $f = 0$, making the private economy's forecasts as accurate as possible, is the optimal policy.

Note that there is a certain paradoxical quality to a test for block-exogeneity of y as a test of the power of rational expectations market-clearing theory. That theory, in the form presented here, does suggest that setting $f = 0$, i.e. setting the level of the money supply according to a non-discretionary rule, would be good policy. In this sense the theory justifies monetarist conclusions. Yet we test the theory by looking for Granger causation of y by m – if we *find* 'causation' of y by m, we *reject* the monetarist theory.[27] An old-fashioned monetarist, used to interpreting regressions of GNP on money as structural equations, would rightly find this conclusion ridiculous. To the extent that money does have important real effects which are not compensated by the operation of frictionless price adjustment and rational expectations, one would expect to find Granger-causality running from m to y. If, however, this is the source of a substantial component of the m-to-y covariance, then monetary stabilization policy has important effects and simple mechanical rules for setting m may be far from optimal.

To summarize, one can interpret block-exogeneity tests within at least three frameworks of maintained hypotheses. Under rational expectations and interia-less prices, rejection of exogeneity of y implies that much cyclical variation is not reaction to monetary shock. Active stabilization policy can never be very helpful in this framework, but with y not exogenous, the implication is that it has not historically been the main source of cyclical variability. A 'standard monetarist' who believed that money was very important but did not accept interia-less prices and rational expectations would find y-exogeneity hard to explain. In fact, the income on money regressions associated with this framework are insupportable as structural relations, unless m, not y, is Granger-causally prior. However this approach implies that mechanical monetary rules are unlikely to be optimal. Finally an unregenerate Keynesian, rejecting not only interia-less prices and market clearing but also the idea that money is a policy instrument of dominant importance, could interpret y-exogeneity as indicative of a completely passive monetary policy, accounting for m-to-y time series correlations without resort to causal effects of autonomous policy-induced change in m on y. Rejection of y-exogeneity thus weakens the 'unregenerate Keynesian' position as well as the 'rational expectations market-clearing' position.

In this case, as I think ought to be the case in most macroeconometric work, the data will obviously not determine directly the outcome of debate

---

[27] Of course, as pointed out above, we don't actually reject the theory as false. As described above, causation of y by m only implies that the rational-expectations monetarist theory must allocate important business cycle variance to serial correlation in an unexplained residual. What is important, then, is not *whether* y-exogeneity is rejected, but by how big a likelihood ratio it is rejected.

between various schools of thought; they do, however, influence the conflict by defining what battlefield positions must be.

The rational expectations market-clearing model involves numerous dubious assumptions. In manipulating it we implicitly or explicitly invoked existence and uniqueness results as well as the obviously false linearity and certainty-equivalence assumptions. By excluding real balances from the G_j, we assumed a strong neutrality property. We also relied on continuous market clearing and a very restrictive (and in my view unrealistic) definition of what policy can accomplish.[28] Finally, it is probably in fact important to take account of private costs of acquiring and processing information, instead of, as in this model, treating 'information sets' as given. It might be that the policy authority can relieve the private sector of some such costs by correctly processing information in setting its policy.

For all these reasons I do not regard this type of model as a null hypothesis with non-zero prior probability. This type of model is bound to be more or less false, probably in important ways. Nonetheless, it is for the time being the only class of model which generates a behavioural theory of the *stochastic* behaviour of economic time series. In interpreting the statistical models we fit in this paper, hypotheses suggested by behavioural models in this class are therefore given special attention.

In neither Germany nor the US is the test for block-exogeneity of the real sector passed. The $\chi^2(32)$ statistic for this hypothesis in the Germany system is 52.10, with a marginal significance level of about 0.01 and for the US data (where the import equation is ignored) we get $\chi^2(24) = 64.63$, with a marginal significance level less than 0.001. This conclusion is of course unsurprising when the strong lagged effects on real variables of price and money innovations in Germany and the US, respectively, are taken into account.

On the other hand, the hypothesis that the time form of the system's response to a money innovation (or to a real innovation) should be invariant to the money supply rule, does have a crude plausibility in the light of this system's results. The reaction of money to other variables in the system is very different in the two countries, as already pointed out, yet in both countries we get in response to a money innovation a rise in real GNP

---

[28] By this I mean that the apparently innocuous assumption that the monetary authority must 'set' money supply on the basis of information it has in hand is not realistic. Surely the monetary authority in the US has the option of 'leaning against the wind' in the presence of variations in the short interest rate produced by shifts in the demand for money. Such a policy would create correction between innovations in the money supply and innovations in $u(t)$ without requiring that the authority be able to observe demand shifts in advance, in the sense of getting published data ahead of anyone else. A similar policy would even be possible relative to variations in unemployment: unemployment insurance claims could be paid in part with new currency, thereby creating an automatic link between money and unemployment innovations.

above trend, a corresponding fall in unemployment, and a rise in the real wage above trend, all lasting $2\frac{1}{2}$–3 years.

It is true that the response in the US is substantially greater in percentage terms in real GNP and smaller in percentage terms in the real wage, and also that the drop in real GNP following the rise is relatively larger (compared to the initial rise) in Germany.

The only instance where the shape of the real variables' response is qualitatively different between countries is the response to an unemployment innovation, and here one has the possible explanation that, due to differences in the nature of the unemployment statistics between the two countries, innovations in unemployment are different things in the two countries. My own best guess, though, is that such measurement error does not account for the differing responses. The differences appear to be naturally explained by the differences in the reaction of money to the innovation, which contradicts the classical rational expectations hypothesis,[29] and unemployment is connected to real GNP in roughly the same way in all the response patterns for both countries, which casts doubt on the measurement error explanation. Unfortunately, to test the hypothesis with data from these two countries we would need to believe the dubious assumption that differences in monetary policy rule are the only difference, rather than one obvious difference, between these two countries. A study across more countries might be able to reach firmer conclusions.

To estimate 'wage and price equations' by single-equation methods and give them a structural interpretation, one needs to believe that the right-hand side variables in such equations are exogenous. Given the strong feedback from prices and money into real variables in the systems we are discussing, it should be apparent that the usual form of such systems, in which unemployment and deviations of output from trend (sometimes called 'capacity utilization') are the main right-hand side variables other than lagged values of prices and wages, are not likely to pass an exogeneity test. Indeed the hypothesis that unemployment and real GNP are jointly exogenous is rejected with a $\chi^2(32) = 58.26$ for the US. In Germany this hypothesis was inadvertently not directly tested, but an implication of that hypothesis, that money has a zero sum of coefficients in the unemployment equation, is rejected at a marginal significance level of less than 0.01.

Though the usual interpretation of wage and price equations as reflecting wage bargaining and price mark-up behaviour is difficult to sustain if

---

[29] That is, the response of real variables to a money innovation in the US appears to be naturally explained as a systematic tendency of money to increase after a positive unemployment innovation, followed by a private-sector reaction to the money increase which parallels the private-sector reaction to a monetary 'surprise'. In classical rational expectations models of the sort discussed above, the private sector should not react to predictable movements in the money supply.

money supply is admitted to these equations, empirical research on these equations including money as an explanatory variable has gone forward recently.[30] The null hypothesis that real GNP, unemployment, and money together form an exogenous block is rejected for Germany with a $\chi^2(36) = 68.27$ and a marginal significance level of less than 0.01. For the US this hypothesis turns out to be acceptable, with $\chi^2(36) = 42.54$ and a marginal significance level of 0.21. This hypothesis amounts to the assertion that for analysing developments in the real aggregate variables we need not pay attention to relative price movements. Money supply by itself, with the real variables, provides an adequate measure of nominal–real interactions. The better fit of this hypothesis to US experience might reflect relatively smaller importance for supply shocks in the US.

E. Conclusions

The foregoing small-scale example should have made clear that one can obtain marcoeconomic models with useful descriptive characteristics, within which tests of economically meaningful hypotheses can be executed, without as much of a burden of maintained hypotheses as is usually imposed in such modelling. A long road remains, however, between what has been displayed here and models in this style that compete seriously with existing large-scale models on their home ground – forecasting and policy projection. Even with a small system like those here, forecasting, especially over relatively long horizons, would probably benefit substantially from use of Bayesian methods or other mean-square-error shrinking devices to improve on what is obtained with raw estimates of 144 unconstrained coefficients. To be of much use in policy projection, models like these would have to include considerably more than the one policy variable which appears in these two models. In expanding the list of variables in the model, practical methods for limiting the growth in number of parameters as sample size increases will have to be developed, perhaps along the lines of index models.

But though the road is long, the opportunity it offers to drop the discouraging baggage of standard, but incredible, assumptions macroeconometricians have been used to carrying may make the road attractive.

---

[30] See Wachter (1976) and Gordon (1977).

Appendix I The Data

Money: In the US this is $M1$, seasonally adjusted, as prepared by the Board of Governors of the Federal Reserve System and published in *Business Statistics* and the *Survey of Current Business* by the Department of Commerce. In West Germany this is defined as Money = Reserve Money in Federal Bank + Demand Deposits in Deposit Money Banks − Currency in Deposit Money Banks − Bankers' Deposits, and is taken from the International Monetary Fund Publication *International Financial Statistics*.

Real GNP: In the US this is the series published in the same sources listed above for $M1$ and prepared by the Department of Commerce. It is seasonally adjusted. In West Germany this is based on a series prepared by the Statistisches Bundesampt/ Wiesbaden and published in *Wirtschaft und Statistik*. Besides involving splicing of series based on different index weights, preparation of this series required interpolation to obtain quarterly from published semi-annual data over much of the sample period. The interpolation was carried out by a regression of observed semi-annual data on monthly values of industrial production for the current and three preceding months. Industrial production was the Index der Industriellen Netto-produktion, from the same source cited above for real GNP. The quarterly data have the form of quarterly estimates of two-quarter moving averages of real GNP.

Unemployment rate: In the US this is the rate for all civilian workers, seasonally adjusted, prepared by the Bureau of Labour Statistics and published in the sources already cited for the US. For West Germany this is a ratio of published numbers of unemployed, the series 'Arbeitlose' in the source cited above, divided by the sum of the number unemployed and the number employed. The series for number employed was spliced together from data in *Statistischer Wochendienst*, published by the same organization cited above. For 1964–76 it was Erwerbstatigkeit (abhangige) (i.e. number employed excluding self-employed and family workers) and for 1952–62 it was Beschaftige Arbeitnehmer (i.e. a similar concept but double-counting some multiple job holders). For the intermediate years, and for splicing the series, the series 'Ewerbstatigkeit', which includes self-employed and family workers, was used.

Wages: For the US this is a seasonally adjusted index of average hourly compensation of all private non-farm employees, prepared by the Bureau of Labour Statistics and published in *Business Conditions Digest* by the Department of Commerce. For West Germany this is Hourly Earnings in Industry as published in *International Financial Statistics* by the International Monetary Fund, using the Monthly Report of the Deutsche Bundesbank as source. Splicing of segments using different norming years was required.

Prices: For the US this is seasonally adjusted price deflator of Gross National Product of the non-farm business sector, as prepared by the Department of Commerce and published in the *Survey of Current Business*. For West Germany these data were constructed as a GNP deflator taking the ratio of current dollar GNP to constant dollar GNP as published in the same source cited for German constant-dollar GNP. As with real GNP, interpolation was required, in this case using monthly data on retail prices (Index der Einzelhandelsprese, Einzelhandel insgesamt, from Wertshaft und Statistik) in the same way as data on industrial production were used for interpolating real GNP. A notable difference between the two procedures was that for prices, residuals from the fit of the GNP deflator to retail trade prices showed substantial serial correlation and were therefore used in interpolation. At an early stage of the work this interpolation was two-sided – interpolated values were predicted values from the regression on retail prices plus an average of residuals from the regression one quarter ahead and one quarter behind. Later, it was decided that this might distort the timing of series, so the interpolation was redone using only lagged residuals. This had no important effect on the estimated equations, and hence not all of the restricted regressions used in forming test statistics were repeated with the data interpolated in the latter way. The plots and tables of moving average representations do, however, reflect the latter 'one-sided' interpolation method.

Import Prices: For the US this is the Unit Value of General Imports as published by the Department of Commerce in the Survey of Current Business. For West Germany this is the series Unit Value of Imports published by the International Monetary Fund in *International Financial Statistics*. Splicing of six overlapping segments reflecting small changes in the definition of the series or changes in base year was required.

Appendix II   Charts

Notes to the Charts: Each chart displays the response of one variable in one country's model to six initial conditions. The model is in each case a vector autoregression, in which each of the six variables in the system is predicted as a linear combination of past values of all six variables in the system. The variables are ordered as M, Y, U, W, P, PM. The jth simulation sets the value at time 0 of the jth variable in this ordering at the estimated residual standard error of a regression of the jth equation autoregression residual on the autoregression residuals from lower-order equations. The initial value of variables ordered lower than j is set to zero, as are all values of all variables for negative t. The $t = 0$ values of variables higher than j in the ordering are set equal to the predicted values for those residuals, given the value of the first j residuals, from a regression of the last $6 - j$ residuals on the first j. More formally, if Σ is the estimated variance-covariance matrix of the residuals in the autoregression, the jth simulation sets the time-zero values of the variables to the jth column of the positive, lower-triangular square root of Σ. Finally, an intuitive description is that the jth simultation pertains to a movement in that part of the innovation of the jth variable which is uncorrelated with innovations in the first $j - 1$ variables, with correlations between this part of the jth innovations and $j + s$th innovations being attributed (for positive s) to causal influence of the jth innovation on the $j + s$th. The six numbered horizontal axes on each chart refer to the six simulations, in the order displayed along the left margin of each chart.

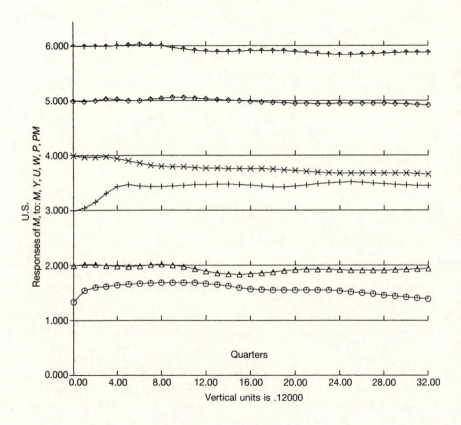

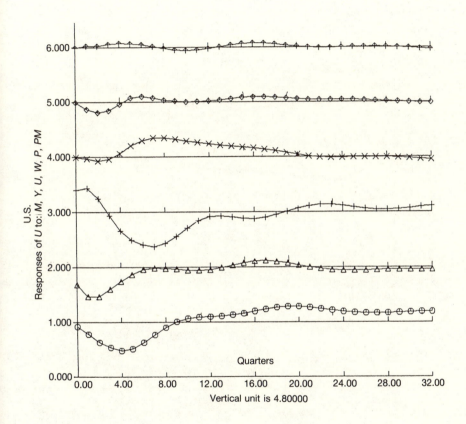

Quarters

Vertical unit is 4.80000

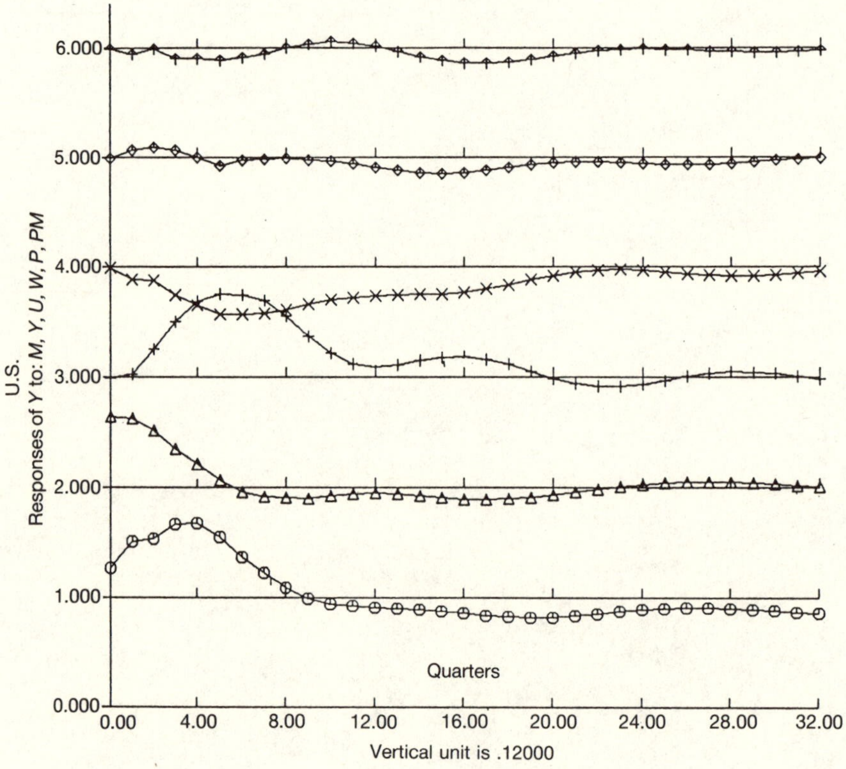
U.S.
Responses of Y to: M, Y, U, W, P, PM
6.000
5.000
4.000
3.000
2.000
1.000
0.000
Quarters
0.00
4.00
8.00
12.00
16.00
20.00
24.00
28.00
32.00
Vertical unit is .12000

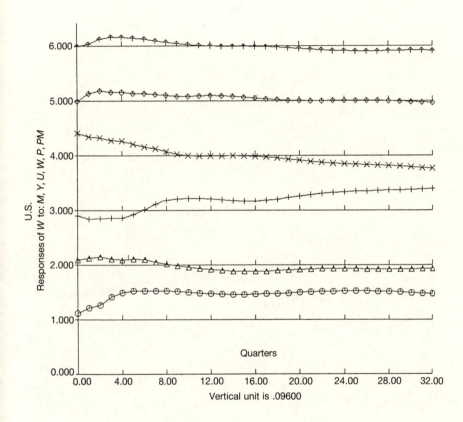

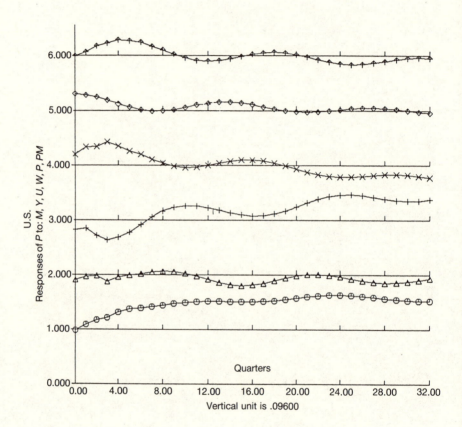

U.S.

Responses of *P* to: *M, Y, U, W, P, PM*

Quarters

Vertical unit is .09600

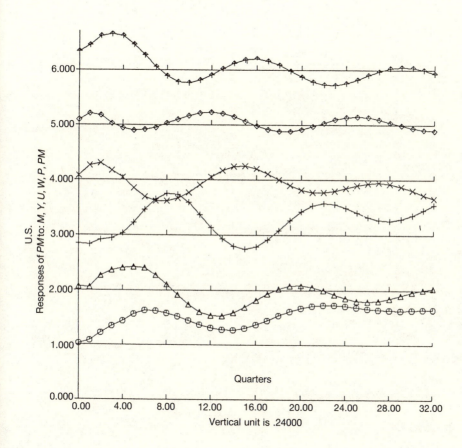

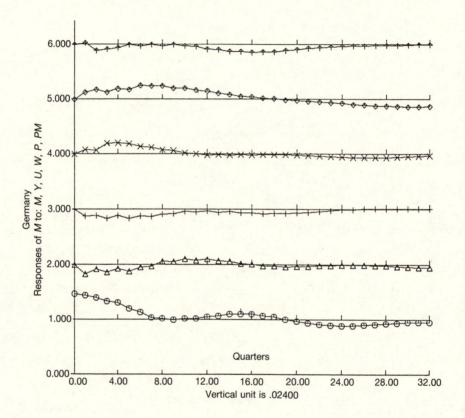

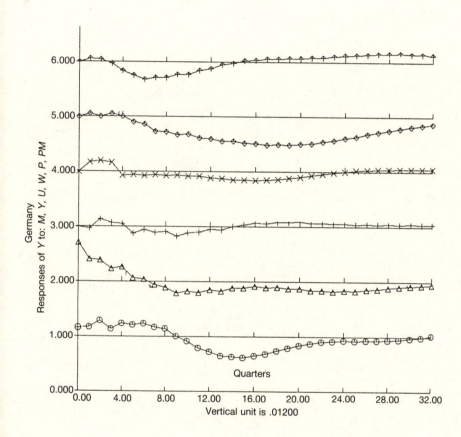

Germany

Responses of *Y* to: *M, Y, U, W, P, PM*

Quarters

Vertical unit is .01200

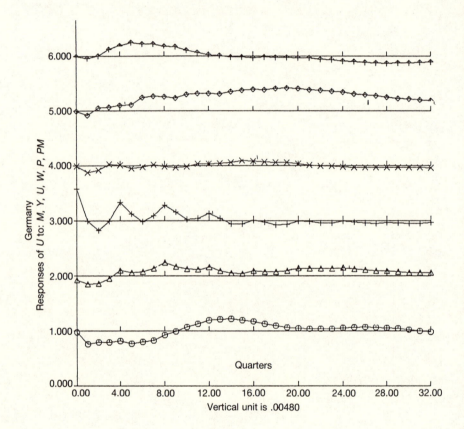

Germany

Responses of *U* to: *M, Y, U, W, P, PM*

Quarters

Vertical unit is .00480

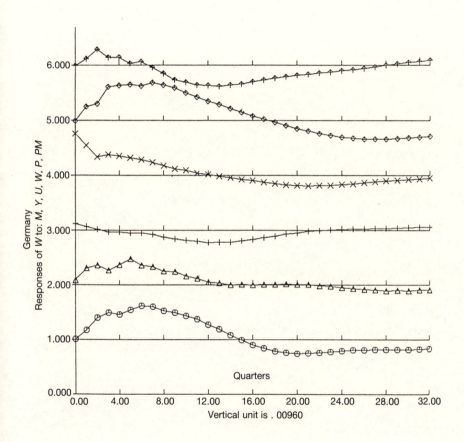

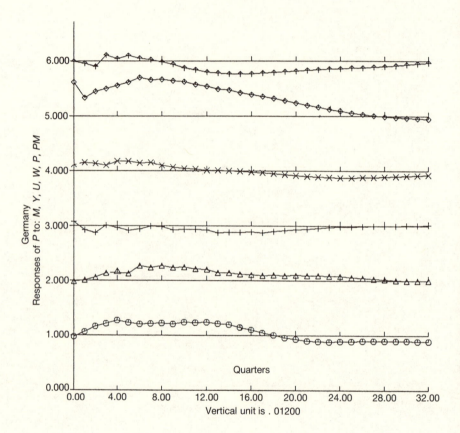

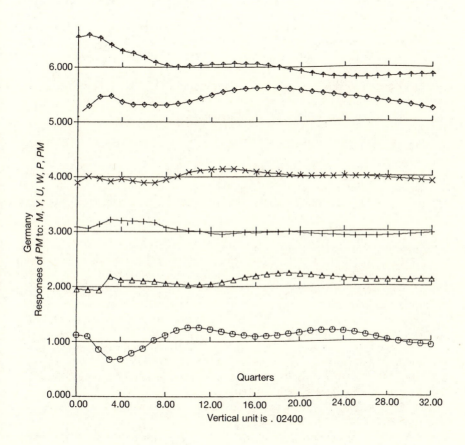

References

Amemiya, Takeshi (1973), Generalized least squares with an estimated auto-covariance matrix, *Econometrica*, 41, 723–32.

Ando, Albert, Modiglani, Franco, and Rasche, Robert (1972), Equations and definitions of variables for the FRB-MIT-Pen econometric model, November 1969, *Econometric Models of Cyclical Behavior*, vol. I, ed. by Bert G. Hickman, NBER *Studies in Income and Wealth*, No. 36. Columbia University Press, New York, pp. 543–600.

Brainard, William C. and Tobin, James (1968), Pitfalls in financial model building, *American Economic Review*, 58, 99–122.

Brillinger, David (1975), *Times Series*. Holt, Rinehart Winston, New York.

Cooper, J. P., and Nelson C. R. (1975), The ex ante prediction performance of the St. Louis and FRB-MIT-Penn econometric models and some results on composite predictors, *Journal of Money, Credit and Banking*, 7, 1–32.

Fair, Ray C. (1976), *A Model of Macroeconomic Activity*. Ballinger, Cambridge, Mass.

Fisher, Irving (1918), *Stabilizing the Dollar in Purchasing Power*. E. P. Dutton & Co.,

Gordon, Robert J. (1977), Can the inflation of the 1970's be explained?, *Brookings Papers on Economic Activity*, 1, 253–79.

Griliches, Zvi (1968), The Brookings Model: a review article, *Review of Economics and Statistics*, 50, 215–34.

Hall, Robert E. (1975), The rigidity of wages and the persistence of unemployment, *Brookings Papers on Economic Activity*, 2, 301–350.

Hatanaka, M. (1975), On the global identification of the dynamic simultaneous equation model with stationary disturbances, *International Economic Review*, 16, 545–54.

Hurwicz, Leonid (1962), On the structural form of interdependent systems. *Logic, Methodology, and the Philosophy of Science*, ed. by E. Nagel et al. Stanford University Press, Stanford.

Koopmans, T. C. and Bausch, Augustus F. (1959), Selected topics in economics involving mathematical reasoning, *SIAM Review*, 1, 138–48.

Leamer, E. E. (1973), Multicollinearity: a Bayesian interpretation, *Review of Economics and Statistics*, 55, 371–80.

Liu, T. C. (1960), Underidentification, structural estimation, and forecasting, *Econometrica*, 28, 855–65.

Lucas, Robert E., Jr (1972), Econometric testing of the natural rate hypothesis, *The Econometrics of Price Determination*, Board of Governors of the Federal Reserve, Washington, DC, pp. 50–59.

Lucas, Robert E., Jr. (1975), Review of *A Model of Macroeconomic Activity,"* *Journal of Economic Literature*, 13, 889–90.

Lucas, Robert E., Jr. (1976) 'Macro-economic Policy Evaluation: A Critique," in *The Phillips Curve and Labour Markets*, ed. by K. Brunner and A. H. Meltzer, Carnegie-Rochester Conference Series on Public Policy, 1. Amsterdam: North-Holland, 1976, pp. 19–46.

McFadden, Daniel (1977), Conditional logit analysis of qualitative choice behavior,

Frontiers in Econometrics, ed. by P. Zarembka. Academic Press, New York, pp. 105–42.

Modigliani, Franco (1977), The monetarist controversy, or, should we forsake stabilization policies, *American Economic Review*, 67, 1–19.

Nelson, C. R. (1972), The prediction performance of the FRB-MIT-Penn model of the U.S. economy, *American Economic Review*, 62, 902–17.

Okun, Arthur (1975): Inflation: its mechanics and welfare costs, *Brookings Papers on Economic Activity*, 2, 351–402.

Prescott, Edward C., and Kydlund Finn E. (1977), Rules rather than discretion: the inconsistency of optimal plans, *Journal of Political Economy*, 85, 473–92.

Priestly, M. B., Rao, T. S. and Tong, H. (1974), Applications of principal component analysis and factor analysis in the identification of multi-variable systems, *IEEE Transactions on Automatic Control*, AC-19, 730–4.

Sargan J. D. (1961), The maximum likelihood estimation of economic relationships with autoregressive residuals, *Econometrica*, 29, 414–26.

Sargent, Thomas J. (1978) Rational expectations, econometric exogeneity, and consumption, *Journal of Political Economy*, 86, 673–700.

Sargent, Thomas J. (1977), The persistence of aggregate employment and neutrality of money. Unpublished manuscript, University of Minnesota.

Sargent, T.J. and Sims C.A. (1977), Business cycle modelling without pretending to have too much a priori economic theory. *New Methods of Business Cycle Research*, ed. by C. A. Sims. Federal Reserve Bank of Minneapolis, Minneapolis.

Sargent, Thomas J. and Wallace, Neil (1975), 'Rational' expectations, the optimal monetary instrument, and the optimal money supply rule, *Journal of Political Economy*, 83, 241–54.

Shiller, Robert L. (1973), A distributed lag estimator derived from smoothness priors, *Econometrica*, 41, 775–88.

Solow, Robert M. (1974), Comment, *Brookings Papers on Economic Activity*, 3, 733.

Wachter, Michael L. (1976), The changing cyclical responsiveness of wage inflation, *Brookings Papers on Economic Activity*, 1, 115–168.

Wallis, Kenneth F. (1980), Econometric implications of the rational expectations hypothesis, *Econometrica*, 48, 49–73.

PART II

Alternative Methodologies

Introduction

There are many possible approaches to modelling. These four papers discuss aspects of four quite different strategies. The most venerable approach uses many equations, a lot of simultaneous relationships and relatively little dynamics, plus a strong reliance on economic theory. This approach is used in the construction of the larger-scale econometric models, which are very influential in the game of economic forecasting. Because of the cost and difficulty in construction of these models they are quite a rare breed, with just a handful in most countries, at most. Some of these models are also linked together to form a world model in Project Link (see, for example, Hickman, 1975). Most of these models are constructed by a team of economists, but Ray Fair produces rather smaller models of this genre largely by himself. His book, *Specification, Estimation and Analysis of Econometric Models*, Harvard University Press, 1984, from which paper 9 is taken, describes a large model, plus a 'smaller' model of only ten equations, and does a careful job of model evaluation, using post-sample forecasting performance as a main ingredient. His paper discusses how economic theory is used in the specification and then reviews five crucial steps: (1) data collection and the choice of variables; (2) the treatment of unobserved variables, including expectations; (3) the specification of the stochastic equations, (4) estimation; and (6) testing and analysis. Altogether it provides a convenient, compact, and interesting account of this particular modelling approach. It should be remembered that only an extract from the book is included here. To completely appreciate the methodology that this paper represents, the full book should be read.

Richard Todd (paper 10) provides a very readable account of an extension of the vector autoregressive modelling procedure, discussed in Sims (paper 8). An obvious problem with the unconstrained VAR is that many parameters have to be estimated, if there are N variables and n lags for each variable, this gives $N^2 n$ parameters. One way of reducing the degrees of freedom problem that results is to use Bayesian priors on the parameters. A sensible set of priors, at least for most sets of macrovariables, were suggested by Robert Litterman. Todd reviews this extension and concentrates on the forecasting use of these models.

The final two papers in this section are also concerned with the use of Bayesian techniques. Bayesians add to the usual information sets by using their own beliefs, knowledge, and accumulated experience in a precise way via prior probabilities. Strong believers in Bayesian methods are amazed that everyone is not a Bayesian and suggest that, in fact, all modellers are at least informal Bayesians. Certainly all modelling strategies involve judgements, and these have to be based on non-numerical information. It is interesting to note that it is a personal choice whether to remain an informal Bayesian or to become a formal one. Both Ed Leamer (paper 11) and Arnold Zellner (paper 12) are forceful advocates of these methods.

Leamer (11) provides an application of techniques that make heavy use of Bayesian ideas and considers alternative determinants of inflation. Starting with a simple, dynamic model of the change in the logarithm of the GNP deflator, the inverse of the percentage unemployed and the level of excess demand, a pair of priors are suggested, called respectively the monetarist and Keynesian priors. The paper is of considerable methodological interest, but does not reach any clear conclusions about the correctness of these alternative theories.

Zellner's paper (12) is a shortened version of his orginal. He puts forward five basic propositions and then issues five challenges designed to focus the discussion and to show the potential superiority of the Bayesian techniques. The part of the paper not reproduced here considers nine specific problems in econometric, statistical, and economic theory, and suggests the Bayesian solution. Although certainly interesting, this part of the paper is not concerned with methodological issues.

Reference

Hickman, B. G. (1975), Project Link, retrospect and prospect. *Modelling the Economy*, ed. by G. A. Renton. Heinemann, London.

9

Macroeconomic Methodology

Ray Fair

1. Macrotheoretical Models and the Role of Theory

A. *Ingredients of Models*

Broadly speaking, an economy consists of people making and carrying out decisions and interacting with each other through markets. Theories provide explanations of how the decisions are made and how the markets work. The ingredients of a theory include the choice of the decision-making units, the decision variables and objective function of each unit, the constraints facing each unit, and the amount of information each unit has at the time the decisions are made. Possible constraints include budget constraints, technological constraints, direct constraints on decision variables, and institutional or legal constraints. If expectations of future values affect current decisions, another ingredient of a theory is an explanation of how expectations are formed.

A theory of how markets work should explain who sets prices and how they are set. If there is the possibility of disequilibrium in certain markets, the theory should explain how quantities are determined each period and why it is that prices are not set to clear the markets. Institutional constraints may play an important role in some markets.

In macroeconomics there are also a number of adding-up constraints that should be met. In particular, balance-sheet and flow-of-funds constraints should be met. An asset of one person is a liability of someone else, and income of one person in a period is an expenditure of someone else in the period. These two constraints are not independent, since any deviation of income from expenditure for an individual in a period corresponds to a change in at least one of his or her assets or liabilities.

B. *The Traditional Role of Theory*

An important issue in the construction of a model is the role that one expects theory to play. If the aim is to use the theoretical model to guide

This article first appeared in Fair, R. (1984), *Specification, Estimation and Analysis of Macroeconometric Models*, Harvard University Press. References to other sections and chapters are to that volume, and not to the present volume.

the specification of an empirical model, the issue is how many restrictions one can expect theory to provide regarding the specification of the equations to be estimated. In practice, the primary role of theory has been to choose the variables that appear with non-zero coefficients in each equation. (Stated another way, the primary role of theory has been to provide 'exclusionary' restrictions on the model; that is, to provide a list of variables *not* to include in each equation.) In most cases theory also chooses the signs of the coefficients. Much less often is theory used to decide things like the functional forms of the estimated equations and the lengths of the lag distributions. (This is not to say that theory could not be used for such purposes, only that it generally has not been.) This role of theory – the choice of the variables to include in each equation – will be called the 'traditional' role or approach.

An interesting question within the traditional approach is whether theory singles out one variable per equation as the obvious dependent or 'left-hand-side' (LHS) variable, where the other variables are then explanatory or 'right-hand-side' (RHS) variables. In this way of looking at the problem, the LHS variable is the decision variable and the RHS variables are the determinants of the decision variable. If the theoretical problem is to explain the decisions of agents, this way seems natural. Each equation is a derived decision equation (derived either in a maximization context or in some other way) with a natural LHS variable. The alternative way of looking at the problem is that theory treats all variables in each equation equally. These two interpretations have important implications for estimation. In particular, full information maximum-likelihood (FIML) treats all variables equally, whereas two-stage least-squares (2SLS) and three-stage least-squares (3SLS) require an LHS variable to be chosen for each equation before estimation (see, for example, Chow, 1964). One might thus be inclined to choose 3SLS over FIML under the first interpretation, although there are other issues to consider in this choice as well. This issue is discussed in more detail in Section 6.3.4, where FIML and 3SLS are compared. For the remainder of this chapter it will be assumed that within the traditional approach the LHS variable is also chosen.

C.   The Hansen–Sargent Approach and Lucas's Point

An alternative role for theory is exemplified by the recent work of Hansen and Sargent (1980). In this work the aim is to estimate the parameters of the objective functions of the decision-making units. In the traditional approach these parameters are never estimated. The parameters of the derived decision equations (rules) are estimated instead, where these parameters are functions of the parameters of the objective function and other things. The Hansen–Sargent approach imposes many more theoretical restrictions on the data than does the traditional approach, especially considering that the traditional approach imposes very few restrictions on the functional forms and the lag structures of the estimated decision equations.

The advantage of the Hansen–Sargent approach is that it estimates structural parameters rather than combinations of structural parameters and other things. The problem with estimating combinations is that if, say, one wants to examine the effects of changing an exogenous variable on the decision variables, there is always the possibility that this change will change something in the combinations. If so, then it is inappropriate to use the estimated decision equations, which are based on fixed estimates of the combinations, to examine the effects of the change. This is the point emphasized by Lucas (1976) in his classic article. (Note that the validity of the point does not depend on expectations being rational. Even if expectations are formed in rather naive ways, it may still be that the coefficient of the decision equations are combinations of things that change when an exogenous variable is changed.)

There are two disadvantages of the Hansen–Sargent approach: one that may be temporary and one that may be more serious. The temporary disadvantage is that it is extremely difficult to set up the problem in such a way that the parameters can be estimated, especially if there is more than one decision variable or if the objective function is not quadratic. Very restrictive assumptions have so far been needed to make the problem tractable. This disadvantage may gradually be lessened as more tools are developed. At the present time, however, this approach is a long way from the development of a complete model of the economy.

A potentially more serious disadvantage, at least as applied to macroeconomic data, is the possibility that the approach imposes restrictions on the data that are poor approximations. Macroeconomic data are highly aggregated, and it is obviously restrictive to assume that one objective function pertains to, say, the entire household sector or the entire firm sector. Although both the traditional approach and the Hansen–Sargent approach are forced to make assumptions like this when dealing with macroeconomic data, the Hansen–Sargent approach is much more restrictive. If because of aggregation problems the assumption that a sector behaves by maximizing an objective function is not correct, models based on both approaches will be misspecified. This misspecification may be more serious for models based on the Hansen–Sargent approach because it uses the assumption in a much stronger way. To put it another way, by not requiring that a particular objective function be specified, the traditional approach may be more robust to errors regarding the maximization assumption.

It is difficult to argue against the Hansen–Sargent approach without sounding as if one is in favour of the use of *ad hoc* theory to explain macroeconomic data. Arguments against theoretical purity are generally not well received in the economics profession. There are, however, as just discussed, different degrees to which theory can be used to guide econometric specifications. There is a middle ground between a completely *ad hoc* approach and the Hansen–Sargent approach, namely what I have called the traditional approach. An example of this approach is given in Chapters 3 and 4.

It should also be noted that the Hansen–Sargent approach can be discussed without reference to how expectations are formed. It is typically assumed within this approach that expectations are rational, but this is not a necessary assumption. It is clearly possible within the context of a maximization problem to assume that expectations of the future variable values that are needed to solve the problem are formed in simple or naive ways. The possible problems with the Hansen–Sargent approach discussed earlier exist independently of the expectational assumptions that are used. The problems are perhaps potentially more serious when the rational expectation assumption is used because of the tighter theoretical restrictions that are implied, but this is only a matter of degree. The treatment of expectations is discussed in Section 2.2.2 in this volume.

Whether the Hansen–Sargent approach will lead to better models of the economy is currently an open question. As noted in Chapter 1, a major theme of this book is that it should be possible in the long run to decide questions like this using methods like the one discussed in Chapter 8. The method in Chapter 8 allows one to compare different models in regard to how well they approximate the true structure. If the Hansen–Sargent approach leads eventually to the construction of complete models of the economy, it should be possible to compare these models to models based on the traditional approach.

If because of the limitations just discussed the Hansen–Sargent approach does not lead to econometric models that are good approximations, this does not invalidate Lucas's point (1976). The point is a logical one. If parameters that are taken to be constant change when an exogenous variable is changed, the estimated effects of the change are clearly in error. The key question for any given experiment with an econometric model is the likely size of this error. There are many potential sources of error, and even the best econometric model in the future (as judged, say, by the method in Chapter 8) will be only an approximation to the structure. It may be that for many experiments the error from the Lucas point is quite small. The question is how much the parameters of estimated decision equations, such as consumption and labour supply equations of the household sector, change when a government policy variable changes. For many policy variables and equations these changes may not be very great. The errors in the multipliers that result from not accounting for the parameter changes may be much smaller than, say, the errors that result from aggregation. At any rate, how important the Lucas point is quantitatively is currently an open question.

One encouraging feature regarding the Lucas point is the following. Assume that for an equation or set of equations the parameters change considerably when a given policy variable changes. Assume also that the policy variable changes frequently. In this case the method in Chapter 8 is likely to weed out a model that includes this equation or set of equations. The model is obviously misspecified, and the method should be able to pick up this misspecification if there have been frequent changes in the policy variable. It is thus unlikely that a model that suffers from the Lucas criticism will be accepted as the best approximation of the structure.

One may, of course, still be misled regarding the Lucas point if the policy variable has changed not at all or very little in the past. In this case the model will still be misspecified, but the misspecification has not been given a chance to be picked up in the data. The model may thus be accepted when in fact it is seriously misspecified with respect to the effects of the policy variable on the endogenous variables. One should thus be wary of drawing conclusions about the effects of seldom-changed policy variables unless one has strong reasons for believing that the Lucas point is not quantitatively important for the particular policy variable in question.

D. The Sims Approach

Another role for theory in the construction of empirical models has been stressed recently by Sims (1980). This role is at the opposite end of the spectrum from that advocated by Hansen and Sargent – namely, it is very limited. Sims does not trust even the exclusionary restrictions imposed by the traditional approach; he argues instead for the specification of vector autoregressive equations, where each variable is specified to be a function of its own lagged values and the lagged values of other variables. (An important early study in this area is that of Phillips, 1959.) Although this approach imposes some restrictions on the data – in particular, the number of variables to use, the lengths of the lags, and (sometimes) cross-equation restrictions on the coefficients – the restrictions are in general less restrictive than the exclusionary ones used by the traditional approach.

Although it is again an open question whether Sims' approach will lead to better models, it should be possible to answer this question by comparing models based on this approach to models based on other approaches. Some results that bear on this question are presented in this book. The method in Chapter 8 is used to compare my US model to two vector autoregressive models. The vector autoregressive models are presented in Section 5.2, and the comparison is discussed in Section 8.5.

E. Long-run Constraints

In much macroeconomic modelling in which theory is used, various long-run constraints are imposed on the model. Consider, for example, the question of the long-run trade-off between inflation and unemployment. Economists with such diverse views as Tobin and Lucas seem to agree with the Friedman-Phelps proposition that there is no long-run trade-off. (See Tobin, 1980, p. 39 and Lucas, 1981, p. 560. For the original discussion of the Friedman–Phelps proposition see Friedman, 1968 and Phelps, 1967.) Accepting this proposition clearly colours the way in which one thinks about macroeconomic issues. Lucas, for example, points out that much of the recent work in macroeconomic theory has been concerned with trying to reconcile this long-run proposition with the observed short-run fluctuations in the economy (1981, p. 561). The imposition of long-run constraints of this type clearly has important effects on the entire modelling exercise, including the modelling of the short run.

Although it is difficult to argue this in the abstract, my feeling is that long-run constraints may be playing too much of a role in recent macro-economic work. Consider the two possible types of errors associated with a particular constraint. The first is that an incorrect constraint is imposed. This error will lead to a misspecified model, and the misspecification may be large if the constraint has had important effects on the specification of the model and if it is a poor approximation. The second type of error is that a correct constraint is not imposed. Depending on the set-up, this type of error may not lead to a misspecified model, but only one in which the coefficient estimates are inefficient. At any rate, it is my feeling that the first type of error may be more serious in practice than the second type, and if this is so, long-run constraints should be imposed with considerable caution. It is not obvious, for example, that the assumption of no long-run trade-off between inflation and unemployment warrants so much con-fidence that it should be imposed on models, given the severe restrictions that it implies.

This argument about long-run constraints will be made clearer in Section 3.1.6 in the discussion of my theoretical model. Again, however, this issue of the imposition of long-run constraints can be tested (in the long run) by comparing models based on different constraints.

F. Theoretical Simulation Models

With the growth of computer technology there has been an increase in the number of theoretical models that are analyzed by simulation techniques.

The main advantage of using these techniques is that much larger and more complicated models can be specified; one need not be restricted by analytic tractability in the specification of the model. A disadvantage of using the techniques is that the properties of the model may depend on the particular set of parameters and functions chosen for the simulation, and one may get a distorted picture of the properties. Although one can guard against this situation somewhat by performing many experiments with different sets of parameters and functions, simulation results are not a perfect substitute for analytic results.

The relationship between simulation exercises and empirical work is not always clearly understood, and it will be useful to consider this issue. If simulation techniques are merely looked upon as a substitute for analytic techniques when the latter are not feasible to use, then the relationship between simulation exercises and empirical work is no different from the relationship between analytic exercises and empirical work. The results of analysing theoretical models are used to guide empirical specifications, and it does not matter how the theoretical model is analysed. An example of the use of simulation techniques in this way is presented in this book. The theoretical model discussed in Chapter 3 is analysed by simulation techniques, and the results from this model are used to guide the specification of the econometric model in Chapter 4. Had it been feasible to analyse the model in Chapter 3 by analytic techniques, this would have been done, and provided no new insights about the model were gained from this, the econometric specifications in Chapter 4 would have been the same. In this way of looking at the issue, the difference between simulation and analytic techniques is not important: the methodology is really the same in both cases.

Note with respect to empirical work that the type of theoretical simulation model just discussed is not an end in itself; it is merely a stepping-stone to the specification of the equations to be estimated. The data are used in the estimation and analysis of the derived empirical model (derived in a loose sense – see Section 2.2) not in the theoretical model itself. This type of theoretical simulation model is quite different from the type that has come to be used in the field of applied general equilibrium analysis. A good discussion of the methodology of this field is contained in Mansur and Whalley (1981), and it will be useful to review this methodology briefly to make sure there is no confusion between it and the methodology generally followed in macroeconomics.

There are two main steps in the construction of an applied general equilibrium model. The first is to construct for a given period (usually a particular year) a 'benchmark equilibrium data set', which is a collection of data in which equilibrium conditions of an assumed underlying equilibrium model are satisfied. Considerable data adjustment is needed in this step because the existing data are generally not detailed enough (and sometimes not conceptually right) for a general equilibrium model. The data, for example, may not be mutually consistent in the sense that the model equilibrium conditions are not satisfied in the data. Most benchmark equilibrium data sets satisfy the following four sets of equilibrium conditions: (1) demand equals supplies for all commodities, (2) non-positive profits are made in all industries, (3) all domestic agents (including the government) have demands that satisfy their budget constraints, and (4) the economy is in zero external balance. Condition (3) usually involves treating the residual profit return to equity as a contractual cost.

The second step is to choose the functional forms and parameter values for the model. These are chosen in such a way that the model is 'calibrated' to the benchmark equilibrium data set. The fundamental assumption involved in this calibration is that the economy is in equilibrium in the particular year. The restriction on the parameter values is that they replicate the 'observed equilibrium' as an equilibrium solution of the model. The values are determined by solving the equations that represent the equilibrium conditions of the model, using the data on prices and quantities that characterize the benchmark equilibirum. Depending on the functional forms used, the observed equilibrium may not be sufficient to determine uniquely the parameter values. If the values are not uniquely determined, some of them must be chosen ahead of time (that is, before the model is solved to get the other values). The values chosen ahead of time are generally various elasticities of substitution; they are often chosen by searching the literature for estimated values.

Once the parameters are chosen, the model is ready to be used for policy analysis. Various exogenous variables can be changed, and the model can be solved for these changes. The differences between the solution values and the values in the data set are the estimates of the effects of the policy change. These estimates are general equilibrium estimates in the sense that the entire general equilibrium model is solved to obtain them.

The difference between this second type of theoretical simulation model and the first type should be clear. The second type is an end in itself with respect to empirical work: models of this type are used to make empirical statements. The main problem with this methodology, as is well known by people in the field, is that there is no obvious way of testing whether the model is a good approximation to the truth. The models are not estimated in the usual sense, and there is no way to use a method like the one in Chapter 8 to compare alternative models. Each model fits the data set perfectly, usually with room to spare in the sense that many parameter values are typically chosen ahead of time. This is contrasted with models of the first type, which can be indirectly tested by testing the empirical models that are derived from them (see the discussion in Section 2.3).

It is unclear at this stage whether the applied general equilibrium models will become more like standard econometric models and thus more capable of being tested, or whether they will remain in their current 'quasi-empirical' state. Whatever the case, the main point for this book is that the methodology followed here is quite different from the methodology currently followed in applied general equilibrium analysis.

2. The Transition from Theoretical to Econometric Models

The transition from theoretical models to empirical models is probably the least satisfying aspect of macroeconomic work. One is usually severely constrained by the quantity and quality of the available data, and many restrictive assumptions are generally needed in the transition from the theory to the data. In other words, considerable 'theorizing' occurs at this point, and it is usually theory that is much less appealing than that of the purely theoretical model. Many examples of this will be seen in Chapter 4 in the discussion of the transition from the theoretical model in Chapter 3 to the econometric model in Chapter 4. This section contains a general discussion of the steps that are usually followed in the construction of an econometric model.

A. Step 1: Data Collection and the Choice of Variables and Identities

The first step is to collect the raw data, create the variables of interest from the raw data, and separate the variables into exogenous variables, endogenous variables explained by identities, and endogenous variables explained by stochastic equations. The data should match as closely as possible the variables in the theoretical model. In macroeconomic work this match is usually not very close because of the highly aggregated nature of the macro data. Theoretical models are usually formulated in terms of individual agents (households, firms, and the like), whereas the macro data pertain to entire sectors (household, firm, and the like). There is little that can be done about this problem, and for some it calls into question the usefulness of using theoretical models of individual agents to guide the specification of macroeconometric models. It may be, in other words, that better macroeconometric models can be developed using less micro-based theories. This is an open question, and it is another example of an issue that can be tested in the long run by comparing different models.

There are many special features and limitations of almost any data base that one should be aware of, and one of the most important aspects of macroeconometric work, perhaps the most important, is to know one's data well. Knowledge of how to deal with data comes in part through experience and in part from reading about how others have done it; it is difficult to learn in the abstract. Appendixes A and B of this book provide an example of the collection of the data for my model.

It is important, if possible, to have the data meet the adding-up constraints that were mentioned at the beginning of this chapter. In addition to such obvious things as having the data satisfy income identities, it is useful to have the data satisfy balance-sheet constraints. For the US data this requires linking the data from the Flow of Funds Accounts to those from the National Income and Product Accounts. This is discussed in Chapter 4 and in Appendix A. The linking of these two data bases is a somewhat tedious task and is a good example of the time-consuming work that is involved in the collection of data.

The data base may be missing observations on variables that are essential for the construction of the model. In such cases, rather than giving up, it may be possible to construct estimates of the missing data. If, for example, the data for a particular variable are annual, whereas quarterly data are needed, it may be possible, using related quarterly variables, to create quarterly data from the annual data by interpolating. There are also more sohisticated procedures for constructing missing observations (see, for example, Chow and Lin, 1971). Appendix B provides a number of examples of the construction of missing data for my multi-country model.

Although it is easiest to think of the division of endogenous variables into those determined by stochastic equations and those determined by identities as being done in the first step, the choice of identities is not independent of the choice of explanatory variables in the stochastic equations. If a given explanatory variable is not exogenous and is not determined by a stochastic equation, it must be determined by an identity. It is thus not possible to list all the identities until the stochastic equations are completely specified.

B.   Step 2: Treatment of Unobserved Variables

Most theoretical models contain unobserved variables, and one of the most difficult aspects of the transition to econometric specifications is dealing with these variables. Much of what is referred to as the '*ad hoc*' nature of macroeconomic modelling occurs at this point. If a theoretical model is explicit about the determinants of the unobserved variables and if the determinants are observed, there is, of course, no real problem. The problem is that many models are not explicit about this, and so 'extra' modelling or theorizing is needed at this point.

Expectations   The most common unobserved variables in macroeconomics are expectations. A common practice in empirical work is to assume that expected future values of a variable are a function of the curent and past values of the variable. The current and past values of the variable are then used as 'proxies' for the expected future values. Given the importance of expectations in most models, it will be useful to consider this procedure in some detail.

Consider first the following example:

$$(1) \qquad y_t = \alpha_0 + \alpha_1 E_{t-1} x_{t+1} + u_t,$$

where $E_{t-1} x_{t+1}$ is the expected value of x_{t+1} based on information through period $t - 1$. A typical assumption is that $E_{t-1} x_{t+1}$ is a function of current and past values of x:

$$(2) \qquad E_{t-1} x_{t+1} = \lambda_1 x_t + \lambda_2 x_{t-1} + \ldots + \lambda_n x_{t-n+1},$$

where it is assumed that x_t is observed at the beginning of period t. Given (2), two procedures can be followed to obtain an estimatable equation. One is to substitrue (2) into (1) and simply regress y_t on the current and past values of x. (Other variables can also be used in (2) and then substituted into (1). If, say, z_t affects $E_{t-1} x_{t+1}$, then z_t would be used as an explanatory variable in the y_t regression.) A priori restrictions on the λ_i coefficients (that is, on the shape of the lag distribution) are sometimes imposed before estimation. Lagged values of time series variables tend to be highly correlated, and it is usually difficult to get estimates of lag distributions that seem sensible without imposing some restrictions. If no restrictions are imposed on the λ_i coefficients, α_1 cannot be identified.

The other procedure is to assume that the lag distribution is geometrically declining, in particular that $\lambda_i = \lambda^i, i = 1, \ldots, \infty$. Given this assumption, one can derive the following equation to estimate:

$$(3) \qquad y_t = \alpha_0(1 - \lambda) + \lambda \alpha_1 x_t + \lambda y_{t-1} + u_t - \lambda u_{t-1}.$$

The coefficient of the lagged dependent variable in this equation, λ, is the coefficient of the lag distribution. It appears both as the coefficient of the lagged dependent variable and as the coefficient of u_{t-1}, and although this restriction should be taken into account in estimation work, it seldom is. Sometimes equations like (3) are estimated under the assumption of serial correlation of the error term (that is, an assumption like $v_t = \varrho v_{t-1} + \varepsilon_t$, where v_t denotes the error term in (3), but this is not the correct way of accounting for the λ restriction.

There is a nonexpectational model that leads to an equation similar to (3), which is the following simple lagged adjustment model. Let y_t^* be the 'desired' value of y_t and assume that it is a linear function of x_t:

$$(4) \qquad y_t^* = \alpha_0 + \alpha_1 x_t.$$

Assume next that y_t only partially adjusts to y_t^* each period, with adjustment coefficient g:

$$(5) \qquad y_t - y_{t-1} = \gamma(y_t^* - y_{t-1}) + u_t.$$

Equations (4) and (5) can be combined to yield

(6) $$y_t = \lambda a_0 + \lambda a_1 x_t + (1 - \gamma)y_{t-1} + u_t.$$

Equation (6) is in the same form as (3) except for the restriction on the error term in (3). As noted earlier, the restriction on the error term in (3) is usually ignored, which means that in practice there is little attempt to distinguish between the expectations model and the lagged adjustment model. It may be for most problems that the data are not capable of distinguishing between the two models. The problem of distinguishing between the two is particularly difficult if the u_t error terms in (1) and (5) are assumed to be serially correlated, because in this case the differences in the properties of the error terms in the derived equations (3) and (6) are fairly subtle. At any rate, it is usually the case that no attempt is made to distinguish between the expectations model and the lagged adjustment model.

Two other points about (3) should be noted. First, if there is another variable in the equation, say z_t, the implicit assumption that is being made when this equation is estimated is that the expectations of z are formed using the same coefficient λ that is used in forming the expectations of x. In other words, the shape of the two lag distributions is assumed to be the same. This may be, of course, a very restrictive assumption. Second, if there is another future expected value of x in (1), say $a_2 E_{t-1} x_{t+2}$, and if this expectation is generated as

(7) $$E_{t-1}x_{t+2} = \lambda E_{t-1}x_{t+1} + \lambda^2 x_t + \lambda^3 x_{t-1} + \ldots,$$

then (3) is unchanged except for a different interpretation of the coefficient of x_t. The coefficient in this case is $\lambda(a_1 + 2a_2\lambda)$ instead of λa_1. The same equation would be estimated in this case, although it is not possible to identify a_1 and a_2.

It should be clear that this treatment of expectations is somewhat unsatisfying. Agents may look at more than merely the current and past values of a variable in forming an expectation of it and, even if they do not, the shapes of the lag distributions may be quite different from the shapes usually imposed in econometric work. The treatment of expectations is clearly an important area for future work. An alternative treatment to the one just presented is the assumption that expectations are rational. This means that agents form expectations by first forming expectations of the exogenous variables (in some manner that must be specified) and then solving the model using these expectations. The predicted values of the endogenous variables from this solution are the expected values. The assumption of rational expectations poses a number of difficult computational problems when one is dealing with large-scale non-linear models, but many of these problems are now capable of solution. Chapter 11 discusses the solution and estimation of rational expectations models.

It is by no means obvious that the assumption that expectations are rational is a good approximation to the way that expectations are actually formed. The assumption implies that agents know the model, and this may not be realistic for many agents. It would be nice to test assumptions that are in between the simple assumption that expectations of a variable are a function of its current and past values and the assumption that expectations are rational. One possibility is to assume that expectations of a variable are a function not only of its current and past values but also of the current and past values of other variables. To implement this, the variable in question could be regressed on a set of variables and the predicted values from this regression taken to be the expected values. In other words, one could estimate a small model of how expectations are formed before estimating the basic model. Expectations are not rational in this case because they are not predictions from the basic model, but they are based on more information than merely the current and past values of one variable. An example of the use of this assumption is presented in Section 4.1.3. Although, as will be seen, this application was not successful, there is clearly room for more tests of this kind.

Other Unobserved Variables   In models in which disequilibrium is a possibility, there is sometimes a distinction between 'unconstrained' and 'constrained' (or 'notional' and 'actual') decisions. An unconstrained decision is one that an agent would make if there were no constraints on its decision variables other than the standard budget constraints. A constrained decision is one in which other constraints are imposed; it is also the actual decision. In the model in Chapter 3, for example, which does allow for the possibility of disequilibrium, a household may be constrained in how much it can work. A household's unconstrained consumption decision is the amount it would consume if the constraint were not binding, and the constrained decision is the amount it actually chooses to consume given the constraint. In models of this type the unconstrained decisions are observed only if the constraints are not binding, and so this is another example of the existence of unobserved variables. The treatment of these variables is a difficult problem in empirical work, and it is also a problem for which no standard procedure exists. The way in which the variables are handled in my model is discussed in Section 4.1.3.

C. Step 3: Specification of the Stochastic Equations

The next step is to specify the stochastic equations, that is, to write down the equations to be estimated. Since the stochastic equations are the key part of any econometric model, this step is of crucial importance. If theory has not indicated the functional forms and lag lengths of the equations, a number of versions of each equation may be written down to be tried, the different versions corresponding to different functional forms and lag lengths. If the theoretical approach is the traditional one, theory has presumably chosen the LHS and RHS variables. The specification of the stochastic equations also relies on the treatment of the unobserved variables from step 2; the extra theorizing in step 2 also guides the choice of the RHS variables.

Theory generally has little to say about the stochastic features of the model, that is, about where and how the error terms enter the equations. The most common procedure is merely to add an error term to each stochastic equation. This is usually done regardless of the functional form of the equation. For example, the term $+ u_{it}$ would be added to equation i regardless of whether the equation were in linear or logarithmic form. If the equation is in log form, this treatment implies that the error term affects the level of the LHS variable multiplicatively. This somewhat cavalier treatment of error terms is generally done for convenience; it is another example of an unsatisfying aspect of the transition to econometric models, although it is probably not as serious as most of the other problems.

D.   Step 4: Estimation

Once the equations of a model have been written down in a form that can be estimated, the next step is to estimate them. Much experimentation usually takes place at this step. Different functional forms and lag lengths are tried, and RHS variables are dropped if they have coefficient estimates of the wrong expected sign. Variables with coefficient estimates of the right sign may also be dropped if the estimates have t-statistics that are less than about two in absolute value, although practice varies on this.

If at this step things are not working out very well in the sense that very few significant coefficient estimates of the correct sign are being obtained, one may go back and rethink the theory or the transition from the theory to the estimated equations. This process may lead to new equations to try, and perhaps to better results. This back-and-forth movement between theory and results can be an important part of the empirical work.

The initial estimation technique that is used is usually a limited information technique, such as 2SLS. These techniques have the advantage that one can experiment with a particular equation without worrying very much about the other equations in the model. Knowledge of the general features of the other equations is used in the choice of the first-stage regressors (FSRs) for the 2SLS technique, for example, but one does not need to know the exact features of each equation when making this choice. If a full information technique is used, it is usually used at the end of the search process to estimate the final version of the model. If the full information estimates are quite different from the limited information ones, it may again be necessary to go back and rethink the theory and the transition. In particular, this may indicate that the version of the model that has been chosen by the limited information searching is seriously misspecified.

Sometimes ordinary least-squares (OLS) is used in the searching process even though the model is simultaneous. This is a cheap but risky method. Because the OLS estimates are inconsistent, one may be led to a version of the model that is seriously misspecified. This problem presumably will be caught when a consistent limited information or full information technique is used, at which point one will be forced to go back and search using the consistent limited information technique. It seems better merely to begin with the latter in the first place and eliminate this potential problem. The extra cost involved in using, say, 2SLS over OLS is small.

E. Step 5: Testing and Analysis

The next step after the model has been estimated is to test and analyse it. This step, it seems to me, is the one that has been the most neglected in macroeconomic research. Procedures for testing and analysing models are discussed in Chapters 7–10; they will not be discussed here except to note the two that have been most commonly used. First, the principal way that models have been tested in the past is by computing predicted values from deterministic simulations, where the accuracy of the predictions is usually examined by calculating root mean squared errors (Sections 8.2 and 8.3). Second, the main way that the properties of models have been examined is by computing multipliers from deterministic simulations (Section 9.2). As will be seen, both of these procedures, especially the first, are subject to criticism.

It may also be the case that things are not working out very well at this testing and analysis step. Poor fits may be obtained, and multipliers that seem (according to one's priori veiws) too large or too small may also be obtained. This may also lead one to rethink the theory, the transition, or both, and perhaps to try alternative specifications. In other words, the back-and-forth movement between theory and results may occur at both the estimation and analysis steps.

F. General Remarks

The back-and-forth movement between theory and results may yield a model that fits the data well and seems on other grounds to be quite good, when it is in fact a poor approximation to the structure. If one searches hard enough, it is usually possible with macro time series data to come up with what seems to be a good model. The searching for models in this way is sometimes called 'data mining' and sometimes 'specification searches', depending on one's mood. A number of examples of this type of searching are presented in Chapter 4. Fortunately, there is a way of testing whether one has mined the data in an inappropriate way, which is to do outside sample tests. If a model is poorly specified, it should not fit well outside of the sample period for which it was estimated, even though it looks good within sample. It is thus possible to test for misspecification by examining outside sample results, and this is what the method in Chapter 8 does in testing for misspecification. (There is, however, a subtle form of data mining that even the method in Chapter 8 cannot account for. This is discussed in Section 8.4.5.)

Because of the dropping of variables with wrong signs and (possibly) the back-and-forth movement from multiplier results to theory, an econometric model is likely to have multiplier properties that are similar to what one expects from the theory. Therefore, the fact that an econometric model has properties that are consistent with the theory is in no way a confirmation of the model. Models must be tested using methods like the one in Chapter 8, not by examining the 'reasonableness' of their multiplier properties.

It should also be emphasized that in many cases the data may not contain enough information to decide a particular issue. If, for example, tax rates have not been changed very much over the sample period, it may not be possible to discriminate between quite different hypotheses regarding the effects of tax rate changes on behaviour. It may also be difficult to discriminate between different functional forms for an equation, such as linear versus logarithmic. In Chapter 4 a number of examples are presented of the inability to discriminate between alternative hypotheses. When this happens there is little that one can do about it except to wait for more data and be cautious about making policy recommendations that are sensitive to the different hypotheses.

3. Testing Theoretical Models

This is a good time to consider the second methodological question mentioned in Chapter 1, namely, what do econometric results have to say about the validity of theories? It should be clear by now that transitions from theoretical models to econometric models are typically not very tight. It may be that more than one theoretical model is consistent with a given econometric model. If this is so, then finding out that an econometric model is, say, the best approximation among all econometric models is not necessarily a finding that a particular theory that is consistent with the model is valid. One may thus be forced to make weaker conclusions about theoretical models than about econometric models.

If it is possible to test the assumptions of a theoretical model directly, it may not be the case that one is forced to make weaker conclusions about theoretical models. The problem in macroeconomics is that very few assumptions seem capable of direct tests. Part of the problem is the aggregation; it is not really possible to test directly assumptions about, say, the way an entire sector chooses its decision variables. A related problem is that many macroeconomic assumptions pertain to the way in which agents interact with each other, and these assumptions are difficult to test in isolation. Assumptions about expectations are also difficult or impossible to test directly because expectations are generally not observed. Even if expectations were observed, however, it would not be possible to test the rational expectations assumption directly. In this case one needs a complete model to test the assumption. One is thus forced in macroeconomics to rely primarily on testing theories by testing econometric models that are derived (however loosely) from them. This procedure of testing theories by testing their implications rather than their assumptions is Friedman's view (1953) about the way theories should be tested. One does not, however, have to subscribe to Friedman's view about economic testing in general in order to believe that it holds for macroeconomics. Macroeconomic theories are tested indirectly not always out of choice, but out of necessity.

Given the indirect testing of theories and the sometimes loose transitions from theories to empirical specifications, it is not clear that one ought to talk in macroeconomics about theories being 'true' or 'false'. Macroeconomics is not like physics, where on average theories are linked more closely to empirical tests. I have suggested (Fair 1974) that it may be better in macroeconomics to talk about theories being 'useful' or 'not useful'. A theory is useful if it aids in the specification of empirical relationships that one would not already have thought of from a simpler theory and that turn out to be good approximations. Otherwise, it is not useful. Although how one wants to label theories is a semantic question, the terms 'useful' and 'not useful' do highlight the fact that theories in macroeconomics are not as closely linked to empirical tests as are many theories in physics.

4.   Expected Quality of Macroeconometric Models in the Long Run

An interesting question is how good one expects macroeconometric models to be in the long run, say in twenty or thirty years. It may be that behaviour is so erratic, and things like aggregation problems so severe, that no model will be very good. This will show up in large estimated variances of prediction errors by the method in Chapter 8 and probably in large estimates of the degree of misspecification. Another way of stating this is that the structure of the economy may be too unstable, or our potential ability to approximate closely a stable structure too poor, to lead to accurate models. If this is true, models will never be of much use for policy purposes. They may be of limited use for short-run forecasting, but even here probably only in conjunction with subjective adjustments.

My research is obviously based on the premise that there is enough structural stability to warrant further work on trying to approximate the structure of the economy well. This is, of course, a premise that can only be verified or refuted in the long run, and there is little more that can be said about it now. It is interesting to note that the extensive use of subjective adjustments by the commercial model-builders and their lack of much scientific research on the models may indicate lack of confidence in a stable structure.

It is also interesting to note, as mentioned in Chapter 1, that the lack of confidence in large-scale models has led to research on much smaller ones. In one sense this may be a reasonable reaction, and in another sense not. If the lack of confidence is a lack of confidence in a stable structure, the reaction does not seem sensible. It seems quite unlikely that the structure would be unstable in such a way as to lead small models to approximate it less poorly than large models. One should instead just give up the game and do something else. If, on the other hand, the lack of confidence in large-scale models is a feeling that they have gone in wrong directions, it may be sensible to back up for a while. In this case the premise is still that the structure is stable, and the issue is merely how best to proceed to try to approximate it well.

References

Chow, Gregory C. (1964), A comparison of alternative estimators for simultaneous equations. *Econometrica*, 32, 532–53.

Chow, Gregory C. and Lin, An-loh (1971), Best linear unbiased interpolation, distribution and extrapolation of time series by related series. *Review of Economics and Statistics*, 53, 372–5.

Fair, Ray (1974), *A Model of Macroeconomic Activity*, Vol. 1: *The Theoretical Model*. Ballinger, Cambridge, Mass.

Friedman, Milton (1953), *Essays in Positive Economics*. University of Chicago Press, Chicago.

Friedman, Milton (1968). The role of monetary policy. *American Economic Review*, 58, 1–17.

Hansen, Lars P. and Sargent, Thomas J. (1980), Formulating and estimating dynamic linear rational expectations models. *Journal of Economic Dynamics and Control*, 2, 7–46.

Lucas, Robert E., Jr (1976). Econometric policy evaluation: critique. *The Phillips Curve and Labor Markets*, ed. by K. Brunner and A. H. Meltzer. North-

Holland, Amsterdam, pp. 19–46.

Lucas, Robert E., Jr (1981), Tobin and monetarism: a review article. *Journal of Economic Literature*, 19, 558–67.

Mansur, Ahsan, and Whalley, John (1981), Numerical specification of applied general equilibrium models: estimation, calibration, and data. Center for the Study of International Economic Relations, Working Paper No. 8106C, University of Western Ontario.

Phelps, Edmund S. (1967), Phillips curves, expectations of inflation and optimal unemployment over time. *Economica*, 34, 254–81.

Phillips, A. W. (1959). Estimation of parameters in a system of stochastic differential equations. *Biometrika*, 46, 67–76.

Sims, Christopher A. (1980), Macroeconomics and reality. *Econometrica*, 48, 1–48.

Tobin, James (1980), *Asset Accumulation and Economic Activity*. University of Chicago Press, Chicago.

10

Improving Economic Forecasting With Bayesian Vector Autoregression

Richard M. Todd

Economic forecasting is often referred to as an art, perhaps because it involves not only data and groups of equations, or statistical *models*, but also the forecaster's personal beliefs about how the economy behaves and where it is heading at any moment. Artistry is an appropriate metaphor for what economic forecasters commonly do: blend data and personal beliefs according to a subjective, undocumented procedure that other forecasters cannot duplicate.[1] This is not the only way to achieve that blend, however. The Bayesian approach to statistics, a general method for combining beliefs with data, suggests an objective procedure for blending beliefs and data in economic forecasting models. This procedure provides a framework that forecasters can use to document and discuss their beliefs, which can help make economic forecasting more of a science and less of an art.

Today's most widely used economic forecasting models are not usually discussed in terms of the Bayesian approach, but they can be. When viewed this way most of them seem too rigid, allowing their human managers to express beliefs within the models only in forms that are often too vague or too precise to accurately represent the managers' true beliefs. This may partly explain why these models' forecasts often seem implausible to the models' managers, and thus why managers often subjectively adjust those forecasts before presenting them to the models' users.

One type of economic forecasting model, known as the *Bayesian vector autoregression* (BVAR) model, has been developed explicitly along Bayesian lines and seems to be an improvement over other types of forecasting models. BVAR procedures give modellers more flexibility in expressing the true nature of their beliefs as well as an objective way to combine those beliefs with the historical record. A specific version of the procedures, developed by Minnesota researchers, has been used to build

---

[1] This practice is well known among economists, but is not often discussed in print. See Litterman and Supel 1983 and Litterman 1984 for some critical comments.

This article first appeared in the Federal Reserve Bank of Minneapolis *Quarterly Review*, Fall 1984, pp. 18–29. The views expressed here are those of the author and not necessarily those of the Federal Bank of Minneapolis or the Federal Reserve System.

models whose unadjusted forecasts seem to be as accurate as the subjectively adjusted forecasts of other common models. The fact that BVAR
models forecast well without subjective adjustment also allows them to
objectively estimate answers to questions about future events and probabilities that subjectively adjusted models cannot as plausibly address.

A Bayesian View of Economic Forecasting

All statistical forecasting models combine, in some way, information from
historical data with information supplied by the builders of the model.
Because modellers must supply at least some information before they
examine data, and because modellers presumably supply information they
think will improve the model's forecasting ability, the information they
supply is known as their *prior beliefs* (or simply their *priors*) about the best
way to forecast. Forecasting techniques differ in how they represent prior
beliefs and how much weight they place on them. BVAR models have
been developed to let modellers represent their beliefs more accurately
and to combine those beliefs with the information in historical data
according to a standard, objective procedure.

Beliefs and Forecasts

At an elementary level, all forecasting procedures clearly rely on at least a
minimal level of prior belief. For example, to forecast any given variable a
modeller must at least suggest which currently known variables are related
to it and might therefore be useful in forecasting it. The final forecasting
model might not use all of the suggested variables, and data may be used to
eliminate some variables from the model. But in picking the candidate
variables for the model, the modeller must rely on beliefs derived from
prior knowledge of the theory and practice of economics and statistics. The
same is true for the types of algebraic formulas that express the relationships among the variables in the model (whether they are linear or quadratic,
for example); data may be used to pick the final types of formulas, but only
from among a set of candidates previously picked by the modeller. The
common transformations of economic data that are used in forecasting
models – such as detrending, deseasonalizing, interpolating, and linearizing
by means of ratios or logarithms – are also chosen in this way.

Beyond this minimal level of prior belief, the modeller might also have
views on the candidate variables or formulas most likely to produce good
forecasts or even on the exact numerical relationships between the variables
in the model and the variables to be forecasted. One major statistical
theory, *Bayesian decision theory*, holds that modellers can be thought of as
having prior beliefs in the form of probabilities about which of the possible

models will forecast best. Bayesian decision theory explains the best way that data can then be used to revise these prior probabilities. Essentially all forecasting procedures, even supposedly non-Bayesian procedures in which the role of prior beliefs is not at first apparent, can be interpreted as at least approximating a Bayesian procedure in which data are used to revise certain implicit prior beliefs.

Complete Ignorance

A forecasting model incorporating only minimal prior beliefs can be constructed by selecting a group, or *vector*, of variables to forecast, allowing all the variables to interact linearly with their own and each other's current and past values, and using historical data to determine the quantitative impact that each variable has on its own future values and the future values of the other variables. Because such a model relates future values of a vector of variables to past values of that vector, it is known as a *vector autoregression* (VAR) model. Because it is only minimally restricted by the modeller's prior beliefs, it is more particularly known as an *unrestricted* vector autoregression (UVAR) model. Economists rarely have enough data to construct UVAR models, especially ones with more than a few variables, that forecast as well as models that supplement the data with more informative prior beliefs.

From a Bayesian point of view, UVAR models more or less let the data speak for themselves. To see this more clearly, consider a simple model built to forecast just the money supply and real output. The UVAR modeller might use economic and statistical knowledge to pick linear formulas for the current and two previous quarterly values of some measure of the money supply (*MONY*) and real (inflation-adjusted) gross national product (*RGNP*) as well as some constant terms (k_m and k_r). Beyond these minimal and relatively uninformative priors, however, the UVAR modeller would essentially claim to be ignorant. Forecasts of each variable in the model would be based on current and past values of all variables in the model, or

(1) $MONY_{t+1} = k_m + a_0 MONY_t + a_1 MONY_{t-1} + a_2 MONY_{t-2}$
$+ b_0 RGNP_t + b_1 RGNP_{t-1} + b_2 RGNP_{t-2} + m_{t+1}$

(2) $RGNP_{t+1} = k_r + c_0 MONY_t + c_1 MONY_{t-1} + c_2 MONY_{t-2}$
$+ d_0 RGNP_t + d_1 RGNP_{t-1} + d_2 RGNP_{t-2} + r_{t+1}$

(where m_{t+1} and r_{t+1} represent the errors that will occur when $MONY_{t+1}$ and $RGNP_{t+1}$, respectively, are predicted from a constant term and the three most recent values of both). Furthermore, from a Bayesian point of view, all possible values of the UVAR model's coefficients [the k's, a's, b's, c's, and d's in equations (1) and (2)], which determine the quantitative impact each variable has on the model's forecasts, would be treated as equally likely. This frequently makes the prior beliefs used in this procedure vaguer than the modeller's true beliefs; most modellers probably don't really believe that all possible values are equally likely even though the UVAR model is estimated as though they are. For example, a modeller might believe that positive values of b_0, b_1, and b_2 are more likely than negative values to lead to good forecasts. Nonetheless, the final values of these coefficients would be chosen without any restrictions to represent these prior beliefs. A simple statistical procedure (ordinary least-squares, or OLS, regression) would pick the coefficient values that best explain the historically observed patterns of interaction among the chosen variables.

Small UVAR models such as the one described above sometimes forecast fairly well, but economists have long recognized that UVAR models with more than a few variables generally do not. Since forecasters are often called upon to forecast large groups of variables and the relationships between them, this is a serious limitation of UVAR models.

The forecasting problems of large UVAR models stem from the fact that economists often have too little data to isolate in a model's coefficients only the stable and dependable relationships among its variables. The statistical procedure used to estimate the coefficients (OLS regression) picks values which best explain the available data, data in which the stable relationships among variables have been obscured by numerous random effects. Furthermore, because current and past values of each variable appear in every equation of a UVAR model, the number of coefficients to be estimated is large compared to the number of observations on the variables. With so many coefficients available to explain so few observations, the estimated coefficients can explain the data very well – too well, in fact. The coefficients are subject to overfitting, a sort of red-herring effect. The statistical procedure chooses the coefficients to explain, or *fit*, not only the most salient features of the historical data, which are often the stable, enduring relationships between variables that are most useful for forecasting. The coefficients are so numerous that the statistical procedure can choose them to also fit many of the less important features of the historical data, features which often reflect merely accidental or random relationships that will not recur and are of no use in forecasting. *Overfitting* refers to this incorporation of useless or misleading relationships in the coefficients of a model. It tends to make large UVAR model forecasts inaccurate and overly sensitive to changes in economic variables.

Complete Certainty or Complete Ignorance

The tranditional solution to the overfitting problem of large UVAR models has been to use prior beliefs to reduce the number of coefficients to be estimated. In the *structural econometric* models that are wisely used for economic forecasting, this is done by including in each equation of the model only a few variables (or lags of variables) that economic theory suggests are most directly related to the variable that the equation forecasts. (This is an attempt to use theory and statistics to recreate the basic structure of the economy; hence the model's name.) Economic theory is thus the main source of priors in structural models, and these priors are built into the model by excluding most variables from most equations.

Note that excluding variables from an equation amounts to certainty that their coefficients are zero. Certainty is an absolute belief, not subject to revision by any amount of historical evidence. So such *exclusion restrictions* also amount to assigning coefficients of zero to the variables regardless of historical evidence. Although these restrictions can prevent overfitting in a structural model, they are often too rigid to accurately express the modeller's true beliefs and tend to cause useful information in the historical data to be ignored.

A given economic theory may imply that some economic variables are related strongly and others are related weakly, or hardly at all. To see how these theoretical implications can be used to overcome overfitting, consider how a modeller using the structural econometric approach might modify the simple UVAR model described above. For example, suppose economic theory and experience led the modeller to believe that next period's real gross national product is mainly affected by that variable's current value, and last period's value of the money supply, while monetary policy generally insulates the money supply from changes in real gross national product. These beliefs would lead the structural modeller to modify the UVAR model (equations (1) and (2)) by excluding all values of RGNP from the MONY equation and excluding all past values of RGNP and all values except the previous period's value of MONY from the RGNP equation. This would be the resulting structural model:

$$(3) \qquad MONY_{t+1} = K_m + A_0 MONY_t + A_1 MONY_{t-1} \\ + A_2 MONY_{t-2} + M_{t+1}$$

$$(4) \qquad RGNP_{t+1} = K_r + C_1 MONY_{t-1} + D_0 RGNP_t + R_{t+1}.$$

Even in so small a model as equations (1) and (2), where overfitting is not nearly as serious as in the large models often used by forecasters, exclusion restrictions cut in half the number of coefficients to be estimated. Because of their smaller number, the coefficients of structural econometric models are less likely than UVAR model coefficients to reflect the useless random relationships among variables. This helps explain why structural econometric models have been the dominant form of large forecasting model for many years.

Although the structural econometric approach does reduce the effects of overfitting, and has been widely used for forecasting, many modellers are likely to find the exclusion restrictions it is based on too extreme and inflexible. Exclusion restrictions probably either overstate or understate the modeller's prior beliefs about the best forecasting model.

On the one hand, by specifying ahead of time that coefficients on excluded variables will be zero no matter what the historical data suggest, the exclusion restrictions imply that the modeller is absolutely confident that the best coefficients for the variables excluded from the equation are zero. This may often exaggerate the modeller's true confidence. The structural modeller above, for example, might have to choose among competing theories about how real gross national product effects the money supply. Even the modeller's preferred theory is unlikely to suggest such sharp distinctions between the effects of current and past values of money and real output on real output as that model's exclusion restrictions imply. Nonetheless, to reduce overfitting the modeller pretends to know for sure that real output doesn't affect money, and that current money and past real output don't affect next period's real output. The data are not allowed to revise these pretended beliefs.

On the other hand, by letting the data completely dictate the coefficients of the included variables, reliance on just exclusion restrictions implies that for those coefficients the structural modeller is as ignorant as a UVAR modeller pretends to be. And here, too, this absolute ignorance about which coefficients lead to good forecasts, or the belief that all of their possible values are equally likely, may often understate the modeller's actual belief. A structural modeller might observe, for example, that in most countries real gross national product rarely changes more than a few per cent per period, even when the money supply has changed a fair amount recently. In the structural model above, these observations might suggest that equation (4)'s coefficient on current RGNP (D_0) should be close to one and its coefficient on past MONY (C_1) should be close to zero. Instead, since the modeller's prior beliefs are only used to restrict the coefficients of the excluded variables (to be exactly zero no matter what), the statistical procedures used to estimate the coefficients of the included variables treat values such as 10 or 10 million to be just as likely as one or zero for these variables.

These statistical procedures are generally similar to OLS regression and also basically pick coefficients, at least for the included variables, so as to best explain the historical data. As a result, serious overfitting of structural model coefficients can still sometimes occur. To avoid this possibility, modellers often estimate several versions of a model (for example, by experimenting with different transformations of the data or different sets of exclusion restrictions) and then pick the one whose combination of plausible coefficients and ability to fit historical data seems best. However, it is hard to document, let alone to evaluate, this highly subjective adaptation of the structural econometric approach.

Besides often distorting the modeller's actual prior beliefs, exclusion restrictions also prevent the modeller from even seeing the historical evidence on the relationship between a forecasted variable and a variable excluded from its equation. In the structural model above, for example, suppose that contrary to the structural modeller's prior belief the historical data would strongly suggest that real gross national product is very useful in forecasting the money supply. If the modeller's belief is expressed as a restriction that excludes RGNP from the equation for MONY, the modeller's chance to be surprised by, and learn from, the data's unexpected information is sharply limited. (This information will show up only indirectly, if at all, in systematic errors in the model's forecasts or in statistics suggesting that the model has not extracted all the useful information in the historical data.)

A More Flexible Expression of Beliefs   Many structural models forecast more accurately than large UVARs, but they still don't satisfy many economists (see, for example, Sims, 1980; Lucas and Sargent, 1981). This has led some to suspect that exclusion restrictions derived from imperfect economic theories may be a barrier to improved forecasting, and that explicitly Bayesian models with the flexibility to more accurately represent prior statistical and economic beliefs might give better forecasts. Bayesian vector autoregression (BVAR) forecasting models have been developed to test this possibility.

At first glance a simple BVAR model might seem to be no different than a simple UVAR model. In both types of models each variable is allowed to depend on the current and past values of all the variables that the modeller has included in the model. The equations of a BVAR model of the money supply and real output, for example, would have the same form as equations (1) and (2).

Although a BVAR model resembles a UVAR model in the form of its equations, it also differs from a UVAR model – and resembles a structural econometric model – by making heavy use of prior beliefs to reduce overfitting. The sources of the prior beliefs and the ways they are used are generally different in a BVAR model than in a structural model, however. Whereas economic theory is the main source of prior beliefs in structural models, it is often secondary to statistical theory and observations in BVAR models. Furthermore, whereas in structural modelling (at least in its textbook form) each coefficient either is set to zero no matter what the data show, or is determined solely by the data no matter what the modeller believes, BVAR modelling doesn't make these sharp distinctions. Instead the BVAR modeller uses prior statistical and economic knowledge to guess which values of all the coefficients will lead to the best forecasts and to specify an extensive system of confidences in each 'guesstimated' coefficient. The modeller then uses a statistical procedure to revise these prior beliefs in light of the evidence in the data and thus to override each of the guesses. The extent to which the data are allowed to revise the modeller's guess about a particular coefficient depends on the modeller's initial confidence in the guess: the more confidence, the less weight given to the patterns in the data and vice-versa.

Thus, unlike structural modellers, BVAR modellers do not try to avoid overfitting by reducing the number of coefficients. Instead, they try to reach that goal by allowing lots of coefficients but reducing the data's influence on them. As long as the BVAR modeller expresses enough confidence in enough coefficient guesses to significantly limit the revisions that accidental patterns in the data can produce, overfitting will generally be limited as well. This is accomplished, however, without preventing important but unexpected historical relationships between variables from being discovered, as when the data strongly override a modeller's guess.[2]

A Close Look at a BVAR Procedure: The Minnesota Prior

Prior beliefs about the coefficients of a forecasting model can come from many sources and take many forms. I have already discussed the sources and forms that are implicitly used in the UVAR and structural modelling approaches. When an explicitly Bayesian approach is used, it becomes clear that the modeller is free to take prior beliefs from many sources and cast them into many forms. Therefore it is impossible to speak of a unique Bayesian or even BVAR approach to forecasting.

In recent years, however, at least one BVAR approach has evolved as an alternative to structural econometric modelling for a variety of economic forecasting applications. This approach is more objective and reproducible than most procedures for combining beliefs and data in forecasting, and it has been described, documented, and evaluated by several researchers (for example, see Litterman, 1980; Kinal and Ratner, 1983; Hoehn, Gruben, and Fomby 1984; Doan et al. 1984; and the technical appendix to the outlook paper by Litterman [in the original journal], available on request to the Research Department, Federal Reserve Bank of Minneapolis). Although this approach was developed with the overfitting problems of

---

[2] The distinctions between structural and BVAR models are sometimes blurred, but usually only slightly. Structural modellers, for example, sometimes also use non-exclusion restrictions and flexible degrees of confidence, though rarely as extensively as BVAR modellers. Exclusion restrictions are also sometimes used in BVAR models, though less extensively and for different reasons than in structural econometric models. Even with their exclusion restrictions, some BVAR models currently used for forecasting still have dozens or even hundreds of variables (including lagged variables) in each equation rather than just the few variables that structural model equations include (see the outlook papers by Litterman and by Amirizadeh and Todd [in the original journal], for example). In BVAR models exclusion restrictions are used mainly to reduce the costs of building and using the models, not to avoid overfitting.

large forecasting models in mind, its essential elements can be illustrated with a BVAR version of the simple money supply and real output model of the previous sections. As yet, this particular system of Bayesian priors has not acquired a particular name to simplify discussions of it. Since it has been developed and used mainly by economists associated with the University of Minnesota and the Federal Reserve Bank of Minneapolis, I will call it the *Minnesota system of prior beliefs* or, even more briefly, the Minnesota prior.

Taking a Random Walk, With Confidence

In general terms we have seen that a Bayesian modeller's prior beliefs take the form of probabilities about which of the possible forecasting models will forecast best. The first step in using the Minnesota prior is the common one of limiting the set of possible models by choosing a group of variables to include in the model and specifying that they will be linked by linear equations. As usual, the choice of variables is dictated in part by which variables the modeller wants to forecast, and is also guided by economic reasoning and experience concerning which other variables are available that might be closely related to the variables to be forecasted. In the simple model discussed above (equations (1) and (2)), for example, *MONY* and *RGNP* are to be forecast by using the current value and the two past values of each (and a constant term). Once the variables have been chosen, the prior beliefs concern the values of the coefficients of each of the variables in each of the linear equations of the model, and they can be expressed in the form of probabilities about which set of values will give the best forecasts. In the Minnesota prior, these probabilities can be described by assigning certain numbers – mainly a best guess and a measure of confidence – to each coefficient in the model. A Minnesota prior for the MONY-RGNP model would include a best guess of the coefficients k_m, k_r, a_0, a_1, a_2, b_0, b_1, b_2, c_0, c_1, c_2, d_0, d_1, and d_2 in equations (1) and (2) as well as a quantitative expression of the modeller's confidence in each of these guesses.[3]

In the Minnesota prior, the best guesses of the coefficients are usually set either exactly or approximately according to the *random walk hypothesis*. This hypothesis capitalizes on a simple statistical observation that is often a forecaster's chief source of embarrassment: many economic (and other) variables seem to behave as though changes in their values are completely unpredictable. For such a variable, the best forecast of its future values is

---

[3] In technical terms, the modeller must specify a *joint probability distribution* for the coefficients of the model, and the Minnesota prior assumes that it is a *multivariate normal* distribution. Many of the means and covariances of this prior distribution are often set at zero, but the variances are generally positive, as indicated later.

just that they will equal its current value. Even for variables whose changes are thought to be partially predictable, these no-change forecasts can be surprisingly difficult to improve upon.

To implement the random walk hypothesis, the best guesses of the Minnesota prior are that, with one exception, all the coefficients in the equation for any given variable are zero. The exception is the coefficient on the most recent value of the given variable, and that is guessed to be one. In the *MONY-RGNP* model, this would mean setting the best guesses of a_0 and d_0 at one and those of all the other coefficients at zero. If all these guesses were right, future values of the variables would differ from their current values only because of completely unpredictable random events (represented by m_{t+1} and r_{t+1} in equations (1) and (2)).

Since it is an explicitly Bayesian procedure, the Minnesota prior does not place unlimited confidence in the best guesses derived from the random walk hypothesis. Instead the modeller must supply a quantitative measure of confidence in each best guess. Although these measures can be expressed in many equivalent ways, in the Minnesota prior they are usually documented and discussed in terms of what a Bayesian statistician would call the *prior variance of the coefficient*. In less technical (and somewhat loose) language, this measures how likely it is that the coefficient is actually close to the best guess and, in particular, how far above and below the best guess the modeller would have to go before being willing to place 2-to-1 odds on the coefficient actually lying between those values. (The distance away from the best guess in either direction equals the square root of the prior variance, which is known as the *prior standard deviation*.) A small prior variance, or equivalently a narrow 2-to-1 *confidence band*, indicates that the modeller is very sure that the coefficient that gives the best forecasts is close to the best guess. A wide band indicates that the best coefficient could easily be very far away from the modeller's best guess. Narrowing the band, or decreasing the prior variance, is known as tightening the prior (around the best guess). Similarly, *loosening* the prior involves widening the band, or increasing the prior variance. A complete description of the modeller's degree of confidence in the best guesses would determine the prior variance of the coefficient of each variable in each equation.

Some BVAR forecasting models have hundreds of coefficients, which means that the number of prior variances to choose is so large that deliberating about each individually is impractical for the modeller. The Minnesota prior includes a system which makes such deliberation unnecessary. It approximates a full set of prior variances almost automatically once the modeller has chosen some of their key features. With one exception, this system proceeds in two stages. First the modeller selects a few restrictions that group the prior variances and mainly determine the relative sizes of the prior variances within each group. Then, for each of those groups, the modeller selects a range of possible values for a scale factor that completes the determination of the prior variances.

The one exception to the two-stage procedure for determining prior variances concerns the prior variances of the constant terms in each equation. (These would be the prior variances of k_m and k_r in the *MONY-RGNP* model of equations (1) and (2).) These variances are often simply set to very large numbers, which amounts to saying that at least over a very large range the modeller regards all possible values of the constant term as almost equally likely, and is willing to let the constant term be determined by the data alone. The constant term represents the average increase per period, or the *drift*, in the variable.[4] Because drift is determined by the data with almost no influence from the modeller's guess of zero for the constant term, the best guesses of the Minnesota prior are sometimes described not as just the random walk hypothesis but as the *random walk plus drift hypothesis*.

Relative Degrees of Confidence

Specification of the rest of the prior variances begins with the selection of restrictions on how the variances are related to each other. BVAR modellers use many different types of restrictions (see Doan et al., 1984, for many examples). Most modellers, however, use two basic and closely related types. Both of them are motivated by the notion that the highly lagged (less recent) values of a variable are less likely to be useful in forecasting than the less highly lagged (more recent) values.

In the equation that forecasts any given variable, the first restriction takes the form of weights that shape the prior variances of the coefficients of current and past values of the given variable. These values are known as the *own lags* (of the variable that the equation forecasts). In the simple *MONY-RGNP* model they are $MONY_t$, $MONY_{t-1}$, and $MONY_{t-2}$ in the money supply equation and $RGNP_t$, $RGNP_{t-1}$, and $RGNP_{t-2}$ in the real output equation.

The Minnesota prior asserts that the less important a variable is believed to be for forecasting, the greater is the modeller's confidence in the best guess of its coefficient. Since the more recent values of a variable are considered more important for forecasting than the less recent ones, the prior variances on the own lags should get smaller, or tighter around the best guess, as the lags become longer (that is, as the variable becomes less recent). As lag length increases, this feature of the Minnesota prior combines with the random walk best guess to express increasing confidence

---

[4] For the many variables in logarithmic form in most BVAR models, the constant term represents average percentage increase per period.

that zero coefficients for own lag variables will lead to good forecasts. The restriction is imposed by weighting each own lag prior variance by $1/(k + 1)$, where k is the length of the lag (the number of periods before the current period). Making the own lag prior variances proportional to $1/(k + 1)$ means that, in the *MONY* equation, for example, the prior variances of the coefficients of $MONY_{t-1}$ and $MONY_{t-2}$ are one-half and one-third, respectively, as large as the prior variance of the coefficient of $MONY_t$.

In the equation that forecasts any given variable, the second restriction takes the form of weights that shape the prior variances of the coefficients of current and past values of all the variables besides the given variable. These values are known as the *cross lags* (of the variable that the equation forecasts). In the simple *MONY-RGNP* and model they are $RGNP_t$, $RGNP_{t-1}$, and $RGNP_{t-2}$ in the money supply equation and $MONY_t$, $MONY_{t-1}$, and $MONY_{t-2}$ in the real output equation. The prior variances of the coefficients of the cross lag variables have the same relative sizes as the coefficients of the own lag variables. In particular, they are weighted by $1/(k + 1)$, so that their prior variances also get tighter (smaller) as the length of their lag increases (and hence as their probable importance for forecasting declines). They are also each weighted by an own-versus-cross variance factor, which gives the cross prior variances units comparable to those of the own prior variances.[5]

The combined effect of the random walk best guesses and the first stage of the determination of the confidence levels is illustrated for the money supply equation of the *MONY-RGNP* model in the accompanying figure. The curves show the relative probabilities attached to the coefficients of the *MONY* and *RGNP* variables in that equation. The curve for the current value of *MONY* has its highest value – the highest probability among the possible values of its coefficient – at one, which is the best guess for that variable. Similarly, the curves for the other variables have their highest values at zero, the best guess for those variables. The curves for current values of variables are broad and low, which means that a wide range of possible values for the coefficient has prior probability not much lower than the best guess, and that even values fairly far from the best guess are not considered to be extremely unlikely. The curves for the lagged values of variables become progressively more peaked and concentrated around

---

[5] The own-versus-cross variance weight is s_o/s_c, where s_o and s_c are the standard errors of estimate from regressions of the own and cross variable, respectively, on several of their past values. It is independent of lag length but specific to a given cross variable. It becomes especially important in larger models, where each equation would have not just one cross variable (and its lags) but rather many. Then the prior variance of each lag of each cross variable is converted to units comparable to the own lag prior variances by the own-versus-cross variance factor (s_o/s_c) specific to that cross variable.

Coefficients on Own Lags
(*MONY* Variables)

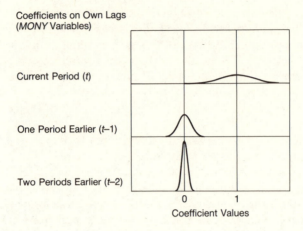

Current Period (*t*)

One Period Earlier (*t*–1)

Two Periods Earlier (*t*–2)

0   1
Coefficient Values

Coefficients on Cross Lags
(*RGNP* Variables)

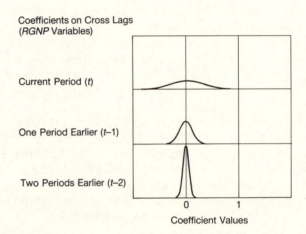

Current Period (*t*)

One Period Earlier (*t*–1)

Two Periods Earlier (*t*–2)

0   1
Coefficient Values

The Minnesota prior's relative degrees of confidence in its random walk, best-guess coefficients.
Hypothetical probabilities on the coefficients in the money supply equation (1)

the best guess, which puts low probability on values outside of that narrow range. This reflects the fact that as lag length increases the modeller becomes increasingly confident that a zero coefficient will be consistent with a model that forecasts well.

Absolute Degrees of Confidence

Restrictions such as the two described above determine many, but not all, features of the prior variances of the coefficients in the model. In particular, they define a few large groups of coefficients and, within each group, determine how the coefficients' prior variances are related to each other. In the *MONY-RGNP* model above I have defined two groups – the own lag coefficients and the cross lag coefficients – and have picked weights that determine the relative sizes of the prior variances within each group.[6]

Once this has been done, all the modeller would need to do to complete the specification of the prior variances is to pick one number, a scale factor called a *hyperparameter*, for each group of coefficients. That hyperparameter would simultaneously multiply all the weights assigned to coefficients in the group and convert these weights from relative to absolute prior variances. For example, if in the *MONY-RGNP* model the hyperparameters H_o and H_c were assigned to the own and cross variable groups of prior variances, respectively, then together with the own and cross lag weights already chosen they would give the prior variances shown in the accompanying table. (In the table, $f_m = s_m/s_r$ and $f_r = s_r/s_m$, where s_m is the standard error of estimate in a regression of *MONY* on several of its past values and s_r is the corresponding figure for *RGNP*.) To be more specific, if H_o equalled $\frac{1}{8}$ and H_c equalled 2, the own lag weights in the table would become $\frac{1}{8}$, $\frac{1}{16}$ and $\frac{1}{24}$, while the cross lag weights would become 2, 1, and $\frac{2}{3}$. Assigning hyperparameters to each group of coefficients is the second stage in specifying prior variances according to the Minnesota prior.

The second stage would be very simple – and the entire procedure a standard Bayesian one – if the modeller had firm beliefs about the hyperparameters, or in other words was certain of the absolute size of at least one of the variances within each group of relative variances. In that case, as in the *MONY-RGNP* example, the appropriate hyperparameter would be assigned to each group, completing the specification of the prior probabilities (best guesses and variances) of the model's coefficients. The the data would be examined with standard Bayesian statistical procedures in order to revise these prior coefficient probabilities and determine the final forecast.

The Minnesota prior, however, generalizes the standard Bayesian approach by not requiring that the modeller have firm beliefs about the hyperparameters. The modeller determines many key features of the prior coefficient probabilities with the best guesses and the restrictions among groups of prior variances. Once that is done, the modeller using the Minnesota prior can claim to be almost ignorant about the absolute levels of the various groups of prior variances. This adds another layer of prior probabilities – probabilities about the few hyperparameters that determine those absolute levels – to the normal Bayesian procedure. In other words, instead of picking a single probability distribution for the model's coef-

---

[6] In this example the groups do not overlap, but in real BVAR models this is not necessary and often not true. See Doan, Litterman, and Sims (1984) for example.

Moving from relative to absolute degrees of confidence in a model's coefficients.
Hypothetical prior variances for the coefficients in the *MONY-RGNP* model[a]

	Equations	
	(1)	(2)
Variables	Money Supply	Real Output
Money supply variables (*MONY*)		
Current period (*t*)	H_o	$H_c f_r$
One period earlier (*t* − 1)	$H_o(\frac{1}{2})$	$H_c(\frac{1}{2})f_r$
Two periods earlier (*t* − 2)	$H_o(\frac{1}{3})$	$H_c(\frac{1}{3})f_r$
Real output variables (*RGNP*)		
Current period (*t*)	$H_c f_m$	H_o
One period earlier (*t* − 1)	$H_c(\frac{1}{2})f_m$	$H_o(\frac{1}{2})$
Two periods earlier (*t* − 2)	$H_c(\frac{1}{3})f_m$	$H_o(\frac{1}{3})$

[a] This is the general formula for the prior variances:

$$
\begin{bmatrix} \text{Absolute confidence} \\ \text{scale factor.} \\ \text{Hyperparameter} \\ (H_o \text{ or } H_c) \end{bmatrix}
\times
\begin{bmatrix} \text{Relative confidence} \\ \text{weight} \\ 1/(k+1) \\ (k = \text{lag length}) \end{bmatrix}
\times
\begin{bmatrix} \text{Own vs. cross} \\ \text{variance factor:} \\ f_m \text{ or } f_r \\ \text{(on cross lags only, to make} \\ \text{units comparable)} \end{bmatrix}
$$

ficients, the modeller specifies a group of similar probability distributions, one for each setting of the hyperparameters, and treats all the distributions within the group as equally likely. Ideally, standard Bayesian statistical procedures would then be applied to the data to compute revised (*posterior*) coefficient probabilities for each possible setting of the hyperparameters. The final coefficient probabilities (and hence the final forecast would be formed as a weighted average of these, with the weight attached to each proportional to the probability that the setting of the hyperparameters that generated it is consistent with the historical data (see Doan et al., 1984).

In principle, adding this ideal weighting process to standard Bayesian statistical procedures should not be difficult, but the great expense of actually computing the average has led most BVAR modellers to use a cheaper approximation. Instead of averaging all the standard models that come from all the possible settings of the hyperparameters, they simply try to find the one set of hyperparameters that leads to the best mock forecasts of the historical data. Under certain assumptions the forecasting model and revised probabilities associated with the best mock forecasts will be close to those formed by the ideal weighted average (Doan et al., 1984). One of those assumptions is that the modeller's beliefs can be thought of (at least approximately) as defining a particular range of hyperparameter values: all values within the range are believed to be equally likely and all values outside it highly unlikely. Another assumption is that within that range the quality of the mock forecasts does not vary too much. This second assumption frequently seems to be satisfied over ranges broad enough to include most plausible hyperparameter values. (See Doan et al., 1984 for one example.) That has made it relatively easy for several BVAR modellers to accept the first assumption as well.[7]

Finding the Final Model

In practice, then, the second stage of specifying prior variances according to the Minnesota prior merges into the selection of a final forecasting model: these are simultaneously determined when the modeller finds the hyperparameters that lead to the model that seems to give the best forecasts. To judge the forecasts associated with a given setting of the hyperparameters, the modeller repeatedly replicates how a model based on those hyperparameters would have forecast in the past.[8] To find the setting that seems to lead to the best forecasts, the modeller simply uses trial-and-error, testing many settings and picking the one that leads to a model whose replicated forecasting errors are smallest (according to whichever of several standards of accuracy the modeller prefers). The final forecasting model, computed as part of the trial-and-error process, uses all available historical data to revise the prior probabilities associated with the best setting of the hyperparameters.

The key step in finding the best setting of the hyperparameters is replicating how a model based on any given set of hyperparameters would have forecast. Because BVAR models are linear and can easily be re-estimated when new data become available, BVAR modellers can address this question by simply recreating hundreds of past forecasts.

Suppose that a BVAR modeller had quarterly data from the first quarter of 1955 to the fourth quarter of 1984, or a total of 120 observations, on the variables on the *MONY-RGNP* model. For any given set of hyperparameters the modeller could use the first 20 observations (the first quarter of 1955 through the fourth quarter of 1959) to estimate a BVAR model, use

[7] An alternative, non-Bayesian interpretation of picking the hyperparameters that lead to the best mock forecasts is that BVAR modellers' restrictions on the relative sizes of prior variances already express a set of prior beliefs strong and clear enough to avoid overfitting. Having done this, the BVAR modeller can just pick the model that seems to forecast most accurately (according to tests on the historical data) without being too concerned that the model's coefficients have been contaminated by accidental patterns in the historical data.

[8] Note that, in the Minnesota prior, hyperparameters are picked according to how well the coefficients they lead to forecast data that were not used to estimate the coefficients. This is known as *out-of-sample* forecasting. A more common procedure for choosing among models is *in-sample* forecasting, where models are judged by how well they explain the same data used to estimate their coefficients. That is not as effective as out-of-sample forecasting at weeding out models whose coefficients have been overfit to the data.

that model to forecast the 21st observation (the first quarter of 1960), and then compute the difference between the forecast and actual values of the 21st observation. This difference is known as the *one-step-ahead forecast error* for the 21st observation, because it is the error in a forecast that extends one quarter beyond the period of historical data used to estimate the forecasting model. It replicates the forecast that a BVAR modeller could actually have made in early 1960, as soon as data for the fourth quarter of 1959 became available. Next the BVAR modeller would use the first 21 observations to compute a one-step-ahead error for the 22nd observation, the first 22 observations to compute a one-step-ahead error for the 23rd observation, and so on until all the observations had been used to compute, in this case, 100 one-step-ahead forecast errors for the given setting of the hyperparameters. The same number of one-step-ahead forecast errors would then be computed for each of a number of other possible settings of the hyperparameters. The setting with the smallest average one-step-ahead forecast errors (by any of several measures) could then be selected as the best, or the modeller might also examine similarly computed two-, four-, or eight-step-ahead forecast errors before selecting the best setting of the hyperparameters. This would complete the selection of the hyperparameters as well as of the final forecasting model.

Once the hyperparameters that lead to the best forecasting model have been chosen, they are usually re-evaluated only every few years or, more likely, when a change is made in the model, such as the addition or deletion of a variable. More frequent updating of the hyperparameters is expensive, and experience in searching for the best settings of the hyperparameters suggests that it would probably make little difference in the average accuracy of the forecasts.

Although the hyperparameters are infrequently revised, the coefficients associated with the chosen hyperparameters are routinely updated every period, as new data become available. The linear relationships between variables in a BVAR model make this simple and inexpensive.

The Minnesota system of prior beliefs is not simple to use, but it does give forecasters a flexible way to express prior beliefs and an objective procedure for combining those beliefs with historical data to produce forecasts. In that sense it represents a move away from traditional forecasting procedures toward Bayesian procedures that seemed, by the late 1970s, more promising to at least some economists.

Improved Method, Improved Results

The accuracy of a forecasting model is generally assessed by some measure of the average distance between its guesses of what the future is most likely to be and what the future actually turns out to be. Although the evidence is limited, BVAR models' guesses about the most likely future appear to be at least as accurate as those of competing forecasting procedures.

As noted earlier, structural econometric models are frequently not accurate enough to satisfy the modellers who manage them, and many of these managers routinely use their own subjective views about where the economy is heading to adjust their models' forecasts. Because of this subjectivity, good evidence on the relative accuracy of forecasts by BVAR models and forecasts by structural modellers is hard to come by. Good evidence would consist of, for example, a history of thousands of comparable forecasts from both of these sources. At first thought it might seem that such evidence could be synthesized by doing with structural models what BVAR modellers do – repeatedly using data up to some previous date to estimate the coefficients of the model, pretending to forecast the ensuing periods, and comparing these pretended forecasts to the actual historical data. However, this would not accurately reproduce structural modellers' forecasts. It omits the subjective adjustment they would have made to the model's forecasts. That adjustment cannot be realistically re-created with hindsight.

Instead of using synthetic forecasting records to compare the forecasts made by BVAR models and structural econometric modellers, generally we must look to the history of their actual forecasts. This history is far too short to give decisive evidence, and the fact that the subjective component in the structural forecasts takes on new properties at least every time a new person begins to manage the model means that in some sense it will always be too short. Nonetheless, the historical record gives no reason to regard BVAR forecasts as less accurate. The longest record of reasonably comparable forecasts includes national economic forecasts from several well-known structural econometric forecasting firms as well as from the first BVAR prototype, a six-variable model constructed at the Federal Reserve Bank of Minneapolis in the late 1970s. This model pioneered the Minnesota prior in an attempt to investigate the usefulness of the BVAR technique. Forecasts from that BVAR prototype, regularly computed over a four-year period with no subjective adjustment or respecification of the model, compare favourably with those from the structural forecasters. Out of a total of over 1100 forecasts, the BVAR model was most accurate for 39 per cent; the next-best model was most accurate for only 23 per cent (see Litterman, 1984).

The explicit documentation of BVAR statistical procedures means that the forecast performance of BVAR models is more likely to improve than that of structural econometric forecasters. Unlike the highly personal procedures for adjusting structural forecasts, the objective BVAR procedures can be improved by economic research and accumulated forecasting experience, and this is already happening. Recent BVAR models of the national economy are much more sophisticated and likely to be accurate than the BVAR prototype that outperformed the commercial forecasting models (see Doan, Litterman, and Sims, 1984).

If accuracy of guesses about the most likely future were the only criterion, some might consider the advantages of BVAR models modest. However, because BVAR models can forecast a large group of variables relatively accurately without subjective adjustment, they are also likely to be more informative than other forecasting procedures. They probably can produce more accurate answers to a wider variety of questions about complicated or unobservable features of the future economy.

Examples of such questions are: How would an unexpected change in the money supply affect real output?; and What are the odds of a recession occurring next year?[9] The accuracy of any answers to such questions is obviously very hard to measure. But a BVAR model's answers are probably more accurate than a structural model's. A BVAR model produces these types of forecasts using only current data and the same explicitly documented statistical procedure whose measured accuracy compares well with that of other procedures. By contrast, as we have seen, a structural model's forecasts – or at least the forecasts that the model's managers actually give to its users – often include adjustments that the managers make according to an undocumented and highly personal procedure. Even if the managers appear to be accurate forecasters of simple observable future values, therefore, there is no guarantee that the subjective adjustments they would make to forecast complicated economic interactions or unobservable probabilities would be determined by procedures consistent with those they use to generate their standard forecasts, whose accuracy can be measured. The procedures they use to forecast anything more complicated than a most likely value are not only generally undocumented but also probably untested and almost untestable.

These abstract arguments for the greater informativeness of BVAR models are mild compared to arguments based on the practical ways BVAR and structural models are actually used. With BVAR models the same model and explicit statistical procedures that produce its accurate forecasts of the most likely values of variables are routinely used to generate answers to a wide variety of more complicated questions, about future probabilities and hypothetical relationships among variables. Structural econometric modellers often avoid forecasting these important but complicated events, or forecast them in ways that defy a rigorous statistical interpretation (see Litterman and Supel, 1983).

---

[9] For examples of the use of BVAR models to answer such questions, see the other papers [in the original journal].

Summary

Research on BVAR models and the Minnesota prior was stimulated in the 1970s by dissatisfaction with the methods and results of structural econometric forecasting, and by hopes that explicitly Bayesian forecasting procedures could improve both. Experience with BVAR models is still limited, but they seem to be realizing the initial hopes to some degree. Forecasts straight from BVAR models seem to be at least as accurate as subjectively adjusted forecasts based on structural econometric models. The ability of BVAR models to forecast accurately without adjustment means they can generate objective answers to complicated questions that structural econometric forecasts usually avoid or evade. The methods used to construct BVAR models combine flexible – and therefore probably more accurate – forms for expressing and documenting personal beliefs about the economy with objective, reproducible statistical procedures for combining those beliefs with historical data. This has made these forecasting procedures relatively open to scientific examination and discussion, a powerful process which has led to some useful refinements already and may well lead to many more.

References

Doan, Thomas, Litterman, Robert and Sims, Christopher (1984), Forecasting and conditional projection using realistic prior distributions. *Econometric Reviews*, 3(1), 1–100.

Hoehn, James G., Gruben, William C. and Fomby, Thomas B. (1984), Some time series methods of forecasting the Texas economy. Preliminary Working Paper, Federal Reserve Bank of Dallas.

Kinal, Terrence and Ratner, Jonathan (1983), A VAR forecasting model of a state economy: Its construction and comparative accuracy. Department of Economics, State University of New York at Albany (manuscript).

Litterman, Robert B. (1980), A Bayesian procedure for forecasting with vector autoregressions. Working Paper, Massachusetts Institute of Technology. Available from the Research Department, Federal Reserve Bank of Minneapolis.

Litterman, Robert B. (1984), Forecasting with Bayesian vector autoregressions – Four years of experience. Paper presented at the American Statistical Association's Annual Meeting, sponsored by the Business and Economic Statistics Section and held at Philadelphia, Penn., 12–14 August. Also, forthcoming in proceedings volume and as Research Department Staff Report, Federal Reserve Bank of Minneapolis.

Litterman, Robert B. and Supel, Thomas M. (1983), Using vector autoregressions to measure the uncertainty in Minnesota's revenue forecasts. Federal Reserve Bank of Minneapolis *Quarterly Review*, 7 (Spring), 10–22.

Lucas, Robert E., Jr and Sargent, Thomas J. (1981), Introduction. *Rational Expectations and Econometric Practice*, Vol. 1, pp. xi–xl. University of Minnesota Press, Minneapolis.

Sims, Christopher A. (1980), Macroeconomics and reality. *Econometrica*, 48, 1–48.

11

A Bayesian Analysis of the Determinants of Inflation

Edward E. Leamer

1. Introduction

The persistence of inflation despite unanimous public opposition reveals that either a secret cabal of policy-makers controls our economy for its own purposes or, for want of ability or knowledge, the determinants of inflation are beyond our control. Perusal of the business sections of the newspapers leads me to believe that lack of knowledge is the culprit.

Keynesians, monetarists, pragmatists, gradualists, antimonetarists, supply-siders, microfoundationists, classicists, rational expecters, random walkers, and so on and on – the macroeconomics landscape is littered with economists carrying different banners and offering different advice. I adopt at the outset the hopeful attitude that empirical evidence, properly employed, could move these disparate sects in the direction of a consensus. I assume that the Bayesian subjective probability model characterizes properly formed opinions. Differences in opinions are then due either to differences in observations or to differences in subjective prior probabilities. Since macroeconomists have access to more or less the same macro data, we must point to differing priors as the source of the disparate opinions.

At a minimum I intend to demonstrate whether or not different priors about the causes of inflation can lead to different inferences from the US post-World War II macro data. But I begin with a more ambitious task in mind. I suspect that much of the source of differing opinions, even after having observed the macro data set, is not due to dogmatically held priors but rather to improper processing of the available data. Empirical economists have not had Bayesian training, and the way they use their priors is to search for a model that yields estimates more or less consistent with prior

This article first appeared in *Model Reliability*, edited by P. A. Belsley and E. Kuh. MIT Press, Cambridge, Mass., 1986, pp. 62–89. Support from NSF Grant SES78–09479 is gratefully acknowledged. Thomas Wolfe provided able research assistance, advice, and constant discouragement. David Blair assisted on an earlier version of the empirical work. Much of the data was supplied to the MIT Center for Computational Research in Economics and Management Science by Robert Gordon for analysis by a group of statisticians and econometricians interested in model choice and model validity issues.

opinion. It is hard to imagine that this would change anyone's mind. Here I will show, for example, how strongly a Keynesian must believe in the irrelevance of monetary policy to conclude, after having seen the data, that money does not matter. If this is a very dogmatically held belief, most of us will draw a different inference from the data set. If the data are reasonably convincing, a consensus may emerge. Thus the ideal outcome of this work would be a decisive statement of the usefulness of empirical evidence for studying this macroeconomics issue.

In order to perform this analysis it is necessary to write down a general macromodel with a parameterization so broad that special parameter values imply models of the Keynesian type, of the monetarist type, and so forth. Then prior distributions for these parameters must be selected to represent the opinions of each of the sects. This is not an easy task.

Theoretical and empirical models of inflation rest implicitly or explicitly on assumptions about market-clearing processes and about the formation of expectations: coordination and information, to use Leijonhufvud's (1981) title. One viewpoint, which is associated with the name of Keynes, is that price increases are preceded by realized excess demands that give rise to unintended reductions of inventories of goods or labourers. Fiscal and monetary policy can affect the rate of inflation only by first affecting the level of excess demand. In terms of mathematical symbols we could write such a system as

$$\Delta \log P = \beta_0 + \beta_1 X, \tag{1}$$

$$X = \gamma_0 + \gamma_1 F + \gamma_2 M \tag{2}$$

where $\Delta \log P$ is the rate of inflation, F is the fiscal policy, M is money, and X is the level of excess demand. Equation (2) summarizes the IS-LM system, and equation (1) can be thought to combine a Phillips curve with a price mark-up rule.

At a theoretical level this Keynesian model leaves much to be desired. The period for which this model is thought to apply is left unspecified. Expectations seem to be myopic. The failure of markets to clear has no stated dynamic implications – that is, notional demands are unaffected by coordination failures. Supply is taken as fixed.

The extreme opposite viewpoint is that markets clear instantaneously and that changes in inventories of goods or labour reflect changes in expectations about the future path of prices and wages. A static version of this viewpoint is summarized by the quantity equation $MV = PQ$. If Q and V are fixed, we would then have a monetarist model of inflation,

$$\Delta \log P = \beta_0 + \beta_1 \Delta \log M, \tag{3}$$

with $\beta_0 = 0$ and $\beta_1 = 1$.

This monetarist model also leaves much to be desired. There are no dynamics in the model, no uncertainty, no reason for inventories of goods or labour.

Given the obvious shortcomings of these two models as characterizations of dynamic processes, it may seem surprising that they serve as foundations for the empirical work on the determinants of inflation. Nevertheless, most studies use one of these two frameworks with a few lagged variables thrown in. These lagged variables are justified as reflecting expectation formation, but it is fair to say that the dynamic empirical models that result do not have a solid theoretical foundation, or at least not a fully articulated one. Since neither my experience nor my desires allow me to specify a complete model of inflation, I will, with a queasy feeling, follow the path of my predecessors and 'dynamize' the model in an ad hoc fashion. The resulting empirical work, though lacking a theoretical foundation, should still appeal to some macroeconomists, who seem not to need one.

The approach that I take is to combine these two models into the composite model

$$\Delta \log P = \beta_0 + \beta_1 X + \beta_2 \Delta \log M, \tag{4}$$

$$X = \gamma_0 + \gamma_1 F + \gamma_2 M, \tag{5}$$

and to characterize the difference between the Keynesian and the monetarist viewpoints in terms of the choice of prior distributions for the parameters in this general model. A Keynesian expects to see β_2 small, whereas a monetarist expects to see β_1, γ_1, and γ_2 small. Keynesians and monetarists are also distinguished by their attitudes towards the dynamics in the system, with the Keynesians generally expecting a relatively sluggish response. In addition a distinction is drawn between classical and Friedmaniac attitudes toward the dynamics in the excess demand equation (5). Though both expect no long-run effect of money ($\gamma_2 = 0$), a Friedmaniac allows short-run effects.

The priors I will be defining will leave most readers uncomfortable. In practice the only prior distribution that does not cause discomfort is the diffuse prior, but the use of a diffuse prior for the analysis of economic data is either a delusion or a deceit. To combat the feeling of discomfort that you properly will feel, I report a global sensitivity analysis. A sensibly inclusive family of priors in the neighbourhood of the hypothesized prior is selected, and the corresponding family of inferences is identified. If all the inferences in this set are essentially the same, we may conclude that inferences from these data are 'resilient', that is, insensitive to the choice of prior. If this set includes substantially different inferences, the conclusions from these data are judged to be 'fragile' and unworthy of attention.

Those of you who are not reading this chapter for its methodological contribution but for the light it sheds on the debate over the inflation/unemployment trade-offs may now terminate reading, since I regret to inform you that virtually all the inferences I report are fragile. A monetarist can find convincing evidence that money growth affects inflation, though a Keynesian remains unconvinced. Both do agree that if unemployment slows inflation, the effect is small. Otherwise, this data set is not particularly useful. Neither Keynesians nor monetarists will find their personal beliefs greatly influenced by it. Nor does it produce anything approaching a consensus.

2.   A General Model of Inflation

The model I will use to illustrate how priors play a role in inferring the determinants of inflation consists of the two equations described in tables 3 and 4. Variables are defined in Table 1. The first difference operator Δ_i and the averaging operator A_i are defined in Table 2. The inflation equation expresses the rate of inflation in terms of six variables, each with its own distributed lag. The first set of explanatory variables are lagged inflation rates. These variables allow 'momentum' in the inflation process, possibly due to the formation of expectations. Inflation rates up to three years earlier are allowed to affect the current rate. A general distributed lag of this length would require thirteen variables, one for each quarter. Computer limitations force an economy of parameterization on any empirical exercise. In this case the number of explanatory variables is limited to at most twenty-five. Accordingly the distributed lag process is characterized in terms of four variables: inflation rates over the past quarter, the past year, the past two years, and the past three years.

The second set of variables in the inflation equation are growth rates of money, with timing similar to the lagged inflation rates. The third set of variables are unemployment rates. The Phillips curve is traditionally expressed in terms of the inverse of the unemployment rate, a form that is also adopted here. This variable is multiplied by 25 to make the derivative of the inflation rate with respect to U evaluated at $U = 5$ equal to the coefficient. This facilitates the formation of prior information, since the size of the coefficient on $25\,U^{-1}$ is the approximate answer to the question: How much would the inflation rate increase if the unemployment rate fell from 5 to 4 per cent?

The fourth variable is the government deficit scaled by GNP. Monetarists do not believe the deficit has a direct impact on the inflation rate. This opinion is well expressed by Meiselman (1981) who, in a report titled 'Are tax cuts inflationary', writes: 'Inflation occurs when the quantity of money expands faster than output. . . . Changes in tax rates, or other provisions of the tax code, will affect inflation if these changes alter output. . . . If a deficit is financed by selling government bonds to the Federal Reserve, the

Table 1.   Variable definitions (all data seasonally adjusted)

Symbol	Description	Source
P	Fixed weight GNP deflator (1972) = 100)	Gordon data set
M	Money: M1B 1959–80 spliced to M1, 1947–58 (splice factor = 0.9845722)	Federal Reserve System data base via San Francisco Federal Bank Librarian
U	Unemployment percentage (0–100) (survey of week including 12th day of month, average over quarter)	Gordon data set
D	Federal government deficit in billions	Dept. of Commerce, BEA, Business Condition Digest
Y	GNP in billions of dollars	
E	Crude oil price per barrel (34° ex Ras al Tanurah)	*Petroleum Economist*
C_1	Price control 'on' dummy equal to 2/3 from 1971 third quarter to 1972 fourth quarter (C_1 sums to 4)	Gordon data set
C_2	Price control 'off' dummy equal to 1 from 1974 second quarter to 1975 first quarter (C_2 sums to 4)	Gordon data set
G	Federal government purchases of goods and services (billions of dollars)	Business Condition Digest
A	G – taxes + transfers + gross private domestic investment – capital consumption allowances + net exports (billions) (Friedman – Meiselman definition)	Dept. of Commerce, NIPA's Survey of Current Business
F	Civilian labour force in millions	Dept. of Commerce, BLS, Business Condition Digest

resulting increase in the supply of money reduces the value of money, which is to say inflation results.' Since the level of money is controlled for in equation (4), the only route for deficits to affect prices is through their impact on output, and the effect will be small according to this monetarist prescription. The Keynesian contrary opinion is not often fully articulated because prices remain in the wings of the Keynesian drama. One view, built on hazy notions of inflexible prices, allows fiscal policy to affect inflation only through the route of excess demand, which is captured by the

Table 2.   Notation

$$x = \log X$$
$$L^n x_t = x_{t-n}$$
$$\Delta_n x_t = 400(x_t - x_{t-n})/n$$
  = average growth at annual rates of X over the previous n quarters
$$A_n x = (x_t + x_{t-1} + \ldots + x_{t-n+1})/n$$
  = average value of x over current and $n - 1$ preceding quarters

Table 3.   Inflation equation

	$\Delta_1 p =$
Intercept	β_0
Lagged inflation	$+ \beta_1 L\Delta_1 p + \beta_2 L\Delta_4 p + \beta_3 L\Delta_8 p + \beta_4 L\Delta_{12} p$
Money	$+\beta_5 \Delta_1 m + \beta_6 \Delta_4 m + \beta_7 \Delta_8 m + \beta_8 \Delta_{12} m$
Unemployment	$+ \beta_9 25U^{-1} + \beta_{10} A_4 25U^{-1} + \beta_{11} A_8 25U^{-1} + \beta_{12} A_{12} 25U^{-1}$
Deficit/GNP	$+ \beta_{13} 100D/Y + \beta_{14} A(100D/Y) + \beta_{15} A_8(100D/Y)$ $+ \beta_{16} A_{12}(100D/Y)$
Oil price	$+ \beta_{17} \Delta_1 e + \beta_{18} \Delta_4 e + \beta_{19} \Delta_8 e + \beta_{20} \Delta_{12} e$
Price controls	$+ \beta_{21} C_1 + \beta_{22} C_2$

Table 4.   Unemployment equation

	$25U^{-1} =$
Intercept	γ_0
Lagged unemployment	$+ \gamma_1 L(25U^{-1}) + \gamma_2 LA_4(25U^{-1}) + \gamma_3 LA_8(25U^{-1})$ $+ \gamma_4 LA_{12}(25U^{-1})$
Money	$+ \gamma_5 m + \gamma_6 \Delta_1 m + \gamma_7 \Delta_4 m + \gamma_8 \Delta_8 m + \gamma_9 \Delta_{12} m$
Prices	$+ \gamma_{10} Lp + \gamma_{11} \Delta_1 p + \gamma_{12} L\Delta_4 p + \gamma_{13} L\Delta_8 p$ $+ \gamma_{14} L\Delta_{12} p$
Real government	$+ \gamma_{15}(G/LP) + \gamma_{16} A_4(G/LP) + \gamma_{17} A_8(G/LP)$ $+ \gamma_{18} A_{12}(G/LP)$
Real autonomous expenditures	$+ \gamma_{19}(A/LP) + \gamma_{20} A_4(A/LP) + \gamma_{21} A_8(A/LP)$ $+ \gamma_{22} A_{12}(A/LP)$
Labour force	$+ \gamma_{23} F$

unemployment variable. Another viewpoint is that fiscal policy affects the level of aggregate demand, which in turn influences both the level of prices and the unemployment rate. My reading of the editorial pages of newspapers makes me believe that most editorial writers are uncertain of the link between deficits and inflation. This view persists even though prominent Keynesians such as Heller (1979) find otherwise: 'Even a cursory inspection of the data on deficits and inflation shows little relation between the two.' It is probably fair to say that Heller expected to see a link, whereas Meiselman (1981) did not. The fact that they both came to the same conclusion from an examination of the data is a very hopeful sign for those who think data can be useful.

The possibility that deficits generate inflation by first affecting the money supply suggests that we should add to our model a third equation describing the determinants of money.[1] It is logically possible to continue to add equations in this way until inflation is traced back to the big bang. The decision to terminate these linkages with money taken as given reflects the belief that money can be controlled or, to put it differently, that the reaction function can be altered. The interpretation of the coefficients in our two-equation model is rendered difficult if these parameters depend on the money supply reaction function, as is suggested by the rational-expectations logic of Lucas (1972) and Lucas and Sargent (1978). In that event an attempt to control inflation by restricting money growth must take into account the effects of the new policy rule on the parameters. In this article, I will ignore this problem and adopt the out-of-fashion attitude that the parameters are invariant to the money rule. Moreover money is treated as if it were exogenous.

The next variable is the price of oil. It would come as a great surprise to me if anyone estimated an inflation equation before 1974 with oil prices as an explanatory variable. The coincidence of the formation of OPEC and the inflation of the 1970s has changed that completely, and energy prices have found their way into the Keynesian price mark-up equations such as those of Frye and Gordon (1980). Quantity theorists would expect to the contrary that increases in the price of imported oil would modestly lower real GNP (oil imports were less than 1 per cent of GNP) and consequently modestly increase the price level. Otherwise, an increase in the price of oil, if the demand for oil is inelastic, would leave less income to spend on other commodities generally and would lower their prices. Okun (1981, p. 3) argues, however: 'No professional economist will ever again insist (as some did early in 1974) that a major rise in the price of oil cannot raise the price level since it merely pushes other prices down', and he generalizes 'that

---

[1] For example, see Barro (1978a, b) or Hamburger and Zwick (1981).

the same truth applies to hikes in indirect taxes, from price supports and minimum wages'.

The last two variables measure the effect of the Nixon price controls. These variables are taken from Frye and Gordon (1980) and are designed to select the period over which the controls were removed (1974.I to 1975.I). Each sums to four so that the estimated coefficients indicate the cumulative effect of the controls programme on the price level.[2]

To make the two-equation system linear, the unemployment equation is expressed in terms of $25U^{-1}$ which greatly facilitates policy analysis. The unemployment rate is allowed to depend on past unemployment rates, on the current labour force, and on distributed lags in money, prices, government, and autonomous expenditures. In writing this equation I have tried to understand the IS-LM model. A version of that model seems to take prices and wages as fixed in the short run (a quarter?). Aggregate demand is then determined by monetary and fiscal policy as well as by the 'autonomous' component: investment plus net exports. If this aggregate demand does not match aggregate supply, measured by the labour force, then unemployment results. The unemployment equation accordingly includes current values of money, prices, government expenditure, autonomous expenditure, and the labour force.

Also included in the unemployment equation are distributed lags of money and prices. The acceleration hypothesis, cited by Frisch (1977, p. 1298), is that only changes in the rate of growth of money have real effects. This viewpoint, which is most often associated with the name of Milton Friedman, is consistent with the proposition of Lucas (1972, 1973) and Barro (1977) that only 'unexpected' money has real effects, if expectations are formed by extrapolating past money growth experience into the future. Barro's (1977) econometric model of unemployment is similar to the one used here, although he estimates a two-equation system, the second equation determining expectations of money growth and the first expressing unemployment as a function of unanticipated money movements.

Prior for the Inflation Equation

A monetarist and a Keynesian prior for the inflation equation are described in Table 5. If the monetarist prior means were imposed exactly, the inflation equation would be $\Delta_1 p = \alpha + \Delta_1 m$: money growth in the quarter causes an equal increase in the price level. If the Keynesian prior means were imposed exactly, the inflation equation would become $\Delta_1 p = \alpha + 75U^{-1}$:

---

[2] Suppose the inflation rate $p_t - p_{t-1} = (1 - L)p_t$ is generated by the process $(1 - L)p_t = \beta x_t$, where x_t is a dummy variable taking on the value n^{-1} in the first n periods and zero otherwise. Then $p_t = \beta x_t/(1 - L) = \beta(x_t + x_{t-1} + x_{t-2} + \ldots)$, and the effect of x on the future price level is $\beta n n^{-1} = \beta$.

Table 5.   Probable values of coefficients, inflation equation: two times prior standard errors (means in parentheses if not zero)

Coefficients		Monetarist prior	Keynesian prior
Prices	β_1	0.4	0.5
	β_2	0.2	0.4
	β_3	0.1	0.3
	β_4	0.05	0.2
Money	β_5	a	0.1
	β_6	0.4	0.08
	β_7	0.2	0.06
	β_8	0.1	0.04
	$\Sigma_1^8 \beta_i$	(1.0)0.2	a
Unemployment	β_9	0.4	a
	β_{10}	0.2	0.10
	β_{11}	0.1	0.08
	β_{12}	0.05	0.06
	$\Sigma_9^{12}\beta_i + 3\Sigma_1^4\beta_i$	a	(3.0)3.0
Deficit	β_{13}	1.0	10.0
	β_{14}	0.5	8.0
	β_{15}	0.25	6.0
	β_{16}	0.125	4.0
Oil prices	β_{17}	0.05	a
	β_{18}	0.025	0.1
	β_{19}	0.0125	0.08
	β_{20}	0.00625	0.06
	$\Sigma_{17}^{20}\beta_i + 0.1\Sigma_1^4\beta_i$	a	(0.1)0.1
Controls	β_{21}	∞	∞
	$\beta_{21} + \beta_{22}$	1	(−5.0)5.0
	β_{22}	∞	∞

[a] Implicit in other prior constraints.

an increase in the unemployment rate from 5 to 6 percent would reduce inflation by 2.5 per cent $(75 \times (6^{-1} - 5^{-1}))$.

The standard errors on these prior means reflect the level of uncertainty that is likely to be attached to these beliefs. For example, the monetarist prior allows some one-quarter momentum in prices, since the coefficient on lagged price can vary from zero by as much as 0.4, in the sense that an a priori 95 per cent interval for β_1 is $(-0.4, 0.4)$. This means that as much as 40 per cent of last quarter's inflation can be carried over into this quarter. The corresponding figures for annual, biannual, and triannual carry-over are 20, 10, and 5 per cent. If these figures seem high, remember the most likely estimates are zero, and these numbers indicate extremes beyond which the coefficients are not expected to go.

The monetarist prior allows some momentum but insists that the system has a short momory in the sense that the coefficients are expected to decline (geometrically) as the lag length increases. The Keynesian prior allows more momentum and less memory loss (at an arithmetic pace).

A monetarist prior constraint $\Sigma_1^8 \beta_1 = 1$ expresses the idea that, in the long run, prices are proportional to money. A constant money growth rate at x per cent in the long run produces inflation at the rate of x times $(\beta_5 + \beta_6 + \beta_7 + \beta_8)/(1 - \beta_1 - \beta_2 - \beta_3 - \beta_4)$, which, when set to one, generates the constraint $\Sigma_1^8 \beta_i = 1$. The standard error on this linear combination is difficult to select because, for example, the opinion that $\theta_1/(1 - \theta_2)$ is close to one is not equivalent to the opinion that $\theta_1 + \theta_2$ is close to one. The former opinion can be expressed by the statement that $[\theta_1(1 - \theta_2)^{-1} - 1]^2$ is small, or equivalently that $(\theta_1 + \theta_2 - 1)^2/(1 - \theta_2)^2$ is small. This could be well approximated by the statement that $(\theta_1 + \theta_2 - 1)^2$ is small if θ_2 is close to zero. Thus the prior that $\Sigma_1^4 \beta_i$ is small allows us to treat the statement that $\Sigma_1^8 \beta_i$ is within 0.2 of 1 as an approximation to the statement that the long-run multiplier $\Sigma_5^8 \beta_i/(1 - \Sigma_1^4 \beta_i)$ is within 0.2 of 1.

In addition to the long-run proportionality between money and prices, the monetarist prior embodies the idea that money is likely to have a rapid impact on prices, since the lagged effects, β_6, β_7, and β_8, all have zero means with declining standard errors. The Keynesian prior, on the other hand, has zero means for all the money variables, with small standard errors that decline relatively slowly with time, thereby reflecting the Keynesian belief that money does not have much of a direct effect on price, and also the belief that the system may be sluggish.

The unemployment variable is treated oppositely with the Keynesian expecting an effect but the monetarist expecting none. The Keynesian prior for the sum $\Sigma_9^{12} \beta_i + 3\Sigma_1^4 \beta_i$ is located at 3, which would mean that an increase in unemployment from 5 to 6 per cent would reduce the rate of inflation by $3 \times 25 \times (6^{-1} - 5^{-1}) = 2.5$ per cent per annum in the long run. The fairly large standard error on this sum allows this effect to be as small as zero or as large as 5 per cent. The Keynesian expects the current unemployment rate to be the conveyor of information about excess demand in the labour market, which drives price changes, and consequently means for the lagged unemployment coefficients are set to 0 with declining standard errors. The monetarist prior has means for all the unemployment coefficients equal to zero with rapidly declining standard errors.

The federal deficit is treated as a doubtful direct cause of inflation by both the monetarist and the Keynesian. If a deficit coefficient were equal to one, a rise in the federal deficit from 0.1 to 0.2 per cent of GNP would raise the rate of inflation by 0.1 per cent, a very small number. This is the upper limit of the monetarist's range of prior estimates. The Keynesian is ten times as uncertain because he thinks fiscal policy determines excess demand which may not be fully captured by the unemployment variable.

A Keynesian using a mark-up model of prices expects to see increases in the cost of oil passed on to the consumer in higher prices. With oil inputs making up about 10 per cent of costs, every percentage increase in oil prices would raise final goods prices by 0.1 per cent. The sum $\Sigma_{17}^{20}\beta_i +$ $0.1\Sigma_1^4\beta_i$ accordingly has mean 0.1 and a large standard error of 0.1/2. The time it takes to pass these costs along is not expected to be a quarter, and the lagged coefficients on oil prices are given large standard errors. The monetarist, in contrast, is fairly certain that oil price increases do not lead to inflation if they are not 'monetized' by expanding money.

The net effect of the price controls $\beta_{21} + \beta_{22}$ is expected by the monetarist to be zero with a small standard error, but is expected by the Keynesian to be minus five with a relatively large standard error.

The Choice of Prior: Unemployment Equation

The formation of a prior for the unemployment equation is more difficult than the inflation equation because neither the monetarist nor the Keynesian model offers much advice about the magnitudes of the coefficients. I adopt the same convention as in the inflation equation that the monetarist expects less momentum and more rapid memory loss than the Keynesian, and I take the prior standard errors on the lagged unemployment rates to be the same as the prior standard errors on lagged inflation rates in the inflation equation.

The Keynesian prior otherwise is built on an IS-LM model of aggregate demand which takes prices as fixed for a period (a quarter) at the level of the previous quarter and generates aggregate demand as a function of the exogenously given levels of money, government expenditures, and autonomous expenditures (investment plus net exports). These expenditure components are deflated by the previous quarter's prices, which means that I am taking as predetermined (independent of current prices) the nominal government and autonomous expenditures. The priors for the coefficients of these two expenditure variables imply that each extra $5000 in expenditure is expected to generate one extra job in the long run.[3] The

---

[3] If E represents the number employed and F the labour force, then $U^{-1} = F/100 (F - E)$ and $\partial(25)U^{-1}/\partial E = (25)F/100(F - E)^2 = 25U^{-1}(F - E)$. Then if the derivative of E with respect to X is taken to be 1/5000, the derivative $\partial 25U^{-1}/\partial X = \partial 25U^{-1}/\partial E)(\partial E/\partial X) = 25U^{-1}/5000(F - E)$. If total unemployment $F - E$ were 100 million and U were 5 per cent, then $\partial 25U^{-1}/\partial X = 10^{-11}$, which is the coefficient on X we would expect if X were measured in dollars. If X is measured in billions (10^9) and is deflated by a price index in the neighbourhood of 100, the expected coefficient is $10^{-11} \times 10^{11} = 1.0$ The proposition that in the long run each $5000 in government expenditure generates one extra job is therefore approximated by the constraint $\Sigma_{15}^{18}\gamma_i/(1 - \Sigma_1^4\gamma_i) = 1$. As described before, the prior on this ratio is approximated by a prior on the sum $\Sigma_{15}^{18}\gamma_i + \Sigma_1^4\gamma_i$ with mean 1 and standard deviation $\frac{1}{2}$.

relatively large standard errors and their slow rate of decay reflect the Keynesian's uncertainty about the precise timing of the job-creating effect of these expenditure variables.

The money variable in the unemployment equation is in logarithmic form, and the Keynesian chooses a prior mean for γ_5 such that a 1 per cent rise in money would lower unemployment from 5.0 to 4.9 per cent. A similar drop in prices in the previous period would have the same beneficial effect on unemployment. (Here I am thinking of the money demand function.) The growth rate variables for money and prices are all treated as doubtful. The coefficient for the labour variable in the Keynesian prior is selected under the assumption that the level of employment is decided by IS-LM analysis independent of the number of job seekers. Unemployment is then just the gap between the number seeking jobs and the number the economy can employ.[4]

Monetarists can be divided into classicists, who think money has no effect on unemployment, and Friedmaniacs, who expect no long-run effects but allow short-run effects. For the Friedmaniacs the sum of the coefficients (the long-run effects) are constrained rather tightly to zero but otherwise the prior is uninformative. The classicist treats all variables as doubtful, with zero prior means. For example, the expenditure variables are thought to affect the allocation of the work force among government, consumer goods, and investment goods, but not to have an impact on measured unemployment. Likewise a large labour force lowers the real wage but leaves unaffected the number of individuals (optimally) searching for a new job. Money influences the price level, not the unemployment rate.

A Bayesian Sensitivity Analysis

Most readers of the previous section on the choice of priors will find themselves amused or irritated by the notion of characterizing precise Keynesian or monetarist priors. It is the incredulity that invariably greets any particular prior probability distribution that in the past has prevented Bayesian analysis from being used routinely. On the other hand, there is little doubt that data analysts, particularly macroeconomists, use prior information as a guide for the selection of variables. There has to be a reason why a formal Bayesian analysis is not used in practice when judgement is so often used and so often reported as the reason for selecting one set of estimates over another. The reason, I believe, is that researchers are unable to form complete prior distributions. The description in the previous section in-

---

[4] If unemployment is $U = 100(F - E)/F$, then $\partial 25^{-1}/\partial F = -25E/100(F - E)^2$. If employment were 10^8 and unemployment 5×10^6, then this derivative would be -10^{-6}, which would be the expected coefficient if F were measured in labourers. But if F is measured in millions of labourers, the expected coefficient becomes -1.

volves so many twists and turns, so many partly arbitrary decisions, that you have to feel uncomfortable with the final product. You ought to be uncomfortable as well with the usual *ad hoc* regression selection procedures, but many people are blissfully ignorant and act as if the equation they select were really the only one that matters anyway.

A sensitivity analysis can be used to combat the arbitrariness associated with the choice of prior distribution. Two forms of sensitivity analysis are used here to study the effect of a change in the prior variance matrix. For the first form of sensitivity analysis, estimates are formed using priors that are either more diffuse or more concentrated than the priors defined in Tables 5 and 6. The prior is altered by multiplying the prior covariance matrix V_0 by a scale factor σ_1^2 that takes on several values between zero and infinity. In the second form of sensitivity analysis the prior covariance matrix V is allowed to take on any value in an interval around V_0: $\lambda^{-2}V_0 \leqslant V \leqslant \lambda^2 V_0$, where λ is a scalar assuming several values exceeding one and where $A \leqslant B$ means $B - A$ is positive semidefinite. Corresponding to this interval of prior covariance matrices is an interval of Bayes estimates from which extreme values are selected to indicate the ambiguity in the estimates associated with the ambiguity in the prior. The second form of sensitivity analysis is often preferred, since it is unlikely that the prior covariance matrix could be selected so that it is known up to a scale factor. For more details see Leamer and Leonard (1983) or Leamer (1978, 1982).

3. Estimation Results

Estimates of the Inflation Equation

Estimates of the inflation equation using the monetarist and the Keynesian priors and data from 1954, quarter two, to 1980, quarter two, are reported in Tables 7 and 8. The second column in these tables, headed by $\sigma_1 = 0$, contains least-squares estimates subject to the constraints in the prior because here the prior covariance matrix has been multiplied by the scalar $\sigma_1 = 0$. The monetarist prior constrains all coefficients to zero except the current money growth rate, with a coefficient of one, and the two dummies for the price controls, which are constrained to have coefficients that sum to zero. As you move to the right in these tables, the prior constraints are imposed with less and less confidence. The column headed by $\sigma_1 = 1$ contains estimates based on the priors defined in Tables 5 and 6. The adjacent columns dilute or sharpen the prior by a factor of two. At the penultimate column the prior is fully diluted, and the estimates are just the unconstrained least-squares values. The corresponding t values are recorded in the last column. Also the row labelled 'Confidence' is the confidence

Table 6. Probable values of coefficients unemployment equation: two times prior standard errors (means in parentheses if not zero)

Coefficients		Keynesian	Classical	Friedmaniac
Unemployment	γ_1	0.5	0.4	0.4
	γ_2	0.4	0.2	0.2
	γ_3	0.3	0.1	0.1
	γ_4	0.2	0.05	0.05
Money	γ_5	(10)10	5	1.0
	γ_6	5	4	∞
	γ_7	4	2	∞
	γ_8	3	1	∞
	γ_9	2	0.5	∞
	$\Sigma_6^9 \gamma_i$	a	a	1.0
Prices	γ_{10}	(−10)10	5	1.0
	γ_{11}	5	4	∞
	γ_{12}	4	2	∞
	γ_{13}	3	1	∞
	γ_{14}	2	0.5	∞
	$\Sigma_{11}^{14} \gamma_i$	a	a	1.0
Government	γ_{15}	a	0.4	∞
	γ_{16}	1.0	0.2	∞
	γ_{17}	0.8	0.1	∞
	γ_{18}	0.6	0.05	∞
	$\Sigma_1^4 \gamma_i + \Sigma_{15}^{18} \gamma_i$	(1)1.0	a	∞
	$\Sigma_{15}^{18} \gamma_i$	a	a	0.1
Autonomous	γ_{19}	a	0.4	∞
	γ_{20}	1.0	0.2	∞
	γ_{21}	0.8	0.1	∞
	γ_{22}	0.6	0.05	∞
	$\Sigma_1^4 \gamma_i + \Sigma_{19}^{22} \gamma_i$	(1)1.0	a	∞
	$\Sigma_{19}^{22} \gamma_i$	a	a	0.1
Labour	γ_{23}	(−1)1	0.1	0.1

[a] Implicit in other prior constraints.

level attaching to the sample ellipsoid on which the corresponding estimate lies.

Examination of the unconstrained least-squares values in the column headed $\sigma_1 = \infty$ and the t values in the last column might lead you to the following conclusion:

(1) The inflation process has a long memory and large momentum, where the momentum is measured by the sum of the coefficients on the lagged inflation terms and the memory is measured by the average lag of

Table 7. Estimates of inflation equation: monetarist prior

	s^b	σ_1 (prior standard error scale factor)					t^c
		0	0.5	1.0	2.0	∞	
Confidence		1.0	0.999	0.996	0.937	0	
Intercept	∞	-0.24	1.07	1.36	1.21	0.96	1.0
$L\Delta_1 p$	0.4	0	0.29	0.20	0.07	-0.19	-1.8
$L\Delta_4 p$	0.2	0	0.11	0.20	0.28	0.11	0.4
$L\Delta_8 p$	0.1	0	0.03	0.06	0.10	-0.06	-0.2
$L\Delta_{12} p$	0.05	0	0.01	0.02	0.06	0.80	2.4
$\Delta_1 m$	a	1.0	0.20	0.11	0.08	0.06	0.8
$\Delta_4 m$	0.4	0	0.21	0.21	0.17	0.43	2.3
$\Delta_8 m$	0.2	0	0.08	0.13	0.16	-0.68	-1.6
$\Delta_{12} m$	0.1	0	0.03	0.05	0.12	0.88	2.3
$25U^{-1}$	0.4	0	-0.15	-0.25	-0.43	-1.05	-2.8
$A_4 25U^{-1}$	0.2	0	-0.01	0.02	0.14	0.96	1.4
$A_8 25U^{-1}$	0.1	0	0	0.01	0.05	0.47	0.5
$A_{12} 25U^{-1}$	0.05	0	0	0	0	-0.67	-1.1
$100D/Y$	1.0	0	-0.43	-0.65	-0.88	-1.15	-5.1
$A_4 100D/Y$	0.5	0	0.05	0.14	0.16	-0.64	-1.5
$A_8 100D/Y$	0.25	0	0.05	0.11	0.22	1.10	1.8
$A_{12} 100D/Y$	0.125	0	0.01	0.01	-0.02	-0.44	-0.9
$\Delta_1 e$	0.05	0	0.01	0.01	0	0.01	-0.8
$\Delta_4 e$	0.025	0	0.01	0.01	0.01	0.01	0.5
$\Delta_8 e$	0.0125	0	0	0.01	0.02	0.09	4.0
$\Delta_{12} e$	0.00625	0	0	0	0	-0.04	-1.3
C_1	–	-5.9	-2.59	-2.25	-2.2	-2.75	-2.2
C_2	–	5.9	2.24	2.24	1.8	-0.55	-0.4

[a] Implicit in other prior constraints.
[b] Twice the prior standard error.
[c] Least-squares t values.

inflation behind its determinants. The three-year average rate of inflation has the largest and most significant coefficient of the lagged inflation rates. The same is true for the money growth coefficients.

(2) The short-run impact of money growth on inflation is small, but the long-run coefficient $(0.06 + 0.43 - 0.68 + 0.88)/(1 + 0.19 - 0.11 + 0.06 - 0.80) = 2.05$ is large enough to embarrass even a monetarist.

(3) High levels of unemployment in the current quarter, rather than suppressing inflation, actually stimulate it. This is in conformity with the quantity equation, since higher levels of unemployment mean lower output and 'fewer goods being chased by the given supply of dollars'. Recall that a coefficient of 3, as expected by the Keynesian, would

Table 8. Estimates of inflation equation: Keynesian prior

| | s^b | σ_1 (prior standard error scale factor) | | | | |
		0	0.5	1.0	2.0	∞
Confidence		1.0	0.997	0.809	0.180	0
Intercept	∞	−12.2	0.98	0.64	0.45	0.96
LA_1p	0.5	0	0.17	0.04	−0.05	−0.19
LA_4p	0.4	0	0.27	0.30	0.19	0.11
LA_8p	0.3	0	0.16	0.26	0.32	−0.06
$LA_{12}p$	0.2	0	0.09	0.18	0.35	0.80
Δ_1m	0.1	0	0.04	0.08	0.11	0.06
Δ_4m	0.08	0	0.02	0.05	0.12	0.43
Δ_8m	0.06	0	0.01	0.02	0.05	−0.68
$\Delta_{12}m$	0.04	0	0	0.01	0.03	0.88
$25U^{-1}$	a	3.0	−0.21	−0.49	−0.77	−1.05
A_425U^{-1}	0.10	0	0.20	0.46	0.69	0.96
A_825U^{-1}	0.08	0	0	0	0	−0.47
$A_{12}25U^{-1}$	0.06	0	0	0	0.01	−0.67
$100D/Y$	10	0	0.18	−1.07	−1.11	−1.14
A_4100D/Y	8	0	0.54	0.05	−0.19	−0.64
A_8100D/Y	6	0	0.07	0.86	1.04	1.10
$A_{12}100D/Y$	4	0	0	−0.16	−0.30	−0.44
Δ_1e	a	0.10	0	0	0	−0.01
Δ_4e	0.1	0	0.02	0.02	0.01	0.01
Δ_8e	0.08	0	0.04	0.06	0.07	0.09
$\Delta_{12}e$	0.06	0	−0.01	−0.03	−0.05	−0.04
C_1	∞	−8.09	−2.47	−2.53	−2.96	−2.75
C_2	∞	3.09	−0.97	−0.30	0.16	−0.55

a Implicit in other prior constraints.
b Two times the prior standard.

mean that an increase in unemployment from 5 to 6 per cent would reduce the rate of inflation by 2.5 per cent per annum. The least-squares estimate of −1.05 for the current quarter means that this increase in the unemployment rate by 1 per cent would increase the rate of inflation by 0.8 per cent. This initial impact is offset as time proceeds so that a two-year sustained high level of unemployment does reduce inflation, but in the long run the estimated effect of $25U^{-1}$ is the small (and statistically insignificant number) − 0.85.

(4) The deficit surprisingly has both short- and long-run negative effects on the inflation rate. The higher the deficit relative to GNP, the lower the inflation rate.

(5) Energy prices do get passed onto other goods in general after a two-year period. The long-run coefficient is 0.15, which means that 15 per cent of energy inflation is passed on.

(6) The Nixon controls lowered the rate of inflation by 2.75 per cent, and the removal of the controls did not cause a burst of pent-up price increases to offset this effect.

Some of these findings seem to conflict with monetarist opinions; others conflict with Keynesian opinions. But what seems apparent from estimates and t values may not actually be there if this data evidence is formally pooled with the prior information. The pooled estimates based on the priors presented earlier are indicated in the columns headed by $\sigma_1 = 1$. These estimates lead to the following conclusions:

(1) In contrast to the least-squares results, the monetarist does not find the level of momentum to be high or the lag length long. Most of the action occurs within a year. The Keynesian, as expected, finds both higher momentum and longer lag length.

(2) The monetarist estimate of the long-run money coefficient is 0.96, and the Keynesian estimate is 0.76. These are both much lower than the least-squares estimate of 2.03. The Keynesian prior in this case is rather sharply altered by the data.

(3) Even a Keynesian with a tighter prior ($\sigma_1 = 0.5$) than the one we are using cannot find the Phillips curve that he expects.

(4) Both the Keynesian and the monetarist find that the federal deficit reduces inflation, although a Keynesian with a tighter prior ($\sigma_1 = 0.5$) does find that the deficit induces inflation.

(5) Both the Keynesian and the monetarist conclude that energy price increases are passed on; the Keynesian long-run coefficient (0.17) is higher than his prior estimate of 0.1. Even the monetarist ends up with a surprisingly large long-run value of 0.045.

(6) The short-run impact of the price control programme is estimated to be about the same by the Keynesian and the monetarist, but the monetarist concludes that the removal of the controls completely offsets the temporary reduction in inflation.

The preceding discussion has to be regarded with a great deal of scepticism because it is all based on rather fanciful and unlikely priors. The unconstrained least-squares estimates use diffuse priors which would be implicitly rejected by researchers when they omit variables in the usual *ad hoc* fashion. The Bayes estimates sensibly omit variables in a 'partial' way, but they are built on highly specialized and therefore unlikely prior notions. If a minor change in the prior leads to a major change in the inference, inference with this data set will have to be regarded as too fragile to be worth serious consideration.

Table 9.   Bounds for estimates of the long-run coefficients, inflation equation: prior variance matrix bounded from above and below ($\lambda^{-2}V_0 \leqslant V \leqslant \lambda^2 V_0$)

		Monetarist bounds				Keynesian bounds		
	Mean	$\lambda = 1$	$\lambda = 2$	$\lambda = 4$	Mean	$\lambda = 1$	$\lambda = 2$	$\lambda = 4$
Money	1.0	1.0	1.5	2.2	0	0.8	1.8	3.0
		1.0	0.5	0		0.8	−0.3	−1.6
Unemployment^{-1}	0	−0.4	0.3	1.2	3.0	−0.2	0.9	2.5
		−0.4	−1.0	−1.7		−0.2	−1.3	−2.7
Deficit	0	−0.8	0.1	1.2	0	−1.5	1.1	4.3
		−0.8	−1.7	−3.0		−1.5	−3.7	−5.8
Oil prices	0	0.1	0.1	0.2	0.1	0.2	0.4	0.5
		0.1	−0.0	−0.1		0.2	−0.0	−0.3

One way to study the fragility of a Bayesian inference to identify a family of priors in the neighbourhood of the hypothesized prior distribution. If all priors in a neighbourhood of credible size lead to essentially the same conclusion, then the inference can be judged to be sturdy. If, on the other hand, it is necessary to employ an incredibly narrow set of priors to obtain a usefully narrow set of estimates, then inferences from these data are too fragile to be useful. The neighbourhood I will study here takes the location of the prior as fixed but lets the prior variance V lie in an interval $\lambda^{-2}V_0 \leqslant V \leqslant \lambda^2 V_0$, where V_0 is the initial hypothesized variance matrix. For example, if $\lambda = 2$, prior standard errors are allowed to be either twice as large or half as small. Given my considerable uncomfortableness in selecting a prior, this seems like a reasonable interval of prior variance matrices.

Extreme estimates for the long-run coefficients using these neighbour-hoods of priors are reported in Table 9. If $\lambda = 1$, the interval of covariance matrices is just a point, and the corresponding interval of Bayes estimates is a point. If $\lambda = 2$, there is only one interval of estimates that does not overlap the origin. Only the inference with the monetarist prior that money matters can be judged to be sturdy. In every other case the inference is fragile, in the sense that the sign of the estimate is indeterminate. (The interval of estimates for energy prices at $\lambda = 2$ is almost strictly positive, and a slightly narrower interval of priors would lead to a determinate sign.)

The prior means for these long-run effects are also reported in Table 9. Almost all of the intervals for $\lambda = 2$ include the corresponding prior mean. Thus neither the Keynesian nor the monetarist need be convinced that his prior estimate is wrong, since each can find a prior covariance matrix close to the initial one which reproduces the prior mean as an estimate. The one exception is that the Keynesian must conclude that the Phillips curve is not as important as he expected since the maximum estimate of the coefficient on unemployment is only 0.9 with the Keynesian prior and with $\lambda = 2$.

These bounds generally include not only the corresponding prior mean but the mean of the other prior distributions as well. For example, the Keynesian interval for money includes the monetarist prior mean of 1.0. Thus the Keynesian is unable to convince himself that the monetarist is incorrect about the role of money. The exceptions are that the monetarist is convinced that the Keynesian is wrong about the effect of money and about the effect of unemployment.

To sum up, most of the inferences that might be made from this macro data set seem excessively fragile. The monetarist may come away from this exercise with a relatively happy feeling because he regards his conclusion that money matters to be resilient, as is his opinion that unemployment does not have much impact on inflation. The Keynesian, in contrast, is unable to find a Phillips curve with nearly the effect he expects, nor is he able to rule out the substantial effect of money expected by the monetarist. The Keynesian is able to find (fragile) estimates of a considerable energy price markup. He is also able to find a Keynesian prior that leads to the conclusion that there is no effect of money on prices.[5]

Estimates of the Unemployment Equation

Estimates of the unemployment equation are reported in Tables 10–12. Examination of the unconstrained least-squares values in the column headed $\sigma_1 = \infty$ and the t values in the next column might lead you to the following conclusions:

(1) The memory in the unemployment process is much shorter than the memory in the inflation process. The coefficient on the previous quarter's unemployment rate is virtually one. The annual and biannual averages have smaller effects, and the triannual average has no effect. The biannual money growth is by far the most important of the money variables. The inflation rates have mixed effects, with the triannual influence being essentially zero. Most of the effects of government expenditure and autonomous expenditure are felt in the first quarter.
(2) High levels of money are associted with high levels of unemployment, though rapid growth over the past two years reduces unemployment.

---

[5] It should be pointed out that the prior covariance matrix that leads the Keynesian to the most substantial coefficient on energy price is not the same covariance matrix that implies the largest unemployment effect. For this reason the preceding discussion may be regarded to be slightly misleading. This suggests the interesting mathematical problem to find the covariance matrix in the interval $\lambda^{-2}V_0 \leq V \leq \lambda^2 V_0$ which implies a Bayes estimate closest to the prior means.

Table 10. Estimates of unemployment equation: classical prior

| | s^b | σ_1 (prior standard error scale factor) | | | | | t^c |
		0	0.5	1.0	2.0	∞	
Confidence		1.0	0.996	0.703	0.061	0	
Intercept		5.2	9.5	8.6	10.3	12.7	1.4
$L25U^{-1}$	0.4	0	0.74	0.92	1.02	1.05	11.4
LA_425U^{-1}	0.2	0	−0.01	−0.14	−0.30	−0.55	−3.6
LA_825U^{-1}	0.1	0	−0.01	−0.00	0.07	0.35	1.4
$LA_{12}25U^{-1}$	0.05	0	−0.01	−0.01	−0.01	−0.01	0
m	5	0	−1.89	−2.83	−5.36	−9.19	−1.8
$\Delta_1 m$	4	0	0.01	0.02	0.03	0.02	1.4
$\Delta_4 m$	2	0	0.10	0.08	0.06	0	0
$\Delta_8 m$	1	0	0.21	0.14	0.14	0.24	2.4
$\Delta_{12} m$	0.5	0	−0.06	−0.02	0.03	0	0
Lp	5	0	0.32	1.48	3.79	7.01	1.5
$L\Delta_1 p$	4	0	0.06	0.06	0.06	0.05	2.4
$L\Delta_4 p$	2	0	0.03	−0.06	−0.08	−0.09	−1.7
$L\Delta_8 p$	1	0	0.01	0.04	0.06	0.07	0.9
$L\Delta_{12} p$	0.5	0	0	0	0	0.02	0.2
G/LP	0.4	0	0.03	0.07	0.23	1.63	1.1
$A_4 G/LP$	0.2	0	0	0	0.01	−0.91	−0.3
$A_8 G/LP$	0.1	0	0	0	0	0.52	0.1
$A_{12} G/LP$	0.05	0	0	0	0	−0.84	−0.3
X/LP	0.4	0	0.08	0.27	0.66	2.06	3.5
$A_4 X/LP$	0.2	0	0.01	0.01	−0.01	−1.00	−0.8
$A_8 X/LP$	0.1	0	0	0	0	0.87	0.5
$A_{12} X/LP$	0.05	0	0.03	0	0	−0.70	−0.4
F	0.1	0	−0.01	−0.01	0	0.03	0.5

[a] Implicit in other prior constraints.
[b] Twice the prior standard error.
[c] Least-squares t values.

(3) High levels of prices (and lower real wages?) tend to reduce unemployment, as do high inflation rates.
(4) The job-creating effect of government and autonomous expenditures in the current quarter is substantial but is partially offset over time.
(5) The level of the labour force does not have an effect on the unemployment rate.

Bayesian estimates based on the classical prior are generally just scaled-down versions of the least-squares estimates, as might be expected since the classical prior treats all coefficients as if they were likely to be small.

Table 11. Estimates of unemployment equation: Friedmaniac prior

	s^b	σ_1 (prior standard error scale factor)				
		0	0.5	1.0	2.0	∞
Confidence		1.0	0.77	0.06	0.0006	0
Intercept		4.81	4.5	4.02	4.75	12.74
$L25U^{-1}$	0.4	0	0.68	0.86	0.99	1.05
LA_425U^{-1}	0.2	0	0.03	-0.09	-0.25	-0.55
LA_825U^{-1}	0.1	0	0.01	0.01	0.05	0.35
$LA_{12}25U^{-1}$	0.05	0	0	0	0	-0.01
m	1	0	-0.12	-0.17	-0.33	-9.19
$\Delta_1 m$	∞	-0.07	0	0.02	0.02	0.02
$\Delta_4 m$	∞	0	0.03	0.03	0.01	0
$\Delta_8 m$	∞	0.06	0.17	0.13	0.12	0.24
$\Delta_{12} m$	∞	0.01	-0.04	-0.06	-0.04	0
Lp	1	0	-0.17	-0.25	-0.38	7.01
$L\Delta_1 p$	∞	-0.01	0.06	0.06	0.06	0.05
$L\Delta_4 p$	∞	0.17	-0.03	-0.05	-0.06	-0.09
$L\Delta_8 p$	∞	0.17	0.09	0.11	0.12	0.07
$L\Delta_{12} p$	∞	-0.33	-0.05	-0.06	-0.07	0.02
G/LP	∞	4.35	4.61	3.63	2.87	1.63
A_4G/LP	∞	6.93	-6.52	-5.78	-4.55	-0.91
A_8G/LP	∞	32.71	6.74	6.17	5.34	0.52
$A_{12}G/LP$	∞	-30.12	-4.82	-4.01	-3.65	-0.84
X/LP	∞	1.39	2.03	2.12	2.06	2.06
A_4X/LP	∞	5.06	-1.07	-1.74	-1.99	-1.00
A_8X/LP	∞	-2.54	-0.14	0.55	0.85	0.87
$A_{12}X/LP$	∞	-3.9	-0.81	-0.92	-0.89	-0.70
F	0.1	0	-0.03	-0.02	-0.01	0.03

[a] Implicit in other prior constraints.
[b] Two times the prior standard error.

Estimates built on the Friedmaniac prior are somewhat different. Remember the Friedmaniac expects no long-run impact of any of the variables but allows an effect in the short run (unexpected events being the cause of unemployment). The major difference between the Friedmaniac estimates and the classical estimates are the coefficients of the expenditure variables, which in the Friedmaniac case allow for substantial unemployment induced by variability in expenditure over time. A prescription for low unemployment is higher levels of real expenditures in the current quarter than over the last year, and higher levels of real expenditure over the last two years than over the last three.

Table 12. Estimates of unemployment equation: Keynesian prior

	s^b	\multicolumn{5}{c}{σ_1 (prior standard error scale factor)}
		0	0.5	1.0	2.0	∞
Confidence		1.0	0.975	0.031	0	0
Intercept		73.9	−3.9	5.12	10.3	12.74
$L25U^{-1}$	0.5	0	0.80	0.96	1.02	1.05
LA_425U^{-1}	0.4	0	−0.03	−0.24	−0.43	−0.55
LA_825U^{-1}	0.3	0	−0.01	0.12	0.27	0.35
$LA_{12}25U^{-1}$	0.2	0	−0.07	−0.07	−0.07	−0.01
m	10	10.0	3.73	−1.56	−5.56	−9.19
$\Delta_1 m$	5	0	0.02	0.02	0.02	0.02
$\Delta_4 m$	4	0	0.05	0.03	0.01	0
$\Delta_8 m$	3	0	0.14	0.14	0.20	0.24
$\Delta_{12} m$	2	0	−0.10	−0.02	0	0
Lp	10	−10.0	−1.28	1.28	3.83	7.01
$L\Delta_1 p$	5	0	0.07	0.06	0.06	0.05
$L\Delta_4 p$	4	0	−0.02	−0.05	−0.07	−0.09
$L\Delta_8 p$	3	0	0.02	0.06	0.07	0.07
$L\Delta_{12} p$	2	0	0.02	0.01	0	0.02
G/LP	a	1.0	0.77	1.03	1.35	1.63
$A_4 G/LP$	1.0	0	−0.16	−0.27	−0.39	−0.91
$A_8 G/LP$	0.8	0	−0.17	−0.24	−0.31	0.52
$A_{12} G/LP$	0.6	0	−0.15	−0.24	−0.32	−0.84
X/LP	a	1.0	0.70	1.32	1.79	2.06
$A_4 X/LP$	1.0	0	−0.24	−0.57	−0.77	−1.00
$A_8 X/LP$	0.8	0	−0.13	−0.24	−0.18	0.87
$A_{12} X/LP$	0.6	0	−0.06	−0.10	−0.11	−0.70
F	1	−1.0	−0.12	−0.04	0.01	0.03

[a] Implicit in other prior constraints.
[b] Two times the prior standard error.

Bayesian estimates based on the Keynesian prior are rather similar to the estimates based on the classical prior. The Keynesian is surprised to find that high levels of money and low levels of prices cause unemployment, but his priors about the effect of current expenditure are confirmed, though the job-creating effects of these expenditure variables are largely offset in the long run.

Extreme estimates of the long-run effects formed from priors in the neighbourhoods of these are reported in Table 13. Almost all of the inferences about the signs of these effects are fragile in the sense that zero is included in the interval of estimates corresponding to the interval of priors

Table 13. Bounds for estimates of the long-run coefficients, unemployment equation: prior variance matrix bounded from above and below ($\lambda^{-2}V_0 \leqslant V \leqslant \lambda^2 V_0$)

	Classical prior				Friedmaniac				Keynesian prior			
	Mean	$\lambda=1$	$\lambda=2$	$\lambda=4$	Mean	$\lambda=1$	$\lambda=2$	$\lambda=4$	Mean	$\lambda=1$	$\lambda=2$	$\lambda=4$
Money	0	-12.4	28.7	85.7	0	-0.8	15.7	49.4	10	-6.5	-60.9	149
		-12.4	-58.4	-123.4		-0.8	17.6	-53.3		-6.5	-68.0	-144
Money growth	0	1.0	2.0	3.5	0	0.6	1.4	2.27	0	0.72	2.1	3.8
		1.0	0	-1.3		0.6	-0.3	-1.86		0.72	-0.7	-2.6
Prices	0	6.5	41.4	94.2	0	-1.2	12.2	36.2	-10	5.34	60.7	132.8
		6.5	-24.3	-71.7		-1.2	-14.5	-37.1		5.34	-50.6	-125.2
Inflation	0	0.17	0.5	1.0	0	0.18	0.7	1.25	0	0.29	1.0	2.1
		0.17	-0.2	-0.7		0.18	-0.3	-1.14		0.29	-0.5	-7.1
Government	0	0.3	6.5	14.5	1.0	0	1.8	6.06	1.0	1.21	9.5	19.5
		0.3	-5.4	-12.4		0	-1.8	-6.05		1.21	-7.0	-16.9
Autonomous	0	1.2	7.9	17.6	1.0	0.1	1.8	5.87	1.0	1.68	12.6	26.4
		1.2	-4.7	-13.3		0.1	-1.7	-5.61		1.68	-8.7	-21.7
Labour force	0	0	0.8	1.7	-1	-0.1	0.4	1.20	-1	-0.15	0.6	1.4
		0	-0.8	-1.6		-0.1	-0.6	-1.31		-0.15	-1.0	-2.1

$V_0/4 \leqslant V \leqslant 4V_0$. The exception is the conclusion by the classicist that high rates of money growth have job-creating effects. This conclusion is surprising to the classicist since his prior mean is zero. In all other cases the bounds at $\lambda = 2$ contain the corresponding prior mean. Moreover the intervals generally include the means of the other two prior distributions. The exceptions are that neither the classicist nor the Friedmaniac can find an estimate for the effect of the labour force which is as negative as the Keynesian expects. Thus there is little in this data set that can be regarded as convincing evidence to a Friedmaniac, a classicist, or a Keynesian.

4. Concluding Remarks

My intention was to show that macro inflation data speak clearly if they are processed in a conceptually clear manner. However, it turns out that ambiguities in the definition of prior information about the inflation process seem not to be substantially eliminated by the data evidence. In general, there are Keynesian priors that yield Keynesian results, but there are also Keynesian priors that yield monetarist results. The same can be said for monetarist priors. I suspect that evidence of a similar degree of fragility could be uncovered for many macroeconomic data analyses. Beyond the obvious fact, then, that data analyses are always to be treated sceptically, the following conclusion emerges: the theoretical honing of macromodels is likely to be a more productive activity than data mining with ill-defined priors.

References

Anderson, L. and Karnosky, D. (1972), The appropriate time frame for controlling monetary aggregates: the St. Louis evidence. *Controlling Monetary Aggregates II: The Implementation*. Conference Series No. 9. Federal Reserve Bank of Boston, Boston, Mass., September.

Barro, R. J. (1977), Unanticipated money growth and unemployment in the United States. *American Economic Review*, 67, (March): 101–15.

Barro, R. J. (1978), Unanticipated money, output and the price level in the United States. *Journal of Political Economy*, 86, (August): 549–80.

Berman, P. I., (1978), *Inflation and the Money Supply in the United States, 1956–1977*. D. C. Heath, Lexington, Mass.

Frisch, II. (1977), Inflation theory, 1963–1975: a second generation 'Survey'. *Journal of Economic Literature*, 15, (December): 1289–1317.

Frye, J., and Gordon, R. J. (1980), The variance and acceleration of inflation in the 1970's: alternative explanatory models and methods. Mimeo.

Gordon, R. J. (1976), Recent developments in the theory of inflation and unemployment. *Journal of Monetary Economics*, 2, (April), 185–220.

Gordon, R. J. (1981), Output fluctuations and gradual price adjustment. *Journal of Economic Literature*, 19, 493–530.

Hamburger, M. J. and Zwick, B. (1981), Deficits, money and inflation. *Journal of Monetary Economics*, 7, 141–50.

Heller, W. W., 1979. Balanced budget fallacies. *Wall Street Journal*, 16 March, p. 22.

Laidler, D. and Parkin, M. (1975), Inflation: a survey. *Economic Journal*, 85, (December), 741–809.

Leamer, E. E. (1978), *Specification Searches*. Wiley, New York.

Leamer, E. E., (1982), Sets of posterior means with bounded variance priors. *Econometrica*, 50, (May): 725–36.

Leamer, E. E. and Leonard, H. (1983), Reporting the fragility of regression estimates. *Review of Economics and Statistics*, 65, (May): 306–17.

Leijonhufvud, A. (1980), What was the matter with IS-LM? Working Paper 186, Department of Economics, UCLA.

Leijonhufvud, A. (1981), *Information and Coordination*. Oxford University Pres, New York.

Lucas, R. E., Jr, (1972), Expectations and the neutrality of money. *Journal of Economic Theory*, 4, (April): 103–124.

Lucas, R. E., Jr, (1973), Some international evidence on output–inflation trade offs. *American Economic Review*, 63, (June): 326–34.

Lucas, R. E., Jr, (1981), Tobin and monetarism: a review article. *Journal of Economic Literature*, 19, (June): 558–67.

Lucas, R. E., Jr, and Sargent T. J. (1978), After Keynesian macroeconomics. *After the Phillips Curve: Persistence of High Inflation and High Unemployment*. Federal Reserve Bank of Boston Conference, Vol. 19. Federal Reserve Bank, Boston.

Meiselman. D. I. (1981), Are tax cuts inflationary? *Manhattan Report on Economic Policy*, Vol. I, pp. 1–3.

Okun, A. (1981), *Prices and Quantities*. Brookings Institution, Washington, DC.

Sargent, T. J. (1976a), The observational equivalence of natural and unnatural rate theories of macroeconomics. *Journal of Policitcal Economy*, 84, 631–40.

Sargent, T. J. (1976), A classical macroeconometric model for the United States. *Journal of Political Economy*, 84, 207–37.

Stein, J. L. (1981), Monetarist, Keynesian, and new classical economics. *American Economic Review*, 71, (May): 139–49.

12

Bayesian Analysis in Econometrics

Arnold Zellner

1.   Introduction

Since the early 1960s there has been a considerable growth in the volume of Bayesian econometric research. This research has been focused on the development and application of Bayesian methods to solve econometric problems. These include general problems of science, namely, describing, understanding and modelling economic phenomena, testing hypotheses suggested by economic theory, using econometric models and methods for prediction and policy analysis, and solving a variety of practical economic and business decision problems. Before the early 1960s almost all econometricians employed non-Bayesian methods in their work in spite of the fact that Edgeworth, an eminent economist and statistician, and Jeffreys, a leading natural scientist, had produced many useful and important Bayesian methods by building on the earlier work of Laplace and others – see, e.g., Bowley (1928), Stigler (1978), Jeffreys (1967/1st ed. 1939 and 1973/1st ed. 1931), Geisser (1980a, b), Good (1980), and Lindley (1980). It appears that the works of Savage (1954), Friedman and Savage (1948, 1952), Raiffa and Schlaifer (1961) and a rediscovery of Jeffreys's work stimulated several econometricians, including Albert Ando, Jacques Drèze, Walter Fisher, Tom Rothenberg, Arnold Zellner, and several others to commence research on Bayesian econometrics in the early 1960s. In Zellner (1984) further information is provided about these Bayesian researchers and their publications.

During the 1960s, Bayesian econometric research progressed rapidly and in 1970 the first meeting of the NBER–NSF Seminar on Bayesian Econometrics was held at the University of Chicago that brought together leading Bayesian econometricians and statisticians. Since 1970, semi-annual meetings of the Seminar have been important in fostering much research in Bayesian econometrics and statistics, some of which has been published in Fienberg and Zellner (1975), Zellner (1980) and Goel and Zellner (1986). Also, since the mid-1960s a number of other Bayesian works have been

The article first appeared in *Journal of Econometrics*, Vol. 37, 1988, pp. 27–50. Section 3 of the original is not reproduced here.

published including Lindley (1965, 1971), DeGroot (1970), Lempers (1971), Morales (1971), Zellner (1971a), Press (1972), Box and Tiao (1973), Aykac and Brumat (1977), Leamer (1978), Bernardo et al. (1980, 1985), Berger (1980), Drèze and Richard (1983), Bauwens (1984), Kadane (1984), Boyer and Kihlstrom (1984), and Broemeling (1985). In addition, current and recent general econometrics textbooks include varying amounts of Bayesian material – see, e.g., Judge et al. (1985), Malinvaud (1980), Maddala (1978), Intriligator (1978), and Theil (1971). These works attest to the remarkable progress that has been made in Bayesian statistics and econometrics. It is accurate to state that the Bayesian approach to inference has had a significant impact on econometrics and that its influence is growing rapidly. Zellner (1984, 1985a) provides additional references to theoretical and applied Bayesian econometric studies.

Since this Conference is concerned with issues in the foundations of statistical inference and their impact on applied statistical work in econometrics and other fields, I shall review some elements of the foundations of Bayesian inference that I have found to be particularly important in econometric applications. Further, some comparisons of particular Bayesian and non-Bayesian solutions to specific estimation, prediction, control and other problems will be provided, in part an extension of the considerations presented in Rothenberg (1975) and Zellner (1975). Finally, I shall state some general propositions that I believe are of key importance for applied work in econometrics and other sciences and issue some challenges relating to them.

2. Foundational Issues and Applied Econometrics

In considering alternative systems of inference for use in econometrics and other sciences, researchers have devoted considerable attention to issues in the philosophy of science. While I shall not attempt to review this vast literature, I shall present some general propositions that I believe have great relevance for applied econometric work. Many references will be made to Jeffreys's work because as Good (1980, p. 32) has written:

In summary, Jeffreys's pioneering work on neo-Bayesian methods, at a time when such methods were very unpopular, was stimulated by his interest in philosophy, mathematics, and physics, and has had a large permanent influence on statistical logic and techniques. In my review (Good (1962)) I said that Jeffreys's book on probability 'is of greater importance for the philosophy of science, and obviously of greater immediate practical importance, than nearly all the books on probability written by professional philosophers *lumped together*'.

Thus, I and many others believe that there is much to be learned about foundational matters in Jeffreys's work that Jaynes (1983, 1984) regards as a direct continuation and extension of Laplace's work on Bayesian philosophy, inference and applications. Note that Laplace, Jeffreys and Jaynes have their roots in the physical sciences which have been on the whole very successful. It is quite probable that foundational propositions that these Bayesians regard as central are worth considering seriously by econometricians, other social scientists, and statisticians. Some of these propositions will be stated and briefly discussed below. To sharpen the discussion, and to provoke further considerations, the propositions will be followed by specific challenges.

PROPOSITION 1   *The Unity of Science Principle (USP) is valid.*

Karl Pearson (1938), Jeffreys (1967) and many others subscribe to the USP that Pearson (1938, p. 16) states as follows: 'The unity of science consists alone in its method, not in its material. . . . It is not the facts themselves which form science, but the methods by which they are dealt with,' Also, Jeffreys (1967, p. 7) remarks:

'No matter what the subject-matter, the fundamental principles of the method must be the same. There must be a uniform standard of validity for all hypotheses, irrespective of the subject. Different laws may hold in different subjects, but they must be tested by the same criteria; otherwise we have no guarantee that our decisions will be those warranted by the data and not merely the result of inadequate analysis or of believing what we want to believe.'

Thus the USP implies that the same inductive methods are to be employed in making inferences in the natural, biological, and social sciences and in experimental and non-experimental sciences. That is, the principles of estimation, testing, prediction, etc. that are employed in learning from data in different areas of science should be the same according to the USP.

CHALLENGE 1   *Demonstrate that fundamentally different inference principles for learning from data, that is fundamentally different principles of testing, estimation, prediction, etc. are required and are fruitful in different areas of science, say in the social sciences as contrasted with the physical and biological sciences.*

A second proposition to which many physical scientists, statisticians, and some econometricians subscribe is the belief that sophisticatedly simple hypotheses or models will probably work well in explaining facts and in prediction. This belief in the efficacy of sophisticatedly simple hypotheses and models is sometimes supported by an appeal to Ockham's Razor, the Principle of Parsimony or the Jeffreys–Wrinch Simplicity Postulate. Jeffreys (1967, p. 47) explains the Simplicity Postulate as follows:

Precise statement of the prior probabilities of the laws in accordance with the condition of convergence requires that they should actually be put in an order of decreasing prior probability. But this corresponds to actual scientific procedure. A physicist would test first whether the whole variation is random as against the existence of a linear trend; then a linear law against a quadratic one, then proceeding in order of increasing complexity. All we have to say is that the simpler laws have the greater prior probabilities. This is what Wrinch and I called the simplicity postulate.

As Jeffreys (1973, pp. 38–9) further explains, scientists cannot consider all possible models at once because they are all not known. What is done is to adopt a simple model that fits the data within a range of error. As new observations are obtained, the model is modified, usually implying greater complexity. However, sometimes this is not the case because a new simple conceptualization is put forward that explains the past data and makes good predictions. Einstein's general theory and quantum theory are cited as examples. With respect to these new theories or laws, Jeffreys (1973, p. 39) writes: 'the very fact that the new laws were simpler than the old ones was widely and influentially claimed to be a reason for accepting them. This amounts to saying that in the absence of observational evidence, the simpler law is the more probable'.

In view of the above considerations, the following proposition is put forward.

PROPOSITION 2 *The Jeffreys–Wrinch Simplicity Postulate (SP) is a very useful working principle in econometrics and other sciences.*

Many natural scientists and statisticians will probably regard Proposition 2 to be 'obvious'. For example, Jaynes (1985, p. 334) writes: 'We keep our model as simple as possible so as not to obscure the point to be made; and also to heed Arnold Zellner's wise advice about "sophisticatedly simple" models.' Also, some leading quantitative economists, including the Nobel Prize winners Jan Tinbergen, Ragnar Frisch, Milton Friedman, Kenneth Arrow, George Stigler, James Tobin, and Theodore Schultz all appear to appreciate the value of sophisticated simplicity in their work. The same can be said for many leading statisticians including George Box, Morris DeGroot, Seymour Geisser, Bruce Hill, George Tiao, and others. However, there are a number of econometricians and economists who believe strongly that complicated models and methods are required and will work better in explaining and predicting economic phenomena than sophisticatedly simple models. Since I have not found this to be the case in my own econometric work on methods and applications, I have issued the following challenge on many occasions:

CHALLENGE II *Demonstrate that a very complicated model in any area of science has performed well in promoting understanding of past data and in predicting as yet unobserved data.*

With respect to very complicated macroeconometric models containing hundreds of non-linear stochastic difference equations and thousands of parameters, the eminent econometrician Christ (1975, p. 59) has written: 'they [the models] disagree so strongly about the effects of important monetary and fiscal policies that they cannot be considered reliable guides to such policy effects, until it can be determined which of them are wrong in this respect and which (if any) are right.' Also Litterman (1980, 1985) and McNees (1985) have compared the forecasting performance of several of these large, complicated macroeconometric models and concluded that it is not superior to that of a relatively simple Bayesian vector autoregressive model developed by Litterman (1980, 1985). It is the author's view that a prior preference for complicated methods and models, not only in macroeconomics but also in other areas, has significantly impeded the progress of econometrics and possibly of other social sciences.

A third proposition which most scientists support is the Prediction Principle (PP), namely that prediction is central in science. Indeed, in a review of philosophical concepts of causality Feigl (1953, p. 408) summarizes philosophers' views by defining causality as predictability according to a law or set of laws. In Zellner (1984), this concept of causality is compared with others and it is concluded that there is no need for a special definition of causality in econometrics in accord with the USP. Further Jeffreys (1967, p. 8) defines induction as follows: 'part [of our knowledge] consists of making inferences from past experience to predict future experience. This part may be called generalization or induction.' Thus prediction is central in science as explained above and leads to the following proposition:

PROPOSITION 3 *The Prediction Principle (PP) that predictive performance is central in evaluating hypotheses and models is of key importance in econometrics and other sciences.*

While the content of Proposition 3 has been emphasized by many, particularly by Friedman (1953) in economics and by Geisser (1980a, b) in statistics, it is a fact that many econometricians and other social scientists apparently are not aware of its importance or are openly opposed to it. As Geisser might put it, they are overly concerned with unobservables, e.g. estimating parameters, and thus neglect and/or fail to appreciate the all-important role of prediction. Further, some of these who work with very complicated models find it difficult or perhaps unwise to implement predictive testing of their models. For these and others who do not stress the importance of prediction, the following challenge is put forward:

CHALLENGE III   *Demonstrate that a principle other than the Prediction Principle has been effective in producing sound results in econometrics and other sciences.*

Above in the statement of the Jeffreys–Wrinch Simplicity Postulate, probabilities were associated with hypotheses and models and such probabilities are not 'objective' or 'frequency-based'. Bayesians interpret such probabilities as measures of degrees of belief. Jeffreys (1967, p. 15) views a numerical probability as measuring 'the degree of confidence that we may reasonably have in a proposition, even though we may not be able to give either a deductive proof or disproof of it.' Savage (1962, p. 163) writes: 'Personal probability is a certain kind of numerical measure of the opinions of somebody about something.' These are subjective concepts of probability that Bayesians find most useful in applied work. On the other hand, many econometricians and other workers claim that they use 'objective' or 'frequency' concepts of probability in their work, a claim that Jeffreys (1967, p. 369) disputes in the following words: 'In practice no statistician ever uses a frequency definition, but . . . all use the notion of degree of reasonable belief, usually without even noticing that they are using it and that by using it they are contradicting the principles they have laid down at the outset.'

With respect to the classical or axiomatic, the Venn limiting frequency and the Fisher hypothetical infinite population definitions of probability, Jeffreys (1967, Ch. 7) provides devastating critiques of these definitions that have been unanswered, perhaps because as some have remarked, they are unanswerable.

In view of the above consideration, I put forward the following proposition:

PROPOSITION 4   *A subjective concept of probability is more useful in research and applied work in econometrics and other sciences than are other concepts of probability.*

Challenges related to Proposition 4 are:

CHALLENGE IV(a)   *Demonstrate that Jeffreys's criticisms of axiomatic, limiting frequency, and hypothetical infinite population concepts of probability are invalid.*

CHALLENGE IV(b)   *Demonstrate that subjective probability concepts are not widely used in econometric and other applied areas of research by non-Bayesians.*

In connection with Challenge IV(b) the following remarks of several leading non-Bayesians are illuminating. Tukey (1978, p. 52) writes:

It is my impression that rather generally, not just in econometrics, it is considered decent to use judgment in choosing a functional form, but indecent to use judgment in choosing a coefficient. If judgment about important things is quite all right, why should it not be used for less important ones as well? Perhaps the real purpose of Bayesian techniques is to let us do the indecent thing while modestly concealed behind a formal apparatus. If so, this would not be a precedent. When Fisher introduced the formalities of the analysis of variance in the early 1920's, its most important function was to conceal the fact that the data was being adjusted for block means, an important step forward which if openly visible would have been considered by too many wiseacres of the time to be 'cooking the data'. If so, let us hope that day will soon come when the role of decent concealment can be freely admitted. . . . The coefficient may be better estimated from one source or another, or, even best, estimated by economic judgment. . .

It seems to me a breach of the statistician's trust not to use judgment when that appears to be enough better than using data.

Freedman (1986, p. 127) expresses his views as follows:

When drawing inferences from data, even the most hardbitten objectivist usually has to introduce assumptions and use prior information. The serious question is how to integrate that information into the inferential process and how to test the assumptions underlying the analysis.

Also, Lehmann (1959, p. 62) writes:

Another consideration that frequently enters into the specification of a significance level is the attitude toward the hypothesis before the experiment is performed. If one firmly believes the hypothesis to be true, extremely convincing evidence will be required before one is willing to give up this belief, and the significance level will accordingly be set very low.

These quotations reveal that leading non-Bayesians use non-frequency, subjective, judgmental information in making inferences in so-called 'objective' or 'frequency-based' approaches.

Finally, Bayesians who use Bayes's Theorem as a learning model in their work find it extremely useful. Cox (1961), Jaynes (1974, 1983, 1984) and others have provided fundamental analysis rationalizing Bayes's Theorem as a coherent model of inductive reasoning. In Boyer and Kihlstrom (1984), many uses of Bayes's Theorem as a learning model in mathematical economics are described. In estimation, testing, prediction, control, design, and other applied problems, the Bayesian learning model has been found to be very useful. This range of considerations leads to the following proposition:

PROPOSITION 5 *The learning model embedded in Bayes's Theorem is very useful in econometrics and other sciences.*

Associated with Proposition 5 is the following challenge:

CHALLENGE V *Demonstrate that some other learning model is more general and useful than the Bayesian learning model in econometrics and other areas of science.*

These then are some basic propositions and challenges that I put forward that relate to foundational issues that appear to me to be of fundamental importance in applied econometrics. In my own applied econometric work I have found it fruitful to abide by the USP. In the applied projects on which I have worked I have found that the best solutions have involved simple formulations in accord with the SP. 'Reality' may appear to be complex, but this seems to me to be no more than saying that understanding is lacking. Appropriate, sophisticatedly simple concepts and formations have been found valuable in accord with the SP. Similarly, the PP has played a vital role in appraising alternative formations and models. Finally, in many applied studies, use of subjective probabilities and Bayes's Theorem has been very useful. Since it would take too long to describe these specific studies in great detail, in the next section I shall just describe selected 'canonical' statistical problems that arise in applied econometrics, provide Bayesian solutions and challenge non-Bayesians to provide better solutions.

.   .   .   .

4. Summary and concluding remarks

In Section 2 several key propositions were put forward that have important implications for the inductive process in econometrics and for foundational considerations in statistics. The present writer finds them compelling and urges others to consider them carefully. In essence, they lead to emphasis on the fruitfulness of the unity of methods in science, sophisticatedly simple models and methods, the predictive criterion, subjective probability and the Bayesian learning model in making inferences and decisions. Then, in Section 3 [not reproduced in this volume] several problems were described and solved using Bayesian methods rather readily even though most of the problems are difficult to solve satisfactorily using non-Bayesian approaches. In the way of an overall conclusion, it is suggested that more wide-spread adherence to the propositions described in Section 2 and further use of Bayesian methods will do much to promote more rapid progress in econometrics and other sciences.

References

Aitchison, J. and Dunsmore, I. R. (1975), *Statistical Prediction Analysis.* Cambridge University Press, Cambridge.

Aykac, A. and Brumat C. (eds) (1977), *New Developments in the Applications of Bayesian Methods.* North-Holland, Amsterdam.

Bauwens, L. (1984), *Bayesian Full Information Analysis of Simultaneous Equation Models using Integration by Monte Carlo.* (Springer-Verlag, Berlin).

Bawa, V. S., Brown, S. J. and Klein, R. W. (1979), *Estimation Risk and Optimal Portfolio Choice.* North-Holland, Amsterdam.

Berger, J. O., (1980), *Statistical Decision Theory*, Springer-Verlag, Berlin, 2nd edn in 1985.

Bernardo, J. M. (1980), A Bayesian analysis of classical hypothesis testing. Bayesian Statistics. Proceedings of the First International Meeting held in Valencia (Spain), 28 May to 2 June, 1979, ed. by J. M. Bernardo et al. University Press, Valencia, Spain, pp. 605–18.

Bernardo, J.M., M. H. DeGroot, D. V. Lindley and A. F. M. Smith (eds) (1980), Bayesian Statistics. Proceedings of the first international meeting held in Valencia (Spain), 28 May to 2 June, 1979. University Press, Valencia, Spain.

Bowley, A. L., (1928), *F. Y. Edgeworth's Contributions to Mathematical Statistics* (Royal Statistical Society, London); reprinted in 1972. Augustus M. Kelley Publishers, Clifton, NJ.

Bowman, H. W. and Laporte, A. M. (1975), Stochastic optimization in recursive equation systems with random parameters with an application to control of the money supply. *Studies in Bayesian Econometrics and Statistics in Honour of Leonard J. Savage* ed. by S.E. Fienberg and A. Zellner. North-Holland, Amsterdam, pp. 441–62.

Box, G. E. P. and Tiao, G. C. (1973), *Bayesian Inference in Statistical Analysis.* Addison-Wesley, Reading, MA.

Boyer, M. and Kihlstrom, R. E. (eds) (1984), *Bayesian Models in Economic Theory.* North-Holland, Amsterdam.

Broemeling, L. D., (1985), *Bayesian Analysis of Linear Models.* Marcel Dekker, New York.

Brown, S. J., (1976), Optimal choice under uncertainty. Unpublished doctoral dissertation, Graduate School of Business, University of Chicago, Chicago, IL.

Brown, S.J., (1978), The portfolio choice problem: Comparison of certainty equivalence and optimal Bayes portfolios. *Communications in Statistics B*, 321–34.

Christ, C. F. (1975), Judging the performance of econometric models of the U.S. economy, *International Economic Review*, 16, 54–74.

Cox, R. T., (1961), *The Algebra of Probable Inference.* Johns Hopkins University Press, Baltimore, MD.

DeGroot, M.H. (1970), *Optimal Statistical Decisions.* McGraw-Hill, New York.

Drèze, J. H. and Richard, J. F. (1983), Bayesian analysis of simultaneous equation systems. Handbook of Econometrics, Vol. 1 ed. by Z. Griliches and M. D. Intriligator. North-Holland, Amsterdam, 517–98.

Feigl, H. (1953), Notes on causality. *Readings in the Philosophy of Science*, ed. by H. Feigl and M. Broadbeck. Appleton-Century-Crofts, New York, pp. 408–18.

Fienberg, S.E. and Zellner, A. (eds) (1975), *Studies in Bayesian Econometrics and Statistics in Honor of Leonard J. Savage*. North-Holland, Amsterdam.

Fisher, W.D. (1962), Estimation in the linear decision model, *International Economic Review*, 3, 1–29.

Freedman, D. A., (1986), Reply. *Journal of Business and Economic Statistics*, 4, 126–7.

Friedman, M., (1953), *Essays in positive Economics*. University of Chicago Press, Chicago, IL.

Friedman, M., (1957), *A Theory of the Consumption Function*. Princeton University Press, Princeton, NJ.

Friedman, M. and Savage, L. J. (1948) The utility analysis of choices involving risk. *Journal of Political Economy*, 56, 279–304.

Friedman, M. and Savage, L. J. (1952), The expected-utility hypothesis and the measurability of utility. *Journal of Political Economy*, 60, 463–74.

Geisser, S., (1980a), The contributions of Sir Harold Jeffreys to Bayesian inference. *Bayesian Analysis in Econometrics and Statistics: Essays in Honour of Harold Jeffreys*, ed. by A. Zellner. North-Holland, Amsterdam, pp. 13–34.

Geisser, S. (1980b), A predictivistic primer. *Bayesian Analysis in Econometrics and Statistics: Essays in Honour of Harold Jeffreys*, ed. by A. Zellner. North-Holland, Amsterdam, pp. 363–82.

Goel, P. K. and Zellner (eds) (1986), *Bayesian Inference and Decision Techniques: Essays in Honor of Bruno de Finetti*. North-Holland, Amsterdam.

Good, I. J. (1962), Review of Harold Jeffreys' 'Theory of probability' (3rd ed.), (*Geophysical Journal of the Royal Astronomical Society*, 6, 555–558;) and *Journal of the Royal Statistical Society A*, 125, 487–9.

Good, I. J., (1980), The contributions of Jeffreys to Bayesian statistics. *Bayesian Analysis in Econometrics and Statistics: Essays in Honour of Harold Jeffreys*, ed. by A. Zellner North-Holland, Amsterdam pp. 21–34.

Harkema, R. (1975), An analytical comparison of certainty equivalence and sequential updating, *Journal of the American Statistical Association*, 70, 348–50.

Intriligator, M.D. (1978), *Econometric Models, Techniques, and Applications*. Prentice-Hall, Englewood Cliffs, NJ.

Jaynes, E.T. (1974), Probability theory with applications in science and engineering: A series of informal lectures. Manuscript (Department of Physics, Washington University, St Louis, MO).

Jaynes, E. T. (1983), *Papers on Probability, Statistics and Statistical Physics*, ed. by R. D. Rosenkrantz. D. Reidel, Dordrecht, Holland.

Jaynes, E. T. (1984), The intuitive inadequacy of classical statistics. *Epistemologia*, VII (special issue on probability, statistics and inductive logic), 43–74.

Jaynes, E. T. (1985), Highly informative priors, *Bayesian Statistics*, vol. 2, ed. by J. M. Bernards et al. North-Holland, Amsterdam, pp. 329–52.

Jeffreys, H. (1967), *Theory of Probability*, 3rd edn. Oxford University Press, London; 1st edn in 1939.

Jeffreys, H. (1973), *Scientific Inference*, Cambridge: Cambridge University Press, 3rd ed. (1st ed., 1931).

Jorion, P. (1983), 'Portfolio Analysis of International Equity Investments,' unpublished doctoral dissertation, Graduate School of Business, University of Chicago.

Jorion, P. (1985), 'International Portfolio Diversification with Estimation Risk,' *Journal of Business*, *58*, 259–78.

Judge, G. G., W. E. Griffiths, R. C. Hill, H. Lütkepohl and T.-C. Lee (1985), *The Theory and Practice of Econometrics*, 2nd ed., New York: John Wiley and Sons, Inc.

Kadane, J. B. (1984), (ed.), *Robustness of Bayesian Analysis*, Amsterdam: North-Holland Publishing Co.

Klein, R. W. and S. J. Brown (1984), 'Model Selection When There Is "Minimal" Prior Information,' *Econometrica*, *52*, 1291–1312.

Leamer, E.E. (1978), *Specification Searches*, New York: John Wiley & Sons, Inc.

Lempers, F. B. (1971), *Posterior Probabilities of Alternative Linear Models*, Rotterdam: Rotterdam University Press.

Lindley, D. V. (1965), 'Introduction to Probability and Statistics from a Bayesian Viewpoint,' (2 vols.), Cambridge: Cambridge University Press.

Lindley, D. V. (1971), *Bayesian Statistics: A Review*, Philadelphia: Society for Industrial and Applied Mathematics.

Lindley, D. V. (1980), 'Jeffreys's Contribution to Modern Statistical Thought,' in A. Zellner (ed.), *Bayesian Analysis in Econometrics and Statistics: Essays in Honour of Harold Jeffreys*, Amsterdam: North-Holland Publishing Co., 35–9.

Litterman, R. B. (1980), 'A Bayesian Procedure for Forecasting with Vector Auto-regressions,' Department of Economics, MIT, Cambridge, MA.

Littreman, R. B. (1985), 'Forecasting with Bayesian Vector Autoregressions: Five Years of Experience,' Tech. Report, Federal Reserve Bank of Minneapolis, Minneapolis, Minnesota, to appear in *Journal of Business and Economic Statistics*, *4* (Jan., 1986).

Maddala, G. S. (1978), *Econometrics*, New York: McGraw-Hill Book Co.

Malinvaud, E. (1980), *Statistical Methods of Econometrics*, Amsterdam: North-Holland Publishing Co., 3rd rev. ed.

McNees, S.K. (1985), 'Forecasting Accuracy of Alternative Techniques: A Comparison of U.S. Macroeconomic Forecasts,' invited paper presented at the ASA Meetings, Las Vegas, Nevada, August 1985 and to be published with invited discussion in *Journal of Business and Economic Statistics*, *4* (Jan., 1986).

Monahan, J. F. (1983), 'Fully Bayesian Analysis of ARMA Time Series Models,' *Journal of Econometrics*, *21*, 307–31.

Morales, J. A. (1971), *Bayesian Full Information Structural Analysis*, Berlin: Springer-Verlag.

Park, S. B. (1982), 'Some Sampling Properties of Minimum Expected Loss (MELO) Estimators of Structural Coefficients,' *Journal of Econometric*, *18*, 295–311.

Pearson, K. (1938), *The Grammar of Science*, London: Everyman Edition.

Prescott, E. C. (1975), 'Adaptive Decision Rules of Macroeconomic Plantning,' in S. E. Fienberg and A. Zellner (eds.), *Studies in Bayesian Econometrics and Statistics in Honour of Leonard J. Savage*, Amsterdam: North-Holland Publishing Co., 427–40.

Press, S. J. (1972), *Applied Multivariate Analysis Including Bayesian Techniques*, New York: Holt, Rinehard, and Winston, Inc.

Raiffa, H. and R. Schlaifer (1961), *Applied Statistical Decision Theory*, Boston: Graduate School of Business Admin., Harvard University.

Richard, J. F. (1973), *Posterior and Predictive Densities for Simultaneous Equation Models*, Berlin: Springer-Verlag.

Rothenberg, T. J. (19175), 'The Bayesian Approach and Alternatives in Econometrics,' in S. E. Fienberg and A. Zellner (eds.), *Studies in Bayesian Econometrics and Statistics in Honour of Leonard J. Savage*, Amsterdam: North-Holland Publishing Co., 55–68.

Savage, L. J. (1954), *The Foundations of Statistics*, New York: John Wiley & Sons, Inc.

Savage, L. J. (1962), 'Bayesian Statistics', in R. F. Machol and P. Gray (eds.), *Recent Developments in Information and Decision Theory*, New York: Macmillan Co., 161–94; reprinted in *The Writings of Leonard Jimmie Savage—A Memorial Selection*, Washington, DC: American Statistical Association and Institute of Mathematical Statistics, 1981.

Schwarz, G. (1978), 'Estimating the Dimension of a Model,' *Annals of Statistics*, 6, 461–4.

Stein, C. and A. Zaman (1980), 'Admissibility of the Bayes Procedure Corresponding to the Uniform Prior Distribution for the Control Problem in Four Dimensions But Not in Five,' Tech. Report No. 324, Department of Statistics, Stanford University.

Stigler, S. M. (1978), 'Francis Ysidro Edgeworth, Statistician,' *Journal of the Royal Statistical Society*, Ser. A., *141*, 287–313.

Swamy, P. A. V. B. (1980), 'A Comparison of Estimators for Undersized Samples,' *Journal of Econometrics*, 14, 161–81.

Swamy, P. A. V. B. and J. S. Mehta (1983), 'Further Results on Zellner's Minimum Expected Loss and Full Information Maximum Likelihood Estimators for Undersized Samples,' *Journal of Business and Economic Statistics*, *1*, 154–62,

Theil H. (1971) *Principles of Econometrics*, New York: John Wiley & Sons, Inc.

Varian, H. R. (1975), 'A Bayesian Approach to Real Estate Assessment,' in S. E. Fienberg and A. Zellner (eds.), *Studies in Bayesian Econometrics and Statistics in Honour of Leonard J. Savage*, Amsterdam: North-Holland Publishing Co., 195–208.

Villegas, C. (1980), 'Comment on "On Some Statistical Paradoxes and Non-Conglomerability" by Bruce M. Hill,' in J. M. Bernardo, et al. (eds.), *Bayesian Statistics: Proceedings of the First International Meeting Held in Valencia (Spain), May 28 to June 2, 1979*, Valencia, Spain: University Press, 53–4.

Wright, R. (1983), 'Measuring the Precision of Statistical Cost Allocations,' *Journal of Business and Economic Statistics*, *1*, 93–100.

Zaman, A. (1918a), 'Estimators Without Moments: The Case of the Reciprocal of a Normal Mean,' *Journal of Econometrics*, *15*, 289–98.

Zaman, A. (1981b), 'A Complete Class Theorem for the Control Problem and Further Results on Admissibility and Inadmissibility,' *Annals of Statistics*, 9, 812–21.

Zellner, A. (1971a), *An Introduction to Bayesian Inference in Econometrics*, New

York: John Wiley & Sons, Inc.

Zellner, A. (1971b), 'Bayesian and Non-Bayesian Analysis of the Log-Normal Distribution and Log-Normal Regression,' *Journal of the American Statistical Association*, 66, 327–30.

Zellner, A. (1973), 'The Quality of Quantitative Economic Policymaking When Targets and Costs of Change are Misspecified,' in W. Sellekart (ed.), *Selected Readings in Econometrics and Economic Theory: Essays in Honour of Jan Tinbergen*, Part II, London; Macmillan, 147–64; reprinted in A. Zellner, *Basic Issues in Econometrics*, Chicago: University of Chicago Press, 1984, 169–83.

Zellner, A. (1975), 'The Bayesian Approach and Alternatives in Econometrics,' in S. E. Fienberg and A. Zellner (eds.), *Studies in Bayesian Econometrics and Statistics in Honour of Leonard J. Savage*, Amsterdam: North-Holland Publishing Co., 39–54.

Zellner, A. (1978), 'Estimation of Functions of Population Means and Regression Coefficients Including Structural Coefficients: A Minimum Expected Loss (MELO) Approach,' *Journal of Econometrics*, 8, 125–58.

Zellner, A. (1980), (ed.), *Bayesian Analysis in Econometrics and Statistics: Essays in Honour of Harold Jeffreys*, Amsterdam: North-Holland Publishing Co.

Zellner, A. (1984), *Basic Issues in Econometrics*, Chicago: University of Chicago Press.

Zellner, A. (1985a), 'Bayesian Econometrics,' *Econometrica*, 53, 253–70 (a written version of my invited Fisher-Schultz Lecture, Econometric Society Meeting, Pisa, Italy, 1983).

Zellner, A. (1985b), 'Bayesian Estimation and Prediction Using Asymmetric Loss Functions,' Tech. Report, H.G. B. Alexander Research Foundation, Graduate School of Business, University of Chicago, to appear in *Journal of the American Statistical Association*.

Zellner, A. (1985c), 'A Tale of Forecasting 1001 Series: The Bayesian Knight Strikes Again,' Tech. Report, H. G. B. Alexander Research Foundation, Graduate School of Business, University of Chicago.

Zellner, A. (1985d), 'Further Results on Bayesian Minimum Expected Loss (MELO) Estimates and Posterior Distributions for Structural Coefficients,' Tech. Report, H. G. B. Alexander Research Foundation, Graduate School of Business, University of Chicago, to appear in D. Slottje (ed.), *Innovations in Quantitative Economics: Essays in Honour of Robert L. Basmann*, JAI Press.

Zellner, A. and V. K. Chetty (1965), 'Prediction and Decision Problems in Regression Models from the Bayesian Point of View,' *Journal of the American Statistical Association*, 60, 608–16.

Zellner, A. and M. S. Geisel (1968), 'Sensitivity of Control to Uncertainty and Form of the Criterion Function,' in D. G. Watts (ed.), *The Future of Statistics*, New York: Academic Press, Inc., 269–89.

Zellner, A. and S. B. Park (1979), 'Minimum Expected Loss (MELO) Estimators for Functions of Parameters and Structural Coefficients of Econometric Models,' *Journal of the American Statistical Association*, 74, 185–93.

Zellner, A. and P. E. Rossi (1984), 'Bayesian Analysis of Dichotomous Quantal Response Models,' *Journal of Econometrics*, 25, 365–93.

Zellner, A. and A. Siow (1980), 'Posterior Odds Ratios for Selected Regression

Hypotheses,' in J. M. Bernardo, et al. (eds.), *Bayesian Statistics: Proceedings of the First International Meeting Held in Valencia (Spain), May 28 to June 2, 1979*, Valencia, Spain: University Press, 585–603.

Zellner, A. and W. Vandaele (1975), 'Bayes–Stein Estimators for k-Means, Regression and Simultaneous Equation Models,' in S. E. Fienberg and A. Zellner (eds.), *Studies in Bayesian Econometrics and Statistics in Honour of Leonard J. Savage*, Amsterdam: North-Holland Publishing Co., 317–43.

PART III

LSE Methodology

Introduction

The LSE methodology is a mid-point between the classical econometrics strategy, with a heavy dependence on economic theory, and the theoretical pure time series techniques which extend the Box–Jenkins approach, such as VAR. Economic theory is used to suggest an initial specification, but then the data are allowed to speak in the process of considering alternative specifications and in the eventual evaluation. The three papers included here give three alternative accounts of this methodology at different levels of technical sophistication. The result is the most comprehensive modelling strategy now available. Where alternative strategies discuss and defend just a few aspects of the problem of how best to model, the LSE approach considers many more of these problems. This does not necessarily mean that the LSE method is one that should be preferred by all applied economists, but it clearly deserves very careful consideration.

Christopher Gilbert (paper 13) begins by finding a difference in modelling approach between the typical British econometrician and the traditional ('North American') methodology. The latter is set up as a straw man, called the average economic regression, which perhaps not coincidentally has the abbreviation AER. Here the model is given exactly by the data; the econometrician's only task is to estimate its parameters. Several well-known early econometrics textbooks took exactly this approach. The alternative LSE procedure starts by considering a data-generating process, an approximation to it called the tentatively adequate conditional data characterization being a fairly general specification and then using a simplification search; thus going from general to simple. As part of the evaluation procedure, six model acceptance criteria are suggested: data admissibility, consistency with theory, weak exogeneity of explanatory variables, constancy of parameters, data coherency, and encompassing of alternative models.

David Hendry and Jean-François Richard (paper 14) cover similar ground, although rather more formally and illustrated by considering the proportion of outstanding mortage loans repaid in a period. The paper proceeds carefully and precisely through various steps in the modelling process, providing fourteen definitions of relevant concepts. The application provides useful insights into the practicality of the methodology. The final section considers critically the usefulness and interpretation of a popular evaluation device known as dynamic simulation.

The final paper, by Aris Spanos (15) attempts a synthesis of various approaches, including the traditional one, pure time series techniques and the LSE approach. A great deal of interplay is allowed between theory and data, at least in the suggested procedure, which is generally presented in a formal rather than a practical manner. The paper places many aspects of the LSE approach on a firmer footing. The formalization enables a number of methodological issues to be resolved within a coherent framework.

13

Professor Hendry's Econometric Methodology

Christopher L. Gilbert

1. The AER Procedure

It is widely acknowledged that there is a substantially different outlook on both the teaching and practice of econometrics in Britain relative to that in the United States.[1] This paper is expositional and does not attempt to provide an historical account of these developments.[2] Instead, it aims to give a simple account of the British approach to econometrics which will be accessible to the non-specialist econometrician.

A clean comparison between the 'British' econometric methodology and the traditional ('North American') methodology is aided by focusing on a single 'representative' econometrician. David Hendry, who is widely known for his work on savings behaviour[3] and also as a critic of Milton Friedman,[4] is the obvious choice. This is, in part because of his substantial participation in these developments, but primarily because he has explicitly addressed the large methodological issues. However, the fact that I associate positions and developments with his name should not be taken as implying that he is the originator of these developments. The comparison is also aided by a certain degree of caricature of the opposing position. I trust that this will be understood as a pedagogic device.

Hendry is concerned with the issues of *model specification* and *validation* in a time series context. I first erect a 'straw man' which I shall oppose to Hendry's view about how one should do econometrics. This straw man will

This paper started as a lecture to final year Oxford PPE undergraduates in early 1984 before appearing in the *Oxford Bulletin of Economics and Statistics*, Vol. 48, No. 3, 1986 pp. 283–307. I am grateful to David Hendry for detailed comments, but the views expressed remain my own, and I take full responsibility for errors and misrepresentations. I have received helpful comments from many friends, colleagues and students on earlier drafts of the paper. However, I should particularly mention Les Godfrey, John Knight, Steve Nickell, Adrian Pagan and Tessa van der Willigen.

[1] The geographical partitioning of views is of course far less precise than this. Many of the positions which I characterize as either 'British' or 'Northern American' are held elsewhere in the world.

[2] I address the historical development of British econometrics in Gilbert (1986).

[3] Davidson et al. (1978), Hendry and von Ungern-Sternberg (1981), Davidson and Hendry (1981), Hendry (1983).

[4] Hendry and Ericsson (1983).

be familiar to many students and ex-students from econometric theory courses. I shall call this straw man the *average economic regression* (AER) view of econometrics. On the AER view, we have a specification derived from theory which we *know* to be correct. For simplicity, we consider the single equation specification

$$y = X\beta + \epsilon$$

The econometrician's task is very simple – it is just to obtain an estimate b of the coefficient vector β. What are the econometrician's problems? He must worry about the *pathology* of his estimators – so he will worry about serial correlation, multicollinearity, heteroscedasticity, simultaneity, and so forth. These pathological *problems* generate the chapters of econometrics textbooks.[5] The problems manifest themselves in applied work in terms of *low* Durbin–Watson statistics, *wrong* signs, *insignificant* co-efficients and so forth. The term 'wrong' is telling – we know what the right sign is; the estimates give us the wrong sign; and the econometrician's response to these pathological manifestations is to respecify his equation in some way – to add or subtract variables, change the definition of variables and so forth – until, eventually, he gets an equation which has all correct signs, statistically significant coefficients, a Durbin–Watson statistic of around 2, a relatively high R^2 and so forth.

The econometrician proceeds to publish his results, but this presents the reader with a problem. She/he reads two articles on the same topic, one written by a Professor A. Smith and the other by a Dr K. Marks. Smith claims that a particular data set supports his theory whilst Marks, who uses the same or a similar data set, estimating a different model, since he has started from a different theory, claims that the data set supports his theory. Which should the reader believe? He may very well conclude that either bourgeois or radical economics, depending on his preferences, is not very scientific, and he probably should conclude that neither is scientific. It certainly cannot be the case that both Smith and Marks are correct. But the AER view of econometrics, shared by bourgeois and radical alike, has not been of much help.

The problem with the AER approach is that we are using econometrics to *illustrate* the theories which we believe independently. The alternative might be to use econometrics to *discover* which views of the economy (or market) are tenable and to test, scientifically, the rival views. Our normal concept of science tends to be based on the natural, and in particular, the physical sciences, and does not obviously translate to the social sciences. This alternative programme for econometrics raises the question of what is

---

[5] For example, Chapter 6 of Wonnacott and Wonnacott (1970) is entitled 'Serial correlation and other *problems*' and Chapter 6 of Surrey (1974) is 'Miscellaneous single-equation *problems*' (italics added).

required for economics to be scientific. Much of Hendry's work may be seen as an attempt to grapple with this issue.

2. Data-generating Processes and Models

Hendry's approach to econometrics is grounded in the concept of the *data-generating process* (DGP) (Hendry and Richard (1982), p. 10, and Hendry and Richard (1983), p. 115). This is nothing more than the joint probability of all the sample data (i.e. on both endogenous and exogenous variables). Thus x_t is the vector of observations on all these variables in period t, and $X_{t-1} = (x_1, \ldots, x_{t-1})'$. The joint probability of the sample x_t may be written as

$$\prod_{t=1}^{T} D(x_t | X_{t-1}; \theta) \tag{1}$$

where θ is a vector of parameters of the joint density function D. This joint density function is on the one hand uncontroversial, but on the other hand so general as to be useless. Econometric modelling consists of judicious simplification of this DGP. The econometrician will do this in four ways (generally iterating backwards and forwards):

(1) he will *marginalize* the DGP with respect to the variables that 'don't matter' (w_t say) in the determination of the variables of current interest;
(2) he will *condition* the endogenous variables (y_t) on the (weakly) exogenous variables (z_t);
(3) he will look for suitable *simple* representations of the conditioned marginalized DGP; and
(4) he will replace the unknown parameters in this representation by estimated values.

Economic theory guides the econometrician in the first three of these steps; econometric estimation theory is concerned with the final operation. Provided that the marginalization and conditioning are valid, this allows the econometrician to replace the very general representation (1) by the much more specific[6]

---

[6] This requires that the DGP in (1) can be written as $D(x_t | X_{t-1}; \theta) = D^1(w_t | X_t, Y_t; \lambda) \cdot D^2(y_t | Y_{t-1}, Z_t; \phi) \cdot D^3(Z_t | Y_{t-1}, Z_{t-1}; \psi)$ D^1 is the component of the DGP that depends on the irrelevant variables w_t; D^2 is the component of interest which relates the variable of interest y_t to the 'regressor' variables z_t, and D^3 is the component which describes the generation of these regressor variables. D^2 is the main object of investigation, but for certain purposes (e.g. forecasting) one will need to know (or to be able to approximate) D^3. Marginalization with respect to W_t involves two components: marginalization with respect to the current values w_t, which is generally unproblematic; and marginalization with respect to the lagged values W_{t-1} which requires Granger non-causality (see footnote 14).

$$\prod_{t=1}^{T} D(y_t|Y_{t-1}; Z_t; \phi). \tag{2}$$

We do not know in advance whether the simplifications we have made in moving from (1) to (2) are valid. Furthermore, the concept of *validity* is not straightforward. Economies are complicated organizations, and this must be reflected in complexity of the general representation of the DGP given as (1). This complexity is reinforced by our inability in macro-economics, and to a lesser extent more generally, to perform controlled experiments. Despite this complexity, limited observation sets typically force us to consider relatively simple models. If one uses test statistics with constant size (i.e. a constant degree of confidence), almost any simple model will be rejected given a sufficiently large data set. The fact that the hypothesis that a particular coefficient is equal to zero cannot be rejected only implies that insufficient data are available to permit this rejection; and any hypothesis can be maintained by testing it on a sufficiently short time series.[7]

This implies that we know for certain that the simplified representation of the DGP (2) cannot be strictly valid. The question therefore becomes one of *adequacy* rather than *validity*. Hendry proposes that we look for a *tentatively adequate conditional data characterization* or what might be called a model which is *congruent* with all the evidence. The conditionality is on the data, and the characterization is only tentatively adequate because we should not be so vain as to suppose that it is impossible to improve upon our work. Models are not right or wrong but are useful or misleading for particular purposes; non-congruent models are open to constructive improvement.

This discussion of the derivation of the model (2) as a tentative simplification of the overall DGP (1) is to be contrasted with the AER procedure in which the model (1) is simply asserted as correct. This has major implications for econometric procedure – in the AER procedure poor test statistics imply problems in consistently and efficiently estimating the parameters of the (axomatically correct) model; in the DGP approach the same statistics, obtained from the same regressions, imply model misspecification.

The AER response to a poorly fitting equation is to add variables or parameters (e.g. autocorrelation parameters) in an attempt to 'patch' the original 'theoretical' model. We may represent this approach as *simple →
general*. In direct opposition, Hendry advocates *general → simple*. Take the consumption function as an example. The AER procedure starts from the textbook representation

---

[7] For this reason, Leamer (1978) proposes that the econometrician should reduce the significance level he uses as his sample size increases.

$$C_t = \beta_0 + \beta_1 Y_t. \tag{3}$$

When this appears inadequate, the specification is altered by, for example, adding C_{t-1} as an additional regressor, or by adding inflation or interest rate regressors. The difficulty with this approach is that, if two investigators start from different simple hypotheses (as is likely to be the case with Smith and Marks) there is no reason to suppose that they will converge on the same final equation and even with the same starting point, investigators may diverge if they adopt different respecifications.

The general-to-simple methodology is less vulnerable to this objection. The investigator starts with a very general hypothesis that is acceptable to all the adversaries and then narrows it down by looking for simplifications that are acceptable on the data. Thus, if it is agreed that we should confine our attention, in the consumption function example, to income, inflation, and liquid asset variables, we might initially specify

$$\ln C_t = \sum_{j=1}^{5} \alpha_j \ln C_{t-j-1} + \sum_{j=1}^{5} \beta_j \ln Y_{t-j} + \sum_{j=1}^{5} \gamma_j \ln P_{t-j}$$
$$\sum_{j=1}^{5} \delta_j \ln L_{t-j-1} + \psi' q_t + \epsilon_t \tag{4}$$

where P is the consumption deflator and L is end-period holdings of liquid assets. q_t is a vector consisting of the constant term, three seasonals and a time trend. (A limit on the length of the lag distributions is forced by degrees of freedom considerations.)[8] One then conducts what Leamer has called a *simplification search* with respect to this general specification (Leamer, 1978). Trivedi (1984) refers to this iterative estimation and testing procedure as 'testimation'.

In moving from the general to the simple, therefore, we confine our attention to specifications that are acceptable, using the classical F-test, as simplifications of the general specification. I shall call such simplifications *F-acceptable*. This criterion alone is likely to rule out the contributions of Professor Smith and Dr Marks – since they have not estimated the general specification they will not have been able to ask whether or not their results might be rejected by more general hypotheses. The estimated general equation may suggest simplifications (if for example, a number of coefficients are near zero), and eliminate (as implausible) other simplifications (those involving deletion of variables with estimated coefficients which are relatively large in relation to their estimated standard errors). Moreover,

---

[8] The greater the number of variables included in the equation, the shorter the lag length that must be imposed. But why five periods? Hendry would argue that this is natural in the analysis of quarterly data, since it allows simplification to include both fourth differenced variables (e.g. $\Delta_4 \ln Y_t$) and the first difference of these fourth differences ($\Delta_1 \Delta_4 \ln Y_t$) – see Davidson et al. (1978) for an example.

the long-run elasticities calculated from the estimated general equation will (as the consequence of collinearity amongst the regressors) have much smaller standard errors than will the individual coefficients, and will not be subject to misspecification bias through the incorrect omission of variables contained in the general data set.

Even within the general-to-simple approach, there are likely to be alternative *F*-acceptable congruent simplifications of the general representation, and we will be forced to choose between these. Which does one choose? There are four distinct questions here:

What criteria must a satisfactory model satisfy?
How do we discover such models?
What features should we design into our models?
What do acceptable models typically look like?

These questions form the agenda of the remainder of this paper. But there is a major issue which we need to address first.

The AER procedure is open to the objection that, since the published regression has been accepted in part because its coefficients all have the correct signs and are statistically significant, these significant coefficients cannot be taken as evidence for or against the hypotheses under investigation.[9] What, one is tempted to ask, about the other 999 regressions which have been consigned to Smith's (Marks') waste bin? Do these also confirm/ reject the same hypotheses? It is this problem which prompts Leamer (1983) to propose that econometricians confine themselves to publishing mappings from prior to posterior distributions, rather than actually making statements about the economy.[10]

The important question in the present context is whether the Hendry methodology is robust in this respect. Leamer (1983) argues that we need to invoke the *axiom of correct specification* in order to justify use of classical statistical methodology on a regression which has been chosen on the basis of regression estimates of competing specifications. This view implies that the use of classical methodology in econometrics is largely an act of faith. A more appealing way to recast Leamer's proposition is as the *axiom of route independence*: the validity or invalidity of a particular specification cannot be dependent on the research strategy that generated the specification. This axiom implies that testing must proceed as if the specification were the first selected. But the implication of Leamer's axiom is reversed: we do not assume that the specification is correct, but test to see whether it is congruent with the data. Tests of the specification relative

---

[9] A regression estimate of an equation specification selected on the basis of a previous regression is known as *pre-test* estimator. The distribution theory of such estimators is complicated – see Judge and Bock (1978).
[10] See McAleer et al. (1985) for a critical discussion of this view.

to the general formulation (perhaps (4)), together with other tests to be discussed in Section 3, establish whether or not this can be maintained. If this is established, then we may tentatively proceed to conduct tests within the specification without the support of the axiom of correct specification.[11]

3. Model Acceptance Criteria

Hendry and Richard (1983) give six criteria for model selection.[12]

(1) Models must be *data admissible*. This is a logical criterion – is it logically possible for the data to have been generated from this model? This concept is best illustrated by giving examples of a data-inadmissible specification. Consider the case of modelling a proportion of agents taking a certain action – for example the proportion of voters voting Conservative. Proportions must lie in the interval [0, 1]. If the dependent variable of the equation is defined so that with non-zero probability it will lie outside this range, it is possible to predict that less than 0 per cent or more than 100 per cent of the electorate will vote Conservative. This violates the data admissibility criterion.

(2) Models must be *consistent with theory*. There may of course be alternative theories, but a satisfactory model must be consistent with at least one theory.

(3) Satisfactory models should have regressors that are (at least) *weakly exogenous*. (In a simultaneous context, this requirement refers to the regressor variables in the reduced form.) Technically, with weakly exogenous regressors, it is valid to condition on the regressor set. If the regressors are not weakly exogenous, then they are endogenous by default and must be jointly modelled (in a simultaneous system). Rather obviously, there is not much point in claiming that one has 'explained' y in terms of x if x, in turn, is 'explained' in terms of y. What is required is a joint explanation of x and y.

For certain purposes weak exogeneity may not be sufficient. Consider the following simple model:

$$y_t = \alpha + \beta x_t + u_t \qquad u_t \sim \text{NID}(0, \sigma_u^2) \tag{5}$$

$$x_t = \gamma + \delta y_{t-1} + v_t \qquad u_t \sim \text{NID}(0, \sigma_v^2) \tag{6}$$

---

[11] A problem with sequential testing is that if each test is conducted at, say, a 5 per cent significance level, the size of the overall sequence of tests is likely to be considerably in excess of 5 per cent. Each component test should therefore be conducted at a lower level of significance if the overall probability of Type 1 errors is to be controlled – see Mizon (1977).

[12] Their order of presentation is somewhat different, but I do not believe that this implies any ordering of priority. Hendry and Richard (1982) give the same list but omit (2), which is discussed earlier in the article, and might be considered to be implied by a reformulation of (4) as the requirement that the parameters of *interest* be constant.

and where $E(u_s v_t) = 0 \ \forall s, t$. x_t is weakly exogenous in relation to β which may therefore be consistently estimated, by for example, OLS[13] but if one proposes to use (5) to forecast more than one period ahead, one will also need to know (6), because any change in one's forecast y_f will alter the value of the 'explanatory' variable x_{f+1} needed to forecast y_{f+1}. Weak exogeneity is sufficient (in most cases) for testing hypotheses, but for forecasting one in general requires *strong exogeneity* which is weak exogeneity plus an absence of feedback.[14] Forecasting models therefore tend to be larger, and often much larger, than the models used to test hypotheses about behaviour in particular sectors of the economy.

An even stronger requirement is *super exogeneity*, which may be required in policy analysis. Suppose, for example, that in the regression

$$y = X\beta + \epsilon \tag{7}$$

one of the theoretical variables relates to agents' expectations about the money stock (or its rate of growth), and that this is modelled by including in the set of X variables lagged values of the money stock. If the monetary authority now changes its monetary growth rule, it is plausible that the relationship between the expectational variables and the lagged money stock variables will be altered, and consequently, the policy change will result in a change in the β coefficients. Given strong exogeneity of X, (7) may forecast perfectly well, but it will in principle be misleading if used to analyse the implications of alternative monetary policies. For this we require that the parameter vector β be independent of the process generating the X variables, and not just of the values of the X variables. This will be the case if (7) is respecified in terms of more fundamental super exogenous variables.[15]

(4) Satisfactory models must exhibit *parameter constancy*. This is essential if the model is to be of any use in forecasting or in policy simulation,

---

[13] Note that variables are not weakly exogenous with respect to other variables, but relative to the parameters of interest. (The same point applies to the less useful concept of *predetermination*). For example, if y_t and z_t are jointly normally distributed, it is valid to regress y_t on z_t, taking z_t as weakly exogenous, but by symmetry, one may equally take z_t to be weakly exogenous and regress z_t on y_t. Whether one decides to follow one or other or neither of these alternatives depends on the parameters of interest, and this is a question which relates to the economic theory relating y_t and x_t, and not to their statistical relationship.

[14] If the z variables are to be strongly exogenous, then D^3 in footnote 6 (above) must specialize to

$$D^3(z_t | Z_{t-1}; \psi)$$

implying that z_t is independent of all (past and present) values of y_t. This latter requirement is the condition that y does not *Granger-cause* z. Strong exogeneity is equivalent to weak exogeneity plus Granger-non-causality. These relationships are very clearly explained in Section 5 of Engle et al. (1983).

[15] This is related to the famous *Lucas critique* (Lucas, 1976). Super exogeneity requires weak exogeneity, and in addition that the parameter vectors ψ and ϕ be independent. Technically, this states that they must lie in non-intersecting spaces Ψ and Φ respectively,

both of which require that the same parameter values apply inside and outside the sample period. A consistent feature of Hendry's applied work is that he uses a number of observations at the end of the sample period for testing the constancy of the estimated model. This may be done using a standard Chow test (Harvey, 1981, p. 181). In the single equation context

$$\xi = (\hat{y}_f - y_f)'[I + X_f(X'X)^{-1}X_f]^{-1}(\hat{y}_f - y_f)/s^2 \sim F(n, T - k) \quad (8)$$

where $\hat{y}_f$ is the vector of forecasts for n post-sample periods conditional upon the values X_f of the regressor variables, y_f are the outcomes, and s^2 is the standard estimate of the error variance. If this test is satisfied, then, however poorly it may forecast, the forecast errors do not betray any evidence of parameter non-constancy. In this case, efficiency then demands that the model be re-estimated over the entire sample (including the final n observations). However, if the model fails this test, it cannot adequately represent the data-generating process, and respecification is required.

(5) A satisfactory model must be *data coherent*. This is the requirement that the differences between the fitted values generated by the model and the actuals should be random, in the sense that they should not be predictable from their own past history. For a model to be satisfactory, it should not be possible to predict how the model will misforecast. If one can make such predictions, then there exists a superior model, which is simply the original model augmented by the process for forecasting the original model's misforecasts.

This has implications for serial correlation, since serial correlation of a model's residuals is just such a systematic departure of a model's forecasts from the out-turns. Here, then, is a radical difference between the AER view and Hendry's methodology. On the AER view the absence of serial correlation is tested for using the Durbin–Watson statistic (which is most powerful against the presence of first-order autocorrelation) and, if found, is corrected by application of the Cochrane–Orcutt transformation. On Hendry's view such correction is entirely inappropriate, since the presence of serial correlation will generally imply a model which cannot be taken to represent the data-generating process, and the remedy to this is a revised specification and not re-estimation.

Most frequently, the required version is the incorporation of one or more of the lagged regressor variables. The specification

$$y_t = \alpha + \beta'x_t + u_t \quad (9)$$

---

but an alternative way of putting this is that there does not exist a lower dimensional vector μ such that $\psi = \psi(\mu)$ and $\phi = \phi(\mu)$. Super exogeneity is a sufficient condition for a parameter vector to be invariant, but it is not necessary since particular parameters of interest may turn out to be invariant with respect to changes in, say, expectations generation, even though other parameters are affected.

with

$$u_t = \varrho u_{t-1} + \epsilon_t$$

where the $\{\epsilon_t\}$ are white noise, may be transformed to

$$y_t = \alpha(1 - \varrho) + \varrho y_{t-1} + \beta' x_t - \varrho \beta' x_{t-1} + \epsilon_t \qquad (10)$$

The unrestricted version of this equation may be written as

$$y_t = \gamma_0 + \gamma_1 y_{t-1} + \gamma_2' x_t + \gamma_3' x_{t-1} + \epsilon_t \qquad (11)$$

The hypothesis of first-order serial correlation is only acceptable if the restriction

$$\gamma_1 \gamma_2 + \gamma_3 = 0 \qquad (12)$$

is satisfied. If this turns out to be the case serial correlation is 'a convenient simplification, not a nuisance,' but more usually the restriction will be rejected, and the statistic indicating serial correlation would be correctly interpreted as pointing to the omission of the relevant lagged variable (Hendry and Mizon, 1978).[16] As will be apparent, this is just an application of the general to simple methodology discussed in Section 2 (serial correlation implies the presence of a 'common factor' in the lag distributions in (11)).

Hendry's view of serial correlation follows from the fact that the properties of the equation disturbance are implied by the model specification. On this view the disturbance ϵ_t is derived from the model. This is to be contrasted with the AER view where one posits $y = X\beta + \epsilon$ and then proceeds to make assumptions about ϵ. This implies a particular process for y, and is indeed how we proceed in Monte Carlo analysis. However, in empirical work, the dependent variable already follows a particular process, and the assumption that $y = X\beta + \epsilon$ implies (if β is constant and X follows a known and independent process) a process for the disturbance ϵ. Rather, in looking for data coherence, one is looking to see whether the derived ϵ process is close to white noise. If it is not, this suggests augmentation or respecification of the equation.[17]

(6) A satisfactory model should *encompass* a wide range of rival

---

[16] There is a complication that some components of x_{t-1} may be exactly collinear with x_t (for example if x_t contains a time trend or seasonal dummies). Let x_{t-1}^* be the sub-vector of x_{t-1} which is not exactly collinear with x_t and partition x_t and γ_2 conformably into x_t^* and x_t^{**} and γ_2^* and γ_2^{**} respectively. Then (9) becomes

$$\gamma_1 \gamma_2^* + \gamma_3 = 0$$

The seminal paper is Sargan (1964), extended in Sargan (1980).

[17] 'Most estimation theory in econometric textbooks is predicated on knowing the "correct" model, while simultaneously, most practitioners are well aware that their models are inevitably inadequate in many respects. Consequently, it seems more useful to try and *design* empirical models such that their residuals are white-noise *innovations* relative to the available information' (Hendry and Richard, 1983, p. 17, author's italics).

models.[18] One model may be said to encompass a second model if it can explain the second model's results. A good model should not only explain the data, but should also explain both the successes and the failures of rival models in accounting for the same data. The Special Theory of Relativity encompasses Newtonian mechanics (which could not explain the Michelson–Morley results), but is itself encompassed by the General Theory of Relativity (as it cannot explain the visibility of the planet Mercury behind the Sun during a solar eclipse).

Suppose Smith believes

$$H_{\text{Smith}}: y = X\alpha + u \quad u \sim N(0, \sigma_u^2 I) \tag{13}$$

whilst Marks asserts

$$H_{\text{Marks}}: y = Z\beta + v \quad v \sim N(0, \sigma_v^2 I) \tag{14}$$

If $X \neq Z$, at most one of these theories can give both a correct and complete description of the economy.[19] In the actual sample there is also a relationship between the X and Z variables, which may be summarized as

$$Z = X\Pi' + w \tag{15}$$

This is uncontentious. Π is simply the set of regression coefficients obtained from regressing the Z variables on the X variables over this sample, and may have no theoretical interpretation. This relationship implies that, on H_{Marks}

$$y = X\Pi'\beta + (v + w\beta). \tag{16}$$

This allows Marks to attempt to predict Smith's results, since equating coefficients in the two equations (14) and (16) relating y to X

$$\alpha = \Pi'\beta \tag{17}$$

and

$$\sigma_u^2 = \sigma_v^2 + \beta'\Sigma_w\beta \tag{18}$$

where Σ_w is the sample variance covariance matrix of w.[20] Note that this implies $\sigma_u^2 > \sigma_v^2$, so there is no point in attempting to encompass a theory with a lower error variance.[21] If H_{Marks} is correct, it can predict the coefficients that will be obtained by fitting the incorrect specification-H_{Smith}, and it will also predict how badly H_{Smith} will fit the data.

---

[18] In Hendry and Richard (1982) *all* rival models are to be encompassed! In practice the data are unlikely to be decisive in all cases. See Mizon (1984) and Mizon and Richard (1985) for more extended discussion of encompassing.

[19] Both may be 'correct' in the limited sense that it can be true that $E(y_t|x_t) = \alpha'x_t$ and $E(y_t|z_t) = \beta'z_t$. However, it cannot be the case that $E(y_t|x_t, z_t) = \alpha'x_t$ and $E(y_t|x_t, z_t) = \beta'z_t$ (for arbitrary values of α and β) unless $x_t = z_t$ (Mizon, 1984).

[20] This requires that v and w be independent. By (weak) exogeneity of Z, $E(Z'v) = 0$. In addition, Smith must claim (weak) exogeneity of X implying $E(X'v) = 0$. But (11) then implies $E(W'v) = 0$.

[21] This comment requires the qualification that in small samples one might have $\hat{\sigma}_v^2 > \hat{\sigma}_u^2$ despite (18) as the consequence of sampling variation.

It is interesting that both of these conditions may be tested by the classical F test on the common nesting hypothesis

$$H_{\text{nesting}}: y = Z\beta + X^*\gamma + e \tag{19}$$

where X^* is a submatrix of X which is not exactly collinear with Z. H_{Marks} simply implies $\gamma = 0$. Thus encompassing may also be seen as an application of general to simple methodology. The role of H_{nesting} is to provide a common distributional framework for H_{Smith} and H_{Marks}, and it is important to note there need be no theory which gives it an interpretation (Mizon, 1984, pp. 142–3). If both H_{Marks} and H_{Smith} are rejected (the latter by formulation of H_{nesting} in terms of Z^* and X), then each theory rejects the other, and more work is required. (It is of course possible that neither theory will be rejected on a given data set.)

I have now listed the six criteria which an acceptable model must satisfy. A model which does satisfy all six criteria is said to be *congruent* with the evidence. It is notable that the major criterion in the AER methodology is absent from this list. This is the criterion of goodness-of-fit. It is possible to characterize an alternative approach to specification as that of selecting *parsimoniously undominated* models (e.g. Amemiya, 1980). A readily recognizable caricature of the econometrician's objective is the maximization of $\bar{R}^2$ subject to Durbin–Watson near 2. In the Hendry methodology, goodness-of-fit is not an explicit criterion for accepting a model as a good representation of the data-generating process. However, the criterion is implicitly present in the encompassing principle, since in a linear framework encompassing implies *variance–dominance* (i.e. the criterion which states that one should accept the model with the lowest variance). Hendry simply notes that this is one of several criteria that one would wish to adopt (Hendry and Richard, 1982, p. 14).

That a model can be acceptable despite having a poor fit is clear. Similarly, the fact that a rival model has a better fit does not *ipso facto* make it a better model. The latter point is perhaps obvious through the phenomenon of over-fitting: R^2s can always be increased by the addition of further 'explanatory' variables, but in general this will result in apparent structural non-constancy as additional data points are added and so parameter constancy will be violated. To illustrate the former point, consider modelling asset prices generated by an efficient market (stock market or foreign exchange prices for example). There is every reason to suppose that, at least to a very good approximation, such prices follow a martingale process, and that the changes in these prices are therefore unpredictable. A random walk model will have zero explanatory power in relation to these price changes, but may nevertheless be a perfectly acceptable statistical representation.[22]

---

[22] The random walk model strengthens the martingale model by the additional imposition of constant variance.

More generally, however, goodness-of-fit is implied by use of the encompassing principle. One representation can only encompass other representations if it has lower error variance than do these alternatives. And, because we are looking for simplifications and have thus implicitly adopted a parsimony principle, if one *F*-acceptable simplification nests another, we adopt the second (more parsimonious) specification. Uniqueness is not guaranteed, but the set of possible representations will be much smaller, and these will all be sustainable in relation to the given data set. Thus it might be possible to claim that a particular asset price follows a martingale process relative to one information set, and is therefore unpredictable from that information set, but this explanation may be encompassed by an alternative that makes the prices predictable relative to an enlarged data set (which includes, for example, insider information).

4. Model Design and Model Discovery

How should the econometrician set about discovering congruent simplifications of the general representation of the DGP (1) (i.e. simplifications which satisfy the six criteria in Section 3)? Hendry offers no advice (Hendry, 1985). Scientific discovery is necessarily an innovative and imaginative process, and cannot be automated.[23]

Nevertheless, the same scientific insight may be expressed in a number of different ways; and there wil be an element of choice as to how a particular hypothesis is incorporated in an econometric model. This is the issue of model design. In looking for counterparts to economics among the natural sciences, engineering science has at least as great a claim as physics, and I shall use an engineering analogy.[24]

One of the most obvious feats of mechanical engineers is bridge-building, and their success in this activity, together with the occasional failure, is apparent to the entire world. Hendry's bridges are econometric models. Bridges are built to serve particular purposes, and so are econometric models. Bridge design rests on the sciences of mechanics and the properties of materials; similarly, the structure of econometric models relies on economic and econometric theory. Bridge designs must be

---

[23] Does the common factor approach, discussed in relation to serial correlation in Section 3 provide a method of automating model discovery? A general procedure based on the Wald test for testing for the number of common factors in an unrestricted representation (like (4)) was developed by Sargan (1980), and is implemented in Hendry and Mizon (1978). The difficulty with this approach is that common factor tests have very low power in samples of the size normally employed in time series econometrics (Mizon and Hendry, 1980). Hendry appears to have retreated from this pure approach, if indeed he ever whole-heartedly adopted it. He sees the general-to-simple approach as providing a testing methodology but not a method of discovery.

[24] This analogy is taken from Hendry's graduate lectures.

thoroughly tested, for example in wind-tunnel experiments, before the
bridge can be built; similarly, econometric models should be thoroughly
tested before being employed in forecasting or policy analysis. Builders of
bridges must submit their plans and their test results to detailed professional and public scrutiny, and the same should be true of econometric
model-builders. Cost is important in building bridges (steel is used where
tungsten would undoubtedly be stronger), and similarly econometric
model-builders must operate within budget constraints. And whilst it is
true that the failure of a bridge is more dramatic than mistaken policies
resulting from the use in forecasting or policy formation of incorrect econometric models, the welfare loss from the latter may also be large. What
then, should a good econometric bridge look like?

Partly, this must depend on what sort of traffic it is to carry. Heavy
lorries require a stronger construction than do pedestrians and cyclists. In
the econometric design process, a vital issue is that the appropriate concept
of exogeneity depends on the use to which the model is to be put – weak
exogeneity will in large measure be sufficient for hypothesis testing; strong
exogeneity is in general required for forecasting; and for policy analysis we
will require super-exogeneity. If one is involved in forecasting or policy
analysis, then the time horizon will be important. Responses which may be
negligible if one's horizon is 12 months may dominate the outcome if one's
horizon is 12 years. In addition, different problems may require different
degrees of disaggregation.

A second criterion that Hendry would adopt is *robustness*. Econometric
models are tested in the wind tunnels of sample data, and, in good professional hands, are also validated against immediate post-sample data (8).
But no firm of civil engineers would gain a bridge contract unless they
could assure the authorities that the bridge would be able to withstand
all reasonable eventualities. What changes from sample conditions should
worry the econometrician? OLS estimates reflect the sample data covariance matrix $T^{-1}X'X$, and the same matrix, projected into some other
space or otherwise transformed will be important in other estimation procedures.[25] Robustness requires that the parameter estimates, and hence
model forecasts and policy prescriptions, are unaffected, if, in the future,
the world throws up a different data covariance matrix. If the weight limit
for lorries rises from 32 tonnes to 36 tonnes, bridges should not need to be
strengthened.

This all relates to the chapter in the AER pathologist's handbook entitled *multicollinearity*. Collinearity is often seen as a problem relating to

[25] $X'\Omega^{-1}X$ in GLS, and $X'P_zX$ in instrumental variables (where P_z is the projection matrix
into the space spanned by the instruments). LIML is asymptotically equivalent to instrumental variables estimation, and so the same point holds as an asymptotic approximation.

the data, and it is obviously true that the correlations in the data are what they are. But equally, the econometrician is free to define his regressor matrix X in any way he likes in relation to this data. In experimental applications, collinearity reflects the experimental design, and in necessarily non-experimental time-series econometrics, collinearity implies failure to exploit efficiently the data which are available. The regression

$$y = W\alpha + \epsilon \tag{20}$$

where $W = XA$ for A square and non-singular, is statistically indistinguishable from the regression

$$y = X\beta + \epsilon \tag{21}$$

However $X'X$ may achieve an arbitrarily high degree of collinearity on any proposal measure, whilst $W'W$ can be as close to orthogonal as one likes.[26] In looking for simplifications of the general hypothesis (e.g. (17)), robustness dictates that we should look for simplifications that involve near-orthogonal variables. Specifically, consider the regression

$$y_t = \beta_0 + \beta_1 X_t + \beta_2 X_{t-1} + \epsilon_t \tag{22}$$

It is likely that X_t and X_{t-1} will be quite highly correlated, but the regression may be equivalently reformulated as

$$y_t = \alpha_0 + \alpha_1 \Delta X_t + \alpha_2 X_{t-1} + \epsilon_t \tag{23}$$

where $\alpha_0 = \beta_0$, $\alpha_1 = \beta_1$ and $\alpha_2 = \beta_1 + \beta_2$. The level variable X_{t-1} and the change variable ΔX_t will be nearly independent when X_t is highly autoregressive. Similarly, a regression involving a distributed lag on X_t, X_{t-1} and X_{t-2} may be reformulated in terms of a level effect (X), a first difference (ΔX) and a second difference $(\Delta^2 X)$. This is essentially the procedure followed by Davidson et al. (DHSY, 1978).[27] The resulting near-orthogonality of the regressor variable set allows valid inferences to be drawn from individual estimated parameters taken in isolation; and

---

[26] Setting A equal to the matrix of eigenvectors of $X'X$ makes $W'W$ diagonal. The columns of W are then the principal components of X. This is not however a sensible transformation of the X variables since the parameters (α) of the principal components in the y regression will not in general be interpretable.

[27] The simplification in Davidson et al (1978) is in terms of seasonal differences $(\Delta_4 Y_t = Y_t - Y_{t-4})$ and the first difference of these differences $(\Delta_1\Delta_4 Y_t)$. Modelling in terms of seasonal differences may be appropriate when using quarterly data if the same quarters in successive years are more closely related than successive quarters in the same year. This would be the case, for example, if families plan their vacation expenditures over a period of years in relation to their permanent income, rather then take whatever vacations they can afford in a given year in relation to their income that year (so that a week in Blackpool in 1985 may be followed by a fortnight in the Bahamas in 1986). But note that in an error correction equation, in which lagged levels variables are included in the regression, the Davidson et al. argument that seasonal differencing allows the seasonal dummies to be dropped (on the grounds that $\Delta_4 q_t = 0$ if q_t is a seasonal dummy) is incorrect – see Hendry and von Ungern-Sternberg (1981).

permits inference about the effects of omitting particular regressors from the equation.

Simplification in terms of near-orthogonal variables may conflict with a further requirement that it is reasonable to seek in econometric models, namely that the parameters of the models are *interpretable* in terms of economic theory. This is not simply a matter of compatibility with theory. Consider for example the contrast between structural and reduced form versions of a model. If the former is compatible with a particular theory, then, *a fortiori*, so must be the latter. But the coefficients of the reduced form model are not (at least directly) interpretable. In relation to collinearity, we can always find data transformations that will give complete orthogonality, but there is no guarantee that these coefficients will be interpretable, and in general they will not.

Why is interpretability important? Two reasons may be proposed. Firstly, although reduced form coefficients may be compatible with theory, it is difficult to know whether or not this is true of any particular set of reduced form coefficients. Secondly, parameters sometimes change, and indeed, in a policy context, the policy may consist of changing parameters (e.g. tax parameters). In order to exploit our knowledge of these changes, we must parameterize in terms of the theoretical (structural) parameters. The DHSY simplification mentioned above must therefore be rationalized not only in terms of the near-orthogonality of the regressor variables, but also in terms of the theoretical interpretability of the DHSY relationship. This is the subject of the next section.

A third criterion which Hendry adopts is *parsimony*. Parsimonious specification is the econometric application of Occam's Razor – if two competing explanations of the same phenomenon have the same explanatory power, then select the simpler. The epistemological justification of the parsimony principle has provoked long debates. There is no convincing reason to suppose that simplicity is an in-built feature of creation; and neither biological nor social evolutionary theories imply a tendency towards simplicity. It is, therefore, unreasonable to suppose that economic DGPs will be simple. But if the DGP is not simple, why should simplicity be a desirable feature of a congruent model?

There are two reasons for valuing parsimony in econometrics, and these both relate to the charaterization of econometric models as *tentatively* adequate. At a practical level, degrees of freedom considerations force simplicity. A given time series will not allow precise estimation of more than a small number of parameters; and, even with the adoption of Hendry's orthogonalization procedure, the econometrician will be forced to choose between omitted variable bias and imprecise estimates resulting from inclusion of too many explanatory variables. Secondly, it is arguable that the human intellect possesses a limited ability to comprehend complex phenomena. Complexity permits *degenerate* research programmes to defend their central propositions by a *protective belt* of auxiliary hypotheses (Lakatos, 1970).[28] These auxiliary hypotheses may be correct, but it is more plausible to suppose that vested professional interests are being protected. Parsimony, on this view, forces scientific honesty.

The econometric modeller must therefore decide on what is important in relation to (1) theory, (2) the characteristics of his sample and (3) the use to which the model is to be put, and seek, within this context, a simple specification satisfying the criteria of Section 3. The resulting model should be specified, according to Hendry, in terms of a near-orthogonal regressor variable set, satisfy exogeneity assumptions sufficiently strong for the uses to which the model will be put, and have coefficients which are both constant and interpretable in terms of economic theory.

5.   Do Acceptable Models Have a Common Structure?

In his applied econometric work over the past decade, Hendry has consistently adopted a specification which has become known as the *error correction model* (ECM). The best known instance is the Davidson et al. (1978) (DHSY) consumption function.

The ECM, which was introduced to economists by Phillips (1954), was first explicitly adopted in applied econometrics in Sargan's (1964) very influential model of UK wage determination. Sargan modelled the quarterly change in wage rates as

$$\Delta \ln w_t = \beta_0 + \beta_1(\ln p_{t-1} - \ln p_{t-4}) - \beta_2 u_{t-1} - \beta_3(\ln w_{t-1} - \ln p_{t-1}) + \beta_4 t + \psi q_t + \epsilon_t \tag{24}$$

where w_t, is the index of wage rates, p_t is the retail price index, u_t is the unemployment rate, and q_t is now a vector of seasonal and other dummies. (The model also included an equation for p_t.) The important term here is $-\beta_3(\ln w_{t-1} - \ln p_{t-1})$, and if we incorporate the time trend, we may write this composite term as

$$-\beta_3\left[\ln\left(\frac{w_{t-1}}{p_{t-1}}\right) - \ln \omega_t\right] \tag{25}$$

where (with suitable adjustment to the intercept)

$$\omega_t = \left(\frac{w_0}{p_0}\right) \exp\left(\frac{\beta_4 t}{\beta_3}\right)$$

We may interpret ω_t as the *target real wage* towards which the actual real wage, w_t/p_t, is adjusting, and, as was natural in a model estimated on a

---

[28] Hendry (1985) appears to place himself deliberately within a Lakatosian framework. See Cross (1982) for a Lakatosian discussion of modern economic theory.

sample which terminated in the mid-1960s, Sargan saw the target real wage as rising steadily over time. To the extent that the actual real wage was in excess of the target, wage settlements would be lower (because of the negative coefficient β_3) but if the actual real wage fell below the target (through the effects, for example, of incomes policy or Sterling devaluation) wage increases would be higher than otherwise. The error correction term in the Sargan wage model is therefore directly interpretable in terms of the target real wage hypothesis. Hendry intoduces analogous terms into his consumption functions, where their presence might have been less expected.

Consider an annual version of the DHSY model (with the inflation terms omitted for simplicity):

$$\Delta \ln C_t = \beta_0 + \beta_1 \Delta \ln Y_t - \beta_2(\ln C_{t-1} - \ln Y_{t-1}) + \epsilon_t \qquad (26)$$

This is the most simple example of an ECM. The change in the dependent variable (the logarithm of consumption) is related to the change in the explanatory variable (log income), and the lagged discrepancy between the dependent and the explanatory variable. In a quarterly version of the model, lagged or higher differences of the explanatory variable are likely to appear, and the final error correction term will often appear with a longer lag length (typically four).

It is straightforward to obtain the long-run consumption-income ratio along a steady state growth path from (26).[29] This is the ratio towards which the actual rate will tend. If the rate of income growth is set to g, this ratio is

$$\ln \left(\frac{C}{Y} \right) = \frac{\beta_0 - (1 - \beta_1)g}{\beta_2} \qquad (27)$$

It is sometimes argued that the ECM should be seen as defining a class of model parameterizations rather than a class of models. To see this, consider a second order general distributed lag linking the logarithm of consumption to the logarithm of income

$$\ln C_t = \alpha + \sum_{j=1}^{2} \beta_j \ln C_{t-j} + \sum_{j=0}^{2} \gamma_j \ln Y_{t-j} + \epsilon_t \qquad (28)$$

Trivially, this may be rewritten, without imposing any restrictions, in terms of current and lagged income and consumption changes, and a set of lagged level variables.

$$\begin{aligned}
\Delta \ln C_t = \alpha &+ (\beta_1 - 1) \Delta \ln C_{t-1} + (2\gamma_0 + \gamma_1) \Delta \ln Y_t \\
&- (\gamma_0 + \gamma_1) \Delta^2 \ln Y_t - (1 - \beta_1 - \beta_2)(\ln C_{t-2} - \ln Y_{t-2}) \\
&+ (\beta_1 + \beta_2 + \gamma_0 + \gamma_1 + \gamma_2 - 1) \ln Y_{t-2}
\end{aligned} \qquad (29)$$

[29] The presence of growth rates in the steady state solution has provoked some discussion – see Currie (1981) and Nickell (1985).

Equation (29) is of the ECM form, but it is observationally equivalent to the unrestricted specification (28). No restrictions have been imposed. However, the ECM parameterization may be useful because the near-orthogonality of the regressors (here $\Delta \ln Y$ and $\Delta^2 \ln Y$) facilitates parsimonious representation of the general distributed lags. This is because the t-statistics on the variables in the unrestricted ECM equation (29) provide a good guide as to the effects of omission of these variables in a simplified equation. But if this were all, the ECM would only define a useful regression strategy, as discussed in the previous section.

In fact, more is implied. In the ECM strategy the investigator is permitted to eliminate and otherwise restrict the influence of the differenced variables at will, but cannot eliminate the lagged level terms since it is these terms that define the equilibrium solution of the model. Equation (29) implies that across steady-state equilibria, the elasticity of consumption to income will be $(\gamma_0 + \gamma_1 + \gamma_2)/(1 - \beta_1 - \beta_2)$. On the permanent income hypothesis this ratio should be equal unity, and this constitutes a test of that model within this framework. In (29) it is immediately testable through the coefficient of $\ln Y_{t-2}$. The premise of the ECM approach to applied econometric modelling is that long run proportionality relationships of this sort (with or without unit coefficients of proportionality) are features that we should expect. If we model entirely in terms of differenced variables, as in the influential Box–Jenkins approach, we cannot say anything about long run relationships; and it is likely that, if there are such relationships, our models will forecast very poorly as the forecast horizon is extended.

The claim that there generally exist long-run relationships between variables may now be recognized as the claim that economic variables are *co-integral* (Engle and Granger, 1985). The statistical theory of co-integral processes postdates much of Hendry's work on ECMs, which is an example of application preceding theory. A variable x is said to be $I(n)$ (integral of order n) if its nth difference $\Delta^n x$ is *weakly stationary* (i.e. if its mean and variance are constant over time). In general, provided we work in logarithms, economic variables are either $I(1)$ or $I(0)$. Consumption and income both grow over time and thus cannot have constant means: we would therefore expect $\ln C$ and $\ln Y$ to be $I(1)$. If two variables x and y are both $I(1)$, then in general any combination of these variables, say $x - \alpha y$, will also be $I(1)$. However, there may exist a singularity, say α^*, such that $x - \alpha^* y$ is $I(0)$. If such a singularity does exist, x and y are co-integral. This implies that, in the long run, although x and y can be arbitarily high or low, they must be proportional to each other with factor of proportionality α^*. The permanent income hypothesis implies exactly this sort of proportionality relationship.[30] Moreover, it is arguable that much of economic

---

[30] Long-run proportionality is dropped in Hendry (1983a).

theory consists of comparative static results which allow comparison of alternative equilibrium positions or paths, and which have little implication for dynamic adjustment. On this view, restrictions should typically be imposed on the equilibrium solutions of econometric equations, and this is facilitated by the ECM formulation.

The appeal of the ECM formulation is that it combines flexibility in dynamic specification with (apparently) desirable long run properties. Engle and Granger (1985) have shown that, if two or more variables are co-integral, there must exist an ECM linking these variables. Hendry's applied work, both on the consumption–income relationship, and on money demand,[31] has assumed co-integration. Recent work on methods for testing for unit roots have brought us to the position where we can test for co-integration prior to embarking on the modelling exercise. The generality of the ECM will become clear once such tests are routinely performed.[32]

This account of the ECM leaves open the economic mechanisms which generate co-integration. A standard way to obtain models of this kind is by invoking *adjustment costs*. Hendry and von Ungern-Sternberg (1981) provide a particularly simple example of this. Consumers have a long-run desired consumption–income ratio K and a long-run desired asset–income ratio of H (which clearly cannot be independent of K). They minimize a myopic loss function[33]

$$\Lambda_t = \lambda_1(a_t - y_t - h)^2 + \lambda_2(c_t - y_t - k)^2 + \lambda_3(c_t - c_{t-1})^2 \qquad (30)$$

where $h = \ln H$, $k = \ln K$, $c_t = \ln C_t$, $y_t = \ln Y_t$ and $a_t = \ln A_t$, and where A_t asset holdings satisfy

$$A_t = A_{t-1} + (Y_t - C_t) \qquad (31)$$

The adjustment cost component of Λ_t is given by the term $\lambda_3(C_t - C_{t-1})^2$. The adjustment path implied by this formulation may be written in the error correction form

$$\Delta c_t = \theta_0 + \theta_1 \Delta y_t - \theta_2(c_{t-1} - y_{t-1}) + \theta_3(a_{t-1} - y_{t-1}) \qquad (32)$$

where the θ_i parameters are functions of the λ_i parameters of (30) together with h and k.

The objective function specified in (30) is for a single period. More generally one would expect agents to minimize a loss function specified as

$$\Lambda_t = \sum_{i=0}^{\infty} \delta^i \Lambda_{t+i} \qquad (33)$$

---

[31] Hendry and Mizon (1978), Hendry (1979), Hendry and Ericsson (1983).

[32] Fuller (1976, pp. 366–82), Dickey and Fuller (1981), Sargan and Bhargava (1983).

[33] Hendry and von Ungern-Stenberg include an additional term $\lambda_4(C_t - C_{t-1})(Y_t - Y_{t-1})$ in their loss function, but this does not alter the form of the control solution (32), although it removes the restriction that $\theta_1 = \theta_2 + \theta_3$.

where $\delta = 1/(1 + \varrho)$ and ϱ is the discount rate. The solution of this model is somewhat more complicated since planned consumption in period t must depend on planned consumption in period $t + 1$, and so forth. Nickell (1985) has provided a systematic analysis of models of this sort.

Suppose that the individual's target consumption in period t is $C_t^* = KY_t$, and that he minimizes a loss function

$$\Lambda = \sum_{i=0}^{\infty} \delta^i [\lambda(c_{t+i} - c_{t+i}^*)^2 + (c_{t+i} - c_{t+i-1})^2] \tag{34}$$

The first term in (34) is the penalty from having an consumption level differing from one's target; the second term is the adjustment cost penalty. Nickell shows that the solution to this minimization problem gives as optimal consumption level for period t

$$\Delta c_t = (1 - \mu) \left[(1 - \delta\mu) \sum_{i=0}^{\infty} (\delta\mu)^i c_{t+i}^* - c_{t-i} \right] \tag{35}$$

where $0 < \mu < 1$. Note the absence of any term in Δc_t^* in (35). As it stands, equation (35) defines a partial adjustment model and not an ECM. The change in the current consumption level is the fraction $1 - \mu$ of the difference between the weighted sum of future target consumption levels and the lagged level. With static income expectations, (35) simplifies to the familiar:

$$\Delta c_t = (1 - \mu)(k + y_t - c_{t-1}) \tag{36}$$

In general, however, income expectations would not reasonably be static. Indeed, under rational expectations the relationship between the current expectation of future income levels and current and past income realizations will depend on the actual income generation process. It turns out that the most satisfactory simple approximation to such processes is obtained by supposing that income follows a second-order autoregression with drift (i.e. that the difference in income follows a first-order autoregression with a non-zero intercept):

$$\Delta y_t = \frac{g}{(1 - \theta)} + \theta \Delta y_{t-1} + \epsilon_t \tag{37}$$

where ϵ_t is white noise. Forming rational expectations of future income levels using (37) and substituting into (35) gives an ECM consumption specification

$$\Delta c_t = \frac{1 - \mu}{1 - \delta\mu} \delta\mu g + \frac{1 - \mu}{1 - \theta\delta\mu} \Delta y_t + (1 - \mu)(k + y_{t-1} - c_{t-1}) \tag{38}$$

Hence the ECM may be expected to arise from partial adjustment of consumption, money stock, etc., to desired values, in conjunction with rational expectations and plausible income-generating processes. There may, of course, be other routes, but adjustment costs and second order autoregressions occur sufficiently widely in economics to suggest a wide application for this class of model.

6.   Conclusions

David Hendry's views on econometrics may be summarized as follows:

(1) The data-generating process underlying a data set is never known. Applied econometrics is therefore in part a process of discovery, and all proposed models must be presumed to be misspecified.
(2) Applied economists should aim to provide structural models which may be taken as approximations to the unknown data-generating process.
(3) Restrictions derived from economic theory will typically relate to the equilibrium solutions to these models, rather than to the short-term dynamics. Such restrictions may frequently be imposed and tested within an error-correction framework. The generality of this model follows from the fact that many important economic series are co-integral.
(4) Any proposed model must be tested within and outside the sample. One needs to ask whether the model adequately characterizes the data, and also whether this characterization is superior to that provided by rival specifications.
(5) Equation specification should be conducted by testing alternative simplifications against a common nesting maintained hypothesis. Tests may be carried out using standard classical statistical procedures, or straightforward generalizations of these procedures.

To a large extent, these views are shared with other practising English econometricians, and are part of a tradition which originated at the London School of Economics in the 1950s and 1960s. In Gilbert (1986) I argued that this tradition derives its power from the combination of the Cowles emphasis on structural modelling with statistical time series analysis methodology. In the United States, by contrast, these two traditions have tended to remain distinct, with the result that structural models compete with VAR (vector autoregression) formulations without any middle ground.

Because much recent British applied econometrics, and in particular Hendry's contributions, differ considerably in style from American studies on the same topics, there is a tendency to suppose that the British approach is, in some sense, extreme. The foregoing analysis suggest that, on the contrary, David Hendry's econometric methodology constitutes a sensible middle ground. The methodology is grounded in prevalence of properly conducted specification searches in econometric practice. It rationalizes much of what econometricians have always done, but also provides guidance as to how these things can be done more efficiently. The most important test of any methodology is, however, the applied research that it generates. In this respect the accumulating body of published articles which utilize the methods discussed in this paper establish this methodology as among the most powerful of the current approaches to applied economics.

References

Amemiya, T. (1980), Selection of regressors, *International Economic Review*, 21, 331–54.

Currie, D. (1981), Some long run features of dynamic time series models, *Economic Journal*, 91, 704–15.

Davidson, J. E. H. and Hendry, D. F. (1981), Interpreting econometric evidence: the behaviour of consumers' expenditure in the UK, *European Economic Review*, 16, 177–92.

Davidson, J. E. H., Hendry, D. F., Srba, F. and Yeo, S. (1978), Econometric modelling of the aggregate time-series relationship between consumers' expenditure and income in the UK, *Economic Journal*, 88, 661–92.

Dickey, J. A. and Fuller, W. A. (1981), Likelihood ratio statistics for autoregressive time series with a unit root, *Econometrica*, 49, 1057–72.

Engle, R. F. and Granger, C. W. J. (1987), Dynamic model specification with equilibrium constraints: cointegration and error correction, *Econometrica*, 55, 251–76.

Engle, R. F., Hendry, D.F. and Richard, J-F. (1983), Exogeneity, *Econometrica*, 51, 277–304.

Fuller, W. A. (1976), *Introduction to Statistical Time Series*. Wiley, New York.

Gilbert, C. L. (1986), The development of British econometrics 1945–85, University of Oxford, Applied Economics Discussion Paper, no. 8.

Hall, R. E. (1978), Stochastic implications of the life cycle–permanent income hypotheses: theory and evidence, *Journal of Political Economy*, 86, 971–87.

Harvey, A. C. (1981), *The Econometric Analysis of Time Series*. Philip Allan, Daddington.

Hendry, D. F. (1979), Predictive failure and econometric modelling in macroeconomics: the transactions demand for money, *Modelling the Economy*, ed. by P. Ormerod. Heinemann, London.

Hendry, D. F. (1983), Econometric modelling: the consumption function in retrospect, *Scottish Journal of Political Economy*, 30, 193–220.

Hendry, D. F. (1985), Econometric methodology. Paper presented to the Econometric Society Fifth World Congress, MIT.

Hendry, D. F. and Ericsson, N. R. (1983), Assertion without empirical basis: an econometric appraisal of 'Monetary trends in...the United Kingdom', by Milton Friedman and Anna Schwartz. In Bank of England Academic Consultants, *Monetary Trends in the United Kingdom*, paper no. 22, pp. 45–101.

Hendry, D. F. and Mizon, G. E. (1978), Serial correlation as a convenient simplification, not a nuisance: a comment on a study of the demand for money by the Bank of England, *Economic Journal*, 88, 549–63.

Hendry, D. F., Pagan, A. R. and Sargan, J. D. (1984), Dynamic specification, *Handbook of Econometrics*, ed. by Z. Griliches and M. D. Intriligator. North-Holland, Amsterdam.

Hendry, D. F. and Richard, J-F. (1982), On the formulation of empirical models in dynamic econometrics, *Journal of Econometrics*, 20, 3–33.

Hendry, D. F. and Richard, J-F. (1983), The econometric analysis of economic time series, *International Statistical Review*, 51, 111–63.

Hendry, D. F. and von Ungern-Sternberg, T. (1981), Liquidity and inflation effects on consumers' expenditure, *Essays in the Theory and Measurement of Consumer Behaviour*, ed. by A. S. Deaton. Cambridge University Press, Cambridge.

Hendry, D. F. and Wallis, K. F. (eds) (1984), *Econometrics and Quantitative Economics*. Basil Blackwell, Oxford.

Judge, G. G. and Bock, M. E. (1978), *The Statistical Implications of Pre-test and Stein-Rule Estimators in Econometrics*. North-Holland, Amsterdam.

Lakatos, I. (1970), Falsification and the methodology of scientific research programmes, *Criticism and the Growth of Knowledge*, ed. by I. Lakatos and A. Musgrave. Cambridge University Press, Cambridge.

Leamer, E. E. (1978), *Specification Searches: Ad Hoc Inference with Non-Experimental Data*. Wiley, New York.

Leamer, E. E. (1983), Let's take the con out of econometrics, *American Economic Review*, 73, 31–43 (reprinted as Chapter 1 in this volume).

Lucas, R. E. (1976), Econometric policy analysis: a critique, *The Phillips Curve and Labour Markets* (*Journal of Monetary Economics*, Supplement, Vol. 1, pp. 19–46), ed. by K. Brunner and A. H. Meltzer.

McAleer, M., Pagan, A. R. and Volker, P. A. (1985), What will take the con out of econometrics?, *American Economic Review*, 75, 293–307 (reprinted as Chapter 2 in this volume).

Mizon, G. E. (1977), Model selection procedures, *Studies in Modern Economic Analysis*, edited by M. J. Artis and A. R. Nobay. Basil Blackwell, Oxford.

Mizon, G. E. (1984), The encompassing principle in econometrics. In Hendry and Wallis (1984), pp. 135–72.

Mizon, G. E. and Hendry, D. F. (1980), An empirical application and Monte Carlo analysis of tests of dynamic specification, *Review of Economic Studies*, 47, 21–46.

Mizon, G. E. and Richard, J-F. (1985), The encompasing principle and its application to non-nested hypotheses, *Econometrica*, 54, 657–78.

Nickell, S. (1985), Error correction, partial adjustment and all that: an expository note, *Oxford Bulletin of Economics and Statistics*, 47, 119–31.

Phillips, A. W. (1954), Stabilization policy in a closed economy, *Economic Journal*, 64, 290–323.

Sargan, J. D. (1964), Wages and prices in the United Kingdom: a study in econometric methodology, *Econometric Analysis for National Economic Planning*, ed. by P. E. Hart et al. Butterworths (reprinted in Hendry and Wallis (1984), pp. 275–314).

Sargan, J. D. (1980), Some tests of dynamic specification for a single equation, *Econometrica*, 48, 879–97.

Sargan, J. D. and Bhargava, A. (1983), Testing residuals from least squares regression for being generated by the Gaussian random walk, *Econometrica*, 51, 153–74.

Surrey, M. J. C. (1974), *An Introduction to Econometrics*. Oxford University Press, Oxford.

Trivedi, P. K. (1984), Uncertain prior information and distributed lag analysis. In Hendry and Wallis (1984), pp. 173–210.

Wonnacott, R. J. and Wonnacott, T. H. (1970), *Econometrics*. Wiley, New York.

14

On the Formulation of Empirical Models in Dynamic Econometrics

David F. Hendry and Jean-François Richard

Abstract. Available information is considered as partitioned into the sets: past, present, and future observations, other data of competing models and theory knowledge. In each case, specific concepts are relevant to empirical model formulation (e.g. innovations for past data, exogeneity for present, encompassing for contending models, etc.) and various properties of such concepts are established (viz. encompassing is transitive and asymmetric). Relationships between concepts are developed (e.g. encompassing entails variance-dominance in linear models), and related to the notion of a progressive research strategy. An empirical model illustrates the various criteria. Model selection by dynamic simulation tracking performance is critically evaluated.

1. Introduction

Notwithstanding the emphasis on 'model building' in econometrics, there does not seem to exist a formal analysis of 'models' and/or of concepts relevant to empirical models in particular. This paper is offered as a step towards developing such an analysis. While it is clearly feasible to undertake a completely formal treatment – corresponding to that of, say, Florens and Mouchart (1980a) for the theory of reduction – initially it seemed most useful and comprehensive to consider the problem more heuristically (and primarily in the context of linear processes).

The framework of the paper is as follows: available information is conceived of as being partitioned into the disjoint sets: past, present, and future observations; other data relevant to contending hypotheses; and theory information. For each item, specific concepts are relevant: viz. 'white noise' for lagged data, 'exogeneity' for present, 'parameter constancy' for future, and 'encompassing' for contending models are some

This article was first published in the *Journal of Econometrics*, Vol. 20, No. 3, 1982, pp. 3–33. The authors are greatly indebted to Frank Srba for undertaking the computations reported below, and to Jean-Pierre Florens, Knud Munk and Aris Spanos for many stimulating discussions on this topic, but do not hold them responsible for the views expressed herein. Financial support from the International Centre for Economics and Related Disciplines and from the Social Science Research Council to the MIME programme at the London School of Economics is gratefully acknowledged.

examples. For each concept, various properties are established; viz. 'encompassing' is asymmetric and transitive and so defines an ordering; and relationships between concepts are developed (e.g. if Model A has a larger residual variance than Model B, then it cannot encompass Model B).

Many widely used concepts arise naturally in the present framework, although the insufficiency of certain of these as a basis for empirical modelling does not seem well known. For example, it is inappropriate to select models by the *sole* criterion that they have white-noise residuals (or that combined with a parsimony condition) as this does not necessarily preclude better-fitting models being developed from the same basic information. Indeed, these could even be more parsimonious than the initial model if the model-building strategy does not ensure that the white noise process is in addition an innovation process relative to the available information. Similarly, simply selecting 'best-fitting' models (again with or without parsimony conditions) does not by itself ensure encompassing. Perhaps less well known, and yet of great practical importance, selecting models by the goodness of their 'dynamic simulation tracking performance' is invalid in general and tells more about the structure of the models than about their correspondence to 'reality'.

It must be stressed that the purpose of the paper is the formulation and preliminary analysis of a number of concepts relevant to the *empirical* econometric analysis of *time-series* observations. In such a framework, economic theory plays a relatively neutral role in the sense that the concepts apply irrespective of the models being based on inadequate (or naive) theories or on sophisticated, general and/or well-established theories (see e.g. the approach in Sargent, 1981). The relationship between theory models and empirical models is discussed in Section 2, followed by an empirical illustration chosen to 'set the scene' for the analysis of Section 4 in which the main concepts and their interrelationships are discussed. The empirical example is reconsidered in Section 5, and Section 6 evaluates the role of dynamic simulation in model selection. Concluding comments are provided in Section 7.

2. Theory Models and Empirical Models

A model of any set of phenomena is a formal representation thereof in which certain features are abstracted while others are ignored with the intent of providing a simpler description of the salient aspects of the chosen phenomenon: 'A model always represents only some but not all the features of the original' (Hayek, 1963, p. 14). Models comprise sets of structures each of which is a well-defined characterization of that which is to be explained. Two classes of model are important: theory models and empirical models. Despite their common aim of seeking an 'accurate' representation of perceived 'reality' and their close interdependence in practice, it is essential to maintain a clear distinction between the two classes in what follows.

Theory models consist of the logically valid implications of sets of initial assertions and qualifying conditions (i.e., *ceteris paribus* clauses) so that, in principle, they are 'free creations of the human mind' (see e.g. Einstein, 1950). Succinctly, theory models postulate theory relationships between latent variables which are defined in the context of the theory using theory connectives such as 'causal dependence' (see e.g. Simon, 1953 and contextual concepts such as 'equilibrium' (see e.g. Spanos, 1981). The empirical relevance or otherwise of the theory follows from the correspondence conditions (or measurement equations) mapping latent on to observable variables (see e.g. Losee, 1980). However, since any given theory may not correctly and completely characterize the perceived world, the perceptibility of *necessary* connections among observed events is open to doubt (following Hume, 1758). Consequently, the unqualified term 'causality' will refer below only to an asymmetric relationship defined in the context of a theory model (for recent discussions of 'causality' in econometrics see *inter alia* Zellner, 1979; Granger, 1980a and Florens and Mouchart, 1981). Of course a major function of any economic theory model in econometrics is to sustain inferences from observed 'empirical regularities' to conjectured 'causal dependencies'. In modern treatments the anticipated presence or absence of certain data correlations is deduced from the causal structure of the theory model, and the outcome used to 'corroborate or refute' the theory model. This obviates the need to try and infer 'causes from correlations', but only by focusing attention on the problem of 'testing' theory models.

Most theories form part of a sequence of formulations all of which are conditional on the empirical validity of many lower-level theories (even if this is usually left implicit in our procedures) and are testable, if at all, only in conjunction with such theories, the *ceteris paribus* clauses, and a particular model implementation. If observed data and theory implications are inconsistent, there is both latitude concerning to which features the inconsistency is attributed, and ample scope for introducing *ad hoc* assumptions to neutralize any anomalies (see Lakatos, 1974). However, an agglomeration of test failures against a background of well-established lower-level theories may lead to the discarding of the sequence of theories in question as 'degenerating' in favour of less suspect alternatives (when such exist) until such time as that theory sequence can account successfully for previous anomalies. Generally, this last step will require explanations to have excess empirical content, some of which is corroborated. Blaug (1980) provides an excellent discussion of such issues in economics using Lakatos's concept of scientific research programmes (see Worrall and

Currie, 1978). Since this last notion evolved precisely because of the impossibility of 'proving' theories combined with the enormous difficulties of 'refuting' them, a primary construct used below is that of a 'progressive' research programme in which novel 'facts' are anticipated by the theory sequence and are later corroborated empirically.

The process of testing a theory model is generally undertaken via an empirical model which comprises relationships between *measured* variables. However, whereas the former may have been a 'free creation', and although it delineates the structure of the latter (which will generally use the same names for the observable counterparts of the latent variables), nevertheless, the use of observed data creates a fundamental distinction between the two classes since an empirical model must, by default, be simply a *recombination of whatever process generated the data*. Which particular recombination is obtained depends on the constraints imposed by the theory and the properties of the underlying data-generation process. In a Monte Carlo context this analysis is trivially obvious: the data-generation process determines the properties of the data set which determines whatever results are obtained on estimating any given relationship by a well-specified method. The implications of this viewpoint for empirical research will be discussed below, following a brief consideration of the role of statistical-theory models in econometrics.

The theory of statistical inference proceeds by postulating various stochastic processes, deducing implications of their behaviour, and using the resulting analysis to interpret observed outcomes: the archetypal example is a coin-tossing 'model' as a Bernoulli trial. Being concerned with the logical study of a hypothetical data-generation process (denoted by DGP below) in statistical theory the maintained theory model is never questioned, and issues of interest concern whether specific structures are identifiable, how 'best' to estimate the parameters of such structures etc. As expressed by Malinvaud (1966, p. 64), inference concerns narrowing the scope of the model in the light of the data. However, conflating the DGP and the model in empirical research provides an unsound basis for inference *until the model in some sense adequately characterizes the data*. The data directly convey information about the DGP (although we may not know how to interpret that information without an appropriate theory) and many features of most models are open to evaluation against the data to investigate how well the model describes that data. But even in the best-formulated instances, the complexity of economic DGPs and the inherent simplicity of econometric models ensure that the axiom of correct specification (see Leamer, 1978, p. 4) is not a sufficient basis for inference. Should that axiom be valid in any particular case, the model simply coincides with the DGP and the potential recombination is an identity mapping, but this seems an unlikely eventuality.

Many of the concepts and issues described above are most easily clarified by examining an empirical illustration which is deliberately formulated to highlight the relevant points and is not claimed to represent in any way *how* econometricians actually conduct empirical research.

3. An Illustration: The Repayment of Mortgage Principal

The theory model is a static-equilibrium world in which all stocks and flows are constant so that in every period a constant proportion ($\mathcal{N}^{-1}$) of the outstanding stock of mortgate loans ($\mathcal{M}$) is repaid each period ($\mathcal{R}$),

$$\mathcal{R} = \mathcal{N}^{-1}\mathcal{M}. \tag{1}$$

Note that the repayment profile for any individual loan is nonetheless non-linear and dependent on the rate of interest ($\mathcal{I}$) even in such a world. Also, (1) is typical of many theory models in economics – it seems logically correct given the assumptions and provides the useful information that $\mathcal{R}/\mathcal{M}$ is independent of $\mathcal{M}$. Next, script letters denote latent variables defined in a static-equilibrium context in which (1) holds in both real and nominal terms, and indeed in various equivalent transformations such as linear-in-logs, first (or, $\forall j < \infty$, jth order) differences etc., as stressed below. Finally, comparing between equilibria, an increase in $\mathcal{M}$ causes an increase in $\mathcal{R}$ (whereas, e.g., an increase in repayments dynamically lowers the remaining mortgage stock *ceteris paribus*).

In the United Kingdom, most mortgages have been provided by building societies (see Hendry and Anderson, 1977 and Mayes, 1979), and for these institutions, excellent quarterly time-series data (R_t, M_t) exist with negligibly small (pure) measurement errors (italic capitals denote the measured 'equivalent' of script variables, lower case denote $\log_e$ of the corresponding capital and $\Delta_j x_t = x_t - x_{t-j}$). However, equivalent theory models do not necessarily yield equivalent empirical models: let $\mathcal{K} = \mathcal{N}^{-1}$, then consider

$$\mathcal{R} = \mathcal{K}\mathcal{M} = \mathcal{K}\mathcal{M}_{-1},$$
$$\mathcal{R}/\mathcal{M}_{-1} = \mathcal{K}$$
$$\mathcal{R}/\mathcal{P} = \mathcal{K}(\mathcal{M}/\mathcal{P})_{-1},$$

where $\mathcal{P}$ denotes an appropriate price index. Without wishing to belabour the point, log-linear equivalents exist of each of these, as do variants in (any order of) differences, and so on. Unfortunately, all of these theory-consistent models (and many more possibilities) can have distinctly different empirical properties in terms of (say) residual variance, heteroscedasticity, autocorrelation, etc. Since almost no repayments of new loans occur within one quarter, for quarterly data lagged M seems preferable to current and logs seem preferable to original units as entailing positivity and a constant percentage residual variance. This suggests estimating

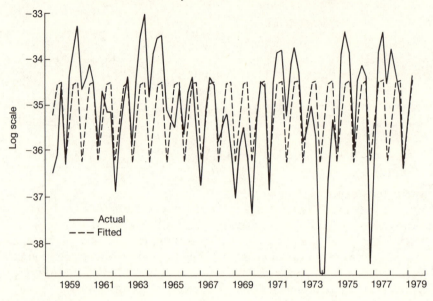

Figure 2 $r_t - m_{t-1}$

DW), so 'refitting' in first differences to remove the trend and auto-correlation,

$$\Delta_1 \hat{r}_t = 0.83 \Delta_1 m_{t-1} + \hat{S}_t, \quad R^2 = 0.65, \quad \hat{\sigma} = 0.067, \quad DW = 1.80.$$
$$(0.23) \tag{4}$$

The null of serially uncorrelated residuals can no longer be rejected against the alternative of first-order autocorrelation, (4) implements another of the theory model equivalents, $\hat{\sigma}$ has fallen considerably, and $\hat{a}_1$ is not 'significantly different from unity'. On such criteria, (4) seems to provide an adequate model.

Appearances can be deceptive, however: if the error on (4) really were an autonomous white-noise process, then $(r_r - m_{t-1})$ would be a random walk, and so could assume any value, rendering (1) a useless theory (see Davidson et al., 1978). Further, DW has been used as a selection criterion and if the only equations reported are those with $DW \approx 2$, it hardly provides useful 'test' information. Moreover, the claim that the residuals in (4) are white noise (even if it were true) does not entail that the equation is an 'adequate description of the data', since, for example, the unit common-factor assumption in (4) could be invalid and hence either or both r_{t-1} and m_{t-2} could be significant if added as regressors (see Sargan, 1980; Hendry and Mizon, 1978). According to (1), we 'know' that $a_1 = 1$, yet after fitting (4) all that can be said is that $(0.37, 1.29)$ provides a 95 per cent confidence interval for a_1!

It seems clear that a formal analysis of the various concepts involved in formulating empirical models, and of their interrelationships, is necessary in order to clarify the problems encountered above. Relating back to Section 2 a crucial issue is that some unknown mechanism generated (r_t, m_t) from which (2) is a derived representation such that ε_t *must* contain everything affecting r_t not explicitly included in (2): the assertion that $\varepsilon_t \sim IN(0, \sigma_\varepsilon^2)$ is tantamount to the claim that (2) is the DGP even though (3) immediately contradicts that by its obvious failure to describe many salient data features. Thus, (a_0, a_1) is a (reduced) reparameterization of the parameters (θ) of the (unknown) underlying DGP, induced by the method of estimation and so is defined implicitly by the auxiliary claims that $\mathscr{E}(\varepsilon_t) = 0$, and $\mathscr{E}(\varepsilon_t m_{t-1}) = 0$. The constancy of θ and the reduction necessary to obtain (2) determine the constancy (or otherwise) of $(\hat{a}_0, \hat{a}_1)$ as T varies, the properties of the residuals, and so on (for a general analysis of the theory of reduction – in a Bayesian framework – see Florens and Mouchart, 1980a).

Relating forward to Section 4, issues meriting consideration are the predictability of white-noise errors, their use as an equation selection criterion and their relationship to goodness-of-fit, the theory consistency of empirical models, the validity of data transformations, and so on. We hope our analysis will allow a useful framework to be developed for formulating and selecting empirical models which do not coincide 1–1 with the actual data-generation process. Also, while (1) is obviously a very rudimentary starting point (to highlight specific issues), similar potential difficulties lurk behind any empirical study, however good its initial theory, the difference being a matter of degree not of kind.

4. An Analysis of Empirical-model Concepts

For notational convenience, the mechanism generating the outcome $X_T^1 = (x_1 \ldots x_T)$ of a k-dimensional time-sequential economic process is assumed continuous with respect to an appropriate measure as in, e.g. Engle et al. (1981), and is therefore described by the density function

$$D(X_T^1|X_0, \theta) = \prod_{t-1}^{T} D(x_t|X_{t-1}, \theta_0, \theta_t), \tag{5}$$

where $\theta = (\theta_0\{\theta_t\}) \in \Theta$ is a finite-dimensional, identifiable, sufficient parameterization (see e.g. Madansky, 1976, ch. 2). Also, θ_0 denotes parameters which are fixed throughout the time horizon T, while θ_t regroups transient parameters (as in, say, Crowder, 1976). X_0 is the matrix of initial conditions and $X_{t-1} = (X_0 X_{t-1}^1)$. To aid the exposition and simplify proofs, the analysis is implicitly restricted to the linear framework, although we conjecture that many of the results apply more generally. If

$\{x_t\}$ is assumed to be strongly mixing and (5) involves a finite lag dependency, then the results in Domowitz and White (1982) seem to provide an adequate basis for a valid asymptotic distribution theory for least-squares approximations to a wide range of models. Below, T is assumed sufficiently large that large sample theory is applicable.

The analysis is based on a partition of the available information (described in Section 1 above) into (1) past (or lagged) data, (2) current data, (3) future data, (4) the separate data of contending hypotheses, and (5) theory information. This ordering is chosen for analytical convenience so that the elements of the partition can be considered cumulatively.

A.   Past Information

DEFINITION 1 $\{e_t\}$ is a (mean) white-noise process if $\mathscr{E}(e_t|E_{t-1}) = \mathscr{E}(e_t)$, $\forall t$, where $E_{t-1} = (E_0 E_{t-1}^1)$. Thus $\{e_t\}$ is not predictable linearly from its past (see Granger, 1986b), beyond its unconditional mean (taken to be zero).

Note that $\{e_t\}$ may be predictable either fully or in part given an extended information set, and indeed may have a temporal structure (see Davidson and Hendry, 1981). Also, $\{e_t\}$ need not be homoscedastic and in particular could follow an ARCH scheme (see Engle, 1982). If $\mathscr{E}(e_t) = 0$, $\forall t$, given Definition 1, then $\{e_t\}$ is a (vector) martingale difference sequence (see Whittle, 1970, Ch. 9). Since from any stochastic process with a rational spectrum a white-noise component can be extracted by an appropriate filter, having a white-noise residual is a *minimal* criteria for an empirical model to satisfy rather than an 'adequate' stopping point in a modelling exercise.

To minimize repetition, it is convenient to allow for the possibility that contemporaneous information might be available even though this sub-section is explicitly concerned only with past data.

DEFINITION 2   (i) $\{v_t\}$ is a mean innovation process (MIP) with respect to an information set $\mathscr{F}_t$ if $\mathscr{E}(v_t|\mathscr{F}_t) = 0$, $\forall t$; and (ii) $\{v_t\}$ is an innovation process with respect to $\mathscr{F}_t$ if it is a MIP and $D(v_t|\mathscr{F}_t) = D(v_t)$, $\forall t$.

Whether or not $\{e_t\}$ is an innovation process critically depends on the information set under consideration. White noise is certainly a MIP relative to its own history and if $\mathscr{F}_t$ contains $\mathscr{V}_{t-1}$, then innovations are also white noise. However, if $\mathscr{F}_t = (E_{t-1}, \mathscr{H}_{t-1})$ where $\mathscr{H}_{t-1}$ describes the past of an additional set of variables η_t, then $\{e_t\}$ is a MIP with respect to $\mathscr{F}_t$ and if η does not Granger-cause e (see Granger, 1969; Engle et al., 1981).

As an example, let y_t be a subvector of x_t, let $v_t = x_t - \mathscr{E}(x_t|Y_{t-1})$ and let $\alpha(L)v_t = \varepsilon_t$ where $\alpha(L)$ is a rational polynomial matrix in the lag operator

L such that $\{\varepsilon_t\}$ is vector white noise, then these conditions are not sufficient to ensure that $\{\varepsilon_t\}$ is a MIP with respect to X_{t-1}. Models with invalid common factors in lag polynomials are an instance of non-innovation white noise. Thus, for any given time series of data, a multiplicity of empirical models can be constructed which have disturbances that are not detectably different from white noise.

Econometric models typically consist of a hypothetical description of the (conditional) process generating a subset of the observable variables, say y_t. Let z_t denote the conditioning ('exogenous') observable variables and let w_t consist of all the other variables in x_t (whether latent or observable) so that x_t is now partitioned into $(w_t y_t z_t)$. Let $S_{t-1} = (Y_{t-1} Z_{t-1})$.

DEFINITION 3   (i) A statistical model of $\{y_t|z_t;\ t = 1,\ldots,T\}$ is any parametric stochastic representation $\{P(y_t|z_t, S_{t-1}, \psi_0, \psi_t);\ t = 1,\ldots,T\}$ where $P(\cdot)$ is a probability density function and $\psi = (\psi_0\{\psi_t\})$ is the corresponding parameterization. (ii) An empirical model of $\{y_t|z_t\}$ is any complete numerical specification of a statistical model thereof.

When no ambiguity arises, the generic 'model' is used as a shorthand below for whichever of these two concepts applies. However, the hypothesized density functions $\{P(y_t|z_t, S_{t-1},.)\}$ should not be confused with the genuine data density functions $\{D(y_t|z_t, S_{t-1},.)\}$ which they are designed to mimic. The latter can be derived, conceptually at least, from the DGP(5) by marginalizing with respect to W_T^1 and sequentially conditioning with respect to $\{z_t\}$ (see Florens and Mouchart, 1980a, b; Hendry and Richard, 1981). In the linear case, such reductions could be conducted analytically, as in Engle et al. (1981), so that, e.g. under the axiom of correct specification, ψ would be an explicit function of θ. More generally, the properties of the pseudo-partial likelihood function,

$$L(\psi; S_T^1) = \prod_{t-1}^{T} P(y_t|z_t, S_{t-1}, \psi_0, \psi_t), \qquad (6)$$

depend on the underlying DGP, as does the behaviour of estimators of ψ. Whichever interpretations model-builders accord to ψ, such 'parameters' are *de facto* those functions of θ which happen to be consistently estimated by the 'estimators' that have been selected on the basis of the statistical model under consideration (see Hendry, 1979; Domowitz and White, 1981).

Let $\mathscr{E}$ and $\mathscr{E}_p$ denote expectations operators with respect to the density functions $D(\cdot)$ and $P(\cdot)$, respectively. The 'errors', $e_t = y_t - \mathscr{E}_p(y_t|z_t, S_{t-1})$, receive considerable attention in econometric modelling, and correctly so, since under the axiom of correct specification, $\{e_t\}$ should be a MIP relative to (z_t, S_{t-1}) and even relative to (z_t, X_{t-1}) if W_{t-1} does not

Granger-cause ($y_t z_t$). In practice, however, $\{e_t\}$ often is not even white noise. Hence we define:

DEFINITION 4   A model is data coherent if the error process $\{e_t\}$ is (at least) white noise.

Thus, the actual and fitted values differ 'randomly' in a data coherent model: this is the notion used, e.g. in Davidson et al. (1978). In effect, the Δ operator in (4) was an adequate filter for achieving residuals that were not first-order autocorrelated. However, $DW \approx 2.0$ does not imply that the residuals are white noise: a 'portmanteau' test for a flat spectrum would be required to throw light on that issue (i.e., non-rejection achieved by low-power[1] tests is hardly persuasive). Further, white noise need not be a MIP. Note that one important aspect of working with a model based on a mean innovation process (even if this is heteroscedastic) is that valid inference about ψ can proceed on the basis of results in Domowitz and White (1981, 1982) for a useful range of stochastic processes relevant to economics data.

Since simply possessing a white-noise error process does not characterize a unique choice of model, let $g(\cdot)$ denote a (scalar) criterion function defined on $\mathscr{A}$, the class of models under consideration (for example, $g(\cdot)$ could denote the negative of the log-likelihood value, or that corrected for the number of estimated parameters or $\{-R^2\}$ or σ^2 or generalized variance for a system, etc.). Then:

DEFINITION 5   The model A_1 g-dominates the model A_2 if and only if $g(A_1) < g(A_2)$ [A_1 and A_2 are g-equivalent if $g(A_1) = g(A_2)$].

Variance-dominance is a major selection criterion in actual empirical research, in part because of the proposition that 'true models' dominate 'false' when the 'model' contains the DGP as a special case (see e.g. Theil, 1971, p. 543; Leamer, 1978, p. 75). It remains to be discussed precisely how useful variance-dominance is when $\mathscr{A}$ does not contain the DGP.

It follows from Definition 5 that g-dominance is an asymmetric relationship and is transitive, both of which are important attributes of a selection criterion. However, *by itself* dominance is not necessarily a decisive criterion since a model based on the union of the regressors of all sub-models (less redundant variables) cannot be variance- or likelihood-dominated in its class, or as noted by Poirier (1981), a nesting model in a class of false models has the highest (large sample) posterior odds. Nevertheless, we state:

THEOREM 1   *Models without mean innovation error processes can be variance-dominated by a model with a mean innovation error on the same data.*

---

[1] Or, of course, incorrectly sized.

This is a well-known result, based on the fact that $\mathscr{E}(y_t|z_t, S_{t-1})$ is the minimum mean square error predictor of y_t given (z_t, S_{t-1}) and that $\varepsilon_t = y_t - \mathscr{E}(y_t|z_t, S_{t-1})$ is a MIP relative to (z_t, S_{t-1}). Theorem 1 provides a partial answer to the question raised above about the usefulness of variance-dominance when $\mathscr{A}$ does not contain the DGP. Moreover, if the set of conditioning variables in A_1 is a subset of those in A_2, then A_1 cannot variance-dominate A_2 thus inducing one variant of a progressive research strategy (see Section 2, above). Indeed, this notion appears to lead naturally to model-building strategies which focus (at some stage) on relatively 'unrestricted' models (in terms of choice of regressor variables and lag lengths) to calibrate the MIP error variance. Parsimony considerations may then induce a simplification search procedure (on these issues, see Sims, 1980; Leamer, 1978; Hendry, 1980). Thus we have:

DEFINITION 6   The model A is g-parsimonious if $\dim(\psi) < \dim(\psi_i)$ for all models A_i which are g-equivalent to A or g-dominated by A.

Much of the so-called 'model selection' literature (in which model choice is based on AIC, FPE or Schwartz criteria, etc. (see Amemiya, 1980; Chow, 1981; Sawyer, 1982) is concerned with selecting 'parsimoniously undominated' models for various choices of $g(\cdot)$, usually subject to a restriction that the residual process be white noise.

As will be seen below, it is unclear that model selection should emphasize 'parsimonious non-dominance' to the exclusion of other important features (such as invariance, encompassing, and so on).

B.   Contemporaneous Information

It is conventional in econometrics to condition analyses on current dated information and this possibility was allowed for above with models being conditional on z_t.

The validity of such conditioning for purposes of inference, prediction, and/or policy has long been a subject of debate in econometrics concerning alternative notions of exogeneity. That important topic is the subject of a separate recent paper (see Engle et al., 1981) and, therefore, will not be reanalysed herein beyond noting that we adopt the definitions and formulations of those authors. However, in order to make the present paper essentially self-contained, we briefly restate their definitions of weak and strong exogeneity as well as in Subsection (C) below that of superexogeneity. Also, since we have already emphasized the distinction between the DGP and models, it is useful to distinguish explicitly between, say, D-exogeneity and P-exogeneity, depending on whether we are discussing exogeneity at the level of the DGP (which is typically unknown but fundamentally determines the empirical findings) or at the level of models thereof. The definition of D-exogeneity is based on the factorization

$$D(y_t, z_t|S_{t-1},.) = D(y_t|z_t, S_{t-1},.)D(z_t|S_{t-1},.), \quad\quad (7)$$

where $D(y_t, z_t|S_{t-1},.)$ is derived from the DGP (5) by marginalizing with respect to W_T^1.

DEFINITION 7 z_t is D-weakly-exogenous for a set of 'parameters of interest' if these are functions of those of the conditional DGP $D(y_t|z_t, S_{t-1},.)$ only, the latter being 'variation-free' with the parameters of the marginal DGP $D(z_t|S_{t-1},.)$. Also, z_t is D-strongly-exogenous, if, in addition, y does not Granger-cause z.

P-exogeneity is defined in a similar way with reference to a hypothetical density function $P(y_t, z_t|S_{t-1},.)$ which typically requires 'completing' the statistical model under consideration by an auxiliary model $P(z_t|S_{t-1},.)$, at least for the purpose of constructing parametric tests of P-exogeneity.

D-weak-exogeneity validates conducting inference on any function of the parameters of the conditional DGP $D(y_t|z_t, S_{t-1},.)$, possibly including some parameters of a mis-specified model thereof, without loss of relevant sample information. However, P-exogeneity is the concept which is *de facto* the object of any modelling exercise and, in particular, specification errors (including errors affecting the auxiliary marginal model for z_t) may lead to a rejection of P-exogeneity even though z_t is D-weakly-exogenous.

C.   Future Observations

This slightly unfortunate terminology is meant to denote that if x_t is the current-dated variable, then $\{x_{t+1}\ldots\}$ comprises future information (even if such values are already known).

DEFINITION 8   A statistical model A has constant parameters if (ψ_0, ψ_t) $= \psi$ for $t = 1,\ldots,T$.

A standard statistic for evaluating parameter constancy is the Chow test (see Chow, 1960) although there exists a large literature on investigating potential parameter variations related to the Kalman filter (for an exposition, see Harvey, 1981). The important issue here, however, is that there is no necessary connection between parameter constancy and the criteria previously discussed. Since constant parameters are of interest for most modelling purposes, the inadequacy of (say) 'parsimonious non-dominance' as the sole selection criterion is clear.

Note that constancy of the parameters of the DGP entails constancy of the parameters of statistical models thereof, however misspecified they may be, insofar as the latter are functions of the former. However, it is a common empirical finding that DGPs are subject to interventions affecting some of their parameters. A typical example is that of control variables which are subject to policy interventions. A critical issue for prediction or policy simulation experiments is the constancy of the parameters of the corresponding conditional DGP (or model thereof) under interventions affecting the DGP of the control variables.

DEFINITION 9   (i) A statistical model has invariant parameters under a class of interventions if its parameters remain constant under such interventions. (ii) z_t is D-super-exogenous if it is D-weakly-exogenous and the conditional model has invariant parameters.

Parameter invariance is a more demanding requirement than just constancy since the latter may simply be the result of chance DGP constancy over the sample period or of invariance with respect to a limited class of interventions (covering those which occurred over the sample period), while the former typically requires parameter constancy under hypothetical interventions and is, therefore, conjectural (see e.g. Lucas, 1976; Sargent, 1981). However, within sample parameter change is sufficient to reject that conjecture.

Finally, to use an invariant empirical model of $\{y_t | z_t, S_{t-1}\}$ (where z_t is weakly exogenous for the parameters of the conditional model) for prediction of Y_T^{t+1} conditional on Z_T^{t+1} requires that z_t be strongly exogenous over the period $[t + 1, T]$. Otherwise, an auxiliary empirical model of $\{z_t | S_{t-1}\}$ is required in order to exploit the feedback of Y_{t-1} on z_t. Likewise, *conditional* simulation experiments (on which see Section 6 below) require strong exogeneity.

D.   Data Relevant to Contending Models

It is rare in economics to obtain a unanimous view on the precise determination of any economic variable, and usually there is a proliferation of rival empirical models. In our framework these all constitute recombinations of the DGP, and hence are not 'independent representations', a point made in the context of time-series versus econometric models by Wallis (1977). Thus, while the underlying theory models may be separate or non-nested, in that none is a special case of any other, the empirical models are all nested within the DGP. This is manifest on attempting Monte Carlo analysis of 'non-nested' models – enough of the DGP must be specified to generate all of the observables, whence the outcome depends on how the DGP was constructed (as well as on which separate hypotheses are postulated).

If the complete DGP were known (as in the Monte Carlo context since 'real' DGPs may be unknowable), then one could deduce what results would obtain on estimating a given set of models, irrespective of whether these were mutually separate or not. Consequently, one can ask of any specific model whether it mimics this property of the DGP in that it can account for the results obtained by other models; if so, then the first model is said to be encompassing.

Encompassing could be defined at a high level of generality where contending models may differ by:

(1) their choices of endogenous variables;
(2) their functional forms;
(3) their choices of conditioning variables.

In view of the scope of the present paper we shall formulate definitions which cover only (2) and (3), and illustrate them with reference to *linear* models which differ solely in their choices of 'regressors'.

Let r_{1t} and r_{2t} be two different subsets of the variables in (z_t, Y_{t-1}, Z_{t-1}) (r_{1t} and r_{2t} may have variables in common, see e.g. Mizon and Richard (1981, Section 4.4), in which case some of the density functions we introduce below are singular and degrees of freedom for test statistics have to be adjusted conformably). Let $A_1 = \{P_1(y_t|r_{1t}, \psi_{1t}); t = 1,\ldots,T\}$ and $A_2 = \{P_2(y_t|r_{2t}, \psi_{2t}); t = 1,\ldots,T\}$ be rival models. It is assumed that the model-builders had access to a common set of data and, accordingly, that

$$P_i(y_t|r_{it}, \psi_{it}) \equiv P_i(y_t|z_t, Y_{t-1}, Z_{t-1}, \psi_{it}), \quad i = 1, 2, \quad t = 1,\ldots,T, \quad (8)$$

which entails that

$$P_1(y_t|r_{1t}, \psi_{1t}) \equiv P_1(y_t|r_{1t}, r_{2t}, \psi_{1t}), \quad (9a)$$
$$P_2(y_t|r_{2t}, \psi_{2t}) \equiv P_2(y_t|r_{1t}, r_{2t}, \psi_{2t}). \quad (9b)$$

DEFINITION 10 A_1 least-squares encompasses A_2 if and only if ψ_{2t} can be derived from ψ_{1t} and the least-squares description of the (data) relationship linking r_{1t} and r_{2t}.

To link A_1 and A_2 essentially requires specifying a set of mutually compatible auxiliary density functions $\{P_1(r_{1t}|r_{2t}, \lambda_t); t = 1,\ldots,T\}$ – and carrying out the following marginalization:

$$P_1(y_t|r_{2t}, \psi_{1t}, \lambda_t) = \int P_1(y_t|r_{1t}, \psi_{1t})P_1(r_{1t}|r_{2t}, \lambda_t)dr_{1t}. \quad (10)$$

However, the weaker form of encompassing in Definition 10 only requires considering least-squares approximations of r_{1t} by r_{2t}.

Note that the validity of (10) requires that of formula (9a). (If (9a) did not hold, then A_1 should first be completed to form a model of y_t conditional on r_{1t} and r_{2t}.) Provided $P_1(y_t|r_{2t}, \psi_{1t}, \lambda_t)$ and $P_2(y_t|r_{2t}, \psi_{2t})$ belong to a common class of parametric density functions, their reconciliation induces a mapping between parameter spaces, say,

$$\psi_{2t} = h(\psi_{1t}, \lambda_t), \quad t = 1,\ldots,T. \quad (11)$$

The application of Definition 10 at the level of empirical models requires checking whether or not (11) holds for the numerical values under consideration (see e.g. Davidson and Hendry, 1981). Alternatively, replacing the unknown parameters in (11) by appropriate estimators may provide the basis of an encompassing test statistic, using a Wald formulation. Mizon and Richard (1981) use another version of encompassing which builds on the pioneering work of Cox (1961). Let ψ_{2t} denote the maximum-likelihood estimator of ψ_{2t} (under A_2) and let $g_T^1(\psi_{1t}) = \mathcal{E}_{p1}(\hat{\psi}_{2t}|r_{1t})$ denote the expectation of $\hat{\psi}_{2t}$ with respect to Y_T^1 under the working assumption that A_1 is the relevant DGP, taking into account (9a).

DEFINITION 11 A_1 Cox-encompasses A_2 if and only if

$$\psi_{2t} = g_T^1(\psi_{1t}), \quad t = 1,\ldots,T.$$

It is easily shown that the two versions of encompassing coincide in linear worlds where the rival models differ only by their choices of regressors and, furthermore, that in a single-equation framework, the conventional *F*-test statistic can be interpreted as an encompassing test statistic (compare Section 6 in Hendry and Richard, 1981 and Section 4.3 in Mizon and Richard, 1981). This interpretation offers the advantage that, in contrast to the conventional Neyman–Pearson framework, the validity of the 'nesting' model based on the union of the two sets of regressors is irrelevant within an encompassing framework.

It can also be shown that in linear worlds, encompassing entails variance dominance. Let Σ_t be the covariance matrix of (y_t, r_{1t}, r_{2t}). Dropping the time subscript (as irrelevant to the essence of the argument) partition Σ conformably with (y, r_1, r_2),

$$\Sigma = \begin{pmatrix} \Sigma_{yy} & & \\ \Sigma_{1y} \Sigma_{11} & \\ \Sigma_{2y} \Sigma_{21} \Sigma_{22} \end{pmatrix}. \tag{12}$$

Let

$$\Sigma_{yy.i} = \Sigma_{yy} - \Sigma_{yi}\Sigma_{ii}^{-1}\Sigma_{iy}, \quad i = 1, 2,$$

where $\Sigma_{yy.i}$ is the covariance matrix of the residuals of the least-squares approximation of y by r_i. We can establish the following lemma:

LEMMA If $\Sigma_{2y} = \Sigma_{21}\Sigma_{11}^{-1}\Sigma_{1y}$, then $\Sigma_{yy.2} \geqslant \Sigma_{yy.1}$.
Proof $a'(\Sigma_{yy.2} - \Sigma_{yy.1})a$
$= a'(\Sigma_{y1}\Sigma_{11}^{-1}\Sigma_{1y} - \Sigma_{y2}\Sigma_{22}^{-1}\Sigma_{2y})a$
$= a'(\Phi\Sigma_{y1}\Sigma_{11}^{-1}\Sigma_{1y} - \Sigma_{y1}\Sigma_{11}^{-1}\Sigma_{12}\Sigma_{22}^{-1}\Sigma_{21}\Sigma_{11}^{-1}\Sigma_{1y})a$
$= (\Sigma_{11}^{-1/2}\Sigma_{1y}a)'[I - (\Sigma_{11}^{-1/2}\Sigma_{12}\Sigma_{22}^{-1/2})(\Sigma_{22}^{-1/2}\Sigma_{21}\Sigma_{11}^{-1/2})](\Sigma_{11}^{-1/2}\Sigma_{1y}a)$
$\geqslant 0.$

Since the assumption that $\Sigma_{2y} = \Sigma_{21}\Sigma_{11}^{-1}\Sigma_{1y}$ is the least-squares counterpart of assumption (9a), the lemma establishes that, in a least-squares framework, encompassing entails variance-dominance. Since in addition encompassing is transitive, the concept is close to that of a 'sufficient model' in a theory of reduction in that knowing the encompassing model, one can forget about other models, deriving them as the need arises (compare the notion of sufficient statistics). If A_1 encompasses A_2 when both models are linear least-squares approximations the converse is false, and if A_2 in turn encompasses A_3 then A_1 encompasses A_3. Thus, encompassing is a central concept in any progressive research strategy, especially in view of the lemma that variance-dominance is necessary but not sufficient: an encompassing model will variance-dominate but a variance-dominating model need not encompass.

Two further consequences follow from this result: firstly, the emphasis on selecting variance-dominating models is somewhat misplaced and should follow automatically from a selection procedure which seeks an encompassing model, rather than being an 'independent' criterion; and secondly, since Cox-type non-nested hypothesis tests simply test for variance-encompassing (see Cox, 1961; Mizon and Richard, 1981), if tests of the dominated model against the dominating do not reject the former, the power of the test is revealed as low. Other intriguing implications can be derived: let A_1 and A_2 be two rival models with claimed constant parameters. If A_1 encompasses A_2 and it is known that the relationship of r_{1t} to r_{2t} has altered over the sample period (a common occurrence in empirical work), the modeller knowing A_1 can deduce by using (11) over different subperiods what parameter change A_2 should exhibit (even though neither investigator has directly tested for such a contingency in A_2!). Similarly for residual autocorrelation: an encompassing model should allow one to predict the magnitude of this in contending models, and so on.

Accounting for all the salient features of rival models may seem at first sight an overly demanding criterion: strictly speaking the DGP is the only model that could encompass *all* its rivals while, at the same time, it is essentially unknowable given limited sample evidence. It is obvious that any model, however good an approximation to the DGP, could be rejected against a rival model expressly designed for that purpose. However, this is a vacuous exercise if it does not lead to the formulation of 'better' models, and so encompassing seems bound to be an essential component of a progressive modelling strategy. In particular, in a subject with many separate models all being advocated as a basis for policy, encompassing seems a reasonable requirement which remains impressive when obtained from a parsimonious specification. Clearly, concepts such as minimal encompassing (with minimal dimension ψ) can be developed, and the notion generalized to systems in which endogenous regressors occur and/or hypotheses differ as to what variables are weakly or strongly exogenous, etc.

E. Theory Information

This plays an essential role in econometric analysis and it is doubtful if one could even define parameters of interest in the absence of an adequately articulated theory. Indeed, the DGP itself may be dependent on currently popular economic theory. In certain theories, ψ is highly constrained (as in, say, rational expectations formulations; see Lucas and Sargent, 1981). A weak condition is:

DEFINITION 12   An empirical model is theory-consistent if it reproduces the theory model under the conditions assumed by the theory.

Lest it be thought that this is vacuous, note that, e.g. in Section 2 above, (4) was not consistent with the static solution (1), from which it was ostensibly derived. As a further example, changes in assumptions about error autocorrelation can alter the consistency of a model with a given dynamic behavioural theory (see e.g. Hendry et al., 1981).

Generally, theories incorporate measurement structures and hence models need to be consistent with whatever data constraints are automatically binding (e.g. identities, positivity, lying between zero and unity, etc.):

DEFINITION 13   An empirical model is data-admissible if its predictions satisfy all data constraints with probability unity.

For example, $0 \leqslant \mathscr{R}/\mathscr{M} \leqslant 1$ holds for the variables in Section 2, so neither (3) nor (4) is data-admissible. Attempting to specify a functional form which is data-admissible often leads to a model specification in which approximate normality of the error process is reasonable. Unfortunately, tractability and admissibility may conflict and/or no function can be found which jointly satisfies two data constraints (e.g. a linear identity and a positivity constraint).

As with admissible estimators, many investigators work with data-inadmissible models or achieve admissibility by artifact (see Brainard and Tobin, 1968), usually for convenience or because the probability of violating constraints is believed to be negligible.

F.   *Representing the DGP*

DEFINITION *14*   A model is a tentatively adequate conditional data characterization (TACD) if:

(1) it encompasses all rival models;
(2) its error process is a MIP relative to the selected data base;
(3) its parameters of interest are constant;
(4) it is data-admissible;
(5) its current conditioning variables are weakly exogenous for the parameters of interest.

A number of points need to be made about the concept of a TACD. Firstly, such a model is not claimed to be the DGP, simply to adequately represent it. Thus, in a Monte Carlo, data generated from the TACD should reproduce all the investigated features of the original data. This does not preclude the development of 'better' TACDs using more information, such that these successively encompass previous results with MIPs having ever smaller variances. Secondly, we have not included 'theory consistency' as a criterion because of the well-known rationalization problem: there always exists some theory consistent with the observed results unless these are mutually contradictory (which hopefully (4) excludes). In any case, Definition 14 is applicable however naive or sophisticated the initial theory may have been.[2] Next, weak-exogeneity assertions often are only indirectly testable but are partially checked by (1) and (3) holding for worlds in which some elements of θ are transients which induce data correlation changes. Fourthly, a sequence of TACDs would seem to characterize a useful research strategy, which would be progressive if the theoretical framework enabled successive improvements to be predicted in advance (rather than as responses to observed anomalies). Further, we believe it is possible to develop TACDs and would cite Davidson et al. (1978) as a potential example. In practice, successively encompassing TACDs also can be generated (see e.g. Davidson and Hendry, 1981). Parenthetically, we note that UK government policy has been based on a model which uses a version of the Davidson et al. equation (see HM Treasury, 1980) so that on this measure the approach is of some use. Finally, if the explanatory variables are all strongly exogenous, Definition 11 can be modified to a tentatively adequate conditional DGP, and if the model is closed, to a tentatively adequate DGP (note that (2) subsumes data coherency).

Two more related issues remain to be discussed: the use of tests as selection criteria, and data mining. Concerning the former, a model would not be advanced as a TACD (by an investigator who intended to develop such a representation) unless appropriate test-statistic values were obtained. Thus diagnostic tests employed in model selection are satisfied by design and do not constitute 'independent checks' on the validity of the model, although new statistics, later data, and/or further rival models can provide genuine tests in so far as the TACD is hazarded to potential rejection. Next, 'data mining' has been used in both dismissive and positive senses, but the latter connotation applies to any methodology aimed at developing TACDs since such an activity involves 'judgement and purpose' (see Leamer, 1978, Ch. 1). The former sense is justified when the modelling is structureless through lack of either a theory context or a search strategy. But we wish to stress that, despite estimating several variants prior to selecting any specific model, *conditional* on its being a TACD, then, e.g.

---

[2] Naturally, one anticipates that 'better' theories will lead to better TACDs or to more rapid development of these.

the quoted parameter standard errors (estimated as in, say, Domowitz and White, 1982) are consistent estimates of the sampling standard deviations of parameters estimated from such a DGP. Such conditional statements seem less than convincing if models are not even TACDs.

G. Parameters of Interest

While a given theory defines what 'parameters' are of general interest, usually it leaves latitude concerning precisely which features are basic and/ or constant (e.g. propensities or elasticities, etc.). Thus, additional considerations must be invoked in designing models and 'orthogonality' and 'parsimony' enter at this stage. By the former is meant a reparameterization based on *prior* considerations such that the associated variables are not highly intercorrelated; data-dependent transformation (such as principal components) are deliberately excluded from our notion. The parameters should have clear-cut interpretations (see e.g. Rothenberg, 1973) and near-orthogonal parameterizations often arise naturally in modelling economic behaviour (see Davidson et al., 1978). Our practical experience is that such parameters tend to be robust to changes in both model specification and data correlations (which of course would follow trivially if 'included' and 'excluded' variables were, and remained, orthogonal).

The latter topic arises again here (see Subsection (A) above) through its link with reparameterizations designed to enhance robustness and facilitate model selection when prior specification is uncertain: it seems a reasonable objective to try and achieve the maximum of explanation with the minimum of factors. Indeed, a data-admissible econometric model with a *parsimonious* specification of constant, interpretable parameters related to a well-formulated theory which still succeeded in encompassing alternative (commensurable) hypotheses must deserve serious consideration in any scientific research strategy. Later models almost certainly will be developed which are in turn encompassing and based on 'sounder' theory, but this does not vitiate adopting the currently best available model. Note that our analysis does not exclude the possibility that an entire sequence of models is wholly misconceived and, after a long progression, is duly replaced by a (perhaps incommensurable) alternative sequence based on a totally different conceptual framework (as occurred, e.g., with Cartesian and Newtonian theories of planetary motion).

5. The Empirical Illustration Reconsidered

The concepts discussed in Section 4 are applicable to the empirical models in Section 3, but it is readily established empirically that these equations fail on almost every criterion. Rather than criticize such simple formulations, however, the purpose of this section is to describe a TACD consistent with (1) which helps exposit our ideas constructively.

The underlying theory is one of dynamic adjustment around a steady state *defined by* (ℓ). The model allows for activity changes in the housing market (most UK mortgages must be repaid on selling the associated house), the consequentially varying age profile of loans (for actuarial reasons, a larger percentage is repaid on longer-standing loans), changes in interest rates (total monthly payments are usually announced so that as ℓ varies the proportion of repayments may alter), and premature repayments out of deposits (presumably from balances excess to liquidity requirements).

The statistical model is an autoregressive-distributed lag of

$$q_t = \log \left[\frac{R_t/M_{t-1}}{1 - R_t/M_{t-1}} \right]$$

on $\Delta_1 p_{t-1}$, $\Delta_1 I_{t-1}$, $\Delta_1 m_{t-1}$, $\Delta_1 d_{t-1}$ with four lags on each variable, plus constant, S_t, m_{t-1}, I_{t-1} and $V \cdot \Delta_1 I_{t-2}$, where P denotes an index of house prices and V is a dummy variable equal to unity till 1974(ii) and zero thereafter, and D denotes building society deposits. Thus, the specification is

$$q_t = \sum_{j=1}^{4} (\alpha_j q_{t-j} + \beta_j \Delta_1 p_{t-j} + \gamma_j \Delta_1 I_{t-j} + \lambda_j \Delta_1 m_{t-j} + \phi_j \Delta_1 d_{t-j}$$

$$+ \delta_2 I_{t-1} + \gamma_0 V \cdot \Delta_1 I_{t-2} + S_t + \delta_0 + \delta_1 m_{t-1} + \varepsilon_t, \tag{13}$$

where $\{\varepsilon_t\}$ is to be a MIP relative to the available information. The logistic form for the dependent variable ensures data-admissibility for the constraints $0 \leqslant R/M \leqslant 1$, although R_t/M_{t-1} is so small that only positivity is relevant in practice. Also, P is included to reflect housing market activity, since demand changes rapidly result in house-price changes given the essentially fixed stock. Initially estimated models implicitly set γ_0 at zero and experienced substantial predictive failure when $\Delta_1 I_{t-2}$ was included as a regressor, posing a conflict between goodness-of-fit and parameter constancy. However, this was diagnosed as due to a change in institutional arrangements in 1974 when continuously rising interest rates forced building societies to demand increases in total monthly payments to maintain positive repayments of principal (note the nadir of q_t in 1974 in Figure 3). Thus, $\gamma_0 V$ is an example of a transient parameter.

The OLS estimates of (13) are not interesting *per se*, but it should be recorded that $\hat{\sigma} = 0.0419$ and that both the Chow (1960) test for parameter constancy (for several periods) and Harvey's (1981) *F*-version of the Lagrange multiplier test for 6th-order autocorrelation (see Godfrey, 1978) were not significant at the 0.05 level (these tests are denoted $\eta_1(\cdot)$ and $\eta_2(\cdot)$ below, with degrees of freedom in parentheses). This evidence is consistent

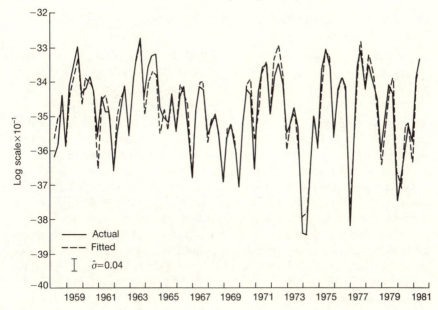

Figure 3 q_t

with $\{\varepsilon_t\}$ being white noise and a MIP on the present information. Next, (13) was simplified by imposing restrictions consistent with (1), reparameterizing any short distributed lags and deleting inessential variables such that the overall F-test of all the restrictions was not significant at the 0.05 level ($\eta_3(\cdot)$ below). Kiviet (1982) presents evidence about the independence of some of the above tests of specification and misspecification (adopting the dichotomy in Mizon, 1977; see also Kiviet, 1981).

The simplified equation thus selected for the period 1960(i) to 1981(iii) is

$$\hat{q}_t = -1.34 + 0.60q_{t-1} - 0.058\Delta_1 I_{t-1} + 0.65\Delta_1 p_{t-1} - 0.78\Delta_4 m_{t-1}$$
$$[0.16] \quad [0.04] \qquad [0.010] \qquad\quad [0.20] \qquad\quad [0.14]$$

$$-0.090V \cdot \Delta_1 I_{t-2} + 2.3\Delta_1 d_{t-1}, \tag{14}$$
$$[0.027] \qquad\quad [0.4]$$

$$T = 94, \quad R^2 = 0.90, \quad \hat{\sigma} = 0.0405, \quad \eta_1(20, 64) = 1.36,$$

$$\eta_2(6, 78) = 0.51, \quad \eta_3(17, 68) = 0.69, \quad \eta_4(1) = 5.1,$$

where the heteroscedasticity-consistent standard errors are given in brakcets (see White, 1980; Domowitz and White, 1982), and $\eta_4(1)$ is the test for first-order ARCH (see Engle, 1982), asymptotically distributed as χ_1^2 on the null of no ARCH effect. It may be noted that the conventionally calculated standard errors are similar to those reported above.

Descriptive statistics relevant to the scaled residuals $\{\hat{\varepsilon}_t/\hat{\sigma}\}$ are

Maximum	Minimum	Skewness	Excess kurtosis
2.10	-2.34	-0.20	-0.53

There are no evident outlier problems, and the first four moments are similar to those of a normal distribution, perhaps being somewhat 'flatter'. Figure 3 shows the graph of $\{q_t\}$ and the corresponding fit.

Equation (14) appears to satisfy our criteria for being a TACD. The residual is white noise (on $\eta_2(\cdot)$) and not significantly different from the residual of (13) (on $\eta_3(\cdot)$), so it is unlikely that this model could be significantly dominated on the present information set although there is evidence of autoregressive conditional heteroscedasticity ($\eta_4(\cdot)$). All the regressors are lagged or non-stochastic, so $\hat{\sigma}$ measures the actual one-step-ahead forecast standard error, which is under 4 per cent of $\bar{R}$, and $\eta_1(\cdot)$ is consistent with constant parameters (in fact, for several horizons). It can be shown that the selected model encompasses both (3) and (4) above (although these are not 'special cases') and the other R_t equations considered in Hendry and Anderson (1977), as well as variance-dominating the equation in Mayes (1979) (we have been unable to conduct a formal encompassing test against this last model, which has a standard error of 7.6 per cent, of $\bar{R}$, but four lagged values of personal disposable income were insignificant at the 0.05 level if added to (13). By construction, (8) is both data-admissible, in that all values of q_t yield $0 \leqslant R_t/M_{t-1} \leqslant 1$, and consistent with (1). The static equilibrium solution yields $N = 7.3$ years, with substantial seasonal variation between 11.3 years and 6.9 years. The parameters are fairly well determined, with anticipated signs and sensible magnitudes, and have clear interpretations, almost all the squared correlations between regressors being negligible (the largest is 0.30 between q_{t-1} and a seasonal dummy). Five variables explain most of the non-seasonal variation in q_t since 1974, over which period the largest quarter-on-quarter change in $(r_t - m_{t-1})$ was 0.40 (about $10\hat{\sigma}$), with the observed variance having increased markedly since 1973. However, an important caveat before regarding the estimated parameters as measures of invariants of housing market behaviour is that we have not included any factors to account for long-run changes in the propensity to move house (e.g. household formation rates, job mobility determinants, etc.); hopefully (14) may provide a useful basis for developing a more general encompassing formulation in due course.

6. Dynamic Simulation

Most large-scale estimated dynamic econometric models have been studied by simulation techniques at some point in their existence. Indeed, simulation tracking performance is often viewed as a major aspect of 'validating'

$$r_t = a_0 + a_1 m_{t-1} + S_t + \varepsilon_t, \quad t = 1,\ldots,T, \tag{2}$$

where S_t denotes three seasonal dummy variables (to allow for known seasonal activity in the housing market), and $a_0 = -\log_e N$ and $a_1 = 1$ are anticipated. Parenthetically, equations like (2) have occurred in many large estimated macroeconometric systems (see e.g. Waelbroeck, 1976) and, since m_{t-1} is 'predetermined', are usually estimated by ordinary least-squares (OLS) on the auxiliary assumption that $\varepsilon_t \sim IN(0, \sigma_\varepsilon^2)$. For UK data from 1958(i) to 1979(iii) OLS estimation yields

$$\hat{r}_t = -3.2 + 0.97\, m_{t-1} + \hat{S}_t, \quad R^2 = 0.98, \quad \hat{\sigma} = 0.097, \quad DW = 0.49,$$
$$(0.1) \quad (0.02) \tag{3}$$

where the estimated standard errors are given in parentheses, $\hat{\sigma}$ is the residual standard error, and DW is the Durbin–Watson statistic. Figure 1 shows the time-series graph of $(r_t, \hat{r}_t)$.

Certainly, $\hat{a}_1 \approx 1$ and $\hat{a}_0$ implies $N \approx 6$ years (close to the mean time between household moves in the UK), but DW rejects the assumption of serial independence in the residuals (so the quoted standard errors are downward biased), although this is easily 'rectified'. However, while the R^2 is 'high', it is only 0.33 when $(r_t - m_{t-1})$ is the regress and – and would be zero for that variable on seasonally adjusted data! Figure 2 highlights this lack of fit, despite being essentially a replot of Figure 1. Granger and Newbold (1974) would describe (3) as a 'classic' spurious regression ($R^2 >$

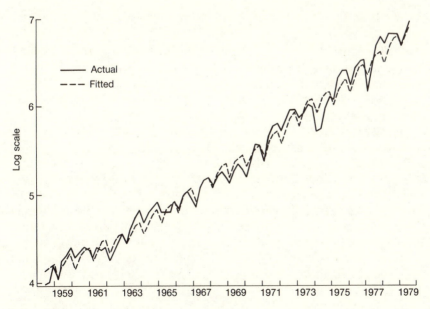

Figure 1 r_t

such models, i.e. of checking their overall correspondence to 'reality' at least as revealed by the observed historical data – see e.g. Sowey (1973) and McNees (1982). Judging by the frequency with which root mean square errors (RMSEs) based on dynamic simulations are quoted, and that small RMSEs seem to be viewed as 'good', it is worthwhile specifically investigating the use of n-step MSEs (denoted by $M(n)$ below) as a dominance criterion for model selection.

Of course, $M(1)$ is the previously considered variance-dominance criterion, but the concern here is with $M(n)$ when n is 'large', to highlight the issues involved. The analysis builds on the work of Haavelmo (1940), but focuses on different aspects of model evaluation than 'spuriously significant' variables. Rather, our concern is with the choice of information set underlying different 'types' of simulation and the bearing that the results of deterministic simulation exercises may have on assessing the usefulness of a model for alternative purposes. The analysis proceeds by means of a simple example which incorporates all the required features; additional complications like non-linearities, omitted variables and unknown/non-constant parameters seem liable to exacerbate the problem.

Consider the linear stationary two-equation process in (15) and (16), where the parameters are *known* and constant and the latent roots lie within the unit circle,

$$y_t = \alpha z_t + \beta y_{t-1} + \varepsilon_t, \qquad \begin{pmatrix} \varepsilon_t \\ \nu_t \end{pmatrix} \approx IN\left[\begin{pmatrix} 0 \\ 0 \end{pmatrix}, \begin{pmatrix} \sigma_\varepsilon^2 & 0 \\ 0 & \sigma_\nu^2 \end{pmatrix} \right], \quad (15)$$

$$z_t = \lambda z_{t-1} + \gamma y_{t-1} + \nu_t, \quad \begin{matrix} 0 \leqslant \beta < 1, \quad 0 \leqslant \lambda < 1, \\ 1 \geqslant \alpha \geqslant 0, \quad -1 < \gamma \leqslant 0. \end{matrix} \quad (16)$$

The one-step-ahead system predictions are computed from

$$\begin{pmatrix} \hat{y}_t \\ \hat{z}_t \end{pmatrix} = \begin{bmatrix} \beta + \alpha\gamma & \alpha\lambda \\ \gamma & \lambda \end{bmatrix} \begin{pmatrix} y_{t-1} \\ z_{t-1} \end{pmatrix}, \quad (17)$$

and so have error variances

$$\begin{pmatrix} \sigma_\varepsilon^2 + \alpha^2\sigma_\nu^2 \\ \sigma_\nu^2 \end{pmatrix} = \begin{pmatrix} \mathrm{var}(y_t | Y_{t-1}, Z_{t-1}) \\ \mathrm{var}(z_t | Y_{t-1}, Z_{t-1}) \end{pmatrix}. \quad (18)$$

By way of contrast,

$$\mathrm{var}(y_t | Y_{t-1}, Z_t) = \sigma_\varepsilon^2 \quad \text{from (15)}.$$

There are two alternative means of computing the deterministic dynamic simulation path for y_t: treating the model as 'open' (so the analysis is conditional on $\{z_t\}$ or as 'closed' (so (y_t, z_t) are jointly simulated) and we denote these by $\tilde{\ }$ and $\bar{\ }$, respectively. Then

$$\tilde{y}_t = \alpha z_t + \beta \tilde{y}_{t-1} = \alpha \sum_{j=0}^{n-1} \beta^j z_{t-j} + \beta^n y_0, \quad t = 1, \ldots, T, \quad \tilde{y}_0 = y_0. (19)$$

For simplicity in what follows, initial conditions are ignored when this clarifies the analysis without misleading the logic. From (19) and (15),

$$y_t - \bar{y}_t = \sum_{i=0}^{n-1} \beta^i \varepsilon_{t-i},\tag{20}$$

and hence

$$\text{var}(y_t - \bar{y}_t) = \sigma_u^2(1 - \beta^{2t}) = \text{var}(y_t|Z_t, Y_0) \quad \text{where} \quad \sigma_u^2 = \sigma_\varepsilon^2/(1 - \beta^2).\tag{21}$$

Note from (20) that $(y_t - \bar{y}_t)$ is autocorrelated and heteroscedastic, although $\{\varepsilon_t\}$ is neither. Also, as $M_y(n)$ is the average of (21) over $t = 1, \ldots, n$, for large n it is approximately equal to σ_u^2, or more generally,

$$M_y(n) = \sigma_u^2(1 - \beta^2(1 - \beta^{2n})/n(1 - \beta^2)).\tag{22}$$

This notation is not fully informative compared to (21), but (22) is the expected value of the usual deterministic simulation MSE *treating z as strongly exogenous*. Of course, if $\gamma \neq 0$ then z is not in fact strongly exogenous, but it is important to realize that (22) does not depend on the actual value of γ, only on the assumption that the model is open.

Next, consider the closed model simulation

$$\begin{pmatrix} \bar{y}_t \\ \bar{z}_t \end{pmatrix} = \begin{bmatrix} \beta + \alpha\gamma & \alpha\lambda \\ \gamma & \lambda \end{bmatrix} \begin{pmatrix} y_{t-1} \\ z_{t-1} \end{pmatrix} \quad \text{with} \quad \begin{pmatrix} \bar{y}_0 \\ \bar{z}_0 \end{pmatrix} = \begin{pmatrix} y_0 \\ z_0 \end{pmatrix}.\tag{23}$$

Thus

$$\begin{pmatrix} \text{var}(y_t - \bar{y}_t) \\ \text{var}(z_t - \bar{z}_t) \end{pmatrix} = \begin{pmatrix} \text{var}(y_t|Y_0, Z_0) \\ \text{var}(z_t|Y_0, Z_0) \end{pmatrix},\tag{24}$$

which yield, for sufficiently large t, the unconditional variances of y_t and z_t given by [derived as in e.g. Hendry (1979)]

$$\sigma_y^2 = [\sigma_\varepsilon^2(1 - \beta\lambda) + \alpha^2(1 + \beta\lambda)\sigma_z^2]/[(1 - \beta\lambda)(1 - \beta^2) - 2\alpha\beta\gamma],$$
$$\sigma_z^2 = [\sigma_\nu^2(1 - \beta\lambda) + \gamma^2(1 + \beta\lambda)\sigma_y^2]/[(1 - \beta\lambda)(1 - \lambda^2) - 2\alpha\gamma\lambda],\tag{25}$$

In the special case that $\gamma = 0$, the unconditional variance of y is

$$\sigma_y^2 = \sigma_u^2 + \{\alpha^2(1 + \beta\lambda)\sigma_{,\nu}^2/(1 - \beta\lambda)(1 - \beta^2)(1 - \lambda^2)\}.\tag{26}$$

Now, it is an inherent property of closed linear, stationary models (which are at least TACDs that their n-step simulation error variance is close to the unconditional data variance for large n or, alternatively expressed, that their deterministic simulation track converges on the unconditional data mean. Consequently, such models appear to track 'very badly' even when they are valid. Conversely, comparing (22) and (26) when $\{z_t\}$ is strongly exogenous, how well the model appears to simulate depends on the extent to which the variance of $\{y_t\}$ is due to $\{z_t\}$ (the term $\{\cdot\}$ in (26)). The crucial difficulty, however, is that (22) is unaffected by the value of γ, so that the 'accuracy' of the simulation track is primarily dependent on the extent to which the selected model attributes data variance to factors which are 'outside the model', *irrespective of whether or not such factors really are strongly exogenous in practice*. Nothing in the analysis of simulating $\{y_t\}$ conditional on Z_T^1 depended on z *being* strongly exogenous (except, of course, the meaningfulness of the procedure!), providing the investigator acted *as if it were*, as is clear from the choice of conditioning sets in (21) and (24). Consequently, the validity of a model cannot be assessed by its *n*-step tracking performance alone.

Rather, $\{1 - M(n)/\sigma_y^2\}$ measures the extent to which the 'explanation' of $\{y_t\}$ is attributed to variables which are treated as if they are strongly exogenous: the validity of the *simulation* is better assessed by tests of all of the strong exogeneity claims, and the validity of the *model* by the criteria discussed in Section 4. This adds a caveat to the analysis in McNees (1982) since it is not appropriate to define exogenous as 'outside the scope of the model', and also points towards techniques for resolving his 'dilemma of model comparisons' by investigating, e.g. encompassing, and the one-step system predictions like (17).

It must be stressed that valid inter-model comparisons cannot be based simply on an *agreement* between modellers as to which variables may be taken as strongly exogenous for computing $M(n)$: even if a unique set is agreed and no other used by any modeller, the model with the lowest $M(n)$ value $(n > 1)$ may have nothing to commend it. For example, consider a comparison between (15) and

$$y_t = \sum_{i=0}^{k} \phi_i z_{t-i} + e_t, \tag{27}$$

with the assertion that $\mathscr{E}(z_{t-i}e_t) = 0$, $\forall i > 0$, where (15) and (27) constitute 'rival hypotheses', when the data generation process is (15) + (16) with $\gamma \neq 0$. By construction, (15) must therefore encompass and $M(1)$ dominate (27), although if $\sigma_v^2/\sigma_\varepsilon^2$ happens to be small, σ_e^2 will be similar in magnitude to σ_ε^2, so that there will be little to choose between the models in terms of $M(1)$. But if both modellers agree to treat z as strongly exogenous, (27) will have a much better simulation track than (15) with error variance still equal to σ_e^2! Yet if (y_t, z_t) are jointly simulated, (15) should perform better, with both having far larger error variances than their equivalent conditional simulations (compare (21) and (24)).

For practical *ex ante* forecasting, the future values of non-deterministic 'exogenous' variables are unknown and have to be projected by auxiliary equations, often of a surprisingly *ad hoc* nature given that the resulting predictions of the endogenous variables will be conditional thereon. Thus, $\mathrm{var}(y_{T+n}|Y_T, Z_T)$ is the relevant *n*-step forecast error variance and this varies from (18) for $n = 1$ to (25) for very large n, but never coincides with (21). It follows that conditional simulations of the form (19) do not help select models which will be best for n-step *ex ante* forecasts either.

There are several important implications of this analysis worth summarizing:

(1) Ranking models by $M(n)$ as a dominance criterion reflects how much of the explanation is attributed to variables not generated in the simulation; and hence
(2) it is not necessarily a criticism of *closed* 'time-series models' that their values of $M(n)$ exceed those of open 'econometric' models for $n > 1$ (nor a virtue for the latter), especially if the former have the smaller $M(1)$ values in post-sample forecast tests;
(3) $M(n)$ values calculated from simulations conditional on assumed known 'strongly exogenous' variables z need reflect neither the operational (*ex ante*) forecasting characteristics of the model (since z_{T+i} are unknown) nor the 'goodness' of the underlying model as a characterization of the DGP (if the z variables are not actually strongly exogenous). It is also worth adding that
(4) stocks will usually appear to simulate 'badly' even when changes in stocks are quite well determined due to the additional dynamic latent root close to unity.

These conclusions are demonstrable by computer experiments in which the DGP is known and alternative models are simulated under valid and invalid strong exogeneity assumptions. It must be stressed, however, that the only point at issue here is the assessment of model validity by dynamic simulation, using $M(n)$ as a *selection criterion*. Comparative simulations – with the model fixed and the inputs perturbated as a numerical method for calculating multipliers – have not been criticized, although it is well known that such counterfactuals depend on assumptions about super-exogeneity instead (see Lucas, 1976; Engle et al., 1981).

7. Conclusion

An analysis of empirical-model concepts suggests that there are pertinent considerations affecting how much models should be designed when available theory is not a complete quantitative characterization of the world. Many of the notions investigated above are well known, but have previously been justified by arguments whose relevance is unclear when the model does not include the data-generation process as a special case. Moreover, the relationships between widely used criteria for model selection do not seem to have been the subject of much previous analysis.

Data modelling advances beyond mere description only if sustained by an associated theory, so we have assumed throughout that the best available theory is adopted. Nevertheless, no economic theory is likely to comprehensively explain all observed phenomena, and some means of ordering empirical models remains desirable. The main ordering discussed above is based on encompassing both, because it offers a more stringent check on model adequacy than that conventionally used (e.g. variance-dominance combined with white-noise errors is only necessary and is not sufficient to ensure encompassing) and because it provides one possible operational implementation of a progressive research strategy.[3] By way of comparison, it does not seem valid to base an ordering on dynamic simulation *n*-step mean square errors (for large *n*) alone.

Our practical experience, despite the turbulence of the 1970s, is that theory-consistent, data-coherent, parsimonious encompassing models can be developed. Further, those that have been proposed tend to manifest relatively constant parameters of interest for quite extensive time periods, despite changes in data correlations (for a recent appraisal of UK consumption functions, see Davis, 1982). The simple empirical example presented to illustrate the analysis is consistent with this view.

---

[3] Even so, we regrettably concur with Blaug (1980), that empirical investigators in economics are unlikely to progress beyond being more handmaidens to theorists.

References

Amemiya, T. (1980), Selection of regressors, *International Economic Review*, 21, 331–54.

Blaug, M. (1980), *The Methodology of Economics: How Economists Explain.* Cambridge University Press, Cambridge.

Brainard, W. and Tobin, J. (1968), Econometric models: Their problems and usefulness, *American Economic Association Papers and Proceedings*, May, pp. 99–149.

Chow, G. C. (1960), Tests of equality between sets of coefficients in two linear regressions, *Econometrica*, 28, 591–605.

Chow, G. C. (1981), Selection of econometric models by the information criteria. *Proceedings of the Econometric Society European Meeting 1979*, ed. by F. G. Charatsis. North-Holland, Amsterdam, Ch. 8.

Cox, D. R. (1961), Tests of separate families of hypotheses. *Proceedings of the Fourth Berkeley Symposium on Mathematical Statistics and Probability*, Vol. 1. University of California Press, Berkeley, CA, pp. 102–23.

Crowder, M. J. (1976), Maximum likelihood estimation for dependent observations. *Journal of the Royal Statistical Society B*, 38, 45–53.

Davidson, J. E. H. and Hendry, D. F. (1981), Interpreting econometric evidence: Consumers' expenditure in the United Kingdom, *European Economic Review*, 16, 177–92.

Davidson, J. E. H., Hendry, D. F., Srba, F. and Yeo, S. (1978), Econometric modelling of the aggregate time-series relationship between consumers' expenditure and income in the United Kingdom. *Economic Journal*, 88, 661–92.

Davis, E. P. (1982), The consumption function in current macro-economic models: a comparative study. Discussion paper. Bank of England, London.

Domowitz, I. and White, H. (1981), Nonlinear regression with dependent observations. Discussion paper no. 81–32. University of California at San Diego, La Jolla, CA.

Domowitz, I. and White, H. (1982), Mis-specified models with dependent observations. *Journal of Econometrics*, 20.

Einstein, A. (1950), *Out of My Later Years*. London.

Engle, R. F. (1982), Autoregressive conditional heteroscedasticity with estimates of the variance of United Kingdom inflations. *Econometrica*, 50, 987–1008.

Engle, R. F., Hendry, D. F. and Richard, J.-F. (1981), Exogeneity, *Econometrica*, 51, 277–304.

Florens, J.-P. and Mouchart, M. (1980a), Initial and sequential reduction of Bayesian experiments CORE discussion paper no. 8015. Université Catholique de Louvain, Louvain-la-Neuve.

Florens, J.-P. and Mouchart, M. (1980b), Conditioning in econometric models. CORE discussion paper no. 8042. Université Catholique de Louvain, Louvain-la-Neuve.

Florens, J.-P. and Mouchart, M. (1981), A linear theory for non-causality, CORE unpublished paper. Université Catholique de Louvain, Louvain-la-Neuve.

Godfrey, L. G. (1978), Testing against general autoregressive and moving average error models when the regressors include lagged dependent variables. *Econometrica*, 46, 1293–1301.

Granger, C. W. J. (1969), Investigating causal relations by econometric models and cross-spectral methods. *Econometrica*, 37, 424–38.

Granger, C. W. J. (1980a), Testing for causality – A personal viewpoint. *Journal of Economic Dynamics and Control*, 2, 329–52.

Granger, C. W. J. (1980b), Forecasting white noise. Discussion paper no. 80–31. University of California at San Diego, La Jolla, CA.

Granger, C. W. J. and Newbold, P. (1974), Spurious regressions in econometrics. *Journal of Econometrics*, 2, 111–20.

Haavelmo, T. (1940), The inadequacy of testing dynamic theory by comparing theoretical solutions and observed cycles. *Econometrica*, 8, 312–21.

Harvey, A. C. (1981), The Kalman filter and its applications in econometrics and time-series analysis. Invited paper presented at the Symposium über Operations Research, Augsburg.

Harvey, A. C. (1981), *The Econometric Analysis of Time Series*. Philip Allen, Oxford.

Hayek, F. A. (1963), *Studies in Philosophy, Politics and Economics*. Routledge & Kegan Paul, London.

Hendry, D. F. (1979), The behaviour of inconsistent instrumental variables estimators in dynamic systems with autocorrelated errors. *Journal of Econometrics*, 9, 295–314. (Also see E. Maasoumi and P. C. B. Phillips, and a Reply in Vol. 19, 1982.)

Hendry, D. F. (1980), Predictive failure and econometric modelling in macro-economics: the transactions demand for money. *Modelling the Economy*, ed. P. Ormerod. Heinemann Educational Books, London.

Hendry, D. F. and Anderson, G. J. (1977), Testing dynamic specification in small simultaneous systems: an application to a model of building society behaviour in the United Kingdom. *Frontiers in Quantitative Economics*, Vol. IIIA, ed. M. D. Intriligator. North-Holland, Amsterdam.

Hendry, D. F. and Mizon, G. E. (1978), Serial correlation as a convenient simplification, not a nuisance: a comment on a study of the demand for money by the Bank of England. *Economic Journal*, 88, 549–63.

Hendry, D. F. and Richard, J.-F. (1981), The econometric analysis of economic time series, *International Statistical Review*, 51, 111–63.

Hendry, D. F., Pagan, A. R. and Sargan, J. D. (1981), Dynamic specification. *Handbook of Econometrics*, ed. Z. Griliches and M. D. Intriligator. North-Holland, Amsterdam.

HM Treasury, (1980), *Macroeconomic Model Technical Manual*. HM Treasury, London.

Hume, D. (1758), *An Enquiry Concerning Human Understanding* (1927 edn). Open Court Publ. Co., Chicago, IL.

Kiviet, J. F. (1981), On the rigour of some specification tests for modelling dynamic relationships. Paper presented to the Conference of Econometric Society, Amsterdam.

Kiviet, J. F. (1982), Size, power and interdependence of tests in sequential procedures for modelling dynamic relationships. Unpublished paper (University of Amsterdam, Amsterdam).

Lakatos, I. (1974), Falsification and the methodology of scientific research programmes. *Criticism and the Growth of Knowledge*, ed. I. Lakatos and A. E. Musgrave. Cambridge University Press, Cambridge.

Leamer, E. E. (1978), *Specification Searches: Ad-hoc Inference with Non-experimental Data*. Wiley, New York.

Losee, J. (1980), *A Historical Introduction to the Philosophy of Science*. Oxford University Press, Oxford.

Lucas, R. E. (1976), Econometric policy evaluation: a critique. *The Phillips Curve and Labour Markets*, ed. K. Brunner and A. H. Meltzer. Carnegie Rochester conference series on public policy, Vol. 1. North-Holland, Amsterdam.

Lucas, R. E. and Sargent, T. J. (eds) (1981), *Rational Expectations and Econometric Practice*. Allen & Unwin, Lodon.

Madansky, A. (1976), *Foundations of Econometrics*. North-Holland, Amsterdam.

Malinvaud, E. (1966), *Statistical Methods of Econometrics*. North-Holland, Amsterdam.

Mayes, D. G. (1979), *The Property Boom*, Martin Robertson, Oxford.

McNees, S. K. (1982), The role of macroeconometric models in forecasting and policy analysis in the United States. *Journal of Forecasting*, 1, 37–48.

Mizon, G. E. (1977), Inferential procedures in non-linear models – an application in a UK industrial cross-section study of factor substitution and returns to scale. *Econometrica*, 45, 1221–42.

Mizon, G. E. and Richard, J.-F. (1981), The encompassing principle and its application to non-nested hypotheses. Discussion paper. Southampton University, Southampton.

Poirier, D. (1981), Posterior odds analysis when all compelling models are false. *Economics Letters*, 8, 135–40.

Rothenberg, T. J. (1973), *Efficient Estimation with A Priori Information*. Cowles Foundation Monograph 23. Yale University Press, New Haven, CT.

Sargan, J. D. (1980), Some tests of dynamic specification for a single equation. *Econometrica*, 48, 879–97.

Sargent, T. J. (1981), Interpreting economic time series. *Journal of Political Economy*, 89, 213–48.

Sawyer, K. P. (1982), Econometric model selection in perspective. Unpublished paper, Australian National University, Canberra.

Simon, H. A. (1953), Causal ordering and identifiability. *Studies in Econometric Method*, ed. W. C. Hood and T. C. Koopmans. Cowles Foundation Monograph 14. Yale University Press, New Haven, CT.

Sims, C. A. (1980), Macroeconomics and reality. *Econometrica*, 48, 1–48.

Sowey, E. R. (1973), Stochastic simulation of macroeconomic models: Methodology and interpretation. *Econometric Studies of Macro and Monetary Relations*, ed. A. A. Powell and R. A. Williams. North-Holland, Amsterdam.

Spanos, A. (1981), Disequilibrium, latent variables and identities. Unpublished paper. Birkbeck College, London.

Theil, H. (1971), *Principles of Econometrics*, Wiley, New York.

Waelbroeck, J. K. (ed.) (1976), *The Models of Project LINK*. North-Holland, Amsterdam.

Wallis, K. F. (1977), Multiple time series analysis and the final form of econometric models. *Econometrica*, 45, 1481–97.

White, H. (1980), A heteroscedastic-consistent covariance matrix estimator and a direct test for heteroscedasticity. *Econometrica*, 48, 421–48.

Whittle, P. (1970), *Probability*. Penguin Library of University Mathematics, Harmondsworth.

Worrall, J. and Currie, C. (eds) (1978), *The Methodology of Scientific Research Programmes*, Vol. 1: *Imre Lakatos*. Cambridge University Press, Cambridge.

Zellner, A. (1979), Causality and econometrics. *Three Aspects of Policy and Policymaking*, ed. K. Brunner and A. H. Meltzer. North-Holland, Amsterdam.

15

Towards a Unifying Methodological Framework for Econometric Modelling

Aris Spanos

1. Introduction

Since the early 1970s the 'textbook' econometric modelling strategy, formalized during the late 1950s and early 1960s, has been increasingly under attack for failing to deliver the initial promises in quantifying theoretical relationships and testing economic hypotheses. A large number of econometric relationships such as the consumption function, the Phillips curve, and the demand for money established in the 1960s, on closer examination were found to be much less robust and stable than initially thought, and invariably misspecified. Despite the huge number of empirical studies in specific areas no consensus seemed to emerge; indeed a plethora of disparate and often contradictory empirical results appeared to coexist (see Hadjimatheou, 1987 for a recent discussion of the literature on the consumption function). Econometric modelling, viewed as a way for testing theories, has failed because theories are revised rather than abandoned purely because of contrary empirical evidence, raising doubts about the value of empirical econometric modelling. In an attempt to construct more adequate empirical models, modellers found themselves resorting to ad hoc procedures giving rise to what Blaug (1980) branded cookbook econometrics:

express a hypothesis in terms of an equation, estimate a variety of forms for that equation, select the best fit, discard the rest, and then adjust the theoretical argument to rationalize the hypothesis that is being tested (p. 257).

Under these circumstances a re-examination of the foundations of econometric modelling became inevitable, and since the mid-1970s has given rise to a number of distinctive viewpoints about alternative research strategies. The economic theory-oriented criticism related to the Lucas critiue (see

This article first appeared in *Economic Notes, Sienna*, No. 1, 1988, pp. 1–28. Revised and updated version of the paper presented at the course 'Recent Advances in Econometric Modelling: Causality, Time Series Methods and Computer Applications' held in Santa Margherita Ligure (Italy), 12–22 November 1984.

Lucas, 1976) and the rational expectations hypothesis (see Lucas and Sargent, 1981) criticized the modelling of expectations and raised serious doubts about the invariance of so-called 'structural' parameters of estimated macro-models. The time series-oriented criticisms questioned the existence of legitimate a priori theoretical information (see Sims, 1980) and stressed the importance of the temporal structure of economic time series (see Granger and Newbold, 1977). The Bayesian-oriented criticism questioned the *ad hoc* nature of 'cook-book' econometrics and prescribed a more formal treatment using Bayesian techniques (see Leamer, 1978, 1983). From the Popperian philosophy of science viewpoint the criticism called mainly for the rejection of the positivist features dominating the 'textbook' approach and the adoption of a more falsificationist approach (see Blaug, 1980). A further criticism of 'cookbook' econometrics followed from the LSE tradition in econometric modelling (see Hendry and Richard, 1982, 1983; McAleer et al. 1985; Gilbert, 1986). This sought to allow the structure of the data an important role in determining the various specification aspects (especially the short-run dynamics) of an empirical model.

The aim of this paper is to formalize a methodological framwork in the spirit of Haavelmo (1944) which combines features from various of the above alternative approaches. In Section 2 the 'textbook' approach is briefly discussed as a prelude to Sections 3 and 4. In Section 3 a number of alternative approaches is briefly considered and contrasted with the 'textbook' approach. No attempt to provide a detailed discussion of these approaches is made, because they are mainly used to motivate the methodological framework discussed in Section 4.

The methodology formalized in Section 4 is not proposed as *the* sole correct procedure to construct empirical models because no such unique procedure could ever exist. As Caldwell (1982) argues:

Just as there is no best way to listen to a Tchaikovsky symphony, or write a book, or to raise a child, there is no best way to investigate social reality. Yet methodology has a role to play in all of this (p. 252)

One of the aims of the formalization is to show how the ingenuity and craftsmanship of individual modellers play an important role in constructing adequate empirical models. Without discounting the descriptive, prescriptive, and the validation aspects of the proposed methodological framework, it should be viewed more as a framework in the context of which empirical modelling can be discussed, analysed, and constructively criticized.

Although the discussion which follows is focused on time-series data the essential features of the formalized methodology apply equally to cross-section and panel data. Some specific features, however, which depend on the nature of the data, need to be changed in order to accommodate different forms of observed data.

2.   The Textbook Approach to Econometric Modelling

One of the few things about the current state of econometric modelling the
various critics agree upon is that the 'textbook' approach is not adequate as
a basis for empirical research. While it has rarely been formalized explicitly
a number of sketches of the 'textbook' approach, similar to Figure 1,
have appeared in various econometric textbooks (see Johnston, 1972;
Koutsoyiannis, 1977, p. 7; Intriligator, 1978, p. 3 *inter alia*). Nevertheless,
it is useful to set up a formal strawman of 'textbook' econometrics because
its difficulties will lead naturally to the formalization adopted in Section 4.
Section 4.

The 'textbook' approach was caricatured by Pagan (1984) as follows:

Four steps almost completely describe it: a model is postulated, data gathered, a
regression run, some *t*-statistics or simulation performance provided and another
'empirical regularity was forged' (p. 103).

The roots of this methodology can be traced back to the seminal work
of Tinbergen (1937, 1939) and the associated well-documented exchange
between Keynes (1939) and Tinbergen (1940). Tinbergen narrowed down
the intended scope of econometric modelling from the Frisch (1933)
definition to 'the quantification of theoretical models in an attempt to test
the empirical validity of theories and a means for policy analysis'. The
role of the econometrician was implicitly confined to the estimation and
empirical evaluation of theoretical relationships (supplied by the theorist)
using both theoretical and statistical criteria. The theoretical criteria were
mainly related to the sign and magnitude of the estimated coefficients as
compared with a priori theoretical information. The statistical criteria were
primarily the value of R^2 and later the *t*-ratios of the individual coefficients
which were subsequently supplemented by a few diagnostics such as the
Durbin–Watson statistic. The same criteria were used to both test theories
or choose between theories. The current 'textbook' approach differs from
the Tinbergen methodology of the 1940s firstly, in so far as the advances

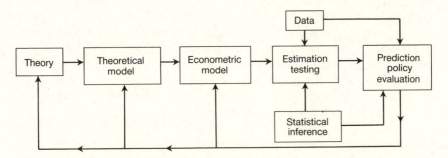

Figure 1   The 'textbook' approach

in computer technology made available more sophisticated methods of estimation and testing and secondly, the well-known exchange between Koopmans and Vining (see Koopmans, 1947; Vining, 1949) on the question of 'measurement without theory' tipped the scales in favour of a priori theoretical information over any information related to the probabilistic structure of the observed data, despite the early and often-cited discussion in Haavelmo (1944). This classic monograph had very little influence on the methodology of econometric modelling because it was immediately filtered through by the Cowles Commission group, which narrowed down its intended scope to that of the probabilistic foundations and the simultaneous equations model (see Spanos, (1987b) for a more extensive discussion). In Section 4 it is argued that some of the main features of the formalized methodology can be traced back to Haavelmo (1944).

To make the discussion less abstract one of the first theoretical relationships to be subjected to the 'textbook' approach, namely the consumption function, is used as an example. Initially, the relevant theory came in the form of Keynes's absolute income hypothesis (AIH), and the aim of empirical modelling was the quantification of the marginal and average propensities to consume. The observed data commonly chosen were time series on aggregate consumers' expenditure and income. In the early empirical literature when the AIH was estimated in the context of the linear regression model the results raised a number of problems whose proposed solutions had a lasting effect on the development of econometric modelling. In the late 1940s and early 1950s the typical scenario was that although the value of the R^2 and t-ratios, as well as the sign and size of the estimated coefficients, were suggesting close corroboration, the predictive ability of the estimated equations left a lot to be desired (see Wallis, 1977). This was initially interpreted as a rejection of the AIH, taking the statistical results at face value. In Spanos (1987a) it is shown that the so-called 'stylized' facts associated with this early literature, on closer examination, turn out to be a long way from being facts necessitating a very different reinterpretation of this literature. The basic problem with this early literature is that most of the estimated models are statistically misspecified, rendering their conclusions unwarranted.

With the development of misspecification tests such as the Durbin–Watson test (see Durbin and Watson, 1950, 1951) this aspect of the problem became apparent, and the modeller considering how to proceed had few options within the 'textbook' approach. Indeed, it can be argued that the restrictive nature of the 'textbook' approach contributed significant to the emergence of 'cookbook' econometrics.

By the mid-1950s it became apparent that neither the Cochrane–Orcutt nor the simultaneous-equations formulations were adequate for the measurement of the AIH, from time-series data. On the other hand the inclusion of lags among the explanatory variables tended to signficantly improve the stability and predictive ability of the estimated model. Within the 'textbook' approach a natural route to account for such lags is by developing and extending the underlying theory, and was one of the stimuli to formulating the habit persistence, life-cycle and permanent income hypotheses (see Thomas, 1985, *inter alia*). In turn these developments raised the problem of matching latent theoretical variables to observed data series and led to the modelling of the dynamics using the adaptive expectations and partial adjustment hypotheses. In a certain sense these fruitful hypotheses delayed the questioning of the methodological under-pinnings of the 'textbook' approach until the early 1970s because they could be used to transform an essentially static theory to a dynamic theoretical relationship. When combined with an allowance for residual autocorrelation and simultaneity, such relationships gave rise to adequate empirical models for over a decade, until a combination of factors such as the oil crises and the end of Bretton-Woods agreement led to the break-down of some of the best-known empirical regularities such as the Phillips curve and the demand for money. Important changes in the economic environment and the general availability of computer packages to calculate numerous new misspecification tests revealed inadequacies in the existing empirical models which were seen to be based on the 'textbook' approach. 'Cookbook' econometrics bore the brunt of the criticism and a general feeling of disenchantment with the state of empirical econometrics emerged by the mid-1970s. Was this state of affairs either necessary or inevitable? The critics agreed that it was not, but they differed in both their diagnosis and their prescribed alternatives.

In the next section a number of the alternatives to the 'textbook' approach suggested since the mid-1970s, are discussed briefly, as a prelude to the discussion in Section 4, where a general methodological framework is formalized.

3. Alternatives to the 'Textbook' Approach

The main tradition in time-series modelling was founded by Wold (1938), who established a link between the autoregressive (AR (p)) and moving average (MA (q)) formulations of Yule and Slutsky, respectively, and the probabilistic structure of stochastic processes formalized by Kolmogorov and Khintchin. This tradition led to the ARMA (p, q) model as the most influential family of models in time domain modelling. Building upon this tradition, Box and Jenkins in a series of papers culminating in their 1970 textbook (see Box and Jenkins, 1976), formalized and popularized time-series modelling in the context of the univariate ARIMA (p, d, q) formu-lation, which extended the ARMA (p, q) model to a certain class of nonstationary processes, known as integrated processes. The aim of their approach was to provide a parsimonious representation of the mechanism generating the data, within the ARIMA family, guided by the probabilistic structure of the data. The Box–Jenkins procedure is summarized in Figure 2, where the word identification in this context is used to denote the determination of the optimal values for *p*, *d* and *q*.

Given the emphasis on forecasting in the large-scale macro-models of the late 1960s, it was perhaps inevitable that the 'textbook' approach would find itself challenged by the Box–Jenkins methods for modelling aggregate time series. In the early 1970s a number of studies compared estimated univariate ARIMA models with the large-scale macro-models on forecasting grounds and the latter were found wanting (see Naylor et al., 1972; Nelson, 1972 and Cooper, 1972, *inter alia*). Although this comparison concentrated on forecasting, it brought out a very important defect in the empirical macro-models; the macro-modellers, preoccupied with simultaneity, were largely ignoring the temporal structure of the time-series data, at their peril (to quote Granger and Newbold, 1977).

An influential extension of the Box–Jenkins approach to allow for the *joint temporal structure* of economic time series was proposed by Sims (see Sargent and Sims, 1977; Sims, 1980, 1982) To let the structure of the data play an important role, and minimize the role of the theory, Sims suggested modelling the economic time series of interest in the form of Vector AR (*m*) models. The VAR representation was chosen by Sims as the most convenient way to parameterize the joint temporal structure of a stationary vector stochastic process and study its (temporal) causality structure (see Geweke, 1984). The estimated VAR model, although lacking a direct economic theoretic interpretation, can nevertheless be used for prediction and policy analysis as an alternative statistical formulation to the simultaneous-equation model for tackling the problem of doubtful a priori restrictions. In Sims's view the theoretical structure imposed on the data through identification restrictions, is simply 'incredible' (to quote from

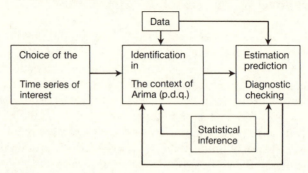

Figure 2   The Box–Jenkins approach

Sims, 1980). Moreover, Sims doubted the validity of most assertions about the exogeneity of any contemporaneous variables. A most widely used rule for the identification of a single equation, using exclusion restrictions, is the order condition, which requires that the number of excluded exogenous variables be no less than the number of included endogenous variables minus one (see Intriligator, 1978, *inter alia*). Since this is only a necessary condition, it is possible to turn an underidentified equation into an apparently identified one by adding more exogenous variables to the rest of the system. Instead, Sims chose to ignore a priori restrictions as well as the endogenous/exogenous distinction. The role played by economic theory in unrestricted VAR modelling, as in the Box–Jenkins approach, is just in choosing the relevant observed data series. The critics of the unrestricted VAR approach argue, however, that the lack of theoretical structure renders these models inappropriate not only for explanation and testing of theories but for policy analysis as well (see Cooley and LeRoy, 1985).

In his attempt to explain the poor forecasting performance of macro-models and the apparent breakdown of a number of empirical regularities forged during the heyday of the 'textbook' approach, Lucas (1976) argued that structural instability was inherent in their construction. Using the examples of consumption and investment functions and the Phillips curve, interpreted as decision rules of economic agents, he showed that under rational expectations the estimated coefficients of these models constitute a mixture of the parameters of the objective function of the agents and the statistical parameters of the stochastic processes involved, including the processes controlled by the government. Consequently, these estimated coefficients are unlikely to be invariant to policy changes and in order to construct structural models which can be used for policy evaluation it is imperative that the two sets of parameters be disentangled. When this is achieved the estimated parameters of the objective function can be used to consider alternative policy rules and their implications for the economy.

This viewpoint gave rise to an alternative approach to empirical econometric time series modelling, with Lucas and Sargent the protagonists (see Lucas and Sargent, 1981). The Lucas–Sargent research strategy differs from the 'textbook' approach in at least three important respects. Firstly, theoretical models are interpreted as decision rules of agents or/and the government and they are consistently derived via dynamic optimization of fully specified objective functions given the relevant constraints. Secondly, the temporal structure of all the stochastic processes involved is explicitly recognized in the interpretion of the estimated parameters. Thirdly, the 'textbook' approach to identification, using exclusion restrictions, plays a much lesser role in this context and instead non-linear cross-equation restrictions, implied by the dynamic optimization and the rational expectations hypothesis, are used extensively.

A Bayesian-oriented criticism of 'cookbook' econometrics was mounted by Leamer (1978). His critique was motivated by the great disparity between the formal 'textbook' approach and its practised counterpart in the form of 'cookbook' econometrics. Leamer's diagnosis is that the main cause of this disparity in the 'axiom of correct specification' (Leamer, 1978, pp. 3–4) which underlies the 'textbook' approach. The alternative proposed by Leamer purports to 'take the con out of econometrics' (to quote Leamer, 1983) by formalizing the *ad hoc* nature of 'cookbook' econometrics using informal Bayesian procedures such as the extreme bounds analysis (EBA) (see Leamer and Leonard, 1983). This is allegedly accomplished by making it difficult for the modeller to hide his/her prejudices and arbitrary use of a priori information. EBA entails generating the complete range of possible coefficient estimates based on the given sample information but using widely different priors. This aims to expose the possible fragility of estimated relationships by testing their robustness to changes in prior information.

McAleer et al. (1985) questioned the value of Leamer's EBA as a method for investigating fragility and suggested that a more effective way to 'reduce the con in econometrics' is to subject the estimated equations to a variety of misspecification tests. Their criticism was based on the methodological approach founded by Sargan (see Maasoumi, 1987), which broke away from the restrictive framework of the 'textbook' approach in a number of respects. Firstly, Sargan did not assume that the form of the empirical model is known at the outset irrespective of the observed data chosen. Indeed, he allowed the temporal structure of the data to play an important role in the specification of the dynamics for his wages and prices equations; an element that can be traced back to Tinbergen (1939). Secondly, he interpreted the estimated behavioural equations as price-adjustment equations which are related to, but do not coincide one-to-one with, the demand/supply functions of the labour and output markets (see the discussion with Ball in Sargan, 1964). Thirdly, by explicitly distinguishing between the empirical and theoretical models, he allowed the theory to influence the specification of the former via its long-run solution.

These departures from the 'textbook' approach introduced by Sargan were pursued further by Hendry and Anderson (1977) and Davidson et al. (1978). The role of the observed data in determining the dynamics of the empirical econometric model was explicitly recognized by Davidson et al. (1978) and formalized in Mizon (1977a, b) and Hendry (1979) as *the general-to-specific* procedure. In this procedure the modeller starts from the general dynamic specification which is transformed into a theoretically meaningful relationship and then tested downwards for a more parsimonious representation (see Gilbert, 1986). As well as raising a number of methodological issues which were previously only informally discussed, Davidson et al. (1978) seemed to have popularized a data-oriented specification for adjustment equations based on the *error-correction* formulation introduced by Sargan (1964). Their paper also demonstrated the usefulness of extensive *misspecification testing* applied to estimated equations, by the continued empirical success of their consumption function model (see Hendry, 1983). In addition, the concept of *encompassing* was introduced at an informal level, requiring the modeller to account for the results of previous studies using his/her estimated empirical model. Finally, the theoretical model was viewed as influencing the form of the empirical model via the latter's long-run solution, with the temporal structure of the data influencing its short-run dynamics. This approach was extended by Hendry (1979, 1983), Sargan (1980) and Hendry and Wallis (1984), *inter alia*.

An attempt to formalize that approach in a coherent framework was made by Hendry and Richard (H-R) (1982, 1983). The H-R formalization is important to the present paper because it introduced a number of features which form the basis of the formalization in Section 4. First, the specification of statistical models is defined directly in terms of the observable random variables involved, and not through the error term. Secondly, the statistical models are viewed as reductions of the joint distribution of the random variables involved using marginalization and conditioning. this enabled them to formalize the concept of statistical exogeneity defined in Engle et al. (1983). Thirdly, they stressed the distinction between a theoretical model, the empirical model, and the actual generating mechanism. Further, they provided a formulation for interpreting the roles of a variety of design and evaluation criteria for econometric models. Finally, they formalized the concept of encompassing extended in Mizon (1984) and Mizon and Richard (1986).

A brief appraisal of the above alternatives as compared with the 'text-book' approach is required in order to relate these approaches to the methodological framework discussed in the next section.

The criticism of econometric modelling from univariate ARIMA exercises, despite its limited scope, exposed an important weakness in the 'text-book' approach since there, the temporal structure of the time-series data had no role to play beyond the one attributed to it by the theory. Thus, an empirical model which utilized the temporal structure of the data in conjunction with the a priori theoretical information and the system structure of the economy should be able to outperform a Box–Jenkins ARIMA model. The theoretical validity of this conjecture was confirmed by a number of papers (see Zellner and Palm, 1974; Prothero and Wallis; 1976, Wallis, 1977, and Zellner, 1979, *inter alia*) by relating the multivariate ARMA formulation with the structural simultaneous-equations form. They showed that any univariate ARMA model could be embeded within the final form of a linear dynamic structural model if the latter is endowed with a sufficiently general dynamic structure. The problem, however, is how to introduce such dynamic structure in the context of the 'textbook' approach where the temporal structure of the data could only be modelled in so far as the dynamics are accounted for by the theory. Below it is argued that this problem could be tackled by changing the methodological framework to allow the structure of the observed data to be modelled at an initial stage unconstrained by the precise form of the theoretical model. This enables us to integrate Sims's unconstrained VAR specification, interpreted as an 'unstructured first-stage model' (see Sims, 1980, p. 15), with the Lucas–Sargent type of theoretical model without leading to any contradictions.

The Lucas–Sargent approach constitutes an improvement over the 'textbook' approach by taking into consideration the temporal structure of the data when specifying dynamic models. Their approach, however, retains the 'textbook' assumption that the theoretical and empirical models coincide. This, viewed as a long-term goal, is commendable, but in practice the theoretical models do not go far enough in order to bridge the gap between what is observed and what the theory suggests ought to be observed.

By the same token Leamer's formalization of *ad hoc* specification searches does not constitute a break from the 'textbook' approach, but offers a formalization of 'cookbook' econometrics. However, Leamer is right in pointing to the 'axiom of correct specification' as the main culprit behind the problems of the 'textbook' approach. In the context of the methodology formalized in the next section it is argued that this axiom, as specified by Leamer (1978), is in fact overly restrictive and unecessary for statistical inference purposes. In specifying statistical models no such assumption is needed. This is based on distinguishing between a statistical and a theoretical model.

The main contribution of the LSE tradition in this debate came in the form of dynamic specification. It brought attention to the fact that empirical models are often dynamically misspecified, a problem which in general renders any statistical arguments based on such models unwarranted. The LSE approach in tackling this problem has in turn been criticized on various grounds. The use of general dynamic specifications advocated by this tradition appeared to be *ad hoc* from both the theoretical and statistical viewpoints. Secondly, there appears to be no formal justification for the general-to-specific methodology. Thirdly, the procedure from the general to the specific empirical econometric model appears to rely more on the modeller's skill and ingenuity rather than the theory or some formally justified statistical procedure. Fourthly, the resulting empirical models have only a tentative connection with the underlying theory. One of the important features of the methodological framework formalized in Section 4 is that these issues can be satisfactorily resolved. In this sense the proposed methodology can be viewed as providing a more coherent framwork for the LSE tradition; a framework which utilizes the complementary features of the above alternative approaches.

4. Towards a Unifying Methodological Framework

One of the main contributing factors to the restrictive nature of the 'text-book' approach is its narrow interpretation of the intended scope of econometric modelling.

The notion of quantifying theoretical relationships assumes that the theoretical model essentially coincides with both the statistical model and the actual generating mechanism, up to a white-noise error term. On closer examination the metamorphosis of the theoretical model into an empirical model reveals a number of questionable implicit presuppositions. First, there is no reason to suppose that the observed data chosen constitute unique measurements of the theoretical variables involved. The history of the empirical consumption function illustrates this non-uniqueness most vividly by the numerous alternative data series used for C and Y. Indeed, the fact that cross-section data tended to give rise to somewhat different estimates of the average and marginal propensities to consume was viewed as a paradox to be explained by the early empirical literature (see Thomas, 1985 *inter alia*). Is the form of the empirical model invariant to the choice of the data? Secondly, the specification of the statistical model is determined by the theory, and it is assumed to hold irrespective of the nature of the observed data chosen (e.g. time series, cross-section or panel data). Whatever the data, they are assumed to have the structure imposed upon them by the form of the theoretical model and the attached error term. If the estimated model turns out to be misspecified any statistical arguments related to the sign, size, or significance of the estimates are commonly unwarranted. Where does this leave the modeller who relies on such criteria? Given that the estimated model cannot be used as a basis of any statistical arguments, misspecification tests cannot be interpreted as tests of the theory either. It has been argued (see Hendry, 1979) that the poor forecasting performance of empirical macro-models and the breakdown of certain empirical relationships in the early 1970s can be explained by more mundane reasons then the Lucas critique–including the effects of simple forms of misspecification. Thirdly, given the direct link between the probabilistic assumptions about the error and the observable random variables, any alterations of the original assumptions potentially affects the interpretation of the theoretical model.

To allow for the structure of the observed data we first need to broaden the scope of econometric modelling into the systematic study of economic phenomena of interest using observed data. This will enable us to relate the empirical econometric model to the actual mechanism underlying the observable phenomena of interest and not just to the theory. As a result the scope of econometric modelling is no longer restricted by the form of the theoretical model, irrespective of the observed data chosen. Both the theory and the observed data have a common denominator in the form of the DGP (data-generating process) which demarcates the framework of analysis. Theories are not constructed for the sake of theorizing, but as possible explanations of economic phenomena of interest. Several aspects of these phenomena are 'observable', and provide the basis for the available observed data. The proposed formalization is schematically represented in Figure 3.

To avoid the problems of the textbook approach raised above we follow Haavelmo (1944) and distinguish at the outset between *theoretical* variables, in terms of which a theoretical model is defined, and the *observed* data (see Spanos, 1987b). *A theoretical model* in the present context is defined to be a mathematical formulation of a *theory*. The latter is viewed as a conceptual construct providing an idealized description of the phenomena within its intended scope (see Spanos, 1982). Concepts such as demand, supply, and decision variables in the context of a theoretical model refer to intentions and plans, and cannot be assumed to coincide with the observed data series under all circumstances and irrespective of the nature of such data series. Often the modeller finds that there is no unique data series corresponding to the theoretical variables of interest even though a multitude of data series is commonly available. For example we rarely have data directly relating to demand, supply, or consumption. The observed data usually available in such cases come in the form of quantities transacted and the corresponding prices.

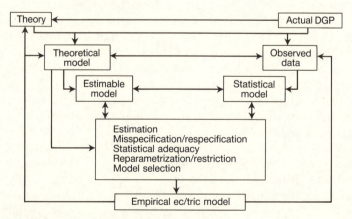

Figure 3   A unifying methodological framework

Thus, the question arises as to how to coalesce the relevant theoretical and sample information in the specification of statistical models. Since the statistical inferences will be bound up with the nature and structure of the observed data, it makes sense to specify statistical models in terms of the observable random variables (the observed data being realizations of such variables) and not some error term being attached to the theoretical model. As emphasized by Haavelmo (1944) so far as statistical inference is concerned 'all come down to the same thing, namely, to study the properties of the joint distribution of the random (observable) variables in a stochastic equation system' (p. 85).

The theory has a role to play in the specification of statistical models but not to the exclusion of all other information. Initially the theory influences the specification of statistical models in so far as it determines the *choice* of the observed data for the modelling in question. Behind every form of observation there is a theory, however rudimentary, which suggests the importance of observing some aspect of a phenomenon of interest. Unfortunately in econometrics what the theory suggests we should observe and what we can observe are commonly different. In view of the non-experimental nature of economic data this implies that what is estimable, given a set of observed data, might not coincide with the theoretical model. Hence, it is advantageous to distinguish between a *theoretical model* and an *estimable model* given a set of observed data; a distinction which can also be traced back to Haavelmo (1944) (see Spanos, 1987b). There are circumstances under which the theoretical and estimable models might coincide; in particular when the circumstances envisaged by the theory coincide with the actual DGP. For example if observations relating to demand can be generated in an experimental-like fashion by asking the agents to register their intentions corresponding to a given set of hypothetical prices, then demand schedules might be directly estimable.

In order to illustrate these concepts reconsider the example of the consumption function. The observable economic phenomenon of interest is the behaviour of aggregate consumers' expenditure in relation to income. For the sake of the argument, retain the absolute income hypothesis (AIH) as the relevant theory. The first decision facing the modeller is the choice of the most appropriate data series in view of the theory and the actual DGP. This decision should not be taken lightly because it will have a bearing upon the form of the estimable model as well as the choice of the statistical model. If we choose the commonly used time series C_t–real consumers' expenditure on non-durables and services and Y_t–real personal disposable income, we need to ascertain their appropriateness as measurements of the theoretical variables consumption (C) and income (Y) as used in the context of the AIH. If, for example, these theoretical variables refer to plans or intentions, we need to allow for the possibility that the estimable model might differ from the theoretical model.

Next, the *statistical model* is specified directly in terms of the observables random variables denoted by $\{Z_t, t \in T\}$, giving rise to the observed data chosen (see Figure 3). The *theory* influences this specification via the choice of the observed data and its estimable form. Another form of information which influences the statistical model specification is the *measurement information* related to the units and system of measurement of the observable random variables Z_t. This form of information also includes any exact relationships among the observed data, such as accounting identities. A third type of information relevant for the specification of the statistical model is the *sample information* related to the nature and probabilistic structure of $\{Z_t, t \in T\}$, stemming from the nature of the data chosen and their sampling methods.

Let the theoretical model for the AIH be:

$$(1) \qquad C = \alpha_0 + \alpha_1 Y, \quad \alpha_0 > 0, \quad 0 < \alpha_1 < 1$$

with measured C_t and Y_t as defined above. The fact that C_t and Y_t are ratio scale variables taking only positive values constitutes important measurement information. Another form of potentially relevant measurement information is the well-known income identity. The relevant sample information comes in the form of the time-series nature of the data which exhibit distinct time trends and temporal dependence. In the context of the 'textbook approach' the theoretical model (1) is often embedded into a statistical model by assuming that C and Y coincide with the observed data chosen and attaching a white-noise error (often normal) term, yielding the linear regression model:

$$(2) \qquad\qquad\qquad y_t = \alpha_0 + \alpha_1 x_t + \epsilon_t$$

$$\epsilon_t \sim N(0, \sigma_\epsilon^2), \ E(\epsilon_t \epsilon_s) = 0 \text{ for } t \neq s, \quad t, s = 1, 2, \dots \text{T}.$$

where $y_t \equiv C_t$ and $x_t \equiv Y_t$.

The implied probabilistic structure for the observed data in this case is that y_t conditional on x_t is normally distributed with linear mean, homoscedastic variance and temporally independent:

$$(3) \qquad E(y_t/x_t) = \alpha_0 + \alpha_1 x_t. \quad \text{Var } (y_t/x_t) = \sigma_\epsilon^2$$

$$\text{and } \mathrm{cov}(y_t y_s/x_t) = 0 \text{ for } t \neq s, \quad t, s = 1, 2 \dots T$$

If any of these assumptions turn out to be invalid any inference related to the estimated coefficients will be misleading. As shown in Spanos (1987a) the statistical model (2) fails all misspecification test for linearity, homosedasticity, and temporal independence for USA annual data. In practice it is important to be able to assess the appropriateness of a statistical model at the outset in order to avoid misleading conclusions.

To be able to assess the appropriateness of (2) as a statistical model in the context of which (1) can be considered we need to take account not only of the theory but the structure of the data as well. This entails relating the implied probabilistic structure for $\{y_t/x_t, t \in T\}$ to the structure of the joint process $\{Z_t, t \in T\}$, where $Z_t = (y_t, x_t)$, because the time plots of these data are related to the joint and not the conditional process. The implied probabilistic structure on the latter, impling (3) for the former, is that $\{Z_t, t \in T\}$ is normal, independent, and identically distributed (NIID):

(4) $\quad Z_t \sim N(m, \Sigma_0)$, $\Sigma_0 > 0$ and cov $(Z_t Z_s) = 0$ for $t \neq s, t, s \in T$

Using (4) we can re-interpret (2) as follows:

(5) $$y_t = E(y_t/x_t) + \epsilon_t$$

where $$\mu_t = E(y_t/x_t) \text{ and } \epsilon_t = y_t - E(y_t/x_t)$$

are viewed as the *systematic* and *non-systematic components* of the specification which are by construction orthogonal $(E(\mu_t\epsilon_t) = 0)$. Moreover the parameters $\theta = (\alpha_0, \alpha_1, \sigma_\epsilon^2)$ are now given a *statistical interpretation* as:

$$\alpha_0 = m_1 - \alpha_1 m_2, \quad \alpha_1 = (\sigma_{12}/\sigma_{22}) \text{ and } \sigma_\epsilon^2 = \sigma_{11} - (\sigma_{12}^2/\sigma_{22}) \text{ where}$$

$m_1 = E(y_t)$, $m_2 = E(x_t)$, $\sigma_{11} = \text{var}(y_t)$, $\sigma_{12} = \text{cov}(y_t x_t)$ and $\sigma_{22} = \text{var}(x_t)$.

Given that the most general description of the sample information is given by the joint distribution of all the observable random variables for the whole of the sample, it makes sense to view statistical models as reductions of the latter.

Following Hendry and Richard (1982) (5) can be viewed as a reduction from $D(Z_1, Z_2, \ldots X_T; \Psi)$ as follows:

(6) $$D(Z_1, Z_2, \ldots Z_T; \Psi) = \prod_{t=1}^{T} D(Z_t; \Psi_t) = \prod_{t=1}^{T} D(Z_t; \Psi)$$
$$= D(y_t/x_t; \Psi_1) D(x_t; \Psi_2)$$

The first and second equalities follow from the independence and identically distributed assumptions, respectively. The normality assumption together with the positive definiteness of Σ_0 imply that Ψ_t and Ψ_2 are variation free, enabling us to concentrate exclusively on $D(y_t/x_t; \Psi_1)$ in specifying (5) (see Engle et al., 1983).

The complete specification for *the linear regression* (LR) *model* in the case of k regressors is as follows:

(I) *Statistical GM:* $\quad y_t = \beta' x_t + x_t + u_t, \quad t \in T$

(1) $\mu_t = E(y_t/D_t) \equiv \beta' x_t$, $u_t = y_t - E(y_t/D_t)$, where $D_t = \{X_t = x_t\}$
(2) Statistical parameters of interest: $\theta = (\beta, \sigma^2)$
$\quad$ where $\beta = \Sigma_{22}^{-1}\sigma_{21}$ and $\sigma^2 = \sigma_{11} - \sigma_{12}\Sigma_{22}^{-1}\sigma_{21}$
(3) X_t is weakly exogenous with respect to θ
(4) No a priori information on θ
(5) Rank $(X) = k$, for all $T > k$.

(II)   Probability model

$$\Phi = \{D(y_t/X_t; \theta) = (1/\sigma\sqrt{2\pi}) \exp[-(1/2\sigma^2)(y_t - \beta' x_t)'(y_t - \beta' x_t)],$$
$$\theta \in \mathrm{IR}^k \times \mathrm{IR}_+\}$$

(6) (i) $D(y_t/X_t; \theta)$ is normal

    (ii) $E(y_t/X_t = x_t) = \beta' x_t$ – linear in x_t

    (iii) $\mathrm{cov}(y_t/X_t = x_t) = \sigma^2$ – homoscedastic

(7) θ is time invariant.

(III)   Sampling model

(8) $Y_T \equiv (y_1, y_2, \ldots y_T)'$ is an independent sample, sequentially drawn from $D(y_t/X_t; \theta)$, $t = 1, \ldots, T$, respectively; see Spanos (1986) for more details.

Although the specification is defined solely in terms of the conditional process $\{y_t/X_t, t \in T\}$ the sufficient conditions in terms of $\{Z_t, t \in T\}$ are of interest because they enable us to assess the appropriateness of the statistical model in question and it is potentially useful in suggesting how to respecify a misspecified model in order to account for the indicated departures. Related to this is the question of relaxing these sufficient conditions without affecting the results associated with the model. In the case of the LR model the identically distributed (ID) assumption for $\{Z_t, t \in T\}$ can be extended to allow for various forms of time-dependent means. In the case where $m(t)$ is a known function of time no special problems arise apart for some caution in deriving the asymptotic results for the estimators of the parameters.

The specification of the LR model as given above brings out the role of the probabilistic structure of Z_t in so far as it influences the definition of the systematic component via the relevant conditioning information set; x_t in this case. Given that $\{Z_t, t \in T\}$ is assumed to be temporally independent it is not surprising that the past history of the process, denoted by $Z_{t-1}^0 = (Z_{t-1}, Z_{t-2}, \ldots)$, incorporates no relevant information for the explanation of y_t. However, for the consumption and income data the assumption of temporal independence is likely to be invalid thus calling into question the appropriateness of the reduction of (6) and the specification (5). Indeed, it is more reasonable to assume that $\{Z_t, t \in T\}$ is temporally correlated, say asymptotically independent:

(7) $Z_t \sim N(m, \Sigma_0)$, $\Sigma_0 > 0$ and $\mathrm{cov}(Z_t Z_s) = \Sigma_{|t-s|} \to 0$ as $|t - s| \to \infty$ $t, s \in T$

This assumption suggests that the past history of the process is potentially relevant and calls for a respecification of the systematic and non-systematic components in (5) to:

$$u_t^* = E(y_t/z_{t-1}^0, x_t),$$
$$u_t^* = y_t - E(y_t/Z_{t-1}^0, x_t).$$

The gives rise to an alternative statistical specification of the form:

(8) $$y_t = c_0 + \beta x_t + \sum_{t-1}^{l} [\alpha_i y_{t-i} + \beta_i x_{t-i}] + u_t$$

for some $l > 0$ ($l < T$). The new statistical parameters $\theta^* = (c_0, \beta, \alpha_i, \beta_i, i = 1,2,\ldots l)$ are directly related to Ψ_1^* in the reduction:

$$D(Z_1, Z_2, \ldots Z_T; \Psi) = \prod_{t=1}^{T} D(Z_t/Z_{t-1}^0; \Psi_t^*) = \prod_{t=1}^{T} D(Z_t/Z_{t-1}^0; \Psi^*)$$

(9) $$= \prod_{t=1}^{T} D(y_t/Z_{t-1}^0, x_t; \Psi_1^*) D(x_t/Z_{t-1}^0; \Psi_2^*)$$

The assumptions of stationarity and asymptotic independence lead to the time-invariance of the parameters in Ψ^* and the existence of the truncation lag l, respectively; see Spanos (1986) Ch. 22–3, for details.

In the context of the above specification we can easily accommodate various forms of non-stationarity such as deterministic trends and stochastic time-dependent means which can be modelled by integrated processes (see Phillips and Durlauf, 1986). In the same context we can consider a variety of questions from Granger causality (see Granger, 1969) to common factors (see Hendry and Mizon, 1978) and co-integration (see Granger, 1986; Engle and Granger, 1987) and how these are related to the structure of $\{Z_t, t \in T\}$ (see Spanos, 1987d, e).

The novelty in the above specification does not lie with its generality but its interpretation in the context of the methodology depicted in Figure 3 and the implications thereof. In postulating the statistical model we do not assume that the statistical GM necessarily coincides with either the theoretical model or the DGP. The statistical GM and the underlying assumptions are viewed as providing a sufficient summary of the sample information in a way which enables us to consider the theoretical model in question in its context. The statistical model underlying (8) is viewed as a hypothesis about the structure of the stochastic process $\{y_t/Z_{t-1}^0, X_t, t \in T\}$ whose validity depends on the probabilistic structure of the observed data chosen and not that of the theory. The theory influences its form in two ways, by suggesting the relevant observable variables and the theoretical parameterization of interest. The statistical parameterization is then chosen in a way which can be transformed into the latter, but at the same time takes account of the data's structure. Before any theoretical questions can be considered we need to ensure the validity of the statistical model chosen. This viewpoint is reflected in assumptions (1)–(4) which are not made in the 'textbook' approach. In assumption (1) we choose the systematic component in a way which ensures that all the systematic information in $D(Z_1, Z_2, \ldots Z_T; \Psi)$ is incorporated in the relevant information set D_t. The error term is defined as the unmodelled part and it is non-systematic relative to D_t. This interpretation of the error term is close to the notion of *noise* in systems theory (see Anderson and Moore, 1979). The main aim in postulating μ_t is to take account of all the relevant information for the mechanism generating y_t in order to reduce u_t. Modelling the error term using say, some ARMA specification, does not arise at this stage because any form of systematic information should be incorporated in μ_t. Indeed, the non-systematic nature of u_t will be instrumental in mis-specification testing. The viewpoint that the statistical GM is not assumed to coincide with either the theoretical model or the actual DGP is emphasized further by assumption (2), which reiterates that the parameters θ should not be interpreted (at this stage) as anything more than statistical parameters in terms of which the statistical GM is defined. They are viewed as functions of the parameters Ψ. The great temptation to interpret these as coinciding with the theoretical (structural) parameters is resisted at this stage.

By deriving the statistical specification from the joint distribution $D(Z_1, Z_2, \ldots Z_T; \Psi)$ we make explicit the need for weak and strong exogeneity assumptions (see Engle et al., 1983). In turn, this enables us to view the problem of endogeneity as an issue related to the parameterization of interest and not as a problem of estimation bias. Moreover, the distinction between a statistical and an empirical model will enable us to view collinearity or near-collinearity (see (5)) as a statistical problem of insufficient sample information related to the statistical and not the theoretical parameterization of interest (see Spanos, 1986).

Looking at the above specification of the LR model we can see that no assumptions relating to the exhaustiveness or uniqueness of the regressors are made. This interpretation of the statistical model enables us to circumvent the 'axiom of correct specification' by interpreting the rejection of the underlying assumptions not as a rejection of the theory but as an indication that the postulated probabilistic structure is inappropriate for the data chosen. Before we can consider any questions related to the theory we need to ensure that the estimated statistical model does have the statistical meaning we assume it has. That is to say, we need to ensure that the estimated statistical model is well-defined statistically.

DEFINITION   A statistical model whose assumptions are tested and not rejected (using conventional significance levels), for the data chosen, is said to be tentatively statistically adequate (TESTA).

A statistically adequate model is interpreted as a statistically meaningful summary of the information in the data chosen, and provides the baseline for any further econometric modelling; without it no valid statistical inference arguments can be used to say anything about the theory in question. How do we proceed in the case where a number of the assumptions underlying the statistical model are rejected?

The question of estimating dozens of regressions by changing the observed data or/and the variables involved does not arise, because the above interpretation of the statistical model does not involve any assumptions of uniqueness or completeness underlying the 'axiom of correct specification' (see Leamer, 1978). The choice of the relevant variables is a matter for the theory or theories in question. The same applies to the practice of 'correcting' for misspecification results such as the presence of heteroscedasticity or/and temporal dependence by modelling the error term. Any systematic information indicated by these departures belongs to the systematic component, not the error. In the context of the methodology depicted in Figure 3 the way to proceed when certain assumptions are rejected is to respecify the statistical model in an attempt to end up with a statistically adequate model. In other words, choose an alternative statistical model which (hopefully) constitutes a more appropriate characterization of the information in the data chosen. This brings us conveniently to the next stage of the modelling procedure, going from a statistically adequate model to an empirical model.

The difference between a statistically adequate model and an empirical econometric model is that the former needs to have only statistical not theoretical meaning, but the latter needs both. The important implication of this is that the modeller should not be inhibited by the form of the estimable model when choosing a statistical model as long as the latter can be used to consider the former in its context, in the sense that the theoretical parameters of interest are derivable from the statistical parameters.

If we were to assume that the statistical model based on (8) with $l = 1$:

$$(10) \qquad y_t = \beta_0 + \beta_1 x_t + \beta_2 y_{t-1} + \beta_3 x_{t-1} + \varepsilon_t$$

turns out to be a statistically adequate model for annual data, we can proceed to consider the question of relating the theoretical with the statistical parameters. A naive way to proceed is to view the theoretical parameters $\alpha = (\alpha_0, \alpha_1)$ as corresponding to $\theta = (\beta_0, \beta_1, \beta_2, -\beta_3)$ subject to the restrictions:

$$(11) \qquad \beta_2 = \beta_3 = 0$$

In this sense the theoretical parameters are viewed as a *reparameterization/ restriction* of the statistical parameters. These restrictions, however, are unlikely to be satisfied in practice, and the question arises as to the possibility of having an estimable form which gives rise to a more reasonable set of restrictions. A widely used example of such an estimable model results when Y in (1) is reinterpreted as permanent income Y_t^* i.e.:

(12) $$C_t = \alpha_0 + \alpha_1 Y_t^*$$

Postulating the additional auxiliary hypothesis of adaptive expectations relating Y_t^* with the observable Y_t:

(13) $$(Y_t^* - Y_{t-1}^*) = \alpha_2 (Y_t - Y_{t-1}^*), \quad 0 < \alpha_2 < 1$$

gives rise to the estimable model:

(14) $$C_t \equiv \alpha_0 \alpha_2 + \alpha_1 \alpha_2 Y_t + (1 - \alpha_2) C_{t-1}$$

In this case the statistical and theoretical parameters are related via:

$$\beta_0 = \alpha_0 \alpha_2, \quad \beta_1 = \alpha_1 \alpha_2, \quad \beta_2 = (1 - \alpha_2), \quad \beta_3 = 0$$

In general if we denote the statistical and theoretical parameters of interest by θ and α, respectively, we assume that the relationship between the two is described by a mapping:

(15) $$H(\cdot) : A \to \theta,$$

which commonly takes the form:

(16) $$\theta = H(\alpha)$$

The theoretical parameter vector α is said to be *identified* iff $H(\cdot)$ is one-to-one (an injection) i.e.:

(17) $$H^{-1}(H(\alpha)) = \{\alpha\}$$

Identification of α in this context amounts to being estimable from the knowledge of θ from which it derives its statistical meaning. In practice, it is often the case that we have fewer theoretical than statistical parameters. In general, the mapping $H(\cdot)$ being an injection satisfies the condition:

(18) $$H(H^{-1}(\theta)) \subseteq \theta$$

From this condition we can distinguish between the cases where α is *over-identified* (when the $H(H^{-1}(\theta)) \subset \theta$) and *just-identified* $(H(H^{-1}(\theta)) = \theta)$. In the latter case $H(\cdot)$ is both an injection and a surjection, i.e. a bijection (one-to-one and onto) describing a simple *reparameterization*. In this case $H(H^{-1}(\cdot))$ imposes restrictions on θ and thus we refer to it as a *restriction*. In this sense the empirical econometric model is viewed as a reparameterization/restriction of a statistical model.

The above formulation of the connection between the statistical and empirical econometric models provides an alternative viewpoint to the problem of *identification* in econometrics. In effect it separates the problem into identification of the statistical parameters first and then the theoretical (structural) parameters. The statistical parameters are identified on the basis of the likelihood function, and the problem is whether the sample information is adequate for the estimation of the statistical parameterization of interest. If $T(\theta)$ refers to the log-likelihood function then θ is said to be *identified* iff the mapping $T(\cdot) : \theta \to R$, defines an injection. That is:

(19) $$\text{for } \theta_1, \theta_2 \in \theta \text{ if } \theta_1 \neq \theta_2 \text{ then } T(\theta_1) \neq T(\theta_2)$$

For further discussion on identification see Spanos (1985a). This enables us to distinguish between insufficient sample information problems such as collinearity or short data and insufficient theoretical information related to the theoretical interpretation of the statistical parameters. The implication of this is that the second identification stage is not considered with respect to some imaginary statistical form irrespective of the data, but to a statistically adequate model based on the data in hand. The two stages, although closely related, can be profitably separated to allow a role for the observed data. In addition, this interpretation of identification enables us to provide a unified treatment of the problem which is applicable to all statistical models in econometrics not just the simultaneous equations model as in the 'textbook' treatment (see Intriligator, 1978, *inter alia*). In the case of the latter the identification problem is posed and solved before any data are even chosen. In terms of the methodology discussed above the structural form of the SEM (see Intriligator, 1978):

$$(20) \qquad \Gamma' y_t + \Delta' X_t = \varepsilon_t$$

is viewed as the theoretical parameterization of interest with α being the unknown elements of Γ and Δ. The relevant statistical GM is not automatically the *derived* reduced form:

$$(21) \qquad y_t = B' X_t + u_t,$$

because if the latter does not take account of the temporal structure of the data it is highly likely that it will be statistically inadequate. In order to avoid that it is advisable at the outset to postulate the dynamic linear regression model (see Spanos, 1986) as the relevant statistical model underlying (20). If the latter turns out to be statistically adequate the identification problem is then considered in the context of the latter and not (21). Note that this view of identification allows the data to play a role as was initially envisaged by Working (1927).

Modelling in such a framework will reduce the problem of arbitrary restrictions. Although alternative theories will suggest different reparameterization of a statistically adequate model, and thus some arbitrariness (in the sense of Sims) in the reparameterization still remains, any over-identifying restrictions should be tested before being imposed. In addition we should also check that the empirical econometric model was not derived at the expense of the statistical properties of the statistically adequate model on which it is based. Testing the validity of the statistical assumptions in the context of the empirical model does not constitute proper mis-specification testing because these assumptions have already been tested and not rejected in the context of the statistical model; hence such testing is referred to as *diagnostic checking*. It purports to ensure that the estimated empirical econometric model is not just theoretically meaningful but also statistically well defined. This is indeed because the model is likely to be used for prediction and simulation purposes. In the case of the simple reparameterization no tests are required because the bijection between the theoretical and statistical parameters ensures that the former are well defined given that the latter are based on a statistically adequate model.

A question which naturally arises at this stage is to what extent is it necessary or useful to go beyond a statistically adequate model. It is often argued that for prediction, and to some extent for simulation purposes, the gains from using the empirical econometric model rather than the statistically adequate model are only marginal (see Sims, 1980, *inter alia*). The answer to this question lies with the functions of empirical models. Empirical econometric models are not used only for prediction and simulation, but for description and explanation as well. A statistically adequate model is largely *data-specific* and hence its value in terms of explanation and description is very limited. On the other hand the more restrictive the empirical econometric model the more informative in terms of explanation. Another important reason, related to this, is that the empirical model purports to model the 'invariant' features of the actual DGP. Indeed, the main reason for the reparameterization/restriction is to capture these 'invariants' in the form of the structural (theoretical) parameters whose estimates are not data-specific. This will ensure the appropriateness of the empirical model for prediction and simulation purposes.

In practice, when the sample size is sufficiently large, reaching a statistically adequate model should not present many difficulties to the modeller, because of the availability of numerous misspecification tests applicable to almost all conceivable cases. The next step, however, from a statistically adequate model to an empirical econometric model is likely to tax the ingenuity and craftsmanship of any modeller, especially in models of regime shifts, integrated, pathogenous processes, and parameter change. This is because there are no ready-made rules or formulae to be applied unless the modeller has a very specific estimable model with a strong theoretical underpinning which, when tested against the statistically adequate model, is not rejected. In this respect the theoretical models suggested by the Lucas–Sargent approach, when reinterpreted in the context of the present methodological framework, can provide good examples of estimable models. More often than not, however, the theoretical models suggested by the theory are not directly estimable, and as a result the theoretical model can only provide rough guidelines for the form of the empirical econometric model. In this respect the development of dynamic estimable models referring to adjustment and processes is of paramount importance for more theoretically coherent empirical models (see Muelbauer and Bover, 1986; Nickell, 1984, *inter alia*). Another way to derive such empirical models is provided by the LSE tradition, where the theory is viewed as relating to the long-run solution of the empirical model. In this case form of the empirical model is determined by theoretical considerations in so far as they restrict the short-run dynamics via its long-run solution. The exact form of the empirical model combines data-oriented parameterization with this form of theoretical considerations (see Sargan, 1964; Davidson et al., 1978; Hendry, 1979, 1983, *inter alia*). A third alternative is to combine the above two approaches by rationalizing the LSE tradition's empirical models as decision rules derived from a coherent dynamic optimization problem (see Alogoskoufis and Nissim, 1981; Nickell, 1985; Muelbauer and Bover, 1986).

Although the parameterization/restriction is not arbitrary there is nothing unique about the mapping $H(\cdot)$ in (16). Numerous alternative empirical econometric models based on different theories are derivable from the same statistically adequate model. This raises the problem of *model selection*, choosing between the alternative empirical econometric models. When all the empirical econometric models are derivable from a common statistically adequate model the problem of model selection becomes easier to tackle, because they are all based on a common statistical model. The need for a common statistical framework in the context of non-nested models and encompassing was emphasized by Mizon (1984) and Mizon and Richard (1986). The discussion of the methodology depicted in Figure 3 suggests that, although empirical models are likely to be non-nested, they are always nestable within a common statistical model. The latter, however, is of little value unless it constitutes a statistically adequate model.

Assuming that the empirical econometric models in question constitute alternative reparameterization/restrictions of a common statistically adequate model a number of the design and evaluation criteria proposed by Hendry and Richard (1982, 1983) can be reinterpreted as model selection criteria in the context of the formalization depicted in Figure 3. These criteria include:

(i) *Theory consistency*,   (ii) *Robustness*   (iii) *Parsimony*,
(iv) *Encompassing*

The other design and evaluation criteria suggested by Hendry and Richard such as *data admissibility* and *coherence*, *valid conditioning*, and *parameter constancy*, when viewed in the context of the methodology formalized above, are better interpreted as related to the statistical model rather than the empirical econometric model. Data admissibility, referring to the property that it should be logically possible for the data to have been generated by the model in question, was classified as part of the measurement information on which the specification of the statistical GM is based. A data-coherent statistical model is more or less equivalent to a statistically adequate model which might include valid conditioning or/and parameter constancy depending on whether these assumptions are actually made in the context of the particular statistical model in question. Statistical models of interest in econometrics might include VAR as well as stochastic parameter models. For alternative categorizations of model selection criteria, see McAleer et al. (1985), Pesaran and Smith (1985), *inter alia.*

The model selection criteria mentioned above, together with the intended purpose of the empirical model (prediction, policy evaluation, description, and explanation) can be used to select an empirical econometric model. The chosen model purports to provide an adequate approximation of the actual DGP, and constitutes the result of the modeller's attempt to come to grips with the observed phenomenon of interest. The estimated model can also be used in order to evaluate the theory, the choice of the observed data, as well as other aspects of the modelling methodology formalized above.

As argued above, the methodology formalized in this section can be viewed as a refinement and extension of the Hendry and Richard (1982, 1983) formalization of the LSE tradition. In terms of Figure 3 the main differences between the above and the H-R formalization come in the form of the additional distinctions between a *theoretical* and an *estimable model*, and between a *statistical* and an *empirical econometric model*. These additional distinctions could be viewed as refinements of the H-R formalization which enables us to resolve a number of methodological issues, as well as gain some additional insight into the role of the theory in determining the estimated form of the empirical model.

The distinction between a theoretical model and its estimable form can be used to rationalize a number of successful empirical econometric models of the LSE tradition as adjustment equations rather than demand/supply functions. This interpretation provides us with additional insight in so far as supply-side variables might be deemed relevant in an adjustment equation. In this context economic theory can be used in order to provide more realistic adjustment equations and thus make the connection between such empirical models and the theory more explicit.

The most important refinement of the H-R formalization comes in the form of the distinction between a statistical and an empirical econometric model. This distinction enables us to delineate a number of problems raised by the H-R formalization. Because of the absence of such a distinction H-R are forced to concede that all the tests they propose in the form of a tentatively adequate conditional data (TACD) characterization are in effect design and evaluation criteria or diagnostic checking. However, using the concept of a statistically adequate model we can differentiate between statistical criteria, which are relative to the statistical model chosen, and evaluation and model selection criteria for empirical econometric models. The distinction is important because, in the context of the statistical model, ensuring the validity of the underlying assumptions is sary to enable us to use statistical arguments for the construction of empirical models, it is not a matter of choice or design. Put in a different way, in the context of the methodology depicted in Figure 3, if two people are given the same data set and similar theories it is highly likely that they will end up with the same choice of a statistical model and a similar statistically adequate model, but it is highly unlikely that they will end up with the same empirical model. This is because the degree of subjectivity in setting up a statistically adequate model is considerably less than in constructing an empirical model. Moreover, testing the underlying assumptions of a particular statistical model is proper misspecification testing. On the other hand, the same tests applied to the chosen empirical econometric model can only be viewed as diagnostic checking. Secondly, the distinction between a statistical and an empirical econometric model enhances our understanding of the concept of encompassing. At the level of the statistical model specification encompassing is not very interesting, because a model with the most observable data series encompasses all the others. At the level of an empirical econometric model, however, encompassing becomes a very powerful concept because it can be used to evaluate different models which are based on the same statistically adequate model. This formulation immediately points to a weakness in the discussion of encompassing (see Mizon, 1984; Mizon and Richard, 1986) in so far as they do not emphasize the importance of statistical adequacy for the encompassing model. An encompassing model which is not statistically adequate is of little value. In the context of the above formalization the criticism of encompassing as leading to theoretically uninteresting models can be seen to be misplaced, because the encompassing model is viewed only as a basic statistical, and not as a theoretical, model.

The distinction between a statistical and an econometric model can also be used to resolve the controversy related to the so-called 'general-to-specific procedure' (see Gilbert, 1986, *inter alia*). The controversy has been over whether 'the general-to-specific' or 'specific-to-general' methodologies provide the best strategy for the construction of empirical econometric models. In the context of the formalized methodology the controversy becomes irrelevant, because the issue is one of establishing a statistically adequate model in order to have a solid statistical foundation upon which to construct an empirical econometric model. In the case of time-series data it is more likely that the most appropriate statistical model will be that of the dynamic linear regression model, which is commonly described as 'general' in this literature, but not necessarily. A simple static statistical GM might turn out to be a statistically adequate model. The real problem in econometric modelling arises when the modelling is based on a mis-specified statistical model trying to derive a more adequate one using theoretical arguments and *erroneous* statistical procedures.

5. Summary and Conclusions

The main aim of the paper has been to formalize a coherent methodological framework for econometric modelling in the spirit of Haavelmo (1944). The proposed framework provides an integration of features from various alternative and seemingly contradictory approaches, and can be viewed as providing a coherent framework for the LSE tradition. The main message from this formalization is that, before any economic theoretical issues can be considered, using valid statistical arguments, it is imperative to establish a statistically adequate model based on the data chosen. A simple test of adequacy for any empirical model is against a more general estimated statistical model which has been established as a statistically adequate model. The proposed formalization enables us to resolve a number of methodological issues in a coherent framework. The perspective also provides additional insight into the process of econometric modelling, by making the modeller aware of a number of problems and issues which are often dealt with by default.

References

Alogoskoufis, G. S., Nissim, J. (1981), Consumption-income dynamics under rational expectations: theory and evidence, *Greek Economic Review*, 3, 128–35.

Anderson, B. D. O., Moore, J. B. (1979), *Optimal Filtering*. Prentice-Hall, Princeton.

Blaug, M. (1980), *The Methodology of Economics*. Cambridge University Press, Cambridge.

Box, G. E. P. and Jenkins, G. M. (1976), *Time Series Analysis: Forecasting and Control* (revised edn). Holden-Day, San Francisco.

Caldwell, B. (1982), *Beyond Positivism: Economic Methodology in the Twentieth Century*. George Allen & Unwin, London.

Cooley, T. F. and LeRoy, S. F. (1985), Atheoretical macroeconomics: a critique, *Journal of Monetary Economics*, 16, 283–308.

Cooper, R. L. (1972), The predictive performance of quarterly econometric models of the United States. *Econometric Models of Cyclical Behavior*, ed. by B. G. Hickman. Columbia University Press, pp. 813–947.

Davidson, J. E. H., Hendry, D. F., Srba, F. and Yeo, S. (1978), Econometric modelling of the aggregate time-series relationship between consumers' expenditure and income in the United Kingdom, *Economic Journal*, 88, 661–92.

Durbin, J. and Watson, G. S. (1950), Testing for serial correlation in least squares regression, I, *Biometrika*, 37, 409–28.

Durbin, J. and Watson, G. S. (1951), Testing for serial correlation in least squares regression, II, *Biometrika*, 38, 159–78.

Engle, R. F., and Granger, C. W. J. (1987), Cointegration and Error-correction: representation, estimation and testing, *Econometrica*, 55, 251–76.

Engle, R. F., Hendry, D. F. and Richard, J. F. (1983), Exogeneity, *Econometrica*, 51, 277–304.

Frisch, R. (1933), Editorial, *Econometrica*, 1, 1–4.

Geweke, J. (1984), Inference and causality in economic time series models, *Handbook of Econometrics*, Vol. II, ed. by Z. Griliches and M. Intriligator. Noth-Holland, Amsterdam, Ch. 19.

Gilbert, C. L. (1986), Professor Hendry's econometric methodology, *Oxford Bulletin of Economics and Statistics*, 48, 283–307.

Gilbert, C. L. (1987), The development of British econometrics 1945–85, *Journal of Economic Literature* (forthcoming).

Granger, C. W. J. (1986), Developments in the study of cointegrated economic variables, *Oxford Bulletin of Economic and Statistics*, 48, 213–27.

Granger, C. W. J. and Newbold, P. (1977), *Forecasting Economic Time Series*. Academic Press, London.

Haavelmo, T. (1944), The probability approach in econometrics, *Econometrica*, 12 (supplement), 1–115.

Hendry, D. F. (1979), Predictive failure and econometric modelling in macroeconomics: the transactions demand for money. *Economic Modelling*, ed. by P. Ormerod. Heinemann, London, pp. 217–42.

Hendry, D. F. (1983), Econometric modelling: the consumption function in retrospect, *Scottish Journal of Political Economy*, 30, 193–220.

Hendry, D. F. and Anderson, G. J. (1977), Testing dynamic specification in small simultaneous systems: an application to a model of building society behaviour in the UK. *Frontiers in Quantitative Economics*, Vol. IIIA, ed. by M. D. Intriligator. North-Holland, Amsterdam.

Hendry, D. F. and Mizon, G. E. (1978), Serial correlation as a convenient simplification not a nuisance: a comment on a study of the demand for money by the Bank of England, *Economic Journal*, 88, 549–63.

Hendry, D. F. and Richard, J.-F. (1982), On the formulation of empirical models in dynamic econometrics, *Journal of Econometrics*, 20, 3–33.

Hendry, D. F. and Richard, J.-F. (1983), The econometric analysis of economic time series, *International Statistical Review*, 51, 111–63.

Hendry, D. F. and Wallis, K. F. (eds) (1984), *Econometrics and Quantitative Economics*. Basil Blackwell, Oxford.

Intriligator, M. D. (1978), *Econometric Models, Techniques and Applications*. North-Holland, Amsterdam.

Keynes, J. M. (1939), Professor Tinbergen's method, *Economic Journal*, 49, 8–68.

Koopmans, T. C. (1947), Measurement without theory, *Review of Economics and Statistics*, 29, 161–72.

Koopmans, T. C., Rubin, H. and Leipnik, R. B. (1950), Measuring the equation systems of dynamic economics, *Statistical Inference in Dynamic Economic Models*, ed. by T. C. Koopmans. Cowles Commission Monograph, no. 10.

Koutsoyannis, A. (1977), *Theory of Econometrics*. Macmillan, London.

Leamer, E. E. (1978), *Specification Searches: Ad Hoc Inference with Non-experimental Data*. John Wiley & Sons, New York.

Leamer, E. E. (1983), Let's take the con out of econometrics, *American Economic Review*, 73, 31–44 (reprinted as Chapter 1 in this volume).

Leamer, E. E. and Leonard, H. B. (1983), Reporting the fragility of regression estimates, *Review of Economics and Statistics*, 65, 306–17.

Lucas, R. E. Jr. (1976), Econometric policy evaluation: a critique, *The Phillips Curve and Labour Markets*, ed. by K. Brunner and A. M. Melzer. Carnegie-Rochester Conference on Public Policy, I, 19–46.

Lucas, R. E. Jr. and Sargent, T. J. (1981), *Rational Expectations and Econometric Practice*. George Allen & Unwin, London.

Maasoumi, E. (1987), *Contributions to Econometrics: J. Denis Sargan*, Vols I, II. Cambridge University Press (forthcoming).

McAleer, M., Pagan, A. R. and Volker, P. A. (1985), What will take the con out of econometrics?, *American Economic Review*, 75, 293–313 (reprinted as Chapter 2 in this volume).

Mizon, G. E. (1977a), Inferential procedures in non-linear models: an application in a UK industrial cross section study of factor substitution and returns to scale, *Econometrica*, 45, 1221–42.

Mizon, G. E. (1977b), Model selection procedure, *Studies in Modern Economic Analysis*, ed. by M. J. Artis and A. R. Nobay. Basil Blackwell, Oxford, Ch. 4.

Mizon, G. E. (1984), The encompassing approach in econometrics, *Econometrics and Quantitative Economics*, ed. by D. F. Hendry and K. F. Wallis. Basil Blackwell, Oxford, Ch. 6.

Mizon, G. E. and Richard, J.-F. (1986), The encompassing principle and its application to testing non-tested hypotheses, *Econometrica*, 54, 657–78.

Muellbauer, J. and Bover, O. (1986), Liquidity constraints and aggregation in the consumption function under uncertainty. Applied economics discussion paper no. 12, Institute of Economics and Statistics, Oxford.

Naylor, T. H., Seaks, T. G. and Wichern, D. W. (1972), Box–Jenkins methods: an alternative to econometric models, *International Statistical Review*, 40, 123–37.

Nelson, C. R. (1972), The prediction performance of the FRB–MIT–PENN model of the US economy, *American Economic Review*, 62, 902–17.

Nickell, S. (1985), Error correction, partial adjustment and all that: an expository note, *Oxford Bulletin of Economics and Statistics*, 47, 119–31.

Nickell, S. (1984), An investigation of the determinants of manufacturing employment in the U.K., *Review of Economic Studies*, LI, 529–57.

Pagan, A. R. (1984), Model evaluation by variable addition, *Econometrics and Quantitative Economics*, ed. by D. F. Hendry and K. F. Wallis. Basil Blackwell, Oxford, Ch. 5.

Pagan, A. R. (1985), Time series behaviour and dynamic specification, *Oxford Bulletin of Economics and Statistics*, 47, 199–211.

Pesaran, M. H. and Smith, R. P. (1985), Evaluation of macroeconometric models, *Economic Modelling*, April, pp. 125–34.

Phillips, P. C. B. and Durlauf, S. N. (1986), Multiple time series regression with integrated processes, *Review of Economics Studies*, LIII, 473–96.

Prothero, D. L. and Wallis, K. F. (1976), Modelling macro-economic time series, *Journal of the Royal Statistical Society*, series A, 139, 468–500.

Richard, J.-F. (1980), Model with several regimes and changes in exogeneity, *Review of Economic Studies*, 47, 1–20.

Sargan, J. D. (1964), Wages and prices in the U.K.: a study in econometric methodology, *Econometric Analysis for National Economic Planning*, ed. by P. E. Hart et al. Butterworths, London (reprinted in Hendry and Wallis, 1984).

Sargan, J. D. (1980a), Some tests of dynamic specification for a single equation, *Econometrica*, 48, 879–97.

Sargan, J. D. (1980b), The consumer price equation in the post war British economy: an exercise in equation specification testing, *Review of Economic Studies*, 47, 113–35.

Sargent, T. J. and Sims, C. A. (1977), Business cycle modelling without pretending to have too much a priori economic theory. In Sims (1977).

Sims, C. A. (ed.) (1977), *New Methods in Business Cycle Research*. Federal Reserve Bank of Minneapolis.

Sims, C. A. (1980), Macroeconomics and reality, *Econometrica*, 48, 1–48.

Sims, C. A. (1982), Policy analysis with econometric models, *Brookings Papers on Economic Activity*, 107–64.

Spanos, A. (1982), Latent variables in dynamic econometric models. London University, Ph.D. thesis.

Spanos, A. (1985), Identification in econometrics: statistical versus theoretical parameters of interest. Birkbeck College (mimeo).

Spanos, A. (1986), *Statistical Foundations of Econometric Modelling*. Cambridge University Press, Cambridge.

Spanos, A. (1987a), Early empirical findings on the consumption function, stylized facts or fiction: a retrospective view. *Oxford Economic Papers* (forthcoming).

Spanos, A. (1987b), On re-reading Haavelmo. Birkbeck College, unpublished paper.

Spanos, A. (1987c), Instrumental variables revisited: A finite sample interpretation, Birkbeck College, discussion paper.

Spanos, A. (1987d), Error-autocorrelation revisited: the AR(I) case, *Econometric Reviews* (forthcoming).

Spanos, A. (1987e), Co-integration and the associated parameterization, a note. Birkbeck College, unpublished paper.

Thomas, R. L. (1985), *Introductory Econometrics: Theory and Application*. Longmans, London.

Tinbergen, J. (1937), *An Econometric Approach to Business Cycle Problems*. Herman and Cie, Paris.

Tinbergen, J. (1939), *Statistical Testing of Business Cycle Theories*, Vols I and II. League of Nations, Geneva.

Tinbergen, J. (1940), On a method of statistical business-cycle research: a reply, *Economic Journal*, 50, 141–54.

Vining, R. (1949), Koopmans on the choice of variables to be studied and of methods of measurement, *Review of Economics and Statistics*, 31, 77–94.

Wallis, K. F. (1977), Multiple time series models and the final form of econometric models, *Econometrica*, 45, 1481–97.

Wold, H. O. (1938), *A Study in the Analysis of Stationary Time Series*. Almquist and Wicksell, Uppsala (2nd edn 1954).

Working, E. J. (1927), What do statistical demand curves show?, *Quarterly Journal of Economics*, 41, 212–35.

Zellner, A. (1979), Statistical analysis of econometric models, *Journal of the American Statistical Association*, 74, 628–43.

Zellner, A. and Palm, F. (1974), Time series analysis and simultaneous equations econometric models, *Journal of Econometrics*, 2, 17–54.

PART IV

Model Evaluation and Selection

Introduction

Throughout this book the importance of evaluation of models has been emphasized. The two papers in this final section take very different viewpoints on this important topic. Hal White (paper 16) discusses the theoretical possibility of building a model which automatically ensures that certain design criteria are obeyed, at least in sample, and so makes in-sample evolution irrelevant. Yock Chong and David Hendry (paper 17) take a more conventional approach, are convincingly critical about some conventional evolution techniques, and emphasize the importance of forecast encompassing for evaluation of systems.

In paper 14 Hendry and Richard proposed a set of criteria that a model should obey for it to be 'congruent' with the data. White uses this list as a starting point, suggests a somewhat revised list and then discusses how one can test that members of a candidate list C of probability models obey these desired criteria. In so doing, one does not necessarily arrive at any acceptable model, in which case a previously agreed plan can be used to suggest further models for testing. Leamer (1988) emphasizes that such contingency plans should be made before any analysis is attempted, but this is rarely done as it is not always possible to predict in what ways the data will reject a model. White's procedure may select a single model, or several models of the candidate set may be acceptable, in which case more stringent criteria may be applied to get to a single model. To illustrate the process four criteria of increasing stringency are considered and relevant tests are suggested. The models considered are either probability models (denoted S), which include a full distribution specification, or are models which describe conditional means (denoted M). The desirable criteria include either encompassing or 'correct specification', which is more stringent. A new class of econometric tests, called m-tests, are found to be particularly relevant. Hal White's new book, *Estimation, Inference and Specification Analysis*, Cambridge University Press, 1989, contains material that leads up to this unpublished paper. His proposals have yet to be applied to real data, and may require further refinement to make them fully practical, but the basic approach is obviously very promising.

There are an enormous number of available ways of evaluating a model or system of models. Many are listed in paper 17 by Yock Chong and David Hendry. They show that some traditional methods of evaluation are not really appropriate, such as dynamic simulation and possibly a simple comparison of forecasting accuracy whilst ignoring forecasting confidence intervals. They discuss four evaluation devices which are fairly new and generally applicable. The first, called forecasting encompassing, tests if the forecasts from one model (M_1) encompass those from another model (M_2), such so that linear combinations of the two forecasts are no better than those from M_1. These ideas can be generalized to multi-step forecasts and many alternative models. The second evaluation procedure suggested looks at n-step forecast confidence intervals, using either conditional or unconditional standard deviations. These intervals are affected by the quality of models' first and second (conditional) moments, and thus evaluates more of the model than is usual.

The other evaluation methods discuss summary statistics for systems and large models plus inter-equation feedbacks. The paper thus discusses various aspects of models that are currently little discussed, and deserve more attention from practical modellers.

16

A Consistent Model Selection Procedure Based on *m*-testing

Halbert White

1. Introduction

Empirical research progresses by formulating one or more theoretical models to explain an observable phenomenon, comparing the predictions of the models to observations on the phenomenon (a process which often involves statistical estimation to resolve details left unspecified by the model), and then rejecting or retaining a particular model based on these comparisons. The purpose of this paper is to present a formal treatment of such a process in a context which, although by no means universal, is nevertheless relevant to econometric practice. We build on recent work of Hendry and Richard (1982) and Hendry (1987) for arriving at a 'congruent' model, i.e. a model correctly specified in a number of precise ways. Our approach is based on the *m*-tests of Newey (1985) and Tauchen (1985); we propose a model selection procedure which selects one or more models meeting particular specification requirements with probability approaching one, and which also rejects models not possessing those with probability approaching one, as the number of observations tends to infinity. Such a model selection procedure is said to be 'consistent'.

2. Specification-based Model Selection

We suppose that we observe a realization of a vector-valued discrete stochastic process $\{X_t: \Omega \to \mathbb{R}^v, t = 1, 2, \ldots; v \in \mathbb{N}\}$, where $(\Omega, \boldsymbol{F})$ is a measurable space. The stochastic behaviour of X_t is governed by the unknown data-generating process (DGP) P_o, a probability measure on $(\Omega, \boldsymbol{F})$. We call a collection of probability measures on $(\Omega, \boldsymbol{F})$ a 'probability model', $\boldsymbol{P}$. The probability model $\boldsymbol{P}$ can be thought of as all probability measures (model elements) which could describe the behaviour of $\{X_t\}$ under a particular theory. Given a collection of probability models $\boldsymbol{P}_i$,

This paper follows on from material contained in *Estimation, Inference and Specification Analysis* (Cambridge University Press, in press). The author is grateful to Clive Granger and David Hendry for helpful discussions. The errors committed here are the author's own. This research was supported by NSF grant SES85-10637.

$i = 1, \ldots, N$ the model selection problem is to choose the model or models (thus, the associated theory) which is in some sense most acceptable, or 'best'.

A 'best' probability model might or might not be required to contain P_o. If $\boldsymbol{P}$ contains P_o, we say that $\boldsymbol{P}$ is correctly specified for $\{X_t\}$. If $\boldsymbol{P}$ does not contain P_o, it is misspecified; however, one or more elements of $\boldsymbol{P}$ may share certain features of P_o. When this is the case, we say that $\boldsymbol{P}$ is correctly specified to some extent; we may be willing to accept as 'best' a probability model which is correctly specified only to some extent.

Generally, the desired extent of correct specification can be expressed in terms of a precise list of criteria which an acceptable model must meet. Failure to meet these criteria is taken to constitute an unacceptable model misspecification. We refer to these criteria as the 'specification requirements'. For convenience, we adopt the following formalism.

DEFINITION 2.1 A *specification-based model selection framework* ($\boldsymbol{C}$, $\boldsymbol{R}$) is defined as a collection of probability models $\boldsymbol{C} = \{\boldsymbol{P}_1, \ldots, \boldsymbol{P}_N\}$ (the 'candidate set') together with a set of specification requirements $\boldsymbol{R}$ which specify precisely properties which a given model must exhibit in order to be acceptable, and which when violated constitute an unacceptable misspecification.

Given a candidate set of models $\boldsymbol{C}$ and a set of specification requirements $\boldsymbol{R}$, an apparently reasonable model selection procedure can be described in the following heuristic manner: for each model, formulate and perform a statistical test designed to detect failure of any of the specification requirements (a specification test). If an unacceptable misspecification is detected, then that model is rejected. Otherwise, the model is retained.

This procedure has three relevant outcomes: (1) no models are retained; (2) exactly one model is retained; or (3) more than one model is retained. In the first instance all of the models are unacceptably misspecified: no model is selected. In the second instance the retained model is viewed as the model 'selected'. In the third instance all the retained models are viewed as being selected. Further testing must be conducted if it is required to select only one model. This testing can be conducted by formulating a more stringent list of specification requirements and repeating the selection procedure.

To illustrate the issues which arise in following such a procedure, consider the criteria proposed by Hendry and Richard (1982) for a model 'congruent with the evidence' (Hendry's (1987) terminology; a 'tentatively adequate conditional characterization of the DGP' in the original terminology). According to Hendry and Richard, a model (element) is congruent if:

(a) it 'encompasses' all rival models;

(b) its error process is a 'mean innovation process' (*MIP*);
(c) its 'parameters of interest' are constant;
(d) it is 'data admissible'; and
(e) its current conditioning variables are 'weakly exogenous for the parameters of interest'.

For convenience, we call a model congruent if it contains a congruent element. Terms in quotation marks are as defined by Hendry and Richard (1982). Below, we discuss the meaning of several of these terms further.

Inspired by Popper (1962), the model-building strategy of Hendry and Richard requires that empirical analysis proceed by arriving at a congruent model. Whenever new data or new models become available, the existing congruent model is to be evaluated against all available models and available data, with a new congruent model (which may or may not be the existing congruent model) ultimately arrived at. The congruent model element is not claimed to be the DGP, but simply an adequate representation given currently available information.

The model-building strategy of Hendry and Richard is thus a 'progressive' research strategy, as the congruent model at any point in time is not only consistent with all empirical evidence (data) so far available but, because of encompassing, is capable of explaining the statistical results associated with any alternative model. Hendry and Richard (1982) provide a compelling discussion of the advantages of such an approach to model-building in econometrics.

Suppose we have a candidate set *C* and wish to arrive at a congruent model. We can conduct the search for a congruent model as a model selection process of the sort described above. (Indeed, this is precisely the sort of process implemented in Hendry's econometric model-building software package GIVE, for the congruence criteria.) To proceed, one must formulate a specification test (or tests) which will detect any failure to meet the specification requirements. Such specification tests should have known statistical properties and be straightforward to compute. The *m*-tests of Newey (1985) and Tauchen (1985), as extended by White (1987, in press) meet these requirements very nicely; in the next section we describe these tests and discuss implementation of a model selection procedure based on m-testing. We shall not need the specifics of the *m*-testing implementation for the present discussion, however. For now, we simply indicate generally relevant specification tests for the specification requirements of a congruent model.

For concreteness, suppose we are deciding whether or not to retain the first model, P_1. Corresponding to requirement (a) of the congruence criteria are the complete parametric encompassing tests of Mizon (1984) and Mizon and Richard (1986). Requirement (b) of the congruence criteria requires that the 'error process is a MIP relative to the selected database'. In many cases this amounts to the requirement that an appropriate residual forms a martingale difference sequence. Corresponding to this requirement are tests for serial correlation, and the dynamic information matrix tests of White (1987, in press).

Corresponding to requirement (c) of the congruence criteria are the Chow (1960) tests for parameter constancy. Here there is a fair amount of latitude, as break-points for the Chow test can be chosen freely.

Requirement (d) imposes the criterion of 'data admissibility'. This is defined by Hendry and Richard (1982, Definition 13) in the following way: 'An empirical model is *data admissible* if [and only if] its predictions satisfy all data constraints with probability unity'. Let $X^t \equiv (X_1, \ldots, X_t)$. Expressed in our terminology, we would say that a model element P_θ is data admissible if and only if $P_o[E_\theta(X_t|X^{t-1}) \in S_t] = 1$, where E_θ is expectation under P_θ and S_t is the minimal support of X_t (so that $P_o[X_t \in S_t] = 1$, $t = 1, 2, \ldots$). A model is data admissible if at least one of its elements is. For example, data admissibility fails when X_t is a Bernoulli random variable $(P_o[X_t = 1] = P_{ot}, P_o[X_t = 0] = 1 - P_{ot}, t = 1, 2, \ldots)$ but a linear probability model is posited $(X_t|X^{t-1} \sim N(X_{t-1}\theta, 1), t = 1, 2, \ldots)$. In this interpretation, data admissibility fails when the conditional expectation of a dependent variable can take on values (in intervals) with positive probability under the model element, but which in fact have zero probability under the DGP. At first sight this appears to be a reasonable specification requirement in that, if it is violated, it leads to unacceptable model misspecification. (For example, most would agree that the linear probability model is unacceptably misspecified for the limited dependent variable DGP when one intends to interpret the resulting parameter estimates as having some economic meaning.) However, the interpretation given above for Hendry and Richard's condition is too stringent. The nonlinear probability model $X_t|X^{t-1} \sim N(\Phi(X_{t-1}\theta), \Phi(X_{t-1}\theta)(1 - \Phi(X_{t-1}\theta))$ yields a stochastic specification such that the model of the conditional mean $\boldsymbol{M} = \{\Phi(X_{t-1}\theta)\}$ is correctly specified for $\{E(X_t|X^{t-1})\}$ when $E(X^{t-1}) = \Phi(X_{t-1}\theta_o)$ for some θ_o in Θ. In this case, $S_t = \{0, 1\}$ and $E_\theta(X_t|X^{t-1}) = \Phi(X_{t-1}\theta)$. However, $P_o[\Phi(X_{t-1}\theta) \in S_t] = 0$ for all $\theta \in \Theta$, so that this model is data inadmissible under the current definition. Even so, this does not result in a useless specification. One still obtains consistent and efficient estimates of θ_o, as well as useful predictions $\hat{X}_t = \Phi(X_{t-1}\hat{\theta}_n)$, even though these predictions generally attain the (data constrained) values 0 and 1 with probability zero.

Instead of attempting a more appropriate reinterpretation of the data admissibility criterion, we treat it simply as a requirement which accomplishes its intended effect by removing from a priori consideration any model which is patently misspecified in an unacceptable manner. Because such models (which we now refer to simply as 'patently misspecified') will not appear in the candidate set **C**, we do not identify specification tests corresponding to 'data admissibility'. It is plausible that any patently unacceptable model which was erroneously included in the candidate set would be strongly detected by the other misspecification tests. Despite the fact that it is inappropriate to include a patently misspecified model in the candidate set, it may nevertheless be desirable to include it in a 'test' set of models, say $\{P_1, \ldots, P_N, P_{N+1}, \ldots, P_{N'}\}$, where $P_{N+1}, \ldots, P_{N'}$ are patently misspecified models which any congruent model should be capable of encompassing. This suggestion was first put forward by Davidson and MacKinnon (1981) in the context of the Cox test for non-nested hypotheses.

In recognition of the futility of selecting a patently misspecified model, but of the possible utility of including it in a test set, for the remainder of this discussion we suppose that the model under consideration (P_1) is not patently misspecified, but that $\{P_1, \ldots, P_N\}$ may include patently misspecified models as 'straw men'. (In some circumstances there may initially be available only such 'straw men'.)

Hendry and Richard (1982, p. 22) explicitly point out that the weak exogeneity requirements of (e) 'are often only indirectly testable, but are partially checked by (a) and (c)'. In addition, particular Lagrange multiplier (e.g. Engle, 1982; Hausman, 1978), and conditional moment (Newey, 1985) tests may be useful in this regard. Again, there is considerable freedom in the choice of these tests.

Once particular specification test statistics corresponding to each specification requirement have been chosen, one can carry out individual or joint tests of the null hypothesis that the specification requirements are met. In order to obtain a test of known size one must carry out a joint test. This is awkward given the various forms of the statistics mentioned above; an advantage of the *m*-testing framework discussed below is that a joint test is straightforward to construct. When a joint test is not practical, (generalized) Bonferroni bounds (Kwerel, 1975a, b) can be applied to obtain tests of specific size asymptotically.

Despite these difficulties, one must be able to perform a test of known or bounded size in order to proceed. With such a test available, one could proceed by selecting a particular critical size and rejecting the model if the test indicates statistical significance at that level. Otherwise, one retains the model. We could proceed in this way through the candidate set until each candidate had been tested. The models remaining would constitute those selected.

A serious problem with this procedure is that it is not guaranteed to produce a congruent model even if the candidate set contains one. Application of the above procedure with a fixed critical value will not select the congruent model(s) with certainty, but with a fixed probability less than one by the amount of the significance level. Fortunately, as we see in the next section, this difficulty can be overcome in a fairly straightforward manner by letting the critical size tend to zero as the sample size tends to infinity.

3. An *m*-testing Framework for Model Selection

The discussion of the previous section makes clear the roles played by the specification requirements and their associated tests, and helps motivate the *m*-testing framework, to which we now turn our attention.

It is important to recognize that no one set of specification requirements will be appropriate in all circumstances. Below we set forth a number of different specification requirements, motivated by those of Hendry and Richard (1982), but different in a variety of particulars. In order to formulate these, we introduce some notation and concepts used by White (in press) in the investigation of maximum-likelihood estimation of possibly misspecified models.

Let $\mathbb{R}^{vt} \equiv \times_{\tau=1}^{t} \mathbb{R}^{v}$. A 'stochastic specification' $\boldsymbol{S}$ is a collection of sequences of functions $f(\theta) \equiv \{f_t(\cdot, \theta) : \mathbb{R}^{vt} \to \mathbb{R}^+, t = 1, 2, \ldots\}$ obtained by letting θ range over $\Theta \subseteq \mathbb{R}^p$, $p \in \mathbb{N}$, i.e. $\boldsymbol{S} \equiv \{f(\theta) : \theta \in \Theta\}$. For convenience, we also write $\boldsymbol{S} = \{f_t\}$. The quasi-maximum likelihood estimator (QMLE) is the solution $\hat{\theta}_n$ to the problem

$$\max_{\theta \in \Theta} L_n(X^n, \theta) \equiv n^{-1} \sum_{t=1}^{n} \log f_t(X^t, \theta).$$

We say that $\hat{\theta} \equiv \{\hat{\theta}_n\}$ is the QMLE 'generated by' $\boldsymbol{S}$. Under regularity conditions (White, in press, Ch. 3), $\hat{\theta}_n - \theta_n^* \to 0$ prob-P_o, where $\{\theta_n^*\}$ is a non-stochastic sequence such that θ_n^* solves the problem

$$\max_{\theta \in \Theta} E(L_n(X^n, \theta)).$$

Partition X_t as $X_t = (Y_t, Z_t)$ where Y_t is $1 \times l$ and let W_t be a $1 \times s_t$ subvector of $\bar{X}^{t-1} = (X^{t-1}, Z_t)$. If for all θ in Θ $f_t(X^t, \theta)$ is measurable-$\sigma(Y_t, W_t)$ (where $\sigma(Y_t, W_t)$ is the σ-field generated by Y_t and W_t) and integrates to unity over the range of Y_t, then we may view $f_t(X^t, \theta)$ as an approximation to the conditional distribution of Y_t given W_t. If for some θ_o in Θ we have that $f_t(X^t, \theta_o)$ is the conditional density implied by P_o for Y_t given W_t, then we say that $\boldsymbol{S}$ is correctly specified for $\{Y_t | W_t\}$. In this case, $\theta_n^* = \theta_o$. Even so, the conditional distribution of Y_t given W_t may differ from that of Y_t given $\bar{X}^{t-1}$ (i.e. W_t omits Granger-causal variables). In this case we say that $\boldsymbol{S}$ exhibits dynamic misspecification.

In some circumstances interest focuses not on the conditional distribution of Y_t given W_t, but only on some aspect of the conditional distribution such as the conditional mean, $E(Y_t|W_t)$. In these cases one may formulate a model of the conditional mean, say $\boldsymbol{M} \equiv \{\mu(\theta): \theta \in \Theta\}$, $\mu(\theta) \equiv \{\mu_t(\cdot, \theta):R^{s_t} \to R^l, l \leqslant v, l \in \mathbb{N}\}$. Quasi-maximum-likelihood estimation is achieved by further specifying $f_t(X^t, \theta) = \exp \psi_t(Y_t, \mu_t(W_t, \theta))$ for some function ψ_t. When for some θ_o in Θ we have $\mu_t(W_t, \theta_o) = E(Y_t|W_t)$, we say that $\boldsymbol{M}$ is correctly specified for $\{E(Y_t|W_t)\}$. In this case we also have $\theta_n^* = \theta_o$ given appropriate regularity conditions (see White, in press, Ch. 5). When W_t omits variables Granger-causal in mean, we have dynamic misspecification in mean.

Now write $\boldsymbol{F}^t = \sigma(X^t)$ and define

$$l_t^* \equiv \nabla_\theta \log f_t(X^t, \theta_n^*)$$
$$\nabla l_t^* \equiv \nabla_\theta^2 \log f_t(X^t, \theta_n^*).$$

Alternative specification requirements $\boldsymbol{R}$ useful in constructing a specification-based model selection framework can be stated as follows:

DEFINITION 3.1
(1) A specification $\boldsymbol{S}(\boldsymbol{M})$ is defined as C_1 if
   (a) $\{l_t^*, \boldsymbol{F}^t\}$ is a martingale difference sequence; and
   (b) $\boldsymbol{S}(\boldsymbol{M})$ parametrically encompasses all rival specifications completely.
(2) A specification $\boldsymbol{S}(\boldsymbol{M})$ is defined as C_2 if
   (a) $\{l_t^*, \boldsymbol{F}^t\}$ is a martingale difference sequence; and
   (b) $\boldsymbol{S}(\boldsymbol{M})$ is correctly specified for $\{Y_t|W_t\}$ ($\{E(Y_t|W_t)\}$).
(3) A specification $\boldsymbol{S}(\boldsymbol{M})$ is defined as C_3 if
   (a) $\{l_t^*, \boldsymbol{F}^t\}$ is a martingale difference sequence; and
   (b) $\{\nabla l_t^* + l_t^* l_t^{*\prime}, \boldsymbol{F}^t\}$ is a martingale difference sequence.
(4) A specification $\boldsymbol{S}(\boldsymbol{M})$ is defined as C_4 if
   (a) $\{l_t^*, \boldsymbol{F}^t\}$ is a martingale difference sequence;
   (b) $\{\nabla l_t^* + l_t^* l_t^{*\prime}, \boldsymbol{F}^t\}$ is a martingale difference sequence; and
   (c) $\boldsymbol{S}(\boldsymbol{M})$ parametrically encompasses all rival specifications completely.

We assume implicitly that the regularity conditions needed to define the objects above are satisfied; we omit them to avoid tedious details. Complete parametric encompassing is as defined by White (in press, Definition 9.14). The designations C_1, C_2, C_3, C_4 are used to distinguish them from Hendry and Richard's original requirements for a congruent model, which we subsequently denote C_0. Note that the requirements are placed on the stochastic specification, rather than on a probability model. This allows us to take advantage of not having to specify a probability model completely. In such circumstances the candidate set $\boldsymbol{C}$ consists of the probability models $\boldsymbol{P}_{S_i}(\boldsymbol{P}_{M_i})$ compatible with specifications $\boldsymbol{S}_i(\boldsymbol{M}_i)$, $i = 1, \ldots, N$. (We say that $\boldsymbol{P}_S(\boldsymbol{P}_M)$ is compatible with $\boldsymbol{S}(\boldsymbol{M})$ if $\boldsymbol{P}_S(\boldsymbol{P}_M)$ is the

collection of all probability measures P^o such that $S(M)$ is correctly speci-
fied for $\{Y_t|W_t\}$ ($\{E(Y_t|W_t)\}$) under P^o.)

Requirement (1b) is Hendry and Richard's encompassing criterion,
while requirement (1a) is the analogue of their requirement that the
'errors' be a MIP. Requirement (1a) holds even in circumstances in which
a generalized residual is not admitted. We have omitted requirements
(c)–(e) for C_0 in formulating C_1. We omit (e), as its failure will typically be
signalled by failure of (1a) and/or (1b); moreover, the concept of weak
exogeneity does not play a central role in the analysis of White (in press).
We omit (d), as we suppose either that patently misspecified models are
excluded a priori from the candidate set, or that patent misspecification
will be signalled by failure of (1a) or (1b). We omit (c) because the heterogeneity which would lead to violation of (c) also typically causes the failure
of (1a). Thus C_1 represents a 'streamlined' version of C_0.

In Definition 3.1(2), we define more stringent criteria which may sometimes be more convenient in applications than those of (1). Specifically, we
see that (2b) replaces the encompassing requirement of (1b) with the
correct specification requirement. As shown by White (in press, Theorem
9.15), correct specification implies encompassing, so that if a model is C_2,
then it is C_1. (We also have necessarily that $\theta_n^* = \theta_o$ for all n, guaranteeing
(c) of C_0.) The reason that the more stringent criterion may be more
convenient in applications is that (2b) can be tested for M using Bierens'
(1987) watertight test (see also White, in press, 9.2.c) which will have many
fewer degrees of freedom than the encompassing tests. An analogous
watertight test for S is not yet available, though it may be possible to
develop one.

The present difficulty of testing (2b) for S in a watertight way, together,
with the practical and theoretical advantages afforded by the information
matrix equality (see White, in press, Ch. 6), motivate the replacement in
(3b) of correct specification for $S(M)$ by the information matrix equality.
This requirement is less stringent than requiring S to be correctly specified,
although typically more stringent than requiring M to be correctly
specified, as correct specification of (a model of) conditional variance is
typically required to ensure that (3b) holds when M is correctly specified.

The most stringent set of requirements is that of C_4, which is the union
of those for C_1 and C_3. In this case both encompassing and the information
matrix equality are required.

These specification requirements are not definitive, but are intended to
be somewhat generally useful, and to illustrate the kinds of requirements
that one may wish to impose. It is recommended that in any empirical application the researcher formulate and clearly enunciate the specification
requirements appropriate to the task at hand; these may or may not coincide with those given here.

Given specification requirements R, we must have some way to construct appropriate specification tests. Because of its generality, flexibility, and convenience in constructing joint tests, we propose using the m-testing framework of Newey (1985) and Tauchen (1985) as extended by White (1987, in press) for constructing the required specification tests.

The idea underlying the m-testing framework is simple, but powerful. Whenever **S** or **M** is correctly specified, it will generally be the case that for a variety of functions $m_t: \mathbb{R}^{vt} \times \Theta \to \mathbb{R}^q$ we have

$$E(m_t(X^t, \theta_o)) = 0 \quad t = 1, 2, \dots.$$

A particular function m_t will be called an 'indicator'. Although both θ_o and the expectation above are unknown, we generally can consistently estimate $n^{-1} \sum_{t=1}^n E(m_t(X^t, \theta_o))$ by

$$\hat{m}_n \equiv n^{-1} \sum_{t=1}^n m_t(X^t, \hat{\theta}_n).$$

Thus, with correct specification $\hat{m}_n$ will be close to zero. A value for $\hat{m}_n$ too far from zero is evidence of misspecification. The question of how far from zero is too far is answered asymptotically by finding the asymptotic distribution for $\hat{m}_n$. This distribution has been obtained for dynamic contexts by White (1987; in press, Ch. 9). Under the null hypothesis of correct specification and appropriate regularity conditions $\sqrt{n}\, \hat{m}_n \overset{A}{\sim} N(0, V_n^*)$. An asymptotic chi-square statistic can then be formed as

$$M_n = n \hat{m}_n' \hat{J}_n^- \hat{m}_n,$$

where $\hat{J}_n$ is a consistent estimator of V_n^*, i.e. $\hat{J}_n - V_n^* \to 0$ prob-P_o. White (1988, Theorem 9.2) also gives the limiting distribution for M_n when $\hat{J}_n$ is not consistent for V_n^*.

The relevance of m-tests for present purposes is that appropriate indicators can be found for each of the specification requirements in C_1, C_2, C_3, and C_4. Specifically, the dynamic information matrix indicators of White (in press, Ch. 10.1.a) are appropriate for 3.1(1a) (as well as (2a), (3a) and (4a)) and the encompassing indicators of White (in press, Ch. 9.2.c) are appropriate for 3.1 (1b) and (1c). The Hausman test indicators for Bierens' watertight test (White, in press, Ch. 9.2) are appropriate for 3.1 (2b), and the (second-order) information matrix indicators of White (in press, Ch. 10.1.b) are appropriate for 3.1(3b) and (4b). Thus, all of the specification requirements can be associated with specific indicators. A great convenience of these indicators is that they can be stacked to yield a joint indicator vector capable of yielding a single test for the null hypothesis that $C_1(C_2, C_3, \text{ or } C_4)$ holds. For details of this theory and the indicators mentioned above, the interested reader is referred to Chapters 9 and 10 of White (in press). We formalize these considerations in the following way.

DEFINITION 3.2 Let $(\boldsymbol{C}, \boldsymbol{R})$ be a specification-based model selection framework. If for each candidate model $\boldsymbol{P}_i$, $i = 1, \dots, N$, each requirement of R (indexed by $j = 1, \ldots, r$, say) can be associated with a miss-pecification indicator sequence $m_{ij} = \{m_{tij}\}$ (with m_{tij} a $q_{ij} \times 1$ vector), then (C, R) *admits an m-testing implementation based on* $m = \{m_1, \ldots, m_N\}$, where $m_i = \{m_{ti} = (m'_{ti1}, \ldots, m'_{tir})'\}$.

This definition explicitly recognizes the latitude available in implementing the model selection procedure by specifying the 'specification requirement indicator set' m. To carry out an implementation based on m, we must compute appropriate m-statistics and perform appropriate significance tests. The following definition formalizes the nature of this implementation.

DEFINITION 3.3 Suppose that (C, R) admits an m-testing implementation based on m, and for each element m_i of m let $M_i = \{M_{ni}\}$ be a sequence of m-statistics $M_{ni} = n \hat{m}'_{ni} \hat{J}^-_{ni} \hat{m}_{ni}$, where $\hat{m}_{ni}$ and $\hat{J}_{ni}$ satisfy the conditions of Theorem 9.2 of White (in press), $i = 1, \ldots, N$. Let $k = \{k_n\}$ be a non-stochastic sequence of positive scalars. A *specification-based model selection procedure based on* m *and implemented by* (M, k), $M \equiv \{M_1, \ldots, M_N\}$, proceeds as follows: reject $P_i = P_{Si}$ (or $= P_{Mi}$) if $M_{ni} > k_n$; otherwise retain P_i, $i = 1, \ldots, N$.

The conditions of Theorem 9.2 of White (in press) are mild regularity conditions that appropriately control the asymptotic distribution of the m-statistics. We refer to White (in press) to avoid tedious details here.

Although it is quite important to be specific about the basis m and the implementation (M, k) used in any particular context, for convenience we refer to such procedures generally as the 'm-testing model selection procedure'. Any models retained by this procedure will be called 'selected models'. As pointed out in the heuristic discussion at the outset, such a procedure may produce any number of models selected from zero to N. More stringent requirements R may be imposed to reduce the number of selected models, or less stringent requirements may be imposed to increase the number of selected models.

In order to state our conclusions concisely, we need to introduce definitions for the local and global alternative models associated with a given indicator sequence $m = \{m_t\}$.

DEFINITION 3.4 The *local alternative to the model underlying the specification test based on indicator sequence* $m = \{m_t\}$ *and* QMLE $\hat{\theta}$ is the collection $P^u_a(m)$ of all probability measures P^o such that:

(1) $\sqrt{n}\, \hat{m}_n = \sqrt{n}\, m^*_n + \nabla_\theta \bar{m}^*_n \sqrt{n}(\hat{\theta}_n - \theta^*_n) + o_{P^o}(1)$, where $\hat{m}_n \equiv n^{-1} \sum_{t=1}^n m_t(X^t, \hat{\theta}_n, \hat{\pi}_n)$, $m^*_n \equiv n^{-1} \sum_{t=1}^n m_t(X^t, \theta^*_n, \pi^*_n)$, $\nabla_\theta \bar{m}^*_n \equiv n^{-1} \sum_{t=1}^n E^o(\nabla_\theta m_t(X^t, \theta^*_n, \pi^*_n))$, $\hat{\pi}_n - \pi^*_n \to 0$ prob$-P^o$ for some non-stochastic vector sequence $\{\pi^*_n\}$, $\sqrt{n}(\hat{\theta}_n - \theta^*_n) + A^{*-1}_n l^*_n \to 0$ prob$-P^o$ for some $O(1)$ non-stochastic sequence of uniformly non-singular $p \times p$ matrices $\{A^*_n\}$ and stochastic sequence of $p \times 1$ vectors $\{l^*_n\}$; and

(2) there exists a non-stochastic $O(1)$ vector sequence $\{a_n^*\}$ and a non-stochastic matrix sequence $\{V_n^* \equiv \text{var}^o[\sqrt{n}(m_n^* - \nabla_\theta \bar{m}_n^* A_n^{*-1} l_n^*)]\}$ $O(1)$ and uniformly positive definite such that

$$\sqrt{n}(m_n^* - \nabla_\theta \bar{m}_n^* A_n^{*-1} l_n^*) \overset{A^o}{\sim} N(a_n^*, V_n^*).$$

Note that the indicators are allowed here to depend on a vector of nuisance parameters π; this is convenient in applications. This definition provides some but not all of the necessary technical detail. Measurability, differentiability, integrability conditions, etc., as well as a definition for convergence in distribution when the limiting distribution depends on n, can be found in White (in press).

The key aspect of $\boldsymbol{P}_a^u(m)$ is that its elements provide enough structure for $\sqrt{n}\hat{m}_n$ to have a normal distribution asymptotically. The local alternative arises because $\{a_n^*\}$ is $O(1)$. When $a_n^* \to 0$ (generally because $\bar{m}_n^* = E(m_n^*)$ $\to 0$) we have the null hypothesis, i.e. no unacceptable misspecification. Local alternatives are obtained with P^o fixed by allowing f_t or m_t to depend implicitly on n. These represent unacceptable misspecifications which vanish asymptotically.

DEFINITION 3.5 The *global alternative to the model underlying the specification test based on indicator sequence $m = \{m_t\}$ and QMLE $\hat{\theta}$* is the collection $\boldsymbol{P}_A^u(m)$ of all probability measures P^o such that $\hat{\theta}_n - \theta_n^* \to 0$ prob–P^o and for some $\varepsilon^o > 0$ and $N^o \in \mathbb{N}$, *we have* $\bar{m}_n^{*\prime} \bar{m}_n^* > \varepsilon^o$ *for all* $n > N^o$.

This global alternative contains any probability measure for which any element of $\bar{m}_n^*$ is eventually bounded away from zero by some (even small) amount, thereby indicating an unacceptable misspecification.

Because of details concerning regularity conditions and the pathologies associated with certain kinds of heterogeneity, the models $\boldsymbol{P}_a^u(m)$ and $\boldsymbol{P}_A^u(m)$ do not account for all probability measures on $(\Omega, \boldsymbol{F})$. Nevertheless, they are those most relevant for our present purposes.

We now have sufficient structure to state our main result: by properly choosing a sequence of critical values $k = \{k_n\}$, a specification-based model selection procedure based on $\boldsymbol{m}$ and implemented by (M, k) is consistent in the sense that models satisfying the specification requirements are retained with probability approaching one, while models failing the specification requirements are rejected with probability approaching one. This can be stated formally in the following way. (The proof is straightforward and is omitted.)

THEOREM 3.6 Given a specification-based model selection framework $(\boldsymbol{C}, \boldsymbol{R})$ and a specification-based model selection procedure based on $\boldsymbol{m}$ and implemented by (M, k), if $\{k_n\} = o(n)$ and $k_n \to \infty$ as $n \to \infty$, then for each $i = 1, \ldots, N$.

(1) If $P_o \in \boldsymbol{P}_{a_i}^u(m_i)$, $P_o[M_{ni} \leqslant k_n] \to 1$;

(2) If $P_o \in \boldsymbol{P}_{A_i}^u(m_i)$, $P_o[M_{ni} > k_n] \rightarrow 1$,

where $\boldsymbol{P}_{a_i}^u(m_i)$ and $\boldsymbol{P}_{A_i}^u(m_i)$ are the local and global alternatives respectively for the model underlying the test based on m_i. (The subscripts on a_i and A_i reflect the possible dependence of these alternatives on $\{\hat{\theta}_{ni}\}$ and $\{\hat{\pi}_{ni}\}$.)

In the result of (1), we require $k_n \rightarrow \infty$. This is violated for k_n constant; indeed with $k_n = k_o$ we generally have $P_o[M_{ni} > k_o] < 1$, so that there is positive probability that no model is selected, even in the presence of a correctly specified model. This would be a highly undesirable property. Instead, by letting $k_n \rightarrow \infty$, we have probability approaching zero of rejecting an acceptable model. To ensure that k_n does not grow so quickly as to invalidate (2) we require that $\{k_n\} = o(n)$. This ensures the applicability of appropriate results of Chapters 9 and 10 of White (in press).

Choices for k_n which satisfy the conditions of Theorem 3.6 are $k_n = \epsilon n^\delta$, $\epsilon > 0$, $0 < \delta < 1$, or $k_n = \epsilon \log n$. Effectively, such choices for k_n permit both the Type I and Type II errors to shrink to zero, in contrast to standard hypothesis-testing procedures which fix the Type I error at an arbitrary level, while the Type II error shrinks to zero with n. Depending on one's viewpoint it is either an advantage or a drawback of the present result that it does not make any explicit use of information about the size of the test. Such information may be exploited to arrive at a particular form for k_n based on desired trade-offs between Type I and Type II errors. This may be investigated using the known tail properties of the asymptotic distribution of M_n, but we will not pursue this here. The theory of large deviations may also be helpful in obtaining more sophisticated results. When the asymptotic size of the test is known, then ϵ (and δ if $k_n = \epsilon n^\delta$) can be determined by setting the size of test desired for samples of one or two different values of n and solving directly.

Note that the selection procedure retains a probability model $\boldsymbol{P}_i = \boldsymbol{P}_{\boldsymbol{S}_i}$ or $\boldsymbol{P}_i = \boldsymbol{P}_{\boldsymbol{M}_i}$ asymptotically whenever $P_o \in \boldsymbol{P}_{a_i}^u(m_i)$. Thus, we face a situation in which the model explicitly tested is in fact not the model actually tested. Instead, the model underlying the test (an implicit null) is tested. For this reason, retaining $\boldsymbol{P}_i$ should be interpreted strictly as retaining $\boldsymbol{P}_{a_i}^u(m_i)$. This also makes clear the dependence of the model selection procedure on the specification requirement indicators used, as different indicators may have different associated underlying models tested.

Because $\hat{J}_n$ is fairly arbitrary it need not be consistent for V_n^*. Moreover, it can be chosen to be block diagonal in such a way that individual m-statistics for particular specification requirements can be added together in arriving at M_{ni}, as if these m-statistics were asymptotically independent. The result of Theorem 3.6 is valid despite possible failure of consistency of $\hat{J}_n$ for V_n^* or the independence assumption. One gains convenience at the sacrifice of precise control over the asymptotic size of the test.

Thus, we have an *m*-testing model selection procedure which rejects sufficiently misspecified models and retains sufficiently correctly specified models with confidence approaching certainty as $n \to \infty$. Use of such procedures has the potential to remove some of the capriciousness associated with certain empirical work in economics and other fields. For this reason we wholeheartedly endorse progressive research strategies such as that of Hendry and Richard (1982) and Hendry (1987) for arriving at sufficiently well specified characterizations of the DGP. We believe the *m*-testing framework set forth here can be a convenient vehicle for such strategies.

4.   Concluding Remarks

In much of empirical economics research the goal is to test hypotheses about parameters to which one wishes to attribute economic meaning. It is our view that this is inappropriate and unjustified without first establishing that the model within which the hypotheses are being tested is congruent with the data to at least some extent. Otherwise, one may only have confidence that one is testing hypotheses about parameters with an information theoretic interpretation (White, 1982, in press); the economic interpretation desired is untenable.

Even when a congruent model is arrived at, the researcher should be quite specific about the specification requirements used to define a congruent model and the specification tests by which these requirements are implemented. The importance of this arises from the necessarity of other researchers being able to replicate results, and from the possible sensitivity of the conclusions drawn to the methods used to obtain them.

Although the procedures of Section 3 provide valid methods for arriving at a congruent model, they do not explicity allow for reformulation of any model or collection of models in response to the observed interaction of the data with the model. The candidate set is fixed; one does not have the option of continually modifying or updating the model in response to empirical observation. But of course this is what one *must* do if a research strategy is to be truly 'progressive'.

For the physical sciences this feature of the approach of Section 3 imposes virtually no limitations. We may apply our procedures to data using some appropriate candidate set of models, observe the outcome, and then adjust our candidate set of models in whatever way we wish. Then we obtain a *fresh* set of data (i.e. data statistically independent of previous observations), frequently by means of experiment, and again apply the methods of Section 3. This permits us to engage unhindered in a dialogue of the sort advocated by Popper (1962); the procedures of Section 3 provide a means of carrying out this dialogue.

It is an inherent and fundamental limitation of economics that economic experiments are difficult to conduct. We are often at nature's mercy: for example, we have only one observation on the post-war United States economy. Nevertheless, we may certainly obtain fresh or nearly fresh data, either through the passage of time, as in macroeconomic or asset market data; by means of a fresh cross-sectional survey; or, increasingly, by conducting controlled experiments, usually microeconomic in nature.

Consequently, we advocate here a methodology in which one confronts a candidate set of models with empirical observations using the tools of Section 3, obtains a model congruent to a specified degree (or not), reformulates the candidate set of models, and confronts this with a fresh set of empirical observations. This process can be repeated at will; it does not appear to have a natural terminus, especially as the process of modifying the theory may suggest the usefulness of collecting new types of data for the purpose of deciding between competing models equally acceptable on the basis of available data.

Such a methodology is extremely arduous, but it is the author's view that only in this or some similar way is there any hope of increasing understanding of economic phenomena through the use of parametric modelling techniques.

References

Chow G. C., Tests for equality between sets of coefficients in two linear regressions, *Econometrica* 28, 591–605.

Davidson, R. and MacKinnon, J. (1981), Several tests for model specification in the presence of alternative hypotheses, *Econometrica*, 49, 781–94.

Engle, R. F. (1982), A general approach to Lagrange multiplier model diagnostics, *Journal of Econometrics*, 20, 83–104.

Hausman, J. A. (1978), Specification tests in econometrics, *Econometrica*, 46, 1251–72.

Hendry, D. F. (1987), Econometric methodology: a personal perspective. *Advances in Econometrics, Fifth World Congress*, Vol. 2, ed. by T. Bewley. Cambridge University Press, New York, pp. 29–48.

Hendry. D. F. and Richard, J.-F. (1982), On the formulation of empirical models in dynamic econometrics, *Journal of Econometrics*, 20, 3–32.

Kwerel, S. (1975a), Bounds on the probability of the union and intersection of m events, *Advances in Applied Probability*, 7, 431–48.

Kwerel, S. (1975b), Most stringent bounds on the probability of the union and intersection of m events for systems partially specified by $S_1, S_2, \ldots, 2 \leqslant k \leqslant m$, *Journal of Applied Probability*, 12, 612–19.

Mizon, G. (1984), The encompassing approach in econometrics. *Econometrics and Quantitative Economics*, ed. by D. F. Hendry and K. F. Wallis. Basil Blackwell, Oxford, pp. 135–172.

Mizon, G. and Richard, J.-F. (1986), The encompassing principle and its application to testing non-nested hypotheses, *Econometrica*, 54, 657–78.

Newey, W. K. (1985), Maximum likelihood specification testing and conditional moment tests, *Econometrica*, 53, 1047–70.

Popper, K. (1962), *Conjectures and Refutations: The Growth of Scientific Knowledge*. Routledge & Kegan Paul, London.

Tauchen, G. (1985), Diagnostic testing and evaluation of maximum likelihood models, *Journal of Econometrics*, 30, 415–44.

White, H. (1982), Maximum likelihood estimation of misspecified models, *Econometrica*, 50, 1–25.

White H. (1987), Specification testing in dynamic models. *Advances in Econometrics, Fifth World Congress*, Vol. 1, ed. by T. Bewley. Cambridge University Press, New York, pp. 1–58.

White, H. (in press), *Estimation, Inference and Specification Analysis*. Cambridge University Press, New York.

17

Econometric Evaluation of Linear Macroeconomic Models

Yock Y. Chong and David F. Hendry

Abstract. Macro economic models are generally designed to achieve a multiplicity of objectives and correspondingly, they have been evaluated using a vast range of statistical, econometric, economic, political and even aesthetic criteria. However, in so far as they claim to represent economic behaviour, empirical macro-economic systems are certainly open to direct evaluation and testing against data information. The last few years have witnessed a substantial growth in the literature on econometric evaluation techniques, but despite important improvements in formalising evaluation procedures and their increased scope, formidable problems confront any investigation of a high dimensional, non-linear, stochastic, dynamic structure. Since *system* characteristics are the prime concern of economy-wide models, it might be the case that the validity of every individual component is not essential to adequate overall performance. While this viewpoint is debatable it does draw attention to the need for *system* evaluation procedures, at which point data limitations pose serious constraints on formal tests. Thus a new 'limited information' test of *forecast encompassing* is proposed, based only on forecasts and requiring no other data from a model's proprietors. The derivation, merits and drawbacks of such a test are presented together with some suggestions for testing entailed relationships and inter-equation feedbacks.

1. Introduction

Macroeconomic models are generally designed to achieve a multiplicity of objectives and correspondingly, they have been evaluated using a vast range of statistical, econometric, economic, political, and even aesthetic criteria. However, in so far as they claim to represent economic behaviour,

This article first appeared in *Review of Economic Studies*, Vd. 53, 1986, pp. 671–90. The research was financed in part by the Higher Studies Fund at Oxford University and by ESRC grants HR8789 and B00220012; we are grateful to the ESRC for its continuing support for this project. Helpful comments from Chris Allsopp, Richard Baillie, Julia Campos, Robert Fildes, Stephen McNees, John Muellbauer, Grayham Mizon, Adrian Pagan, Jean-Francois Richard, and the participants of the 1984 International Symposium on Forecasting and the 1985 Warwick University Summer Workshop are gratefully acknowledged. We are indebted to Neil Ericsson, Jon Faust, Frank Srba, and especially Adrian Neale, for invaluable research assistance, and to the DAP Support Unit at Queen Mary College London for their help with, and advice on, calculating the small sample properties of dynamic forecast confidence intervals. This is a revised and extended version of Hendry (1983b).

empirical macroeconomic systems are certainly open to direct evaluation and testing against data information. While this aspect is only one of several necessary conditions for establishing their 'validity', some degree of adequacy on model evaluation procedures has always featured prominently in the justification for, and credibility of, claimed empirical relationships.

Nevertheless, surprisingly little attention has been paid to appraising the evaluation *procedures* generally adopted by the proprietors of macro-econometric systems. As documented in Section 2 below, most of the currently popular approaches are problematical and it is unclear what light they have thrown on model validity. Indeed, without considerable care, there is a grave danger of seriously *incorrect* inferences being drawn about model choice using (say) dynamic simulation tracking performance or forecasting track records.

At the same time, the past few years have witnessed a substantial growth in the literature on econometric evaluation techniques: see *inter alia* the many papers in Kmenta and Ramsey (1980, 1981), Chow and Corsi (1982), the studies of Klein and Bray in Ormerod (1979) and the Bank of England Paper (1982), as well as Chow (1981), Pagan (1981), Artis (1982), McNees (1982), Hendry (1982), Hendry and Richard (1982) and Smith (1984). This list makes no claims as to exhaustiveness, since most work on model evaluation in general is relevant to systems of equations (with suitable extensions or modifications). Thus, bibliographic completenes would mean including research on misspecification, diagnostic testing, and inter-model tests (see, for example, White, 1980; Breusch and Pagan, 1980; Engle, 1982; Pagan, 1984; and MacKinnon, 1983). Moreover, several earlier studies commented perceptively on the problems of evaluation and validation (see in particular the excellent paper of Dhrymes et al., 1972, and the papers by Klein and Naylor in Intriligator, 1971).

Despite the important improvements in formalizing evaluation procedures and their increased scope, formidable problems confront any investigation of a high-dimensional, non-linear, stochastic, dynamic structure. Certainly, individual equations can be tested using the techniques described in the references above, and certain of these methods could be extended directly to small systems or sectors by formulating the appropriate likelihood-based statistics. The exemplar considered below is n-step forecast tests ($n > 1$) given that forecasting is a major function of macro-models. One caveat might be the adequacy of asymptotic analysis to characterize the finite sample performance of tests applied to systems. Consequently, in Section 3 Monte Carlo methods are used to calibrate tests based on the multi-period forecasts from a small linear system.

A rather different facet is that since *system* characteristics are the prime concern of economy-wide models, it might be the case that the validity of every individual component is not essential to adequate overall performance. While this viewpoint is debatable, it does draw attention to the need for *system* evaluation procedures, at which point data limitations pose serious constraints on formal tests. Thus a new 'limited information' test of *forecast encompassing* is proposed, based only on forecasts and requiring no other data from a model's proprietors. The derivation, merits, and drawbacks of such a test are also presented in Section 3, together with some suggestions for testing entailed relationships and inter-equation feedbacks. Section 4 concludes the paper.

As noted above, a complete evaluation of a macroeconometric system would require far more than just the statistical considerations described below. For example, the 'microeconomic theory foundations' of the system might be thought important, the internal consistency of the economic analysis is clearly relevant, and the theoretical rationales for equation specifications may influence their 'credibility', etc. Even so, an econometric assessment remains a necessary ingredient, albeit that there may occur conflicts between different criteria in the present state of modelling practice.

For expositional simplicity, only the linear case is considered here. Almost all extant systems are actually non-linear, so notation and analysis are more complex than described below, but the main principles seem unaffected. Where linearity is too restrictive, or is likely to mislead, special note is taken.

2. A Brief Critique of Some Present Procedures

Denote the theoretical formulation of the model to be estimated as:

$$By_t + Cy_{t-1} + Dz_t = \epsilon_t, \quad t = 1, \ldots, T. \tag{1}$$

where contemporaneous variables y_t, z_t are *treated* respectively as endogenous and extraneous (i.e. to be and not to be explained respectively) and ϵ_t is an error term defined by its being unrelated to (y_{t-1}, z_t). One lag imposes no loss of generality, since either (1) could be viewed as a companion form system, or general lag operator notation could be used. It is assumed that any error autocorrelation anticipated by the investigator has been removed by appropriate lag transformations embodied in (1). Although interpreting a formulation such as (1) as a companion form means that the covariance matrix of $\{\epsilon_t\}$ will be singular, the presence of a National Accounting framework entails that $\{\epsilon_t\}$ has a degenerate distribution anyway in most cases. Despite its practical importance, neither the conventional nor the proper treatment of seasonality will be discussed here for space reasons: throughout, it is assumed that unadjusted data are used and that z_t correctly captures all relevant seasonal variation.

Descriptive and inferential statistics relevant to many aspects of the evaluation of (1) are sporadically reported for most estimated models in support of their 'adequate' performance. In 'best practice' models many such statistics are recorded for individual equations, together with some evidence concerning system performance. The latter is the focus of this section since 'conventional wisdom' seems to be that the crucial validation procedures for *overall* system adequacy are:

(1) dynamic simulation tracking accuracy.
(2) the historical record of genuine forecast outcomes; and
(3) the economic plausibility of the estimated system (see e.g. the survey reported in Kmenta and Ramsey, 1981); these three procedures will be considered in turn.

A.   Dynamic Simulation Performance

This is widely argued to be a major method of model evaluation (see e.g. Kmenta and Ramsey, 1981; Klein and Young, 1982; Sowey, 1973; Mc-Nees, 1982, *inter alia*). Because models differ in their choices of endogenous and extraneous variables, inter-model comparisons are difficult to conduct and McNees (1982) has dubbed this the 'dilemma of model comparisons'. However, as shown in Hendry and Richard (1982), the problem is far worse than just being a 'dilemma'. For example, the dilemma cannot be resolved simply by having all model-builders agree on a common set of 'exogenous' variables. In fact, what dynamic simulation tracking accuracy mainly reflects is the extent to which the *explanation of the data is attributed to non-modelled variables*. Since the outcome of such a simulation depends only on the *assertion* of 'exogeneity', independently of its validity, it can reveal nothing about relative model goodness unless the relevant variables are exogenous in the strong sense defined by Engle et al. (1983) (so there is no influence of past y's on current z's). Consequently, feedback of y_{t-1} onto z_t should be tested to assess the validity of the *simulation*.

Even then, it is essential to realize the limitations of dynamic simulation as a device for selecting *between models*. Consider the conditioning sets pertinent to the various aspects of modelling, using the categorization in Hendry and Richard (1983). Let $X_{t-1}^1 = (x_1, \ldots, x_{t-1})$ for any variable $\{x_t\}$; then letting $x_t = (y_t z_t)$, the relevant conditioning sets are:

$$\begin{aligned}
\textit{Estimating:} \quad & (z_t, x_{t-1}) \text{ (for a model specified as (1))};\\
\textit{Testing:} \quad & (z_t, X_{t-1}^1) \text{ (or sometimes only } X_{t-1}^1);\\
\textit{Forecasting:} \quad & X_{t-n}^1 \text{ (for } n\text{-step ex ante forecasts of } y_t);\\
\textit{or:} \quad & (Z_t^{t-n+1}, X_{t-n}^1) \text{ (for } n\text{-step conditional forecasts)};\\
\textit{Dynamic simulation:} \quad & Y_0, Z_T^1 \text{ (for the whole historical record)}.
\end{aligned}$$

Direct comparison reveals, therefore, that the last cannot discriminate between models in terms of the validity of their estimated parameters, nor their congruency with the sample evidence, nor in terms of their *operational* characteristics for ex-ante forecasting *except for t-step forecasts when* Z_t^1 *is known*! One must conclude that despite its 'face validity', dynamic simulation is not a sensible model *selection* criterion if one wishes to choose models for forecasting, or policy, or testing economic theories. Alternatively expressed, to optimize dynamic simulation performance, maximal use should be made of the (pretended) knowledge of Z_T^1 in that mode (not available for forecasting) even if the actual mechanism is one in which y_{t-1} summarizes all past information.

Moreover, as shown in Box and Tiao (1976), and stressed by Pagan (1985), for a *fixed* model specification, the dynamic simulation errors $\tilde{U} = (\tilde{u}_1, \ldots, \tilde{u}_T)$ are a non-singular transformation H (dependent on the coefficients of y_{t-1}) of the usual one-step ahead reduced form errors $\hat{U}$, so that:

$$\tilde{U} = H\hat{U}. \tag{2}$$

As a consequence, not only are the $\{\tilde{u}_t\}$ autocorrelated and heteroscedastic (see Hendry and Richard, 1982), any appropriate tests based on them would need to 'undo' the H transform, thereby being reduced to tests on the innovation errors $\{\hat{u}_t\}$. Thus, the procedure is redundant for generating tests as well: it seems time to downgrade the role of dynamic tracking performance in model evaluation.

A caveat to this criticism of the evaluation and model selection roles of dynamic simulation is that the procedure could be useful to evaluate theory consistency, or in stochastic mode to investigate data inadmissibility (e.g. negative prices or 110 per cent unemployment rates). Note, also, that intra-model comparative simulations as a numerical device either for calculating multipliers or for assessing dynamic stability are not subject to the preceding critique, but depend instead on either super or strong exogeneity assertions respectively, the former issue, of course, being much discussed since Haavelmo (1944) (recently rekindled by Lucas, 1976).

B.   Forecasting Accuracy

Inter-model records of the *ex-ante* forecasting success of macroeconometric systems are certainly of interest to their prospective clients and appear presently to be the main way of publicly 'ranking' such models *qua* systems. Nevertheless, problems persist. Firstly, as is well-known, since *ex-ante* forecasts are jointly determined by the modeller and the model, the evaluation is a joint one of the modeller and the system, and cannot uniquely reveal the goodness of the system *per se*, which is the relevant issue here. Next, while one might anticipate that larger (supposedly more informative) systems should forecast 'better', cost-effectiveness must not be ignored: small models may be 'best buys' even if they do not 'win' on the criterion of absolute accuracy. Finally, while absolute accuracy is desirable it is only weakly associated with validity. For example, misspecified models could forecast well (if the process remained constant) or good models could forecast poorly (if the data variance was high). Consequently, *ex-ante* confidence intervals also need to be calculated both to establish likely forecast accuracy and to test for an excess frequency of forecast errors lying outside the expected region. Useful models must have 'small' forecast confidence regions, which are in practice exceeded only 100α per cent of the time for an α-level choice.

Denote by the *predictive form* of the model that which utilizes only lagged information:

$$y_t = Q_1 y_{t-1} + Q_2 z_{t-1} + Q_3 w_{t-1} + \xi_t \tag{3}$$

where the variates w_{t-1} are introduced on eliminating z_t from the reduced form of (1). Note that (3) entails an implicit model for $\{z_t\}$. Let $f(\cdot)$ denote a scalar comparison function (of which many alternatives are possible and sensible, including the negative of the log-likelihood function, that adjusted for parsimony, posterior odds etc.). Then of two models M_1 and M_2; M_1 is said to g-dominate M_2 if $g(M_1) < g(M_2)$. A frequently used example is a ranking by $|\mathrm{var}\,(\xi_t)|$ which helps reveal within-sample relative one-step forecast accuracy.

The real dilemma of model evaluation is as follows: as discussed in e.g. Hendry (1983a) and Hendry and Mizon (1985), models often can be designed to ensure $\{\xi_t\}$ which apparently satisfy all the required properties for data coherency and have excellent one-step ahead characteristics which are g-dominant for interesting choices of $g(\cdot)$. Nevertheless, such models need not adequately represent the 'physical situation' (e.g. known properties of economies) nor have good n-step forecasts for $n > 1$ (where the last must be based on available information only). This suggests formally evaluating n-step forecasting performance, as will be considered in the next section.

C. Economic Plausibility

Finally, the only aspect of 'economic plausibility' which can be considered here in the absence of a specific economic theory is that relating to the consistency of the model with the believed theory. Since economists differ greatly in what they consider as plausible, evaluation of consistency reverts back to checking a further aspect of design, and can shed little light on invalidity *per se*. Moreover, corroboration is a minimal criterion for model adequacy (see e.g. Ahumada, 1985). Since there is remarkably little model evaluation information to be gleaned from what presently seem the major approaches, we turn instead to other methods which might prove more informative.

3.   Some Alternative Proposals for Model Evaluation

Models which are built to serve specific purposes naturally must be evaluated for their adequacy in performing the given tasks. Thus, if a fully articulated loss function is available, alternative models can be compared directly in terms of their losses. This is not a common situation in macro-economics: rather, systems are constructed to provide quantitative mimics of economic theories, to forecast a wide range of variables, to assist in scenario studies, and as an input to policy-making agencies. Multi-purpose use requires multi-criterion evaluation.

Consequently, in this section it is assumed that all aspects of a model's performance are legitimate targets for critical appraisal. In particular, we assume that the information are all available, and hence all of the reduction assumptions underlying the system may be investigated to the extent that they are testable. For single-equation evaluation, a huge literature exists on tests for various specific hypotheses (see e.g. Chow, 1960; Engle, 1982; Godfrey, 1978; Granger, 1969; Harvey, 1982; Kiviet, 1985; Pagan and Hall, 1983; Sargan, 1964; and White, 1980; and for more general discussions, see Zellner, 1979; Breusch and Pagan, 1980; Engle, 1984; Hendry and Richard, 1982, 1983). Here, we are only concerned with system evaluation. While many of the available tests can be applied to small systems (see e.g. Hendry, 1974), few are directly applicable to large models treated as integrated systems. Nevertheless, satisfying the relevant single-equation or small sub-block criteria seems necessary, if not sufficient, for useful systems to emerge. Below it is assumed that models are indeed acceptable at the single-equation level; if not, there seems little point in applying the following procedures as evaluation devices for systems already known to be composed of flawed components.

Four main evaluation devices are proposed:

(a) forecast encompassing;
(b) *n*-step forecast tests ($n > 1$);
(c) long-run properties; and
(d) inter-equation feedbacks.

This selection is not intended to imply that other methods of model evaluation are not useful. In particular, optimal control analyses seem capable of yielding considerable insight into the properties of systems, and frequently highlight 'gaps', 'quirks', and even the data inadmissibility of extant models (see e.g. Artis and Karakitsos, 1981). Rather, such approaches are well known and have already been tried (see e.g. Chow, 1981 and Chow and Corsi, 1982) whereas the four areas considered here have received little attention as practical tools (although, as noted below, a substantial literature does exist relevant to the theory of (b)). We consider (a)–(d) in turn.

A. Forecast Encompassing

Models which claim to congruently represent a data-generation process must be able to account for the findings of rival models (irrespective of whether these are nested or separate alternatives). A failure by one model M_1 to encompass some salient features of any rival model M_2 reveals the latter to incorporate information relevant to explaining the observed data, which information is excluded from M_1. This is so whether M_1 fails to encompass M_2 by (e.g.) over- or under-predicting its goodness-of-fit, since by knowing the data-generation process one could correctly deduce the fit of M_2. In practice, however, there are additional sampling complications.

Now, one could seek to encompass some or all of the features of rival models (e.g. their coefficients, error variances, residual non-sphericity, forecasts, etc.), and appropriate tests could be of a large-sample variety or be adjusted (approximately) for degrees of freedom. For nested rivals, encompassing of the simple model by the general specification is automatic, independently of the goodness of specification of the nesting model, and hence is uninteresting. However, the reverse of parsimonious-encompassing of the general model by a special case is far from automatic (for an exposition, see Hendry, 1983a and for a formal development Mizon, 1984). As one example, Sargan's (1964) test for the validity of instrumental variables is also a Wald test of parsimonious encompassing by the restricted or the unrestricted reduced form. A wide variety of encompassing-type tests has been suggested for single equations (see *inter alia* MacKinnon (1983) for a survey of non-nested tests – following Cox (1961) and Pesaran (1974) – Mizon and Richard (1984) for the generating equation for encompassing tests, Mizon (1984) for an exposition, and Ericsson (1983) for appropriate instrumental variables generalizations). The informational requirements of encompassing and its relation to Cox-tests are discussed by Hendry and Richard (1982, 1983). Doubts have been cast on the applicability of this type of test to systems (see Dhrymes et al, 1972) due to computational cost and programming complexity (as in (say) Pesaran and Deaton (1978) for non-linear reduced form models). However, the Davidson–MacKinnon (1981) C-test suggests a possible test form for systems, closely related to the apparently separate literature on pooling of forecasts (see e.g. Granger and Newbold, 1977, and Winkler, 1983).

A prior issue, however, is: what features of rival systems might one hope to encompass? Complete parametric encompassing is too ambitious – sample sizes are too small and most systems too large and non-linear to allow full information maximum-likelihood (FIML) estimation, and the data requirements seem to be too demanding (a complete matching of endogenous variables and full knowledge of all the observations used in the rival models).

However, testing for outside-estimation-sample forecast encompassing seems feasible in principle, and to avoid being too demanding of sample information about the rival model, we restrict the admissible class of tests to those based on forecasts only. To exposit the idea, consider two 'contending' single-equation models for stationary stochastic data with *claimed* formulations:

$$H_1: \quad y_t = x'_{1t}\beta + u_t, \qquad u_t \sim IN(0, \sigma_{uu}) \tag{4}$$

$$H_2: \quad y_t = x'_{2t}\gamma + \epsilon_t, \qquad \epsilon_t \sim IN(0, \sigma_{\epsilon\epsilon}). \tag{5}$$

For large estimation samples, sample estimators within each hypothesis ($\hat{\beta}$ and $\bar{\gamma}$) will be close to their respective 'population' values β and γ defined by $E(y_t|x_{1t}, x_{2t}) = x'_{1t}\beta$ and $E(y_t|x_{2t}) = x'_{2t}\gamma$. Generally, $\hat{\beta}$, $\bar{\gamma}$ have sampling variances of $O(T^{-1})$, but for most macro systems the variances of the reduced form parameters are not even computed. Consequently, we investigate the usefulness of forecast encompassing tests which *neglect the variation due to β, γ being estimated*. Let the one-step ahead forecasts generated over the period $t = T + 1, \ldots, T+n$ be denoted: $\hat{y}_t = x'_{1t}\beta$ and $\bar{y}_t = x'_{2t}\gamma$ (where x_{1t}, x_{2t} can be *known* at time t so that (4) and (5) are already in predictive form). Then the 'composite artificial model':

$$y_t = (1 - \alpha)x'_{1t}\beta + \alpha x'_{2t}\gamma + u_t \tag{6}$$

which might be considered for forecast encompassing essentially coincides with the 'pooling of forecasts' formula:

$$y_t = \alpha_1 \hat{y}_t + \alpha_2 \bar{y}_t + u_t \tag{7}$$

(though often $\alpha_1 + \alpha_2$ is not restricted to be unity in (7): see Bates and Granger, 1968 and Winkler, 1983). A very simple forecast-encompassing test of H_1 is that $\alpha = 0$; and of H_2 is that $\alpha = 1$ (respectively: ($\alpha_1 = 1$, $\alpha_2 = 0$) and ($\alpha_2 = 1$, $\alpha_1 = 0$) for (7)), any other outcome showing that neither model encompasses the other, although these only test a necessary condition for parameter encompassing. Note that the *need* to pool forecasts is prima-facie evidence of a failure to encompass, and if H_1 is an econometric model and H_2 a univariate time-series model (say) then if H_1 does not encompass H_2 it seems highly suggestive of the possibility that H_1 is dynamically misspecified (that being the only information available to H_2).

To obtain a test requires the distribution under H_1 of the least-squares estimate of α in (6) or of α_2 in (7). When H_1 holds, then $\alpha_1 = 1$, $\alpha_2 = 0$ so for (7):

$$y_t - \hat{y}_t = u_t = \alpha_2 \bar{y}_t + e_t \quad \text{where } \alpha_2 = 0. \tag{8}$$

This expresses the test in a 'residual diagnostics' form (see Pagan and Hall, 1983). Then:

$$\hat{\alpha}_2 = \left(\sum_{t=T+1}^{T+n} \bar{y}_t^2 \right)^{-1} \sum_{t=T+1}^{T+n} \bar{y}_t u_t \tag{9}$$

Note that (9) requires $x'_{2t}\gamma \neq 0$ and so $\gamma \neq 0$ which means that if H_1 holds then $M_{12} = T^{-1}\sum_{t=1}^{T} x_{1t}x'_{2t} \neq 0$. This follows because on H_1:

$$E(y_t|x_{1t}, x_{2t}) = x'_{1t}\beta, \tag{10}$$

so that letting the projection of x_1 on x_2 define P:

$$x_{1t} = Px_{2t} + w_t \text{ (say)}, \quad \text{where } \text{plim}_{T\to\infty} T^{-1} \sum x_{2t}w'_t = 0, \tag{11}$$

then on substituting (11) into (4) and equating to (5): $\gamma = P'\beta$. Thus, conditional on strongly exogenous variables x_{1t}, x_{2t}, known parameters, and given (4):

$$\hat{\alpha}_2|X^1_{1T+n}, X^1_{2T+n} \sim N\left(0, \sigma_{22}\left(\gamma' \sum_{t=T+1}^{T+n} (x_{2t}x'_{2t})\gamma\right)^{-1}\right). \tag{12}$$

This functions as a baseline case.

More generally, for cases where (x_{1t}, x_{2t}) are only weakly exogenous for β (but still abstracting from the parameter estimation issue):

$$\text{plim}_{n\to\infty} \hat{\alpha}_2 = \text{plim}\left(\frac{1}{n} \sum \gamma'x_{2t}x'_{2t}\gamma\right)^{-1} \text{plim}\left(\frac{1}{n} \sum \gamma'x_{2t}u_t\right). \tag{13}$$

Let $\text{plim}(1/n)\sum x_{2t}x'_{2t} = M_{22}$, then from (10) the last term in (13) is zero and so:

$$\text{plim } \hat{\alpha}_2 = (\gamma'M_{22}\gamma)^{-1} \cdot 0 = 0 \tag{14}$$

Next:

$$\sqrt{n}\hat{\alpha}_2 = \left(\frac{1}{n} \sum \gamma'x_{2t}x'_{2t}\gamma\right)^{-1} \gamma' \frac{1}{\sqrt{n}} \sum x_{2t}u_t$$

$$= (\gamma'M_{22}\gamma)^{-1}\gamma' \frac{\sum x_{2t}u_t}{\sqrt{n}} + o_p(1) \quad \text{by Cramer's theorem.} \tag{15}$$

Since $E(x_{2t}u_t) = 0$ and $E(x_{2t}x'_{2t}u_t^2) = \alpha_{uu}M_{22}$ (on H_1):

$$\frac{1}{\sqrt{n}} \sum_{t=T+1}^{T+n} x_{2t}u_t \xrightarrow{D} N(0, \sigma_{uu}M_{22})$$

and hence on H_1:

$$\sqrt{n}\hat{\alpha}_2 \xrightarrow{D} N(0, \sigma_{uu}(\gamma'M_{22}\gamma)^{-1}). \tag{16}$$

Finally, $\text{plim }(1/n)\sum \bar{y}_t^2 = (\gamma'M_{22}\gamma)$. These are *large-forecast-sample* equivalents to (12) for stochastic x's. Consequently, the usual least-squares standard errors of $\hat{\alpha}_2$ in (8) are asymptotically valid for known β, P, even though no information is used on the actual values of $\{x_{1t}\}$ and/or

$\{x_{2t}\}$. In the practical case where $\hat{\beta}, \bar{\gamma}$ are used, the approximations are also subject to a term of $O(T^{-1})$ which clearly could be important in some (or even many) situations. If $\{x_{1t}\}$ is available, then the J-test (see Davidson and MacKinnon, 1981) could be used: otherwise, if testing is to proceed in the limited information setting of $(\hat{y}_t, \bar{y}_t)$ *only*, Monte Carlo simulation studies should help reveal potential difficulties arising from the $O(T^{-1})$ approximations adopted, noting that $(\hat{\beta}, \bar{\gamma})$ is independent of $\{u_{T+j}\}$ $(j > 0)$ under H_1. Such a straightforward outcome contrasts markedly with the use of analogous formulae to (8) *within* estimation samples, since then the limit of the conventional least-squares calculated standard error is not equal to the asymptotic standard error of $\sqrt{T}\ \bar{a}_2$ (see Davidson and MacKinnon (1981) and the J-test they propose instead; also, Durbin (1970) addresses the general problem when deriving his h-test in place of the Durbin–Watson statistic).

The converse derivation for regressing $(y_t - x'_{2t}\gamma)$ on $x'_{1t}\beta$ follows directly and allows the power function of the test to be obtained when H_1 is valid and H_2 is not (more generally, the power function can be obtained for a given H_3 of which H_1 and H_2 are reductions). In the case of strongly exogenous regressors and known parameters, for the test based on:

$$(y_t - \bar{y}_t) = \phi\hat{y}_t + v_t \text{ (say)},$$

$$\text{with } \hat{\phi} = \left(\sum_{t=T+1}^{T+n} \hat{y}_t^2 \right)^{-1} \sum_{t=T+1}^{T+n} \hat{y}_t(y_t - \bar{y}_t)$$

then:

$$E(\hat{\phi}|\cdot) = 1 - (\beta' \sum x_{1t}x'_{1t}\beta)^{-1}\beta' \sum x_{1t}x_{2t}\gamma = \phi \qquad (17)$$
$$E(\hat{\phi} - \phi)^2 = \sigma_{uu}/(\beta' \sum x_{1t}x_{1t}\beta)$$

so that a non-central 't' results (more generally, the error variance will not coincide with σ_{uu}). The asymptotic power can be computed from these formulae as in Mizon and Hendry (1980).

It is surprising that for forecast encompassing of large systems any test (although very approximate) as simple and as easily implemented as the Student 't'-statistic on $\hat{a}_2$ in (8) should result, providing that *ex-ante* one-step forecasts are used. However, when T is small the variances of $\hat{\beta}$ and $\bar{\gamma}$ will almost certainly affect the behaviour of such a test (analogous to the issues raised by Kiviet (1982, 1986) for Chow versus other forecast tests), but we are investigating this issue via Monte Carlo simulation. Given published predictions from systems, forecast encompassing tests should not prove difficult to implement, although a failure to encompass a model with 'intercept adjustments' needs careful interpretation – the forecasts then reflect both modeller and model, whereas the test is legitimate only if the former plays no role. Thus, progress in evaluation may require access to *unadjusted* forecasts, based on lagged (or at least available) information only. This may exacerbate the finite sample problems discussed by Kiviet (also see Kiviet, 1985). While much hard analytical and simulation research remains to be done to derive the distributions of forecast encompassing tests for 'realistic' systems, econometric theory could yield useful returns by producing simple tests which are not informationally taxing or computationally demanding; and deriving the approximate distribution of $\tilde{\alpha}_2$ for a univariate regression like (8) despite the models being large and non-linear may provide such a test. For non-linear models, stochastic simulation averages (preferably using antithetic variates) may be necessary when computing $\hat{y}$ and $\bar{y}$ to avoid the well-established prediction bias of deterministic forecasts (see e.g. Brown and Mariano, 1983 and Mariano and Brown, 1983). Also, to merit calculating such a test at all, neither model should have already experienced predictive failure, as this would confound parameter change with encompassing. This leads directly to the topic of within-model forecast evaluation (although practical applications should proceed in the opposite order).

B. n-*step Forecast Confidence Intervals*

Forecast standard errors provide useful information on the operational properties of models. Since most econometrics' forecasts are obtained, in effect, from the derived reduced forms of structural systems estimated by non-likelihood methods, parameter uncertainty can increase greatly in the solution process inducing great sensitivity of forecasts to minor changes in 'assumptions' or in 'exogenous' variables values, implying large forecast confidence intervals. It would seem hazardous to place much faith in a 'policy recommendation' based on such a model. Moreover, the arduous 'rounds' of model adjustment through which forecasters seem wont to go may in part reflect the sensitivity of the outcome to the inputs and hence the need to carefully select the latter if 'absurd' forecasts are to be avoided. Thus, forecasts are modified towards some 'prior expectation', so that even if a model could warn of large impending problems, it is not allowed to do so. A 95 per cent confidence interval which covered more than plus or minus two *unconditional* standard deviations of a variable to be forecast would reveal the weakness of any point forecast. This holds especially so in practice, since the forecast standard errors will not reflect such sources of uncertainty as model selection variability, increased measurement errors in the latest (provisional) data, etc. However, an alternative interpretation of the role of intercept corrections is discussed below.

The neat idea in Calzolari (1981) allows the computation of forecast variances for one-step predictions even for quite large systems. This simplified formula has been implemented in FIML from AUTOREG (see Hendry and Srba, 1980) for linear systems and has proved very inexpensive for six- to eight-equation subsystems.

For operational and policy purposes, n-step *ex-ante* forecast confidence intervals are required where n may be around 8–12. For linear models a number of analytical results have been established for forecast error variances (see, *inter alia*, Schmidt, 1974; Baillie, 1979, 1981; Spitzer and Baillie, 1983).

The class we have chosen to consider in detail is the stationary closed linear system written in companion form as:

$$y_t = Ay_{t-1} + v_t \quad \text{with } v_t \sim IN(0, \Omega) \tag{18}$$

where y_t ($m \times 1$) comprises all variables and relevant lags (except the longest) and hence Ω is generally singular. The actual subset of current dated variables to be forecast is selected by the matrix S into $S'y_t$. Let T denote the estimation sample size, n the forecast horizon and $\sim$ an estimate and/or forecast. A is a linear function of a subset of parameters θ such that:

$$\sqrt{T}(\tilde{\theta} - \theta) \overset{D}{\to} N(0, \Psi) \quad \text{and} \quad \theta = P'\alpha, \tag{19}$$

where P' is the parameter selection matrix, $\alpha = A^v$, and $(\ )^v$ is a column vectoring operator.

An n-step forecast is given by:

$$\tilde{y}_{T+n} = \tilde{A}^n y_T \tag{20}$$

whereas from (18):

$$y_{T+n} = A^n y_T + \sum_{i=0}^{n-1} A^i v_{T+n-i} \tag{21}$$

Consequently:

$$(y_{T+n} - \tilde{y}_{T+n}) = \sum_{i=0}^{n-1} A^i v_{T+n-i} + (A^n - \tilde{A}^n) y_T. \tag{22}$$

Assuming that $E(A^n - \tilde{A}^n)$ is negligible relative to terms retained, then from Baillie (1979), letting $\tilde{g}_{T+n} = S'(y_{T+n} - \tilde{y}_{T+n})$, we have:

$$\text{Var}(\tilde{g}_{T+n}|y_T) = S'\left\{\sum_{i=0}^{n-1} A^i \Omega A^{i'}\right\}S + T^{-1}(I \otimes y_T')D(n)'\Gamma D(n)(I \otimes y_T) \tag{23}$$

and from (19):

$$\sqrt{T}(\tilde{\alpha} - \alpha) \overset{D}{\to} N(0, \Gamma) \quad \text{with } \Psi = P'\Gamma P \tag{24}$$

$$D(n)' = \frac{\partial(S'A^n)}{\partial \alpha'} = (S' \otimes I)\left\{\sum_{i=0}^{n-1} A^i \otimes A'^{n-i-1}\right\} \tag{25}$$

Note that P selects elements of α for which derivatives exist, so that its columns are the kth column from a unit matrix if α_k is variable, and hence $D(n)'P'$ selects derivatives with respect to θ. Below, A is unrestricted and $P = I$.

The calculations are similar for covariances ($n \geqslant h$, $k = n - h$):

$$\text{Cov}(\tilde{g}_{T+n}, \tilde{g}_{T+h} | y_T) = S' \left\{ \sum_{i=0}^{h-1} A^{i+k} \Omega A^{i'} \right\} S \tag{26}$$
$$+ T^{-1}(I \otimes y_T')D(n)'\Gamma D(h)(I \otimes y_T)$$
$$= C_{nh}.$$

Let

$$C = ((C_{jh})) \quad \text{for } j, h = 1, \ldots, n \quad \text{and} \quad \tilde{g}' = (\tilde{g}_{T+1}' \ldots \tilde{g}_{T+n}').$$

Then under the assumptions of (18):

$$\tilde{g} \underset{app}{\sim} N(0, C). \tag{27}$$

Let $\tilde{C}$ denote the $mn \times mn$ matrix C evaluated at $\tilde{A}$, $\tilde{\Omega}$ and $\tilde{\Gamma}$ where there are m current-dated variables to be forecast. Previous simulation studies of $\tilde{C}$ include Schmidt (1977) and Spitzer and Baillie (1983), both of whom accord an important role to the second term in (26), even though it is $O(T^{-1})$. Also Nicholls and Pagan (1982) propose computing forecast confidence intervals using repeated least-squares with constructed variables.

As well as considering one n-step forecast test based on (27), n one-step or k h-step ($hk = n$) forecasts could have been calculated. To the order of approximation adopted here, most such tests are equivalent (assuming parameter estimates are not updated). For example, taking the case of known parameters for expositional simplicity, one-step forecasts are given by:

$$\hat{y}_{T+i+1} = A y_{T+i} \quad \text{with } v_{T+i+1} = y_{T+i+1} - A y_{T+i} \tag{28}$$
$$= \hat{f}_{T+i+1} \quad \text{(say)}$$

whereas, for h-step forecasts (for arbitrary h):

$$\tilde{y}_{T+h} = A^h y_T \quad \text{with } \tilde{f}_{T+h} = \sum_{j=0}^{h} A^j v_{T+h-j}. \tag{29}$$

Thus letting $\tilde{f} = (\tilde{f}_{T+1} \ldots \tilde{f}_{T+n})$:

$$\tilde{f} = H\hat{f} \quad \text{where } H = \begin{pmatrix} I & 0 & \ldots & 0 & 0 \\ A & I & \ldots & 0 & 0 \\ A^{n-1} & A^{n-2} & \ldots & A & I \end{pmatrix} \tag{30}$$

This is the result already noted in Section 3, and shows that, *ex-post*, nothing is gained by analysing $\tilde{f}$ over $\hat{f}$; *ex-ante*, however, only the former can be calculated for $n > 1$ and hence the accuracy in finite samples of formulae like C in (26) merits investigation. Nevertheless, there are some non-equivalent tests, of which the most natural (for quarterly models) are those based on annual averages. With $n = 8$ and an observation frequency of 4, two average forecast errors result of the form:

$$\frac{1}{4} \sum_{l=1}^{4} (y_{T+l+I} - \bar{y}_{T+l+I}) \quad \text{for } I = 0 \text{ or } 4.$$

Consequently, for $n = 8$ (relative to the latest available information), such forecasts are a linear function of $\bar{f}$, say $\tilde{f} = Q\bar{f}$ where Q is 2×8 and hence $\tilde{f}$ $\sim_{app} N(0, QCQ')$ under (18). Then tests based on $\tilde{f}$ will have different size and power characteristics from those based on $\bar{f}$. To investigate these possible evaluation procedures, a Monte Carlo study was undertaken.

The most suitable computer was the ICL Distributed Array Processor (DAP) located at Queen Mary College, London. This is a 64×64 array of microprocessors of the single-instruction-multiple-input variety, each processor having access to about two kilobytes of fast memory. Thus 4096 calculations could proceed *simultaneously*. The model chosen was constrained to fit within 2K so that 4096 *replications* of the experiment could be conducted simultaneously, providing a large number of trials at minimal cost (effectively for the cost of one replication on a sequential computer). This resurrects the old idea of simple distribution sampling (see Student 1908), but efficiently exploits the new computer 'architecture' (see Sylwestrowicz, 1981 and Parkinson and Sylwestrowicz, 1982).

The program was written in DAP-FORTRAN by the first author. At first sight, obtaining 4096 *independent* streams of random numbers appears to pose an awkward problem. Fortunately, the algorithm developed by Smith et al. (1984) solves this difficulty using the fact that if $x_{n+i} = kx_n$ mod m, then the sequences: $x_{n+i} = k^\alpha x_n$ mod m are α apart (i.e. every αth of the original sequence is picked). Setting $\alpha = 4096$ (and cleverly calculating k^α mod m using DAP arithmetic) yields 4096 streams from the vector seed $X_0 = (x_0, \ldots, x_{4095})$.

The primary focus of the study was on tests based on $\bar{f}$ and $\tilde{f}$, viewed as summary statistics for the accuracy of C and the adequacy of the asymptotic approximations. These two statistics are:

$$\eta_1(\tilde{A}) = \bar{f}'\bar{C}^{-1} \xrightarrow{D} \chi^2(mn, \psi_1^2) \tag{31}$$

where ψ_1^2 is the non-centrality parameter ($= 0$ under the null) and

$$\eta_2(\tilde{A}) = \bar{f}'Q'(Q\bar{C}Q')^{-1}Q\bar{f} \xrightarrow{D} \chi^2(mn/4, \psi_2^2). \tag{32}$$

Note that the forecast variance matrix is 16×16 even for $m = 2$ and $n = 8$ and so is very difficult to summarize across a range of experiments. While there are many other interesting results produced by the Monte Carlo (viz. finite sample behaviour of first order vector autoregressive processes in two variables), these are incidental to the present study and will not be reported.

The specific system adopted for study was:

$$\begin{pmatrix} 1 & -\alpha \\ 0 & 1 \end{pmatrix} \begin{pmatrix} y_{1t} \\ y_{2t} \end{pmatrix} = \begin{pmatrix} \beta & 0 \\ \gamma & \lambda \end{pmatrix} \begin{pmatrix} y_{1t-1} \\ y_{2t-1} \end{pmatrix} + \begin{pmatrix} v_{1t} \\ v_{2t} \end{pmatrix} + \begin{pmatrix} \delta_{1t}^{*} \\ \delta_{2t}^{*} \end{pmatrix} \qquad (33)$$

or

$$By_t = \Gamma y_{t-1} + v_t + \delta^{*}{}_t \qquad (34)$$

where $B^{-1} v_t \sim IN(0, \Omega)$. This is a just-identified two-equation model such that unrestricted reduced form estimates are efficient when $\theta = (\alpha, \beta, \gamma, \lambda)$ and Ω are unconstrained, and the reduced form and companion form coincide.

The design space comprised $T = (36, 81)$, $\lambda = 0.75$ $\alpha = 1$, $\gamma = (0.0, -0.4)$ ('feed-back'), $\beta = (0.5, 0.9)$ ('dynamics'), with $\Omega = \begin{pmatrix} \sigma_e^2 & K \\ K & 1 \end{pmatrix}$ where $\sigma_e^2 = (1, 4)$ ('noise') and $K = (0, 0.5)$ ('simultaneity'). This generated 32 models; note that the structural error variance matrix varies over a wide range of values, being an induced parameter in the design. Throughout, even if $\gamma = 0$, A was estimated unrestrictedly.

Two forecast horizons and four states of nature were considered as follows:

$n = (8, 4)$ and $\delta_t = 0$ $(t = 1, \ldots, T)$ with $\delta_{T+1}, \ldots, \delta_{T+n}$ (the reduced form equivalents of δ_{T+i}^{*}: $\delta_{T+i} = B^{-1} \delta_{i+i}^{*})$ being:

(i) $\delta_{T+i} = \begin{pmatrix} 0 \\ 0 \end{pmatrix}$ $(i = 1, \ldots, n)$ [null]

(ii) $\delta_{T+1} = \begin{pmatrix} 1.5 \\ 0 \end{pmatrix}$ $(\delta_{T+2}, \ldots, \delta_{T+n} = 0)$ [impulse]

(iii) $\delta_{T+i} = \begin{pmatrix} 1 \\ 1 \end{pmatrix}$ $(i = 1, \ldots, n)$ [step]

(iv) $\delta_{T+i} = \begin{pmatrix} 0.5i \\ 0 \end{pmatrix}$ $(i = 1, \ldots, n)$ [trend]

These values were chosen to span the range of test powers.

Since $A = B^{-1}\Gamma$ is known to the experimenters, we could investigate the performance of $\eta_1(A)$ and $\eta_2(A)$ which should be precisely χ^2-distributed (given the generation of normal random numbers) and hence act as a check on the validity of the simulation study as well as a potential control across experiments for fluctuations due to the random sampling. In the four experiments with $h = 8$, $\sigma_e^2 = 4$, $K = 0.5$, and $T = 36$, the inaccuracy of calculating $D(8)$ on the DAP posed occasional numerical problems and we doubt the wisdom of evaluating C for substantially larger values of n in practical models.[1]

---

[1] Several algorithms and factorizations were tried, none of which was fully satisfactory; these experiments are excluded from the response surface analyses reported below.

Given the average value of C across 4096 replications, the non-centralities of the test statistics were calculated. Note that these are the *average conditional* variances (given the y_T's of each replication) rather than the unconditional variances but must be extremely close to the latter; in particular, they reflected the well-known property of the latter of being monotonic in the forecast horizon. From the non-centralities thus calculated, an 'anticipated' large-sample power $P^* = \Pr(\chi^2(r, \psi^2) \geqq CR)$ was calculated where r equals the degrees of freedom of the test, CR is the appropriate critical value to achieve a 5 per cent anticipated rejection frequency under the null and ψ^2 is the non-centrality parameter. As a check, the P_i^* should be very close to the empirical rejection frequencies of the associated $\eta_i(A)$ tests.

The power response surfaces chosen to summarise the experimental outcomes were based on Mizon and Hendry (1980):

$$H[\mathcal{L}(\hat{P}) - \mathcal{L}(P^*)] = HT^{-1}f(\theta, \Omega, T, n) + v \tag{35}$$

where $\mathcal{L}(x) = \log(x/(1 - x))$, $\hat{P}$ is the empirical rejection frequency, P^* the corresponding asymptotic power, $H = (N \cdot \hat{P}(1 - \hat{P}))^{1/2}$ for $N = 4096$ replications and hence $E(v^2) = 1$ if $T^{-1}f(\cdot)$ is appropriately formulated.[2] While tests based on both $\hat{A}$ and A were calculated, only the former are reported below (as the latter acted primarily as a control on the experiments). Moreover, only one equation was selected to characterise both the 64 experiments in the design and the four states of nature (null, impulse, step and trend shocks) but separately for $\eta_1(\cdot)$ and $\eta_2(\cdot)$.

Table 1 summarizes the mean rejection frequencies of the tests in each state averaged over the 64 design points, as well as the matching P^* values. Throughout, $\hat{P}[\eta_i(A)] \simeq P^*[\eta_i(A)] \geqq P^*[\eta_i(\hat{A})]$, as anticipated given the second term in (23). However, $\hat{P}[\eta_i(\hat{A})|H_0] > 0.05$, to a sufficient extent that $P[\eta_i(\hat{A})] > P[\eta_i(A)]$ in many experiments, revealing the need for a better significance level calibration (critical values CR_i such that $\hat{P}(\eta_i(\hat{A}) \geqq CR_i) = 0.5$ were calculated). Also, again as expected, $\eta_2(\cdot)$ was 'less powerful' than $\eta_1(\cdot)$ for an impulse shock, but more powerful otherwise, considerably so for a step change.

Despite the importance of terms of $O(1/T)$ in the response surfaces under both null and alternative, P^* accounted for the vast majority of the inter-experiment variation in the $\hat{P}$ values. For example, regressions of $H\mathcal{L}(\hat{P})$ on $H\mathcal{L}(P^*)$ usually yielded $R^2 > 0.99$ with a unit coefficient for that regressor. For $\eta_i(A)$, $\hat{\sigma}_v^2 = 1$, but for $\eta_i(\hat{A})$ it proved extremely difficult to develop simple response surfaces with acceptable values of $\hat{\sigma}_v$.

Since the unit coefficient on $H\mathcal{L}(P^*)$ was acceptable, the formulation in

---

[2] $\mathcal{L}(\cdot)$ was corrected by $\frac{1}{2}N$, and 12 (16) experiments where $\hat{P}$ or P^* was unity were eliminated for η_1 and η_2 respectively ($H = 0$ for these cases anyway).

Table 1   Average empirical ($\hat{P}$) and theoretical (P^*) rejection frequencies

	Null (i)		Impulse (ii)		Step (iii)		Trend (iv)	
	$\hat{P}$	P^*	$\hat{P}$	P^*	$\hat{P}$	P^*	$\hat{P}$	P^*
$P[\eta_1(\hat{A})]$	0.078	0.05	0.138	0.104	0.396	0.321	0.478	0.394
$P[\eta_1(A)]$	0.051	0.05	0.107	0.107	0.412	0.409	0.517	0.515
$P[\eta_2(\hat{A})]$	0.061	0.05	0.091	0.077	0.506	0.464	0.507	0.458
$P[\eta_2(A)]$	0.050	0.05	0.089	0.089	0.581	0.576	0.534	0.531

(35) was retained and, as shown, much of the deviation of $\mathscr{L}(\hat{P})$ from $\mathscr{L}(P^*)$ could be explained by terms of $O(1/T)$.

For $\eta_1(\hat{A})$, let $\hat{\mathscr{L}}_1 = H\mathscr{L}\{\hat{P}(\eta_1(\hat{A}))\}$ and $\mathscr{L}_1^* = H\mathscr{L}\{P^*(\eta_1(\hat{A}))\}$, then:

$$(\hat{\mathscr{L}}_1 - \mathscr{L}_1^*) = 4.1Hn/T + 22H(1 - \mu^2)/T - 9.8H\psi^2\mu(1 - \mu)$$
$$\quad\;\;(0.2) \qquad\quad (2) \qquad\qquad\quad (1.2)$$

$$+ 20H\gamma D_1/T + 3.3\mathscr{L}_1^* D_2/T - 0.15HD_3 \qquad (36)$$
$$\quad (3) \qquad\qquad (0.6) \qquad\qquad (0.02)$$

$$M = 240, \quad R^2 = 0.94, \quad \hat{\sigma}_v = 2.6, \quad \xi_1(2) = 77, \quad \xi_2(2, 232) = 12.2$$
$$\xi_3(27, 207) = 6.6, \quad \text{(i)} = 1.7, \quad \text{(ii)} = 1.6, \quad \text{(iii)} = 2.9, \quad \text{(iv)} = 3.2.$$

In (36), ψ^2 is the non-centrality parameter, μ is the largest modulus of the latent roots of A, and the $\{D_i\}$ are dummy variables defined by:

$$D_1 = \begin{cases} 1 & \text{for (iii), (iv)} \\ 0 & \text{otherwise} \end{cases}, \quad D_2 = \begin{cases} 1 & \text{for (i), (ii), (iv)} \\ 0 & \text{otherwise} \end{cases},$$

$$D_3 = \begin{cases} 1 & \text{for (ii)} \\ -1 & \text{for (iv)} \\ 0 & \text{otherwise} \end{cases}$$

Also, heteroscedastic-consistent standard errors are reported and $\xi_3(\cdot)$ is an F-test for heteroscedasticity/functional form misspecification (see White, 1980), $\xi_1(2)$ is the Jarque-Bera (1980) $\chi^2(2)$ test for normality, and $\xi_2(\cdot)$ is the RESET F-test (see Ramsey, 1969) for 2nd and 3rd moments; the remaining values denoted '$(\cdot) = $' are for $\hat{\sigma}_v$ in the four subsets of 64 experiments within each state. The values of $\hat{\sigma}_v$ and the $\xi_i(\cdot)$ reveal substantial misspecification in (36) although no simple form removing this could be designed. Even so, the equation explains 94 per cent of the variation of $\hat{P}$ around P^* for $\eta_1(\hat{A})$ and $\hat{\sigma}_v$ is not particularly large given that $N = 4096$. The coefficients of the selected regressors were relatively constant across admissible subgroups although $\hat{\sigma}_v$ varied considerably (the lowest within-group R^2 was 0.92 for (iv)).

Turning to the interpretation of (36), the horizon length relative to T is the most important factor accounting for why $\hat{P}$ exceeds P^* (called the 'excess rejection'), under both null and alternative (n/T varies from 0.22 to 0.05), cautioning against using n-step forecast tests based on (23) for large n. Next, the 'excess rejection' falls as μ increases, but for μ close to unity the derivations of asymptotic approximations could be radically altered. Under the null, $\mathcal{L}^*/T$ is the only other term and again the excess rejection rises as T falls. Under the alternatives (ii)–(iv) the non-centrality parameter interacts with μ to lower the excess rejection, as does the presence of feedback ($\gamma < 0$) for step and trend shocks. Finally, for impulse shocks the excess is lower, and for trend shocks higher, than anticipated. No independent role was found for K, σ_ε^2, or β beyond their affecting $\mathcal{L}^*$, μ, and ψ_1.

Despite its manifest limitations, (36) offers a convenient summary of a vast amount of experimental evidence, highlighting the dominant roles of P^*, n, T, γ and μ in determining $\hat{P}$. The simulation thus reveals that even for simple linear stationary models, $\hat{C}$ is an imperfect measure of ex ante n-step forecast error variances, but that $\eta_1(\hat{A})$ has power to detect a range of structural breaks.

Similar findings were obtained for $\eta_2(\hat{A})$ as summarized in (37):

$$(\hat{\mathcal{L}}_2 - \mathcal{L}_2^*) = 2.3Hn/T - 6.5H\mu^2/T + 9.5H\gamma D_1/T - 19H\gamma(1 - D_1)/T$$
$$\quad (0.2) \qquad\quad (1.5) \qquad\quad (2.4) \qquad\quad (2)$$

$$+ 9.3\mathcal{L}_2^* D_2/T - 0.10HD_3 \tag{37}$$
$$\quad (0.7) \qquad\quad (0.02)$$

$$M = 236, \quad R^2 = 0.81, \quad \hat{\sigma}_\nu = 2.9, \quad \xi_1(2) = 72,$$
$$\xi_2(2, 228) = 10.7, \quad \xi_3(24, 206) = 4.0.$$

There is no direct effect of $1/T$ but n/T and $\mathcal{L}_2^* D_2/T$ enter positively, and μ^2/T and D_3 negatively as before. The influence of γ/T is surprising, having the *opposite* sign in (i) and (ii) to that in (iii) and (iv). R^2 is lower than for (36), but the coefficient of $\mathcal{L}_2^*$ was not significantly different from unity in the unrestricted regression with $\hat{\mathcal{L}}_2$ as regressand.

Overall, $\eta_2(\hat{A})$ and the corresponding confidence intervals seem to merit further investigation, especially if 'within-year robustness' is desired with reasonable power properties between-years for quarterly models.

Finally it should be noted that the conditional forecast variances of the form C are *NOT* generally monotonic in the forecast horizon. This is most easily seen in the scalar case, $m = 1$, $A = \varrho$ where $|\varrho| < 1$ and (see e.g. Harvey, 1981, p. 214):

$$C_{hh} = \frac{(1 - \varrho^{2h})}{1 - \varrho^2} \sigma_e^2 + T^{-1}h^2 y_{TQ}^2 \varrho^{2(h-1)}(1 - \varrho^2) \tag{38}$$

using var $(\hat{\varrho}) = (1 - \varrho^2)/T$. Now, $h^2\varrho^{2(h-1)}$ reaches a maximum at $h =$

$-1/\log \varrho$ so that the second term is certainly non-monotonic, and even though the first is monotonic, their sum need not be. For example, if $\sigma_e^2 = 1$ (without loss of generality, noting the units of y_t), $T = 40$ and $\varrho = 0.72$ for $y_T = 3$, then C_{hh} is largest at 2.21 when $h = 5$ and *drops* monotonically to the *unconditional* variance 2.08 thereafter. Note how C_{hh} can *exceed the unconditional variance*: $\sigma_y^2 = \sigma_e^2/(1 - \varrho^2)$ (compare Granger's interpretation in Kmenta and Ramsey, 1981). Moreover, the region of maximum excess (for scalar processes where it is easily calculated) seems to be that of primary policy interest (four to twelve quarters, say).

While such a finding is initially disappointing, it potentially provides a scientific justification for intercept corrections ('add factors', etc.). If C_{hh} exceeds σ_y^2 one might find a weighted average of conditional and unconditional predictions which has smaller variance than either alone (compare Bollerslev, 1985); a plausible unconditional predictor is the relevant 'long-run growth rate' and many intercept corrections seem to involve shrinkage towards such values (though the relative weights do not reflect the associated forecast accuracy). We conjecture that a formal procedure could be derived from this notion which greatly reduces the apparent arbitariness of present practices.

C. Summary Statistics for Large Models

This general area also has witnessed a great deal of research effort (see e.g. Malgrange and Muet, 1984 and Sheinin and Klein, 1981), and the present focus on 'long-run' properties is again not meant to detract from other approaches, but to emphasize further ideas as yet little developed. Traditionally, 'multipliers' have been used as 'ready reckoners', but these are high-dimensional and vary with the lag time (as well as with the levels of the variables and the sizes of the perturbations in non-linear systems). Properly designed 'scenario studies' could play a powerful summarizing role since, from (1):

$$\Delta \hat{y}_t = \hat{\pi}_1 \Delta y_{t-1} + \hat{\pi}_2 \Delta z_t, \quad t = 1, \dots, n \tag{39}$$

so that $\{\Delta \hat{y}_t\}$ is a linear combination of the impact multipliers with weights given by the perturbations under study. Replacing Δy_{t-1} by $\Delta \hat{y}_{t-1}$ generates cumulative effects. Such combinations often may be more useful summaries than the multipliers themselves if specific combinations of shocks merit consideration. For non-linear systems, mean stochastic simulation values would be needed for computing scenario statistics out of comparative runs; for one-off shocks, these are often reported.

Underlying (1) is a hypothetical, deterministic, steady-state 'equilibrium' corresponding to a world in which change is constant at some mutually consistent vector of growth rates (g_y, g_z):

$$y = (I - \pi_1)^{-1}\pi_2 z + f(g_y, g_z) = \prod z + f(g_z) \qquad (40)$$

since $g_y = \prod g_z$.

Often, $\prod$ is denoted the 'long-run' multiplier and for linear systems is simple to compute and e.g. standard errors of $\hat{\prod}$ are also easily calculated in FIML. Since $\prod$ can be obtained by setting all changes to zero and re-arranging the coefficients of (1), it may prove analytically tractable for large blocks of non-linear structures, leaving only a small amount of itera-tion or linear approximation to complete the solution. Alternatively, it may prove easier to obtain a more 'structural' equilibrium of the form:

$$(B + C)y = -Dz. \qquad (41)$$

Each endogenous variable would then be expressed in a more parsimoni-ous way as a function of a few other endogenous and some 'exogenous' variables.

From (41) the theory consistency of the estimated system could be checked to ensure no inadvertent theory misspecifications have arisen. More interestingly, given the *implied* 'long-run' in (17.41), direct tests of the *existence* of such relationships are possible for evolutionary time series using the results of Granger and Engle (1985) (also see Granger and Weiss, 1983 and Granger, 1981, 1986). If the data on the y, z variables need dif-ferencing once to be stationary, then the series are denoted $I(1)$ and in principle have unbounded variances in levels. If several $I(1)$ variables are claimed to define a relationship, then a minimal requirement seems to be that the deviations from that relationship have a bounded variance (i.e. are $I(0)$ – it is hard to attach much significance to a claim that e.g. x_{1t} and x_{2t} are related but can be infinitely far apart). If a set of $I(1)$ variables linked by a vector of non-zero coefficients has a finite variance error, then they are said to be co-integrated. There is at most one co-integrating vector of constants in any minimal subset of variables since changing any constant by epsilon would add an unbounded variance component to the error (of course, if two sets of co-integrable variables exist, as both are $I(0)$ by hypothesis, components of either *set* may be added to the error without it becoming $I(1)$, so it is important to note the qualifer 'minimal' above).

Hence, it should be relatively easy to test quilibrium assertions directly (preferably prior to spending resources on modelling the non-existent!), using information on whether errors from static relationships have bounded variances. The class of tests envisaged by Granger and Engle is that for unit roots in autoregressive representations of the errors $\{v_t\}$ from *data* equivalents of (41):

$$(B + C)y_t + Dz_t = v_t. \qquad (42)$$

If the hypothesis of a unit root in $\{v_t\}$ cannot be rejected when the relevant elements of (y_t, z_t) are I(1), then the underlying relationships seem some-what tenous (on this topic see Gould and Nelson, 1974; Fuller, 1976; Dickey and Fuller, 1979, 1981; Evans and Savin, 1981, 1984; Sargan and

Bhargava, 1983; and Bhargava, 1983). Again, much further research is needed, but some incisive results on model adequacy may be forthcoming from this approach. Often, underspecification may be the cause of random walk components of $\{v_t\}$, rather than non-existence. This notion is closely linked to the issue of data inadmissibility and also leads directly to the final proposal.

D.   Investigating Inter-equation Feedbacks

While the specification of systems as a unitary structure – rather than piecemeal, an equation at a time – is a reasonable goal and may be attainable for sub-blocks, in practice *ad hocery* (common sense?) tends to rule. Thus, having designed a myriad of separate equations each to satisfy all the requisite selection criteria in isolation, a large question mark usually hangs over how the whole will interact. Sometimes the results are disappointing – in dynamic simulation or under control optimization mode, data inadmissibility appears (e.g. negative interest rates, etc.). Such findings suggest that inadequate attention has been paid to between-equation error corrections (see e.g. Davidson, 1983; Longbottom, 1983; and the Second Report of the Treasury and Civil Service Committee on International Monetary Arrangements, 1983).

For example, equations determining interest rates are usually linear for theoretical reasons, even though one might regard negative rates as infeasible. To ensure non-negative predictions from systems may require feedbacks with an ever-increasing effect as an inadmissibility region is neared. Likewise for unemployment, although here an alternative solution is a logit-transformation if an unemployment equation is explicitly incorporated in a model. As Davidson (1983) notes, system error-corrections can be designed to deliver results like (40) or (41) directly, and could incorporate adjustment mechanisms to minimize the chance of predicting impossible values. For an empirical example relating 'mark-up' behaviour to reserves, see Anderson and Hendry (1984).

As earlier, an implicit assumption is that closely interacting small subsystems already have been rigorously tested for parameter constancy, the validity of over-identifying restrictions, and the absence of residual autocorrelation (note the easily implemented suggestion of Harvey (1982) for the latter). Failure on any of these tests could arise from inadequate modelling of inter-equation interactions, but that is only one possible constructive response.

IV.   Conclusion

Following a critique of dynamic simulation, forecasting records and economic 'plausibility' which appear to be the most widely used evaluation criteria in modelling macroeconomic systems, several new alternatives are discussed. Tests for forecast encompassing and for the existence of long-run relationships, the calculation of forecast confidence intervals and tests based thereon presently seem both feasible and more promising than conventionally used tools. Although it is premature to draw any conclusions on the best, or even a good, approach to evaluating econometric systems, further research on evaluation procedures looks like paying handsome dividends. Both analytical and Monte Carlo studies can help appraise evaluation procedures prior to their application. This would help avoid a repetition of the difficulties arising in earlier instances, such as judging models by their historical dynamic simulation tracking performance.

References

Ahumada, H. (1985), An encompassing test of two models of the balance of trade for Argentina, *Oxford Bulletin of Economics and Statistics*, 47, 51–70.

Anderson, G. J. and Hendry, D. F. (1984), An econometric model of United Kingdom building societies, *Oxford Bulletin of Economics and Statistics*, 46, 175–210.

Artis, M. J. (1982), Why do forecasts differ? (Bank of England Panel of Academic Consultants, Paper 17).

Artis, M. J. and Karakitsos, E. (1982), Monetary and exchange rate targets in an optimal control setting. Discussion Paper, Manchester University.

Baillie, R. T. (1979), Asymptotic prediction mean squared error for vector auto-regressive models", *Biometrika,* 66, 675–8.

Baillie, R. T. (1981), Prediction from the dynamic simultaneous equations model with vector autoregressive errors, *Econometrica*, 49, 1331–7.

Bank of England (1982), The usefulness of macroeconomic models. Bank of England Paper 14.

Bates, J. M. and Granger, C. W. J. (1968), The combination of forecasts, *Operational Research Quarterly*, 20, 451–68.

Bhargava, A. (1983), On the theory of testing for unit roots in observed time series. DP83/67, International Centre for Economics and Related Disciplines, London Shool of Economics.

Bollerslev, T. (1984), Reduced asymptotic mean square prediction errors in a non-linear simultaneous systems. Discussion Paper, University of Califorina, San Diego.

Box, G. E. P. and Jenkins, G. M. (1970), *Time Series Analysis, Forecasting and Control.* Holden Day, San Francisco.

Box, G. E. P. and Tiao, G. (1976), Comparison of forecast and actuality, *Journal of the Royal Statistical Society, C*, 195–200.

Breusch, T. S. and Pagan, A. R. (1980), The Lagrange multiplier test and its applications to model specification in econometrics, *Review of Economic Studies*, 47, 239–53.

Brown, B. W. and Mariano, R. S. (1983), Residual-based procedures for prediction and estimation in a nonlinear simultaneous system, *Econometrica*, 52, 321–43.

Calzolari, G. (1981), 'A note on the variance of ex post forecasts in econometric models, *Econometrica*, 49, 1593–6.

Chow, G. C. (1960), Tests of equality between sets of coefficients in two linear regressions, *Econometrica*, 28, 591–605.

Chow, G. C. (1981) *Econometric Analysis by Control Methods*. John Wiley & Sons, New York.

Chow, G. C. and Corsi, P. (eds) (1982), *Evaluating The Reliability of Macro-Economic Models*. John Wiley & Sons, New York.

Cox, D. R. (1961), Tests of separate families of hypotheses. *Proceedings of The Fourth Berkeley symposium on Mathematical Statistics and Probability*, Vol. 1. University of California Press, Berkeley, pp. 105–23.

Davidson, J. E. H. (1983), Error correction systems. Unpublished Paper, London School of Economics.

Davidson, R. and MacKinnon, J. G. (1981), Several tests of model specification in the presence of alternative hypotheses, *Econometrica*, 49, 781–93.

Dhrymes, P. et al. (1972), Criteria for evaluation of econometric models, *Annals of Economic and Social Measurement*, 1, 291–324.

Dickey, D. A. and Fuller, W. A. (1979), Distributions of the estimators for auto-regressive time series with a unit root, *Journal of the American Statistical Association*, 74, 427–31.

Dickey D. A. and Fuller, W. A. (1981), Likelihood ratio statistics for autoregressive time series with a unit root, *Econometrica*, 49, 1057–72.

Durbin, J. (1970), Testing for serial correlation in least squares regression when some of the regressors are lagged dependent variables, *Econometrica*, 38, 410–21.

Effron, B. (1982) *The Jack-Knife, the Bootstrap and Other Resampling Plans*. SIAM, Philadelphia.

Engle, R. F. (1982), A general approach to Lagrange multiplier model diagnostics, *Journal of Econometrics*, 20, 83–104.

Engle, R. F. (1984), Wald, likelihood ratio and Lagrange multiplier tests in econometrics. *Handbook of Econometrics*, ed. by Z. Griliches and M. D. Intriligator. North-Holland, Amsterdam.

Engle, R. F., Hendry, D. F. and Richard, J-F. (1983), Exogeneity. *Econometrica*, 51, 277–304.

Ericsson, N. R. (1983), Asymptotic properties of instrumental variables statistics for testing non-nested hypotheses, *Review of Economic Studies*, 50, 287–304.

Evans, G. B. A. and Savin, N. E. (1981), Testing for unit roots 1, *Econometrica*, 49, 753–77.

Evans, G. B. A. and Savin, N. E. (1984), Testing for unit roots 2, *Econometrica*, 52, 1241–69.

Godfrey, L. G. (1978), Testing against general autoregressive and moving average error models when the regressors include lagged dependent variables, *Econometrica*, 46, 1293–1301.

Gould, J. P. and Nelson, C. R. (1974), The stochastic structure of the velocity of money, *American Economic Review*, 64, 405–17.

Granger, C. W. J. (1969), Investigating causal relations by econometric models and cross-spectral methods, *Econometrica*, 37, 424–38.

Granger, C. W. J. (1981), Some properties of time series data and their use in econometric model specification, *Journal of Econometrics*, 16, 121–30.

Granger, C. W. J. (1986), Developments in the study of co-integrated economic variables, *Oxford Bulletin of Economics and Statistics*, 48, 213–28.

Granger, C. W. J. and Engle, R. F. (1983), Dynamic specification with equilibrium constraints: co-integration and error correction. Discussion Paper, University of California, San Diego.

Granger, C. W. J. and Newbold, P. (1977) *Forecasting Economics Time Series*. Academic Press, New York.

Granger, C. W. J. and Weiss, A. A. (1983), Time series analysis of error-correction models. *Studies in Econometrics, Time Series and Multivariate Statistics*, ed. by S. Karlin et al. Academic Press, New York.

Haavelmo, T. (1944), The probability approach in econometrics, Supplement to Econometrica, 12.

Harvey, A. C. (1981) *The Econometric Analysis of Time-Series*. Philip Allan, Oxford.

Harvey, A. C. (1982), A test of misspecification for systems of equations. Discussion Paper, A31, LSE.

Hendry, D. F. (1974), Stochastic specification in an aggregate demand model of the United Kingdom, *Econometrica*, 42, 559–78.

Hendry, D. F. (1982), The role of econometrics in macro-economic analysis, *U.K. Economic Prospect*, pp. 26–38.

Hendry, D. F. (1983a), Econometric modelling: the consumption function in retrospect, *Scottish Journal of Political Economy*, 30, 193–220.

Hendry, D. F. (1983b), Evaluating macro-econometric models. Paper presented to the ISF Conference.

Hendry, D. F. and Mizon, G. E. (1985), Procrustean econometrics: or stretching and squeezing data. Discussion Paper, Centre for Economic Policy Research, London (reprinted as Chapter 7 in this volume).

Hendry, D. F. and Richard, J-F. (1982), On the formulation of empirical models in dynamic econometrics, *Journal of Econometrics*, 20, 3–33.

Hendry, D. F. and Richard, J. F. (1983), The econometric analysis of economic time series (with discussion), *International Statistical Review*, 51, 111–63.

Hendry, D. F. and Srba, F. (1980), AUTOREG: A computer program library for dynamic econometric models with autoregressive errors, *Journal of Econometrics*, 12, 85–102.

Hendry, D. F. and Wallis, K. F. (1984) *Econometrics and Quantitative Economics*. Basil Blackwell, Oxford.

Intriligator, M. D. (ed.) (1971) Frontiers of Quantitative Economics. North-Holland, Amsterdam.

Jarque, C. M. and Bera, A. K. (1980), Efficient tests for normality, homoscedasticity and serial independence of regression residuals, *Economics Letters*, 6, 255–9.

Kiviet, J. F. (1982), Size, power and interdependence of tests in sequential procedures for modelling dynamic relationships. Unpublished paper, University of Amsterdam.

Kiviet, J. F. (1985), Model selection test procedures in a single linear equation of a dynamic simultaneous system and their defects in small samples, *Journal of Econometrics,* 28(3), 327–62.

Kiviet, J. F. (1986), On the rigour of some specification tests for modelling dynamic relationships, *Review of Economic Studies,* 53, 241–62.

Klein, L. R. and Young, R. M. (1982), *An Introduction to Econometric Forecasting and Forecasting Models.* Lexington Books, Lexington.

Kmenta, J. and Ramsey, J. B. (eds) (1980), *Evaluation of Econometric Models.* Academic Press, New York.

Kmenta, J. and Ramsey, J. B. (eds) (1981), *Large Scale Macro-Econometric Models.* North-Holland, Amsterdam.

Longbottom, A. (1983), The use of dynamic equations in economic model building: some further problems. Economic Forecasting Unit Discussion Paper, London Business School.

Lucas, R. E. (1976), Econometric policy evaluation: a critique. *The Philips Curve and Labour Markets,* ed. by K. Brunner and A. H. Meltzer. Carnegie-Rochester Conference Series on Public Policy, Vol. 1. North-Holland, Amsterdam, pp. 19–46.

Mackinnon, J. G. (1983), Model specification tests against non-nested alternatives (with discussion), *Econometric Reviews,* 2(1), 85–158.

Malgrange, P. and Muet, P-A. (1984) *Contemporary Macroeconomic Modelling.* Basil Blackwell, Oxford.

Mariano, R. S. and Brown, B. W. (1983), Asymptotic behaviour of predictors in a non-linear simultaneous system, *International Economic Review*, 21, 253–36.

McNees, S. K. (1982), The role of macroeconometric models in forecasting and policy analysis in the United States, *Journal of Forecasting*, 1, 37–48.

Mizon, G. E. (1984), The encompassing approach in econometrics. *Econometrics and Quantitative Economics,* ed. by D. F. Hendry and K. F. Wallis. Basil Blackwell, Oxford, pp. 135–72.

Mizon, G. E. and Hendry, D. F. (1980), An empirical application and Monte Carlo analysis of tests of dynamic specification, *Review of Economic Studies*, 47, 21–46.

Mizon, G. E. and Richard, J-F. (1986), The encompassing principle and its application to non-nested hypotheses, *Econometrica,* 54, 657–78.

Nicholls, D. F. and Pagan, A. R. (1982), Estimating predictions, prediction errors, and their standard errors, using constructed variables. Mimeo, Australian National University.

Ormerod, P. (ed.) (1979), *Economic Modelling.* Heinemann, London.

Pagan, A. R. (1981), Reflections on Australian macro-modelling. Working Paper 048, Australian National University.

Pagan, A. R. (1984), Model evaluation by variable addition. *Econometrics and Quantitative Economics*, ed. by D. F. Hendry and K. F. Wallis. Basil Blackwell, Oxford, pp. 103–33.

Pagan, A. R. (1985), What can we learn from a dynamic simulation. Discussion Paper, Warwick University.

Pagan, A. R. and Hall, A.D. (1983), Diagnostic tests as residual analysis, *Econometric Reviews*, 2, 159–218.

Parkinson, D. and Sylwestrowicz, J. D. (eds) (1982), *DAP In Action*. Queen Mary College, London.

Pesaran, M. H. (1974), On the general problem of model selection, *Review of Economic Studies*, 41, 153–71.

Pesaran, M. H. and Deaton, A. S. (1978), Testing non-nested, non-linear regression models, *Econometrica*, 46, 677–94.

Ramsey, J. B. (1969), Tests for specification errors in classical least squares regression analysis, *Journal of the Royal Statistical Society, B*, 31, 350–71.

Sargan, J. D. (1964), Wages and prices in the United Kindgom: a study in econometric methodology, *Econometric Analysis for National Economic Planning*, ed. by P.E. Hart et al. Butterworths, London.

Sargan, J. D. and Bhargava, A. (1983), Testing residuals from least squares regression for being generated by the Gaussian random walk, *Econometrica*, 51, 153–64.

Schmidt, P. (1974), The asymptotic distribution of forecasts in the dynamic simulation of an econometric model, *Econometrica*, 42, 303–9.

Schmidt, P. (1977), Some small sample evidence on the distribution of dynamic simulation forecasts, *Econometrica*, 45, 997–1005.

Sheinin, Y. and Klein, L. R. (1981) *Wharton Mini Growth Model of the U.S. Economy*. Wharton Econometric Forecasting Associates, Philadelphia.

Smith, R. P. (1984), The evaluation and comparison of large macroeconomic models. *Contemporary Macroeconomic Modelling*, ed. by P. Malgrange and P. A. Muet. Basil Blackwell, Oxford, pp.

Smith, K. A., Reddaway, S. F. and Scott, D. M. (1984), Very high performance pseudo-random number generation on DAP. Mimeo, Queen Mary College, London.

Sowey, E. R. (1973), Stochastic simulation of macroeconomic models: methodology and interpretation. *Econometric Studies of Macro and Monetary Relations*, ed. by A. A. Powell and R. A. Williams. North-Holland, Amsterdam.

Spitzer, J. J. and Baillie, R. T. (1983), Small sample properties of predictions from the regression model with autoregressive errors, *Journal of the American Statistical Association*, 78, 258–63.

'Student' (1908), On the probable error of a mean, *Biometrika*, 6, 1–25.

Sylwestrowicz, J. D. (1981), Applications of the ICL DAP in econometric computations, *ICL Technical Journal*, 2, 280–5.

Treasury and Civil Service Select Committee of the House of Commons (1983), *Second Special Report on International Monetary Arrangement*. HMSO, London.

White, H. (1980), A heteroscedastic-consistent covariance matrix estimator and a direct test for heteroscedasticity, *Econometrica*, 48, 421–48.

Winkler, R. L. (1983), Combining forecasts. Paper presented to the Third International Symposium on Forecasting, Philadelphia.

Zellner, A. (1979), Statistical analysis of econometric models, *Journal of the American Statistical Association*, 74, 628–43.

Subject Index

Name Index